Praise for *Educating the WholeHearted Child*

Educating the WholeHearted Child gives biblical direction to parents amidst the myriad of false voices. Thanks for staying true to the course set before us as described in the Word of God. The highest calling for a Christian is discipleship, and *Educating the WholeHearted Child* is setting parents on this course.

David Quine
Cornerstone Curriculum, www.CornerstoneCurriculum.com

After a quarter century of homeschooling, it is easy to become jaded regarding new home education products. There is a sense that one has seen it all. Not so with this new edition of *Educating the WholeHearted Child*. This is a book for anyone wanting to understand how to *do life*. It is densely packed with wisdom, instruction, practical ideas, inspirational quotations, tools for identifying your child's learning style, book lists, and much more.

Even just a casual perusal will reveal that Clay and Sally are students of life. They have been careful observers of children, education, and culture. Not only have they gleaned from the wisdom of the Bible, but they are also well read, and they know and understand the culture in which we are living and how best to prepare our children for a future in the real world. There is nothing formulaic about their approach, and those who desire nice boxed answers to the enigmas and mysteries of life and education won't find them here. This is a book to encourage you on a journey of discovery in your home life, in education, and in faith. Those who embrace the spirit of this book will find that living *wholeheartedly* is the key to a life well lived.

Rea Berg
Beautiful Feet Books, www.bfbooks.com

Once in a great while, we open a book that reveals a marvelous, beckoning world where treasure and adventures await. This is one of those books. And the world is real.

Sharing insights gained over a lifetime of ministering, teaching, and parenting, Clay and Sally Clarkson speak deeply and practically to the desire of every Christian homeschooling parent to raise their children in a godly home. *Educating the WholeHearted Child* describes clearly what this approach means—both in theory and in day-to-day practice—and leads the reader step-by-step into the richness and possibilities of the wholehearted learner. Most importantly, this book rests on the uniquely biblical foundation of following God's leading in life and in learning. It teaches us how to "nurture, disciple, and educate your children *by faith*." I gladly recommend this wondrous resource to you all.

Diana Waring
History Revealed, www.DianaWaring.com

When I reviewed the first edition of *Educating the WholeHearted Child* in 1994, I noted, "Glory! Now I don't have to write this book!" I have felt the same way with each updated edition. And the 130 new pages make it better than ever!

Clay and Sally Clarkson build a firm foundation for family life—showing how to make the home a nurturing environment where discipleship and education are woven together. The Clarksons don't tell readers what to do; they share their wisdom and tested ideas, then point them to the Holy Spirit for divine guidance. Their strategies are simple, yet inspiring. Although the book focuses on four-to-fourteen-year-olds, a new section "WholeHearted Learning Youth: Beyond the WholeHearted Child" is worth the price of the book. I love the "In Our Home" sidebars, presenting real-life Clarkson family experiences.

Educating the WholeHearted Child is a must-have for all families, especially those educating with living books and classics. It is a great mixture of philosophy and practicality, answering home educators' most common questions. Excellent reading suggestions for all ages, as well as applicable quotes and scriptures, are incorporated throughout. Thank you, Clay, for blessing families with your *magnum opus*. Highly recommended!

Tina Farewell
Cofounder, Lifetime Books and Gifts, www.BobandTinaFarewell.com

The newest edition of *Educating the WholeHearted Child* will prove a rich resource for Christian families exploring homeschooling. Clay and Sally Clarkson are wise guides. They have distilled years of practical experience in raising their own children. They have deep insights about what it means to carry out the high calling of Christian parents: to disciple our children and help them grow up to be godly men and women—in short, to educate and shape their whole hearts.

Rob Shearer
Greenleaf Press & Francis Schaeffer Study Center, www.GreenleafPress.com

Educating the Wholehearted Child is overflowing with practical insights. It is written for parents who wish to create an inspiring home education that will bless well into the next generation.

Karen Andreola
A Charlotte Mason Companion, www.CharlotteMason.com

In *Educating the Wholehearted Child*, Clay and Sally Clarkson emphasize the training and care of the child's heart and cover just about everything one needs to start (and continue) homeschooling a Christian child. They discuss education in terms of generating a love for learning so that it's real, beginning at the truest foundation of teaching and discipling—fostering an environment where children long for the Lord Himself. If we can shape our children's hearts and minds to live for Christ, the rest comes easy; the basis for homeschooling is strong.

What grabbed my interest with this incredibly in-depth, thick book is the vast amount of resources the Clarksons lay before the reader. They cover methods of teaching, delve deeply into areas of study (subjects), and provide lists like children's chores and important books to read. This book is gold for the homeschool mama! I wish I had had it when I began my own homeschool journey. Five stars for a "how to homeschool" resource. I recommend it to every new and veteran homeschooler.

Gena Suarez
Publisher, *The Old Schoolhouse*® Magazine, www.TheHomeschoolMagazine.com

There are many educational resources that come across my desk, but every once in a while one stands out above the rest. *Educating the WholeHearted Child* is a perfect title because it reflects a wholehearted author who writes with the intensity and thoroughness of genuine scholarship. Clay Clarkson is not your typical homeschool author, nor is he your typical educator. Clay approaches his subject material with the skills of a surgeon, leaving no stone unturned. In a culture that is addicted to mediocrity, *Educating the WholeHearted Child* raises the bar of excellence, offering parents and educators a powerful resource from which to build a solid educational foundation that is woven with biblical scholarship and insights.

Mark Hamby
Lamplighter Publishing, www.LamplighterPublishing.com

I'm shocked that so much detail, vision, and practical advice could be packed into one book. This is one reference book every homeschool family needs. Their heart-based model is described and punctuated with advice from years of experience that will benefit the new homeschooler as well as those who have been educating at home for years.

Dr. Scott Turansky
National Center for Biblical Parenting, www.BiblicalParenting.org

As a brand-new homeschooling mom of young children, I'm often burdened with guilt from well-meaning sources making me feel I need to be more rigid, regulated, and regimented in our homeschooling, home management, and child training. *Educating the Wholehearted Child* was a breath of fresh air filling my soul and spirit with encouragement, hope, and resolve. Thank you, Clay and Sally, for reminding me that nurturing my children's hearts by providing a haven of learning and love in our home is what matters much more than a "perfect" curriculum, schedule, or child-training method.

Crystal Paine
Money Saving Mom®, www.MoneySavingMom.com

Educating the WholeHearted Child has long been one of the first books I recommend to new homeschoolers, so I was delighted to have the privilege of editing this revised and expanded edition. My enthusiastic recommendation still stands.

Mary Jo Tate
How Do You Do It All, www.MaryJoTate.com

I recommend *Educating the WholeHearted Child* to every new homeschooler I meet. More importantly, I recommend it to seasoned homeschool mothers who need encouragement to stay the course. This book was a lifeline to me as my children transitioned out of the easy elementary years—a time when a lot of homeschoolers struggle. It spans the entire journey of homeschooling and reminds us of the higher calling and true goal of our adventure of raising—and educating—our kids at home: wholehearted kids becoming wholehearted adults!

Heather Solsbery
The Homeschool Post, www.hsbapost.com

For thirteen years, *Educating the WholeHearted Child* has influenced my life more than any other parenting or education book. I remember well the first summer I read it, and I revisit it every year for fresh inspiration. This new edition is astounding in its scope with much wisdom, candor, and inspiration. It reflects Clay and Sally's journey and their desire to mentor a whole new generation (and teach a thing or two more to those of us who began the journey years ago). I especially appreciate their perspective on WholeHearted Learning beyond childhood and into a God-centered youth. The depth and breadth of this book are unparalleled in any other book of its kind. Now, instead of dedicating a week to a reread, I look forward to spending the entire summer with this new edition, reigniting a passion for putting my whole heart into learning with my children at home.

Elizabeth Foss
Real Learning: Education in the Heart of the Home, www.ElizabethFoss.com

Educating the WholeHearted Child

Educating the
WholeHearted Child

A Handbook for Christian Home Education

Clay Clarkson

with Sally Clarkson

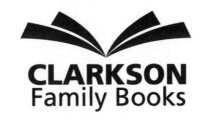

EDUCATING THE WHOLEHEARTED CHILD

Published by Apologia
a Clarkson Family Book,
an imprint of Apologia Press,
a division of Apologia Educational Ministries, Inc.
1106 Meridian Plaza, Suite 220/340
Anderson, IN 46016
www.apologia.com

© 1994, 1996, 2011 by Clay Clarkson

ISBN: 978-1-932012-95-8

Cover design: Alpha Advertising, Sidell, IL
Book design: Clay Clarkson

Printed in the United States of America
by Bang Printing, Brainerd, MN

Third Edition
Sixth Printing: February 2016

Note on Style: Pronouns in reference to God are lowercase, following the style of the NIV.

— Dedication —

Dedicated to the many wholehearted mothers and fathers who since 1994 have followed and affirmed our vision for nurturing, discipling, and educating their children at home, and to their wholehearted children who will faithfully carry Christ's light into the next generation.

Also dedicated to our own wholehearted children— Sarah, Joel, Nathan, and Joy. May you all "shine like stars in the universe as you hold out the word of life" to your own generation and to your children's children. We love you and thank God for each of you. We are blessed.

Table of Contents

— Preface —
A WholeHearted Journey for Home

Solomon had it right when he said, "Of making many books there is no end, and much study wearies the body" (Ecclesiastes 12:12). But in his day of scrolls and scribes, he couldn't even begin to imagine the bookmaking deluge unleashed first by the printing press and movable type and now by the advent of computers and digital type. It wearies the body just trying to figure out which books (not to mention magazines, newspapers, e-books, websites, and e-mails) are worthy to be read. All of which begs the question—why this book? What will you, a homeschooling parent, find of value in *Educating the WholeHearted Child*?

The answer to that question is simple—you will find a model for home education that will help you sort out the books and materials that weary you (and your children) from the ones that will enrich you and your children. The WholeHearted Learning model explained in this book will show you how your home can become a heart-filling, rich, and lively learning environment where your children will love to learn as naturally as they love to play.

Many people would consider Solomon's life worth emulating—great intelligence and wisdom, immense power, worldwide fame, and vast wealth. He seemed to have it all. What he did not have, though, was a wholehearted devotion to God. God filled Solomon's mind with supernatural wisdom, but Solomon's heart was divided. He did not prepare his own sons to be God's wholehearted, single-minded leaders because he was not one himself. Solomon's divided heart resulted in a divided kingdom and, eventually, God's judgment on the nation of Israel. David, Solomon's father and a man after God's own heart, knew the condition of his son's heart. Near the end of his life, David prophetically admonished Solomon to serve God "with wholehearted devotion." Had Solomon listened, perhaps Israel's history would have been different:

> *...acknowledge the God of your father, and serve him with wholehearted devotion and with a willing mind, for the Lord searches every heart and understands every motive behind the thoughts. If you seek him, he will be found by you; but if you forsake him, he will reject you forever.* (1 Chronicles 28:9)

Like David, we have very simple goals for our children. We want them to be wholeheartedly devoted to our God and to have willing minds that seek and serve him. That is what we mean by the "WholeHearted Child." It is not difficult today to set our parenting goals on making our children successful by the world's standards. But if their hearts and minds are not turned wholeheartedly toward God, we will miss the mark by God's standards.

While the world may judge our children against the temporal standards of intelligence, appearance, money, power, and fame, God will judge them by their hearts—"The LORD does not look at the things man looks at. Man looks at the outward appearance, but the LORD looks at the heart" (1 Samuel 16:7b). We are raising our children for God's approval. If you are reading this book, it is likely you share our vision for Christian parenting. You have considered the costs and committed yourself to the most important stewardship God will ever entrust to your care—your children. That is why you are homeschooling—to make sure, as far as you are able, that you give back to God children who are wholeheartedly devoted to him.

* * *

Since you are reading this book, you are probably in one of three groups of parents. The first group is the wholehearted parents who know about our ministry, have used our products, or have been touched by Sally's books or conferences for mothers. We are so thankful you are still walking with us on this journey of Christian parenting. The second group is the many seasoned, veteran homeschooling parents who are looking for new insights, fresh encouragement and inspiration, or just someone to affirm the choices and convictions that have shaped their homeschool journey with God. We are so glad you have found us, and we pray you will find encouragement and refreshment in these pages.

The third group is new homeschooling families who are just getting started on the journey and seeking wisdom and direction. You are part of a new generation of Christian homeschooling families, and God has put you on our hearts. In a time when you are faced with a confusing and often frustrating array of educational choices for how to homeschool, we simply want to share our vision of WholeHearted Learning—a biblical, commonsense, discipleship-based lifestyle of home education using real books, real life, and real relationships. Whatever model of homeschooling you choose for your family, we hope this book can help infuse your life at home with the colors of faith, family, and freedom.

We knew from the beginning that we could never say everything about homeschooling that you would need to know. Still, this book probably contains more information, resources, and suggestions than you will ever actually use. That's by design, so feel free to let go of any notions that you have to do everything in this book. What we have tried to do is create a fully developed, fully biblical homeschooling model that you can easily and effectively implement in your home. The WholeHearted Learning model is a thoughtful and life-tested approach to Christian homeschooling that can give you confidence as a parent that you are walking by faith in the right direction. With God's help and a clear path to follow, you can raise a wholehearted child.

* * *

Reprints too often are just the old content in a new package. Not in this case. This new third edition of *Educating the WholeHearted Child* is an extensive revision and expansion of the 1996 edition, not only because content and references needed to be updated, but also because God has updated us since that edition. We simply have much more to share about what we have learned in the past fifteen years about homeschooling and parenting. Consequently, 252 pages grew into 384 pages. There are well over 100 pages of all-new material, and a high percentage of the original material has been rewritten as well. This edition is like an Extreme Makeover—Book Edition.

We have never written books just to have something more to sell. We write because we have something more to say. God has always put messages and ministries on our hearts and in our minds, and the books and resources we write are simply those convictions worked out into tangible form. We would even like to think that a hundred years from now, someone will rediscover this book and make its content available for a whole new generation of Christian parents looking for a better way to raise wholehearted Christian children. We hope those future families will find in these pages more than just a nostalgic or historic record of Christian homeschooling from the early twenty-first century. We want them to find the same truths we hope you will find—eternal ideas of God's design for home and children that will still be as relevant then as they are today.

* * *

We are indebted to all those who have encouraged us along our way, listened to our ideas, influenced our thinking, challenged our convictions, and shaped our direction. And we are grateful for all the families who have joined us on this journey of parenting by faith—it is for you that we have dedicated our lives to this ministry. We look forward to rejoicing with you all some day as we look back on the legacy of Christian faith passed on through generations of wholehearted Christian families. For you and your children, we pray with Paul "that you may become blameless and pure, children of God without fault in a crooked and depraved generation, in which you shine like stars in the universe as you hold out the word of life" (Philippians 2:15-16a).

This book is designed to give you, a Christian parent and home educator, greater confidence in the stewardship of your children. The WholeHearted Learning model is a natural, home-centered way to nurture, disciple, and educate your children—to raise each one to be a wholehearted child. By the grace of God, you will see your children graduate from your homeschool to take places of Christian leadership in the church and in the world as mature Christian adults, serving God "with wholehearted devotion and with a willing mind." In God's timing, they will marry and begin their own families to carry on all that you have taught them, and to raise their own wholehearted children. May we all live to see that day.

With our whole hearts,

Clay and Sally Clarkson
April 2011

— Introduction —

Christian Homeschooling: Taking a Step of Faith toward Home

It's Your Decision

"We homeschool." Those two words change everything. Either you will or you won't, but deciding that you will homeschool will change the course of your life and your children's lives. It's not overly dramatic to say that it is a decision of epic proportions, so make sure you make it for the right reasons. Whatever else influences your decision, there is really only one reason in the end that should settle and seal it—that in your heart, before God and by faith, you know that being at home with your children is the right thing to do.

When you declare your independence from conventional schooling and establish a new outpost of spiritual, personal, and academic freedom within the walls of your home, you can do so with faith and confidence that you have made the right decision. But soon, faced with the task of home education, you will start asking a whole new round of questions: How can I be sure my children will learn all they need to know? What curriculum should I use? What will we do all day? Can I really do this? What do I do now?!

Home vs. School

It is at this point that many new, and even veteran, homeschoolers, having chosen the right thing to do, choose the wrong way to do it. Having chosen to be at home with their children, they then look outside the home and begin to pattern their homeschooling after the traditional classroom model. They simply fall into the default mode of teaching and learning that they grew up with—classrooms, teachers, textbooks, and curricula. But a home is not a school! Men designed schools, but God designed the home. God did not somehow forget to mention school in the Bible; it simply wasn't needed. There are only three divinely established institutions—family (referred to as the home or household in Scripture), government, and the church—and the home is the only institution designed and provided by God in Scripture for training children. It doesn't make sense to try to impose elements of an institution of man, such as public school, upon an institution of God.

A home-centered, wholehearted approach to learning is a biblical lifestyle, not an institutional experiment in education. It is a renewed expression of living and learning within the trusted biblical institution of the home. When you move toward it in faith, you might hear echoes of God's words in Isaiah, "Behold, I will do something new" (43:19). More and more families are saying the old way has gone—no more formal classrooms, graded curricula, tedious textbooks, wearisome workbooks, and long lectures. In their place, a new way has come—the home, a God-designed dynamic learning environment, full of real books, real life, and real relationships. This book is all about converting to that new way of seeing and thinking about home education.

I have no greater joy than to hear that my children are walking in the truth.

— 3 John 1:4

We proclaim Christ, admonishing and teaching our children with all wisdom, so that we may present all of our children whole and complete in Christ. To this end we labor as parents, struggling with all the energy Christ provides through his Spirit, which so powerfully works in us as fathers and mothers.

— Colossians 1:28-29 (adapted from NIV text)

We know truth, not only by the reason, but also by the heart.

— Blaise Pascal (1623-1662), French scientist, philosopher, and theologian, from *Pensées*

A little Learning is a dang'rous Thing;
Drink deep, or taste not the Pierian Spring:
There shallow Draughts intoxicate the Brain,
And drinking largely sobers us again.

— Alexander Pope (1688-1744), English poet, from "Essay on Criticism"

He is educated who knows how to find out what he doesn't know.

— Georg Simmel (1858-1918), German philosopher

The Liberation of Learning

Your home can and should be a warm, vibrant place where your children love to learn as freely and as naturally as they love to play. In fact, education should be the natural activity of every Christian home. That is what God intended in his design for home and family. For many homeschooling families, though, the tyranny of textbooks and the rigid rules of school have stolen the joy of homeschooling. The freedom that homeschooling should bring is held captive by an artificial formality and the constant demands of age-graded curricula. Families with the right intentions become enslaved to the wrong educational methods—methods designed for human institutions, not for the home.

That was briefly our experience, too, until we realized that dry textbooks and formal curricula could too easily become artificial means of education. Rather than unleashing learning potential, they often held it back. For us as parents, the common tools of conventional classroom schooling created a false security that we were doing enough and a false confidence that our children were really learning. For our children, those tools created an unhealthy dependence on formal methods of learning and a misguided distinction between learning and living. We began to see how conventional classroom curricula diluted the wonder and joy of real learning and too often turned it into a tedious and burdensome task unrelated to real life at home. This was not how God intended children to learn and grow! On the other hand, our children naturally loved reading and being read to, talking about their own insights and ideas, learning through real life, and having time to explore and learn on their own. We knew instinctively this was how God intended our children to live and learn. It was the liberation of learning in our home!

Cooperating with God's Design

Since then we have been fully invested in a home-centered, wholehearted approach to learning using real books and real life. Every day we see more clearly how natural and normal it is. For our family, it has been more than just finding the best way to home educate—choosing one out of many other good ways. It has been more like finding the right way—the commonsense way that we sensed must be out there all along. At last we feel like we are actually cooperating with God's design for our home and children. There is great freedom in knowing that what we are doing is going along with a pattern that is already built into the very fabric and rhythm of life. We have come to the place where we can honestly say that there is no distinction in our homeschool between home and school—we are living to learn and learning to live, all at the same time. That is what should happen in a home.

You may ask how we know we are cooperating with God's design when the term "homeschooling" is never mentioned in Scripture. It's because home education is not our primary goal—home nurture and discipleship are, and home education is simply the natural extension of those biblical priorities. If we are nurturing the life of Christ in our children's spirits to want to know and follow him and we are discipling our children to be used by God in his church and kingdom work, then that process will also naturally include preparing them intellectually to be thoughtful, productive, and competent adults in the world in which they will live, work, and raise a family. Since biblical nurture and discipleship are relational processes, then education must be a relational process, too.

When we follow God's biblical patterns and principles for home, the natural and normal fruit should be not just spiritual growth and maturity, but intellectual growth and maturity as well. Scripture suggests no other process or institution for raising and training children—only the family. Your home is a dynamic living and learning environment designed by God for the very purpose of raising your children to become mature, useful disciples of Jesus. When you begin to understand the biblical priority and the spiritual dynamic of home and family, you will begin to find a freedom you never knew was possible in your home education. It is not God's design for a school to be the center of your children's lives for twelve years. The purpose of this book is to help you discover the full dynamic of wholehearted learning so you can see how your home, by God's design, will actually work for you in nurturing, discipling, and educating your children.

Therefore, teaching, talk and tale, however lucid or fascinating, effect nothing until self-activity be set up; that is, self-education is the only possible education; the rest is mere veneer laid on the surface of a child's nature.

— Charlotte Mason, *Towards a Philosophy of Education*, 1925

The WholeHearted Learning model is not just a new perspective on your home and family, though; it is also a new perspective on your children. Not only did God design home to be a living and learning environment, but he also designed and prepared your children to learn naturally within that environment. Children made in God's image are prewired to be intelligent, creative, and curious. No matter what you do (or don't do!), God has already put within your children the drive to question, explore, discover, and learn. They do not learn because you enable them to make sense of things; they make sense of things because they are able to learn! Your role as a home-educating parent, then, is to provide a rich and lively living and learning environment in which your children can exercise their God-given drive to learn and then to biblically train and instruct your children within the natural context of your home and family life. It's that simple.

WholeHearted Learning

WholeHearted Learning, as described in the rest of this book, is not meant to be an educational program that you implement and maintain, as though we have the only right way to homeschool. We are very comfortable saying that what is right for one family may not be right for another. How we express WholeHearted Learning in our home will be, and in fact should be, different from how you express it in yours. Our aim in this book is not to tell you what we think is right for your family. Only you can determine that. We don't even want to tell you what books you should read to your children at what age or in what order. You are the best judge of what books your children should read and when. Neither have we any desire to become yet one more curriculum.

You don't need to become dependent on others telling you what to do, whether it is us or someone else. God has given you all you need to train and educate your children at home—it's in real books, real life, and real relationships. We want to equip you and other home-educating parents to homeschool with confidence in yourself, in your home, and in God, with a minimum of curricular safety nets. We simply want to come alongside your family and share some of the things we have learned. You can take it from there.

Our goal in this book is uncomplicated: to give you a larger vision for what God can do in your home and to provide a model of home education that gives you the freedom to follow the Holy Spirit for what your children need most. WholeHearted Learning is simply cooperating with God's eternal design for your family, home, and children. It is really just an old model with a new face that is bringing freedom to home-educating families. May you find that freedom in your home.

All your sons will be taught by the LORD, and great will be your children's peace.

— Isaiah 54:13

I have no greater joy than to hear that my children are walking in the truth.

— 3 John 4

Keeping Faith in Your Family

There are many doors of entry into the world of Christian homeschooling. We'll look at a number of them in this book, but our goal is to help you understand the adventure of faith and family that lies behind the WholeHearted Learning door. We are motivated by God to point you toward that path, but not just because we love homeschooling and want you to experience the same joy and fulfillment it has brought to our family. That would be enough for a book like this, but we're motivated by a vision for family that is bigger than just homeschooling: We want to encourage and equip you to build a biblical home for your children. You have taken a giant step of faith toward home by choosing, or even just considering, homeschooling, and we have written this book to affirm and support your decision. But we also want to strengthen your faith to see the strategic and eternal importance of your home in God's plan. Our vision is to help you keep faith in your family. That's really what *Educating the WholeHearted Child* is all about. We want you to be a truly faith-based and faith-building homeschooling family!

In the rest of this book, we will look at four key components that define the WholeHearted Learning homeschool approach: home, learning, methods, and living. In the "Home" section, you'll learn why Christian homeschooling must be built upon the foundation of a Christian home. You'll learn about biblical and practical reasons for homeschooling and then review the three biblical priorities of building a Christian home—home nurture, home discipleship, and home education. In the "Learning" section, you'll find out what makes WholeHearted Learning unique as a model for Christian homeschooling, how to organize your home for learning so it will work for you, how to understand your children's learning styles, and how to think about the young adult years. In the "Methods" section, you will be inundated with ideas and suggestions for how to implement the WholeHearted Learning model in a wide range of subject areas and topics. In the "Living" section, you will gain insight on how to live the homeschooling life with grace and faith. You'll find helpful suggestions for planning, organization, support, and family life. Finally, in the "Resources" section at the end of the book you will find lists, information, and forms you can use.

The writer of Hebrews said, "And without faith it is impossible to please God, because anyone who comes to him must believe that he exists and that he rewards those who earnestly seek him" (Hebrews 11:6). You have taken a step of faith toward home, but you will need to remind yourself daily that faith doesn't stop when the homeschooling begins. If you get caught up in the works of curricula, workbooks, and age/grade demands, you'll soon wonder what faith has to do with homeschooling. However, we are convinced that when you truly liberate learning in your home with the ideas and principles in this book and you begin to taste the fruits of homeschooling by faith, you'll never want to go back to old-school ways of learning. WholeHearted Learning will radically change the way you view your home, your children, and how God meant for you to live and learn. Even more, you will sense the presence of God in your home in a fresh new way. If you seek him in your home and homeschool, you will find the reward of his blessing.

So open the door into WholeHearted Learning and begin to explore and experience the joy of living and learning at home. We hope you find in it all that your heart is hoping for in your decision to take a step of faith toward home and homeschooling.

Section 1

Home

— Chapter 1 —

The Christian Home: Learning to Be at Home with Christ

Home Is Where Their Hearts Are

It has often been said that there is a God-shaped vacuum in the heart of every person that can be filled only by God. However, we believe there is also a home-shaped vacuum in the heart of every child that can be filled only by a biblical, godly home. In the same way that we seek after God until we find him, children will seek after the kind of home and family life that they instinctively desire, even though they are too young to do anything about it. Every child bears the image of God, their Creator, in their soul. Since the ideal of a godly home and family was part of God's original creation before the Fall and an expression of his creative nature, we believe it is etched in every child's heart. Your child is made for and naturally longs for the home that you can provide. If a child finds that kind of home, the vacuum will be filled and they will be more likely to find contentment and fulfillment that will shape the rest of their lives; if they do not find it, they will be more likely to seek to fill that vacuum with substitutes and counterfeits, and that futile search will shape the rest of their restless lives.

There is a reason that Moses, before Israel crossed the Jordan to enter the Promised Land, exhorted all of the people (Deuteronomy 6:1-9) to love God with their whole beings, to have his commandments on their hearts, and to diligently teach them to their children at rest and at work, in the evening and in the morning. (In colloquial Hebrew, he meant everywhere and all the time.) There was a God- and home-shaped vacuum in the heart of every child in Israel that needed to be filled with God's reality and God's truth. That, and only that, would create a generation that would find its fulfillment and purpose in God. Moses was writing the prescription for the future health of Israel. Unfortunately, the people of Israel did not love God wholeheartedly or have his truth on their hearts, and they soon forgot Moses' admonition and even Joshua's "as for me and my household" challenge to serve God after they were in the land (Joshua 24:15). It should not be surprising that the next generation did not know God, forsook him, and served other gods (Judges 2:10-13). The vacuum was never filled in the hearts of their children, who grew up and filled them with substitutes and counterfeits.

We must not underestimate the importance of building a godly, Christian home. We are no different from the parents of Moses' day, and his exhortation is just as fresh for us today as it was for those undoubtedly well-meaning parents 3,500 years ago. Though we are not building a physical nation, we are nonetheless building a spiritual one, and the health of the future body of Christ and his kingdom will be affected by whether or not Christian parents heed the admonition of Moses concerning our children and of the Apostle Paul to "bring them up in the training and instruction of the Lord" (Ephesians 6:4). We still must choose whom to serve and to build our homes for Christ.

Hear, O Israel! The LORD is our God, the LORD is one! You shall love the LORD your God with all your heart and with all your soul and with all your might. These words, which I am commanding you today, shall be on your heart. You shall teach them diligently to your sons and shall talk of them when you sit in your house and when you walk by the way and when you lie down and when you rise up. You shall bind them as a sign on your hand and they shall be as frontals on your forehead. You shall write them on the doorposts of your house and on your gates.

— Deuteronomy 6:4-9 (NASB)

...choose for yourselves this day whom you will serve...But as for me and my household, we will serve the LORD.

— Joshua 24:15

You have made us for yourself, O Lord, and our hearts are restless until they rest in you.

— St. Augustine of Hippo (354-430), Christian theologian and philosopher, from *Confessions*, ca. 397

Unless the LORD builds the house, they labor in vain who build it.

— Psalm 127:1a (NASB)

Parents! The work entrusted to us is holier than we know. The precious instrument, so delicate, so wonderfully made, so marred by sin already, and so exposed to its power, is of such inconceivable worth. To take charge of an immortal soul, to train a will for God and eternity, surely we ought to shrink from it. But we cannot. If we are parents, the duty is laid upon us. But, thank God! Sufficient grace is prepared and promised, too. If we do but give up our home and our life to God for Him to come in and rule, He will Himself take possession, and by the gentle influence of His Holy Spirit bow their will to Himself.

— Rev. Andrew Murray, *The Children for Christ*, 1887

It ought to be so, in every well-ordered home, that a child can find more pleasure at home than away from home...Wiser parents secure to their children such home amusements as cannot be indulged in to the same advantage outside of that home.

— H. Clay Trumbull, *Hints on Child-Training*, 1890

Three Priorities of a Christian Home

Every Christian parent will readily affirm that their children are being raised in a Christian home. Probe a little deeper, though, and you'll find that often what they really mean is that their children are being raised in a Christian culture. Let me state what should be obvious, but isn't: Christian activities and interests do not make a home Christian. A Christian home is never defined by what the children are doing; it is defined by what the parents are doing. Your child could study the Bible every day, listen only to Christian music, watch only Christian videos, read missionary biographies, know a zillion memory verses, and never miss Sunday School or Bible Club, yet still not live in a Christian home. Simply deciding as a Christian parent to homeschool your children does not mean they will be raised in a Christian home. You can bring your children home for the right reasons, but without the right biblical perspective you might be just adding another activity to their lives and to yours. As good as homeschooling can be, it's only part of the picture.

A Christian home is one in which the parents purposefully keep Jesus Christ at the center of every area of family life. You choose to build your house upon the rock of Christ and his words and then to bring up your children "in the training and instruction of the Lord." That is why this book is about much more than just homeschooling; it is about building a Christian home. Even though most of the book is about home education, you cannot really understand that priority without understanding it as one of the three biblical priorities that we believe define a Christian home: home nurture, home discipleship, and home education. Each of these three priorities builds upon the one before it and supports the one following it. Each is necessary if you are committed to becoming a Christian homeschooling family in a well-balanced Christian home. Each is critical for shepherding, shaping, and strengthening your child for God.

HOME NURTURE: Shepherding Your Child's Spirit to Long for God

Home nurture is bringing the life of Christ into your home. Many Christian parents mistakenly believe this is accomplished only by adopting a Christian lifestyle. While certainly part of the process, the heart of home nurture is bringing the living Christ into all that you do through the life of the Holy Spirit and through the living and active Word of God. A Christian lifestyle alone might cause your children to long for Christianity, but only regular exposure to the living God will cause them to long for Christ. When you understand the power of home nurture, you realize you are shepherding your children's hearts and planting seeds of longing for the living God. You are giving them life.

HOME DISCIPLESHIP: Shaping Your Child's Heart to Live for God

Home discipleship is the process of leading your children to follow and serve Christ as Lord. It is one thing to know the language and lifestyle of Christianity, but it is quite another to know Christ. Home discipleship is how you as a parent not only instruct your children about Christ but also model the life of Christ for them and lead them into a relationship and daily walk with him. You do that by studying Scripture together, reading and discussing inspiring and challenging Christian books, and getting involved in church and community ministry as a family. It is the process of walking with your children on God's path of life until they begin to walk that path on their own with God.

HOME EDUCATION: Strengthening Your Child's Mind to Learn for God

Home education, then, is the natural outgrowth of home nurture and home discipleship. Your goal is not just an educated child, good SAT scores, and college or even a career with a good salary. Those may be fruits of your efforts, but your overriding goal should be to raise spiritually mature children who have both the will and the skill to learn and the desire and ability to keep learning. That is the goal of WholeHearted Learning. Your goal in home education should be to raise well-rounded, spiritually grounded, truth-founded Christian children whose goal in life is to make a difference for the kingdom of God, whatever life path they choose. You're actually raising future Christian adults.

It's important to understand, though, that there is no biblical formula for building a Christian home. We can define the principles that we believe provide the major building blocks of a Christian home, but like everything else in the Christian life, how you express and live out those principles is all by faith. At its simplest, it is really just a relational process of loving God and loving your children. In fact, like the Christian life, most of the process of building a Christian home is simply a matter of walking daily in the power of the Holy Spirit, praying for wisdom, and stepping out in faith. That is what will define your home as a Christian home—that you, the parents, with God's help, are nurturing, discipling, and educating your children at home for Christ.

Home for Good, Home for God

When you decide to keep or bring your children home for good, you are saying two things: (1) that your home is where they should be and (2) that your home is a source of goodness in their lives. You don't have to look very long or hard at the state of culture to see a rapid deterioration of truth, values, and morality. You rightly worry about so many negative influences that could lead your precious children away from God's goodness and grace and even away from you. Home is a place, by God's design, where you can shield them from those negative influences, protect their innocence, and preserve the good in their hearts and minds. Home is good, but that's only half the solution.

When you also bring your children home for God, you are saying two more things: (1) that your home will give God the most undistracted access to their hearts and minds and (2) that your home will give you the greatest freedom to influence them for God for their entire childhood. When your children are home, they are in the best place to experience the presence of God in their lives, either directly in a childlike-faith kind of way under your guidance or indirectly through watching, listening to, and learning from your own relationship with God. You can limit negative and unnecessary influences that would distract them from God, and you have complete freedom to speak God's love, grace, and truth into their lives without competition from voices that do not share your convictions. Bringing your children home for good keeps out the negative influences that could lead them away from God's path of life, and bringing them home for God puts in the positive influences that will keep them on the path of life with God.

This book is mostly about home education. But we want to help you see that the home life you are seeking is also about home nurture and home discipleship. When all three of those priorities come together in one place in your home, you'll be able to say with confidence that you brought your children home for good and home for God.

Fathers, do not exasperate your children; instead, bring them up in the training and instruction of the Lord.

— Ephesians 6:4

How many parents there are...who are readier to provide playthings for their children than to share the delights of their children with those playthings; readier to set their children at knowledge-seeking, than to have a part in their children's surprises and enjoyments of knowledge-attaining; readier to make good, as far as they can, all losses to their children, than to grieve with their children over those losses. And what a loss of power to those parents as parents, is this lack of sympathy with their children as children.

— H. Clay Trumbull, Hints on Child-Training, 1890

Your statutes are wonderful; therefore I obey them. The unfolding of your words gives light; it gives understanding to the simple. I open my mouth and pant, longing for your commands. Turn to me and have mercy on me, as you always do to those who love your name. Direct my footsteps according to your word; let no sin rule over me. Redeem me from the oppression of men, that I may obey your precepts. Make your face shine upon your servant and teach me your decrees. Streams of tears flow from my eyes, for your law is not obeyed.

— Psalm 119:129-136

For the word of God is living and active. Sharper than any double-edged sword, it penetrates even to dividing soul and spirit, joints and marrow; it judges the thoughts and attitudes of the heart. Nothing in all creation is hidden from God's sight. Everything is uncovered and laid bare before the eyes of him to whom we must give account.

— Hebrews 4:12-13

Homeschooling by the Book

As *Educating the WholeHearted Child* grew from workshop and seminar notes into its first incarnation in 1994, it became clear to us very early on that this was not going to be a "passionate defense of homeschooling as an alternative education" kind of book. We were never driven by the need to marshal all the evidence to prove that homeschooling is a valid educational alternative or to argue why it is more desirable than its public and private counterparts. Frankly, many other writers have done a much better job of making those kinds of arguments than we can or will. We simply assumed the validity and desirability of homeschooling from the beginning. We realized that what we were writing was not just about why to choose homeschooling over other more conventional educational options but even more about why to choose homeschooling because it is the fullest expression of a biblical Christian family lifestyle. Rather than being the discovery of something new, we saw homeschooling as the recovery of something old—the recovery of the biblical home as God had designed it to be his primary institution for spreading his righteousness from one generation to the next. Rather than writing about homeschooling by the numbers, as though there were some simple formula for success, we were writing about homeschooling by the Book and the challenge to live by faith by the biblical design, principles, and vision of a wholehearted Christian home.

You will find some content in this chapter and throughout the book that sounds like a defense of homeschooling, but in reality it is there to provide insight and perspective that you can use to gain confidence as a Christian homeschooling parent that what you are doing is God's will for your family and is a sound biblical choice for building a Christian home. If you think all you need is a simple pro/con analysis of homeschooling, public schooling, and private schooling so you can pick the one with the most plus marks or the highest score, then this book might be somewhat frustrating unless you're willing to add all the biblical and spiritual arguments into your analysis chart. We wrote this book to give Christian homeschooling families not just a reasoned justification for their choice for bringing their children home but a truly biblical vision and foundation for it. We are convinced that homeschooling is a movement of God in our times, and our heart is to spread that vision for Christian homeschooling to other families.

It is not our intention to suggest that there is a definable or defensible doctrine or theology of homeschooling in the Bible. However, Scripture is filled with principles and truths that inform, undergird, suggest, reflect, and reinforce homeschooling beliefs and practices. What it teaches, admonishes, and illustrates about children, parents, home, and family is consistent with biblically based expressions of Christian homeschooling, such as the WholeHearted Learning model. When all of the relevant scriptures are taken as a whole and taken seriously, it is difficult to deny their affirmation of Christian home education as a major component of the fullest expression of a Christian home.

The rest of this chapter is a suggestive, but certainly not exhaustive, collection of scriptures you can consider as confirmations of your choice to homeschool your children. Each page represents a different perspective on why homeschooling is a biblical choice for your family. You can study each page individually or discuss it as a couple or family. Some of the scriptures are specific, others more general. Let the Word of God direct your heart as you consider making homeschooling a part of your Christian home.

Ten Good Biblical Reasons for Homeschooling

1. Homeschooling best reflects the Old Testament model for family that is closest to God's original design.

> Deuteronomy 5:16, 6:4-9; Psalm 78:1-8; Psalm 127:3-5

2. Homeschooling best reflects the New Testament principles of Christian home and family roles and relationships.

> Ephesians 6:1-4; Titus 2:3-5; 1 Thessalonians 2:7-12

3. Homeschooling allows the greatest opportunity for emphasizing the Word of God in a child's life.

> 2 Timothy 3:16-17; Hebrews 4:12-13; 1 Thessalonians 2:13

4. Homeschooling allows the greatest opportunity for building wisdom and discernment in a child's life.

> Proverbs 1:1-9; Matthew 7:24-27; James 1:5-8

5. Homeschooling allows the greatest opportunity for strategic discipleship influence in a child's life.

> Luke 6:40; Matthew 28:18-20; Colossians 2:6-7; 2 Timothy 2:2

6. Homeschooling provides the best setting for personalized learning through natural, biblical relationships.

> Philippians 4:8-9; 2 Timothy 3:14-15; 1 Thessalonians 2:7-12

7. Homeschooling provides the best setting for self-motivated learning through reading and real books.

> Joshua 1:8; Psalm 1; 2 Timothy 4:13

8. Homeschooling provides the best setting for dynamic learning through exposure to real-life experiences.

> James 1:2-4, 19-27; Proverbs

9. Homeschooling provides the best setting for discovering and developing spiritual gifts and personal skills and talents.

> 1 Peter 4:10-11; Colossians 3:17; 2 Timothy 1:6-7

10. Homeschooling is the best way to live out the biblical picture of walking with your children on God's path of life until they walk it on their own.

> Proverbs 4:1-19, 22:6; John 14:6; Ephesians 5:1-2

NOTE: The scriptures listed for the ten points are meant to be suggestive only, not exhaustive. There are many more scriptures that could be added to each point.

All Scripture is God-breathed and is useful for teaching, rebuking, correcting and training in righteousness, so that the man of God may be thoroughly equipped for every good work.
— 2 Timothy 3:16-17

I tell you the truth, unless a kernel of wheat falls to the ground and dies, it remains only a single seed. But if it dies, it produces many seeds. The man who loves his life will lose it, while the man who hates his life in this world will keep it for eternal life. Whoever serves me must follow me; and where I am, my servant also will be. My Father will honor the one who serves me.

— John 12:24-26

Then Jesus said to his disciples, "If anyone would come after me, he must deny himself and take up his cross and follow me. For whoever wants to save his life will lose it, but whoever loses his life for me will find it. What good will it be for a man if he gains the whole world, yet forfeits his soul? Or what can a man give in exchange for his soul? For the Son of Man is going to come in his Father's glory with his angels, and then he will reward each person according to what he has done.

— Matthew 16:24-27

Suppose one of you wants to build a tower. Will he not first sit down and estimate the cost to see if he has enough money to complete it? For if he lays the foundation and is not able to finish it, everyone who sees it will ridicule him, saying, "This fellow began to build and was not able to finish." Or suppose a king is about to go to war against another king. Will he not first sit down and consider whether he is able with ten thousand men to oppose the one coming against him with twenty thousand? If he is not able, he will send a delegation while the other is still a long way off and will ask for terms of peace. In the same way, any of you who does not give up everything he has cannot be my disciple.

— Luke 14:28-33

Counting the Cost Before You Begin

Christianity is not neutral. Neither is Christian home education. There is always a cost to accepting the cross, whether it is in your career, marriage, lifestyle, family, or your homeschool. If you decide to keep or bring your children home, you will have to make some sacrifices—there will be a cost. However, the temporal and eternal benefits in your family's life will be worth the sacrifices you will make.

Home education is a ministry of discipleship with much the same concerns as Jesus addressed. You are building your child into a disciple, so you must be committed to finishing what you start. You are heading into a battle, so you must be prepared to face and fight that battle wisely. Whether building or battling, you are taking up the cross for the sake of your children, and the cross always has a cost. Before you take the step into Christian home education, be sure you have honestly counted the cost.

The Cost of Ministry (John 12:24-26)

Am I willing to minister to my children...to become a servant like Jesus, giving up my own life for my children?

Christian home education is a ministry of discipleship and education to your children. It is a powerful biblical way for you to "bring them up in the training and instruction of the Lord." For ministry-minded Christian parents, home education is not simply an educational alternative. Rather, it is an issue of obedience and submission to God's will for their family. Home education is the natural and logical extension of what God, from the beginning, designed the family to be and to do.

The Cost of Lifestyle (Matthew 16:24-27)

Am I willing to accept, along with the joys and blessings, the limitations and sacrifices of the homeschooling lifestyle?

Home education will change your life...literally. The good news is that you will be blessed because of it. The not-so-good news is that you will have to make sacrifices. To be a successful home-educating family, you must be ready to continually, and sometimes radically, adjust your lifestyle to the realities of home education. It will impact every area of your life: home life, church involvement, leisure time, income, adult social life, your children's friendships, housekeeping, and more. It is not small change.

The Cost of Commitment (Luke 14:28-33)

Am I willing to take a step of faith, trusting God to provide and intending in my heart to persevere in that decision?

Home education is not something you casually fit into your calendar or make room for in your schedule. It is a commitment you make to God and to your family that will require perseverance, energy, and patience. You cannot buy a homeschooling kit that will make you instantly and easily successful. It is a long-term learning process, both for you and for your children. Only a prayerful, deliberate commitment before God will sustain you through the difficulties and challenges you will face in that process.

Be Sure It Is God's Will for Your Family

If you have counted the cost, then you are ready to decide if Christian home education is God's will for your family. Be sure that your decision is a matter of conviction that has come from earnestly seeking God and hearing him speak to your heart through his Word. If home education is not a matter of faith for you, then you very likely will not last as a Christian home educator. If it is a matter of God's will for you, then step out in faith, without doubting, and do it (James 1:2-8). God will honor your faith and enable you to do his will.

The pages that follow contain some selected scriptures to help you gain biblical perspective and insight as you seek to discern God's will concerning home education for you and your family. Listen to and carefully consider what God has to say to you about your children's Christian training, home life, and education. If you're not sure about what it means to know God's will for your life, first take some time to consider the scriptures in the sidebar and the biblical insights below.

God's will is not something hidden that needs to be found; it is something revealed that waits to be done.

The Holy Spirit — The first step in knowing God's will is to know Christ as your personal Savior and to be filled with the Holy Spirit. The Holy Spirit gives us the mind of Christ. You cannot know and do God's will if you are walking in the flesh. You must walk in the Spirit. (Romans 8:5-8; 1 Corinthians 2:11-16; Galatians 5:16; 1 Peter 4:6)

Stewardship — In the case of home education, God's will is mostly a matter of stewardship: What is the best stewardship of the home and children that God has entrusted to you? Regardless of your feelings or circumstances, Scripture calls you to be a good steward or manager of all God has entrusted to your care. Your home and children are certainly among your most valuable possessions in this life. (Romans 12:1-2; 1 Timothy 6:17-19)

Obedience — What is God saying to you through his Word? Are you sensing the conviction of the Holy Spirit in the area of becoming a more godly parent? Are there direct commands of Scripture concerning your children that you need to obey? If you sense God's leading in your life, it will become an issue of obedience. (John 14:15-17)

Discernment — Determining God's will is primarily the exercise of godly discernment concerning the choices and decisions you make. God's Word and his Spirit are his means to help you develop spiritual discernment and wisdom. The more you study the Word of God and walk in the Spirit, the more discerning you will become. (Philippians 1:9-10)

Prayer — Doing God's will always involves persistent prayer—asking God for wisdom, discernment, and direction. As God speaks to you through his Word, you speak to him in prayer about what he is saying to you. That ongoing prayer relationship is essential to the process of decision making. (Philippians 4:6-7)

Wise Counsel — God will often speak through other godly, wise Christians to make his will clear to you—to clarify confusion, affirm a conviction, or confirm a decision you have made. Seek out the insights of trusted friends, godly homeschoolers, and wise counselors. Ask them to pray for you. Listen to their counsel. (Proverbs 15:22)

If any of you lacks wisdom, he should ask God, who gives generously to all without finding fault, and it will be given to him. But when he asks, he must believe and not doubt, because he who doubts is like a wave of the sea, blown and tossed by the wind.

— James 1:5-6

Be very careful, then, how you live—not as unwise but as wise, making the most of every opportunity, because the days are evil. Therefore do not be foolish, but understand what the Lord's will is.

— Ephesians 5:15-17

Trust in the LORD with all your heart and lean not on your own understanding; in all your ways acknowledge him, and he will make your paths straight.

— Proverbs 3:5-6

But seek first his kingdom and his righteousness, and all these things will be given to you as well. Therefore do not worry about tomorrow, for tomorrow will worry about itself. Each day has enough trouble of its own.

— Matthew 6:33-34

Do not conform any longer to the pattern of this world, but be transformed by the renewing of your mind. Then you will be able to test and approve what God's will is—his good, pleasing and perfect will.

— Romans 12:2

Therefore everyone who hears these words of mine and puts them into practice is like a wise man who built his house on the rock. The rain came down, the streams rose, and the winds blew and beat against that house; yet it did not fall, because it had its foundation on the rock.

— Matthew 7:24-25

Do not be deceived: God cannot be mocked. A man reaps what he sows. The one who sows to please his sinful nature, from that nature will reap destruction; the one who sows to please the Spirit, from the Spirit will reap eternal life. Let us not become weary in doing good, for at the proper time we will reap a harvest if we do not give up.

— Galatians 6:7-9

Do not store up for yourselves treasures on earth, where moth and rust destroy, and where thieves break in and steal. But store up for yourselves treasures in heaven, where moth and rust do not destroy, and where thieves do not break in and steal. For where your treasure is, there your heart will be also.

— Matthew 6:19-21

I am not saying this because I am in need, for I have learned to be content whatever the circumstances. I know what it is to be in need, and I know what it is to have plenty. I have learned the secret of being content in any and every situation, whether well fed or hungry, whether living in plenty or in want. I can do everything through him who gives me strength.

— Philippians 4:11-13

Biblical Principles to Consider

Renew your mind. (Romans 12:1-2)

Most people's thinking about education is influenced and shaped by, and often conformed to, the philosophies and thinking of the world. Despite many successful alternative approaches, public education is still the default standard by which any educational models or materials are evaluated. But God commands us to be transformed by renewing our minds with his truth so we can think like he thinks. He doesn't want us thinking about anything by default. And that includes our thinking about parenting and education.

Build on truth. (Matthew 7:24-27)

Some very dangerous cultural storms are looming on the horizon. You will face some as a home-educating parent, and your children will face them as adults. These storms will tear apart many families who are unprepared. You and your children, though, can stand strong and stay faithful in the face of them if you build your house on the secure foundation of God and his Word. Any foundation other than God's truth will be sandy ground that will wash away in the storms and floods of life. Your house wouldn't stand a chance. But God's truth is solid rock. Build the house of your family on truth and stand.

Sow for the Spirit. (Galatians 6:7-9)

You will reap in your children's lives exactly what you sow in them as a parent. If you want to reap secure, mature adults, you must sow by the Spirit the seeds of time, togetherness, and training. If you want to reap a godly heritage, you must sow by the Spirit the seeds of godly influence. If you want to reap godly character, you must sow by the Spirit the seeds of a good example. You can no longer sow to please your own desires, but to please Christ. Only he can cause your seed to grow and produce a harvest of blessing. You are sowing for temporal fruit with eternity in mind.

Value the eternal. (Matthew 6:19-24)

Your children are your most valuable assets. They are priceless, eternal treasures entrusted to you by God. They are yours for a short time, after which you will present them back to God. He has given them to you to invest for eternity. If you treasure those young lives, that is where your heart will be—reproduced in their hearts. If you treasure the things of this world, though, you will have missed the opportunity to touch their hearts for God. You must decide what, or who, is going to matter most to you this side of eternity. For "where your treasure is, there your heart will be also." In other words, the designs of your mind will define the desires of your heart.

Be content in Christ. (Philippians 4:10-13)

A decision to homeschool is also a decision to accept limitations on your life. Your expectations of adult life will be greatly limited by the realities of home education. The more you resist those limitations, the less content you will be. Contentedness grows as you learn to submit to those limitations. God has promised that you can do everything through Christ, who gives you strength. You can sacrifice, serve, and learn to be content with whatever lifestyle God has for you. You can be content as a home educator.

Specific Scriptures to Consider

About Parenting

Ephesians 6:4; Colossians 3:21 — How can I make sure that I am obeying God's commands to raise my children for him and to train them in righteousness?

Deuteronomy 6:4-9 — How can I make sure that my children's training in righteousness is consistent and continuous and that it is a whole-life, "everywhere, all the time" process?

Psalm 78:1-7 — How can I make sure that I pass on a godly and righteous heritage to my children and to their children and that nothing of eternal value is hidden from them?

Psalm 127:3-5 — How can I make sure that my children know they are valued blessings in my house, not burdens, and that they are arrows of God's truth to the world?

1 Timothy 3:4; Titus 1:6 — How can I make sure that my household is managed well and my children are "under control" as a testimony of my maturity?

About Your Children

Proverbs 2:11-12, 22:6 — How can I make sure that my children are disciplined to go in the way they should go so that they will not be misled off the path of righteousness?

Matthew 18:5-6 — How can I make sure that I am not putting my children in situations where they will be tempted to sin, or even worse, which will cause them to sin?

Proverbs 13:20; 1 Corinthians 15:33 — How can I make sure that my children walk with "the wise" and do not become harmed as the "companion of fools"?

2 Corinthians 6:14 — How can I make sure that my children do not become spiritually, emotionally, or socially "yoked together with unbelievers" as light with darkness?

2 Timothy 2:16-19 — How can I make sure that my children are not under the authority and influence of false teachers or false teaching that would lead them to ungodliness?

About the Christian Life

Romans 12:1-2 — How can I make sure that my children do not become conformed to the world (its ways of thinking), but are transformed by the renewing of their minds?

1 John 2:15-17 — How can I make sure that my children are taught to love God and to do his will and are not taught to love the world or anything in the world?

Proverbs 4:23 — How can I make sure that I am guarding my children's hearts against all ungodly influences that can adversely shape their beliefs and attitudes?

Ephesians 5:11-12 — How can I make sure that my children are not enticed by the "fruitless deeds of darkness" or exposed to those things God calls "shameful"?

Philippians 4:8 — How can I make sure that my children's minds are filled with and trained to think about only those things that God considers excellent and worthy of praise?

Children, obey your parents in everything, for this pleases the Lord. Fathers, do not embitter your children, or they will become discouraged..

— Colossians 3:20-21

We will not hide them from their children; we will tell the next generation the praiseworthy deeds of the LORD, his power, and the wonders he has done.

— Psalm 78:4

My son, do not reject the discipline of the LORD or loathe His reproof, for whom the Lord loves He reproves, even as a father corrects the son in whom he delights.

— Proverbs 2:11-12 (NASB)

Train a child in the way he should go, and when he is old he will not turn from it.

— Proverbs 22:6 (NASB)

So do not throw away your confidence; it will be richly rewarded. You need to persevere so that when you have done the will of God, you will receive what he has promised. For in just a very little while, "He who is coming will come and will not delay. But my righteous one will live by faith. And if he shrinks back, I will not be pleased with him." But we are not of those who shrink back and are destroyed, but of those who believe and are saved.

— Hebrews 10:35-39

Now faith is being sure of what we hope for and certain of what we do not see...And without faith it is impossible to please God, because anyone who comes to him must believe that he exists and that he rewards those who earnestly seek him.

— Hebrews 11:1, 6

All these people were still living by faith when they died. They did not receive the things promised; they only saw them and welcomed them from a distance. And they admitted that they were aliens and strangers on earth. People who say such things show that they are looking for a country of their own...Therefore God is not ashamed to be called their God, for he has prepared a city for them.

— Hebrews 11:13-14, 16b

Therefore, since we are surrounded by such a great cloud of witnesses, let us throw off everything that hinders and the sin that so easily entangles, and let us run with perseverance the race marked out for us. Let us fix our eyes on Jesus, the author and perfecter of our faith, who for the joy set before him endured the cross, scorning its shame, and sat down at the right hand of the throne of God. Consider him who endured such opposition from sinful men, so that you will not grow weary and lose heart.

— Hebrews 12:1-3

Be Ready to Live by Faith

There are many reasoned and rational arguments you can make to justify and defend homeschooling. There's only one, though, that closes off debate: "We searched the Scriptures, prayed about it, and determined it is God's will for our family to homeschool." At that point, it is no longer an opinion but an issue of conviction, obedience, and faith. Good arguments alone will not carry you very far as a home educator. When you're up to your eyeballs with children, housework, home business, activities, responsibilities, bills, broken appliances, car problems, and you-don't-know-the-troubles-I've-seen circumstances, those nicely reasoned arguments will ring pretty hollow. When you're pushed to the limits, only a tested and seasoned faith will take you beyond.

That was where many Jews found themselves as new Christians after being scattered throughout Israel in the persecution that followed Stephen's martyrdom. For a time, they lived by their newfound faith, holding on to the apostles' teachings. But then they began to grow weary and to shrink back from the life of faith. There probably will come a time when you, too, will be tempted to shrink back from what God has called you to do in your family. If that happens, read Hebrews 10-12 and then come back to this page to do this study so you can hear God say to you, as he said to those first Christians: "So do not throw away your confidence; it will be richly rewarded. You need to persevere so that when you have done the will of God, you will receive what he has promised."

Hebrews 10:35-39 — Perseverance: The Mark of Faith

What could cause you to want to throw away your confidence in God's presence and work in your life? In what ways do you need to persevere in doing the will of God? How does the promise of Christ's return and his rewards affect your faith?

Hebrews 11:1, 6 — Belief: The Proof of Faith

What do you hope for with a surety that affects how you live? What spiritual realities are you certain about even though you do not see them? When is your faith enough to please God? Do you really believe that God exists? How, exactly, do you seek him?

Hebrews 11:1-38 — Faithfulness: The Example of Faith

Which examples of living by faith mentioned in this chapter touch your spirit? Why? What can you learn from them? What would you want to be said about you?

Hebrews 11:39-40 — Hope: The Promise of Faith

What was the promise that kept all those mentioned in chapter 11 living by faith (see verses 1, 2, 9, 10, 13-16)? What does that promise mean to you? How does it affect the way you live? Do your children know what the promise means to you?

Hebrews 12:1-3 — Endurance: The Strength of Faith

Are you encouraged by the testimonies of the great cloud of witnesses in chapter 11? What hindrances slow you down in your race? What sins, big or little, entangle you and trip you up? Do you fix your eyes on Jesus or on the distractions around you? Do you think about him when you grow weary and lose heart? Fix your eyes on Jesus!

— Chapter 2—

The Christian Homeschool: Learning at Home to Be with Christ

Starting with a Heart for Home Education

It has been interesting over the years to observe the responses of Christian parents who do not homeschool when they learn that we do homeschool. Though we rarely initiate the topic, they almost always volunteer an assessment of themselves, as though our just being there compels them to say something. There are generally three kinds: (1) those who approve of homeschooling, (2) those who do not approve (whether reasonably or unreasonably), and (3) those who say, "Oh, I could never do that." Most in that third group are sincere and generally are not negative about homeschooling, but they are expressing a myth that keeps many good families from ever even considering homeschooling. It is the myth of qualification: "I don't know enough to homeschool my children."

The myth that you must have some kind of higher education in order to give your children a good education suggests that being smart is more important in homeschooling than being committed. It isn't. When we were on staff with a large Christian organization, we often heard that the real standard of our qualifications to serve others was being FAT: Faithful, Available, and Teachable. That is true of the Christian homeschooling parent as well. To really serve your children, you will need to be faithful to God's ideals for your family, available to God and to your children, and, yes, teachable. You need to be ready to learn new things. It doesn't matter that you don't know everything about all that you want to teach your children (none of us does), but it matters much that you are ready and willing to learn with them. Your influence in your children's lives is not derived from how smart you are, but rather from how committed you are to becoming all that you need to be in order to help them become all that God wants them to be. It is not your responsibility only to give them an education; it is your vision and privilege to guide them into learning, growing, and becoming...with you.

Whatever you do for your children's education, it should be clear from the previous chapter that at the very least you need to be committed to building a Christian home. Christian homeschooling is about having a heart for building a home that includes learning together as a family, knowing that process will bring you together in a way nothing else can. Making that commitment, though, requires you to have the heart attitude that you are just as excited about what you can learn as a home-educating parent as you are about what your children can learn at home. Your confidence will not be shaken by the myth of qualification. Your vision will not be blurred by the challenge of growing personally to be a better home educator. Your commitment will not be weakened by fears or feelings of inadequacy. This chapter will help to strengthen your confidence in homeschooling, but never lose sight of the bigger vision—that you are choosing to learn at home so you can experience Christ more as a family.

I am much afraid that schools will prove the great gates of hell unless they diligently labor in explaining the Holy Scriptures, engraving them in the hearts of youth. I advise no one to place his child where the Scriptures do not reign paramount. Every institution in which men are not increasingly occupied with the Word of God must become corrupt.

— Martin Luther (1483-1546), German priest and theology professor, founder of the Protestant Reformation

Just as the family is the only secure basis of the state, so is it the only safe basis of true education...In a happy-go-lucky way we have become accustomed to think of school and study as something to which the child must inevitably proceed at the earliest possible moment. In the same measure we have lost sight of the fact that the school is burdened with parental responsibility because home training in our day is grossly neglected. Susanna Wesley taught her children at home, for twenty years carrying on this instruction daily, "not so much," she said, "to train their minds as to save their souls."

— Ella Frances Lynch, *Educating the Child at Home*, 1914

29

You as a parent have a big advantage in teaching your child simply because you are the parent. The most significant people in a young child's life are usually his mom and dad...You may think that you're something less than the world's best parent. You might also think that you can't possibly educate your child as well as a state certified teacher might. But because, subjectively, you are the most significant and important person in the world to your child, you have greater credibility with him and can get more mileage out of instructional time than anyone else could. And that is an objective reality.

— Gregg Harris, *The Christian Home School*, Wolgemuth & Hyatt Publishers, 1988

Be Confident as a Homeschooling Parent

The Scriptures are the basis of your confidence, whatever you do in life. We have found that the best way to make sure that you raise your children according to the principles of Scripture listed in the previous chapter is nurturing, discipling, and educating your children at home. If home education is biblical and you have determined it is God's will for your family, then you can homeschool with confidence. There is no biblical argument for putting your children under the shaping influence of other authorities during the most formative and impressionable years of their lives. American cultural norms notwithstanding, doing so runs counter to the biblical concept of the family, and it is in conflict with how we are wired as mothers and fathers by God. If family is God's design for raising children, then a spiritually sensitive parent should not be surprised to feel conflict when faced with the choice to allow others to raise them for half or more of their childhood waking hours. It should be natural to want to keep your children home to raise them.

On the other hand, keeping your children at home only because you want to keep them protected from the negative influences of the public school is shortsighted. Home education is not just a reaction to the moral decay in our culture—it is a proactive decision about what is the best way to raise and educate children. The best motivation for home educating is that you have decided, before God, that it is the right thing to do for your family. Again, the Scriptures should be your confidence, not the latest statistics on public schools' moral and academic failure. More than just a reactionary decision, home education is a gift you give to your children. You give them the opportunity to experience childhood and growing up the way God intended them to be, all within the context of home and family. You give them a sense of wholeness and rightness that only a Christian home can provide. You give them time and space, with you beside them, to become secure, mature Christian adults. If your family is reasonably mature and stable, you can be confident—without doubts or apologies—that your children will be better off at home with you. God designed your home for your children, and it is right that they should live and learn there until they are ready to leave home.

God's principles are like a strong river flowing through your children's lives and yours. If you ignore those principles and attempt to swim against their current, you will make little progress. If, however, you submit to those principles and swim with the current, you will find a natural strength and power as you are carried along in the flow. As you cooperate with God's eternal design—built into our very nature as fathers, mothers, sons, and daughters—you will experience an undeniable sense of rightness and release. You will know, deep down, that home education is the right thing to do because it is what God designed you to do. Unfortunately, even though you may be going with the flow, you'll soon discover some rocks in your river: critics, skeptics, and sometimes just people with honest questions. The knowledge that you home educate your children will draw several predictable responses from non-home-educators. If you have made your decision to home educate based on the Scriptures, you have no reason to let criticism shake your confidence. The following pages explore five of the most common questions raised about homeschooling and present a confident home educator's response and defense. You don't need to win the argument; just make the point gently and with the confidence that you are doing God's will for your family.

Know What to Do When Cornered by a Critic

Most people who have questions about homeschooling simply want to understand it better. They are curious, but not critical. However, you will also run into the occasional true critic. Always remember that these vocal adversaries of homeschooling are not neutral. You can generally assume their criticisms have been cooking for some time, and you just happen to be the one who gets to taste what's in their mental oven. You don't have to swallow their arguments, but don't throw them back in their face either. Your "gentle answer" may help convert a critic into a an inquirer and maybe even a friend. Here's what to do when cornered by a critic:

- **Be open.** Above all, be patient and attentive. Let them have their say. Simply listening to a critic may be the first step toward winning them over.

- **Be instructive.** Consider it an opportunity to gently educate. If they are receptive, suggest a noncontroversial book about family or homeschooling they might want to read. If they are resistant, simply ask about their family and move on.

- **Be self-controlled.** Stay in control of your emotions. Becoming defensive and angry will only polarize the issues and convince your critic that homeschoolers are extremists. If you answer gently and patiently but with conviction, you may not win the immediate debate, but you won't lose the opportunity for future discussion.

- **Be humble.** Don't be overzealous to defend homeschooling. Offer responses to criticisms only if there is sufficient time for discussion and you can do so confidently and knowledgeably. Otherwise, suggest getting together later to discuss it over a meal.

- **Be restrained.** Don't let an itchy trigger finger unload on your critic with all your best-shot arguments for homeschooling. They'll start shooting back, and you'll both end up emotionally wounded and angered by the exchange.

- **Be thick-skinned.** Don't take your critic's criticism personally. Depersonalize and generalize your response as much as possible. Listen patiently and politely, and share your own thoughts gently and graciously. "A gentle answer turns away wrath."

IN OUR HOME

It doesn't happen that often, but occasionally we will have a guest in our home who feels comfortable letting us know that they really question homeschooling. Rather than engaging them in the debate or giving them a guided tour of our learning room, library, and discovery corners, we simply redirect the discussion and give a positive testimony about our own experience. We might talk about a recent novel we read out loud as a family together, an especially interesting field trip, or a musical event we attended. But the best way we have found to quell any questions is to have our children in the room. We train them early how to engage in conversation with adults, ask good questions, listen well, and be polite. In comparison to the average child or teen, they really are our best arguments for the positive benefits of homeschooling.

A gentle answer turns away wrath, but a harsh word stirs up anger.

— Proverbs 15:1

But in your hearts set apart Christ as Lord. Always be prepared to give an answer to everyone who asks you to give the reason for the hope that you have. But do this with gentleness and respect, keeping a clear conscience, so that those who speak maliciously against your good behavior in Christ may be ashamed of their slander. It is better, if it is God's will, to suffer for doing good than for doing evil.

— 1 Peter 3:15-17

Good philosophy must exist, if for no other reason, because bad philosophy needs to be answered.

— C. S. Lewis (1898-1963), British author, academic, and Christian apologist

Why Homeschool?

According to a 2007 study by the National Center for Education Statistics (U.S. Department of Education, Institute of Education Sciences), homeschooling parents were asked which one of their selected reasons for homeschooling was the most important. (Most parents homeschool for a variety of reasons.) The top three were:

- Provide religious or moral instruction, 36 percent
- Concern about the school environment, 21 percent
- Dissatisfaction with the academic instruction available at other schools, 17 percent

Understand the Questions and the Answers

Let's be realistic. Homeschooling can seem pretty radical to the average person. It is a nonconformist educational movement in a culture that has invested heavily for at least six generations in first a common school and then a public school system that requires conformity for it to work well. Institutional or public (government-run) schooling is now so entrenched in our American experience and mindset that most citizens never even think to question its existence or its effectiveness. The modern homeschool movement will likely require a few more generations of success and integration into culture before it will be widely acknowledged as a valid form of education with the same level of acceptance that public and private schooling now enjoy.

Given its relatively short history since the early 1980s, it is quite natural for people to have questions about homeschooling. Of course, there are those in the national educational establishment who are opposed to even the idea of homeschooling, which by its nature elevates the role of untrained parents in education above that of trained, professional teachers. Homeschooling challenges an entrenched system of education, cultural values, and history. However, most average people have real, reasonable questions about homeschooling. You have an opportunity to sway their opinion and perhaps even win a follower if you can offer good, thoughtful answers to their questions.

The Legislation Question

"It's not right to keep children out of school. Shouldn't the government ensure that every child gets a full and proper education in a good school?"

The Education Question

"You can't really give your children all the benefits at home that they would have in a school. Aren't you depriving them of a much better education?"

The Socialization Question

"Homeschooled children seem so isolated at home. How will your children ever be able to function in the real world unless they are in school?"

The Qualification Question

"I don't think being a good parent is enough for a child. How can you possibly provide as good an education as a professionally trained teacher?"

The Reputation Question

"I hear so many disturbing news stories about homeschooling families. Don't you think homeschooling is an unusual and extreme thing to do?"

The remainder of this chapter presents some of the answers you can give to these inevitable questions. Due to space limitations, they will be very brief answers, but they will nonetheless provide a starting point for you to give a good answer to people with questions as well as to undergird your own convictions about home education.

Answering the Legislation Question

"Home education is legal in all fifty states. It is widely recognized as a valid educational choice."

Home education has been legal in all fifty states since the mid-nineties, although specific regulatory policies differ widely from state to state. In some states there is essentially no regulation; in others there is much more restrictive regulation. The issues of legality and validity may be largely settled, but regulation of home education will be a continuing concern. The ongoing battle against governmental intrusion into your private family life intensifies with the choice to home educate your children. The regulatory tools of intrusion that might be wielded against home educators are myriad—written reports, curriculum review and approval, home visits, attendance and instructional time record keeping, required testing, and on and on. There is no end to the meddling of bureaucrats, regulatory agents, and politicians with our constitutional freedoms and with our children! Regardless of legal conditions, however, home education is always a legitimate form of educating our children. It may not always be fully validated by the state, but it is certainly validated by Scripture, history, experience, and common sense.

There are two areas are of special concern as the homeschooling movement matures. The first is the possibility of state or federal legislation that would attempt to regulate home educators through teacher qualification requirements, mandatory testing, standards-based educational goals, or other intrusions. This is an ongoing battle at every level of the educational, political, and legal system. The courts are fast becoming a new battleground for the future of homeschooling. The National Education Association, the very powerful and influential U.S. public school teachers' union, is on record opposing home education. The NEA lobby will surely continue its campaign to regulate homeschooling. The second area of concern is the real threat of state social and child protective services agencies initiating actions against homeschooling families. In many areas, these agencies can be relatively unaccountable and able to act on unsubstantiated and anonymous charges. They can be aggressive and intimidating, and they have authority to remove children from the home. The courts are beginning to recognize the unconstitutional scope and power of these agencies, but it is likely to be years before effective safeguards are in place to protect our freedoms.

Because home education is only a tenuous freedom, we strongly recommend all that home-educating families become members of Home School Legal Defense Association (HSLDA). Since 1983 these dedicated Christian home educators have been fighting the legal battles in every state in order to win and secure our freedoms to teach our children at home without governmental intrusion. The very low annual fee (reduced through most state organizations) is not only reasonable; it's a bargain. If you find yourself unexpectedly on the defensive against an aggressive governmental or educational system, your legal representation and fees are completely covered. HSLDA will handle your case. Even if you never need their services, your fees are a small contribution to the ongoing fight for your freedom to home educate. You are contributing to a greater cause and helping other families like yours fight the legal battles that you don't have to fight. Those battles will help win the war for your freedom to homeschool.

Freedom is a fragile commodity. It must be won. It must be maintained. Freedom is not a guarantee. It is something we earn. Earning freedom starts with doing a good job training our children academically, socially, spiritually and morally. Home schooling freedom will continue to advance so long as we continue to pursue excellence in all that we do.

— Michael Farris, "Marking the Milestones: HSLDA 1983-1993"

State Regulations

Don't begin to homeschool or withdraw your children from public school until you know for certain what is required for you to be in compliance with the regulations in your state. State requirements vary greatly, so before taking your first step, call your local and state homeschool organizations, and then call Home School Legal Defense Association (www.HSLDA.org). Don't stay home without them!

My son, if you accept my words and store up my commands within you, turning your ear to wisdom and applying your heart to understanding, and if you call out for insight and cry aloud for understanding, and if you look for it as for silver and search for it as for hidden treasure, then you will understand the fear of the LORD and find the knowledge of God.

— Proverbs 2:1-5

I would rather my child had a limited curriculum and access to limited educational resources, and yet learned by basking in the atmosphere of someone who had true pleasure in the books that were pursued, than that he should go to some well-equipped and soulless situation where, theoretically, he could "learn" at optimum speed.

— Susan Schaeffer Macaulay, *For the Children's Sake*, Crossway, 1984

The purpose of education and the schools is to change the thoughts, feelings and actions of students.

— Prof. Benjamin Bloom, the "father of O.B.E." (Outcome-Based Education, a comprehensive secular methodology that emphasizes attitudinal and values conformity over traditional educational goals), *All Our Children Learning*, 1981

Answering the Education Question

"There is no better learning environment than a loving home and a personal tutor. My children are home because I want them to have the very best education."

Those who question homeschooling often raise the issue of what kind of education your child will receive. Skeptics and critics usually imply, but often blatantly assert, that you are sentencing your child to a second-rate education since you cannot possibly, at home, attain the high standards of education provided by conventional schools. Though you almost certainly will not be able to convert critics through argument, no matter how well-reasoned your position, your children will ultimately be your defense (Psalm 127:5). You can be confident, if you use the educational strengths of your home to their fullest, that your children will graduate from your homeschool not just intellectually prepared, but spiritually and personally prepared too. Against a well-educated, wholehearted homeschool graduate, critics have no defense.

To expose the illogic of the education question, simply turn it around. Why should anyone believe that a depersonalized, institutionalized classroom setting is somehow a superior learning environment? On the contrary, it is the least effective setting for developing self-motivated, free-thinking learners. Age grading (placing at a grade level by birth date) is a necessary element of conventional classroom educational strategy, but it is primarily an administrative standard that is used only to maintain order, which has very little to do with true learning. It results in children being routinely advanced in grade by age without achieving the competencies required for learning in the next grade. Only the average child (whichever one that is) is served by grade-level education. Motivated learners are frustrated by the slow pace, struggling learners by the fast pace. The conventional classroom too easily becomes a controlled environment with little or no freedom or flexibility, in which the noisiest and the neediest 10 percent get most of the teacher's personal attention, while the rest of the students are left to fend for themselves. In most conventional classrooms, whether public or private, there is a great deal of wasted time trying to keep children busy, a default reliance on textbooks and workbooks, and a self-perpetuating dependence on the teacher for learning. This system may be efficient for the classroom, but not for the child.

Your homeschool, in stark contrast, has all the potential to be an ideal learning environment for your child. Remember—God designed homes, not schools, to be the living and learning center of a child's life. When you tap into the natural dynamics of your home, you will liberate learning to be all that God intended it to be for your child. You can balance control and flexibility to meet each child's individual learning needs. You can fill their lives with the best books and resources. You can turn them loose to learn whatever they desire. You can determine readiness for and pace of learning, holding off or jumping ahead of grade level without concern. Because you are training your children for life, not just preparing them to make a living, you can use all of life as a classroom. Real life is always within easy reach. If you use the natural learning environment of your home and family, your homeschool graduates will be exceptional people—well-educated disciples, ready to live godly and productive lives. They deserve the best—your home.

Classroom Education	Home Education
CHILD: Children are part of the group. Classroom education focuses on helping the child conform to group and age-grade standards in order to learn certain things at certain times in certain ways, with limited regard to maturity or ability.	CHILD: Each child is an individual. Home education focuses on the development of the whole person, responsiveness to individual learning needs and desires, and guidance in growing in Christian maturity unrestrained by age/grade limitations.
SETTING: Learning structures are created with a teacher's needs for order, conformity, regimen, and control in mind. Formality is demotivating and stifles children's curiosity, creativity, and natural desire to learn.	SETTING: Learning structures are created with the interests of the child, the home, and the family in mind. Unrestricted time and freedom unleash opportunities to exercise children's curiosity, creativity, and natural desire to learn.
INSTRUCTION: Instruction is often simplified to accommodate the poorest learners in the class. Motivated learners are frustrated by the slow pace, struggling learners by the fast pace. Average learners learn to stay average (to keep the teacher's pace of instruction). Slow learners are stigmatized, and fast learners are ostracized.	INSTRUCTION: Instruction is aimed high to challenge all in the homeschool. Learning abilities can vary without any attached meaning or stigma. All children advance at their own pace. Each child advances according to his own level of learning and motivation. Each child is treated as an individual without reference to others.
ATTENTION: Each child receives only limited individual attention in a class of 20-30 children. A single teacher is not able to respond to every child's individual needs and interests. Concentration can be hindered by the high distraction factor in a noisy, uncomfortable, or open classroom.	ATTENTION: Parents are able to give each child unlimited individual attention in a one-on-one tutoring relationship and to respond to each child's individual needs and interests. Concentration is reinforced by the ability to control and even eliminate distractions to optimal learning.
AUTHORITY: Children learn how to please various teachers. The authority relationships are generally unnatural and formal.	AUTHORITY: Children instinctively want to please their parents. The authority relationship is natural and loving.
MATERIALS: Teacher routinely relies on approved textbooks and workbooks. The teacher is the educational authority. The classroom setting results in a self-perpetuating and necessary dependence on the teacher for learning progress.	MATERIALS: Parents are free to choose the best living books and curricula available. Parents are learning facilitators. Children are trained and expected to depend on their own independent learning abilities and skills to advance.
TIME: Much time is wasted in order to keep students occupied and under control. No real-life learning occurs sitting at a student desk. The instructor teaches much less material in much more time. Most graduate at 18 years of age.	TIME: No time is wasted. All of life is a classroom, so every activity or involvement is a learning opportunity. Parents can teach much more in much less time. Not difficult to graduate several years earlier than standard age/grade.
PROGRESS: Children advance in studies on the basis of age and grade with limited regard for knowledge or competence.	PROGRESS: Children advance in studies on the basis of knowledge and competence without regard for age or grade.
TESTING: Children are tested primarily for short-term linear knowledge (ability to recall facts and information). Retention is low. Written tests, though less effective, are easier to administer and grade; oral testing is generally avoided.	TESTING: Children are tested primarily for long-term global knowledge (ability to grasp ideas and concepts). Retention is high. Written tests are unnecessary; oral testing is more effective and a better indicator of learning.
HOMEWORK: Homework is necessary because of the teaching and learning constraints of conventional schooling.	HOMEWORK: Homework is largely unnecessary because of the integration of home and education, living and learning.
GRADES: Grades are necessary for teachers to be able to control and track the progress of a large class of students.	GRADES: Grades are largely irrelevant. Parents work with the child until the knowledge or skill is acquired.

He who walks with the wise grows wise, but a companion of fools suffers harm.

— Proverbs 13:20

Do not be misled: "Bad company corrupts good character."

— 1 Corinthians 15:33

What about Socialization?

Research studies by educator John Wesley Taylor, Psychologist Mona Maarse Delahooke, and others affirm that home-educated students, in relation to public-school-educated students, are *not* socially deprived. On the contrary, research by Dr. Larry Shyers, Dr. Norma Hedin, Dr. Linda Montgomery, and others reveals a significant advantage for homeschooled children for key social development indicators—they are socially adept, possess a positive self-image, and are active in areas that develop leadership skills. In a 1992 controlled study, Thomas Smedley concluded: "...the home educated children in this sample were significantly better socialized and more mature than those in public school." (Dr. Brian Ray, "Marching to the Beat of Their Own Drum! A Profile of Home Education Research," National Home Education Research Institute, 1992). Nonetheless, a 1995 survey of public school superintendents reported that 92 percent did not believe homeschooled students received adequate socialization experiences.

Answering the Socialization Question

"The family is God's primary institution for the socialization of children. If the goal of socialization is greater maturity, that comes from being around mature adults who love the child."

Every home-educating parent hears it with numbing regularity: "But aren't you afraid they won't get enough socialization?" First, you must understand what is being said. To most non-homeschoolers, socialization really means simply learning to enjoy and get along with friends and classmates of the same age and grade. It's about an experience. To the sociologist or educationalist, it means the process of learning one's culture and how to live within it. It's about conforming. To the biblically-informed Christian homeschooling parent, though, socialization should be about the development of biblical character, personal confidence, and social competence for relating appropriately with grace to other people in any situation. It is about Christian maturity. A properly socialized child, then, knows how to relate well to other people, whether young or old, male or female, rich or poor, different or similar. You can be confident that the Christian home is a far better socializing environment than any form of traditional school. In fact, the conventional classroom gets very poor marks for socialization. Research and testing have consistently shown homeschooled children to be significantly above traditional testing norms for social skills and development and for self-esteem.

The reason seems clear. In the homeschool, the primary models for effective relationships are mature adults—father, mother, grandparents, family, friends. This kind of age-integrated socialization simply does not take place in a traditional school setting, where the models are primarily other foolish, immature children and where there is minimal supervision and intervention by mature adults. In the home, in contrast, social skills are constantly and consistently modeled, trained, and corrected by loving parents. Poor social skills are not allowed to become habituated, and good ones are regularly reinforced.

As to interaction with other children, one wonders how much is enough. Who decided that four to eight hours per day in a school should be the norm for socialization? Why not much more or much less? It really seems like common sense, but studies show that constant and excessive interactions and activities (such as in a school) have a negative impact on children, while limited interactional environments (such as a home) have a positive impact. Homeschooling families can easily find opportunities for interaction with other children through church, field trips, support groups, lessons, sports, service, and many other activities. And all of that time is under the loving supervision of mature adults who have a vested interest in the social development of their children. There is no credible evidence or argument that children are better off socially being in an age-segregated, overactive, unsupervised social setting up to eight hours per day. They are better off at home.

Those who say that homeschooled children aren't in the real world just aren't thinking straight. School is the false world. Never in the rest of their lives will a child be forced to live and interact with twenty to thirty age-mates in a sterile, isolated classroom totally segregated from real living experiences. The true real world of home, family, work, and ministry prepares children to work with people of all ages in actual situations that they will experience as adults. School can't even counterfeit that kind of real-life experience.

Conventional School Socialization	Home School Socialization
GOAL: To ensure that a child conforms to the social norms and knowledge of his age-mates and school. Other relationships, if addressed at all, are peripheral.	GOAL: To teach and train a child how to relate graciously and effectively to other people in all kinds of relationships: siblings, parents, other adults, friends, peers, church.
SCOPE: Relational experiences with school age-mates and a teacher with limited involvement or supervision. Extremely limited range of relational settings.	SCOPE: Relational experiences with family, friends, work, ministry, church, neighborhood, community with high involvement and supervision. Wide variety of relational settings.
MODELS: Primarily other immature children.	MODELS: Primarily parents and other mature adults.
QUALITY: Peer relationships are generally shallow and uncertain. The atmosphere is often cool and always competitive. Family is not a factor.	QUALITY: Family relationships are generally stable and close. The atmosphere is warm and non-competitive. Peer relationships are incorporated into the family.
IDENTITY: Child's identity is developed and reinforced by attempting to be accepted by peers. Acceptance is based on popularity and judged mostly by appearance, intelligence, and abilities. Child becomes dependent upon and wants to become like peers. Child feels false security or false pride.	IDENTITY: Child's identity is developed and reinforced as a member of his family. Acceptance is based on the mutual, unconditional love of a Christian family. Child wants to become like his parents. Child feels secure and significant as a family member and is able to act independently of peers.
VALUES: Christian values are often in conflict with the values of other children and of the school. The Christian child can be isolated, rejected, or ridiculed apart from family support.	VALUES: Christian and family values are taught, modeled, and reinforced without conflict. Any rejection of a child's Christian values is shared with the whole family unit.
OTHER FACTORS: Respect for authority is routinely challenged among peers. Interaction with other children is rarely supervised; adult intervention is rare.	OTHER FACTORS: Respect for authority is constantly reinforced. Interaction with other children is supervised by mature adults; adult intervention is immediate.
RESULT: This child is a "companion of fools" and "suffers harm." The child becomes like other children.	RESULT: This child "walks with the wise" and "grows wise." The child becomes like an adult.

IN OUR HOME

We believe in family style socialization. We try to make our home and family life as entertaining, enriching, and enjoyable as we can. We want our children to become family dependent rather than peer dependent, and to prefer our home to any other place they might go. We work hard and make some social sacrifices to build strong family ties. We have a weekly weekend family night with pizza and activities or a movie, a weekly tea time on Sunday afternoon, fun family Bible times on some weeknights, game nights with popcorn and hot chocolate, and of course special traditions and foods for the holidays. All of this, of course, is in addition to play times with friends, support group activities, and church activities. We make our home a magnet so other children will be drawn to the life they see at the Clarksons' house. We want to do all we can to win our children's hearts so that they will value and prefer our home and family over any other.

I've seen kids dismantle one another while parents and teachers stood passively by and observed the "socialization" process. I've then watched the recipients of this pressure begin to develop defense mechanisms and coping strategies that should never be necessary in a young child.

— Dr. James Dobson, former President of Focus on the Family, in a letter to a colleague (quoted in a letter to ministry supporters)

But the LORD said to Samuel, "Do not consider his appearance or his height, for I have rejected him. The LORD does not look at the things man looks at. Man looks at the outward appearance, but the LORD looks at the heart."

— 1 Samuel 16:7

Learning Happens

The Family Research Council evaluated research on learning and found that what happens at home is the single most important factor in determining student success ("The One-House Schoolroom," *Family Policy*, Sept. 1995). It is interesting to note that none of the top-ranked factors, which could be considered typical qualities of the homeschooling lifestyle, involved either curricula or teaching qualifications. The study, which did not evaluate homeschooling, nonetheless concluded that academic success in school is most likely when there is:

- Commitment to family routines and meal times
- A limit on outside activities
- An emphasis on self-discipline and hard work
- A high but realistic expectation of achievement
- Parental involvement in the learning process
- Family reading, writing, and discussion
- A wide variety of books and other learning tools readily available
- An involvement with community resources

Teacher Certification?

A 2008 study of 11,739 homeschooling families (Dr. Brian Ray, NHERI) found that previous or current teacher certification of one or both parents created no statistically significant impact on higher achievement test scores. In fact, students with never-certified parents received slightly higher scores.

Answering the Qualification Question

"I am fully qualified to teach my children in my home. They couldn't have a better teacher than a loving parent committed to their best interests."

Those within the public school system have persistently called for certification of homeschooling parent-teachers. However, given the steady success rate of homeschooling students as compared with their peers in traditional schools, the true intent of the push for certification seems obvious—the regulation of homeschools. Educational associations and lobbying groups opposed to homeschooling argue that state or federally mandated certification is the only way to ensure that every American child receives a quality education. However, there is no reputable research to support the claim that a teaching degree or certificate makes an individual a better teacher. A teaching certificate is simply a state-issued license to teach, not a certificate of knowledge or ability. In reality, much of the training and certification a professional teacher goes through has as much to do with classroom control and the administrative and political aspects of teaching as it has to do with knowing how or what to teach. As a loving, committed parent, you are already certified by God to teach your children. You do not need the state to tell you whether or not you are qualified to train and instruct your children. You are.

You may be tempted to deny your natural qualifications to teach your child or to think that there is just too much to teach and subjects that you might not know much about. The real issue, though, is not how much you don't know, but how much you do know. If you are a parent of average intelligence, are reasonably mature, can speak, read, write, and do math, and love your children, then you are qualified to instruct them. Many traditional school teachers do not meet those qualifications! With only a good library and minimal curricula for teaching the basics, you can take your children much further than a certified teacher ever could in an average classroom setting. There are many exceptional teachers, to be sure, but there are also unfortunately many whose teaching consists mostly of passing out textbooks and workbooks and giving and grading tests. As a parent, you are qualified to do much more. Your goal as a Christian home educator is not just to make your children good test-takers but rather to shape their hearts and strengthen their minds to become self-motivated, independent learners. And because you have a personal, God-given, one-on-one relationship with each of your children, you are much better qualified and equipped to reach that goal than a classroom teacher whose attention is divided between your child and twenty or more other children.

In the same way that objective studies on socialization support the homeschooling model, numerous studies on qualifications and teaching skills have shown that certification does not guarantee or indicate teaching effectiveness and that it may even have a negative effect. The educational background of the parent has minimal effect on the learning of the child. The primary factor is the parent's commitment. Don't confuse qualifications with certification. Education at home is a learning process as much for the parents as it is for the children. Unfamiliar subject areas and problems that you are not able to solve do not reflect on your qualifications to teach your children. They are no more and no less than opportunities for you to learn together. You are qualified. It is not difficult to teach your child. This book will show you how to become an excellent home educator using the principles in the WholeHearted Learning model.

Classroom School Teacher	Home School Parent-Teacher
QUALIFICATIONS: Usually a college degree, certification, competency requirements, and/or professional experience.	QUALIFICATIONS: Maturity, willingness, leading of the Holy Spirit, life experience, self-directed training and learning.
METHODS: Limited to more formal, group-oriented teaching methods that are suited to the classroom setting.	METHODS: No limitation on methods. Able to use informal, individualized teaching methods suited to each child.
GOALS: Goal of instruction is mostly head knowledge with a focus on the right answer. Due to class size, learning is measured mostly by knowledge of facts.	GOALS: Goal of instruction is head and heart knowledge with a focus on understanding. Learning is measured by both knowledge of facts and understanding of ideas.
CONTROL: Must be able to maintain constant control of a classroom of 20-30 children, many of whom are often untrained and undisciplined.	CONTROL: Control is already a natural and normal part of the parent-child relationship. Training and discipline are naturally integrated with learning.
RESOURCES: Mostly limited to the use of approved materials. Not always able to use the best resources available due to budget restrictions, time limitations, or class size.	RESOURCES: Unlimited opportunity to use the very best resources available. Only consideration is the family budget and lack of access to some materials.
CURRICULA: Must use a uniform curriculum and materials with all children in the class, regardless of individual needs, interests, capabilities, or learning style.	CURRICULA: Free to use a variety of curricula and materials, personally tailored to address each individual child's needs, interests, capabilities, and learning style.
CONTENT: Limitations on what can be taught and discussed with students.	CONTENT: No limitations on what can be taught or discussed with children.
TIME: Time with students is limited to the time spent in the classroom. Problem students receive the most individual attention. Unable to adjust the pace of instruction—must keep on tight schedule.	TIME: Unlimited time with children in wide variety of learning situations. All receive individualized attention. Can adjust the pace of instruction as needed—scheduling is flexible and non-restricting.
EVALUATION: Evaluating and directing student progress is limited primarily to testing and grading. Due to class size, evaluation is an impersonal process that necessarily excludes learning readiness, maturity, understanding, and other individualized factors.	EVALUATION: Children's progress is guided through personal interaction and direction. Evaluation is a very personal process that considers all factors that relate to learning in a particular area of study. Testing and grading, if needed at all, are optional tools for evaluation.
DISCIPLINE: Limited disciplinary methods due to legal restrictions. Because there are no natural bonds, discipline must be formal, strict, and authoritarian in most cases. Discipline is mostly for punishment of unacceptable behavior.	DISCIPLINE: Able to use whatever disciplinary method is most effective. Discipline is always done in love within the bonds of the parent-child relationship. Discipline is mostly for the purpose of training in character, conduct, and attitude.
CREATIVITY: Limited opportunities to cultivate creativity in students due to need for structured learning environment and emphasis on right answers. Students learn to stay in seats and answer questions.	CREATIVITY: Able to cultivate maximum creativity in children by providing a dynamic, hands-on learning environment at home. Children learn to explore, discover, ask questions, and seek out answers.
MOTIVATION: Varies greatly. It might be a chosen profession, a love of teaching, or just a job.	MOTIVATION: Most parents are motivated by love, obedience to God, and desire for better education at home.

Homeschool Success Then

In a 1994-1995 study of 16,311 homeschooled students in grades K-12 from all 50 states, the overall average for the basic battery (the three Rs) was the 77th percentile—73rd percentile in language and mathematics and 79th percentile in reading. The national average for all students is 50th percentile. The sample was composed of all students who took the Iowa Tests of Basic Skills. The study was commissioned by Home School Legal Defense Association (HSLDA) and analyzed by Dr. Brian Ray of the National Home Education Research Institute (NHERI).

Homeschool Success Now

In spring 2008, Dr. Brian Ray conducted a new study, commissioned by HSLDA, of 11,739 participants from all 50 states, Guam, and Puerto Rico. The results showed homeschool students excelling in comparison to their public school counterparts, averaging 34-39 percentile points higher than standardized achievement test norms—84th percentile in language, math, and social studies and 89th percentile in reading. The study further revealed that factors commonly thought to influence success and create higher achievement test scores had no statistically significant impact on the results—family background, socioeconomic level, teacher certification, state regulations, number of years homeschooled, or even style of homeschooling (degree of structure, amount of time in parent-directed learning activities, or enrollment in a comprehensive curriculum plan). Males and females performed almost the same at all grade levels. In the study sample, 82.4 percent were Protestant, 12.4 percent Roman Catholic, and 5.2 percent of other persuasions. Homeschooling parents' formal education level was above average, with a correlation between higher test scores and higher levels of parental education, just as there is in institutional schools.

Answering the Reputation Question

"Home education is a rapidly growing and successful educational movement. To many it is a blessing; to some it is a curiosity; to a few it is a threat. To all it is a reality."

An objective observer of the homeschool movement will see a steadily growing forest that is strong and healthy. A biased observer will see one or two diseased trees and then condemn the entire forest. The best response to biased criticism that attempts to attack the reputation of home education, usually based on isolated negative examples, is to change the point of view. Don't allow a detractor to focus on one or two unstable fringe families who give homeschooling a bad name. Gently remind them that public and private schools have their bad trees too. Then, turn their attention to the tens of thousands of normal families (just like them!) who are making genuine sacrifices to obey God's will for their families. They are the solid center and healthy forest of homeschooling, the true measure of the movement's reputation. The best defense is a positive offense. With a positive, nonconfrontational spirit, simply point out the scope and reach of the homeschooling movement by emphasizing the factors that underscore its continuing growth and strength.

- **National, state, and local organizations defend, support, and assist homeschooling families.** There is no formal "national" home education association at this time, and it is unlikely there will be in the near future. However, though they vary widely in scope and purpose, state organizations protect and promote the interests of home educators in the individual states. They often lobby for better homeschooling legislation and cultivate relationships with the educational establishment when possible. These spokespersons, leaders, and organizations also sponsor curriculum fairs and homeschool conferences with special speakers and parent-teacher training seminars. Other spokespersons and organizations, such as HSLDA (see page 31), fight the political and legal battles for the right to homeschool freely.

- **Hundreds of thousands of Christian families choose to homeschool.** Home education is growing annually. Although precise figures are difficult to come by, estimates exceed two million homeschooling children in America. Convention attendance, magazine subscriptions, organizational memberships, product sales, and market research all point to a strong rate of growth and a relatively low attrition rate. Though homeschooling started as a predominantly Christian movement, any family can homeschool, regardless of their religious beliefs. Research indicates the movement is broadening every year.

- **The nationwide network of homeschool support groups is growing.** Many, if not most, urban and near-urban areas have thriving support groups for home educators. Groups vary widely in purpose, scope, structure, size, and quality, but all share common goals and purposes—to provide fellowship for homeschooling families and to help and encourage one another. Most support groups usually led by parent volunteers hold regular meetings, plan field trips and other activities, and provide other cooperative services. Some provide supplemental classes for children and teens for a variety of subject areas, keep academic records (depending on the state), or offer parent-teacher training classes and events.

- **Professional publications, publishers, and ministries keep home educators informed and supplied.** A wide variety of print and digital resources is available for homeschool families. Most are very personal and practical. These resources help homeschool parents stay informed about news, speakers, instructional ideas, and new products. They provide informal teacher training as well as fellowship in print. Curriculum publishers, product catalogs, and other ministries keep a steady stream of new, high-quality materials flowing into the homeschool community. There is already a rich sea of good educational resources, and it expands and deepens every year.

- **More and more homeschoolers and homeschool graduates are gaining national recognition for achievements.** Homeschoolers have gained national attention in televised spelling and geography bees, but that is minor compared to the impact of homeschooling children, teens, and graduates in many fields of endeavor, from education to politics to business to social work to entertainment and media to Christian ministry and much more. As homeschooling has become more mainstream, homeschoolers have become newsworthy for their achievements and influence.

Guarding the Reputation of Homeschooling

To paraphrase a famous line, "No homeschooling family is an island unto itself." Whether you want to be or not, you and your children are public relations representatives for homeschooling. It is important to remember some simple guidelines that will help your family be a positive testimony for homeschooling. Your good example can do more to promote the reputation of homeschooling than any other single factor. Don't underestimate or undervalue the importance of a good witness!

- **Be discreet.** Don't hide the fact that you homeschool, but don't flaunt it either. Give a defense when appropriate, but don't create an offense by unnecessarily making it an issue. Channel your strong convictions into making your case to political and educational leaders, not into winning arguments with friends and neighbors.

- **Be friendly.** Get to know your neighbors and let them know you and your children. Invite them into your home, greet them when you see them, and have your children deliver cookie plates to them at holidays. Be open and friendly.

- **Be aware.** Keep your children under control whenever you're out in public. Like it or not, fair or not, expectations are higher for homeschooled children.

- **Be sensible.** Limit out-of-the-house activities during public school hours to educational functions, such as support group meetings, co-op classes, field trips, and outings. When possible, let shopping with your children wait until after school hours.

- **Be discerning.** Use discretion about outdoor play during regular school hours. It is the perception ("their kids are not in school") and not the reality ("they must be finished with their school work") that some people will see and believe.

- **Be involved.** Church can be a seedbed of conflict over homeschooling. Support the pastor and ministries of the church whenever possible. Reach out in some way to homeschool critics in the body. Serve quietly and faithfully with your children.

How Many Homeschoolers?

There were no statistics then but some have estimated that there were 30,000 homeschooling families at the beginning of the movement in the early 1980s. A 1992 survey by Patricia Lines, Dr. Brian Ray, and HSLDA suggested that a decade later there were as many as 500,000 home-educated children in America (K-12). A 2007 study by the National Center for Education Statistics estimated that 1.5 million students between the ages of 5 and 17 were being home educated in the U.S. (up from 850,000 in 1999 and 1.1 million in 2003). A 2009 study by the National Home Education Research Institute put the number at about 2 million, and a January 2011 study at 2.04 million. According to the U.S. Census Bureau, there were an estimated 54 million K-12 children in the U.S. in spring 2010, suggesting that nearly 4 percent of the school-age population (about 1 in 25) are homeschoolers. Attrition rates among homeschoolers are unknown, but home education appears to be growing between 5 and 12 percent per year and has increased by a whopping 300 percent since 1992. All the trends are up.

Private Schools

Private Christian schools play an important role in the education of Christian children. One cannot write a history of Christianity in America without taking into account the enormous positive impact and influence of private Christian schools. Though the commitment of private Christian education to biblical content and leadership is commendable, in most cases it is still the same institutionalized classroom setting that plagues the public school. Consider just a few of the issues, besides the cost savings, that make home education a more attractive choice. When you choose a private school:

- You are still giving up your ability and privilege to be the primary influence in every area of your children's lives—heart, spirit, and mind.
- Your children will still be restricted by unnatural formality and control at a time when their natural curiosity and creativity are at their peak.
- Individualized attention and real-life learning will be minimal due to the nature of the classroom.
- Even with a heavy dose of discipline, most Christian private schools must deal with children from non-Christian homes.
- Most schools still rely on tedious textbooks and workbooks, time-wasting seatwork, and unnecessary homework.
- Your children will still have to run in the age/grade treadmill with little or no opportunity or encouragement to linger or advance at their own pace.

Regarding Your Reputation as a Christian Homeschooler

One of the most subtle temptations that you will face as a homeschooling parent will be to judge your homeschool, and yourself, by whatever you perceive the world's standards of educational excellence to be. You may fret that your children don't know enough, or that you missed a subject area one year, or that their achievement test scores were too low, or that you aren't using the best materials, or...you get the picture. And if that doesn't give you enough to fret about, you may also be tempted to compare yourself and your children with other Christian homeschooling parents. You may judge yourself as not keeping up or not doing enough and begin to feel inadequate and inferior. You may think that you are not able to keep a good reputation as a homeschooling parent and that you should really just quit and put your children in school.

Here's the truth: You will never be able to live up to either the real or imagined expectations you place on yourself and your children. Don't even try! Make it your goal to please God in your homeschool, not other people. If you are truly seeking to please God in all that you do at home, that is the reputation that matters to him and the one that should matter most to you. If you are being faithful to do what is best for your children out of your love for God and for them, and if you are doing it with "all your heart" (Luke 10:27), then don't worry or fret about your reputation. Let your reputation be that you are faithful to God, known for "good deeds" (1 Timothy 5:10), "full of the Spirit and of wisdom" (Acts 6:3), and that you "seek first his kingdom and his righteousness" (Matthew 6:33). If that is truly your reputation, then you will better be able to keep homeschooling in a more realistic perspective.

IN OUR HOME

Looking back now, it was pretty tame, but in our first year of homeschooling it was a reputation challenge to us. Clay was the new guy on the pastoral staff of what in those days (1988) was a southern California megachurch of 1,500. He was expected to put in seventy hours a week, and Sally was expected to work outside the home like all the other pastoral wives. (Neither of us did.) The only other homeschool family in the church was leaving. We tried to keep our family life under the radar, but we became a blip. When Sally was asked to speak to the women's ministry, the president of the group—an outspoken homeschooling critic—stood up at the front and left the room when Sally got up to speak, and returned only when she had finished. This same woman discussed with other women leaders at the church that Joel, who was playing alone one morning in Sunday School, was obviously a homeschooled child because he was not well socialized. He was three years old! The associate pastor took Clay to lunch and confronted him with research from his doctoral dissertation to defend public schooling and explain why he considered homeschooling elitist. One woman, a stranger, came up to Sally at a meeting and started loudly criticizing homeschooling. We didn't last long at that church, but it was a providential time that crystallized our convictions about family, home, and homeschooling. Whole Heart Ministries was born out of those challenges to our homeschooling reputation.

Moving in the Right Direction

God moves in history at different times and in different ways. We both were involved with Campus Crusade for Christ in college in the 1970s and then as staff members after graduation. The evangelical Christian student movement that started in the early 1950s, the demographic wave of Baby Boom youth in the 1960s, and the Jesus movement of the 1970s all had a profound impact on the church and on Christian culture in America that is still felt today. We knew we were part of a movement of God for our times, and this shaped our convictions and visions about ministry for the rest of our lives.

Thirty-something years later, when we look for that same kind of movement of God in a new generation, we see it in Christian homeschooling. The seeds were planted in the mid-1970s with books by national educators questioning the presumed superiority of classroom education and recommending schooling at home. By the early 1980s, homeschooling rapidly shifted from the fringes to the mainstream to become a national phenomenon defined almost exclusively as a Christian movement. In the years since, though the percentage of Christian homeschoolers has been reduced by the influx of non-Christian homeschooling families, the sense of God's hand continues to be a unifying reality among the still-growing Christian homeschooling community. Christian homeschoolers share a common vision and motivation that is rooted in the desire to be a biblical family. The absence of a single, national organization of Christian homeschoolers has prevented the institutionalization that can slow and weaken a movement of God over time. Christian homeschooling is largely the work of conviction-led, independent, Christian families who simply want to follow God and teach their children to follow God.

After over thirty years of Christian ministry in a wide variety of Christian and cultural settings, we believe God's next great mission field will be the family. For two generations, the family has been fragmented on a scale and at a pace unprecedented in modern times. Even in Christian homes, children are increasingly being raised by parenting surrogates—day care, schools, churches, activities, sports, media, online social networks, and peers. Parents have moved from being central and present to being peripheral and often absent or transient—from being fully engaged, hands-on directors of their children's lives to being disengaged, hands-off observers. We are seeing the fruit of that fragmentation in a new generation, not just in the moral confusion and rejection of absolute truths but also in young Christians entering adulthood and starting new families while adrift on a sea of uncertainty about what a family should be and do.

We feel strongly that Christian homeschooling is a movement of God's Spirit to restore and strengthen the family. When our first child, Sarah, was born in 1984, our first thoughts—born of our years in campus ministry—were about how we would disciple her. We had begun reading books and articles about home education in 1982, and we quickly made the connection with discipleship. We started our homeschooling journey in earnest in 1988 and found ourselves caught up again in a movement of God. This book, first released in 1994, was as much a call to Christian families to be a part of this new movement of God's Spirit as it was an attempt to provide a discipleship-based, biblical model for homeschooling. This new version, after twenty-two years of home education and discipleship, is an even stronger call for Christian parents to see homeschooling as a movement of God to restore the family.

Moving Movements

The essence of an ideologically motivated movement is change. It is not successful unless it can bring about social, political, or religious change, usually on a culture-wide level. It does that by defining its vision or cause, engaging culture, and gathering a growing following of committed individuals and groups. Many movements are well defined but attract few followers and change little or nothing; other movements are broadly defined but attract many followers and change everything. In contrast, homeschooling is a successful and growing national and international educational and family movement that is well-defined, is engaged with culture, and has many committed followers and advocates. It also encompasses all three areas of ideological cultural change—social, political, and religious. It is still growing and gathering momentum, but it has the potential to be a major historical and culture-changing movement of the twentieth and twenty-first centuries. In terms of its impact on culture, homeschooling should be counted among the other major American movements of the past 150 years:

- Public Schools
- Sunday School
- Women's Suffrage (Vote)
- Communism/Socialism
- Labor Movement
- Social Gospel
- Fundamentalism
- Prohibition
- Progressivism/Liberalism
- Private Schools
- Evangelicalism
- Student Movement
- Conservatism
- Civil Rights
- Women's Liberation
- Gay Rights
- Conservationalism
- Environmentalism
- Globalism

O my people, hear my teaching; listen to the words of my mouth. I will open my mouth in parables, I will utter hidden things, things from of old—what we have heard and known, what our fathers have told us. We will not hide them from their children; we will tell the next generation the praiseworthy deeds of the LORD, his power, and the wonders he has done. He decreed statutes for Jacob and established the law in Israel, which he commanded our forefathers to teach their children, so the next generation would know them, even the children yet to be born, and they in turn would tell their children. Then they would put their trust in God and would not forget his deeds but would keep his commands. They would not be like their forefathers—a stubborn and rebellious generation, whose hearts were not loyal to God, whose spirits were not faithful to him.

— Psalm 78:1-8

The heart of parenting is not just about raising an obedient, well-behaved child, but about shaping your child's heart to follow God and placing his feet on the same path of life that you and those before you have walked. Your faith and teaching will live on in generations to come through the hearts of your children, and their children, who hear the call of God to "follow Me."

— Clay Clarkson, *Heartfelt Discipline*, WaterBrook Press, 2003

You Are Teaching Future Generations Today

There is a much bigger picture to being a Christian homeschooling family, though. We so easily get caught up in the day-to-day details, disciplines, and demands of the homeschooling lifestyle, and before we know it we slip into the error of thinking that home education is the big picture of our lives. It's not. In fact, homeschooling is only a small part of the much bigger picture in which God wants us to see ourselves and our children. So much of what we do is temporal and passing, but what we are doing with our children is eternal—we are creating a link in a chain of godly families that will become, by God's grace, a long, strong chain representing many generations of righteousness. Christian homeschooling should not be only about our children getting good test scores, going to college, and getting a job or career. Those are the temporal, not eternal, goals. If those become the focus of what homeschooling means in your family and you miss the bigger picture of passing on a righteous heritage for generations to come, then you've missed it all. You could become the weak link in your own chain of righteousness.

Psalm 78 presents the big picture. The psalmist is looking back to the command God gave to the Israelites many generations earlier as they prepared to cross the Jordan into the Promised Land. Moses commanded them to "teach [God's truth] diligently" to their children (Deuteronomy 6:7a, NASB). The psalmist is reminding the Israelites that the reason they are still a nation of God's people is that their fathers had told their children, who had told their children, and the chain of righteousness and truth had continued right down to the present. They, now, should do the same so that future generations, even ones "yet to be born," would "put their trust in God and would not forget his deeds but would keep his commands." What a great passage for godly families today! But there is a caveat: The chain can be broken (vs. 8). When one generation is "stubborn and rebellious" because it does not "prepare its heart" and has a spirit that is "not faithful to God," they will break the chain of righteousness. Some families, sadly, will fall away.

Psalm 78 speaks directly and powerfully to Christian homeschooling families today. We are part of the chain of righteousness it describes, and we are diligently teaching our children the truth of God so they can teach their children and even the children yet to be born. The highest and holiest motivation and vision for Christian homeschooling is that each family would be a visual sermon, an illustration in life, of the truth and power of Psalm 78:1-8 and Deuteronomy 6:4-9. What we are doing in our homes should be about much more than just educational methodology; it should be about generational theology. We are on this earth for such a short time, but we have the opportunity to make a difference in eternity. If we fail to be truly committed to God's generational plan ("a generation that did not prepare its heart") or if we simply allow our spirit to be distracted by this world and become unfaithful to God's plan ("whose spirit was not faithful to God"), we will miss the opportunity to fill heaven with righteous generations. However, if we are committed and faithful, God will honor and bless homeschooling.

That is the big picture. But who knows how long this window of opportunity will remain open allowing us freely and faithfully to homeschool our children? Our hearts' conviction and burden is to call Christian homeschooling families to the bigger picture, to the vision of strengthening and extending the chain of righteousness into future generations. That is a homeschooling movement worth all the effort and sacrifice.

— Chapter 3 —

Home Nurture: Shepherding Your Child's Spirit to Long for God

Signs of Life at Home

Have you ever visited a church and caught yourself thinking, "The spirit here seems so lifeless"? There can be stimulating teaching, pleasant fellowship, and even enjoyable worship, and yet something is missing. The right things are done, and things are done right, but the Spirit of God does not seem to be alive and moving in that place.

The same can be true of many Christian homes. A home can be filled with praise-worthy Christian things and activities and yet still seem lifeless. It just doesn't seem as though the Spirit of Christ is alive there. Good Christian parents can be highly committed to their children and even be very skilled home educators, yet they still may fail to bring the life of God into their home in a way that their children sense his presence and reality there every day. That is why we consider nurture to be the first, and perhaps most essential, step to building a biblical Christian home. Although it is not a concept you will hear much about in relation to the more measurable and visible priorities of discipleship and education, we are convinced it is the missing priority in many Christian homes.

Like a shepherd who leads his sheep to life-giving water and pasture, your first responsibility as a parent is to lead your children to the life-giving presence and reality of Christ in your heart and home. Your desire should be to implant a longing in their spirits for God that can be satisfied only with the water and bread of life in Christ. No matter how good your church may be, a few hours each week cannot create the longing for Christ that God has uniquely designed you to impart to your children. You are to be the primary life-giving presence of Christ to your children, through his Spirit living and working in your life as a Christian parent and through his Word, just as Christ imparted life to those who came in contact with him: "The words I have spoken to you are spirit and are life."

Having been around homeschooling for over twenty-five years, we have seen parents who focus almost exclusively on formal approaches to discipleship and education, turning them into daily disciplines and duties for their children. They do not consider nurturing the life of the spirit a necessary part of their home program. Accomplishing goals is the goal. As the first generation of homeschool children are now entering adulthood, we are sadly seeing the bitter fruit of children whose spirits were not nurtured and whose families and homes were not life-giving. We are seeing far too many children raised in "good Christian homes" become moral casualties and spiritual dropouts and reject the homeschooling lifestyle. It is our growing conviction, though, that homeschooling was not the problem. Rather, it was the failure to make home nurture a nonnegotiable priority. Children who grow up in a home that is alive with the Spirit of God and whose spirits are nurtured and fed will become life-living and life-giving adults. It's all about nurture.

As the deer pants for streams of water, so my soul pants for you, O God.
— Psalm 42:1

For the bread of God is he who comes down from heaven and gives life to the world.
— John 6:33

It is the Spirit who gives life; the flesh profits nothing; the words that I have spoken to you are spirit and are life.
— John 6:63 (NASB)

45

Fathers, do not exasperate your children; instead, bring them up in the training and instruction of the Lord.

— Ephesians 6:4

...but we were gentle among you, like a mother caring for her little children. We loved you so much that we were delighted to share with you not only the gospel of God but our lives as well, because you had become so dear to us...For you know that we dealt with each of you as a father deals with his own children, encouraging, comforting and urging you to live lives worthy of God, who calls you into his kingdom and glory.

— 1 Thessalonians 2:7-12

Fathers Are Parents

Although all the major Bible versions translate the first word of Ephesians 6:4 as "fathers," the Greek term, *pateres*, when used in the plural, can also correctly be translated "parents." Mothers are welcome to receive Paul's admonition as well.

The Biblical Case for Home Nurture

If you search a Bible concordance for "nurture," you won't find much. The word occurs only rarely in English translations. However, the reason we consider nurture to be a high priority is that it is so closely tied to a key New Testament verse on parenting, even though you don't see it at first in the translation. In his letter to the Ephesians, Paul admonishes each member of a typical Jewish or Roman household to fulfill their role in God's plan for a family. In Ephesians 6:4, he addresses fathers directly: "Fathers, do not exasperate your children; instead, bring them up in the training and instruction of the Lord." What you need to know about this verse is that the Greek word for "bring...up" is used only twice in this form in the New Testament. Just eight verses earlier, in 5:29, Paul explains how husbands should love their wives: "After all, no one ever hated his own body, but he feeds and cares for it, just as Christ does the church." The word for "bring...up" and for "feeds" is the same Greek term, *ektrepho*. It is a compound of "out of" and "to feed." Literally, it means to "feed from." However, it can be translated "to nourish" or "to nurture."

Here's what Paul is saying: In the same way that a husband is to see his wife as a living being that he needs to feed and care for, a father needs to nourish and feed his children. Please do not ever again think this verse is about just being sure your children are raised in a "good Christian home"! This verse is about your responsibility to nurture the life of Christ in them. Literally, the force of the entire admonition is, "Stop exasperating your children! Instead, nurture them in the training and instruction of the Lord." The children were exasperated and literally "provoked to anger" because they were not being nurtured! They were created by God to need and expect that nurture, and they were left frustrated and angry without it. Paul strongly commands the Ephesian fathers to stop that! Right now! How? By being sure they feed their children's spirits with godly training (*paideia*) and with loving and personal instruction or admonition (*nouthesia*). And it was to be "of the Lord," coming from the life of God already in their own hearts (a direct reflection of Deuteronomy 6:6). From the life of Christ in their hearts, they were to spiritually feed and nourish their children. That's what nurture is. In arguably the most important passage in the New Testament that speaks directly to parenting, the key concept is nurture. And just in case you missed it, it is a "do it now, today" command—nurture your children!

In 1 Thessalonians 2:7-12, Paul reminds those believers how he was gentle among them, "like a mother caring for her little children" and "as a father deals with his own children, encouraging, comforting, and urging [them] to live lives worthy of God." He uses nurturing language that pictures a parent cultivating the life of Christ in a child. This is the clearest picture in the New Testament of Paul's idea of what a Christian mother and father should be like. It is a word portrait of nurturing parents! Other passages emphasize this quality of parental nurture and how Christ, the Spirit, and the Word are the spiritual life that we as parents are to be feeding to our children from our own hearts. We already have that life—Christ dwells in us, the Spirit empowers us, and the Word instructs us—and our children are designed by God to receive it from us. God commands us to feed them with the life of God that fills our own lives. When biblical nurture is neglected, children can become frustrated and discouraged. Children who are nurtured in Christ's life by a loving parent will receive his grace to grow strong.

The Grace of Nurture

There is no life in Christ apart from God's grace. There can be no spiritual life in your Christian home apart from God's grace. However hard you may try, even the best activities and efforts alone are powerless to bring God's grace into your family's lives. The Apostle Paul made it very clear: "For by grace you have been saved through faith; and that not of yourselves, it is the gift of God; not as a result of works, so that no one may boast" (Ephesians 2:8-9, NASB). If the purpose of biblical nurture is to feed your children with God's life, then it must involve more than just doing Christian things at home. Biblical nurture opens windows for God's life-giving grace to enter your children's hearts.

Grace in the New Testament is the Greek term *charis*—a favor or benefit bestowed on another with no expectation. It is a gift from God—not earned by works but simply accepted by faith. It is also a life-transforming work of the Holy Spirit in our daily lives. Grace breaks the grip of law—the temptation to earn God's favor through our own efforts—and releases us to live by faith in the power of the Spirit. The ultimate result of nurturing your children is to give them the gift of freedom in Christ. You will be making sure they know God's grace and truth in Jesus Christ (John 1:17). Here are some of the best ways to open windows for God's grace.

- **The Word of God** — Always let your children know that you believe that the Word of God is "living and active" (Hebrews 4:12). It is not just words on a page but is alive with the Spirit of God. When you read the Bible, let them know it is God speaking to you as a family. Look to the Scriptures for God's guidance and believe its promises as coming directly from the Father to you. Scripture is grace in print.

- **Prayer** — Guard against prayer becoming ritual and rote. Remind your children that prayer is a conversation with the living God who is present with you in your home. Keep prayer "living and active" by praying the words of Scripture as a family. Use the Psalms as your own language for praise and prayer. Prayer is grace in words.

- **Fellowship** — Bring other like-minded believing families into your home so you can bear one another's burdens and "spur one another on toward love and good deeds." Your children need to receive grace from you and others who have the life of God in them and see that they too have grace to give to others. Fellowship is grace in person.

IN OUR HOME

As a homeschooling family, we find it relatively easy to saturate our home with God's truth and to have many opportunities for prayer as a family and with individual children. We have had to work a bit harder, though, at creating the kind of godly fellowship in our home that will be a source of grace for our children's hearts. There is always the challenge to balance fun and faith, but we regularly have other families over and dedicate part of our evening to talking about the Lord, sharing testimonies, singing hymns and praise songs, and praying together. Even if we keep the time short, it still creates an indelible mark on our children's spirits. Even now that they are older, they still remember times of significant spiritual fellowship, if only because such times are becoming more rare in our isolated culture.

For of His fullness we have all received, and grace upon grace. For the Law was given through Moses; grace and truth were realized through Jesus Christ.

— John 1:16-17 (NASB)

For the word of God is living and active. Sharper than any double-edged sword, it penetrates even to dividing soul and spirit, joints and marrow; it judges the thoughts and attitudes of the heart.

— Hebrews 4:12-13

Let us then approach the throne of grace with confidence, so that we may receive mercy and find grace to help us in our time of need.

— Hebrews 4:16

And let us consider how we may spur one another on toward love and good deeds. Let us not give up meeting together, as some are in the habit of doing, but let us encourage one another—and all the more as you see the Day approaching.

— Hebrews 10:24-25

Observe, it is the parent, who has himself already experienced the salvation of God, who is appointed to lead the child to know God. The knowledge of God is no mere matter of the understanding; it is to love Him, to live in Him, to experience the power of His presence and His blessing. It is evident that the man who would teach others to know God must be able to speak by personal experience of Him, must prove by the warmth of love and devotion that he loves this God, and has his life from Him.

— Rev. Andrew Murray, *The Children for Christ*, 1887

Keeping the GIFTS idea in mind as I went about my daily tasks helped me a lot. But I still found myself floundering sometimes, and one question often led to another. What I really needed was a practical model to help me apply our plan to my daily life. Then the obvious answer struck me: Jesus was the model I was looking for. A big part of his ministry, after all, was teaching his disciples...just as I was trying to teach my children. He ministered to them, and he prepared them for ministry. He taught them with words, and he taught them with his actions. Jesus gave his disciples...the very gifts Clay and I wanted to give our children.

— Sally Clarkson, *The Ministry of Motherhood*, WaterBrook Press, 2004

LifeGIFTS: A Model for Home Nurture

There is a tendency to view nurture as a kind of home version of "Random Acts of Kindness." It's not often viewed as something that necessarily needs to be planned for ahead of time, but rather as the spontaneous, by-the-Spirit acting out of life-giving love and good deeds. Spiritual spontaneity is a commendable characteristic for any Christian home, but a full expression of home nurture requires more. If nurture is about feeding your children's spirits so they will grow in their longing for God, then you need to approach that task with the same forethought that you would a garden. If you want to nurture something to grow, you have to go about it thoughtfully and deliberately.

When we were starting our family, we realized early on that we wanted a simple model to help us give to our children gifts of life—gifts that would enable them to become life-givers to a world of life-seekers. That thought gave birth to LifeGIFTS, an acronym reminder of the five gifts of life we wanted to be sure we were passing on to our children—Grace, Inspiration, Faith, Training, and Service. LifeGIFTS became a simple model to help us actively nurture and disciple our children. The illustration below visualizes the balance of the five priorities among head (knowledge), heart (faith), and hands (actions), with one side fostering desire, the other ability. The result is that LifeGIFTS instill desire-ability in your children.

The five pages that follow expand on each individual priority, explaining how to implement each gift in your own family. Each gift can be given through one or all of three relational forms of nurture: training, instruction, and modeling. Some of these concepts are also expressed in other sections of the book, but the five gifts and the three nurturing tasks will provide a lens through which to evaluate and assess your nurturing efforts.

- **Training** — Training or discipline is the process of influencing your children's actions and attitudes. Your goal as a trainer is to build godly character and habits in your children. (Proverbs 22:6)

- **Instruction** — Instruction or teaching is imparting Bible truth to your children. Through instruction, you are helping your children grow in understanding, wisdom, discernment, and faith. (Ephesians 6:4)

- **Modeling** — Modeling is being a living example of your training and instruction. You are showing your children what Christian maturity looks like and encouraging them to imitate your example. (Luke 6:40)

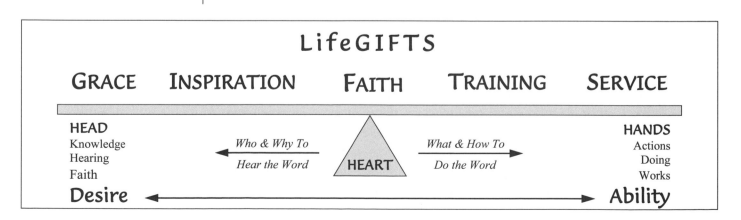

Grace

The gift of grace is the desire and ability to relate personally and purposefully to God and people.

The gift of grace prepares your children to become channels of God's grace and love to other people. A person who cannot relate personally and purposefully to God or to people will, without fail, be handicapped or even hindered in life and ministry. A faithful message and a fruitful ministry are effective and powerful only to the degree that they are characterized by grace in the messenger and minister. In order to be channels of grace, your children must not only know how to receive grace from God, but they also must know how to give God's grace to others. The quality of graciousness (being a grace giver) will make your children equally at home with both commoners and kings and will make others they come in contact with feel accepted and valuable. Even simple courtesies become powerful tools of God's grace. Graciousness removes barriers and builds bridges. It affirms the worth and value of another person. It opens the channel by which the light of God's grace and truth can flow into a darkened world through your children.

- **Training** — Help with personal devotions. Train in gracious behavior (manners). Value and pursue priority relationships. Train your children how to pray. Train them how to listen to God's voice in his Word.

- **Instruction** — About our relationship with God. About God's unconditional love and forgiveness. About God's grace and forgiveness. About our identity in Christ. About the power of the Holy Spirit.

- **Modeling** — Have regular personal and family devotions. Be gracious and kind to family members. Show loyalty to your spouse. Pray spontaneously for needs. Show grace and love to strangers.

IN OUR HOME

We view the ministry of hospitality in our home as God's tool for us to train our children in graciousness. When someone comes to our home, our children know that we expect them to be gracious and quick to serve. That means welcoming adult guests properly, asking if there is something they can get for them, taking their coat, or whatever is appropriate to the visit. (Hospitality drills are a helpful way to train them in this area.) Our children know that being well-mannered and gracious is more than just a cultural formality...it is the way we show respect to another person, affirm their value as a person made in God's image, and strengthen our testimony to them not only as a Christian family but also as a homeschooling family. It is the practical expression of treating others the way you want to be treated, regarding others as more important than yourself, and looking out for the interests of others. Even when we go to someone else's house, we still practice hospitality. We rehearse with the kids before they leave the car how to be gracious guests who are polite, respectful, and helpful.

Jesus replied: Love the Lord your God with all your heart and with all your soul and with all your mind. This is the first and greatest commandment. And the second is like it: Love your neighbor as yourself.

— Matthew 22:37-39

Let no unwholesome word proceed from your mouth, but only such a word as is good for edification according to the need of the moment, so that it will give grace to those who hear.

— Ephesians 4:29 (NASB)

Unless a man is courteous toward others, he is at a disadvantage in the world, even though he be the possessor of every other good trait and quality possible to humanity...Courtesy is the external manifestation of a right spirit toward others.

— H. Clay Trumbull, *Hints on Child Training*, 1890

And without faith it is impossible to please God, because anyone who comes to him must believe that he exists and that he rewards those who earnestly seek him.

— Hebrews 11:6

Therefore, since we are surrounded by such a great cloud of witnesses, let us throw off everything that hinders and the sin that so easily entangles, and let us run with perseverance the race marked out for us.

— Hebrews 12:1

God's faithfulness inspires that of man, and therefore demands and rewards it...To know God's purpose, to believe God's promise, to adore God's unchanging faithfulness, communicates to the soul the very spirit of that faithfulness, and binds us firmly to Him, so that He who is all in all can work out His purpose in us.

— Rev. Andrew Murray, *The Children for Christ*, 1887

Inspiration

The gift of inspiration is the desire and ability to view all of life in the light of God's sovereignty and purpose.

The gift of inspiration prepares your children to live with hope in a fallen world. It enables them to view their lives through the unclouded lens of God's past faithfulness, his present sovereignty, and his future purposes. It enables them to see by faith, with the eyes of their hearts, that the God of eternity is at work in the everyday events of this world and their lives. Inspiration enables your children to see themselves as a part of God's plan for the world—to understand that the same God who created them and provides for them has gifted them for his use and has a special purpose for their lives. It gives them confidence to know that what God has done throughout history in the lives of other great Christians and heroes of the faith, he can do in their lives as well. It gives them the sense that they have a family heritage to share, a legacy of faith to carry on, and a place in history. Inspiration is the flame of faith that burns in their hearts with the truth that they will "believe that he exists and that he rewards those who earnestly seek him" (Hebrews 11:6).

- **Training** — Have an annual Family Day (remembering God's faithfulness). Read Christian history and biographies. Create a Family History and Heritage album. Play "God's Hands" (I saw God's hands when he...). Pray about current events.

- **Instruction** — About God's sovereignty and providence. About God's unique gifts and plan for each person. About God's purpose and design for the family. About the nature of faith and belief. About God's eternal plan of salvation (Ephesians 1:3-14).

- **Modeling** — Share answers to prayer with your family. Trust God for something beyond your current means. Thank God often for his faithfulness. Talk about the reality of heaven and eternal life. Share a verse of Scripture that inspires your faith.

IN OUR HOME

Planting seeds of inspiration in our young children is a continual process. We look for opportunities to affirm areas of giftedness and talent in their lives that God is using or could use for his glory. We use storytelling to create pictures in our children's minds of them as Christian leaders as youths and adults. They especially enjoy stories that have them acting heroically or sacrificing for others. Because there are very few Christian heroes—real or imaginary—for them to emulate today, we diligently search out books and videos that provide good Christian role models. Whenever possible, we try to find stories about people that match one of their current interests (such as music, sports, nature, or others). Inspirational fiction provides many good examples of noble Christian character to imitate. We want to secure in their minds that God uses ordinary people to do extraordinary things and that he can use them too. Literary stories have the power to help them understand and visualize their own lives as part of a larger story that God is writing. That's what Sarah calls being "story-formed."

Faith

The gift of faith is the desire and ability to study God's Word and apply its truths to every area of life.

The gift of faith prepares your children to bring the truth and wisdom of Scripture to bear on all areas of their lives. Grace and inspiration are about head knowledge, training and service are about hands-on action, and faith is about the heart. It is heart-centered faith that energizes everything in our lives. Faith is both objective and subjective. It is both what we believe and whom we believe. Paul called it "the faith," the revealed truths of God that needed to be guarded and passed down to others. But he also said faith is "being sure of what we hope for and certain of what we do not see" (Hebrews 11:1). When you strengthen your children's faith, you give them confidence that both God's truth and his presence are worth believing in. You give them the ability to hear and believe the voice of God in the Scriptures and to see and believe the hand of God in their lives. You give them the understanding that faith is active—that it actively seeks out the truth of God and believes in it and that it actively seeks out the God of truth and believes in him.

- **Training** — Teach your children how to study the Bible. Have a weekly Scripture memory challenge or drill. Have Table Talks about biblical subjects. Take advantage of any teachable moments. Talk about what you believe.

- **Instruction** — About all areas of Bible truth, history, and wisdom. About Bible promises. About the reliability of the Scriptures. About the Bible (authors, order, themes, dates, etc.). About God's presence and activity in your daily lives.

- **Modeling** — Talk about what you are learning from Scripture. Explain a verse or passage to your children. Share how you believe God answered a prayer. Take your children to your adult Bible study. Start a blog to journal God's hand in your life.

So then, just as you received Christ Jesus as Lord, continue to live in him, rooted and built up in him, strengthened in the faith as you were taught, and overflowing with thankfulness.

— Colossians 2:6,7

But you, man of God, flee from all this, and pursue righteousness, godliness, faith, love, endurance and gentleness. Fight the good fight of the faith. Take hold of the eternal life to which you were called when you made your good confession in the presence of many witnesses.

— 1 Timothy 6:11-12

From the very beginning the child can take in the great truths concerning God's nature, and the scope of God's power, as fully as a theologian can take them in. Therefore there need be no fear that too much is proffered to the child's mind in this sphere, if only it all be proffered in simplicity as explicit truth, without any attempt at its explanation.

— H. Clay Trumbull, *Hints on Child Training*, 1890

IN OUR HOME

As an occasional alternative to church Bible clubs, we created our own home Bible club that we liked to call Pathkeepers. Our homemade club centered around memorizing Scripture based on various themes (Christian life, character, doctrine, promises, etc.). We would open with some kind of fun activity and singing. Then one of us would teach a brief lesson for the children, including a review of previously memorized Scriptures and work on new verses. We closed the time with prayer and a favorite dessert. As much as we wanted to think it was the Scriptures that excited them about Pathkeepers, we realized what made it especially attractive to the kids was the awards and prizes we offered for completing memory goals—books, games, software, and such. Our stuff was much better than the typical Bible club awards stuff. We didn't have all the uniforms, pins, and badges, but it was still fun and family centered. In reality, it was really just a fancy family night with prizes. However, it gave us the opportunity to build our children's faith in an enjoyable and memorable way as a family.

Train a child in the way he should go, and when he is old he will not turn from it.

— Proverbs 22:6

Fathers, do not exasperate your children; instead, bring them up in the training and instruction of the Lord.

— Ephesians 6:4

For the grace of God that brings salvation has appeared to all men. It teaches us to say "No" to ungodliness and worldly passions, and to live self-controlled, upright and godly lives in this present age.

— Titus 2:11-12

Parents, do you wish to see your children happy? Take care then that you train them to obey when they are spoken to,—to do as they are bid...Teach them to obey while young, or else they will be fretting against God all their lives long, and wear themselves out with the vain idea of being independent of His control.

— J. C. Ryle, *The Upper Room*, 1888

Training

The gift of training is the desire and ability to grow in Christian maturity in the power of the Holy Spirit.

The gift of training prepares your children to live godly lives. You are doing much more than just training them to do what is right, though—you are also training them to choose what is right to do. You are putting into their hearts the Word of God that, through the Spirit, will teach them and enable them to say no to "ungodliness and worldly passions" and instead to choose to live "self-controlled, upright, and godly lives" by the grace of God (Titus 2:11-12). You are giving your children the gift of a trained spirit. You are enabling them to grow in Christian maturity and to live each day in the power of the Holy Spirit, who is our only source of true Christian character (Galatians 5:25). You are giving them the ability to be self-disciplined or self-governing in their Christian walk, not needing others to rule over them in order to do what they know is right. You are instilling in them the biblical values and Christian character that will keep them on God's path of life and righteousness throughout their lives.

- **Training** — Develop your own list of family values. Create opportunities to exercise godly character. Affirm and reinforce expressions of maturity. Gradually enlarge their areas of stewardship and responsibility. Memorize verses about the Spirit.

- **Instruction** — About honoring and submitting to authority. About walking in the power of the Holy Spirit. About growing in Christlike character. About being a good steward. About biblical characteristics of spiritual maturity.

- **Modeling** — Demonstrate a controlled spirit when under stress. Practice any family values or rules. Talk about stewardship of family finances. Explain a choice or decision you had to make. Talk about how the Spirit helps you live in a godly manner.

IN OUR HOME

Clay wrote Our 24 Family Ways Family Devotional Guide *to address six areas of family life: authority, relationships, possessions, work, attitudes, and choices. Rather than just rules, we wanted to give our children the language of family values that they could easily remember and that we could easily use in training them in righteousness. For example, the following are the ways, or values, that relate to work habits:*

13. We are diligent to complete a task promptly and thoroughly when asked.

14. We take initiative to do all of our own work without needing to be told.

15. We work with a cooperative spirit, freely giving and receiving help.

16. We take personal responsibility to keep our home neat and clean at all times.

The 24 Family Ways help us teach biblical principles, create a common language, and provide some objective standards of behavior for our family. They allow us to avoid nagging and to focus more on positive training. Each way also has a related character quality and a Scripture memory verse.

Service

The gift of service is the desire and ability to minister God's grace and truth to the needs of others.

The gift of service prepares your children to consider it natural to always look for ways that they can be involved in meaningful ministry to others for Christ's sake. It is giving your children eyes that can see needs, hands willing to help meet those needs, and hearts willing to sacrifice, serve, and give generously in the name of Christ. It is easy to be self-centered and unaware of needs beyond our own in the insular world of Christian activities. Without trying, we can soon find ourselves looking out only for our own interests, rather than for the needs of others. But Christ wants our families to serve others. He wants us to be servants, like him, who look out for the needs and interests of others. If our children will one day lead, then they first must learn to serve. They can learn that first at home in a family that serves one another and also serves others—whether helping the poor, reaching the lost, or building up the body of Christ. Service is the natural expression of grace, which brings the GIFTS back to the beginning.

- **Training** — Get involved in a regular service project. Volunteer as a family for a church ministry. Train your children to show hospitality at home. Minister to missionaries (care packages, pen pals, etc.). Always give to the needy.

- **Instruction** — About personal testimony and witness. About God's heart for the poor and needy. About the ministry of the church. About the Great Commission and missions. About the biblical topics of giving and generosity.

- **Modeling** — Create opportunities for expressing hospitality to others. Pray for friends, missionaries, and the unsaved. Serve your spouse whenever possible. Be involved in a ministry in your church. Be generous with tips and giving to the homeless.

The man who loves his life will lose it, while the man who hates his life in this world will keep it for eternal life. Whoever serves me must follow me; and where I am, my servant also will be. My Father will honor the one who serves me.

— John 12:25-26

Do nothing out of selfish ambition or vain conceit, but in humility consider others better than yourselves. Each of you should look not only to your own interests, but also to the interests of others.

— Philippians 2:3-4

If anyone serves, he should do it with the strength God provides, so that in all things God may be praised through Jesus Christ.

— 1 Peter 4:11b

IN OUR HOME

We have always believed that ministry must begin at home: If we don't minister in our home, then we won't minister away from home. So we come full circle back to the first of the GIFTS, grace, in the LifeGIFTS model because the ministry of gracious hospitality we practice at home is the pattern for our ministry and service as a family outside the home— it is God's way for us to practice serving others in Christ's name. During holiday seasons, we go as a family to sing and serve at local nursing homes. After singing, we all visit with the residents. One Christmas, we took our support group choir to a homeless shelter to minister to homeless mothers and children. We filled stockings with useful and fun items to give away and included a pocket Bible or other spiritually encouraging materials. We also try to keep fast-food restaurant gift certificates in our cars that the kids can give to the "work for food" homeless people we come in contact with. Throughout the year, we look for similar ways to meet needs, bear burdens, remember the poor and oppressed, encourage the faithful, and use our gifts as a family for God.

These commandments that I give you today are to be upon your hearts. Impress them on your children. Talk about them when you sit at home and when you walk along the road, when you lie down and when you get up.

— Deuteronomy 6:6-7

Instruction, and advice, and commands will profit little, unless they are backed up by the pattern of your own life. Your children will never believe you are in earnest, and really wish them to obey you, so long as your actions contradict your counsel...Think not your children will practise what they do not see you do. You are their model picture, and they will copy what you are...[Your children] will seldom learn habits which they see you despise, or walk in paths in which you do not walk yourself.

— J. C. Ryle, *The Upper Room*, 1888

It All Starts in Your Heart

Before they were to cross the Jordan into the land God had promised to them, Moses gathered all the people of Israel together. He admonished them to love and serve God, to obey his commands and teachings, and to "impress them on your children." But there was one stipulation: "These commandments that I give you today are to be upon your hearts" (Deuteronomy 6:6-7). They were to be on the parents' hearts first. It wouldn't be enough for them only to tell their children how to live; they must also show them. Simply put, you cannot impress on your children's hearts what is not already on your own.

But what exactly does it mean that you are to impress the truths of God on your children's hearts? The Hebrew word translated "impress" (*sanan*) in the NIV is translated "diligently teach" or an equivalent in most other modern versions. In eight other uses in the Old Testament, though, it is translated "sharpen" or "whet." If that meaning is brought to this passage, then parents are to take the word of God which they have accepted into their own hearts (vs. 6) and use it literally to sharpen or whet their children's hearts. It is as though your child's heart is a dull, unsharpened knife, and it is your responsibility to use the Word of God to put a sharp edge on it. You are sharpening their spirits so they will be useful for God. You are giving them an edge so they can cut into life with God's truth. You are impressing the very words of God on their hearts, diligently teaching them, but even more you are using that truth to whet their hearts, to take away all that is dull and useless in order to leave a sharp edge of God's truth.

Christian home education may be a spiritual awakening through which God is restoring families and preparing for revival. The homeschooling movement may be the first fruits of a greater movement of God's Spirit in our country that is yet to come, and our children may be the seeds of a new and godly generation. Our children may become the sharp edge of truth that God will use to cut through the false beliefs of their generation. However, if our children are to be sharpened for their generation, we must be sharp for ours. If, indeed, we are preparing our children to become the Christian leaders of the next generation, then our goal must be no less than to raise up godly men and women who will be totally, wholeheartedly devoted to loving God and his Word and to living only to please him. We need, then, to seriously consider what qualities of godliness we want to develop in our children. Whatever goals we set for our children, we must also set for ourselves. Whatever we want to be on our children's hearts must first be on ours. Their sharpness will be determined by the quality of the whetting stone that puts an edge of truth on their hearts. We are that whetting stone.

Even though many teachers casually recite the axiom "Christianity is more caught than taught," the truth is more accurately expressed as "Christianity is best caught when taught." A passive Christian example pales in power and impact in relation to an active, verbal one. If you want to provide a true biblical model, whatever is on your heart must also be on your tongue. If biblical character and values are on your heart, then biblical teaching about them will be on your tongue in instructing your children. Wholehearted Christian children come from homes led by wholehearted Christian fathers and mothers. We must take the gospel to the nations, but the home will always be God's primary tool for reproducing believers in the world. And it all starts with your heart.

Feed Your Children with Fish and Bread

In Matthew 7:9-12, Jesus pictures God as a good father. A child who asks for a fish knows he will receive a fish, not a snake. A child who asks for bread knows he will receive bread, not a stone. Your children are asking you to give them a taste of real spiritual life—the same life of the Spirit that they see at work in your own heart. They want to learn from you not just how to live for Christ, but also how they can have the life of Christ they see in you in their own lives. If you are not actively imparting that life to them, then your passivity is the same as a snake or a stone to your child. Decide what you will give them and then determine to provide it. Like the five loaves and the two fishes offered in simple faith by a young boy, God will take what you have to give and multiply it to spiritually feed your children.

LifeGIFTS is a helpful tool for making sure that happens. But just to add a little creativity to your life-giving, you can also use the following acronyms, created from the words "fish" and "bread," to help you think strategically about nurturing your children with the life of the Spirit. Use the words below to provide some simple goals for imparting Christian character (what is important about me) and values (what is important to me) to your children. Be sure you're cultivating those traits in your own heart first, though, and then you can begin to impress them on your children's hearts.

FISH: Christian Character

- **Faithfulness** — To God, to his Word, to his cause, to your family, to your church, to his will for your family, to ministry, to witness.

- **Integrity** — In personal character, in family matters, in work, in finances, in ministry, in relationships, in agreements, in difficulties.

- **Self-Discipline** — To live righteously, to be contented, to persevere under trial, to resist temptation, to fulfill responsibilities.

- **Humility** — In relationships, in disagreements, in serving others, in being available, in being teachable, in asking forgiveness.

BREAD: Christian Values

- **Bible** — Reading it, studying it, memorizing it, talking about it, obeying it, believing it, trusting in its promises.

- **Relationships** — Spending time with your family, enjoying your children, fellowshipping with friends, reaching out to lost people.

- **Eternal Perspective** — Having a biblical worldview, trusting God for daily and future needs, longing for heaven.

- **Authority** — Submitting to authorities, taking biblical authority seriously, speaking positively of leaders, submitting to elders.

- **Disciplines** — Having regular devotions, praying alone and with children, worshipping God, serving others, confessing sins.

For the eyes of the LORD range throughout the earth to strengthen those whose hearts are fully committed to him.

— 2 Chronicles 16:9a

Which of you, if his son asks for bread, will give him a stone? Or if he asks for a fish, will give him a snake? If you, then, though you are evil, know how to give good gifts to your children, how much more will your Father in heaven give good gifts to those who ask him! So in everything, do to others what you would have them do to you, for this sums up the Law and the Prophets.

— Matthew 7:9-12

His divine power has given us everything we need for life and godliness through our knowledge of him who called us by his own glory and goodness. Through these he has given us his very great and precious promises, so that through them you may participate in the divine nature and escape the corruption in the world caused by evil desires.

For this very reason, make every effort to add to your faith goodness; and to goodness, knowledge; and to knowledge, self-control; and to self-control, perseverance; and to perseverance, godliness; and to godliness, brotherly kindness; and to brotherly kindness, love.

For if you possess these qualities in increasing measure, they will keep you from being ineffective and unproductive in your knowledge of our Lord Jesus Christ. But if anyone does not have them, he is nearsighted and blind, and has forgotten that he has been cleansed from his past sins.

Therefore, my brothers, be all the more eager to make your calling and election sure. For if you do these things, you will never fall, and you will receive a rich welcome into the eternal kingdom of our Lord and Savior Jesus Christ.

— 2 Peter 1:3-11

It All Ends in Your Child's Heart

There is perhaps no better picture of the power of nurture than in Peter's opening words in his second pastoral letter (2 Peter 1:3-11). Yes, it was written to adults, but the truths and principles can apply directly to parents and their children, as do the two resulting promises that every Christian parent wants to claim for their children.

Peter starts by declaring that we have everything we need for "life and godliness" and that it is found in Christ. It is all given so that we can "participate in the divine nature" and experience the life of God. That is all the language of nurture. Then Peter describes the process that will enable any person to find that life. He offers not just random qualities and commitments, but a progressive picture of biblical nurture. Faith is the foundation upon which everything else will be built, and each quality builds on the one before it. This is how biblical nurture should work. To faith, add...

- **Goodness** — because faith leads to pursuing morality and goodness.
- **Knowledge** — because goodness leads to desiring more divine truth.
- **Self-Control** — because truth leads to exercising more self-control.
- **Perseverance** — because self-control leads to the need to persevere.
- **Godliness** — because perseverance leads to pursuing godliness.
- **Brotherly Kindness** — because godliness leads to fellowship (*philia*, love).
- **Love** — because fellowship leads to unconditional love (*agape*, love).

If you, as a Christian parent, are growing in these qualities and you are adding them to your children's lives in order to nurture the life of Christ in them, Peter lets you know that you can claim two promises. First, these qualities will keep you and your children "from being ineffective and unproductive" in your knowledge of Christ. As you nurture your children and impart the life of Christ to them, you can be assured that they will grow in their spiritual maturity. Second, these qualities come with the promise that "if you do these things, you will never fall, and you will receive a rich welcome into the eternal kingdom of our Lord and Savior Jesus Christ." Although every child will grow by learning how to overcome temptation and sin, no godly parent ever wants their children to have to learn from failure that leads to a fall. Peter is saying that when you add the seven qualities and virtues to your children's faith, you are strengthening them so they will not fall into a pattern of sin or fall away from God. That is a biblical promise to pursue!

We started this chapter with the observation that too many homeschooled children, raised in "good Christian homes," are falling away from their faith. Peter's words, though, are a strong biblical assurance that this does not have to happen. We strongly believe the key is understanding the power of biblical nurture—shepherding your children's spirits to long for God and imparting the life of Christ into their hearts. It starts with your heart, but it will end with your child's heart. Based on Peter's promise, the end can and should be a good one. We want you to finish well as a homeschooling parent and be able to rejoice as you see your child graduate into adulthood with a heart beating strongly for God and his kingdom. You don't have to grieve over a fallen child; God's principles will work. Start today—make nurture the first priority of your Christian home.

— Chapter 4 —

Home Discipleship: Shaping Your Child's Heart to Live for God

Following You as You Follow Jesus

If you use the term "discipleship" to describe something you want to happen with your children at home, then you need to understand what it really means biblically. Since the middle of the twentieth century, discipleship has come to mean much more than just its biblical references. It is a relatively recent collective term created to express a process that Jesus and the Bible describe but never fully define—the process of becoming and growing as a follower of Jesus. Today, the process called discipleship is often expressed in church programs, personal ministry strategies, curriculum packages, and teaching conferences. And yet there is no universally accepted definition of discipleship.

In Jesus' day, though, everyone understood exactly what it meant to be a disciple. Both Greek and Jewish teachers would gather disciples, who would follow, learn from, and become like their teachers. When Jesus called his followers disciples, he was not creating something new, but rather infusing the common Jewish rabbinical model of making disciples with new meaning. His disciples would become like him not only externally, but also internally through the power of the Holy Spirit (John 14:15ff). The Spirit would teach them after he was gone (John 15:26-27), and they would be known not just for their knowledge, but also by their love for one another (John 13:35). After his resurrection, Jesus instructed his followers to "go and make disciples," by teaching them and baptizing them into the new community of believers, all of whom would be filled with the Spirit (Matthew 28:19-20; Acts 1:4-8). But as Christianity moved into the Roman world, the language of discipleship was dropped—put aside midway through the book of Acts (11:26) and never used in any of the New Testament letters. It was not an important term for Paul, Peter, John, or any of the epistolary writers. As Christianity spread and grew, other terms took its place—church (*ekklesia*), fellowship (*koinonia*), family, and body.

So, what do we mean by home discipleship? As we saw in chapter 3, home nurture is about shepherding your child's spirit to long for God. Home discipleship is the next step—it is shaping your child's heart to live for God. It is taking the sensitivity you have cultivated in their spirit to know God and experience his life and building on that to help them to know more about God's truth and what it means to live for him. Simply put, discipleship is the process of beginning to walk on God's path of life and to follow Christ. Although it will involve some studies and reading and perhaps even some curriculum, it is at its core a relational process, just as it was in Jesus' day. Only now, you as the parent play the role of Jesus. You are inviting your children to walk with you and with Jesus, who lives within you, so they can begin to follow, learn from, and be like Jesus. Your children are not your disciples—you are both disciples of Jesus, learning together to follow him and be like him. When that happens at home, it is home discipleship.

A student is not above his teacher, but everyone who is fully trained will be like his teacher.

— Luke 6:40

Parenting is a much bigger part of the Christian life than most of us care to admit. Under your care are eternal beings whose courses for eternity will be set, in large measure, by what you do. Who and what they become will be shaped by how you relate to them, discipline them, instruct them, counsel them, and love them. What they believe and think about God will be influenced by the God they see in you...When I think about this, I'm struck by how utterly dependent I need to be on God. I want as much of Him in my parenting as possible.

— Clay Clarkson, *Heartfelt Discipline*, WaterBrook Press, 2003

Disciplined Discipleship

You may have heard someone teach that the terms "discipline" and "disciple" are related because they share the same linguistic roots. That may be true in English, but it is not true for the New Testament Greek terms. In Greek, the two word families are completely unrelated.

- *Mathetes* (n) — a disciple, follower, pupil, student
- *Manthano* (v) — to learn, to acquire knowledge
- *Paideia* (n) — discipline, training, upbringing, instruction
- *Paideuo* (v) — to discipline, train, bring up, instruct

Listen, my son, accept what I say, and the years of your life will be many. I guide you in the way of wisdom and lead you along straight paths. When you walk, your steps will not be hampered; when you run, you will not stumble...The path of the righteous is like the first gleam of dawn, shining ever brighter till the full light of day. But the way of the wicked is like deep darkness; they do not know what makes them stumble...Let your eyes look straight ahead, fix your gaze directly before you. Make level paths for your feet and take only ways that are firm. Do not swerve to the right or the left; keep your foot from evil.

— Proverbs 4:10-12, 18-19, 25-27

Trust in the LORD with all your heart and lean not on your own understanding; in all your ways acknowledge him, and he will make your paths straight.

— Proverbs 3:5-6

The root [of the Hebrew word for discipline] denotes correction that contributes to education. Biblical discipline (chastisement) is goal oriented: it seeks to develop a godly person who is responsive to the Lord and who walks in his ways.

— Dr. Lawrence O. Richards, *Expository Dictionary of Biblical Words,* Zondervan, 1985

Parenting on the Path of Life

When Jesus said, "I am the way and the truth and the life," he was not only saying he was the only way to God, but also alluding to being the fulfillment of the Old Testament concept of the way of life or the way of righteousness. In fact, Jesus' statement could be rendered, "I am the way, even the truth and the life" (John 14:6, NET). Paul, before his conversion, referred to the followers of Jesus as "the Way" (Acts 9:2), a name that was still in use twenty years later (Acts 24:14, 22). Jesus is the way, the path of life.

From the early days of Israel's existence as a nation, Hebrew parents and children understood the imagery of the path of life. It captured for them the whole process of godly discipline, a term in Hebrew that encompasses much more than just punishment or correction and that is roughly synonymous with what we now call discipleship. Discipline was the process of one person leading another into a righteous life pleasing to God. The book of Proverbs is all about that kind of life-directing discipline. In the first nine chapters of Proverbs, Solomon appeals regularly to God's path of life as he admonishes his sons as a father to follow his and their mother's instruction and lives—to acquire wisdom and discernment, to avoid the path of sinners and the way of fools, and to choose to walk on God's path of life. The path of life was not just an abstract theological concept for Hebrew parents, but a powerful picture of truth.

The path, or way, is an analogy for life that almost any child can understand from a very early age, and one that becomes even more meaningful and internalized as they grow older. The power for young children is in the concreteness of the image it evokes. They can understand in an uncomplicated way that they need to stay on the path God has provided for them in order to be safe from evil and harm. As young adults, they will understand more fully what the righteousness is that defines the path, what the temptations really are that can lure them off God's path, and what it really means to be lost in sin. If you "train a child in the way he should go" when he is young, then "when he is old he will not turn from it" because he will know "the way" (Proverbs 22:6). Once the picture of the path of life is implanted in a child's mind, it will be there the rest of their adult life.

For that reason, we are using the language of the path of life in this chapter to describe three priorities of home discipleship—direction, correction, and protection. You must first give your children direction so they know which way they are to go. When they wander off the path, they will need correction to bring them back to it. As they journey further along the path, they will need protection from temptations and unrighteous influences that can draw them away from God. You walk with your children on the path, and they look to you to be their guide. That is what it means to disciple your children—to help them stay on the path. Home discipleship is what happens as you walk with them.

There is always the temptation to reduce discipleship to a program, a project, a course of study, or a set of rules. This may be especially true in a curriculum-driven homeschooling community. The danger when that happens is not about doing something biblically wrong, but about missing the biblical dynamic and fulfillment of home discipleship as it could be—the influence of personal relationships, the leading and power of the Holy Spirit, and the joy of the journey exploring God's path of life together. Understanding the path of life can help preserve the spiritual dynamic of home discipleship.

DIRECTION — Moving Along on the Path

The first priority of home discipleship is direction. In order to "train a child in the way he should go," you need to have a clear understanding of what the way to go is. Wandering along a path without any sense of direction is a sure way at best to go nowhere, and at worst to get lost. Fortunately, there is a Path of Life Guide Book, the Bible, that spells out how to make sure you're moving along the path in the right direction.

But that book takes much study to master, so your children need a good guide who knows the Guide Book, who studies its insights and instructions, and who knows where to look when there is a question or the need for direction Being a good guide, though, is more than being only a personal repository of Guide Book facts and information that you dispassionately dispense from somewhere down the path out in front of everyone else. A good guide walks beside the ones he is guiding, understanding that this is a new experience for them, and that they are not all that confident yet. He sympathizes with them, encourages them, and loves them. And into that relationship a good guide is then able to inject instruction from the Guide Book that will help those he is guiding. Real guidance is about much more than just useful content—it is about relationships.

As Christian parents, you are the guides that God has appointed for your children. He trusts you to be able to do the job—there is no heavenly hand-wringing wondering if he has chosen the best guides for your children. Everything you'll need to know to be a faithful and fruitful guide is in God's Word—all the directions and instructions you will need to make sure you and your children keep moving along the path. Your children are excited and ready to make the journey, knowing that you will be walking beside them, sympathizing, encouraging, loving, and instructing them all the way.

Those are, in fact, the qualities that will make your children want to follow your leadership as you move along together on the path of life. Being a good guide and giving good direction is not a static, by-the-numbers formal procedure, but rather a dynamic, always-changing relational process. The further you move along the path, the more your direction will be shaped by the four qualities of leadership in the following pages. Choose to lead your children with sympathy, encouragement, love, and instruction.

Even a child is known by his actions, by whether his conduct is pure and right.

— Proverbs 20:11

Where the believing parent seeks not only to form the habits of obedience, but in prayer and faith to mould and guide and strengthen the will of the child in the way of the Lord, he may count upon the workings of God's Holy Spirit to do what God alone can do. In covenant with God...he does not shrink back from this highest and holiest of tasks, the training of that mighty power, a will made after the image of God's will, and now under the power of sin. He reckons on a Divine wisdom to guide him; he counts on a Divine strength to work with him and for him; he trusts in a Divine faithfulness to make the word true and sure in all its fulness, "Train up a child in the way he should go; when he is old, he will not depart from it."

— Rev. Andrew Murray, *The Children for Christ*, 1887

IN OUR HOME

The "path of life" has been part of our family language from the time our children were very small. We have even had various pictures of families on paths through the years to visualize it for our children. Proverbs 4:18-19 planted the image in our minds as parents, and we knew immediately we would use it with our children. We talked about how we would direct them to stay on God's path of life, which was good and safe. However, they knew that when they wandered off that path, we would correct them to bring them back, not because we were mad at them, but because we wanted them to be safe. We all liked talking about "weeds of wickedness" and the "dark forest of sin" that lay beyond the path. And, of course, we talked of how we would protect them from bad influences trying to lure them off the path (flowering weeds with thorns, and the like). None of us will forget the way!

It is unquestionably true that in no way can any parent gain such power over his child for the shaping of the child's character and habits of life as by having and showing sympathy with that child.

— H. Clay Trumbull, *Hints on Child Training*, 1890

Endeavour by your own tranquillity, gentleness, and kindliness to promote the same feelings in the child. Count upon the wonderful ascendency and influence over children that sympathy gives, in both its aspects. Throw yourself in sympathy into their interests, entering into their state of mind and feeling. Expect them—for their nature is as keenly susceptible of sympathy for others as from others—to enter into your spirit and temper, and instinctively to yield themselves to its influence.

— Rev. Andrew Murray, *The Children for Christ*, 1887

Love should be the silver thread that runs through all your conduct. Kindness, gentleness, longsuffering, forbearance, patience, sympathy, a willingness to enter into childish troubles, a readiness to take part in childish joys, —these are the cords by which a child may be led most easily,— these are the clues you must follow if you would find the way to his heart.

— J. C. Ryle, *The Upper Room*, 1888

Direction: Leading with SYMPATHY (vs. Strictness)

It is common for Christian parents today to proclaim to others, "Oh, I'm definitely a strict disciplinarian." The suggestion, of course, is that they are in control of their children. You probably would not hear someone argue back, "Yeah, well, I'm a sympathetic disciplinarian." They might as well write "permissive" on their forehead, that pejorative of parenting shame tied to the rejected 1950s philosophy of Dr. Benjamin Spock. And yet, just over one hundred years ago, the idea of sympathy was a guiding principle of biblical child training among noted Christian writers and teachers. To them, sympathy was not about permissiveness, and it did not suggest weakness in parenting. Rather, it was the willingness to understand and validate a child's thoughts and feelings, in order to create a channel to the inside of that child's heart. Sympathy, for them, was a powerful and strategic means of gaining a child's heart in order to direct their lives.

For young children (roughly up to about age 12), when they are mentioned in Scripture, there really is no defensible argument to justify what we call "strict discipline" as some kind of biblical mandate or pattern. What little is said about young children in Scripture (as distinct from young adults) views them as vulnerable, maturing, and in need of direction. When you read the views of some of those nineteenth-century Christian teachers, it's clear they relied on sympathy as an important part of their parenting skill set. Giving direction to their children's lives required sympathy.

Even though it sounds a bit counterintuitive in today's culture, sympathy is a key quality of leading your children. As a homeschooling parent who is with your children all day every day, you have much more opportunity than most parents to win your children's hearts. You have time to ask questions and talk about life, interests, amusements, concerns, fears, and delights, and to respond to your child's heart needs. Every child is an individual who needs a different voice of discipline, a different touch of mercy, and a different word of encouragement, and each has special potential that you, as a sympathetic parent, are uniquely and divinely situated to see, affirm, and direct.

Sympathy is the first priority of direction for a reason—it is what will turn you toward your child's heart so that your child's heart will turn toward yours. If you start your homeschooling journey with that dynamic, you will be well on your way to a life of blessing and fruitfulness. Sympathy is not a time-efficient quality, and it will require more commitment and sacrifice from you as a parent, but it will result in a greater reward as your children give you their hearts and want to follow your direction.

IN OUR HOME

As parents, we do not always express our love for our children according to biblical principles and patterns. Occasionally one of us will "lose it" and unload verbally on our kids. Like when Mom gives work assignments three times that don't get done. Or when Dad finds his tools left in the yard overnight in the rain. Like most normal parents, we have our "bad discipline" days when our gentle, sympathetic, loving spirits seem to go into hiding. Fortunately, our children know it's a passing phase (although they do get very obedient very quickly on those days). We recover quickly because we know their hearts, and they know ours.

Direction: Leading with ENCOURAGEMENT (vs. Guilt)

You can turn your child's heart toward yours with sympathy, but then you are faced with the challenge of how to motivate that heart to move forward and how to instill in your child the self-motivation that will cause them to want to reach for more, to desire to walk on the path of life, and to choose wisdom over foolishness, right over wrong. That is the purpose of the second leadership quality of direction—to give your children encouragement (literally, to instill courage and boldness into them). The problem is, real encouragement takes a lot of time, and it is easier for us when we're in a rush to just motivate by fear and guilt, rather than by encouragement. It is much easier to say, "Stop acting like such a child!" than it is to take the time to encourage that child in a positive, biblical way to want to grow or get better at something. Guilt is the enemy of encouragement.

Life is just beginning to stretch out before your children with all of its possibilities, mysteries, and struggles, and they are looking to you for confidence. Whether you are aware of it or not, you need to give your children reasons to believe that there really is a God, that their journey through this life has purpose and meaning, and that there is an eternal home after death. They need to hear you affirm their developing maturity, even though they know they are inconsistent, immature, and weak. They need to know that you are proud of their efforts and achievements in homeschooling, whether learning comes easily or with difficulty for them. They need to know that you see their potential—that you believe that God will use their emerging skills and interests.

If sympathy is an expression of love that focuses on the present moment, then encouragement looks to the future. The aim of encouragement is to strengthen the heart and bolster the spirit—to point your child to God and to God's Word. The best language for encouragement is the words of Scripture itself; the next best is the words that your child knows are from your heart. A child who is regularly encouraged personally and biblically will naturally grow in confidence, and will have a hopeful outlook on the future. And rather than being driven away by guilt messages to look for encouragement elsewhere, whether real or counterfeit, your children will see you as their best source of encouragement and will gladly keep coming to you for direction. If they have hope, they will be self-motivated to follow your direction for the path of life. As you walk along the path with them, yours will be the hand of encouragement reaching back to help them up the difficult or rocky parts of the road. You are the encouragement they need.

IN OUR HOME

Every year on each child's birthday, usually after a special breakfast with Sally's cinnamon rolls, we take time to have each person in the family tell the birthday child (or parent) what they think is special about them and how they have seen them grow in the past year. It is a time of encouragement and affirmation of personality, gifts, abilities, and skills. Then we all pray for that person for the year ahead. The time is important not only for all the encouragement the birthday person receives, but also for how it helps us all learn how to communicate meaningful encouragement to others. We all want others to say things that make us feel more positive and hopeful, but we also want our children to be able to give that encouragement to others.

For everything that was written in the past was written to teach us, so that through endurance and the encouragement of the Scriptures we might have hope.

— Romans 15:4

And let us consider how we may spur one another on toward love and good deeds. Let us not give up meeting together, as some are in the habit of doing, but let us encourage one another—and all the more as you see the Day approaching.

— Hebrews 10:24-25

In the struggle between good and evil that goes on in the child, there is nothing so much needed as that he should be encouraged to believe that the victory of the good is within his reach, that goodness is possible and pleasant. To inspire a child with a holy confidence in what, by God's grace and the aid of his parents, he can accomplish, is one of the blessed secrets of success in training.

— Rev. Andrew Murray, *The Children for Christ,* 1887

That the child may never be discouraged by thinking that its weakness is not taken account of, that its little reasonings are not regarded, that it has not received the pity or the help or the justice it expects, will need a love which children all too little receive, and a thoughtfulness which parents all to little bestow...And as you seek to maintain the rule of love, —not the mere love of natural instinct, but of love as a principle of action, earnestly sought in prayer from above, and carefully cultivated in all your family life, —you will find how the children will catch its spirit, and become your helpers in making your home the reflection of the life of love in which the Heavenly Father guides and trains His children.

— Rev. Andrew Murray, *The Children for Christ*, 1887

It has been said that the essence of teaching is causing another to know. *It may similarly be said that the essence of training is causing another to* do. *Teaching gives knowledge. Training gives skill. Teaching fills the mind. Training shapes the habits...The parent who does not recognize the possibility of training his children as well as instructing them, misses one of his highest privileges as a parent, and fails of his most important work for his children.*

— H. Clay Trumbull, *Hints on Child Training*, 1890

Direction: Leading with LOVE (vs. Neglect)

When they are led with sympathy, your children will want to step onto the path of life with you; leading with encouragement will motivate them to want to move ahead on the path; leading with love will give them a reason to follow you on the path. "Love" can be an abstract term, so let's use the two Greek words for love used in the New Testament. *Philia* we'll call "familial love," the kind that will cause your children to say, "I really love our family." *Agape* we'll call "parental love," the kind that will cause you to make whatever sacrifices are necessary to create the kind of home you know God wants you to provide for your children. *Philia* love is the two-way brotherly love Jesus shared with his disciples; *agape* love is the one-way sacrificial love that took Jesus to the cross to die for our sins. Both kinds of biblical love are necessary as you give your children direction.

God has designed your children's hearts to expect love from their parents. When they don't receive familial and parental love, it is a kind of neglect of their spiritual and emotional nourishment, in the same way that not receiving food would neglect their physical nourishment. A child whose need for love is neglected will begin to close their heart and emotions out of self-protection. But God designed a child's heart with an expectation that you will give them the love they desire, so you would be the greatest spiritual influence in their developing heart. Not only that, but your commitment to loving your children is the purest confirmation that home discipleship is occurring, just as Jesus said, "By this all men will know that you are my disciples, if you love (*agape*) one another." If you are committed to directing your children, you must love them as Christ loves you.

Direction: Leading with INSTRUCTION (vs. Information)

Finally, as you secure the openness of their hearts to your influence through sympathy, encouragement, and love, you will then be able to speak into their lives biblical instruction. This is the true heart of providing direction for your children—instructing them in the words and ways of God so they will walk faithfully and fruitfully on the path of life as children, then as young adults, and ultimately as adults. Your instruction in providing direction for their lives will take many forms, including life lessons, stories, and great books. But the instruction that will have the greatest impact will be the direction you give them from the Word of God—the wisdom of Proverbs, the teachings of Jesus and Paul, the doctrines of truth about God and man, the inspiration of the Psalms, the examples of men and women of faith, the encouragement of prophecy, the reasons for our faith, the hope of the gospel, the power of the resurrection.

Biblical instruction is more than just dispensing impersonal information—it is divine revelation that leads to personal transformation. The "God-breathed" Scripture that is the content of your instruction will be "useful for teaching, rebuking, correcting and training in righteousness, so that the man of God may be thoroughly equipped for every good work" (2 Timothy 3:16-17). Into their open hearts, especially during the childhood years, you have the opportunity to pour in transforming instruction that will direct and set the course of their lives. That is the ultimate goal of home discipleship—to prepare your children to live faithfully as truth-transformed adults. (See chapter 10 for practical ideas for Bible instruction.)

CORRECTION — Getting Back on the Path

Correction is the heart of biblical discipline, but Scripture does not define one way to do it. In this chapter, we'll suggest four biblical training methods for correcting your children when discipline is needed—different methods for different needs. You may be more comfortable with some methods of training than with others, but you should know how to use them all and how to discern which is the best training method for different discipline needs. And because these are God's methods of training, you should know how to use them all in the same way he corrects you—with grace, gentleness, and love.

It is your responsibility to teach and train your children to honor you with proper attitudes (Ephesians 6:1-3) and obey you with proper actions (Colossians 3:20). If they will not honor and obey you, they will be handicapped in understanding how to honor and obey God, and thus in growing in maturity as a Christian. Some parents can fall into a pattern of demanding obedience, but not honor. They can make a child stop a wrong or unwanted behavior ("Stop whining right now!"), but ignore the dishonor in the child's heart (pouting, sulking, anger). Although your children must learn to obey regardless of their feelings, training for obedience does not mean that every situation must become a "me parent...you child" confrontation of wills. It also means learning to be sensitive to issues of age, personality, and circumstances, not expecting the same kind of obedience from a five-year-old that you would from a ten-year-old or demanding perfect obedience when your children are tired or overstimulated. Your children's obedience is the way they will show their love for God (John 14:15). Your job is to help them love God better.

Correction is about reaching your child's heart. In the over 900 references to "heart" in Scripture, the meaning is consistent—heart is who I am. Heart is the "inner man" that is the conscious awareness of everything that defines a person—spirit, intellect, emotion, volition, and reason. The heart is fallen and sinful (we want to sin), but God changes hearts by his grace to respond to him, and that is the purpose of biblical discipline—to train the heart of your child to respond to God and his grace. Paul told Titus that the "grace of God that brings salvation" also "teaches us to say 'No' to ungodliness and worldly passions, and to live self-controlled, upright and godly lives" (Titus 2:11-12). God's grace is a teacher, just like you—it is an inner parent. If you want grace to teach your child's heart, then you must be taught and led by grace yourself. As you understand the impact of God's grace in your own life—his patience, mercy, and gentleness toward you as a sinner—you will be able to extend that same grace to your child when correcting their sins. Correction that expresses God's grace will reach the heart of your child.

Your child's misbehavior is like a PowerPoint presentation of whatever is directing their heart. Jesus said that a person speaks from the overflow of whatever is in their heart, whether it is good or evil (Luke 6:45). Your role as a parent is to fill your child's heart with as much good as you can, and then to train them to choose the PowerPoint slides of behavior that please God. It is the principle that God sets before us a blessing and a curse—we can choose the blessing which leads to life or the curse which leads to death. As you exercise discipline as a parent, you are rearranging the slides of your child's heart, putting the "good" ones at the front (blessings), and pushing the "bad" ones to the back (curses). What you are doing is, literally, "heart work," but as you work to change your child's heart, and their behavior, you are doing sacred work for God.

Children, obey your parents in the Lord, for this is right. "Honor your father and mother"—which is the first commandment with a promise—"that it may go well with you and that you may enjoy long life on the earth."

— Ephesians 6:1-3

Children, obey your parents in everything, for this pleases the Lord. Fathers, do not embitter your children, or they will become discouraged.

— Colossians 3:20-21

Only at home can children be trained in the chivalrous temper of "proud submission and dignified obedience;" and if the parents do not inspire and foster deference, reverence and loyalty, how shall these crowning graces of character thrive in a hard and emulous world?

— Charlotte Mason, *Parents and Children*, 1896

No Lost Hearts

Paul tells the Colossian fathers, "do not exasperate your children, so that they will not lose heart" (3:21, NASB). Literally, he says "don't stir up anger" in your children, and the context is harshness (3:19), and even fairness and justice (4:1). When a father, or parent, is harsh and judgmental with a child, it has the effect of first stirring up their anger or passionate feelings, but then leaving them discouraged and spent, or "without passion." Being harsh has two effects— you lose their hearts, and they lose their hearts. You cannot win and influence a child's heart by being harsh and judgmental. If you want to reach the heart of your child, your heart must be filled with the fruit of the Spirit (Galatians 5:22).

But the fruit of the Spirit is love, joy, peace, patience, kindness, goodness, faithfulness, gentleness and self-control. Against such things there is no law.

— Galatians 5:22

Walking in the Spirit

Walking in the Spirit is not a magic formula that will make you spiritual, but simply living by faith. Here are some simple, biblical steps you can take to begin walking in the Spirit.

- **Confess** — Confess any known sins in your heart and life to God. Agree with God and accept his forgiveness and cleansing. (1 John 1:9)
- **Submit** — No longer sin, but present yourself to God as an "instrument of righteousness" ready to do his will. (Romans 6:12-14)
- **Read** — Read the Scripture daily and diligently. The Holy Spirit speaks to your heart mainly through God's Word. (Hebrews 4:12-13)
- **Pray** — Talk to God throughout the day. Learn to listen for his voice. God hears your thoughts and is listening all the time. (Ephesians 6:18-20)
- **Fellowship** — Spend regular time with other Christians who will encourage you in the Spirit to be faithful and strong. (Hebrews 10:23-25)
- **Trust** — You can say you believe that God is alive and actively involved in your life, but trusting is acting on that truth. (Philippians 4:4-7)

Correction: Training with SPIRITUAL DISCIPLINE

Spiritual discipline acknowledges that correction is a spiritual event, not just a parental act—it is about correcting the inward "thoughts and attitudes of the heart" (Hebrews 4:12), not just controlling outward behavior. It is not generally recognized as an actual method of training or correction, but it is literally the heart of true biblical discipline. If my first impulse is to think about which proven method of discipline will achieve the results I want with my children, then I am probably not thinking about trusting God to change my children's hearts. What I do with this first training method of correction could say a great deal about whether or not I believe God is intimately involved in my discipline and whether or not I am intimately involved with his. If I want my correction to impact my child's heart, I must first, before anything else, ask God, the heavenly parent, to be involved in the process with me.

The active element in spiritual discipline is God's grace—the presence and power of God flowing into and through your family. Because your children are young and still immature, you are by God's design the primary channel of his grace into their hearts. In one sense, much more than being only a method of training, spiritual discipline is the oil of grace that will make the other three methods more effective. In order to apply that oil, though, you need to be receiving God's grace into your own life (see page 47). When you receive grace through God's Word, you can use it in your correction to seek guidance, claim promises, or become the language of your discipline. When you receive grace through prayer, you can pray with your child for the Spirit to work in their spirit. When you receive grace through fellowship, you can bring other voices and other examples of godliness into your correction. Grace ensures that your correction begins with the "inner man" of your child. That is the real goal of spiritual discipline—to change your child's heart so their behavior is changed from the inside out.

You can choose to parent by any of five basic motivations: by the flesh (depending on yourself); by fear (depending on others); by feeling (depending on your emotions); by formula (depending on methods); or you can parent by faith (depending on God). In our early years of parenting, we felt obligated to use "proven" training and discipline methods created by others, but over time found ourselves blindly using methods that didn't always work, put us under a burden of performance and guilt, and treated our children like part of a formula rather than as persons of dignity made in God's image. When we learned how to parent in the power of the Holy Spirit, we discovered the grace and freedom that Christ promised. And more important, our children experienced God's grace through us.

Parenting by faith can be a difficult biblical truth for many parents to grasp. We all want to believe there is a proven biblical method of childhood training and discipline that will make us successful parents. But that is a myth. God did not define a method in Scripture because he would give us something better—the Holy Spirit. The ultimate success of your parenting is not just up to you; it is up to God. If you are faithfully and prayerfully parenting in the power of the Holy Spirit, you can leave the results in his hands. He gave us his Spirit so we can live by his grace, rather than by man-made laws, methods, and rules. If you want your children to see the presence of God in your life and to know his grace, then you must learn what it means to walk each day in the power of the Holy Spirit. Practicing spiritual discipline requires a spiritual parent who is led by the Holy Spirit.

Correction: Training with VERBAL DISCIPLINE

The second tool of correction is one that is always talked about (literally) because it is the first-response level of correction. Parents don't need an expert to teach them how to say "No!" or "Stop that!" to a child. Verbal discipline comes naturally. However, biblical verbal discipline only comes *super*naturally. True verbal discipline requires more of you as a parent than the ability to verbalize a command; it requires you to know the Scriptures, be able to recall them, and discern how to apply them for correction.

When Paul wrote to Timothy that the Word of God teaches, rebukes, corrects, and trains in righteousness (2 Timothy 3:16), he was describing the goals of verbal discipline. Scripture should be consistently taught, talked about, and learned in your home so the standard for all right and wrong behavior is God's words, not just parental opinions or pronouncements. Verbal discipline that includes the Word of God affirms to your children that you are their earthly authority, but even more that God is their ultimate authority. Your authority, though, should never be expressed as parental power that lords it over your children with harsh words or demands (Matthew 20:25-28).

Christlike love is critical to effective verbal discipline. When you confront and correct your children's wrongdoing, think about how Jesus would speak to them. He would be gentle, but authoritative; loving, but truthful; gracious, but firm. Verbal gentleness creates a positive atmosphere of grace, even though discipline might be hard. Your verbal discipline should be characterized by the fruit of the Spirit, which is really the character of Jesus—"love, joy, peace, patience, kindness, goodness, faithfulness, gentleness and self-control" (Galatians 5:22-23). In contrast, strictness, harshness, anger, and judgmentalism create an atmosphere of legalism. Yelling, nagging, blaming, and shaming may result in temporarily desirable results, but few parents really want their children to obey out of fear and guilt. Gentleness keeps verbal discipline in the realm of grace, where children learn to obey from the heart, for the right reasons—to please God and their parents. Consider some Scriptures that balance both discipline and gentleness:

- **1 Corinthians 4:21** — What do you desire? Shall I come to you with a rod, or with love and a spirit of gentleness? (NASB; Paul's implied answer is the latter.)

- **Galatians 6:1** — Brethren, even if anyone is caught in any trespass, you who are spiritual, restore such a one in a spirit of gentleness. (NASB)

- **Romans 2:4** — Or do you show contempt for the riches of his kindness, tolerance and patience, not realizing that God's kindness leads you toward repentance?

- **Matthew 11:29** — Take my yoke upon you and learn from me, for I am gentle and humble in heart, and you will find rest for your souls.

- **1 Thessalonians 2:7** — But we proved to be gentle among you, as a nursing mother tenderly cares for her own children. (NASB)

- **2 Timothy 2:24-25** — And the Lord's servant must not quarrel; instead, he must be kind to everyone, able to teach, not resentful. Those who oppose him he must gently instruct, in the hope that God will grant them repentance leading them to a knowledge of the truth.

For the word of God is living and active. Sharper than any double-edged sword, it penetrates even to dividing soul and spirit, joints and marrow; it judges the thoughts and attitudes of the heart. Nothing in all creation is hidden from God's sight. Everything is uncovered and laid bare before the eyes of him to whom we must give account.

— Hebrews 4:12-13

But as for you, continue in what you have learned and have become convinced of, because you know those from whom you learned it, and how from infancy you have known the holy Scriptures, which are able to make you wise for salvation through faith in Christ Jesus. All Scripture is God-breathed and is useful for teaching, rebuking, correcting and training in righteousness, so that the man of God may be thoroughly equipped for every good work.

— 2 Timothy 3:14-17

There are times, indeed, when words may be multiplied to advantage in explaining to a child the nature and consequences of his offense, and the reasons why he should do differently in the future; but such words should always be spoken in gentleness, and in self-controlled earnestness. Scolding—rapidly spoken censure and protest, in the exhibit of strong feeling—is never in order as a means of training and directing a child.

— H. Clay Trumbull, *Hints On Child Training*, 1890

No discipline seems pleasant at the time, but painful. Later on, however, it produces a harvest of righteousness and peace for those who have been trained by it.

— Hebrews 12:11

Every child ought to be trained to conform his will to the demands of duty; but that is bending his will, not breaking it... Training a child's will is bringing such influences to bear upon the child that he is ready to choose or decide in favor of the right course of action...The final responsibility of a choice and of its consequences rests with the child, and not with the parent... Merely to force one will into subjection to the other is...an injury both to the one who forces and to the one who submits.

— H. Clay Trumbull, *Hints on Child Training*, 1890

Beyond Discipline

There will be times when there is more to your child's behavior than meets the "I won't!" Be sensitive to influences that might explain uncharacteristically challenging behavior. Don't make unreasonable excuses, but do make reasonable allowances when there is an identifiable influence. Remember that your child is not an adult. Here are just a few "beyond discipline" kinds of influences to consider:

- Tiredness
- Overstimulation
- Hunger
- Illness (fever, aches)
- Medication
- Stress
- Irritability (bad day)
- Relationship issues
- Imitative behavior
- Immaturity or childishness
- Condition (dyslexia, hearing)
- Physiology (pain, discomfort)
- Hormones
- Fears (irrational, phobia)
- Disorders (ADHD, OCD)
- Abuse (hidden or repressed)

Correction: Training with BEHAVIORAL DISCIPLINE

Behavioral discipline, the third tool of correction, is the easiest to understand, but it is also a multifunction tool that invites an almost limitless range of creativity in how it is used. Its purpose is always the same—to make your children accountable for their own behavioral actions and choices—but its implementation will almost never be the same. It is the if-then method of corrective discipline ("If you do that, then this will happen"), and it even has its own book in the Bible—Proverbs, which is all about the consequences of choosing either foolishness or wisdom. Behavioral discipline is not always negative, and it can also provide incentives to encourage rightdoing, but it more often provides consequences to discourage wrongdoing (Galatians 6:7-8). The most common expressions of behavioral discipline are natural consequences and logical consequences.

- **Natural consequences** — This follows general foolishness and wrongdoing when there has been no prior agreement concerning a behavior. For example, if a child drops an ice cream cone because he was behaving in a way he knew was foolish, then the natural consequence would be losing the ice cream. If two children are fussing, then they must sit quietly without speaking to one another for thirty minutes. You might also use time-outs, loss of privileges, additional work, or other natural responses. Generally use a measured response and a consequence that you feel is suited to the misbehavior. An objectively applied natural consequence teaches your children that they are always responsible for their own behavioral choices.

- **Logical consequences** — This follows specific wrongdoing when there has been a prior agreement concerning certain behaviors. In other words, your child knows what will happen if they choose to behave in a certain way. For example, if a child says unkind words to a sibling, then the logical consequence might be a previously agreed upon assignment to write ten times a Bible verse about kind words. If chores are not performed on time, then additional previously agreed upon chores would be added. Whatever the logical consequence, the effect is to make your children personally accountable for their own actions and choices. There is, however, a greater responsibility for you to be consistent in carrying out a previously agreed upon logical consequence to avoid sending the message that you don't really mean what you say. It is also best to apply a consequence quickly to emphasize that it is not you, the parent, imposing discipline—rather, it is your child who has chosen the consequence by choosing to disobey. It teaches them to accept the consequences of their own choices and actions and reminds them that obedience is more attractive than disobedience.

You can begin using behavioral discipline as a tool of correction as soon as your child can understand what you are saying: "If you continue crying, then Mommy will not listen to you....If you leave your toys outside, then you won't be able to play with them for a week....If you don't complete your assignment, then you will not go on the field trip." In every case, you are helping your child learn to take personal responsibility for their own behaviors. It is their choice. The key to making it effective is consistency and follow-through from the very first. Behavioral discipline is essentially will-training—teaching your children to control their impulses and desires, not just during their childhood years, but even more during their young adult years, when the consequences become stronger because the results of their foolish choices and actions become more serious.

Correction: Training with PHYSICAL DISCIPLINE

The fourth training method of correction—physical discipline—generates by far the most discussion. It is probably more accurate to consider it the most serious expression of behavioral discipline, but I have given it a place as a method due to its mention in Scripture. Some Christian teachers assert not only that physical discipline of young children is taught in the Bible, but that it is commanded by God and that failure to use physical discipline on a young child is parental disobedience to God and will harm the child. However, I am convinced by careful study that Scripture nowhere mandates physical discipline as a means of correction for young children (in Proverbs, it is for the *naar*, the young man). However, it is also clear that neither does Scripture directly prohibit it. The question of whether or not to use physical discipline as a method of correction for a young child is a matter of freedom in the Spirit—parents are free in Christ to determine what is best for their child.

Our view is that if spanking is used, it should be considered only a method of correction of last resort, never of first response. The practice we all call spanking is never actually mentioned in Scripture—it is entirely a cultural method of discipline, not a biblical one. Spanking is often associated with the rod of Proverbs, but careful exegesis of those passages does not allow for a symbolic interpretation. And even more to the point, physical discipline is never associated in Scripture with young children—only with young men, adults, and nations. Spanking has a long history in both religious and secular contexts and the rod, which has been used widely in other religious and pagan cultures, is certainly not unique to the Bible in ancient history. In my opinion, if you choose to use spanking on your young child as a means of discipline or punishment, you should understand that you are using an extrabiblical method of correction, and you should apply godly common sense and wisdom guided by love and grace.

Discipline is not an option for Christian parents (Ephesians 6:4), but there is not one divinely-mandated method—God gives parents great freedom in the methods of training and correction of children. Some parents believe that spanking is preferable because it is effective—it usually stops disobedience. Remember, the goal of biblical discipline of children is not just to stop misbehavior or to punish wrongdoing—it is to reach and train their hearts. You should use physical discipline only because you have determined, by Scripture and the guidance of the Holy Spirit, that it will be the best way to reach your child's heart. God has entrusted you with the freedom to make a wise and loving decision.

IN OUR HOME

We both came to parenting believing that spanking was God's mandated method for discipline and correction. We wanted to be biblical and obedient, so we applied the "board of correction" when discipline was needed. We didn't question; we just spanked. But as my children grew, I (Clay) began to question the biblical exegesis and interpretation that elevated spanking to a divine mandate. My study of the Scriptures led me to a new understanding of what God's Word has to say about physical discipline, and especially as to whether it applied to young children. It ended up in a book, of course (Heartfelt Discipline), but mostly it ended up in our family life.

As a rule, a child ought not to be punished except for an offense that, at the time of its committal, was known by the child to be an offense deserving of punishment...And if a child understands, when he does a wrong, that he must expect a fixed punishment as its penalty, there is little danger of his feeling that his parent is unjust in administering that punishment.

— H. Clay Trumbull, *Hints on Child Training*, 1890

It is my personal conviction that the radical teachings of Christ on love and forgiveness, and Paul's further teachings on grace and freedom, must be applied as seriously to childhood discipline as they are applied to relationships in the body of Christ.

— Clay Clarkson, *Heartfelt Discipline*, WaterBrook Press, 2003

If You Choose to Spank

Recognize the difference between interventional spanking (hand slap, bottom swat), and punitive spanking (with an object). Neither should be misused, but the latter should be used with constraints in mind:

- It should be used rarely and with restraint.
- It should be clear to the child why they are being spanked.
- It should be done only with a calm and reassuring manner.
- It should be done with love and acceptance expressed verbally and physically.
- It should never cause excessive pain or bruising, only temporary discomfort.
- It should never be done in anger or in haste.
- It should never be done in public or in front of others.
- It should never be done to demean or shame a child.

Heartfelt Discipline

This subject is explored in depth in *Heartfelt Discipline* by Clay Clarkson.

We would be sadly mistaken if we assumed that the cultural invasion is mainly a conflict of abstract ideas. It is a major front in the battle for the soul of modern man, and as such it necessarily entails elements of spiritual combat...The invasion reaches into very young minds, relaxing children's instinctive aversion to what is truly frightening. It begins there, but we must understand that it will not end there, for its logical end is a culture that exalts the diabolical.

— Michael O'Brien, *A Landscape with Dragons*, Ignatius, 1998

Filtered but Not Forgotten

We have tried a variety of filters and blockers designed to turn unacceptable media into more family–friendly versions. They work to some degree, but the resulting language corrections and edits can be almost comical in their awkwardness, often creating humor in what should be a dramatic or serious moment. The edits, being all too obvious even to young ears, also invite the imagination to fill in the blanked out or sanitized words with the "real" words, many times the imagination writing a script actually worse than the original. That pretty much defeats the purpose of the filter. Even devices that use sophisticated technology to create edited versions of movie scenes, such as adding modest clothing, only encourage the imagination to do the unedit. What we finally realized is that, if the unedited original is not something we would watch as a family, we probably shouldn't watch the morally re-imagined version either.

PROTECTION — Staying Safe on the Path

Home discipleship is the process of walking on God's path of life with your children. In this chapter we've talked about two parental priorities for home discipleship—direction and correction—which brings us to the third and final priority, protection. As you disciple your children, one of your more important and active responsibilities is to protect them from influences that could draw them away from God and his ways. Your role, quite literally, is to keep them safe as they walk with you on the path of life.

Homeschooling parents are often criticized for being overprotective of their children, an apparently bad thing to do in the world's way of thinking. That caricature, though, originates in a culture of passive parental neglect that is almost dysfunctionally underprotective of its children. Even though it is a pejorative term in secular parenting lingo, you should not be reluctant to bear it as a badge of honor as a caring and committed Christian parent. God wants you to be an overprotective parent! Your children, by God's design, need an overprotector, a parent who will stand over them to protect them—to guard their innocence and purity, to prevent spiritual wounds and sinful footholds, and to teach discernment and sensitivity to sin. In God's design for families, overprotecting your children is a good thing.

Still, the enemy is very good at infiltrating even good Christian homes with corrupting influences, and homeschooling families are not immune. With technologies such as cable and satellite TV, computers, and the Internet, a constant river of information, images, and ideas can flow freely into your home, much of it good, but too much of it ungodly and corrupt. You can control that flow, but when your children interact in the community with other children, those children all too often are deeply influenced, informed, and indoctrinated by the same river—often without controls on its flow of the worst that culture has to offer—and they will offer it freely to your children. The only thing that is standing between those and other influences, and your child's heart and mind, is a committed overprotector—you! If you don't have a heart that beats strongly with a passion to protect your children against unhealthy appetites, unwise relationships, and ungodly secular media, you can be certain that the enemy stands ready to take full advantage of any holes in your commitment and to exploit your children's innocence, vulnerability, and receptiveness. Diligence is the price you pay for staying safe on the path.

The discipleship priority of protection is necessarily mostly about negatives—protecting your children from negative influences in the areas of appetites, relationships, and media. But parental paranoia about and overreaction to negative influences can become unhealthy and even counterproductive. If you are always overly worried and fearful, your children will learn to view life through your lens of fearfulness. Protect them from the bad stuff, but don't infect them with fear! Exercise parental protection, but remember that a good offense is also a good defense. Protection is about keeping bad things out of your children's lives, but it is also about letting good things in. Each of the three danger areas covered in this section has a positive side, too. Be diligent to protect against unhealthy appetites, but even more to encourage and cultivate healthy ones. Protect against unwise relationships, but provide many good and godly wise friends. Keep ungodly media out of your home, but be creative to find godly, quality media that will give your children biblical and positive images of life. Keep protection in balance.

Protection: Guarding against UNHEALTHY APPETITES

In Proverbs 4:23, Solomon counsels his son, "Watch over your heart with all diligence, for from it flow the springs of life" (NASB). The words in Hebrew suggest a guard or watchman standing on a wall guarding a city from undesirable influences gaining entrance. The word for "springs" is consistently translated in twenty-four other Old Testament texts to express the extremities or borders of a piece of land. With those ideas in view, the verse could be loosely paraphrased, "Work very hard to keep out anything that doesn't belong in your heart, for that is what will define the borders of your life." Whatever you let into your children's hearts will influence or define who they become.

When it comes to discipline, most parents concentrate their efforts on guarding what is coming out of their children's hearts and minds. They assume an adversarial role as a parent, focusing on restraining and correcting every sin. Discipline and correction are obviously priorities of home discipleship, but our greater desire is to be advocates of our children and to focus on what is going into their hearts and minds—the things that will establish the borders and boundaries of their lives and shape who and what they will become. Keeping out unhealthy influences and appetites now will help to ensure that there is room in their hearts for healthy, godly appetites as they grow. In a sense, it is proactive discipline that protects their hearts from bad influences. We want them to think of their parents as advocates who are for them in that process, not as adversaries.

Appetites are also called in Scripture the "desires of your heart." There can be worldly desires (1 John 2:15-17) or godly desires (Psalm 37:4), and Jesus was clear that wherever your desires (your treasures) are, that is where your heart will be (Matthew 6:19-21). Many, if not most, of the desires and appetites that will shape the rest of your child's life will be formed and fueled during childhood. Fortunately, God included in Scripture a kind of universal standards checklist for what we should allow into our children's hearts and minds—if it is true, noble, right, pure, lovely, admirable, excellent, or praiseworthy, then it can go in (Philippians 4:8). Those are things that Paul commands the Philippians to think (consider, ponder, reflect) about. Paul even promises that a heart and mind that thinks on those things will know the peace of God's presence. That is an incredibly positive promise to claim for your children. Watch what goes in, and you can protect your children from forming unhealthy desires and appetites from the things they read, watch, listen to, or are amused by. You are their guardian and advocate, bringing peace.

Above all else, guard your heart, for it is the wellspring of life.
— Proverbs 4:23

For where your treasure is, there your heart will be also.
— Matthew 6:21

But seek first his kingdom and his righteousness, and all these things will be given to you as well.
— Matthew 6:33 (NASB)

Finally, brothers, whatever is true, whatever is noble, whatever is right, whatever is pure, whatever is lovely, whatever is admirable—if anything is excellent or praiseworthy—think about such things. Whatever you have learned or received or heard from me, or seen in me—put it into practice. And the God of peace will be with you.
— Philippians 4:8-9

IN OUR HOME

We are always on the lookout in early years for imitative behavior that can lead to an unwanted appetite. When we were in The Promise *(an amphitheater production), we had to be careful about our young children's behavior and desires being influenced by others in the cast. However, we also loved the imitative behavior that reflected the influence of the dramatic musical production itself when one child would be a prophet, John the Baptist, or Jesus, and another would be a Jewish girl dancing before the Lord as he entered Jerusalem on a donkey. Joy, who was still a toddler but very observant, would be Mary, with a shawl over her head and always holding a stuffed lamb. Now that kind of imitative behavior is great!*

He who walks with the wise grows wise, but a companion of fools suffers harm.

— Proverbs 13:20

It is a parent's duty to know who are his child's companions, and to know the character, and course of conduct, and influence upon his child, of every one of those companions separately. Here is where a parent's chief work is called for in the matter of guiding and controlling his child's companionships...To neglect this agency of a child's training, would be to endanger his entire career in life, whatever else were done in his behalf.

— H. Clay Trumbull, *Hints on Child Training,* 1890

Protection: Guarding against UNWISE RELATIONSHIPS

In Romans 12:2, Paul admonishes Christians to stop being conformed to the "pattern of this world." Literally, he is saying, "Stop agreeing with the way your culture thinks!" Nowhere is that more relevant for Christian homeschooling families than in the area of relationships. Even if you rightly reject the secularist thinking that socialization by schooling is a basic need of all children (see pages 36-37), your children will not be homeschool hermits—they will be in many social situations, with a wide range of child and adult relationships. The right kinds of relationships are a critical, biblical need for your children's growth and maturity, but unwise relationships can quickly undo some or all of the good you do for them. Your children's personalities, values, and spirits are powerfully influenced by their relationships. In any situation, younger children should always be supervised by mature adults, older siblings, or trustworthy young adults. Your first priority of protection is to seek out relationships with what we called "good and godly" friends—well-trained children from trustworthy Christian families. Your second priority of protection is defensive—to be on guard against four kinds of dangerous relationships:

- **Fools** — Don't leave your children in the company of other unsupervised, untrained, or immature children and especially not with someone you would consider to be a foolish adult. Always monitor your children's relationships and activities and screen the adults in their lives. Foolish people are not safe. (Proverbs 13:20)

- **Unbelievers** — Don't allow your children to become emotionally or spiritually yoked to an unbelieving child, even in the absence of other godly friends. Your children will grow by waiting and trusting God for a friend. Be very cautious about leaving your children with unbelieving adults. (2 Corinthians 6:14)

- **Immoral** — Don't put your children in the company of anyone of any age you know to be immoral. If you have any suspicions or concerns, it is best to err on the side of caution. Their language, attitudes, and behaviors can be emotionally and spiritually corrosive. You cannot easily erase their effects. (1 Corinthians 15:33)

- **False teachers** — Don't put your children under the authority of an adult you know to be, or even suspect of being, a false teacher. Children cannot easily discern false teaching or untruth, especially when it is presented and promoted by an adult in authority they have been told to listen to and obey. (2 Timothy 2:16-19)

IN OUR HOME

When Sarah was younger, we lived in a city that had a wonderful nature center with great programs for children. Yet we learned that even good situations can turn bad with very little warning. She was in a group of pre-teen girls who were doing a nature walk and talk. Rather than the normal adult leader, a teen girl was put in charge that day. When the girls stopped for snacks, the teen regaled them with the story of a knife-wielding rapist who broke into the place where she was staying. It was a frightening tale, especially for young girls. It disturbed Sarah for several days, generating irrational (though certainly not unreasonable) fears, as well as bad dreams. The incident passed, but the memory stayed with Sarah for a long time.

Protection: Guarding against UNGODLY MEDIA

Paul asks, "For what do righteousness and wickedness have in common? Or what fellowship can light have with darkness?" (2 Corinthians 6:14). Whenever your children are exposed to secular media—even if for a "good" show—there is the risk of visual, verbal, and spiritual assault by an industry saturated with wickedness and darkness. There is light, to be sure, but the dark side of secular media overflows with occult and supernatural images and ideas, God-free science fiction, graphic violence, casual and graphic sexuality, coarse language, and dysfunctional and degenerate lifestyles. Most popular media routinely violate biblical standards of what God says we should think about or allow (Psalm 101:2-3a, 6; Philippians 4:8) and instead offer for entertainment what God admonishes us to expose and avoid (Ephesians 5:8-14). The goal is not to turn your children into Pharisees who condemn all media but to teach them discernment and self-control. There are plenty of alternatives, but secular media require your protective oversight.

- **Television** — Set a high standard for your children and yourself. Never allow them to watch commercial TV unsupervised or to channel surf with the remote. Make it a family rule and habit to mute (or turn off) the commercials. The TV world is mostly violent, sexual, crude, and pagan, so search for and record the good shows to watch later or invest in good DVDs or digital downloads. Here's the hard part—as a parent, you should be just as disciplined with the television as you want your children to be.

- **Digital media** — E-mail, the Internet, computer and video games, digital devices, cell phones, and all the other forms of digital media are both promising and potentially problematic. Be especially protective of your children's access to the Internet (the Worldly Wild Web). There are many exceptional websites that Christians and homeschoolers can explore, but there are also very dangerous places that are easily accessible, either by choice or by accident. You must always monitor the monitor.

- **Movies** — Become an informed and highly selective movie consumer. Don't go to or rent movies just because they are popular, reviewed well, or recommended by friends or other families. And don't trust the movie ratings—today's PG movies can be surprisingly underrated. Remember that movies are messages in film, no matter how innocuous the subject may seem. Most leave God out of the picture...literally. Set a biblical standard of excellence and be wise in movie viewing.

- **Music** — Secular radio fills the airwaves with songs with unbiblical lyrics sung by artists with unbiblical lifestyles. Music is a powerful medium that can go deep into your children's hearts and minds and stay there for a lifetime. Encourage listening to classical music and quality Christian music. Be careful with young children not to create an appetite too early for pop or rock styles. Music can be a powerful tool for discipleship (Colossians 3:16), but you must use it wisely.

- **Print media** — Be thoughtful about what you leave on the coffee table. Images and ideas can imprint on the brain for life, so put away most secular magazines and the newspaper. Keep your coffee table covered with quality Christian books and resources, selected children's illustrated storybooks, beautiful art and history books, nature photography books, Christian publications, and the like. Beware of danger zones: supermarket check-outs, newsstands, and video rental stores.

I will set before my eyes no vile thing. The deeds of faithless men I hate; they will not cling to me. Men of perverse heart shall be far from me; I will have nothing to do with evil.

— Psalm 101:3-4

Have nothing to do with the fruitless deeds of darkness, but rather expose them. For it is shameful even to mention what the disobedient do in secret.

— Ephesians 5:11-12

The center of companionships in a child's amusements ought to be the parents themselves...No companionship should be permitted to a child in his amusements that is likely to lower his moral tone, or to vitiate his moral taste.

— H. Clay Trumbull, *Hints on Child Training*, 1890

I didn't even dream it would be so good. I would never let my children even come close to the thing.

— Vladimir Zworykin, quoted on his 92nd birthday about his invention, the television, *New York Times*, July 31, 1981

The fear of the LORD is the beginning of knowledge, but fools despise wisdom and discipline.

— Proverbs 1:7

See, I will send you the prophet Elijah before that great and dreadful day of the LORD comes. He will turn the hearts of the fathers to their children, and the hearts of the children to their fathers; or else I will come and strike the land with a curse.

— Malachi 4:5-6

He who knows how to teach a child, is not competent for the oversight of a child's education unless he also knows how to train a child.

— H. Clay Trumbull, *Hints on Child Training*, 1890

It is, therefore, largely a child's training that settles the question [of what kind of person he will become]...In all these things his course indicates what his training has been; or it suggests the training that he needed, but has missed.

— H. Clay Trumbull, *Hints on Child Training*, 1890

Walking on the PATH

Walk on the path of life confidently with your children using this acronym of PATH:

- **P** — Pray for your children regularly.
- **A** — Accept your children unconditionally.
- **T** — Teach and train your children diligently.
- **H** — Honor your children purposefully.

Setting Your Child's Feet on the Path of Life

Solomon knew where the lines were drawn between the heart and the mind. At the very beginning of his book of Proverbs, he says, "The fear of the Lord is the beginning of knowledge, but fools despise wisdom and discipline." Solomon told his son that knowledge is useless unless it is acquired by a heart that fears God. He goes on to tell him that the way to shape a heart that fears God is through wisdom and discipline. If that sounds a lot like the New Testament concept of discipleship—instruction and training—that's no coincidence. God is consistent, and though the terminology may change over time, the methodology does not. In the parable of the seed and the sower, Jesus made it clear that the good soil for the seed of his Word is a noble and good heart. In other words, God's truth makes its way into the mind only through a heart that fears him.

That is why your responsibility to disciple your children is so foundational to your responsibility to educate them. If you desire to teach your children effectively, their hearts must first be turned to God. Until your children submit their hearts to God and to your authority, you cannot effectively educate their minds. In fact, in view of eternity, it is far more important that your children become wholehearted disciples of Jesus Christ than that they become well educated. A mature disciple of Jesus Christ with the will and skill to learn is much more useful to God's kingdom work in this world than a well-educated but immature Christian who is indifferent to the things of God. Discipleship of your children is a priority task for a Christian parent—to shape their hearts to live for God.

Jesus commanded us to "make disciples" (Matthew 28:19), and that certainly includes children. Paul, using the language of discipleship, commanded fathers concerning their children to "bring them up in the training and instruction of the Lord" (Ephesians 6:4). Discipleship is not a responsibility you can put off or turn over to someone else. It is a biblical priority. When you make home discipleship the priority in your family that God intended it to be, you will find that home education will follow naturally. Educating your child is simply the fullest and most fulfilling expression of discipling your child. It is living out the truth at home that "the fear of the Lord is the beginning of knowledge."

If these concepts are new to you or you're just beginning your journey on the path of life as a parent, you don't need to sprint! Paths are made to be enjoyed, and the journey is as important as the destination. Your children need to know that they can expect to enjoy the journey on the path of life with you. If you're walking (not running!) with the Spirit, he will set the right pace for you and your family.

Remember to keep your eyes looking up at the path ahead, not down at the path below. If you've ever hiked a path or trail, you know how easy it is to get in the habit of looking down at your feet to make sure every step is right or to get really serious about making good progress with your "don't bother me; I'm hiking" face. If you do that, though, you miss all the scenery God has along the path, and your children will get discouraged trying to keep up with you. Don't get caught up in whether or not you're doing everything you think you're supposed to be doing. Above all, just remember that God is with you on your journey of Christian parenting, and he wants more than anything for you and your children to enjoy his company along your path. Home discipleship is an exciting and rewarding journey on the path of life with your children.

— Chapter 5 —

Home Education: Strengthening Your Child's Mind to Learn for God

The Heart and Soul of Learning

Learning is a mysterious process. Researchers examine and describe it, scholars attempt to understand and explain it, and teachers try to stimulate and influence it, yet no one except God knows exactly how we learn. He has created us with an innate ability to learn, yet we know very little about such an essential quality of our being. For our purposes, we will limit our examination of learning to two views that summarize the crowded spectrum of educational philosophies and methodologies—secular and biblical. Ask a proponent of each about learning, and you will receive two very different answers.

If you asked a proponent of secular education about learning theory, he would likely describe learning as a mental process centered on the child's material brain and measured by the retention of discrete facts and information. He would emphasize the role of the teacher and the acquisition of knowledge. The purely secular educator or theorist would acknowledge neither the existence of a Creator God nor the existence of an immaterial soul, or spirit, in the process of learning. The educator might describe the child as a wonderful and complex human organism, but when all the educational rhetoric is stripped away, the child is still considered just a smart animal—the product of evolution in a godless, material universe that just happened by cosmic chance. There are, to be sure, many dedicated Christians teaching in otherwise secular settings, but their biblical view of learning is often at odds with the system they serve.

As a Christian home educator with a biblical view of education, your answer to the same question about learning theory should be very different. You would describe learning as a personal process involving both the material brain and the immaterial heart and mind that is measured by wisdom, understanding, and knowledge of truth. You would emphasize the role of the child as a whole person with an innate, natural appetite for knowledge and a limitless capacity to learn. You would be more concerned with your child's understanding of important ideas and concepts than with the accumulation of knowledge. Your child is not just a soulless brain that needs to be filled up with facts by a teacher but a person in relationship with you and God who has eternal value, dignity, and purpose because they are made in the image and likeness of their Creator.

Contrary to the secular educator's view, a child is not educated just because he has logged enough time in classrooms, performed well on certain tests, or completed a formal curriculum. In God's economy, to be educated is not a matter of something you know or have achieved. Rather, to be educated is something you become. A truly educated child is one who has the desire and the ability to learn and to grow as a whole person. The desire to learn (will) is from the heart; the ability to learn (skill) is in the mind.

For all the most important things in education we have an inside track, since we reckon with the whole person, including heart and soul.

— Ruth Beechick, *A Biblical Psychology of Learning*, Accent, 1982

The fundamental idea is, that children are persons and are therefore moved by the same springs of conduct as their elders. Among these is the Desire of Knowledge, knowledge-hunger being natural to everybody.

— Charlotte Mason, *Towards a Philosophy of Education*, 1925

Homeschool History

- **Before 1850** — Children are taught privately, by tutors, or at home. Literacy is high.
- **1850-1900** — Common and compulsory schooling are introduced and spread quickly, accelerated by the Industrial Revolution. Many are still taught at home.
- **1900-1930** — Variations on classroom philosophies (Charlotte Mason, Montessori) are introduced, but public schools are by now well established. Several books defend and promote the idea of home-based learning.
- **1930-1970** — Private and parochial schools rise but the compulsory public schools become more entrenched. School at home is an underground concept fueled mostly by anti-school and anti-bureaucracy motivations.
- **1970-1980** — Popular books by educational theorists are critical of public schooling. Raymond and Dorothy Moore write *Better Late Than Early* (1975) and embrace homeschooling in *Home Grown Kids* (1981). John Holt writes *Instead of Education* (1976), starts *Growing Without Schooling* magazine (1977), and introduces unschooling (1981).
- **1980-2000** — Rapid emergence of a diverse but national Christian homeschooling movement is fueled by, among many others, speaker Gregg Harris (Christian Life Workshops), attorney Michael Farris (HSLDA), *The Teaching Home* magazine, and volunteer leaders in new state and regional organizations. By the mid-1990s, homeschooling is legal in all fifty states. Non-Christian segments grow steadily, but homeschooling remains a predominantly Christian movement.
- **2000-Today** — Homeschooling remains diverse and strong in the face of cultural change and the challenges that come with growth.

Leaving the Old School Behind

Homeschooling is now officially a second-generation movement as children of the first wave in the 1980s have grown up, had children, and begun to homeschool them. Yet despite the presence of that second wave, most families coming into the movement are still first-generation homeschooling parents who are products of institutional schooling, whether government or private. Like those of us who started in the 1980s, many come to homeschooling with a school and classroom paradigm and with some unfortunate secular influences that must be recognized and rejected in order to start fresh.

Before 1850, children learned through a wide variety of means—most either at home or with tutors. Horace Mann, a Unitarian educational activist, started the Common School movement in the mid-1800s. His views that all students should receive the same content and that it should be neutral as to values and beliefs were the first steps toward secularizing public schools. By 1870 all states provided free elective elementary schooling, and by 1918 it was compulsory nationwide. Compulsory schooling gradually incorporated high school, and any alternative forms of education, such as learning at home, were marginalized as radical or even illegal.

From the beginning, the inevitable philosophical trajectory of public education was always toward a nonreligious secularism. Leading educational theorists during the twentieth century advocated ideas that would strengthen the secularizing trends. Jean Piaget's views of cognitive development influenced age/grade standards based on a naturalist view of learning and of moral development through social and peer group interaction. John Dewey's pragmatic view of learning elevated the role of experience in education, laid the foundations for outcome- and standards-based education, and contributed to the progressive education movement that, among other things, would transform schools into social formation tools of the government. Dewey was also one of the thirty-two signers of the first *Humanist Manifesto* (1933), which set forth a humanist social vision for America which included the promulgation of humanist beliefs through public education. B. F. Skinner, one of the most influential psychologists of the twentieth century, was a signer of the *Humanist Manifesto II* (1973). As a leading proponent of behaviorist psychology, he taught that personhood is formed in a child entirely by circumstances, experiences, and conditioning. That defining belief of behaviorism—that nurture, not nature, is the dominant influence—has become a de facto credo of American public education.

When you come home, be sure you leave the philosophical and psychological baggage of public education outside your door. You are not raising your children just so they can conform to the common beliefs of society and not make waves; you are raising your children to be independent, biblically informed, critical thinkers who are able to be strong voices within a lost culture for what is right and good. Your children are not the products of a godless, naturalistic universe who need to be conditioned and programmed so they can be tolerant of all beliefs and useful to society; they are creations of a personal God who bear his image and whose spirits, by nature, are prepared to respond to and follow him. You are called, through nurture, to fill their hearts and minds with God's truth so they can call people in their generation out of darkness into light. When you come home with your children, you are free to follow a whole new path, the path of life. You have left the old school behind, and nothing but real life is ahead of you.

Building Mental Muscles

Our culture is obsessed with measuring learning—achievement testing, PSAT, SAT, ACT, IQ, test grades, report cards. The problem with all this measuring is that it has convinced us as a culture that we should compare our children to other children when it comes to learning. That is not only an unreliable means of assessing progress and a heavy and unfair burden on children, but it is also a poor measure of true education.

The true test of a child's education is not what they know at any one time relative to what other children know (or don't know). It is whether or not the child is growing stronger in all of the most important learning skills—the skills that enable them to acquire knowledge, insight, and ability and to educate themselves independently. We have found it helpful to think of those skills in terms of muscles. In the same way we want our children to develop their physical muscles, we also want them to develop their mental muscles. But just as children have varying physical abilities, they also have varying mental abilities. Some children have stronger leg muscles than others, some stronger arm muscles than others, but it does no good to compare all children's arm muscles.

Neither should we compare and judge all children on the basis of one or two mental muscles only. For instance, IQ can be a helpful measurement, but it is limited mostly to measuring reasoning abilities. Just as some say there are several kinds of intelligence (not just IQ), we believe there are several important mental muscles. The goal should be to exercise all of a child's mental muscles so they enter adulthood with a strong mind and the will and skill to learn whatever is necessary. Schools do not have the time or the resources necessary to give each child the individual attention such a goal requires. Instead, they focus on the measurable goal of knowledge retention. However, a home is an ideal environment to build your child's mental muscles.

Mental strength is not the same as mental capacity. In fact, you probably know adults whose mental capacity for knowledge is adequate, maybe even exceptional, but who are nonetheless mentally weak—they cannot make a decision, present an idea, or be creative. Regardless of your children's mental capacity, it is the strength of their mental muscles that will have the greatest impact on their success in life. In the same way that stronger physical muscles enable you to do more, strong mental muscles will enable your children to learn more and even to expand their mental capacity. The goal of education is not to raise a child who does well on the tests of secular educators; rather it is to raise a child who does well on the tests of real life. When they need to research an issue, they will have the discipline and ability to find and analyze relevant information. When they need to present an argument, they will know how to use language persuasively. When mediating a problem at church, they will know how to apply wisdom and find a creative solution.

Learning is far too complex to reduce it to just seven mental muscles. Nonetheless, they can provide a useful way of looking at your children that can free you from the culturally conditioned dependence on testing to evaluate your child's progress. Your children are persons made in God's image, not just products of an educational system. When you release your children into adulthood, measurements and tests will be of less importance than how you have shaped their hearts to live for God and strengthened their minds to learn for him. Strong mental muscles will prepare them for living in the real world.

There is no education but self-education and as soon as a young child begins his education he does so as a student. Our business is to give him mind-stuff, and both quality and quantity are essential.

— Charlotte Mason, *Towards a Philosophy of Education*, 1925

Growing Mental Muscles

Here is a helpful perspective on the seven mental muscles if you relate to a gardening metaphor more than a body one. Language is the rich soil in which each of the mental muscles will grow—it provides the ground for roots to grow in and nutrients for fruit to grow from. Each root is about understanding (with the head), and each fruit is about expression (with the heart). Here's what it looks like:

- Soil: Language
- Root: Appetites
- Fruit: Habits
- Root: Curiosity
- Fruit: Creativity
- Root: Reason
- Fruit: Wisdom

An inadequate vocabulary sometimes equals an inadequate comprehension of spiritual reality. God formed our brains to be molded by words. He, the living Word who spoke existence into being, created us to be a people of words, both written and spoken. He gave us both Truth and great literature with His gift of the Bible. He designed us to be able to express and record every idea through our words. A young intellect nourished by a feast of words can tackle any concept—whether mathematical, scientific, spiritual, or imaginative—with confidence.

— Sarah Clarkson, *Read for the Heart*, Apologia Press, 2009

We think because we have words, not the other way around. The more words we have, the better we are able to think conceptually.

— Madeleine L'Engle, *Walking on Water,* Shaw, 2001

The newer and broader picture suggests that the child emerges into literacy by actively speaking, reading, and writing in the context of real life, not through filling out phonics worksheets or memorizing [lists of look-say] words.

— Thomas Armstrong, Ph.D., *Awakening Your Child's Natural Genius*, Tarcher/Putnam, 1991

Mental Muscle #1: Language

Your children may grow up to become faithful followers of Jesus Christ, but if they arrive at adulthood unable to articulate or communicate what they know, then you will have provided an incomplete education. You will have given your children a message but failed to make them messengers. It would be like having a battery for your car with no terminals to which you could attach the cables—plenty of power but no way to release it to its intended use. Developing the mental muscle of language is like putting terminals on the battery of your children's minds. Language skill will allow your children to release their spiritual and intellectual power to noble use under the control of the Holy Spirit.

Language development in children is an innate mental ability designed by God, who is the source of all language. How else, with no real instruction, can a child learn such a complex skill? In a few short years beginning at around age two, children experiment with and expand their language abilities almost exponentially. That a young child can cover such an enormous amount of linguistic ground so rapidly is almost miraculous. But that is just the beginning.

Think about the fact that God himself is our model for language: God first spoke his Word, and then it became his written Word. The ability to communicate, especially through the spoken word, is one of God's most important gifts to mankind. Without language—whether spoken or written—there would be no Word of God, no Great Commission to preach to the world, no means to edify and encourage other believers, and no gospel message. With the gift of spoken language, you can proclaim hope, teach truth, encourage others, move multitudes, affirm love, condemn evil, and inspire God's people. With the gift of written language, you can move people in other places and in other times, many miles and years from the sound of your voice, just as God's Word does. With the gift of language you will influence and shape your child's life for God.

It's not enough simply to teach your child to say words, read words, or write words. The power of God's gift of language is in the ability to use words to move people—to cause another person to learn, to change, to act, to resist, to believe, to follow. We all use language as a utilitarian means of information exchange, but those who understand its power use it to change lives and even influence history. Whatever impact your children will have for God—how they will change lives and make their mark on history—will be because of the power of language you give to them. Here are some ways to strengthen their mental muscle of language.

- **Create a verbal environment.** Your children's verbal skills will grow in proportion to the amount of verbal stimulation they receive at home. The more they hear language used and the more they are stimulated to use language, the more their language skills will grow. Begin talking to your children in full sentences very early, even in responding to baby talk. Talk with them, not just at them. As they grow, engage your children in conversation whenever possible, especially at mealtimes when everyone is relaxed. Discuss interesting topics on trips in the car. Look for opportunities to ask open-ended questions: What did you think about the sermon? Why do you want to be a fireman? What would you do if that happened to you? What do you think Jesus meant by "seek first the kingdom"? Make life a verbal adventure.

- **Create a print-rich environment.** Research shows that one of the common characteristics of gifted children is that they are raised with many materials, resources, and books easily available to them (*Encyclopedia of Creativity*, Academic Press, 1999). Don't be stingy on your library—have as many books at home as you possibly can. Have a wide variety of kinds of books. Leave them at strategic reading spots throughout the house. Make all of your books accessible (based on appropriateness, of course). Every time a child opens a book to read, it is a lesson in language—how someone else used words to express a thought, story, idea, or insight.

- **Read, read, read!** The single best way to strengthen your children's language muscles and even expand their capacity for language is to read aloud to them and have them narrate back what they have heard you read. The combination of hearing well-written language spoken aloud, internalizing those words, and then verbally restating what has been heard is an almost ideal language learning method. And it is not just for while your children are young, but for all through their childhood and teens. Also encourage them to read as much as possible or to listen to well-read audiobooks.

- **Write on!** Give your children real-life reasons to write—devotional thoughts, a daily journal, a nature notebook, letters, blogs, e-mails. Writing develops their language skills by helping them to think about what they want to say in an orderly and understandable way. Writing poetry is also a richly rewarding language-building exercise. Writing of any kind is the best way to foster and fine-tune language skills.

- **Limit television.** It is tempting to think that television, as a verbal medium, would strengthen children's language muscles. Just the opposite is true. Because it is totally passive, television actually retards language development because it requires nothing from the child and has been shown to slow down brain function. Without verbal interaction, verbal skills are neither exercised nor strengthened. Limit the tube.

IN OUR HOME

When we lived in Nashville, we became friends with Dean and Karen Andreola, and our children often played together until they moved away to the East. One day we received an audiotape in the mail. When we played it, we were so surprised to hear a perfectly lovely child's voice with a delicate British accent (just like Karen's) reading aloud from a good book. She read well, with appropriate expression and dramatic timing. "That's Sophia! She's a good reader," someone offered. Soon, another sweet voice came on with another wonderful reading. "That's Yolanda! Isn't she great?" We were captivated by their readings—we could count on one hand the number of children we knew whose language skills were so evident. But we really weren't all that surprised. These children were raised on good literature read aloud to them by their mother and father. Their home was full of verbal interaction and good language. We were simply seeing the fruit of that verbally enriched environment. Our children soon were motivated to create their own tape of similarly skillful verbal offerings. The whole episode was a real-life confirmation of the effectiveness of a verbal environment for building language skills. We could hear it with our own ears!

Word Games

There is a definite link between vocabulary and intelligence. The best way to increase your children's vocabulary is to read good books aloud. However, you can also have fun learning new words with any of the many available vocabulary builder products, calendars, or lists. After you've introduced a word a day for a month, start a game of Catch Word. The challenge is to use a word from the list in normal conversation without being caught using it. The contest grows daily because any word from the growing list can be used. Everyone keeps score by earning one point for each time a word is used without it being noticed. If you can use it three times without being caught, you score an extra point and the word is retired. You pick a new word and the game continues. Another good game is Root, using a resource that identifies the common Greek and Latin roots of English words. Points are scored for hearing any words during the day that use the same root words studied that morning. First one to yell "Root!" gets the point.

Verbal Books

We have observed that children who are raised in a verbally enriched environment are not put off by books with a bigger vocabulary than their own. As they listen to them read aloud or read them alone, they may not comprehend all the vocabulary, yet it is going into their minds as food. It is like adding nutrients to the soil of your garden. You won't see immediate results, but the eventual fruit will be much more bountiful than if you had not enriched the soil. Here are some books that we have found uniquely enrich our children's language:

- Charles and Mary Lamb's *Tales From Shakespeare*
- *Dangerous Journey* (a retelling of *Pilgrim's Progress*)
- *The Wind in the Willows*
- James Herriott's *Treasury for Children*

Finally, brothers, whatever is true, whatever is noble, whatever is right, whatever is pure, whatever is lovely, whatever is admirable—if anything is excellent or praiseworthy—think about such things. Whatever you have learned or received or heard from me, or seen in me—put it into practice. And the God of peace will be with you.

— Philippians 4:8-9

A love of reading is an acquired taste, not an instinctive preference. The habit of reading is formed in childhood; and a child's taste in reading is formed in the right direction or in the wrong one while he is under the influence of his parents; and they are directly responsible for the shaping and cultivating of that taste.

— H. Clay Trumbull, *Hints on Child Training*, 1890

We have never been so rich in books. But there has never been a generation when there is so much twaddle in print for children.

— Susan Schaeffer Macaulay, *For the Children's Sake*, Crossway, 1984

Mental Muscle #2: Appetites

Appetites in education are closely related to influences in discipleship. Whatever you encourage your children to consume is what will train their appetites or tastes. A child's mind has a natural appetite for all knowledge, yet too often we satiate our children's intellectual appetites with nutritionless mental junk food that appeals only to their immature childishness rather than to their developing maturity. With adults, you are what you eat; children become what you feed them. Appetites tend to be cross-promotional, so developing a good appetite for quality music can also have a refining influence on developing good appetites for literature. Always keep in mind, though, that your children will pick up many of their appetites from what they see that you value, not just from what you want them to value. If you want to cultivate their appetites to prefer the best foods for learning then you too must value the best foods.

In matters of appetites, a guiding biblical principle is found in Paul's instruction in Philippians 4:8-9. The ultimate goal is to train your children's spirits not only to desire but also to discern these qualities in the appetites they allow to grow in their hearts: whatever is true, rather than counterfeit or false; whatever is noble, rather than common and vulgar; whatever is right, rather than unrighteous and wrong; whatever is pure, rather than corrupt and unholy; whatever is lovely, rather than base and ugly; whatever is admirable, rather than cheap or coarse. You are training your children's appetites to prefer excellence over mediocrity and praiseworthiness over market-worthiness. The close relationship between discernment and appetites has been likened to the training federal agents receive for recognizing counterfeit bills. Rather than studying the counterfeits, they intensely study real bills. They instinctively know a counterfeit bill when they encounter one because it falls so far short of the real thing. You are training your children's appetites to discern the real from the counterfeit. Here are just some of the appetites needing training:

- **Feast on literature.** Great literature is the natural food for your child's mind. It is complete (a whole book), satisfying (real words and ideas; complete sentences and thoughts), and interesting (a complete, complex, well-told story). You do not have to convince or bribe a child to like good literature. Even appetites trained on inferior books will turn very quickly to feed on good literature if given the opportunity. Children have an innate desire for good literature that can be trained into an appetite.

- **Live on living books.** Books on a wide variety of interesting subjects can be either lifeless or living. Lifeless books dwell on dry facts and details, reducing their subjects to snippets of often disconnected information. Living books relate their subjects to real life and real experiences, drawing the reader into a slice of life. Pieces of information will soon be forgotten, but real-life insights from a living book will be locked into a child's memory. Living books live on in a child's mind.

- **Savor art.** Children already have a natural appetite for and appreciation of art and beauty. However, the relentless barrage of mass-produced art, digital art, and commercial media dulls their artistic senses. They need a steady diet of high-quality and classic art to grow in their ability to distinguish good art from mediocre and to enjoy the full range of artistic styles and abilities. As that ability is sharpened, their appetite and taste for high-quality art grows and deepens.

- **Delight in music.** There is a growing sea of children's music today, but it is not often very deep. However, there is a deep ocean of great, inspiring music, whether it is classical, praise and worship, inspirational, hymns, acoustic and folk artists, acoustic instrumental, or other genres. You have the power to shape your children's musical appetites by defining the standards of excellent music in your home and feasting often on the best. It may not be what they will listen to as young adults or adults, but cultivating an appetite for beautiful and uplifting music early will influence later choices in the right direction.

- **Taste video.** If ever there were a vast wasteland of childishness, it is the desert filled with poorly written, cheaply produced children's videos. There are, however, some excellent video products for children that are mentally stimulating high-quality productions. Even so, limit video viewing. As a totally passive medium that has a dulling effect on mental faculties, too many videos can create a negative effect on other habits and appetites as well. Use your TV, computer, and video players sparingly. Focus on exceptional video products and learning opportunities, and use movies and entertaining videos only at strategic times or for special privileges. Video is the medium of the future, but you must control it, not the other way around.

- **Pick poetry.** Reading and writing poetry is a lost art, and your children are impoverished by its absence. Poetry is the most complex expression of language that exercises mental abilities and expands mental capacities. Whether reading, hearing, writing, or reciting it, quality poetry is the power food of the English language. Since you probably were not raised on poetry, you will need to overcome your own linguistic inertia to add poetry to your children's lives. When you do, you'll not only enrich your children's minds, but you will also enrich your life as a family.

IN OUR HOME

Music is always in the air in the Clarkson home. Although we have very discriminating tastes, we try to avoid a negative "That's not good music" approach in our home and instead shape our children's musical tastes and appetites with a more positive "That's good music!" approach. We started them all out young listening to a variety of good Christian, classical, and instrumental music at bedtime. Throughout the day, we listen to a wide variety of genres and artists ranging from classical to praise and worship to folk to Celtic to cowboy to acoustic artists to a cappella. We insist on quality of composition, performance, and production, which sparks discussions that sharpen our children's faculties for discerning what is mediocre from what is excellent. We also apply those same kinds of standards to our video viewing. We might loosen the production and performance standards for a movie with a good or godly story, but offensive content becomes more of an issue with video. Thankfully, it has become so much easier in recent years to build a video library of good family-friendly movies, Christian productions, science series, historical productions, good PBS and BBC productions, and feature-length animated shows. Video will be a part of our children's lives, so we are training their appetites now to guide their choices as adults.

I will sing of your love and justice; to you, O LORD, I will sing praise. I will be careful to lead a blameless life—when will you come to me? I will walk in my house with a blameless heart. I will set before my eyes no vile thing.

— Psalm 101:1-3

Image and Imagination

Feeding an appetite in your children with the entrancing images of video and television can suppress and distort their appetites for works of good literature that engage the imagination. Consider how image subtly overrules imagination with, for example, *Anne of Green Gables*. Who can read about Anne Shirley now without seeing Megan Follows—the actress from the mini-series—in their mind? Anne Shirley, who is a champion of imagination, is no longer left up to the imagination. The images of the films have programmed the imagination so that it is no longer fully engaged when the book is read. The effect is that the imagination can become lazy so that it doesn't have to do the work of visualizing in the mind what is being read from the page. Also, a growing body of research is showing that television has a hypnotic, dulling effect on children that actually depresses mental functioning (*Endangered Minds: Why Children Don't Think and What We Can Do About It* by Jane M. Healy). A steady diet of images that require no mental work will eventually weaken the imagination, which needs effort to function well. Let video be the occasional fun food, but never the main course. Feed your children's hungry imaginations with feasts of good literature, art, and poetry.

Hardly anything can be more important in the mental training of a child than the bringing him to do what he ought to do, and to do it in its proper time, whether he enjoys it or not. The measure of a child's ability to do this becomes, in the long run, the measure of his practical efficiency in whatever sphere of life he labors."

— H. Clay Trumbull, *Hints on Child Training*, 1890

No intellectual habit is so valuable as that of attention; it is a mere habit but it is also the hallmark of an educated person. Use is second nature, we are told; it is not too much to say that "habit is ten natures"...We have lost sight of the fact that habit is to life what rails are to transport cars. It follows that lines of habit must be laid down towards given ends and after careful survey, or the joltings and delays of life become insupportable. More, habit is inevitable. If we fail to ease life by laying down habits of right thinking and right acting, habits of wrong thinking and wrong acting fix themselves of their own accord.

— Charlotte Mason, *Towards a Philosophy of Education*, 1925

Mental Muscle #3: Habits

The process of forming habits begins as soon as your child enters the world. The development of physical habits as an infant and emotional habits as a toddler lays the foundation for the next step—the cultivation of mental habits as a child. That process is, in many respects, the first lesson plan of your homeschooling journey.

Mental habit is the ability to act upon common duties or tasks without the necessity of deliberation or external motivation. It is doing what you know should be done without having to think about it or have someone else make you do it. Of all the mental muscles, habit is arguably the most noticeable, regardless of whether it is weak or strong. You know quickly whether a child has formed good mental habits or not. Most good habits are the end-product of discipleship and discipline of your children. Once formed, though, they can become powerful drives in the learning process, even stronger than many natural drives. Successful homeschooling depends on good habits.

Whatever the habit may be, though, it is not really the child who forms habits; rather, it is the parents who form habits in the young child. Whether actively or passively, knowingly or not, it is in your power to form habits—both good and bad—in your child. To the degree that you fail to instill good mental habits, you will find yourself needing to govern your child's mental habits where they are yet undeveloped or underdeveloped. Like the untrained child in a classroom who takes up most of a teacher's attention and time, the unformed and bad mental habits in your child's life will require the lion's share of your attention until they are corrected. Your child needs strong mental habits in order to become self-governing, which ultimately is the goal of your homeschooling efforts—to raise your child to be a self-motivated learner. The following are just a few of the more important habits related to an effective education.

- **Be attentive to attention.** The habit of attention enables your child, for example, to listen, hear, and retain information without your having to reread, question, or summarize. You can, in fact, train your child to a habit of inattentiveness by allowing any more than a single reading. Your child has an enormous capacity for attention and retention, but it must be trained into a habit in order to be harnessed for learning. Attention is both external (eye contact, body control) and internal (focused thoughts).

- **Concentrate on concentration.** The habit of concentration is an internal control that enables your child to focus mentally on a task. Concentration on reading, for instance, is being able to read a book or article and think about what it is saying without the mind wandering off in other directions and losing the train of thought. If your child has difficulty focusing or concentrating, start with some small tasks requiring less concentration and build up incrementally to more demanding tasks.

- **Respond to responsibility.** Responsibility is, perhaps, the ultimate habit and in some ways the collective expression of all the habits. A child with an internal sense of responsibility will be responsive to your directions as a homeschooling parent. However, few children are naturally responsible, and it is a habit that usually requires consistent training and reminding of what it looks like. Rewarding unsolicited acts of responsibility will affirm your child's responsible choices, even if it's as simple as a certificate posted on the refrigerator or an unexpected treat or privilege.

- **Expect excellence.** The habit of excellence expresses itself in an unwillingness to do less than your best. You develop this habit in your child by not excusing poor work (less than the child's ability) and by expecting and affirming real personal effort, whether in reading, writing, math, art, music, or any other subject. It is best not to judge your child's efforts in any area against what other children can do but rather against what you believe your child is capable of doing or achieving. The idea of excelling is to reach beyond the norm, but the goal needs to be within reach.

- **Order up orderliness.** The habit of orderliness and neatness is expressed not only in doing written reports and projects carefully and neatly, but also in the proper use and storage of materials, the careful use of books from your library, and care for the home (cleaning up messes from studies or projects, carefulness when using paints and glues). Though personality will be a strong factor, you can train your child in habits of orderliness and neatness even if they seem messy and sloppy by nature.

- **Seek out truthfulness.** The habit of truthfulness is not only a necessary Christian character quality, but it also affects your child's attitude toward learning and knowledge. It is necessary to train the habit of being truthful about what is actually known or not known, what was accomplished correctly or poorly, and so on. It is easy for a child to fall into the negative habit of self-deceit concerning self-evaluation of what they have actually learned or done. Whatever the reason (immaturity, fear, laziness), the simple solution is to always check their work and always expect honesty.

- **Push for self-control.** The habit of self-control enables your child to do work, even when it seems hard or he doesn't feel like doing it. Temporary diversions can be helpful and sometimes necessary for allowing the mind to rest, but the habit of self-control enables your child to return to the task willingly without complaint. It is the ability to govern your inner thoughts and feelings to do what needs to be done.

- **Do it with diligence.** The habit of diligence keeps a child moving forward with studies or reading, even when there are distractions or attractive diversions (such as television, friends, or a hobby). Diligence will spur them on to work harder, rather than doing just enough to get by. A child with the habit of diligence generally will not need to be reminded often to do his work. Diligence is difficult to cultivate in some children, but even some progress will be worth the effort.

IN OUR HOME

God was very generous in giving us Joy for our fourth child. With a gap of six years after Nathan and a new season of life for her parents, we had some trepidation about going back to the basics of homeschooling a young child. But Joy has been a joy to teach because she wants to learn and is naturally self-motivated. Even though she doesn't like every subject, she has cultivated good mental habits of getting her work done and even setting her own schedule. Sally has made a morning time with Joy an anchor in her day to help build and model the habit of spiritual discipline, which is a critical component for all of the other mental habits. If Joy keeps up the habits she's already developed, she'll just homeschool herself!

Habituality

Be creative in helping your children look at each day through the lens of habits. Rather than always telling them what must be done (which makes them dependent upon you), make it your own habit to ask your children what is the next thing to do. Be positive about your home routines to give your children a sense of achievement in ordering their hours. Once you have created a good rhythm for your home life, begin to expect your children to learn your routine—especially for homeschooling and chores—and to follow that routine without needing to be reminded. If your routine changes for a new season in life, make it a challenge to learn and master the new routines. Your goal is to give your children ownership of their own habits and routines.

Spirituality

Much of what we might call spirituality in a Christian is really just the practice of devotional habits. They are often called spiritual disciplines, but a discipline is really just a habit of devotion. In our WholeHearted Learning model, the first focused study area is Discipleship Studies. It is the foundation of our model. We make it a discipline, a habit, to start every day with the reading and study of God's Word. No one ever has to ask, "What do we do first?" In our family routine, the Bible is always first.

Feed-a-Habit Challenge

Let your child identify a particular habit or routine they want to develop (that you also want them to develop). Create a simple check-off chart for one to two weeks (longer for older children). At the end, write the child's choice of a favorite meal or restaurant. To earn the reward, the child must faithfully do the habit every day and check the list...without needing to be reminded. Miss a day, and it starts over.

Children are born with creative potential, and time spent playing video games is time wasted insofar as developing and preserving that potential. It is also time spent learning how to avoid being creative, and practicing the "skill" of operating without being creative. Creative thinking is like a muscle, and it needs to be stretched and flexed, or it will atrophy...Contemporary parenting styles may create overly programmed lives for children, by over-protecting them and over-scheduling them, which has the effect of denying children opportunities to discover for themselves as much as in previous eras.

— Kyung Hee Kim, associate professor at the College of William & Mary, "Explaining the Decline of Creativity in American Children: A Reply to Readers," Britannica Blog, December 23, 2010, www.britannica.com

Creativity Is God's Idea

God's pattern of creation in Genesis 1 provides a four-step model for our own creativity. Each day of creation is characterized by four kinds of creative activity that we can imitate. This example uses the decision to build a birdhouse.

- **Information** — First, there must be information or knowledge upon which to draw. ("The earth was formless and empty.") Ex: What different kinds of birdhouses can I build?
- **Imagination** — Second, imagination is engaged to consider possible solutions or actions. ("Let there be.") Ex.: This is the kind of birdhouse that I would like to build.
- **Realization** — Third, the new idea must be realized or expressed so that it becomes a reality. ("And it was so.") Ex.: Build the birdhouse.
- **Evaluation** — Fourth, there must be evaluation of the realized idea to determine its validity and usefulness and, if necessary, to improve it. ("It was good.") Ex.: What can I do to improve my birdhouse?

Mental Muscle #4: Creativity

Your children are creative. In fact, all children are innately endowed with creativity. As image-bearers of the Creator God, we all reflect a part of his creative nature and power, even though that reflection is distorted by sin. Redeemed creativity, though, is a powerful mental muscle that allows even children to reflect the glory of God, not just through artistic expressions, but through any endeavor of life. Never allow yourself to think, "My child just isn't creative." There is no such thing as a "creative personality" that some children possess and others do not. Every personality is capable of different expressions of being creative. Your child is creative, but that creativity must be nurtured if it is to grow and be expressed. It is your job to show your child how to be creative.

A common notion of creativity seems to be that it is some kind of mysterious, mystical inspiration that exudes from certain individuals. It is true that some people are endowed with more natural intuition than others, but even intuitive insights do not break upon the imagination *ex nihilo*—they do not come from nothing. Creativity never really produces something new that never was before—that is what God alone could do, and did at creation. True creativity draws upon what already exists and finds a new or better way of doing something. Far from being a mysterious special gift, it is a process that can be cultivated, encouraged, and even trained in all children.

Children given freedom to explore their own interests will naturally find ways to express their innate creative drive. Sadly, though, research shows a steady decline in creativity since 1990 in K-6 public school children ("The Creativity Crisis," *Newsweek*, July 10, 2010). Perhaps the regimented, limited, only-one-right-answer classroom environment is neutralizing their creativity. Rather than following their creative instincts, they learn to follow their instincts to be acceptable to friends and teachers by conforming to classroom expectations. Fortunately, the home environment is naturally suited to give children freedom to be creative. The more opportunities they have to exercise creativity, the more their creative tanks will stay full. Similarly, the more knowledge, experience, and skill they acquire, the more productive their creative process will become. The following are ways you can strengthen the mental muscle of creativity in your children.

- **Provide tools.** Like any skill, creativity requires good tools. For children, the tools may be simple, but they are necessary for expressing creativity: a good library of books and resources; good computer applications; creative writing materials; arts and crafts materials; creative play resources (such as plastic bricks and blocks); musical instruments; cooking utensils, gardening tools; carpentry tools; sewing materials; science and nature equipment; dress-up clothes and costumes.

- **Allow free time.** One of the most basic characteristics of creativity that research always confirms is the need for lots of free time. Creativity needs time to incubate in the mind before it is hatched. Along with that free time, your children also need freedom—to explore, to try out different creative ideas, and to simply enjoy the creative process. Creativity is not a totally unstructured process, so you can provide structure and guidelines to be sure they are using materials correctly and safely and aren't expressing ungodly ideas (such as violence or murder). However, be sure to give your children lots of freedom beyond those reasonable limitations.

- **Develop imagination.** Imagination is the internal work of the creative process. It is mental vision—the ability to see with your mind's eye. Some children have a more active imagination than others, but all must engage the imagination when listening to a story, wondering about a far-off land, or thinking about how to solve a problem. However, unbridled imagination can lead to an unbiblical thought life, so the imagination must be kept subject to the Spirit and to biblical principles. Reading is the single best way to exercise the imagination in a positive way. Your child cannot read or listen to a book without engaging the imagination in some way. Let the book provide an arena for their imagination so they can envision what the people, life, and times of the book were like. Especially read the kinds of books that will feed their moral imagination with positive role models of virtue, sacrifice, faithfulness, courage, and character. Your goal is to keep your child's imagination active so that it can be called into service for the creative process. A dormant imagination will cripple creativity.

- **Give guidance.** Guide your children into areas of creative expression that you see developing in their lives. Be sensitive to their feelings and certainly don't push your children into something that they do not seem interested in, but suggest different creative areas to them and then give them an opportunity to try them on to see if they fit. If they don't, try on something else. Encourage their creative expressions by displaying them, using them, or recording or photographing them. You may not always be able to praise your child's creative product, but you can always affirm the creative process that brought about the creation. When a creative delight emerges as a potential skill or long-term interest, invest in lessons to develop it.

- **Model creativity.** If you don't value the creative process, it is not likely your children will. Choose an enjoyable hobby or pastime that exercises your own creative gifts. (Yes, you do have them.) Display, perform, or use your creations just like you would your children's. If you are artistic, draw or paint something and put it out for all to see. If you are a songwriter or singer, perform or record your song. If you are good at crafts, make things to use or that your children can give to neighbors for holidays. If you are a scrapbooker, get everyone involved in your projects. If you are a writer, create a book and read it out loud. Creativity should be a family experience.

IN OUR HOME

Despite the need for precautions, the computer has been an incredible tool for releasing creativity in our family. When our boys were in their midteens, they spent many hours with a Whole Heart staff family's kids making short-form digital video productions that were very creative and sometimes surprisingly good. Each child added something different to the creative mix that included scriptwriting, acting, directing, photography (for still shots), videography (digital filming), composing, scoring, and editing (with effects). They also created many photographic slide shows to visualize original music they wrote and performed. Not surprisingly, Andrew Price is now studying video production, Joel is studying music and composition, and Nathan is interested in acting. Though it was all just for fun at the time, it was also building creative confidence for the future.

[Every] child should leave school with at least a couple of hundred pictures by great masters hanging permanently in the halls of his imagination, to say nothing of great buildings, sculpture, beauty of form and colour in things he sees. Perhaps we might secure at least a hundred lovely landscapes, too—sunsets, cloudscapes, star-light nights. At any rate he should go forth well furnished because imagination has the property of magical expansion, the more it holds the more it will hold.

— Charlotte Mason, *Towards a Philosophy of Education*, 1925

Creativity is a God-given ability to take something ordinary and make it into something special. It is an openness to doing old things in new ways...The creative spirit is part of our heritage as children of the One who created all things. And nurturing our creativity is part of our responsibility as stewards of God's good gifts.

— Emilie Barnes, *The Spirit of Loveliness*, Harvest House, 1994

This Is Creative?

Your children may express their creativity in ways that are annoying to you as an adult— messy paintings, noisy instruments, outdoor eyesores, piles of plastic blocks, smelly nature finds—but it's all a part of the creative process. In the beginning, it may seem "formless and void" to you, but it is the necessary first step for your child. Just hold your critique, or your nose, and give it some creative time.

Test everything. Hold on to the good.

— 1 Thessalonians 5:21

Equally strong, equally natural, equally sure of awakening a responsive stir in the young soul, is the divinely implanted principle of curiosity. The child wants to know: wants to know incessantly, desperately; asks all manner of questions about everything he comes across, plagues his elders and betters, and is told not to bother, and to be a good boy and not ask questions. But this only sometimes. For the most part we lay ourselves out to answer [the child's] questions so far as we are able, and are sadly ashamed that we are so soon floored by his insatiable curiosity about natural objects and phenomena.

— Charlotte Mason, *Parents and Children*, 1896

The teacher's first aim is to arouse curiosity, for curiosity is there in every child, just waiting to be stirred. The second is to foster curiosity until it prompts exploration. The third, and most difficult, is to allow the child to make his own discoveries.

— Margaretta R. Vorhees, *The Atlantic Readers, Vol. 1*, 1926

Mental Muscle #5: Curiosity

God has put into children a nearly unquenchable thirst for knowledge. As a parent, you want your children to have a strong mental muscle of curiosity that compels them to become self-directed learners. Curiosity—the drive to know—is in many ways the source of all learning. However, because children lack the natural discernment that comes with maturity, curiosity is a thirst that can lead them to drink from contaminated wells as readily as from mountain springs. You must learn how to channel that God-given curiosity into pure, clean waters. What we choose to know, whether good or bad, determines what we want to know. This is especially true for your children. If you let them choose to know about great missionaries, then the more they will want to know about missionaries and the worlds they live in. If you let your children choose to know about movie and music celebrities, the more they will want to know about celebrities and the world they live in. The more deeply your children drink from any well of knowledge, the more they will want to drink. Ultimately, the knowledge that your curious children retain will shape what they become. We are what we think about! So carefully satisfy their thirst for knowledge by directing them to the best wells.

God is concerned not just about the quality or purity of knowledge, but also about the kind of knowledge we pursue. Too much knowledge "puffs up" with pride, but it does not "build up" with wisdom (1 Corinthians 8:1-3), and it may even keep a person from coming to "acknowledge the truth" (2 Timothy 3:7). Any pursuit of knowledge can become empty and vain if it does not lead back in some way to a knowledge of God as the source of all that is good and true. Even Bible knowledge can become a source of prideful puffery if it becomes separated from the God who spoke it. That is why discipleship (shaping the heart to live for God) must undergird education (strengthening the mind to learn for God). It is the heart that directs the pursuit of knowledge, and the heart must be turned to God so that curiosity is channeled into knowledge that builds up. "The fear of the Lord is the beginning of knowledge" (Proverbs 1:7).

To switch metaphors for a moment, curiosity is also like the nuclear reactor core of learning, discovery, and invention. Curiosity works like nuclear fission, setting off a chain reaction of ideas, observations, and insights that collide and split and releasing great amounts of creative energy that fuel the investigation into the object of the curiosity. It needs to be contained, just like a nuclear reaction, but when it is contained and channeled toward a specific end, curiosity is powerful mental energy. If your children have a strong mental muscle of curiosity, they will never lack for subjects to study. The following are some ways you can strengthen your children's mental muscle of curiosity.

- **Give permission to be curious.** Cultivate your children's curiosity by giving them lots of room and resources to explore and discover. Let them take apart old dead appliances to see what is inside them. Crack the case on the computer and give them a tour through its insides. Get some science kits to play with—magnets, electrical circuits, and chemistry are always interesting. Have a star-watching party during the Perseid meteor shower. Help them plant an herb garden. Give them the tools necessary to make digital videos, record music, and put it all together. Create a Curiosity Shop in a basement, garage, or shed and fill it with things to do and to explore. Do whatever will stimulate their curiosity and desire to know more.

- **Model discerning curiosity.** Be curious about life and invite your children to seek out knowledge with you about new things that are of special interest to you—news stories, how something works, historical events, a new computer skill. This can be a good way to lead them on some curiosity journeys into places where you might be reluctant to send them alone (such as an Internet search). Discuss with them the meaning and impact of what you learn on your life as a Christian.

- **Provide lots of resources.** Fill your home with lots of good cisterns of knowledge from which your children can drink—interesting books, an encyclopedia, how-to books, hands-on projects, computer with Internet, science experiments, telescope, microscope, and the like. If your child is curious about something in particular, create a Discovery Corner (see page 127) dedicated to the object of their curiosity, fill it up with as many resources as you can, and turn them loose on it.

- **Create directed studies.** Look for areas of interest in your children. Harness their curiosity about that area by creating a unit or context study that will broaden their understanding of it and apply it to their lives as Christians. Be as curious about the subject as they are. Find experts who can tell you more, rent DVDs that explore the subject, and do online research with your children.

- **Plan strategic field trips.** Plan specific field trips that will tap into areas of your children's curiosity that you perceive are ripe for exercise. Use the field trip as an opportunity to focus on one object of curiosity or to open up new topics to investigate (such as going to a museum). Have interesting resources available after the field trip to stimulate curiosity about what they learned on it and to open related channels into which their curiosity can naturally flow. Discuss their interest in the subject.

- **Use teachable moments.** Be on the lookout every day for teachable moments during which you can exercise curiosity about new things you see or discover. For example, if you discover a new insect, make observations and ask questions about it and invite your child to do the same. If you are going on a vacation, plan ahead for side trips to places that will stimulate curiosity about historical events and people, how nature works, or architectural and engineering wonders. Be creative and be curious.

I keep six honest serving men (They taught me all I knew); Their names are What and Why and When And How and Where and Who.

— Rudyard Kipling (1865-1936), British author and poet

Go on a Curiosity Safari

Set aside an evening over hot chocolate and s'mores for a Curiosity Safari. Tell your children you're taking a journey into the unexplored realms of Curiositia, deep in the mysterious regions of I-Wonderland. You can start by suggesting a topic or take suggestions and have the family vote. Encourage everyone to ask questions. A simple example would be a safari into a mountain lake: How does the water get there? Where did the fish come from? Why don't the fish freeze in the winter? What would it be like to swim in the lake? Can you drink the water? Write down each question and discuss it. If the discussion is really lively, you can even use it for your homeschooling the next day. You can even keep a Safari journal to record your journey.

IN OUR HOME

Joy recently became interested in gardening. Since we live at 7,500 feet altitude in dry Colorado—not exactly prime gardening conditions—we were curious about what she could do with that interest. We gave her permission to pursue her twelve-year-old curiosity, and soon we found her with tools borrowed from the garage in the front yard beds planting bulbs. No one was more excited than Joy when some daffodils popped up, even though they were rudely covered by a spring snow the next day. Next we found her transplanting some spilled wheat that was sprouting. After redirecting her digging efforts from next to an electrical box (!), Clay helped her find an 8x10 patch of mountain ground to experiment on and fenced it with some chicken wire, and Joy began cultivating some veggies and other plants. Her garden will be a fun summer project grown from a seed of curiosity.

The man without the Spirit does not accept the things that come from the Spirit of God, for they are foolishness to him, and he cannot understand them, because they are spiritually discerned. The spiritual man makes judgments about all things, but he himself is not subject to any man's judgment: "For who has known the mind of the Lord that he may instruct him?" But we have the mind of Christ.

— 1 Corinthians 2:14-16

The child must think, get at the reason-why of things for himself, every day of his life, and more each day than the day before. Children and parents both are given to invert this educational process. The child asks "Why?" and the parent answers, rather proud of this evidence of thought in his child. There is some slight show of speculation even in wondering "Why?" but it is the slightest and most superficial effort the thinking brain produces. Let the parent ask "Why?" and the child produce the answer, if he can. After he has turned the matter over and over in his mind, there is no harm in telling him—and he will remember it—the reason why.

— Charlotte Mason, *Home Education*, 1886

God does not expect us to submit our faith to him without reason, but the very limits of our reason make faith a necessity.

— Augustine (354-430), church father

The faith that does not come from reason is to be doubted, and the reason that does not lead to faith is to be feared.

— G. Campbell Morgan (1863-1945), English pastor and teacher, with D. L. Moody

Mental Muscle #6: Reason

Language and reason are the arms and legs of the mental muscles. Language is the ability to reach out; reason is the ability to go in the right direction. We don't consciously think about the importance of reason that much, any more than we think about the importance of our legs while we are walking, yet we are exercising reason all the time—evaluating options, making decisions, weighing alternatives, arguing a point, planning a meal, reading an article, explaining something to a child.

Sometimes, when we just can't seem to break through with our children about how reasonable our parental opinion of a matter is, we are apt to think that they must have missed out on some reasoning genes at conception. Yet God designed within them an innate reasoning ability which is the imprimatur of his image in us as his creations. Our children are born with the capacity to reason—it is a part of God's image that sets us apart from the rest of creation. It grows quietly throughout childhood, showing itself only in less mature incarnations until around eleven or twelve years of age, when it breaks the surface and shows itself more forcefully. Still, it must be fed and strengthened from birth if it is to become a strong and useful mental muscle in adulthood.

The New Testament verb for "reason" is also an accounting term. It means to take account of all that is real (not speculative or unknown) and make a judgment. The term is derived from the Greek word *logos*, which John uses to describe Jesus as the divine Word who is the full expression of the plan of God. Paul said there is a time when we think and reason "like a child" (1 Corinthians 13:11), but we grow up and leave childish things behind. Here's what that all suggests: Reason is the process of accounting for what we know is real and true in light of our knowledge of Jesus and the gospel. Your children still reason childishly but are moving toward a time when they will choose to reason as adults. Maturation happens, but maturity is a choice. Your role is to be an example of godly reason to your children so they will be ready to make that choice without any doubt.

What makes that process so critical is the nature of the world children will live in as young adults and adults. It will be a culture that reasons based on scientific rationalism, materialistic naturalism, subjective spiritualism, and pluralistic relativism. Few people in the culture they inherit will reason based on objective, absolute, revealed truth. God, the divine Word, has spoken to us, and any attempt at reason—any attempt at accounting for reality—apart from his truth is shadow and darkness. What you are doing in strengthening your children's mental muscle of reason is about much more than just educating them—it is about preparing them to be persuasive messengers of God, who will "appear as lights in the world" in the midst of a "crooked and perverse generation" as they are "holding fast the word of life." If you do that, then you can say with Paul that you have "reason to glory because I did not run in vain nor toil in vain" (Philippians 2:14-16, NASB).

Home education is uniquely suited to strengthening reason. You can provide for your children a great pool of ideas, concepts, and knowledge on which their growing reason can draw, and you can train their powers of reason in the context of their homeschooling. As you demonstrate to them how reason comes into play in every area of life and learning, they will begin to see the patterns that they will use as they begin to reason more on their own. The following are some ways you can reinforce reason at home.

- **Discuss and dialogue.** Talk with your children about their concerns and questions—choices they are making, spiritual questions, their observations about life. Resist the temptation to be the answer-man-or-mom and instead gently probe your children to do their own reasoning. Dialogue with them as they think aloud about their concerns and ask them probing or leading questions that will help them discover reasonable answers on their own. Encourage and help them to reason biblically.

- **Solve problems together.** When you have a real-life problem to solve—how many gallons of paint to paint the garage, how to double a recipe, what kind of car to buy, planning a room addition—get your children involved in the process. Ask them to develop their own suggestions for solutions. Let them present and defend their ideas, but always encourage team problem solving too. When possible, use everyone's input to craft a group solution.

- **Form their opinions.** Even a child experiences the personal satisfaction of having a reasonable opinion on a matter. Encourage your children to think about their opinions, and then give them the opportunity to persuade you why they think their view of a matter is correct. Depending on their age, the argument may be childish reasoning, but always affirm the process nonetheless. (Avoid giving the impression that you think their opinion is childish, even if it is.) Let them have a voice in discussions as long as they honor and respect you and agree to submit to whatever you decide.

- **Exercise thinking skills.** Most children enjoy mental challenges. There are many good workbooks that will stretch their thinking and reasoning skills. They are like mental workouts that help strengthen reason through analogies, sequences, similarities and differences, spatial reasoning, deduction, and logic. They are, in some ways, IQ practice books, but without the stress of being timed. Some children will be faster with these kinds of exercises than others, but verbally value the reasoning itself, not the speed of the reasoning. Make it fun and affirming.

IN OUR HOME

When a controversial book for children came out, there was much discussion among Christians about whether or not it was acceptable. At the time, our children were about 14, 12, 10, and 4—right in the book's demographic bull's-eye. Rather than make an ex cathedra declaration one way or the other, I (Clay) decided to use the occasion as a learning opportunity. We talked about the book's subject matter at the dinner table one night in the very energetic style that often characterizes our dinnertime debates and dialogues. I finally had to end discussion and told the three older kids that I wanted them to read some articles about the book, do some research and thinking about the biblical issues involved, and come back next week ready to discuss the controversy surrounding the book. I would do the same, and together we would decide whether or not it was a book our family would read. We had a great conversation the next week, with reasonable arguments from all perspectives. It ended up being not so much about the book as it was about strengthening our reasoning muscles and having a great family discussion.

Reflect on what I am saying, for the Lord will give you insight into all this.

— 2 Timothy 2:7

Though the will affects all our actions and all our thoughts, its direct action is confined to a very little place, to that postern at either side of which stand conscience and reason, and at which ideas must needs present themselves. Shall we take an idea in or reject it? Conscience and reason have their say, but will is supreme and the behaviour of will is determined by all the principles we have gathered, all the opinions we have formed.

— Charlotte Mason, *Towards a Philosophy of Education*, 1925

Two-Minute Mysteries

Someone sets up the story: "A man lives on the twelfth floor of his apartment building. On sunny days, he gets off at the sixth floor and then uses the stairs. On rainy days, he goes all the way to the twelfth floor. Why?" Everyone then tries to solve the mystery by asking only Yes or No kinds of questions. The two-minute mystery, which usually goes much longer, is a mini-mental workout of almost pure reasoning, but that is also pure delight for children. Everyone wants to be the one who solves the mystery. You can find books with lots of these brain-busters, or if you're really good you can make up your own. Two-Minute Mysteries are a great way to pass the time on long car trips. Oh, and the answer to the mystery above? The man is very short. He can only reach the sixth-floor button without help, but on days when it rains, he can reach the twelfth-floor button with his umbrella.

For the foolishness of God is wiser than man's wisdom, and the weakness of God is stronger than man's strength.

— 1 Corinthians 1:25

The man without the Spirit does not accept the things that come from the Spirit of God, for they are foolishness to him, and he cannot understand them, because they are spiritually discerned. The spiritual man makes judgments about all things, but he himself is not subject to any man's judgment: "For who has known the mind of the Lord that he may instruct him?" But we have the mind of Christ.

— 1 Corinthians 2:14-16

If any of you lacks wisdom, he should ask God, who gives generously to all without finding fault, and it will be given to him...Who is wise and understanding among you? Let him show it by his good life, by deeds done in the humility that comes from wisdom...But the wisdom that comes from heaven is first of all pure; then peace-loving, considerate, submissive, full of mercy and good fruit, impartial and sincere.

— James 1:5, 3:13, 17

Wisdom to Match

Children love a simple search and match game, so why not turn it into a search and learn game? You can use 3x5 index cards. Choose eighteen Proverbs, and create two identical cards for each verse (36 cards)—print the verse reference in bold at the top, and the Proverb text beneath it. To add visual clues, use a particular color for each pair of cards or add a simple line drawing to each card that illustrates the Proverb. Mix the cards and lay them out face down in a 6x6 grid. Whenever you or your child turns over the first card of a match attempt, read the verse on that card out loud together. If you make a match, read it again, remove the cards from the grid, and place in front of the winner.

Mental Muscle #7: Wisdom

Jesus grew in it. Paul preached it. Solomon sought after it. James asked for it. It is more precious than wealth, available to all, a supernatural gift, but only for the humble. It is eternal, but acquired by study. It comes from God. What is it? If you said "wisdom," you're only partially correct. It is godly wisdom—not just the world's wisdom, but God's wisdom. Children can learn the world's wisdom and be very intelligent, knowledgeable, and bright, but only the world will be impressed, not God (Jeremiah 9:23-24).

Most discussions of wisdom focus on it as a godly character quality that is the result of training and discipleship. However, that is not all there is to wisdom. You cannot train into your children all the wisdom necessary to address every situation they will face in life. When they enter young adulthood and you're not always there to help them, they will need to know how to seek out wisdom and apply it to their lives on their own. Wisdom is a mental muscle that must be exercised and strengthened!

In the Old Testament, wisdom is the ability both to live skillfully and to live a life that is pleasing to God. The wise person walks on the path of life, light, and righteousness; in contrast, the foolish person walks on the path of death, darkness, and wickedness. In the New Testament, wisdom (*sophia*) is internal. Godly wisdom begins with a redeemed heart—the heart is turned to God, bondage to sin is broken, and the Holy Spirit indwells the new believer, making him a new creation with the mind of Christ. But receiving the mind of Christ is not the same as receiving God's wisdom. The former must be exercised for the latter to grow. As a new creation, you are set free from sin in order to choose to listen to and learn from God, rather than from the world. Making that choice every day requires a mental fitness beyond just knowing a few precepts and principles of Scripture. It requires an ongoing renewal of the mind to prevent conformity with the world. That ongoing "renewing of your mind" (Romans 12:2) is the daily exercise and strengthening of the mental muscle of wisdom in your children.

The wisdom we have from God through the Spirit is in contrast to the wisdom of the world. Godly wisdom is even considered foolish to the world. Perhaps even more than just growing in godly wisdom, your children need to know that it will be ridiculed and rejected in a world that does not recognize its truth and power. Part of your challenge in strengthening their wisdom muscle is to prepare them for this conflict, reminding them of Paul's words: "Brothers, think of what you were when you were called. Not many of you were wise by human standards...But God chose the foolish things of the world to shame the wise; God chose the weak things of the world to shame the strong" (1 Corinthians 1:26-27). God can use the godly wisdom your children learn at home to change the minds and lives of those living by the world's wisdom.

When Moses prayed that God would "teach us to number our days aright, that we may gain a heart of wisdom" (Psalm 90:12), he was acknowledging that godly wisdom takes work and discipline and that we have only a few days on this earth, in view of eternity, to acquire it. Your task as a parent is to number your children's days to ensure that they gain a heart of wisdom while in your home. The stronger the wisdom muscle you give them, the higher they can hold up the light of truth in their generation. The following are some of the ways you can help your children grow in wisdom.

- **Be discerning.** The most fundamental quality of wisdom is the ability to discern right from wrong, what is pleasing to God from what is not, what is biblical from what is not. Teach your children how to use a concordance and a topical Bible to do their own search of the Scriptures for godly discernment on various subjects such as friends, television, money, music, and activities. For practice, have them create a topical index of the book of Proverbs or the parables of Jesus.

- **Seek understanding.** There is a connection between wisdom and humility. It is the admission that others know more than you and that you can learn from them. It drives the search for understanding: "How blessed is the man who finds wisdom and the man who gains understanding" (Proverbs 3:13, NASB). Books and commentaries can help deepen understanding of a subject, but whenever possible, help your child locate a knowledgeable person to learn from with humility. "The fear of the Lord is the instruction for wisdom, and before honor comes humility" (Proverbs 15:33, NASB).

- **Walk wisely.** Train your children how to seek wisdom from other godly, wise people. "He who walks with the wise grows wise" (Proverbs 13:20). Have them interview a mature believer to learn more about living wisely for God—relationships, work, walk with the Lord, and more. Beyond just knowledge and understanding, teach your children how to listen for the wisdom that comes with experience and age. Have them start a quotables book to record any jewels of wisdom they hear.

- **Pray wisely.** Encourage your children to pray for wisdom (James 1:5) before they do anything else. Have them start a journal to record wisdom they learn in answer to their prayers. Model praying for wisdom for your family, especially when facing major life decisions, but even in just navigating the choices in a normal day.

- **Spend wisely.** Give your children gradually expanding stewardships to exercise their wisdom, such as in the area of money. After the kingdom, Jesus teaches more about money and the use of money than any other subject. How a person uses money is a good indicator of their level of wisdom or foolishness. Study what Scripture says about money with your children, then help them develop a budget and justify where they apportion the monies they receive.

IN OUR HOME

Sarah, our first child, read almost every book in our library before she graduated. She wrote her first book, Journeys of Faithfulness, *when she was sixteen. Her book* Read for the Heart: Whole Books for the WholeHearted Family *is a companion to this book. She is a self-taught authority on classic children's literature of the Victorian era. When she had the opportunity to learn more from Dr. Joe Wheeler, she jumped at the chance. Dr. Wheeler taught English literature at Vanderbilt University for many years and is known for his anthologies of stories from the nineteenth and early twentieth centuries and as an editor of classic books. Sarah visited Dr. Wheeler and his wife in their home in the Colorado Rockies and was thrilled to accept his assignment to read great new books and write reports about them. Sarah was walking with the wise and gaining understanding at the same time.*

Do not conform any longer to the pattern of this world, but be transformed by the renewing of your mind. Then you will be able to test and approve what God's will is—his good, pleasing and perfect will.

— Romans 12:2

For though we live in the world, we do not wage war as the world does. The weapons we fight with are not the weapons of the world. On the contrary, they have divine power to demolish strongholds. We demolish arguments and every pretension that sets itself up against the knowledge of God, and we take captive every thought to make it obedient to Christ.

— 2 Corinthians 10:3-5

Wisdom Wars

Find some good quote books or go online to one of the many quotation websites and start writing down wisdom quotes of all kinds on 3x5 index cards—words spoken, axioms, and proverbs about life and living. Be sure to record the name and any background about the person to whom the quote is attributed, if it is known. Check reference works for interesting facts that will put the quote in context. When you have a good stack of quotes, gather the family for a session for some Wisdom Wars (see 2 Corinthians 10:3-5 above). Read the quote and ask, "Is this worldly wisdom or Wordly wisdom?" The object is to determine if the quote reflects the wisdom of man (world-ly) or the wisdom of God (Word-ly). You can award points for any Scriptures quoted to validate a judgment. Write down the choice on each quote, along with any Scripture references quoted.

Though the will affects all our actions and all our thoughts, its direct action is confined to a very little place, to that postern at either side of which stand conscience and reason, and at which ideas must needs present themselves. Shall we take an idea in or reject it? Conscience and reason have their say, but will is supreme and the behaviour of will is determined by all the principles we have gathered, all the opinions we have formed.

— Charlotte Mason, *Towards a Philosophy of Education*, 1925

As often as the work of instructing the children upon earth threatens to become a burden or a weariness, thou mayst be sure it is a token of something wrong within: the love to God in heaven, or the delight in His word, has been fading. As often as thou seekest for fresh vigour to perform thy work hopefully and joyfully, thou hast but to turn to the words, that reveal the secret of a godly education, and thou shalt experience that, as for thy children so for thyself, there is an unspeakable blessing in the wisdom that has so inseparably connected the heart's secret love with the mouth's spoken words: "Thou shalt love the Lord thy God with all thy heart. And these words shall be in thy heart. And thou shalt teach them to thy children."

— Rev. Andrew Murray, *The Children for Christ*, 1887

Cultivating a Positive Learning Attitude

You cannot possibly teach your children everything they need to know. Just to reassure you, neither can any school. The reality of learning is that exposure to ideas and information can be extremely wide, but depth of knowledge in specific areas is necessarily selective. Learning retention for any topic will vary greatly depending upon the emphasis given in the educational process and the amount of individual attention given to the child. That is what gives home education such a decided advantage over conventional schooling—you are able to affirm and feed your children's specific learning interests, and you can give them unlimited individual attention. That tells your children that the subjects they want to learn about are important and that their desire to know more is important to you, the teacher. Still, they will never be able to learn everything they need to know, even in your homeschool, but that is not the purpose of education.

The ultimate purpose of true education is to create a strong foundation for a lifetime of learning. You do not need to teach them everything, but the one thing you can give them will be the key to learning everything they need to know in order to be successful in life: a positive learning attitude. The attitude that you give your children about learning will stay with them the rest of their lives, and it begins at the earliest ages of childhood. A child with a positive learning attitude will naturally become a self-motivated learner and will more quickly become a self-educating student. The following are some ways you can cultivate a positive learning attitude in your children.

- **Have a positive attitude about learning yourself.** Your attitude and example are the greatest influences on your children's attitude. If you grimace when it's time to study math or any other subject, you are telling your children they can feel the same way.

- **Let your love of books be infectious and consistent.** Build a good library, read many wonderful books to your children from a young age, get excited when new books arrive in the mail, and make book ownership a high value in your home.

- **Believe in your children.** Affirm their worth to you and God. Affirm the great potential that you see in them. Observe the positive qualities and strengths of their personality types, and notice and encourage their natural gifts and talents.

- **Give your children freedom to explore and discover.** Interact with them about what they are learning—ask questions, acknowledge good insights, provide more resources, invite them to tell you more, and make life a journey of discovery.

- **Don't rush learning.** Discern the correct pace for each child, and let them know they're doing fine. Don't always tell them they are either behind or ahead, which are false standards. Focus on what they know, not on what they don't know.

- **Express genuine interest in whatever interests your children.** If something captures your child's mind or imagination, harness that delight and turn it into a learning opportunity. Your child is already excited and motivated—use that.

- **Give your children freedom to ask questions.** No matter how simple or inane a child's question may seem, answer it fully and then help your child frame a better question. Always respond seriously (but appropriately) to serious questions.

Cultivating a Positive Teaching Attitude

You can exhort, cajole, and harangue your children all day long about getting regular exercise to have fit bodies, but if they don't see you exercising, you'll be fighting a losing battle. It is the same with education. If you want your children to value and pursue learning—to build strong mental muscles—then you must set the pace for their learning by providing a good example. Your example will be both a model and a motivation.

One of the extra benefits of homeschooling is that it restores to the whole family the excitement and pleasure of learning—fathers, mothers, daughters, and sons all learning and growing together. God never intended for parents to retire from learning. In the biblical family model, parents continue to learn and pass their learning on to their children in the course of everyday life. We can read Proverbs in an offhanded, detached sort of way that doesn't let the truth sink in, but the exhortations to youth in Proverbs chapters 1-9—to seek out and value wisdom, knowledge, and understanding—were spoken by a parent. Solomon was holding up his own lifelong commitment to learning and wisdom as an example for his sons. God wants us to be willing and fervent learners all of our lives.

God never meant for learning to become a burden, either for children or for parents. He meant it to be a natural, enjoyable part of family life. Our culture has wrested education from families and turned it into an unnatural, tedious drudgery of classrooms, textbooks, and tests. As the roots of learning are severed from the family tree, children's minds and hearts can wilt under the conformity of conventional schooling, and parents likewise can wither intellectually. As you bring education back home, bring with it the joy of learning. If your children see that you value and enjoy learning, they will follow your heart and example. And if you are strengthening their minds to learn for God, then you can be confident that education will happen naturally in your home. As you talk to your children about what it means to become a strong learner, be sure to talk to yourself about your own mental muscles and heart for learning. Ask yourself these questions:

- **Am I developing good mental habits?** Do your children see you working to strengthen your habits?

- **Am I feeding good mental appetites?** Do your children see you choosing what is excellent over what is mediocre?

- **Am I improving my language skills?** Do your children see you speaking with increasing expression and conviction?

- **Am I expressing creativity in my life?** Do your children see you enjoying a creative pursuit and sharing your creations?

- **Am I cultivating curiosity?** Do your children see you seeking out knowledge about areas of interest?

- **Am I strengthening my powers of reason?** Do your children hear you reasoning through problems and issues?

- **Am I growing in wisdom?** Do your children see you seeking God's wisdom on important questions in your life?

Children need to learn how to do things which they do not want to do, when those things ought to be done. Older people have to do a great many things from a sense of duty. Unless children are trained to recognize duty as more binding than inclination, they will suffer all their lives through from their lack of discipline in this direction.

— H. Clay Trumbull, *Hints on Child Training*, 1890

The entrance of Divine truth into the mind and heart, the formation of habit and the training of character, these are not attained by sudden and isolated efforts, but by regular and unceasing repetition. This is the law of all growth in nature, and of this law God seeks to make use in the kingdom of grace, in dependence upon and subservient to the power of the Holy Spirit. This is the principle that is so beautifully applied by Moses to parental duty. The instruction he had enjoined was not to be by means of set times, and stated formal lectures; the whole life with all its duties has to be interwoven with the lessons of God's presence and God's service. With a heart full of God's love and God's word, the ordinary avocations of daily life were to be no hindrance, but helps to lead the youthful hearts heavenwards.

— Rev. Andrew Murray, *The Children for Christ*, 1887

Shifting the Paradigm

The generally accepted paradigm (model or pattern) for home education, fostered through many years of public schooling, has been the classroom. However, a shift is taking place for many who are beginning to recognize the validity of the home itself as a paradigm for home education. Here's a snapshot of what characterizes the primary differences between a classroom paradigm and a home paradigm:

Classroom Paradigm

- **Learning** — The best learning happens through formal instructional procedure.
- **Focus** — The focus is on the teacher and the instructional dynamics of the classroom.
- **Goal** — The goal of learning is to know certain prescribed facts and information.
- **Means** — Textbooks, curricula, and teachers are the primary sources of learning.
- **Child** — A child must be told what to think and what to know in order to learn.

Home Paradigm

- **Learning** —The best learning happens through an informal relational process.
- **Focus** — The focus is on the child and the learning dynamics of the home.
- **Goal** — The goal of learning is to become conversant with many ideas and concepts.
- **Means** — Real books, real life, and family are the primary sources of learning.
- **Child** — A child can be trusted to seek out knowledge and to learn—it is his nature.

It's All There in Christian Home Education

Families have always homeschooled. Even in the heyday of the public schooling movement, some families somewhere were breaking the rules to keep their children out of school and at home. Numbed by years of cultural conformity, the rest of us didn't know we could be dissatisfied with the public schools, and even if we were, we didn't think we had permission to consider something else. Christians, who had the best reasons to look for an alternative, had only the restrictively expensive private school option. But then, almost without warning, the curtains were pulled back and the windows thrown open by educators questioning the classroom model, by families experimenting with learning at home, and by Christians sensing the call of God to come home with their children. We saw the educational light and ran toward it. A new movement was born.

From the beginning, the Christian homeschooling movement has been more than just an educational alternative for many Christians. We married in 1981 and decided in 1983 that we would homeschool our children, even though Sarah would not be born until 1984. It was a lifestyle decision, not just an educational one. It was never just about schooling for us, but about three distinctive priorities that guided our hearts:

- **Christian** — We were committed to a fully biblical Christian lifestyle. We knew instinctively that we could not biblically justify giving our children to others to raise during the most formative years of their lives. We were jealous for the spirits, hearts, and minds of our children. Homeschooling was the answer.

- **Home** — The more we studied Scripture together, the more we became convinced that home and family were at the heart of God's plan of redemption and the Christian life. And now, for the first time, there was a real choice for our children that would give full expression to the divine design for the home.

- **Education** — The more we learned and thought about this new homeschooling option, the more our spirits were drawn to it, not because it was alternative education but because it was exciting to think about our children learning with us as a whole family. It was a clearly biblical way to raise children.

Since the early 1980s, many have replaced the term "homeschooling" with the more descriptive language of "Christian home education." It is who we are—Christians who are using our homes to educate our children, not just for this world, but for God and eternity. Home education is the final of the three priorities we have been exploring of what it means to build a truly Christian home. The first is home nurture, shepherding your child's spirit to long for God. The second is home discipleship, shaping your child's heart to live for God. The third is home education, strengthening your child's mind to learn for God. After years of being held hostage by the public school juggernaut, Christians are at last able to break free to pursue and build a fully Christian home. No one knows how long we will enjoy this freedom or even what God's greater purpose is for allowing it at this particular time in history. But those with eyes to see that Christian home education is more than just an educational movement are acting on faith and responding to God's invitation. They are coming home to be the family that God designed them to be. And one day, looking back from eternity, we will rejoice to see how God used us in his plan.

Section 2

Learning

— Chapter 6 —

The WholeHearted Learning Model: Living and Learning Together at Home

Giving Your Child a Designer Education

Christian home education is the ultimate designer education, not only because it can be tailored to fit any child's needs, but even more because it bears the imprimatur of God, the original Designer. It draws its identity, though, not from some extrapolated biblical design for education but rather from the clear biblical teaching that God's design for the home and family is foundational to all learning and education. Before there was any other instituted order on the earth, God designed family. It is an expression of his divine nature, the spiritual DNA that affects every aspect of our lives, and the language and analogue by which we are able to understand and relate to the eternal, divine Trinity. Family is the institutional cornerstone of the life God created for us on this earth; he introduced it and gave it purpose in the perfection of Eden before the Fall brought corruption into the world. The institutions of government and church would be needed to bring civil and moral order to the post-Edenic world, but they would be dependent on family.

In thinking about institutions created by God, it is also helpful to consider what was *not* created. Nowhere in Scripture did God directly institute the idea of a school as being his divinely designed method for the education of children. He certainly gave mankind the freedom to create educational entities, but school is nowhere found to be part of God's eternal plan for his creation. Instead, he instituted the family. It is clear from Scripture that education is at the very heart of his design for the family: The training and instruction of children is laid in the lap of the family, placed in the hands of parents.

However, in the same way that governments and the church are fluid institutions, families have great freedom and latitude in expressing what it means to train and instruct children. There are some biblical nonnegotiables, of course, but every homeschool can be custom-designed from a wide range of learning structures to suit the unique educational needs of each individual child in the home. Your homeschool will differ in some degree from every other homeschool because your family, children, and home are different. Some families insist on a structured, formal curriculum, and some resist any kind of predesigned approach. You are free to choose the best resources and methods to create an educational model to fit the unique needs and desires of your family.

We wrote this book to guide you in implementing what we call WholeHearted Learning, a biblically based approach to home education that integrates learning and educational goals for children into God's design for the family. Because it is designed to be both comprehensive and flexible, the WholeHearted Learning model can be implemented in any home setting. It is a one-size-fits-all designer (and Designer) educational model for the Christian home. It is, we believe, a full reflection of what God intended for the family.

Apply your heart to instruction and your ears to words of knowledge. My son, if your heart is wise, then my heart will be glad; my inmost being will rejoice when your lips speak what is right. Do not let your heart envy sinners, but always be zealous for the fear of the LORD. There is surely a future hope for you, and your hope will not be cut off. Listen, my son, and be wise, and keep your heart on the right path.

— Proverbs 23:12, 15-19

...the truth is mothers—and fathers—exert far more influence over their children's intellectual development than is commonly realized. In fact, more than three decades of research shows that families have greater influence over a child's academic performance than any other factor—including schools.

— Family Research Council, "The One-House Schoolroom," *Family Policy* (Sept. 1995), remarks by William R. Mattox, Jr. to the World Congress of Families II

Hear, O Israel: The LORD our God, the LORD is one. Love the LORD your God with all your heart and with all your soul and with all your strength. These commandments that I give you today are to be on your hearts. Impress them on your children. Talk about them when you sit at home and when you walk along the road, when you lie down and when you get up.

— Deuteronomy 6:4-7

Moreover, unlike teaching in our culture, teaching as envisioned in the OT does not presuppose a classroom. Rather, the OT presupposes a distinctive community and a distinctive interpersonal setting for teaching and learning ...That is, as life is lived by adult and child, the recurrent experiences they share are to be constantly interpreted by the divine Word. Thus, learning does not take place in classrooms but in the cycle of ordinary events..

— Lawrence O. Richards, *Expository Dictionary of Bible Words*, Zondervan, 1985

Know Your Designer's Purposes

The natural instinct of any parent is to instruct their children. However, it seems that most parents sublimate their instinct to instruct, default to the public or private school system, and delegate the task to an institution. Some of those parents are more involved with their children's education than others, but none fully directs it or owns it. You, though, are reading this book because you want to instruct your children at home. You own your instinct to instruct, you see it as part of God's design for your family, and now you're just trying to figure out how to go about doing it. Before you make the leap into one homeschooling model or methodology over another, though, you should take some time to think carefully about how God designed children to learn.

What was unquestionably implicit in the pre-Fall created order in Genesis 1-3 is made explicit in Deuteronomy 6:4-9, Psalm 78:1-8, and Ephesians 6:4—God designed children to be taught and to learn in the context of family and community and designed parents to be their primary instructors. Don't miss the impact of Moses' words in the Deuteronomy passage. As Israel is about to enter the land God promised them and to realize after all their years of captivity and wandering the completion of God's promise to make them—Abraham's descendants—into a great nation of the earth, Moses addresses them as families (6:2). Not just as a nation, not as individuals, but as families of the new nation Israel and of the community of God's people. He has just read the Ten Commandments to them (5:1-21), and now he elaborates on them for all the families and parents of Israel: Serve the Lord God only, love the Lord God completely, and teach your children to serve and love the Lord God (6:4-9). This passage, still recited daily by pious Jews, would become the foundational identity statement of Israel. At the very heart of the history of Israel is God's design that parents must diligently teach their children the things of God, not just on the Sabbath but at all times, in all places, and in all ways. Parents instructing their children within the context of a close family living within the broader context of the whole community of faith was and still is a nonnegotiable. God is real, God has spoken, and parents must speak God's words to their children.

That is the starting point for figuring out the how of homeschooling. Whatever model or methodology you choose, it must be characterized first by those two life-changing truths—God is real and he has spoken. Those truths, though, are often tagged in our modern culture as being spiritual matters and are commonly separated from the more intellectual matters that are often called a child's education. Yet nowhere in Scripture is that kind of bifurcation of a child's life and development even hinted at. Rather, the parent is always the instructor, and the instruction always begins with the acknowledgment of God's presence and revelation. That is why Christian homeschooling is not something new but rather a recovery of what God intended from the beginning. Home and family are his ideal for how and where children should learn all they need to know to live well and successfully for him. When you choose a homeschooling model or methodology, don't be tempted or fooled by presumptuous promises of educational excellence and academic advantage if those claims are not integrated tightly with God's reality and revelation. Homeschooling is not only about one part of your child's life, as though you can raise a mind; it is about their whole life—heart, mind, and spirit. Whatever model you choose, make sure it enables you to raise a whole child. That was God's purpose from the beginning of creation for home and family.

Know Your Homeschooling Design's Purposes

God's purpose for family as revealed in the Old Testament will not change. It is part of his divine design for the created order, which does not change with changing times and cultures. However, "in these last days [God] has spoken to us by his Son" (Hebrews 1:2), and that has changed everything. Jesus instituted a new covenant of grace and brought a new revelation of truth, and that changed forever the identity and the instruction of those whom God would call his people. Under the previous covenant, God's people were defined by their adherence to a written, external Law, mediated by priests. Under the new covenant, instituted on the cross, a new "people of God" (1 Peter 2:9-10) are defined by their faith in Christ and his work of grace on the cross (Ephesians 2:8-9). God's law is now written directly on the heart by the Spirit of God (Jeremiah 31:31-34), and we are led by the Spirit of Christ (Romans 8:1-4).

So, for two thousand years, those who follow Christ have affirmed the life-changing reality of the incarnation (God is real) and revelation of the gospel of salvation by grace through faith (God has spoken). The Apostle John sums up in the prologue of his gospel the change wrought by Christ's coming: "For we have all received from his fullness one gracious gift after another. For the law was given through Moses, but grace and truth came about through Jesus Christ" (John 1:16-17, NET). In light of John's words, Jesus should be the living center of every Christian homeschool—the eternal "Word [that] became flesh and made his dwelling among us" (John 1:14). Your family and homeschool should affirm and reflect the grace and truth realized in Christ—that God is real and has spoken. That sounds pretty straightforward and easy, but the reality is more complex.

Christians can still find themselves drawn in by the principle of law. Just like the early church, we still can be tempted to think that following formulas and keeping rules will make us better Christians or even better Christian homeschoolers. But the grace and truth realized through Jesus have freed us from the Law and the principle of law in our relationship with God. Jesus said, "So if the Son sets you free, you will be free indeed" (John 8:36). Paul said, "It is for freedom that Christ set us free" (Galatians 5:1). If you feel homeschooling is a burden rather than a blessing, you are not free. You can trust the Holy Spirit to lead you to a model or method of Christian homeschooling that is right for you and that allows you freedom in Christ to let his grace and truth shine from your home. Be sure that is the purpose and the promise of the design you choose.

IN OUR HOME

In our early years of homeschooling, we tried to follow laws of behavior to be more acceptable to God and others; we tried to conform to laws of belief in order to fit into movements or groups. Rather than sensing a freedom in the Spirit, though, we would end up feeling, in Paul's words, "burdened again by a yoke of slavery" (Galatians 5:1). We wish we had discovered the biblical truth of our freedom in Christ earlier. Rather than depending on man-made Christian formulas and rules, we rediscovered the ministry of the Holy Spirit to guide us in our homeschooling days and decisions. We began teaching others to let the Holy Spirit be their confidence, and that teaching became this book.

In the past God spoke to our forefathers through the prophets at many times and in various ways, but in these last days he has spoken to us by his Son, whom he appointed heir of all things, and through whom he made the universe.

— Hebrews 1:1-2

But you are a chosen people, a royal priesthood, a holy nation, a people belonging to God, that you may declare the praises of him who called you out of darkness into his wonderful light. Once you were not a people, but now you are the people of God; once you had not received mercy, but now you have received mercy.

— 1 Peter 2:9-10

"This is the covenant I will make with the house of Israel after that time," declares the LORD. "I will put my law in their minds and write it on their hearts. I will be their God, and they will be my people."

— Jeremiah 31:33

For it is by grace you have been saved, through faith—and this not from yourselves, it is the gift of God—not by works, so that no one can boast. For we are God's workmanship, created in Christ Jesus to do good works, which God prepared in advance for us to do.

— Ephesians 2:8-10

Therefore, there is now no condemnation for those who are in Christ Jesus, because through Christ Jesus the law of the Spirit of life set me free from the law of sin and death.

— Romans 8:1-2

The Education Nation

Primary and secondary education seems at first blush to be a monolithic enterprise with one overarching purpose—to make sure all children get a basic education that will prepare them to get a better education that will prepare them to get a good job. Secular public education in America has evolved into what is essentially an elaborate employment preparation and social indoctrination mechanism. "Educate" is derived from the Latin term *educare*, which means to "bring up," and from a related term which means to "bring out." Education is not only about job and career training but also about bringing up a child in order to bring out their unique skills, abilities, and character. True education is not about making a living but about making a life. Homeschooling is the only schooling option that allows making a life to be fully explored and expressed. If your education is about making a life, then making a living will follow naturally. Don't sacrifice your child's life on the cultural altar of education as the path to making a good living. It will not get you or your child where you want to go.

Schools of Schooling

Until around 1980, there were essentially two schools of education in America—public and private. Although some public schools still reflected Judeo-Christian beliefs and values, only private schools were free to pursue a religious form of schooling. With the advent of homeschooling, Christian families found the freedom to educate their children with their own beliefs and values. As the Christian homeschooling movement rapidly grew, the secularization of public schools advanced just as rapidly. With few exceptions, public schools are now nearly universally secular. Of the four schools of education described below, three are still free to pursue religious beliefs and values. Only public schooling offers no real freedom in regard to religion. As American culture and government become even more secularized, separation of church and state issues in the government-run public school system can be expected to increase, as can government encroachment into the educational freedoms of homeschooling. In order to fully understand homeschooling in America, it is helpful to put it in its proper educational context.

- **Public Schooling** — Public schooling is the system of state-funded and state-run educational institutions for kindergarten through twelfth grade. Although public schools are funded and operated at the state and local level, the system is shaped and influenced by the federal government through legislation, oversight agencies, program initiatives, and strategic funding incentives. It has become almost irreversibly secular in its leadership, union involvement, and teaching content. The introduction of charter schools has added some diversity, but they are still under state authority.

- **Private Schooling** — In order to be free of government restrictions on content or control of educational standards, private schools accept no public funding. Nearly 10 percent of American primary and secondary students attend private schools, the majority of those being Christian schools operating either independently or as part of a denomination or organization. The high cost of most private schools has been a barrier for many parents. Homeschooling provides an affordable alternative, yet most parents unable to afford private schooling choose public.

- **Independent Schooling** — Independent schooling is an emerging form of schooling characterized by parental choice from among a variety of options. Some independent schools combine traditional, remote classroom learning with a home-based learning component. As long as the parent is still considered the primary teacher, the child technically is being homeschooled. However, schooling that requires three or more days a week of classroom learning outside of the home with assignments to be done at home should not be considered homeschooling. It's a fine line, but when most of the schooling occurs outside the home, it should be considered independent schooling.

- **Homeschooling** — Homeschooling is education of a child that takes place predominantly in a home context and is directed solely by the child's parents. Aside from state regulatory requirements, the homeschooling family is independent of formal accountability to any outside authorities or programs to validate the parent-directed learning in the home. Although some age-graded curriculum publishers may require informal accountability, if it is voluntary and nonbinding and if coursework can be completed at home, it is still homeschooling. The home is the key.

Schools of Homeschooling

One of the hallmarks of homeschooling is the diversity of approaches for what and how to teach your children at home. Since there is no centralized homeschooling authority and every family is free to choose a learning model or method that suits them, theoretically there can be as many approaches as there are homeschooling families. This freedom has naturally resulted in a free-market system of educational providers competing for each of those families' allegiance. In their search for an approach that will best fit their own convictions, beliefs, and lifestyle, homeschooling families must navigate a confusing ocean of educational alternatives. Many drift from one approach to another, often being pulled into a new wave or current that takes them in a direction they eventually realize they didn't want to go. Sadly, many end up committed to an approach not necessarily out of a considered decision, but simply out of convenience or even resignation.

Homeschool conventions and book fairs can play a key role in the free-market home educational experience. They bring together respected homeschooling speakers and leaders and provide exhibit areas for homeschool publishers, businesses, associations, groups, and services. Some are large home education tradeshows in convention centers; others are small home education ministries in churches; all are dedicated to helping homeschool families. They can be helpful resources for new and veteran homeschoolers, yet they can also be overwhelming and confusing. The abundance of educational options can cause "deer in the headlights book fair syndrome" if you're not prepared. Do your research first to determine what approach and materials suit you best. If you know why you're there and what you need before you get there, then you can browse the booths and listen to the speakers with discernment.

Families that begin homeschooling with a sense of conviction and confidence about the approach they want to pursue are better equipped to navigate the ocean of options and to avoid uncertainty and drifting. Our heart is to help homeschooling families find that confidence and certainty. The first step is understanding the main schools of homeschooling. We have identified four of these based not on similarity of content or method, but rather on focus and intent. Representative approaches within each of the schools of homeschooling are briefly examined in the rest of this chapter.

- **Curriculum-Centered Homeschooling** — The focus of these approaches is a structured, age-graded (scope and sequence), formal curriculum centered on course materials, textbooks and workbooks, completing assignments, and assessing competence.

- **Content-Centered Homeschooling** — These approaches are typically curriculum-centered but focus on unique content or pedagogy that is integral to the curriculum. The focus is on formal instruction that promulgates or promotes the unique content.

- **Child-Centered Homeschooling** — These approaches are typically informal and unstructured, focusing on the learning experience and the intellectual and character development of the child more than on the actual content of the instruction.

- **Home-Centered Homeschooling** — Home-centered approaches start with the learning environment of home and family and how God designed a child to learn and grow. The focus is on real books, real life, and real relationships within a home.

For this reason we owe it to every child to put him in communication with great minds that he may get at great thoughts; with the minds, that is, of those who have left us great works; and the only vital method of education appears to be that children should read worthy books, many worthy books.

— Charlotte Mason, *Towards a Philosophy of Education*, 1925

Preparing for Book-Fairing

Homeschool conventions and book fairs often have many good speakers and over 100 vendors and are very crowded. Here are a few suggestions for how to get the most out of the experience.

- **Be selective.** If the event includes speakers, plan ahead to select those who will best reinforce your approach to homeschooling. It is better to be encouraged by a few good speakers than to be overwhelmed by too many.

- **Be intentional.** Know what kinds of books and materials you need. If you're open to everything, you'll be easily distracted. Plan ahead what booths you will browse and products you will consider. Stick to a budget.

- **Be prepared.** Take a small notebook and pen to record books, products, and prices at different booths. If you plan to buy materials at the event, it's best to have cash, checks, and credit cards since vendors vary on kinds of payments they will take.

- **Go early.** The first day is the busiest day but also the best day. Get there early and take some time to study the exhibit area map. If you know some items you definitely want, go to those booths first.

- **Go solo.** If possible, make other arrangements for your children. If you're there alone, you'll be freer to follow your own plans, make decisions without distractions, and enjoy the event.

We desperately need to recover a sense of the fundamental purpose of education, which is to provide for the intellectual and moral education of the young. From the ancient Greeks to the founding fathers, moral instruction was the central task of education.

— William Bennett, former U.S. Secretary of Education under President Ronald Reagan, from "America through Foreign Eyes" speech at Hillsdale College, April 1995

Curriculum-Centered Homeschooling

Publishers of age-graded, scope-and-sequence-based curricula are part of a multi-million-dollar industry that serves both Christian private schools and homeschoolers. The curriculum-centered methodology is really a classroom approach that has migrated into the home. Most curriculum publishers employ textbook- and workbook-intensive methods that were designed for age-graded, large classroom schooling conditions. Advocates of curricular studies promote their approach as being a tested, proven, effective way to teach your child that is comprehensive, systematic, and self-contained. It is the ultimate "homeschool in a box" approach.

Printed Curriculum

This traditional schooling approach is highly structured and formal. It relies nearly entirely on age-graded textbooks and workbooks. Many new homeschooling families choose a printed curriculum approach more by default than by design since it is what they are most familiar with from their own school experience or because they place special trust in the publisher or source of the materials. For others, formal curriculum represents a safe choice at a time when they are unconfident about nontraditional choices or they simply are not familiar with all the other options. Formal curriculum is almost always age-graded, with a scope and sequence based upon generally accepted public and private school subject areas and standards. Each Christian curriculum generally reflects a particular doctrinal or theological viewpoint, and many private Christian schools use these as their primary curricula. Textbooks are generally fact-oriented, making up in breadth for what they are not able to provide in depth. In the same way that a classroom teacher is required to plan and guide curricular studies to ensure that all the material is adequately covered and understanding of the material is properly assessed, the parent-teacher is expected to ensure steady progress through the material. Some curriculum publishers use consumable workbooks or worktexts that contain both instructional text and lessons designed for independent pacing and study. These require somewhat less preparation and supervision than a textbook-only approach, yet the parent-teacher is still expected to direct progress to completion and test for competence. Some companies adapt and sell classic curricula from the eighteenth and early nineteenth centuries.

Many of the other approaches to homeschooling use printed curriculum of some kind for subjects requiring more structured study. The caveat with any formal, printed curriculum is always to master the method and not be mastered by it. Some parents will say that a structured curricular approach ends up managing them, rather than them managing it—especially when there are multiple ages and grades in a home. Some parents may feel a pressure to keep up that can detract from the homeschooling experience by encouraging an emphasis on completion of the material over sensitivity to the child's actual learning needs. Some also feel that structured curriculum can overemphasize formal study goals at the expense of spontaneity and creativity, which are critical in giving a child a love for learning and for strengthening independent thinking and problem solving.

Examples: Bob Jones University Press, A Beka, Alpha Omega, Christian Liberty, Calvert School, Rod and Staff, A.C.E. Lighthouse

Virtual Learning

The virtualization of structured learning is still primarily a subset of the current curriculum publishing industry, but it is the rapidly emerging and inevitable dominant future delivery system for curriculum. "Virtual learning" is a collective term to describe the panoply of digital media challenging the dominance of printed curriculum—live streaming and on-demand audio and video, interactive web digital broadcast/cable/satellite, MP3 audio, cell phones and mobile connectivity, proprietary digital devices, VoIP telephony, PDFs, e-book readers, tablet computers, apps, and many more still on the horizon. For many homeschooling families, the personal home computer is a supplemental learning tool used to enhance print-based curricula and study, such as with math and language arts programs, or as a research and writing tool. For a growing percentage of homeschool families, though, virtual learning is the center of their homeschooling program, even for a complete K-12 curriculum. Virtual schools on the Internet are rapidly becoming a "homeschool in a digital box" solution that requires nothing more than a broadband connection (now affordable and universal) and a computer (more younger children have their own desktop or laptop). Virtual learning advocates suggest it is in their children's best interest to become confident and competent computer users, to have access to a literal World Wide Web of knowledge and information, and to be able to self-direct their own learning process and progress with minimal parental involvement.

Although most virtual learning programs do not require Internet access beyond a dedicated portal, some parents are concerned about accidental exposure of children to undesirable online elements and about creating appetites too early for what they feel is a potentially addictive medium. Others point out that more research is needed on the impact of prolonged exposure to video images on the brain development of a child. Watching moving images on a monitor, even video images of words or numbers, is a wholly different mental process than reading words from a page in a book, requiring different brain functions. We are still learning what is lost or gained in that process. Finally, some parents consider the passive and impersonal nature of interacting with a computer or monitor to be unnatural and potentially detrimental to a child's development. Even so, most families will use some form of virtual learning with their children.

Examples: School of Tomorrow, A-Plus, The Grace Academy, K12, BJU Press Online

Online programs increase access to learning opportunities; they don't reduce academic rigor...Indeed, successful online students must be, if anything, more engaged with the material than are students in traditional classrooms, for although the online teacher still provides guidance and support, students must take greater responsibility for managing their time and completing assignments.

— Bruce Friend, "Online Learning: Truth in Advertising?", www.homeedirectory.com/blog, undated post

When used by itself, online learning appears to be as effective as conventional classroom instruction, but not more so... Another consideration is that various online learning implementation practices may have differing effectiveness for K-12 learners than they do for older students.

— U.S. Department of Education, "Evaluation of Evidence-Based Practices in Online Learning: A Meta-Analysis and Review of Online Learning Studies," revised September 2010

IN OUR HOME

We were committed homeschoolers in 1982...two years before our first child, Sarah, would enter the world! In fact, Sally taught a course on homeschooling for our church before she was even pregnant with Sarah. I (Clay) now have to admit that in those early years, my initial uncorrected vision for homeschooling focused on the only schooling concepts I knew—classrooms, curricula, and all the trappings of traditional, institutional school. Fortunately, Sally had more intuitive insight than I did. As we read books and articles and talked about discipleship, family, and the home, our convictions gelled, and any ideas of traditional, curriculum-centered education of our children disappeared. By the time Sarah started homeschooling, we were wholehearted whole-book home educators.

For we let our young men and women go out unarmed in a day when armor was never so necessary. By teaching them all to read, we have left them at the mercy of the printed word...They do not know what the words mean; they do not know how to ward them off or blunt their edge or fling them back; they are a prey to words in their emotions instead of being the masters of them in their intellects...We have lost the tools of learning—the axe and the wedge, the hammer and the saw, the chisel and the plane—that were so adaptable to all tasks. Instead of them, we have merely a set of complicated jigs, each of which will do but one task and no more, and in using which eye and hand receive no training, so that no man ever sees the work as a whole or "looks to the end of the work." What use is it to pile task on task and prolong the days of labor, if at the close the chief object is left unattained?

— Dorothy Sayers, "The Lost Tools of Learning," paper read at Oxford University, 1947

Christ-Centered Homeschool

Someone might look at the schools of homeschooling categories and ask, "What about Christ-centered homeschooling?" Our answer is that being Christ-centered is not about education, but rather it is about orientation. Any of the schools or approaches to homeschooling can be Christ-centered if they acknowledge, affirm, or teach the grace and truth found only in Christ. Being Christ-centered is about viewing and teaching about life through the lens of biblical truth and the gospel of Christ. Any approach that claims to be a uniquely Christ-centered homeschooling model would fit best under the content-centered homeschooling category. Calling a model Christ-centered does not necessarily make it more Christian than any other approach based on biblical truth and grace. Any approach to homeschooling can be Christ-centered if the parents are Christ-centered.

Content-Centered Homeschooling

Some have suggested that childhood education is a science, governed by identifiable laws of learning, mental development, and sociology. In reality, childhood education theories are as diverse and complicated as civil government. Those that work gain validity and followers; those that don't dissipate or disappear. That is also true in the homeschooling movement. In many ways, the history of modern homeschooling has been a rush of educational theories and approaches all vying for validation, credibility, and adherents. Many of those approaches have been characterized and shaped by a unique set of convictions, beliefs, or theological views held by their founders and followers. These content-centered approaches to homeschooling are often highly developed and generate committed communities of users. They often become significant movements within homeschooling.

Some feel that a content-centered approach can make the unique content seem more important than the child or that rigid adherence to a particular pedagogy or methodology may seem more important than the actual learning experience of the child. Although they are to be admired for their adherence to their distinct message or method, a content-centered approach may seem narrow and exclusive to those who are not followers. Here are some representative examples of content-centered homeschooling.

The Classical Approach

The classical model of education has produced many of the world's greatest scholars. Its goal is to teach children how to think. Its distinctives include Latin at an early age and conversation with great minds of the past through extensive reading of great literature. The classical approach revives a medieval form of education that taught children under 16 years of age the tools of learning in a three-stage process known as the Trivium. The grammar stage (ages 6-10) focuses on mastery of facts to grow in knowledge. The student studies the fundamentals of reading, writing, spelling, Latin, memorization, thinking skills, Bible, history, and math. These studies are the foundation upon which all future studies will be built. The logic or dialectic stage (ages 10-14) focuses on the study of logic and reason in order to understand the relationships between facts. The student learns to discuss, debate, interpret, critique, draw out correct conclusions supported by facts, and discern fallacies in an argument. He continues Latin study and adds Greek, Hebrew, interpretive history, higher math, and theology. The rhetoric stage (ages 14 and up) focuses on the use of language to apply in real life what has been studied and comprehended. The student develops proficiency and wisdom in the use of written and spoken language to express himself with eloquence and persuasion. The Trivium is said to parallel the normal stages of development for a child, moving from facts (who, what, when, where) to understanding (why) to wisdom (how). The classical model, specifically the Trivium, can be expressed in either a formal or an informal curriculum or even adapted to other approaches. Classical education requires parent-teachers who will be highly engaged and involved as both learners and instructors.

Examples: Dorothy Sayers (1893-1967), Douglas Wilson, Trivium Pursuit (Harvey and Laurie Bluedorn), The Well-Trained Mind *(Jessie Wise and Susan Wise Bauer), Veritas Press (Marlin and Laurie Detweiler), Tapestry of Grace (Marcia Somerville)*

Unit Studies

Unit studies integrate and relate several areas of study around one common theme, subject, or project. One topic can be studied intensively over a period of time and cover language arts, math, science, nature, history, social studies, fine arts, and whatever other subject areas might apply. This kind of unified approach also allows the opportunity to explain all of the lessons from a biblical worldview. Advocates of unit studies believe that it is more natural to study one topic from several related perspectives than to study several unrelated subjects in isolation from one another. They argue that knowledge is more easily learned and remembered when interrelated and that unit studies feed an appreciation for the unity and interrelatedness of all truth. Unit studies work well in home schools because they can be easily adapted for age-integrated learning, where each child can learn at their own level. Unit studies can also be used to supplement other approaches (such as doing a two-week unit on the human body). The amount of preparation and time involved in unit studies varies depending on the level of complexity and activity you create or plan. However, unit studies tend to be more time- and preparation-intensive than other approaches. Unit studies by Christian publishers are typically organized around Bible chronology, Bible themes, passages of Scripture, Christian character, and history, among other themes. If you design your own unit study, you can determine whatever theme you desire or think may be of interest to your child. Unit studies are very flexible and can be used as a completely self-contained methodology or can be adapted and used within any of the other approaches. Whether lessons are planned and created by the parent or provided by a unit study publisher, the approach requires significant parental planning and involvement.

Examples: KONOS (Jessica Hulcy, Carole Thaxton), History Revealed (Diana Waring), Five in a Row (Jane Claire Lambert, Becky Jane Lambert), Heart of Dakota Publishing (Carrie Austin), The Weaver Curriculum (Alpha Omega)

The Principle Approach

The principle approach attempts to restore three vital concepts to American Christianity: knowledge of our Christian history, understanding of our role in spreading Christianity, and the ability to live according to the Christian principles upon which our country was founded. Subjects are studied in the light of one or more of seven key life principles (biblically based educational values and beliefs). Students learn to think governmentally to determine who or what is creating, preserving, guiding, nurturing, controlling, restraining, directing, or regulating any area of life. The student learns to take responsibility for his own learning and life, with the goal of becoming self-governing. Study of any subject involves recording in a notebook the 4Rs: researching God's Word to identify biblical principles and purpose; reasoning from the biblical truths and principles; relating truths to personal life, character, self-government, and stewardships; and recording conclusions reached about the subject. The student creates an individual notebook for each subject area studied. There are published curricula using this approach, or the teaching parent can easily create lessons. The notebook method of learning can be applied to other approaches.

Examples: James Rose, Stephen McDowell, Rosalie Slater (F.A.C.E.), The Pilgrim Institute, The Mayflower Institute, The Providence Foundation

Basic school subjects are studied in light of a particular topic, theme, or historical time period instead of studying eight or more isolated subjects. Children are able to grasp the wholeness of truth as they see how these subjects relate to one another. Studies are approached from a biblical philosophy of education. Lesson planning is simplified because all ages study a topic together. Families are strengthened through this unity. Field trips, projects, and games all center around a particular unit. Basic skills are taught in an informal manner while engaged in the study of a particular unit.

— Valerie Bendt, *How to Create Your Own Unit Study*, Common Sense Press, 1990

If we want children to be excellent writers and readers, we start with hands-on experiences that build concepts and hold the child's attention. The unit studies method integrates hands-on experiences with reading and writing, locking the child's mind on the wavelength of the unit.

— Jessica Hulcy, "Teaching the Basics with Unit Studies," *Practical Homeschooling Magazine*, #24, 1998

The need is for a generation of American Christians who know God and His Word, and by their own scholarship know how to implement their knowledge. One of the aims of Christian education should be a Biblical mentality by which every sphere of activity is controlled. This mentality stems from a schooling in Biblical principles able to detect and reject everything contrary to Christ and Christianity. It was the Biblical reasoning of the Founding Father generation that produced the only historical alternative to tyranny and oppression of the individual, and which promoted the fullest expression of Christian liberty, rather than pagan license.

— Katherine Dang, Pilgrim Institute, quoted in Elijah Co. catalog

What children need is not new and better curricula but access to more and more of the real world; plenty of time and space to think over their experiences, and to use fantasy and play to make meaning out of them; and advice, road maps, guidebooks, to make it easier for them to get where they want to go (not where we think they ought to go), and to find out what they want to find out.

— John Holt, *Teach Your Own*, Delacorte, 1981

Waldorf Education

Rudolf Steiner (1861-1925) was an Austrian philosopher and educator. The Waldorf Education model he developed in 1919 is still in use today around the world but not as well known in North America. Waldorf Education methods resemble other child-centered approaches, and they have attracted a small following of homeschoolers. Steiner, who viewed education as an art, recognized three developmental phases: 0-7 (no academics), 7-14 (self-directed learning), and 14-18 (more rigorous study). While the method may seem attractive to some for its child-centered approach, Steiner's philosophical views fall outside biblical Christianity. His New Age-like, syncretistic beliefs that he called "spiritual science" and his man-centered philosophical system called Anthroposophy—a view of human development incorporating elements of existentialism, evolutionism, spiritualism, moral relativism, and reincarnation—raise red flags of legitimate concern about the learning methods associated with those views.

Child-Centered Homeschooling

Most traditional, curriculum-centered approaches to childhood education tend to focus on a particular methodology or pedagogy that promises effective results if used correctly. Typically, their underlying assumption is that children are unable to learn without a teacher to teach them. In contrast are child-centered approaches that start with the assumption that a child is intelligent, capable of learning, and will learn naturally if given a good environment and quality resources. These child-centered approaches to homeschooling start with facts and observations about the nature of childhood and childhood development and build a philosophy and methodology around those realities. The focus is more on the learning process and experience of the child, rather than on the teaching role of the parent. The amount and nature of the parent's involvement varies greatly among child-centered approaches.

Child-centered distinctives are certainly not unique to these approaches. Many of the practices are simply a normal, commonsense part of most homeschool families' typical days. Those suspicious of child-centered approaches might affirm the idea of trusting a child's natural drive to learn, yet also emphasize a parent's natural drive to instruct. They point out that parents are admonished in Scripture to bring up their children "in the training and instruction of the Lord" (Ephesians 6:4), and they suggest that a strictly child-centered approach can diminish the importance of that biblical command. Others will argue that giving a child some or even a great deal of direction in their learning activities, in contrast to a more child-centered approach, is a positive interaction that can stimulate new learning. Here are some representative examples of child-centered homeschooling.

Unschooling

The ultimate example of a child-centered approach to homeschooling is unschooling, a term almost certainly given life by John Holt, the father of unschooling, in the 1970s. In contrast to the structure and formality of traditional curriculum-centered educational models, unschooling is by design unstructured and informal. John Holt (1923-1985) was an educator and an author (*How Children Learn*, 1967; *Instead of Education*, 1976; *Teach Your Own*, 1981; *Growing Without Schooling* magazine, 1977-2001) whose insights and influence helped launch the modern home education movement. He believed children possess an innate desire and natural curiosity that can be trusted and that will drive them to learn on their own, in their own way, following their own interests, and in their own time. Holt held that conventional methods of teaching dissipate and destroy a child's natural desire to learn. He advocated instead using minimal structure, instruction, or intervention in order to allow children maximum time, freedom, and creativity to learn whatever they feel they need or want to learn. The distinctives of this approach include free access to good books and learning resources, trust in the child's innate ability and desire to learn, interaction with adults and real life, and formal academics only when the child indicates interest or need. Although it is not as popular among the Christian homeschooling movement as it once was, unschooling still has a committed following. John Holt's ideas about how children learn still influence other models of homeschooling.

Examples: John Holt, John Taylor Gatto, Patrick Farenga, Home Education Magazine

The Moore Formula

Many Christian homeschoolers trace their start in homeschooling to Dr. Raymond and Dorothy Moore's books on childhood education (*Better Late Than Early*, 1975; *Home Grown Kids*, 1981; *The Successful Homeschool Family Handbook*, 1985). Dr. Moore (1915-2007) was an educator and advocate of delaying formal education, especially for boys. His research led him to conclude that children are not ready for the stress of academic studies until 8-12 years of age (different times for different children). Until the child matured physically and emotionally to a point of readiness, he instructed parents to focus on reading good literature and developing good habits, routines, and responsibility. When children are ready to learn, Dr. Moore recommended using multisensory learning resources and unit studies, in addition to drill and review. According to Dr. Moore, children will catch up on learning in a very short period of time once they signal their readiness to learn. The Moore Formula of homeschooling grew out of his views that learning should not be stressful for either the parent or the child and that children need lots of love, discipline, real-life experiences, and time to explore and learn. The Moore Formula is based on three broad priorities of the homeschooling family: (1) study—daily, based on the child's needs and readiness, (2) work—at least as much as study, doing real work at home that is rewarding, confidence-building, and entrepreneurial, and (3) service—daily for an hour, serving others in the home, neighborhood, and community. Dr. Moore believed every child has a specific area of genius or giftedness that needs to be nurtured and encouraged. Many Christian homeschoolers are still attracted to the simplicity, sensibleness, and biblical principles expressed in the Moore Formula, and Dr. Moore's insights continue to influence thinking about home education.

Examples: Dr. and Mrs. Raymond Moore, The Moore Foundation

Montessori Method

In 1895 Maria Montessori (1870-1952) became one of the first women physicians in Italy. She was also a dedicated educator who developed a model of childhood education now known as the Montessori method. Although her child-centered ideas were developed primarily in and for the classroom, some homeschoolers have adapted her educational principles to the home setting with the help of community co-ops. Montessori advocated self-directed, interactive learning characterized by a learning environment specially adapted to the child's developmental level, with hands-on activities designed to help the child understand abstract concepts and develop practical skills. Montessori developed autodidactic learning devices and materials that allowed the child to self-correct without the intervention of a teacher, which she believed interrupted the child's natural learning processes. (She observed that most children learned best left alone in times of intense concentration.) The teacher's role is not to lecture but to introduce the child to the materials and then be a silent presence as an observer. Montessori classrooms are designed with lots of open space to allow a child freedom to move about and explore and to self-select learning activities from several resource-rich areas: practical life, sensorial (senses), language, mathematics, geography, science, and art. Adapting the method to homeschooling requires creativity and often involves cooperation with other Montessori families.

Examples: Dr. Maria Montessori, Kathy Von Duyke, Barbara Curtis

---

For the first eight to ten years at least—until their values are formed—most parents, even average parents, are by far the best people for their children...In general the best teacher or caregiver cannot match a parent of even ordinary education and experience...Children under eight are seldom, if ever, able to reason consistently about why they should or should not behave as parents see best, and sometimes cannot do so until eleven or twelve. So a reasonably consistent, continuing adult example is important if they are to get on a track toward sound character and personality values.

— Raymond Moore, *Home Grown Kids*, Word, 1981

We cannot know the consequences of suppressing a child's spontaneity when he is just beginning to be active. We may even suffocate life itself. That humanity which is revealed in all its intellectual splendor during the sweet and tender age of childhood should be respected with a kind of religious veneration. It is like the sun which appears at dawn or a flower just beginning to bloom. Education cannot be effective unless it helps a child to open up himself to life.

— Maria Montessori (1870-1952), Italian physician, educator, philosopher, devout Catholic, *The Discovery of the Child*, Ballantine, 1980

No use to shout at them to pay attention. If the situations, the materials, the problems before the child do not interest him, his attention will slip off to what does interest him, and no amount of exhortation or threats will bring it back.

— John Holt (1923-1985), American author and educator

No public provision for education can be made which will prove a substitute for parental teaching. The best school system ever devised is the Home School System, which began in the beginning of society, and which must continue while children look up with confidence and questioning to parents who love their children, and who love to guide them in the pursuit of knowledge and in the development of character. Father and Mother ought to be the very best associated principals in this splendid System of Education.

— John H. Vincent, *The Church at Home*, 1893

Just as the family is the only secure basis of the state, so is it the only safe basis of true educaton. If the mother will consider the many difficulties in the way of successful teaching in a large school and will then set against these in the balance the positive and unquestionable advantages of home instruction to the child she will be disposed to wonder why any child having a good home is sent to school before the age of ten...Susanna Wesley taught her children at home, for twenty years carrying on this instruction daily, "not so much," she said, "to train their minds as to save their souls."

— Ella Frances Lynch, *Educating the Child at Home*, 1914

Home-Centered Homeschooling

"Homeschooling" is an unfortunate term. It certainly captured the initial impulse of the movement, which was to move the physical locus of childhood learning from the institutional school to the familial home. However, the term inadvertently promoted the idea that homeschooling was about bringing the classroom into the living room, replete with all the artifacts of schooling such as curricula, desks, and lectures. More general terms such as home education, family learning, or home-centered learning would have helped avoid this implication, but homeschool was a more convenient term and easily won the lexical competition. Like it or not, we are all homeschoolers now.

Home-centered homeschooling approaches, in contrast to the idea of bringing school into the home, start with the home as God designed it and build an educational model from there. These approaches begin not by looking at public and private schools to see what is missing at home by comparison but by looking at Scripture to see what we have missed in comparison to God's design for home. WholeHearted Learning is one such home-centered approach, but there are others. Let me repeat myself from an earlier chapter: God designed the home; man designed the school. God did not forget to include school in his design; he designed the home to provide everything children need to be prepared for life. When parents understand what that really means, they stop thinking about what should happen in a school and start thinking about what should happen in a home. They stop thinking only about living up to the world's standards of education and start thinking about living up to God's standards for his families.

The idea of being home-centered assumes that the home is more than just a physical structure where people live. Secular approaches to homeschooling tend to view home as just a different but better place for children to learn. But a biblical, Christian approach to homeschooling should view the home as the best and primary place for children to learn—a spiritual environment, designed by God as part of the created order, where God intended children to be trained and instructed by godly parents to become wholehearted Christian adults. In the same way that God is present in the church when his spiritual family gathers, God is present in the home when his families gather to follow him. Home is a spiritual place. That is what home-centered homeschooling affirms.

IN OUR HOME

We were both well-trained in the ways of institutional schooling. Sally attended thirteen years of public school and earned a B.A. with a double major in English and speech. Clay attended eleven years of public and two years of private school and earned a B.J. in advertising and an M.Div. from Denver Seminary. But we were also influenced by ministry both during and after college. We both were immersed in the idea of relational discipleship and biblical influence. As we began to have children, we saw them not as students but as future disciples of Christ, and we realized our home was God's ministry field for our family. The idea of home-centered learning quickly displaced any default notions of man-made education for our children. Teaching was a part of parenting. This was God's business.

Whole-Book Method (Living Books)

When we wrote the first version of *Educating the WholeHearted Child*, we called our model "home-centered learning" and described it as "how to use real books and real life to make your home a vibrant center of living and learning for you and your child." As a kind of shorthand to describe our approach, we would call ourselves "whole-bookers." Over the next decade, we noticed other families all across the U.S. calling themselves whole-book homeschooling families. We found that the term had currency with families drawn to a natural, commonsense, real-books and real-life approach to homeschooling. The terms "eclectic homeschooling" and "living books approach" have also been used, but it was always "whole book" that we heard the most in our contacts and conversations.

Using whole books is a convenient conceptual umbrella under which we gather a disparate but distinctive group of homeschooling approaches. Each has its own unique emphases and content, but they all draw from common influences, such as Charlotte Mason, and they all share a common commitment to the priorities of the home, living books, and real-life experiences. What makes them home-centered is their strong commitment to the home as the biblical center of a child's life; what makes them whole-book is their commitment to the priority of living books. The following are representative examples:

- *Beautiful Feet Books* (Russ and Rea Berg) — Their "History Through Literature" and other study guides are good examples of whole-book learning. They have brought many good books back into print and are strongly influenced by Charlotte Mason.

- *Charlotte Mason Research & Supply Company* (Dean and Karen Andreola) — The Andreolas' original and reprinted resources for a Charlotte Mason education provide easy and effective ways to emphasize whole books in any homeschool.

- *Cornerstone Curriculum* (David and Shirley Quine) —With training in curriculum design, David Quine created a comprehensive family of curricula, studies, guides, and books built around Charlotte Mason principles and Christian worldview training.

- *Five in a Row* (Jane Claire Lambert and Becky Jane Lambert) — Five in a Row lesson plans provide a full unit-study program of early learning for children up to age twelve, as well as character studies, all centered on outstanding living books.

- *Greenleaf Press* (Rob and Cyndy Shearer) — Greenleaf Study Guides, reprints, and resources draw on Charlotte Mason principles and classical sources to provide a comprehensive whole-book, home-centered homeschool approach.

- *History Revealed* (Diana Waring) — History Revealed study guides and CDs provide a narrative journey through history accented with recommended whole and living books that bring to literary life the stories of people and events.

- *Ruth Beechick Books* (Dr. Ruth Beechick) — Dr. Beechick, a devoted Christian and educator, advocates a home-centered, natural learning approach that emphasizes the basics, quality books, and empowering parents with confidence.

Other examples: All through the Ages *(Christine Miller),* My Father's World *(David and Marie Hazell),* Relaxed Homeschooling *(Dr. Mary Hood),* Sonlight *(John and Sarita Holzmann),* TruthQuest History *(Michelle Miller)*

Whole Book Fever

This affliction is common throughout the homeschooling community. It is contracted through frequent contact with whole books. There is no known cure. Symptoms include but are not limited to the following:

- You lose the motor function needed to close a good book and put it down.
- You have an irresistible desire to browse through your friends' bookshelves.
- You hyperventilate upon finding a complete set of Landmark books in mint condition with dust jackets at a garage sale.
- You are physically unable to pass by a stack of old books without stopping to look at them.
- You schedule your vacation around the annual community used book sale.
- You begin stacking books horizontally in your bookshelves to make room for more books.
- You hesitate telling a friend about a library sale because you both collect the same book series.
- You buy a fourth copy of *Johnny Tremain* at a library sale because you forgot you had the three others.
- You actually worry about which child will get which books from your home library when you die.
- You start a retail book business just so you can buy more books at dealer's cost.

We hold that the child's mind is no mere sac to hold ideas; but is rather...a spiritual organism, with an appetite for all knowledge. This is its proper diet...(we take) care only that all knowledge offered him is vital, that is, that facts are not presented without their informing ideas... Our business is to give children the great ideas of life, of religion, history, science; but it is the ideas we must give, clothed upon the facts as they occur, and must leave the child to deal with these as he chooses.

— Charlotte Mason, *Towards a Philosophy of Education*, 1925

Children no more come into the world without provisions for dealing with knowledge than without provision for dealing with food. They bring with them not only that intellectual appetite, the desire of knowledge, but also an enormous, and unlimited power of attention to which the power of retention (memory) seems to be attached, as one digestive process succeeds another, until the final assimilation.

— Charlotte Mason, *Towards a Philosophy of Education*, 1925

Charlotte Mason Online

Charlotte Mason (CM) sites abound on the Internet. Here are some of the best for Christian homeschooling families.

- www.CharlotteMason.com — books, resources, and articles by CM experts and pioneers Dean and Karen Andreola
- www.SimplyCharlotteMason.com — CM curriculum guides, books, workbooks, Bible studies, and much more for Christian homeschoolers
- www.AmblesideOnline.org — free CM curriculum guide, booklist, and downloads created and managed by Christian homeschooling mothers
- www.ChildLightUSA.org — dedicated to presenting and preserving a CM education through research, events, publications, blog, and more

Charlotte Mason Method

Charlotte Mason (1842-1923) was a turn-of-the-century educator who had great influence on British education in her time. Her books (see sidebar on page 109) explained an original approach to education and learning that gave rise to her PNEU (Parents' National Education Union) schools and many reforms. We give her ideas more attention because of their importance to our WholeHearted Learning model, but also because of the influence of her ideas about literature and learning on Christian homeschooling in America. The current whole-book movement was birthed mostly out of her extensive writings. Her ideas and principles of education are the seeds from which numerous new expressions of whole-book education have grown.

Children as Persons

Charlotte Mason rejected the traditional, institutional education of her day in England as a soulless system that depersonalized children by viewing them only as containers to be filled with bare facts. She asserted in her writings that information is not education. She eschewed the British system's reliance upon textbooks full of predigested bits of information she called "snippets," inferior and dull books she labeled "twaddle," and unnatural, artificial learning methods. In contrast, she viewed education as the "science of relations." While British culture tended to view children as sub-persons who needed to be formed and civilized, Mason viewed each child as a whole, maturing person with an active intelligence and an enormous capacity for learning. The role of education was to lead children into learning through the many natural relationships with things, thoughts, people, and ideas they were already exploring.

Mason emphasized character development (habits), basic learning skills (reading, writing, arithmetic), the reading of many living books, the study of the fine arts (art, music, poetry), and learning through real-life experiences (nature, museums). She stressed reading alone and reading aloud, as well as the regular practice of narration and dictation—saying back or writing what has been read or heard. She rightly saw in narration a proven instructional method that helped internalize and personalize learning and that also developed attending, thinking, and speaking abilities. She required daily Bible reading, discussion, memorization, and recitation.

Children in her schools were given ample opportunities to interact with the very best literature, art, and music. She believed children had a God-given thirst for knowledge no different than an adult had. Instead of lifeless, pedantic textbooks and workbooks that expected children only to remember the right answer, she insisted on reading living books that made literature, history, geography, and science come alive and that focused more on insights and ideas about the subject than on dry and lifeless facts. Nature study was a regular part of her students' education—long outdoor walks observing nature and wildlife, collecting specimens, and keeping a nature journal of their observations, including sketches. She saw in children an unlimited capacity to learn that needed to be nurtured and stimulated, not controlled and conformed. Her school was ordered and directed, but she believed that traditional structured classrooms and teacher-dependent education got in the way of learning, impoverished children's intellectual development, and prevented them from pursuing their own innate and natural desire to learn and from drawing their own conclusions about what they were learning.

Masterly Inactivity

Charlotte Mason encouraged what she called "masterly inactivity" as a teaching methodology. She believed that adults do not really teach children anything and may even hamper their natural desire to learn by making them dependent upon textbooks and teachers to tell them what to think. She insisted that children possess the same appetite for ideas as adults and viewed the teacher's role as a guide into learning. Mason taught that once an idea was received it would naturally find expression in the child's life with little help from the teacher. Masterly inactivity means providing children with a rich pool of books, arts, experiences, and ideas and then getting out of their way—trusting them to search out knowledge that is meaningful to them and to come to their own conclusions about what they are learning. Mason rejected grading in favor of internal motivations.

Instruments of Education

Mason emphasized teaching children the "Way of the Will" and the "Way of Reason." Her motto for students was "I am, I can, I ought, I will." She also recognized that every educational methodology was limited to some degree because of the many differences in children's personalities. She proposed three instruments of education that would apply to all children regardless of individual personality: an atmosphere, a discipline, and a life. For Mason, these three words defined the truest essence of education.

- **Atmosphere** (the atmosphere of environment) — Education requires an atmosphere in which the child is accepted and valuable; that is nonjudgmental and realistic; and that is stimulating, positive, and enjoyable. Mason rejected the idea of dumbing down education to a "child's level" as crippling to a child's natural desire to learn. Education should look to the home, which is a natural learning environment. Her vision for education foresaw teachers who understood that no artificial motivations were necessary to draw out the best work from children—their natural love of knowledge was sufficient to motivate them to learn and excel.

- **Discipline** (the discipline of habit) — Education requires disciplined habits. A critical part of education is the intentional formation of good habits, both mental and physical. No matter how strong or weak the natural tendencies, Mason taught that habit is stronger than nature. Key disciplines or habits include attention, concentration, truthfulness, self-control, unselfishness, and others. She believed that the habit of attention was the most valuable and the truest mark of an educated person.

- **Life** (the presentation of living ideas) — Education and learning are a continuous process that happens in real life, not just in isolated, artificial classroom experiences. All of life is meant to be used for learning. Children will learn to feed their own minds with the best intellectual food—literature, art, music, history, science, and nature—and come to their own conclusions without being told what to think. Mason taught that "education is a life" and that to sustain the child's inner life of the mind and spirit it needed to be fed and nourished with the food of ideas. She considered ideas to be spiritual in origin, from God who created us to feed one another through spoken word, written word, Scripture, and music.

Examples: Charlotte Mason, Susan Schaeffer Macaulay, Dean & Karen Andreola, David Quine, Catherine Levinson

This broad view of true education as the sum of all of life meant that Charlotte Mason first turned her attention to the parents. She believed that they had the most interesting and valuable vocation that exists among mankind. Into their love, care, and responsibility this person was placed. Charlotte Mason never spoke of education as merely taking place behind the walls of the schoolroom. She saw the home as the basic educational environment.

— Susan Schaeffer Macaulay, *For the Children's Sake*, Crossway, 1984

Charlotte Mason's Books

The writings of Charlotte M. Mason (1842-1923) include primary textbooks and a six-volume study of the life and teachings of Jesus, but she is best known for her six books on education written and published over a span of nearly four decades. Collected first as the "Home Education Series" and later as "The Original Home Schooling Series," the books together form a complete record of Mason's views on education. The books are now in the public domain and available for digital download on the Internet.

- Volume 1 — *Home Education* (1886)
- Volume 2 — *Parents and Children* (1896)
- Volume 3 — *School Education* (1904)
- Volume 4 — *Ourselves* (1904)
- Volume 5 — *Formation of Character* (1905)
- Volume 6 — *Towards a Philosophy of Education* (1925)

Charlotte Mason in Print

Dean and Karen Andreola introduced American homeschoolers to the complete works of Charlotte Mason in 1989. Through their publishing company, Charlotte Mason Research & Supply, they have kept the six-volume set of *The Original Homeschooling Series* in print.

It is not enough for parents to have a lofty ideal for their children, and to instruct and train those children in the direction of that ideal. They must see to it that the atmosphere of their home is such as to foster and develop in their children those traits of character which their loftiest ideal embodies. That atmosphere must be full of the pure oxygen of love to God and love to man. It must be neither too hot in its intensity of social activities, nor too cold in its expressions of family affection, but balmy and refreshing in its uniform temperature of household living and being. It must be gentle and peaceful in its manner and movement of sympathetic discourse. All this it may be. All this it ought to be.

— H. Clay Trumbull, *Hints on Child Training*, 1890

WholeHearted Learning

Very few educational theories—whether they have already come and gone or are still around or new—are wholly original. Those that pass the tests of time do so because they successfully reflect universal principles and practices of education that parents and teachers deem to be acceptable and believable. Judging whether a given theory is actually as effective as it claims to be is more difficult, but at the very least the theory must fit with reality and reason—it should make sense. Perhaps that is why most educational theories borrow the best ideas from one another and share common ground, even though their emphases and designs differ. Solomon was right that there is "nothing new under the sun" (Ecclesiastes 1:9), especially in education.

Like so many other educational theories, the WholeHearted Learning model that is presented in the following pages is a mixture of old and new ideas. It has been grown in soil enriched by most of the approaches discussed on the previous pages, borrowing old and proven principles and practices but expressing them in a new home-centered way. WholeHearted Learning draws most deeply from Charlotte Mason's ideas, as well as from newer whole-book principles. Our approach integrates these various influences and elements with its own original ideas and expresses them in a fresh and vital way in a new comprehensive model of home education.

To fully understand the purpose of the WholeHearted Learning model, it is helpful to know the values and principles that it reflects and integrates. We have identified twelve pillars or distinctives of our model; they are discussed on the next three pages. The first six are principles of living and the last six of learning. More than just foundational ideas for an educational model, they are also convictions about what a child needs in a Christian home to become a wholehearted Christian adult.

IN OUR HOME

The WholeHearted Learning model was birthed in a season of transition and uncertainty. We had moved to family property in central Texas in the spring of 1993 to pray and wait on the Lord's direction for a ministry. Our children were 9, 6, and 4, so we were in the thick of moving in and homeschooling for the next year. At some point in the following spring, it hit us—we wanted to help families raise children with whole hearts who would follow God wholeheartedly. That was the ministry message that God would have us offer. We had been in singles ministries and had seen the broken and divided hearts from the fragmentation of families. But we had been homeschooling for six years at that point and had seen that the home, just as he designed it, was God's divine tool for raising wholehearted children. The WholeHearted Learning model simply came to life out of what we had already been doing. It was biblical, and it made sense. About twenty people crowded into our living room for the first WholeHearted Child workshop that April. The first Educating the WholeHearted Child *appeared that summer, then a better version that fall. Out of it all came Whole Heart Ministries. It was never just about education, though. It's always been about family life lived with God.*

12 Pillars of WholeHearted Learning

1. Children need a home and family.

God designed families to raise children. As we saw in chapter 1, there is a home-shaped vacuum in the heart of every child that can be filled only by a father and a mother. It is natural and normal for children to look to you for their moral, social, spiritual, and intellectual direction and to want to stay with their parents until they are grown. It is *un*natural and *ab*normal to believe others should or must raise your children for you and to divide your child's heart between home and family and other authorities. The love and stability of a godly family can best provide the solid center that all children need, deserve, and are designed by God to expect, and that will enable them to grow up wise and godly, with whole hearts and whole minds.

2. Children need to be discipled by their parents.

Your first responsibility as a Christian parent before God is to make disciples of your children, determining to "bring them up in the training and instruction of the Lord" (Ephesians 6:4). As your child's heart is turned toward God and his feet are put on the path of life, his mind will begin to grow in godly wisdom, knowledge, and discernment. Discipleship is the process of training, instructing, and modeling the Christian life to your children so they will choose, by faith, to follow the Jesus you follow. It is only as your child's heart is growing in submission to you and to God that you will be able to effectively educate your child's mind. "The fear of the Lord is the beginning of wisdom" (Psalm 111:10).

3. Children need to be accepted as persons.

Your child, though young, is nonetheless a whole person by virtue of the image of God. Everything that defines person-ness—intelligence, curiosity, creativity, reason, will—is present in your child. Even though the qualities are nascent or developing, there is nothing incomplete or partial about the image of God in your child. Your child deserves respect as a person based on their emerging maturity and God-given capacity to learn and grow rather than belittlement based on their childish immaturity. Parents are divinely designed to communicate and demonstrate a child's worth in their eyes and in God's eyes.

4. Children need eternal purpose and hope.

Christian home education is the shaping of a life, not just preparation for a living. Your children need to see that home education is preparing them for a higher purpose in life and that their real hope is heaven, not the riches of this world. They need to know that their purpose in life is to serve God, not to make money and buy things. If you set their hearts and minds on things above, not on earthly things, they will find fulfillment in whatever they do in this life because it is a means of serving God. If they understand that God is building his spiritual kingdom in this world and expanding his rule and reign over the hearts of people, then even as children they can understand that God can use them in his kingdom work. You can best help them see they are on earth for a purpose.

It is not merely that the child is to be [someday] the possessor of a marked and distinctive individuality, and that therefore he is to be honored for his possibilities in that direction; but it is that he already is [now] the possessor of such an individuality, and that he is worthy of honor for that which he has and is at the present time.

— H. Clay Trumbull, *Hints on Child Training*, 1890

If we have not proved that a child is born a person with a mind as complete and as beautiful as his beautiful little body, we can at least show that he always has all the mind he requires for his occasions: that is, that his mind is the instrument of his education and that his education does not produce his mind.

— Charlotte Mason, *Towards a Philosophy of Education*, 1925

5. Children need many relationships.

Life is a series of relationships, and we learn from all of them—God, family, siblings, spouse, friends, church, teachers, employers, employees, customers, and on and on. Exposure to many kinds of relationships prepares a child to better relate to and learn from others as an adult. Education that is isolated in a classroom and separated from real relationships in the real world is a waste of a child's learning potential. We are designed by God to live and learn in relationship with others. Only family-based education provides the fullest expression of relational learning.

6. Children naturally love to learn.

Children do not have to be told to want to learn—they already possess an innate, God-given appetite for knowledge, understanding, and ideas. If that appetite is nourished properly on the best mental foods, children can be trusted to learn. They will innately pursue knowledge without constantly being made to think or told what to think. The key to their learning is to create an environment rich with whole books and real life that provides opportunities to exercise their natural desire for knowledge. Learning should never be segregated from living, as though they are somehow two separate pursuits. Your child can grow up living to learn and learning to live and never knowing the difference.

7. Children will learn at their own pace.

The great fallacy of the institutional school industry is that learning is an essentially static process that can be measured, controlled, and managed. The age/grade system that defines most public and private schools assumes that every child learns the same things at the same times. It does not make room for individuality; in fact, it tends to stigmatize nonconformity. But the reality is that your child is not a learning machine. Human learning is a dynamic process. If the freedom of that process is managed and controlled, true learning is quickly replaced by conformity and restraint. Your children, though, have the opportunity to learn at their own pace, without reference to unnatural, man-made learning standards. Forget learning slowly or quickly; just let them learn.

8. Children will learn in their own ways.

Conformity is the enemy of true learning. Yet in order to maintain control of twenty to thirty students, conformity is considered a virtue in the institutional school classroom. Young minds eager to explore and acquire knowledge are taught that there are only certain ways and times at which that knowledge can be obtained and that the price of obtaining it is conformity for hours every day to the expectations of the classroom setting. It's no wonder that studies show that by the third grade, children have lost most of their innate sense of creativity and have learned to conform to the expectations of the teacher. The child educated at home, in contrast, has freedom to explore learning in all its varied facets and expressions, without worrying about conforming to an unnatural classroom. God has made each child with a unique personality, special abilities, and learning style that needs freedom and time to be discovered and to find full expression. The home provides the best place for children to learn how they will best learn. Freedom is the friend of true learning.

9. Children learn from real life.

Seeing and holding a garden snake discovered on a nature walk is infinitely more interesting and educational to a child than being told in a classroom what a garden snake is like and looking at two-dimensional pictures of a garden snake. There is more to learn from observing or doing real tasks than from only reading about or hearing someone else's experience. To enjoy and benefit from that kind of real-life learning, children need lots of free and flexible time to explore, think, play, research, and observe. Real-life learning cannot be replicated in a classroom or achieved in controlled outings that do not allow time for or toleration of freedom and exploration. By God's design, home and family is the freest, most flexible, and richest environment for a child. Home life is real life.

10. Children learn from real books.

It is natural for a child to prefer a whole, living book—one that contains real ideas that are challenging and thought-provoking, not just predigested bits of information disconnected from real life. One of the keys to true education is to feed a child's natural desire for knowledge with lots of good wholesome food rather than starve it with bits of inferior, tasteless food. Whole and living books are deeply satisfying to children because they assume that the child is a real person, not just an average age/grade target audience. When children are allowed to taste and sample a wide selection of real books, their appetites will be trained to prefer the best books. Real books will nourish their minds.

11. Children learn from art, music, and poetry.

Many schools consider the fine arts an elective, and therefore dispensable, area of study. Yet many studies affirm that the fine arts and creative arts contribute directly and uniquely to a child's intellectual development and capacities. They express the passion, power, and beauty of life through the eyes of artists, musicians, and poets. The integration of intellect and emotion in the fine arts is a dim but true reflection of God's creative nature that is part of his image in man. Children learn to express it as they become more aware of it in others. God has expressed his goodness in the world he created both ethically and aesthetically. Studying the arts opens your child's mind and spirit to the fullness of God's goodness. Art is "grace and truth" (John 1:17) for the heart and mind.

12. Children feed on truth, ideas, stories, and facts.

In a typical classroom, learning success is considered to be the ability to remember facts in order to do well on written tests. Teaching, then, becomes predominantly the process of pouring those facts into children's minds, and learning becomes the process of mastering those facts for the tests. Common sense readily sees the flaws in that approach to education. A steady intake of lifeless facts and data will dull a child's mind and senses. Emphasis on knowing the right answers reduces education to little more than human data processing. Children, like adults, think and feel deeply—they need to feed mentally on ideas that help them to understand and make sense of their world. Without the ideas that give them meaning, facts add little to a child's growth. Without the stories that gives it human dimension, truth finds no anchor in a child's spirit.

Therefore, the selection of their first lesson-books is a matter of grave importance, because it rests with these to give children the idea that knowledge is supremely attractive and that reading is delightful. Once the habit of reading his lesson-books with delight is set up in a child, his education is not completed, but ensured; he will go on for himself in spite of the obstructions which school too commonly throws in his way.

— Charlotte Mason, *Home Education*, 1886

With approximately 2.5 million children receiving their education at home in this country, several specific methodologies of imparting knowledge have sprung up over the years. Why? One reason is that all children are created uniquely, and unlike a teacher conducting classes for a roomful of thirty children, parents instinctively know their children well. They know that their young ones are different from each other. Each learns at his or her own pace; each grasps concepts and learns needed skills in his or her own way...There is no cookie-cutter method for teaching and learning, not in homeschool anyway.

— Paul & Gena Suarez, eds., *Homeschooling Methods*, B&H, 2006

The Truth about Educational Models

Educational models are, if you'll pardon the pun, a paradigm a dozen. There's no reason to be an educational expert or learning engineer (and they are legion) if you can't come up with a decent paradigm or model. Since education is decidedly not a science, theories and models abound that try to explain the mysterious-to-us-but-not-to-God process that children go through to acquire knowledge, understanding, and wisdom. Each model is simply a different way of looking at the process of learning and instruction. The WholeHearted Learning model is part of that grand history of model-making, with one significant difference—it attempts to describe the learning process centered in a home rather than in a classroom.

We make no claims to the scientific validity of our model since it is based on common sense and observation rather than on research. The only claims we make are that it makes sense, it is easy to use, and it works in our home. Though we are educated, we are not educational experts. We are Christian, home-educating parents with a heart and vision for the home, not just as a living environment but also as a dynamic learning environment designed by God. We offer this model with fear and trembling (and much prayer), knowing that many will adopt it as their own home education model. That is a humbling realization. We ask only that you see it for what it is—a simple model to help you subdue your home domain as you bring your children home to live and learn.

The WholeHearted Learning model is designed to enable you to provide a range of coordinated learning experiences for your children, moving from more structured learning to more unstructured learning and from more teacher-directed learning to more child-directed learning. This kind of balanced approach allows you to have input and direction at any level in your children's lives while at the same time giving them freedom to explore and discover on their own. That balance is important for your children to develop a self-motivated desire to learn, independent of always being told what they must think and study or at the other extreme simply being left mostly alone to learn whatever they might learn. It gives them the freedom to discover and express the unique people that God is making them to be, but it also retains the biblical priority of parents as their instructors and trainers. WholeHearted Learning is about everyone in the home, not just your children. Home education is a family affair.

IN OUR HOME

The idea of a wholehearted child came to life out of the soil of our years in discipleship ministry, in church ministry to single adults, and from our own search for a homeschooling model that made sense. Ministry with Campus Crusade for Christ ingrained in us the importance of making disciples; singles ministry in southern California showed us the impact of broken homes on young men and women. Our search for a homeschooling model convinced us that a biblical home education was much more than just bringing school into the home. We realized one day that homeschooling was really about raising wholehearted children who would follow Christ. Homeschooling was about educating a wholehearted child. Aha!

WholeHearted Learning: The Educational Model

God has given you a family and a home. A home is a place where a family is grown, just as soil is where a tree is grown. Your task is to use your home to its fullest measure—to make it the richest and best soil that you possibly can cultivate—in order to ensure that you will grow children who will be spiritually, emotionally, and intellectually strong and healthy, who will bear much fruit, and who will stand strong and long for God. The WholeHearted Learning model describes one way to cultivate that kind of soil in order to use your home to disciple and educate your children by God's principles. There is, of course, much more to biblical family life than is contained only in this Christian homeschooling model. Nonetheless, if you are committed to educating your children at home, this model provides a wholistic, comprehensive way of looking at your home as the center of living and learning for your children. It will provide rich soil for growing mature, well-educated disciples of Jesus Christ.

WholeHearted Learning is structured much like a house. First, a house needs a strong and stable foundation on which to stand, and your children need a strong spiritual foundation to be stable as you prepare them for life, just as Jesus taught about building our house on the rock so it would not fall in the storms of life. That is Discipleship Studies. Then, just as the interior of a house is built with different rooms for different purposes, your children's mental interiors have different but connected rooms of learning. One room, Disciplined Studies, is for more structured learning; another, Discussion Studies, is for more relational learning; and another, Discovery Studies, is for more self-directed learning. Finally, just as the roof completes and unifies the house, Discretionary Studies complete and unify your children as they express their own unique gifts and skills that will bring all their learning together under one roof.

WholeHearted Learning?

We have been asked many times, "How would you describe WholeHearted Learning?" The answer to that question typically involves talking about several of the Pillars of WholeHearted Learning, the key convictions and commitments of our homeschooling model. It's not hard to describe what we do. However, we are also asked to define what we do and that's a bit harder. The following definition attempts to capture the essence and spirit of what we do: "The WholeHearted Learning model is a discipleship-based, home-centered, whole-book approach to Christian home education that integrates real books, real life, and real relationships in a life-giving expression of God's biblical design for the family."

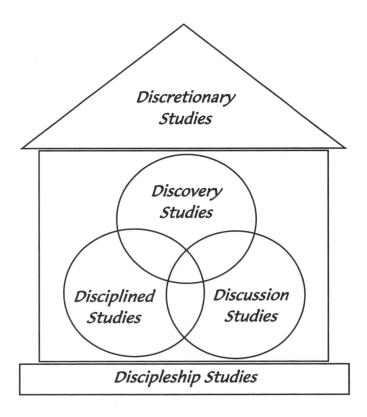

115

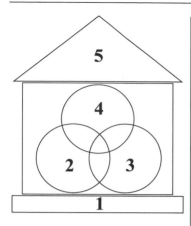

The WholeHearted Learning Model

Recommended Resources

- *Read for the Heart: Whole Books for WholeHearted Families* (Sarah Clarkson)
- *A Charlotte Mason Companion* (Karen Andreola)
- *For the Children's Sake* (Susan Schaeffer Macaulay)
- *A Biblical Home Education* by (Ruth Beechick)
- *Beyond Survival* (Diana Waring)

Five Focused Study Areas

The five focused study areas of the WholeHearted Learning model provide an integrated and comprehensive plan for home education. The house illustration on the previous page shows how the five areas work together. The pages that follow describe each of the five focused study areas in more detail. The lists on each page are only representative, not comprehensive. The "Suggested Methods" section for each area guides you to the relevant methods in section 3.

1. Discipleship Studies

- The solid foundation of the house
- The study of the Bible
- Content: doctrine, wisdom, Bible knowledge
- Purpose: to shape your children's hearts to love and serve God and to study and know his Word

2. Disciplined Studies

- The first interior central study focus (structured learning)
- The study of the basics
- Content: learning skills (reading, writing, math, thinking)
- Purpose: to develop your children's foundational learning skills and competence in language arts, math, and reasoning

3. Discussion Studies

- The second interior central study focus (relational learning)
- The study of ideas and ideals
- Content: literature, history, fine arts
- Purpose: to feed your children's minds by giving them the best in living books and the fine arts

4. Discovery Studies

- The third interior central study focus (self-directed learning)
- The study of learning
- Content: nature, science, creative arts, all interests
- Purpose: to stimulate your children's love for learning by creating opportunities for curiosity, creativity, and discovery

5. Discretionary Studies

- The unique roof of the house
- The study of living
- Content: home, church, and community life, field trips, life skills
- Purpose: to direct your children in developing a range of skills and abilities for adult life according to their gifts and your family's circumstances and resources

DISCIPLESHIP STUDIES

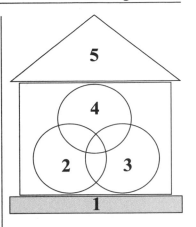

All true education begins with God, who is the source of all that is true. Discipleship Studies are the foundation of the WholeHearted Learning model upon which the rest of the house is built (Matthew 7:24-27). The emphasis of Discipleship Studies is more than just Bible knowledge, though—it is developing a vital relationship with God through his revealed Word. It includes understanding the Bible as a book, studying it as truth from God, and reading it devotionally to hear God speak through it. The goal of Discipleship Studies is to train your children's hearts to seek God and his truth. You are building a secure foundation so the house you build—your child's life—will stand strong.

Focus: The study of the Bible

Content: Doctrine, wisdom, Bible knowledge

Purpose: To shape your children's hearts to love and serve God and to study and know his Word

Discipleship Studies: The Study of the Bible

Learning Objectives:

- To read the Scriptures regularly
- To develop devotional habits
- To memorize selected scriptures
- To understand basic Bible truths
- To know Bible facts
- To know how to study the Bible

Suggested Resources

- *The Holy Bible,* King James Version
- *The Holy Bible,* New King James Version
- *The Holy Bible,* New International Version
- *New American Standard Bible®*
- *The Child's Story Bible* (Catherine F. Vos)
- *The Jesus Storybook Bible* (Sally Lloyd-Jones)
- *The Children's Illustrated Bible* (Selina Hastings)
- *Our 24 Family Ways* (Clay Clarkson)
- *Leading Little Ones to God* (Marian M. Schoolland)
- *Parenting with Scripture: A Topical Guide for Teachable Moments* (Kara Durbin)

Suggested Methods (see section 3):

- Bible knowledge
- Bible reading
- Bible devotions
- Bible study
- Bible instruction
- Reading aloud
- Reading alone
- Narration

- History
- The fine arts
- Memorization and recitation
- Speaking and presentation
- Storytelling
- The creative arts
- Drawing and coloring
- Living and learning notebooks

Suggested Materials:

- Personal Bible
- Other Bible translations
- Bible study notebook
- Devotional notebook or journal
- Bible study reference library (concordance, Bible dictionary, Bible handbook, Bible atlas)

- Scripture memory resources
- Topical Bible study resources
- Family devotional guide
- Bible reading guide for reading through the Bible
- Christian book library (church history, biography, inspirational)

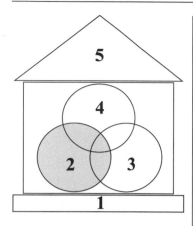

**Disciplined Studies:
The Study of the Basics**

Suggested Resources

- *Reading Made Easy: A Guide to Teach Your Child to Read* (Valerie Bendt)
- *Mommy, Teach Me to Read!* (Barbara Curtis)
- *The Three R's* (Ruth Beechick)
- *Teach Your Child to Read in 100 Easy Lessons* (Siegfried Englemann, Phyllis Haddox, and Elaine Bruner)
- *You Can Teach Your Child Successfully: Grades 4-8* (Ruth Beechick)
- *Mommy, Teach Me!* (Barbara Curtis)
- *Learning Language Arts through Literature* (Common Sense Press)
- *Simply Grammar—An Illustrated Primer* (Karen Andreola)
- *Italic Handwriting Series* (Continuing Education Press)
- *Wordsmith* series (Janie B. Cheaney)
- *How to Teach Any Child to Spell* (Gayle Graham)
- *Making Math Meaningful* series (David Quine)
- *CalcuLadder Math Drills* (Providence Project)
- *The Thinking Toolbox* (Nathaniel and Hans Bluedorn)

DISCIPLINED STUDIES

Learning begins in earnest when a child acquires the basic skills of reading, writing, and arithmetic (the 3 Rs), which open a world of information and ideas. Disciplined Studies focus on developing the foundational skills and competencies required for education and learning—language arts, math, and reasoning. They are called Disciplined Studies because they require a significant amount of commitment and work from both the parent and the child. Disciplined study of these basic learning skills will set the pace for the self-motivated learning that is to come.

Focus: The study of the basics (structured learning)

Content: Learning skills (reading, writing, math, thinking)

Purpose: To develop your children's foundational learning skills and competencies in language arts, math, and reasoning

Learning Objectives:

- To learn to read phonetically
- To develop reading skills
- To strengthen language arts skills
- To develop handwriting skills
- To develop compositional skills
- To master basic math skills
- To strengthen thinking skills

Suggested Methods (see section 3):

- Beginning reading
- Reading aloud
- Reading alone
- Language arts
- Writing and composition
- Math
- Thinking skills
- Asking questions

- The library
- Study groups
- Private lessons and mentors
- Living and learning notebooks
- Standardized tests

Suggested Materials:

- Beginning reading resources
- Lots of good reading books
- Illustrated storybooks
- Handwriting workbooks
- Math workbook or notebook
- Math manipulatives
- Math flashcards

- Drill and review helps
- Language arts workbooks
- Thinking skills workbooks
- Lined writing paper
- Chalk and marker boards

DISCUSSION STUDIES

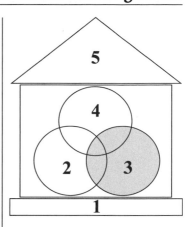

Once your children have acquired the skills of reading and language, they will need good food in order to satisfy new intellectual appetites and to grow. Discussion Studies provide the very best food for their growing hearts and minds through what are generally called the humanities—the best of literature, poetry, art, and music. These are called Discussion Studies because, through discussion and narration, your children learn to express back verbally what they are reading, hearing, and observing. It is a wholistic method of learning that naturally integrates the written and spoken word and internalizes learning. It is the heart and soul of your home education program.

Focus: The study of ideas and ideals (relational learning)

Content: Literature, history, fine arts (art, music, poetry)

Purpose: To feed your children's minds by giving them the best in living books and the fine arts

Discussion Studies: The Study of the Humanities

Learning Objectives:

- To read and discuss great literature
- To read and discuss historical literature
- To study and discuss world history
- To study and discuss American history
- To read and discuss poetry
- To study and discuss music and art

Suggested Methods (see section 3):

- Reading aloud
- Reading alone
- Narration
- History
- The fine arts
- The creative arts
- Drawing and coloring
- Unit study

- Context study
- Memorization and recitation
- Speaking and presentation
- Storytelling
- The library
- Study groups
- Living and learning notebooks

Suggested Materials:

- Home library
- Public library
- Chalk and marker boards
- Drawing and coloring resources
- History visual aids
- History timelines
- Geography visual aids

- Poetry books and collections
- Classical music recordings
- Fine arts videos
- Art posters and books
- Notebooking materials

Suggested Resources

- *Read for the Heart: Whole Books for WholeHearted Families* (Sarah Clarkson)
- *Books Children Love* (Elizabeth Wilson)
- *How to Grow a Young Reader* (Kathryn Lindskoog and Ranelda Mack Hunsicker)
- *Honey for a Child's Heart* (Gladys Hunt)
- *History through Literature* study guides (Rea Berg)
- *Greenleaf Guides* to world history (Rob and Cyndy Shearer)
- *Classical Kids* CD series (Children's Book Store Distribution)
- *Come Look With Me* art book series (Gladys S. Blizzard)

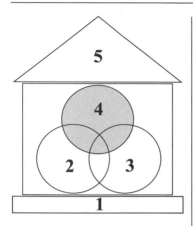

Discovery Studies:
The Study of Learning

Suggested Resources

- Audiobooks (unabridged)
- *Your Story Hour* living history tapes
- Moody Science videos
- Pocket-sized field guides (various publishers)
- *How Great Thou ART* drawing and painting workbooks (Barry Stebbing)
- Mark Kistler drawing workbooks
- Apologia science books and resources

DISCOVERY STUDIES

The desire and ability to learn are instinctual but need to be cultivated. Discovery Studies are directed experiences in self-learning. They are opportunities for your children to discover the world around them through independent exploration, research, experimentation, observation, and study. There are many ways to learn, so freedom is built into Discovery Studies to allow your children to pursue their own learning interests. Creativity and curiosity are allowed fuller expression. Discovery corners in the home provide resources for self-directed learning, and field trips expand the scope of discovery. The goal is to cultivate in your child a natural excitement about and love for learning.

Focus: The study of learning (self-directed learning)

Content: Nature, science, creative arts, all interests

Purpose: To stimulate in your children a love for learning by creating opportunities for curiosity, creativity, and discovery

Learning Objectives:

- To experience, explore, and discover
- To develop and express creativity
- To cultivate self-directed learning
- To know how to use a library
- To know how to use learning tools
- To know how to do simple research

Suggested Methods (see section 3):

- Reading alone
- The creative arts
- Nature study
- Creation science
- Hands-on science
- Computer
- Internet
- Audio/video production

- Speaking and presentation
- Unit study
- Context study
- The library
- Field trips
- Study groups
- Home workshops
- Living and learning notebooks

Suggested Materials:

- Home library
- CD, DVD, MP3 players
- Musical instruments
- Computer and peripherals
- Educational games and puzzles
- Models and kits
- Drawing and coloring materials

- Arts and crafts materials
- Historical dress-up costumes
- Work bench with tools
- Nature museum display shelves
- Field gear (binoculars, pick, shovel, specimen holders)
- Field guides

DISCRETIONARY STUDIES

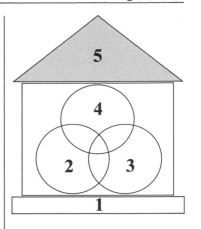

Every child is different. Every family is different. That is why these are called Discretionary Studies: It is up to your discretion as to how to develop the unique gifts, talents, and abilities of your children. Family circumstances and resources differ from one family to another, but God has put your children in your family for a purpose. He has given you the responsibility to prayerfully determine a direction and then marshal the resources available to you to prepare your children for adult life. Your goal is to give each child a broad experience in a wide range of life skills and to help them discover, release, and develop the unique gifts and talents that God has given to them.

Focus: The study of living

Content: Home, church, and community life, field trips, life skills

Purpose: To direct your children in developing a range of skills and abilities for adult life according to their gifts and your family's circumstances and resources

Discretionary Studies: The Study of Living

Learning Objectives:

- To affirm and encourage personal interests
- To develop emerging gifts, skills, and abilities
- To develop general life and living skills
- To study occupations and careers
- To understand how to make/earn money
- To prepare for future educational opportunities

Suggested Resources

- How-to books (areas of interest, age-appropriate)
- Books on children's business ideas
- Private lessons (music, art, programming, etc.)
- Community resource people (experts)

Suggested Methods (see section 3):

- Reading alone
- Speaking and presentation
- The creative arts
- Real-life learning
- Private lessons and mentors
- The library
- Field trips
- Study groups
- Home workshops
- Living and learning notebooks
- Computer
- Internet
- Audio/video production

Suggested Materials:

The materials you need will depend entirely upon what you pursue. A few general examples include:

- Musical instrument(s)
- Science supplies and equipment
- Audio/video gear and software
- Sport supplies and equipment
- Garden supplies and equipment
- Cooking supplies and equipment
- Computer supplies and equipment
- Sewing supplies and equipment
- Special study courses or classes
- Special lessons or instructors
- Special field trips

The truly educated person has only had many doors of interest opened. He knows that life will not be long enough to follow everything through fully.

— Susan Schaeffer Macaulay, *For the Children's Sake*, Crossway, 1984

God wants us to live by faith in Christ, instructed by his Word and guided by his Holy Spirit, not in an immature dependence upon others to tell us how to live. He wants us to live by faith, in mature dependence upon him for the wisdom that he "gives generously to all without finding fault" (James 1:5).

— Sally Clarkson, *Seasons of a Mother's Heart*, Apologia Press, 2009

At Home with the WholeHearted Learning Model

At this point, many homeschool parents are apt to respond, "I understand the model—now just tell me what to do! What is the daily lesson plan I need to follow?" We have to make the distinction that WholeHearted Learning is not an educational curriculum; it is a model. It was never our intent to create a WholeHearted Learning curriculum with daily lesson plans to tell a homeschooling parent which lesson to do from which resource, which books to read at what age, what music and art your family should enjoy and when, or how to schedule your schooling. Frankly, if we were to create a daily lesson plan for each age and grade, we could certainly sell many more books. But that would defeat the very purpose of this book and undermine the unique advantages and strengths of the WholeHearted Learning model.

Perhaps a helpful metaphor is that WholeHearted Learning model is a lens, not a photograph. A photograph is static and unchanging. You can study it and try to recreate it in your home, but it offers only a limited perspective through the eyes of the one who took the photograph. A lens, though, is dynamic—you look through it to find the best picture from your own perspective. A lens brings into clear focus the unique picture that you want to create and even lets you look at your home from a variety of perspectives. We wrote this book to give homeschooling parents a lens to see their homes and lives in a whole new way—a wholehearted way. A curriculum approach, rather than offering freedom and confidence, often causes parents to become dependent on the lesson plan rather than on God. It would be only about studying a static photograph, not using the lens.

Every home and family is different, and our heart is to encourage and help homeschooling parents to listen to the Holy Spirit to determine what is best for their own family, rather than depending on someone else to tell them what to do. How the Clarkson family expresses the WholeHearted Learning model should look different from how you express it in your home. Our experiences, skills, personalities, and training are unique to us. Our children's personalities, drives, abilities, and gifts are unique to them. You will not use all the methods we use or in the way we use them because your family is different and unique. It's not about duplicating what God has done in our family but about discovering what God wants to do in your family. That will be the best way for you.

Many homeschool parents lack confidence to create their own expression of homeschooling from just a model, and they insist they cannot homeschool without a detailed lesson plan to tell them what to do and curriculum to provide instruction. We have all felt like that at some point along the homeschooling journey. However, if Christian homeschooling is truly the fullest expression of our biblical mission to make disciples of our children, then it must be a dynamic process characterized by relationship and wisdom, not a static procedure characterized by routine and information. If homeschooling is only an educational formula to follow, then we no longer have to live that part of our lives by faith or walk each day as a homeschooling parent in the power of the Holy Spirit. It is not too strong to say that how you choose to homeschool, as a Christian, is less a matter of educational methodology than it is an issue of faith. God is much more concerned that you learn how to nurture, disciple, and educate your children by faith, in the power of his Holy Spirit, than he is about what curriculum or methodology you choose. The WholeHearted Learning model is a sincere attempt to encourage and equip you to homeschool by faith.

— Chapter 7 —

The WholeHearted Learning Home: Creating a Home You Can Learn Within

Creating a Home Where Learning Happens

A house is more than just a place where you live. If that is your concept of home, then your vision for what happens there will be limited to form and function—what works best where. WholeHearted Learning, in contrast, asks you to add faith and freedom to your vision—to see your entire home as a dynamic living and learning environment, designed by God to work for you to help you achieve your home education goals.

The image of homeschooling at the kitchen or dining room table emerged early in the movement and continues to be reinforced to some degree by images in both Christian and secular media. It is a relatively harmless stereotype, but it does not represent the reality of the more mature homeschooling movement of today. Home education should not be relegated to temporary, transient locations in your home. The not-so-subtle message to your children is that what they are studying must not be that important if it must be done quickly between meals on the kitchen counter or dining room table. "Hurry up and finish your math so we can set the table for dinner!" says loudly and clearly that dinner is the higher priority, not math. However, when one entire room or area is permanently dedicated to home education and other dedicated learning places are strategically located throughout the house, it speaks volumes to your children that their learning is so important that you want to give them special places for it. Learning is something that goes on all the time and in many places. When you begin to see your entire home as a means for learning, home education takes on a whole new meaning. It is not just education done at home; it is education done with the home. Home is not just a place where education happens—it is an important tool and means of education. When you cooperate with God's design for family, your home will work for you in home education.

Creating a learning environment is the key. Make your entire home an exciting, vibrant place where learning is happening all the time—a place where loving to learn is as natural a part of your children's everyday existence as loving to play. Make it a child-friendly environment that is rich in interesting, inspiring, mentally stimulating options at every turn. Use every part of your home to engage your children's senses in the learning process and to strengthen their emotional ties to the home—the smell of fresh bread baking, the sounds of Baroque chamber music, the sights of beautiful Scripture calligraphy and interesting artwork. Your entire home should reflect your homeschooling values from the way you arrange your furniture to the books you leave out on tables to the pictures and verses you hang on the wall to the way you use your kitchen. There should be no discernible dividing lines between home and education. The natural atmosphere of your home should be alive with learning and life.

But home should be more of a school than it is. It should give lessons and hear recitations. It should be a Sunday school with week day sessions, with songs and readings, the Bible the textbook, the father the superintendent, the mother the chief teacher. Such a school would be a great help to all the kinds of work which home has to do. It would promote politeness, gentleness, and mutual forbearance...It would fill the memory of children with Scripture passages, church hymns, wise proverbs, and rules for everyday living. It would give topics to talk about at table or fireside... Dull hours would be filled in with humor, wisdom, and religion. Day school would be worth more, and Sunday school would be far more precious and useful, because of Home school.

— John H. Vincent, *The Church at Home*, 1893

By wisdom a house is built, and through understanding it is established; through knowledge its rooms are filled with rare and beautiful treasures.

— Proverbs 24:3-4

Books are delightful society. If you go into a room and find it full of books—even without taking them from the shelves they seem to speak to you, to bid you welcome.

— William Gladstone (1809-1898), British statesman and scholar, prime minister four times (more than any other)

Books are the quietest and most constant of friends; they are the most accessible and wisest of counselors, and the most patient of teachers.

— Charles W. Eliot (1834-1926), American academic, President of Harvard 1869-1909

Designate a Learning Room

If you were building a house today, you would expect to find certain kinds of rooms in most floor plans—living room, great room, family room, recreation room, bonus room, or something similar. Because family togetherness is a value for most families with young children, today's homes reflect the need to have more space designed especially for family activities. (Sorry, but home theater doesn't make that list in our book.) If you are a homeschooling family, though, it's time to consider another room for the basic family house plan—a learning room.

If you are committed to discipling and educating your children at home, you should consider creating a designated room dedicated to home education. Ideally, it should be comfortable, roomy, well-lighted, and have storage for books, materials, and other learning resources. You or your classroom-deprived younger children might think that individual student desks (the kind with the attached writing surface and storage shelf) would be a fun addition to your learning room. However, they are not necessary and may even be counterproductive for wholehearted learning, and the novelty grows thin quickly. (They're just vestiges of public school rooms.) Instead, there should be several writing, reading, and drawing spaces available with plenty of tabletop areas for spreading out books, papers, and projects. Rectangular utility tables work well, are easy to move, and are relatively inexpensive. A big, inviting couch or some overstuffed chairs allow everyone to get comfortable for reading aloud or reading alone. If the floor is hard for easier clean-up, be sure to provide a thick, comfortable rug or other floor covering that will allow your children to stretch out on the floor. Make the room child-friendly.

Other rooms in your home can and should be used for education, too, but a learning room is like the hub of a wheel—everything centers around that room, emanates from it, and returns to it. A learning room sends the message to your children that your family takes home learning seriously.

IN OUR HOME

We've learned a lot about creating an atmosphere in the fifteen homes we have lived in since we were married. When Sarah was approaching school age, we began the practice of setting aside one room as a learning room. Now it is the center of our homeschool. Our learning room contains our primary library (thousands of books and growing), our big couch, and personal study areas for each child. It also has several discovery corners—computer and printer, music (keyboard, guitar, rhythm instruments), creative corner (Lego lab, games, puzzles, and more), a writing and drawing corner, and a fine arts corner. (We keep art books open on the coffee table and on mini-easels to display interesting pieces of art.) We have other discovery corners elsewhere inside and outside of the house—piano, music and video, arts and crafts, workbench—but everything flows out of and back into our primary learning room. The great thing is, our children are learning all the time they're there and we don't even have to tell them to. It's as natural to them as breathing. Learning is the atmosphere of our home.

If You Build It, They Will Learn

When learning becomes truly home-centered, then the environment you have created begins to work for you. Your children enjoy learning and discovering because that is what happens in a home by God's design. You know that when they are in your learning room or they are actively engaged in one of the discovery corners you have created for them, home education is happening without you. Learning is what should happen naturally in a home, and you have simply created the means and opportunities for it in your home. However, there may be hurdles to clear on your way to a wholehearted home.

Homeschoolers, in general, are no strangers to sacrifice. Moms sacrifice their expectations for the sake of their children. Most homeschooling families sacrifice financially by choosing a one-income lifestyle. Many homeschoolers have larger families and cheerfully accept the accompanying financial and space sacrifices. Many also sacrifice the ability to have a larger home with adequate space for learning and living. A separate learning room is an ideal that may not be possible for some homeschooling families with smaller homes and no ability to expand. However, you can still accomplish it in principle if you're willing to look at your home creatively and to accept a little bit more sacrifice or ask your children to. Is there an area in one room that can be carved out and dedicated to home education? Can your children sleep together in one room to free up a bedroom that can become your learning room? Can some furniture or other possessions be stored or sold to make additional room? Whatever your situation, with a little creativity and ingenuity, you can turn your home into a vibrant learning center for your children. If homeschooling is God's will for your family, then he will provide a way for you to do it effectively. Whatever God has entrusted to you, he will show you how to use it.

Since you can't declare a tax on your neighbors to pay for your children's education at home, you will have to purchase supplies and resources yourself. One basic rule of thumb in supplying your home is this: Don't try to do and buy everything all at once. Think of your home learning environment as a flower garden you are just beginning to plant. At first, it's going to look a bit thin, but it's going to grow over the years into a beautiful, colorful, growing showplace. There is no need to rush out and buy everything you need to stock every discovery corner you want to have. You will only end up spending more money than you need to on things you might not yet need. Slowly, but steadily, cultivate your home environment and let each new discovery corner bloom over time. The reality is that your home environment is never really completed but is always a work in progress. We are continually cultivating, pruning, and improving our discovery corners. Christmas and birthday gifts add to the discovery corners, as do special finds in garage sales and clearances. When we can afford it, we do a little bit more; when we can't, we wait. But we're always planning and moving ahead.

The real measure of success in building a wholehearted learning environment in your home is not perfection or even completion. It is consistency. If you have a picture in your mind of what it means to create a learning room and discovery corners and you are always moving faithfully toward that vision, you are practicing wholehearted learning. And, to paraphrase a line from a popular movie, "If you build it, they will learn." As you consistently work at creating the kind of wholehearted home you envision, your children will catch your enthusiasm.

Learning Tools

Create a basic reference section in your home library to keep important information within easy reach:

- Bibles (NIV, KJV, NKJV, NASB, ESV)
- NIV, KJV, NASB Concordances
- Topical Bibles
- Children's Bible handbook
- Children's Bible dictionary
- Children's Bible atlas
- Children's dictionary
- Children's thesaurus
- Advanced dictionary and thesaurus
- Atlas, almanac, and globe
- Child-friendly encyclopedia
- Informative topical books
- Historical reference books
- Nature guides (wildlife, plants, weather, stars, etc.)

Organizing Tools

Keep some basic organizational helps on hand to help keep order in the learning room:

- Desktop hanging files (for misc. drawings and papers)
- Desktop and drawer organizers (for pencils, pens, etc.)
- Horizontal or flat files (for various kinds of blank paper)
- Paper boxes (for bulk paper)
- Organizers (for each child's current work)
- Metal bookends (for library)
- Wastebaskets

Hang It on Your Wall!

Learning room walls should say, "Look at me and learn!"

- History timeline
- Posters of historical events and people
- Scripture verses, books of the Bible
- Fine art and music posters
- Maps—world, U.S., Holy Land, historical
- Language arts posters

Visual Aids

Teaching that engages the senses hooks what is learned more effectively in a child's long-term memory. For example: looking at pictures of the Swiss Alps (visual aid) and listening to Swiss folk music (auditory aid) when reading *Heidi*. All children benefit from added visual and auditory dimensions, as well as tactile, smell, and taste. Sensory teaching aids can include audio, video, pictures, manipulatives, foods, maps and globes, items to examine, actions to perform, or items from nature.

- **Keep them simple.** When using sensory teaching aids, keep them simple and relate them as closely as possible to the topic being studied. Avoid sensory overload or creating an increasing appetite for sensory stimulation.

- **Natural is better.** When possible, use real life for aids rather than artificial substitutes. Nature abounds with natural aids; the kitchen is full of them. Use your imagination before resorting to typical classroom aids.

- **Stimulate learning.** Good sensory aids should do more than just stimulate the senses—they should stimulate learning through the senses. An aid is never an end in itself, but rather a means to an end. It simplifies, clarifies, or amplifies the book or topic being discussed.

- **Look at books.** Visual books such as the Eyewitness and Usborne series that offer interesting information and illustrations are excellent teaching aids. Use them often.

- **Search the Internet.** Instructional aids abound online with photos, illustrations, audio, video, and more.

- **Write it on a board.** An old but proven and powerful instructional aid is the venerable chalk or marker board. Use it to illustrate, make notes, solve problems, write out quotes, and more.

Cultivate a Learning Environment

Setting up your house for wholehearted learning is a little like decorating your home, as opposed to only furnishing it. You can put all the right things in all the right places and get the job done, or you can look at your house as a whole and work to create a living and learning environment where everything works together to enhance the unity of that environment. *Webster's Collegiate Dictionary* defines "environment" as "the circumstances, objects, or conditions by which one is surrounded." In your home environment, you want to consider how to surround your children with circumstances that stimulate and invite their inquiry and investigation, objects that reinforce truth and knowledge they are learning, and conditions that motivate them to want to learn. It is helpful, too, to make a distinction between the environment and the atmosphere of your home—environment is the physical surroundings of your home, the space you inhabit; atmosphere is the emotional surroundings of your home, the air you breathe. The following are ways you can cultivate the living and learning environment in your home.

- **Walls** — What hangs on the walls in your home is a good indicator of a Whole-Hearted Learning environment: Scripture calligraphy, historical timelines, maps, artistic creations, calendars and goal planners, classical artwork posters, nature posters, visual aids for learning, family-affirming art, and so on. Use your walls to their maximum and periodically draw your children's attention to what is there. Walls are one of your best teaching tools.

- **Furniture** — Furniture should be comfortable, inviting, and child-friendly. If your children feel like certain furniture is more important to you than they are, they will mentally cordon off and avoid those parts of the home, which will be lost as areas of living and learning. Arrange the furniture to allow maximum movement for naturally energetic children—don't inadvertently create obstacles or hazards that make them fearful of being children in your home. If you are able, make room where they can be more active and mobile, even if you have to move or store some furniture.

- **Tabletops** — Make maximum use of your tabletop spaces. Tastefully display art books, special reading books, and appropriate child-friendly magazines on coffee tables for casual reading. Decorate your dining room table with a centerpiece that reinforces a current holiday or area of study. In your learning room, leave out reference and reading books for current areas of study. Display an open art book flat or on a book easel on a corner table. The idea is to view every table top as a potential display space for environment-building books and objects.

- **Yard** — From a child's perspective, the home environment extends beyond the four walls of your house to the unseen walls that enclose your property (including the garage). Your yard can become an important part of the living and learning environment of your home. Aside from recreational areas, create areas for learning and creativity: a kids' vegetable garden, a place for building materials, a workbench with tools and discarded machines and appliances, birdhouses and feeders for observation, and so on. It should also be, as much as possible, a fun place to play—with a fort or play area, rope swing, basketball goal, and other popular play options.

Create Discovery Corners

Cultivating a learning environment in your home means helping learning happen in every nook and cranny...and corner. A discovery corner is a space dedicated to one general learning focus. The more discovery corners you create in your home, the more choices your children will have for pursuing Discovery Studies that encourage self-motivated, self-directed learning. Although several discovery corners will likely be in your learning room, they can be located anywhere in your house. Each should be a distinct place, well-supplied for the learning activity to which it is dedicated, comfortable, and well-lighted. It is best to have them in public areas of the house so you can monitor your children's learning activities. The following are just a few examples. Be creative in coming up with your own ideas, and let your children decide on some.

- **Drawing and Design Corner** — A tabletop area supplied with paper, pencils, colored pencils, crayons, stencils, coloring books, sketch and tracing books, rulers, easel, chalk board, marker board, and more. Use wall space to display work.

- **Computer/Electronic Media Corner** — Computer with educational and creativity software, a scanner, and a color printer. Filtered or restricted Internet access to web-based learning sites, museum sites, maps, history, country sites, and much more.

- **Creative Play Corner** — Legos, Duplos, wooden blocks, educational games, puzzles, Lincoln Logs, positive historical play sets (soldiers, pioneers, knights, biblical), puppets, and other creative play items.

- **Audio Corner** — CD, DVD, or cassette players to listen to dramatized Bible, history, and biography; classic children's books; classical music; selected popular music; character and adventure stories; Christian and missions testimonies.

- **Music Making Corner** — Piano, keyboard, guitar, dulcimer, autoharp, recorders, rhythm instruments, and whatever other musical instruments are handy; sheet music, songbooks, and "fake" books. A karaoke will encourage singing and performance.

- **History Dress-Up Corner** — A trunk or box full of historical dress-up clothes, uniforms, and accessories for creative play and historical role-playing.

- **Geography Corner** — Globe, maps, atlases, and geography books that tell the stories of different lands; geography drill devices, games, and puzzles; blank maps.

- **Crafts Corner** — An easily-cleaned area stocked with a wide variety of craft books, materials, and tools. Essential to include: freedom to make a mess!

- **Carpentry Corner** — Don't forget to use the garage! Set up a long workbench with tools, scrap wood, nails, and fasteners. You can also put broken appliances there to be fixed, studied, or recycled in new creations.

- **Nature Study Corner** — Nature books, field guides (birds, trees, plants, insects), creation science books, display cases, nature journal and sketch books.

- **And Many More** — Science, astronomy, writing and editing, sewing and other needlework, videography and film editing, composing and songwriting, ad infinitum.

Discovering Audiobooks

Listening to recorded books combines the learning value of hearing with the enjoyment of a good book read well. Use audiobooks only to supplement, not to replace, reading aloud in your home. You can have your children narrate an audiobook formally or informally by eliciting their thoughts and comments about the reading.

- A family audiobook library can be used for many years. Digital downloads will make it even easier. Be sure to try to find books read by the author or by good readers.

- As the world of audio converts to digital, the opportunities increase to find great audiobooks in older media (cassette, CD) for very little cost. Check the library, used book stores, online auctions, and other such outlets.

- Don't forget the audio Bible. Listen before you buy—some are exceptional professional productions with multi-cast dramatic readings, music, and effects; some are straight dramatic readings by a single narrator with music; some are no-frills readings that tend to be dull and unappealing, especially for children.

Digital Audiobooks

With the ubiquity of personal digital devices, audiobooks are only a download away. Here is a short list of current audiobook websites. Many also offer affordable rentals:

- www.iTunes.com
- www.Audible.com
- www.Amazon.com
- www.eMusic.com/ audiobooks
- www.Audiobooks.com
- www.SimplyAudiobooks.com
- www.BooksFree.com
- www.eAudioSource.com (Christian)
- www.ChristianAudio.com
- www.FamilyAudioLibrary. com
- www.ChristianBook.com/ audiobooks

Book Search & Rescue

The Internet revolutionized book search, taking it out of the hands of antiquarian bookstores and putting it into the hands of the consumer. It's fast, easy, and fun. First do an Internet search for any e-book or digitized versions that might already be available in an online virtual library for a free download or reasonable fee. Then search all the best book search sites and auctions. You can also try an interlibrary loan (ILL) search at your local library or search WorldCat to see which libraries around the world have a copy and contact them. If the book is dated 1923 or before, it is probably in the public domain (PD), which would allow you to photocopy or scan the book and print it out for reading. Here are a few of the best online places to start your book search adventure.

- www.AbeBooks.com — searches used book sellers' inventories worldwide
- www.AddALL.com — searches all major book search sites (metasearch)
- www.Amazon.com — huge repository of printed, digital (Kindle), and PD books
- www.BookFinder.com — searches all major book search sites (metasearch)
- www.CCEL.org — the Christian Classics Ethereal Library (Calvin College) of PD e-books; free downloads
- www.eBay.com — many used book dealers with regular auctions; subscribe to your favorites
- http://books.Google.com — Google's searchable database of scanned library books
- www.Gutenberg.org — PD e-books; free downloads
- www.Half.com — large inventory of new and used books (subsidiary of eBay)
- http://Onlinebooks.library. upenn.edu — PD e-books
- www.WorldCat.org — searchable database of all U.S. and international library catalogs

Build a Home Library

A growing home library is absolutely essential for a WholeHearted Learning approach to home education. Erasmus said it first, but it is all too true of many homeschool booklovers that when the paycheck arrives, they buy books first, and if anything is left over, they buy food and clothing! Building a home library is a way of life and a way of thinking (and a way of frustration if you don't have adequate bookshelf space). Just remember, books are an investment. They have intellectual asset value. They are nonconsumable curricula that can be used with every child, then with their children, and passed on to succeeding generations. Books are worth it. Here are a few tips for building and maintaining your home library.

- **Become book smart.** Get to know the antiquarian and used bookstores in your area, www.Amazon.com, www.AbeBooks.com, and specialty book catalogs. Mark your calendar for when library sales and used book fairs are held, and check newspapers for garage and estate sales. Ask your parents about unused books in their libraries.

- **Buy and trade.** Start a book cooperative. Members gather to discuss books in their libraries, trade and sell books, and share useful information on the various catalogs and suppliers. Start an annual used books and curriculum fair in your area.

- **Make a book wish list.** Ask parents and relatives to give you and your children books for Christmas and birthday gifts. (Plastic toys last a few months; books last a lifetime!) Be bold—give them a list of special books you want for your home library. Make a Wish List of wanted books public on www.Amazon.com.

- **Lend books wisely.** Your books are special, so lend them out with due caution. Keep a list or a 3x5 file to record who borrowed which book when. Make sure every book that leaves your house has your name in it. Be especially cautious when lending out-of-print, rare, or hard-to-find books that cannot be easily replaced!

- **Don't do Dewey Decimal.** Unless you have the heart and patience of a librarian, organize simply. You want your children to use your home library and enjoy it, not to admire it or be intimidated by it. Just get the books in general categories and you'll be in good shape: literature, illustrated storybooks, world history, American history, geography, family reading, classic children's books, fiction, Bible-related, Christian stories, reference, science/nature, art, preschool/early reader, and so on. Make it easy for your children to find books they want or to browse for books in areas of interest.

- **Plan ahead for more.** Inevitably you will acquire more books than you need so plan to periodically purge your shelves (you'll need space for the next round of books anyway). Sell them, store them, trade them, or give them away. Consider a garage sale, trade with a used bookstore, put them on consignment, or sell them at homeschool events. Donate some to your church library, an overseas mission, a public school reading program, or a local charity that needs books.

- **Support homeschooling.** Support home-based businesses and ministries by buying from homeschool family-owned-and-run book catalogs whenever possible. Keep your money in the family!

Create a Print-Rich Environment

We have observed that many families rightly attempt to create an enriched learning environment in their homes, yet they often miss or neglect the single most enriching element. They might add lots of quality educational toys and materials, have fact-filled and interesting posters on the walls, and provide lots of good things to do, watch, and listen to, but books get short shrift. As we have read through the years about the effects of books and reading on the intellectual development of children, we have observed what seems to be a common experience: Intelligent children seem to grow up in print-rich home environments—in other words, in homes where lots of books and reading materials are always within easy reach. We like all the other things, too, but to make sure our home learning environment is enriched with the best resources, we have made books a priority. We aim to create what we call a 4-A book environment in our home. We want books to be:

- **Available** — Our first priority is to provide a wide range of books to meet any reading or research desire. If a child has a question, a project, a topic to research, or just a desire for a good novel, we want it to be available in our home. We want to feed intellectual hunger when it strikes, not have to put it off until later.

- **Accessible** — Public libraries are wonderful, but sometimes the books there don't seem very accessible to children. We keep interesting and relevant books within easy reach so they are easy to find. Child-friendly organization by topics and categories makes it easy for a child to browse our bookshelves or go right to a needed book.

- **Appropriate** — Of course, the books we make available and accessible to our children are also appropriate. We add books to our library collection that are suited to our children's current needs, interests, and ages and that reflect our beliefs and values. Generally, books for when they are a bit older are higher on the shelf.

- **Abundant** — This is the most challenging commitment. We try to provide as many good books as we can and as our bookshelves will hold. We want our children to have an abundance of good choices when they go to search out a book. Of course, abundance requires more management of books, but it's worth it.

IN OUR HOME

We do whatever we can to encourage our children to think very positively about book ownership. They enjoy building their own libraries, so we give special books for birthdays and for Christmas. When we get new books, we spend a long time handling, admiring, and talking about them. (We stop short of bibliolatry.) Our children naturally let us know which books they want to read first without our prompting. We will sometimes talk up a really good book but wait to read it, saving it for a rainy day or a trip or as a reward for finishing a project. By the time we get around to reading it, everyone is champing at the bit. With older children, books get read, passed around, and finally discussed. And, of course, library day is a big deal. I think we hold the record for most books checked out in a single visit! And it's all for the love of books.

Give us a house furnished with books rather than furniture! Both, if you can, but books at any rate!...Books are the windows through which the soul looks out. A house without books is like a room without windows. No man has a right to bring up his children without surrounding them with books, if he has the means to buy them. It is a wrong to his family. He cheats them! Children learn to read by being in the presence of books. The love of knowledge comes with reading and grows upon it. And the love of knowledge, in a young mind, is almost a warrant against the inferior excitement of passions and vices...Let us pity these poor rich men who live barrenly in great, bookless houses!...A little library growing larger every year is an honourable part of a young man's history. It is a man's duty to have books. A library is not a luxury, but one of the necessities of life.

— Henry Ward Beecher, *Eyes and Ears*, 1862

Lost in (No) Space

If you plan to start building a library of good books, then plan to build a library of good bookshelves. You need shelf space! Built-ins of some kind will give you the most bookshelf space for the buck, but not everyone has the room, money, and/or inclination to go that route. Finished or unfinished wood or veneer bookshelf units are an alternative to built-ins if you value quality and beauty. KD (knock-down) bookshelves of laminated particle board are heavy as bricks, but they are movable, affordable, and easily sold if you decide later to go for built-ins. Bricks and boards will do in a pinch, but for a starter library only. Other handyman variations work too, depending on just how handy the man in your house is. As a very last resort, you can use Bankers Boxes, corners, and tables, but it's much harder on the books and on you.

[There] is no education but self-education, and as soon as a young child begins his education he does so as a student. Our business is to give him mind-stuff, and both quality and quantity are essential. Naturally each of us possesses this mind-stuff only in limited measure, but we know where to procure it; for the best thought the world possesses is stored in books; we must open books to children, the best books; our own concern is abundant provision and orderly serving.

— Charlotte Mason, *Towards a Philosophy of Education*, 1925

A child's taste in reading is formed in the right direction or in the wrong one while he is under the influence of his parents; and they are directly responsible for shaping and cultivating that taste.

— H. Clay Trumbull, *Hints on Child Training*, 1890

To a genuine lover of books no house is completely furnished which has not a good many of them, not arranged formally in one room, but scattered all over the house.

— Margaret E. Sangster (1838-1912), American Christian author and magazine editor

Acquire Good Books

Occasionally someone will ask, "Why books?" There is a great deal of discussion and data that fuels the debate about the efficacy and power of reading, whether aloud or alone, in the intellectual development of a child. But the question still remains: Why? We believe the answer is a spiritual one, and it elevates the importance of books and reading in a Christian homeschool far beyond even the most convincing secular arguments. God created us to be people of his book, the Bible. We are hardwired from creation with the ability to learn how to speak and read for one reason—so we can learn and know about God through his spoken and written revelation.

God's direct revelation was passed along orally at first, but God's ultimate purpose was to create a holy book, the written Word, that would be eternal and even written on our hearts. By God's divine design, we are made to be a people of words so that we can read his holy Word. When you consider the biblical reality of the Lamb's Book of Life (Revelation 21:27)—a physical book with names written on its real pages—you can begin to understand a little better the "why?" of books and reading. They are, quite literally, a part of the image of God within us. Because he is a God of spoken and written language, we are a people of spoken and written language. It is part of our spiritual nature.

It is our conviction that reading is not just one of the three Rs of a basic education but a fundamental activity for spiritual maturity. Reading God's Word is the highest priority, but a child who develops a love of books and an ability to read well will be a better student of the Word and of the world in which he lives. That love of reading and books is best created during the window of childhood and young adulthood when your children's hearts and minds are most open to you. Exposure to many good books during that time will not only develop your children intellectually (thinking, vocabulary, writing, and much more), but it will also be a critical component in their spiritual development as Christians. It is not overstating the case to say that Christian parents have an obligation before God to instill a love of reading and books in their children.

IN OUR HOME

It wasn't until we started formally homeschooling Sarah in 1988 that we began our whole-book journey. We read books, talked with friends, listened to speakers, discussed for many hours, used whole-book methods, and developed convictions about the use and effectiveness of books and reading for learning. There were many influences in our lives over the next five to six years that shaped much of what we came to believe— Charlotte Mason's writings, Ruth Beechick, the Andreolas, the Quines, Beautiful Feet Books, Lifetime Books & Gifts, The Elijah Company, Greenleaf Press, and others. That period from the late 1980s through the 1990s was the Golden Age of what we like to call the whole-book movement.. Although it has never coalesced into a widely-recognized school of homeschooling, whenever we meet other homeschooling parents who share our passion for books, we know the whole-book movement lives. WholeHearted Learning is our attempt to keep the whole-books heart beating for another generation.

What Qualities to Look for in a Good Book

A popular t-shirt maxim declares, "So many books...so little time." With so little time in a lifetime to read so many books, there is no time to waste on mediocre or meaningless books. This truth is even more important during the brief years of childhood, when the spirit and mind are being shaped and appetites are being established. Older teens and adults will need to read a wide variety of literature, but childhood is the time to feed developing hearts with the best of literature that will create a high standard of goodness and godliness for wider reading later in life. Saturate their minds with good books and avoid lesser books that would dilute the standard of goodness. Here are some qualities that help define a "good book" for your children.

- **Ageless** — The story and/or illustrations are appealing to both children and adults. The book possesses a distinctive verbal power, visual beauty, or both, that is recognizable by an eight-year-old or an eighty-year-old reader.

- **Timeless** — The characters and themes of the book transcend time and culture. It appeals to the higher ideals and virtues of the human heart, mind, and experience that are meaningful from one generation to another. It is not dated by too many passing cultural terms and references.

- **Living** — It is filled with concepts and ideas that touch the heart and mind. Whether fiction or nonfiction, it holds up a mirror to real life and living ideas. It makes its subject come alive with enlightening insights about real people, real places, and real things. It captures the imagination.

- **Literary** — It is well written with a natural flow of narrative, dialogue, and description. The writing is engaging, clear, and grammatically acceptable. It is a worthy model of the English language used well.

- **Whole** — It tells a complete story that is interesting and satisfying. The characters are developed and believable, the plot is clear and understandable, and there is a satisfying story arc that carries the reader from beginning to ending and ties together the characters and plot. It appeals to both the heart and the mind. There is a sense of satisfaction and closure when it is finished.

- **Redemptive** — The best books reveal literary glimpses of redemption, even if the author is not overtly Christian. Those who reject the redemptive end up with despair, nihilism, or empty humanism. Redemptive literature communicates an underlying reality of hope and the enduring power of good over evil.

- **Inspiring** — A good book is morally uplifting and provides literary models of sound moral character. It feeds the moral imagination and inspires the reader to higher ideals and virtues. It touches the Christian's spirit, regardless of its Christian-ness as a literary work, because it depicts true, honorable, and noble ideas.

- **Creative** — It stimulates the imagination through a creatively developed concept, characters, plot, and action. It reflects the creative spirit of the image of the Creator God in the writer. The author's creative use of words, themes, metaphors, description, and writing style draws in the reader.

Ideas must reach us directly from the mind of the thinker, and it is chiefly by the means of the books they have written that we get in touch with the best minds.

— Charlotte Mason, *Towards a Philosophy of Education*, 1925

But neither fancy nor fiction is to be tolerated in a child's reading in such a form as to excite the mind, or to vitiate the taste of the child. And for the limitation of such reading by a child the child's parent must hold himself always responsible. No pains should be spared to guard the child from mental as well as from physical poison....A child must be led to have an intelligent interest in books that are likely to be helpful to him; and this task calls for skill and tact, as well as patience and persistency on the parent's part. Good books must be looked up by the parent, and when they are put into the child's hand it must be with such words of commendation and explanation as to awaken in the child's mind a desire to become possessed of their contents.

— H. Clay Trumbull, *Hints on Child Training*, 1890

If we want the mind of a child to come alive, we feed him living ideas. Ideas reside in living books, which I think has something to do with the intermingling of story, fact, and author's opinion or viewpoint...Living books, unlike the compressed compilations of textbooks, are laced with emotion, saturated with ideas, and they convey information as well.

— Karen Andreola, *Charlotte Mason Companion,* CMR&S Co., 1998

The fact is, a work of literature should give us ourselves idealized and in a dream, all we wished to be but could not be, all we hoped for but missed. True literature rounds out our lives, gives us consolation for our failures, rebuke for our vices, suggestions for our ambition, hope, and love, and appreciation. To do that it should have truth, nobility, and beauty in a high degree, and our first test of a work of literature should be to ask the three questions, Is it beautiful? Is it true? Is it noble?

— Sherwin Cody, *The Art of Writing and Speaking the English Language,* 1906 (quoted in *The Parents' Review,* Fall 1995)

People's beliefs and priorities and behaviors are affected by what they read and see and hear. They are inclined toward the standards dramatized and advocated in the cultural materials they ingest...It was once understood that great art is that art which inspires and elevates and ennobles its readers and viewers. If society subsists on trashy literature and trashy entertainment, it must be noted that the trash receptacles are the minds and hearts and souls of the people.

— Dr. John A. Howard, founder of Rockford Institute, quoted in *Ft. Worth Star-Telegram* editorial, December 17, 1995

What Makes a Living Book Alive

The current emphasis on whole-book education has grown out of a renewed interest in the writings of Charlotte Mason. She was an articulate promoter and defender of what she called "living books" or books with literary power. She considered living books the worthiest intellectual food for the minds and hearts of children hungry to learn. Her language about books has become a part of the homeschool community, but the question arises, "What makes a living book alive?" A living book is the literary expression of insights and ideas in a single work by a single author who knows and loves the subject about which he or she writes. It is a living book because the author touches the heart of the reader—it speaks to the whole person. In contrast to living books, Miss Mason excoriated textbooks as lifeless, fragmented collections crammed with bare facts and boring information, all at the expense of the ideas that give facts meaning. Textbooks typically lack the touch of human emotion and spirit. Children are sustained by ideas, and ideas are found in living books written by individuals with something to say, not in textbooks written by committees with something to design.

- **Living Classics** — All of the great literary classics are whole, living books. They contain stories that feed the moral imagination, touch the heart, and challenge the intellect. They are classics not simply because someone decided they should be but because each is an enduring story with a life of its own. They are classics because they are living books, not the other way around. They are still alive because they were always alive.

- **Living Whole** — Much of today's literature for children may be whole books, but they often are not living books. Even a literary work by a single author may not touch the heart or emotions. This is true of much of today's juvenile fiction. History can become a mind-numbing, lifeless factualism. In contrast, living history includes lively accounts full of narrative, dialogue, and description.

- **Signs of Life** — If a book is new to you, whether it is fiction or nonfiction, the easiest way to test it for signs of life is a one-page reading. Read the first page aloud to your children. If they show an interest and want to hear more, then it has touched something in their hearts and it shows signs of life. Keep on reading. By the end of the first chapter, you will know for sure if it is a living book worth reading.

Living Book	Textbook
The book is written by a single author, who is a real and knowable person.	The book is written by various authors or contributors, often unknown.
It is the literary expression of the author's own ideas and love of the subject.	Usually a non-literary expression of collected facts about a subject.
It is personal in tone and feel, touching the heart and emotions as well as the intellect.	It is impersonal in tone and feel, dispassionately addressing primarily the intellect.
The author addresses the reader as an intelligent and capable thinker.	The book assumes that the reader needs to be informed or instructed.
Ideas are presented creatively in a way that stimulates the imagination.	Information is presented factually in a way that deadens the imagination.

What Kinds of Books to Avoid

In our media- and marketing-saturated culture, adults and children are inundated with options for what to read. Because packaging and promotion can make even the most vapid reading material seem acceptable ("You can't judge a book by its cover"), it is important to establish some filters and nonnegotiable standards to apply when deciding what to acquire or what to read. Here are some we have found helpful.

- **Abridged Classics** — If you are trying to decide between an abridgment and a whole book, always read the whole book! An abridgment tends to take out the literary qualities that make the book both whole and good, leaving only the bare bones of the story. It strips a classic book of the qualities that made it a classic in the first place. Abridgments also tend to remove spiritual and Christian elements—such as testimonies, biblical references, and prayers—in order to focus primarily on the action. In a *textual abridgment*, both language and concepts are rewritten and dumbed down for easy reading. Avoid these mutilations. In a *condensed abridgment*, the original text, style, and language of the author are retained while nonessential content is either condensed or left out. These are often acceptable for unconfident readers, though not necessary and not desirable. Your best choice? Always the whole book.

- **Formula Fiction** — Don't waste your children's time and minds and your money on mass market and serial fiction. More often than not, it is literary junk food. Assiduously avoid modern romance or feminist themes for your daughters and violent or unrealistic action/adventure themes for your sons. The feminine and masculine types they promote are flawed and fleshly at best, pagan and unbiblical at worst. The tastes and appetites they create are enduring and hard to satisfy. Be cautious even about Christian and historical fiction series.

- **Science Fiction** — In general, it would be wise to avoid science fiction or science fantasy for children, especially stories involving intelligent life from other planets, UFOs or aliens of any kind, the occult, or the supernatural. Reading science fiction too early can lead to a very strong appetite for stories that could, potentially, lead your child away from God. Stick with the good and godly in childhood.

- **Commercial Books** — Just say no to all the cartoon and media character books that are just thinly-veiled advertisements for tie-in products, publications, and productions. They are cheap, mass-produced products for the consumer market. Don't be fooled— labeling twaddle as "educational" or even as "Christian" (and there is a lot of Christian twaddle!) will not make it any less twaddly. If it's about a cartoon character, a movie, a band, a singer, or a celebrity, it's probably not for your library.

- **Basal Readers** — Basal readers are typically a series of graded stories and exercises that progress through levels of base reading skills. No matter how cute or popular some of those readers may seem, your children do not need basal readers to learn how to read. They are sugar to minds that need protein. Your children need to hear and read real language in age-appropriate whole books or in collections of real stories and excerpts. If you use basal readers for beginning reading lessons, do not make the mistake of believing you must finish what you start with the entire series. As soon as your child is reading confidently, ditch the basal readers and start reading real books.

Where the children's story is simply the right form for what the author has to say, then of course readers who want to hear that will read the story or re-read it, at any age...I am almost inclined to set it up as a canon that a children's story which is enjoyed only by children is a bad children's story. The good ones last.

— C. S. Lewis, "On Three Ways of Writing for Children," from *On Stories,* Harcourt Books, 1982, 1966

You have to write the book that wants to be written. And if the book will be too difficult for grown-ups, then you write it for children.

— Madeleine L'Engle (1918-2007), American author and Christian

Rewarding Books

When it's time to spend money on a book, remember: It is the content, not the accolades, that makes a book worthy of your library. However, awards point to recognized quality worth considering. Some of the more visible awards include:

- The Caldecott Medal (Gold), for illustration
- Caldecott Honor Book (Silver), for illustration
- John Newbery Medal, for children's literature
- Parents' Choice Awards, by the Parents' Choice Foundation
- Reading Rainbow Book, featured on the PBS series (1983-2006)
- The Horn Book Award, by *Horn Book Magazine* and the *Boston Globe*
- ABBY, by American Booksellers Assoc./International Reading Assoc.
- Book Sense Award (previously IBBY Honour List), by the International Board on Books for Young People

And I think it possible that by confining your child to blameless stories of child life in which nothing at all alarming ever happens, you would fail to banish the terrors, and would succeed in banishing all that can ennoble them or make them endurable. For in the fairy tales, side by side with the terrible figures, we find the immemorial comforters and protectors, the radiant ones; and the terrible figures are not merely terrible, but sublime.

— C. S. Lewis, "On Three Ways of Writing for Children," from *On Stories,* Harcourt Books, 1982, 1966

We have come from God, and inevitably the myths woven by us, though they contain error, will also reflect a splintered fragment of the true light, the eternal truth that is with God. Indeed only by myth-making, only by becoming "sub-creator" and inventing stories, can Man aspire to the state of perfection that he knew before the Fall. Our myths may be misguided, but they steer however shakily towards the true harbour, while materialistic "progress" leads only to the abyss and the power of evil.

— J. R. R. Tolkien (1892-1973), British author, poet, academic

Fairy tales, then, are not responsible for producing in children fear, or any of the shapes of fear; fairy tales do not give the child the idea of the evil or the ugly; that is in the child already, because it is in the world already., Fairy tales do not give a child his first idea of bogey. What fairy tales give the child is his first clear idea of the possible defeat of bogey. The baby has known the dragon intimately ever since he had an imagination. What the fairy tale provides for him is a St. George to kill the dragon..

— G. K. Chesterton, *Tremendous Trifles,* 1920

How to Evaluate Imaginative Literature

Up until about the middle of the nineteenth century, imaginative literature was not considered appropriate for young children. A child's imagination was carefully guarded, and the only books printed specifically for children were biblical instruction, moral stories, fairy tales, or very childish stories. That would change as the Golden Age of children's literature during the Victorian era brought a flood of classic children's books exploring all imaginative writing styles and genres. Even so, innocence and nobility were still revered. That is all gone now, as are restraints on guarding a child's imagination.

Today, every family will have a slightly different level of tolerance or contempt for various forms of imaginative literature. However, the real issue is rarely the form but rather the content of the work. Whatever the literary form or genre may be—fantasy, fairy tale, fable, myth, allegory—Scripture provides a general principle you can apply to help you evaluate the appropriateness of the content of imaginative literature for your children. Paul provides a useful standard in Philippians 4:8—taken as a whole, is the work characterized by "whatever is true, whatever is noble, whatever is right, whatever is pure, whatever is lovely, whatever is admirable—if anything is excellent or praiseworthy"? Paul admonishes his readers to "think about such things" rather than lesser things. That standard certainly applies to the books we give to our children to read and think about.

However, creating that kind of good and godly standard for your children's reading does not mean they should read only books with no evil characters and no examples of human sinfulness. That would be a very unrealistic and unsatisfying story! Nor does it mean that a few objectionable words or scenes necessarily condemn the whole work. Rather, it means that the book is one in which the main story line is about a character who represents good, the lines of good and evil are sharply drawn, and the symbols and images used are clear and unconfused (e.g., witches and serpents are always evil; angels and lambs are always good). Train your children to look for red flags in the content of various forms of imaginative literature—not just bad words but, more important, bad ideas. When you are evaluating imaginative books, talk with your children about what would make a book's content appropriate or not. The following are some of the popular forms of imaginative literature that you will encounter in family reading.

IN OUR HOME

We love imaginative literature in our home. One of the first things Sarah read at around age six was all seven of C.S. Lewis's Chronicles of Narnia. *We also read them as a family, and the characters inspired role-playing family dramatization, as well as long discussions about the deeper meanings of characters, events, and symbols. As a family of creatives, we are drawn naturally to the ideas, ideals, and insights in the best of imaginative literature. When our children began reading authors like J.R.R. Tolkien, George MacDonald, and others, we often found ourselves embroiled in deep discussions until late at night about God and life which were inspired by the reading of great imaginative books. God made us to respond to stories, and the classic stories of great imaginative literature demand response.*

- **Fable** — A fable is a "little story" (Latin) in prose or verse employing animals, nature, or objects given human qualities (anthropomorphized) to illustrate or teach a timely lesson or a timeless truth. They often end with a memorable maxim or moral that summarizes the lesson. Because fables are simple, usually less sophisticated expressions of wisdom, it is rare to find unacceptable ones. In addition to the venerable *Aesop's Fables*, classic children's stories such as Beatrix Potter's animal fables fall in this category. It is an excellent literary form for teaching biblical truth and wisdom and a good exercise of your young child's moral imagination. The parables of Jesus are similar to fables in form, but they use real people and events.

- **Allegory** — All forms of imaginative literature can use symbolism. Allegory, in its purest literary form, is a story in which symbolic elements, actions, and characters (often personified animals) are used to represent real things, events, ideas, and persons. The purpose of allegory is almost always to illustrate or instruct. The strength of allegory is its ability to communicate more than the words on the page in a way that the reader can understand the deeper meaning. *The Pilgrim's Progress*, John Bunyan's timeless allegory of the Christian life, has lost none of its power over 300 years later. *The Gold Thread* by Norman Macleod (1861) is an allegory of the life of faith for children. The parables of Jesus often employed the symbolic elements of allegory.

- **Fairy Tale** — The fairy tale is a story populated with imagined creatures and elements that takes place in a true-to-life setting. In the typical fairy tale, a supernatural world of some kind intersects with the real world in an incredible story. It employs archetypal characters (kings, princesses, witches) and concepts (good vs. evil). As a bridge to truth, a fairy tale can help children learn to think about spiritual realities that they cannot see; as a wall, it might confuse a younger child about spiritual realities. Hans Christian Andersen used fairy tales to creatively teach Christian truths and values. George MacDonald's fairy tales, such as *The Light Princess*, are examples of great literature imbued with Christian concepts and truths.

- **Fantasy** — Fantasy, like fairy tale, is populated by imagined creatures, but its story usually takes place in an imaginary setting as well. This detachment from reality makes fantasy more difficult to evaluate. Pure fantasy that provides no overlap with the real world of a child or with Christian ideas should raise caution flags for childhood reading. Use of Christian or moral symbolism might bring balance to an otherwise pure fantasy story for your child. Because an appetite for fantasy is difficult to satisfy, it should be only one part of a balanced literary diet during childhood. However, mature fantasy, as a literary form, can powerfully illustrate great truths and provide heartfelt literary examples of character for older children and young adults.

- **Myth** — Myth, legend, epic, and folklore are bigger-than-life stories that usually find their origins in an oral storytelling tradition. They can be historical, instructive, or just for fun, or they might provide insights into an ancient culture's beliefs and false views of God and man. Exposure to some mythologies can contribute to your child's cultural literacy and understanding of mythological allusions in literature, but because they often contain unbiblical supernatural and spiritual elements and beings, they are best studied later in middle and high school. Selected legends and folklore can be interesting in limited doses, but good literature is better.

The only imaginative works we ought to grow out of are those which it would have been better not to have read at all.

— C. S. Lewis (1898-1963), British author, academic, and Christian apologist

It is only a novel...or, in short, only some work in which the greatest powers of the mind are displayed, in which the most thorough knowledge of human nature, the happiest delineation of its varieties, the liveliest effusions of wit and humour, are conveyed to the world in the best-chosen language.

— Jane Austen, *Northanger Abbey*, 1882

An Allegory Story

The Pilgrim's Progress by John Bunyan was first published in 1678. It is the quintessential Christian allegory, written for an adult audience. Despite the widespread acceptance of Bunyan's tale, it would be nearly two hundred years before there would be a Christian allegory written specifically for children, who were at that time limited to moralistic tales, pedagogical works, fairy tales, and innocent stories. Norman Macleod (1812-1872), Queen Victoria's favorite chaplain for fifteen years and pastor of his Glasgow church for twenty-seven years, originally wrote *The Gold Thread: A Story for the Young* for his own beloved children to encourage them to live by faith. It was serialized in 1860 in the first year of *Good Words*, a groundbreaking Christian periodical for the common man and families in England for which Macleod was the first editor. The following year, in 1861, it was released as an illustrated book with engravings by some of England's best illustrators. It would stay continuously in print for over fifty years. Its publication, along with other books for children at the time, marks the beginning of what would become the Golden Age of children's literature.

Children's Classics

There are many more titles that could be included under the collective category of "children's classics," but these are representative of the genre:

- *Heidi*
- *At the Back of the North Wind*
- *Black Beauty*
- *Little Women*
- *Anne of Green Gables*
- *Hans Brinker, or The Silver Skates*
- *The Water-Babies*
- *The Secret Garden*
- *A Little Princess*
- *Kidnapped*
- *Treasure Island*
- *Just David*
- *Pollyanna*
- *The Prince and the Pauper*
- *Rebecca of Sunnybrook Farm*

New Children's Fiction

There are many beloved children's stories written since 1920 that should be on your reading list. Here are a few:

- *The Chronicles of Narnia*
- *Treasures of the Snow*
- *Where the Red Fern Grows*
- *Little Britches*
- *Little House on the Prairie*
- *Charlotte's Web*
- *A Wrinkle in Time*

Historical Fiction

Historical fiction is a rich vein of both good stories well-told and good writing. Examples include:

- *The Bronze Bow*
- *The Door in the Wall*
- *The Trumpeter of Krakow*
- *The Courage of Sarah Noble*
- *The Matchlock Gun*
- *Amos Fortune, Free Man*
- *Carry On, Mr. Bowditch*
- *Johnny Tremain*
- *Caddie Woodlawn*
- *Sarah, Plain and Tall*
- *Across Three Aprils*
- *Thee, Hannah*

How to Evaluate Fictional Literature

A work of fiction, most commonly in the form of the novel, is an imaginative work of literature that tells a complete story with narrative, dialogue, characterization, and plot. Classic children's literature is written for children yet also enjoyed by adults. Novels are most often recognized for their literary qualities, as well as for their well-conceived and well-told stories. They are often examples of the best use of the English language. Stories have the power to teach important lessons, illustrate good character and godliness, and impact the heart for good. Selecting and reading the right kinds of fiction for your children can plant in their hearts literary models of nobility, courage, sacrifice, and other virtues that will stay with them their entire lives.

- **Classic Children's Literature** — Classic children's literature, most of which was written between 1860 and 1920, is unique in its literary quality, characterizations, and narrative power. The best writers of the day wrote to a new publishing market for children, before other media and markets drew them away in the early twentieth century. It truly was a Golden Age for children's literature, and much of it was imbued with Christian truth, virtues, and principles that reflected the values of the Victorian age. Though interest will vary with age, the content is almost always acceptable.

- **Contemporary Children's Fiction** — Many good books have been written for children in the last hundred years, but stories reflecting Christian values and virtues that were more culturally common in the Golden Age are now rarer, replaced by a secularized vision of a child's world that often disdains Victorian innocence as outdated. There are wonderful works of Christian fiction for children that will stand the literary tests of time, but they are seldom popular and might require extra effort to find.

- **Historical Fiction** — This genre has generated some wonderful books for children. It seems like the serious writers are often drawn more to historical fiction for children than to general fiction, perhaps because it is a bigger market (schools) and there are fewer constraints when writing about real people and events. Christians can be accurately portrayed in historical fiction, whether it is about real events (fictionalized history) or imagined ones (historical fiction). This is a rich genre of great reading for your children, with wonderful stories that capture the imagination and teach history.

- **Action/Adventure** — If you look for the best literary examples of action and adventure stories, this can be a great genre of fiction for your children. Young boys, especially, respond enthusiastically to hearing or reading a great adventure yarn, and that can be an incentive to help get them started on reading. There are children's classics like Robert Louis Stevenson's books, but even modern adventure fables like the Redwall series by Brian Jacques will keep children reading and wanting more.

- **Moral Story** — The moral story, a Christian form of storytelling, became popular during the Victorian era of the family circle. The purpose of the moral story is to teach a lesson about Christian virtue, wisdom, character, or godliness. The story can be based on actual events, but most are fictional stories set in real life. It is similar to a parable in its function of instructing the young and teaching a lesson, but it typically contains no symbolic or imaginative elements. Moral stories were written to be easily read and understood by children, so they are not often examples of literary quality.

Manage Home Media

Your children will grow up in a media-saturated world. You can and should build their appetites and learning first and foremost around reading and books. Books are always the priority of a wholehearted learning home. However, media is also a rich source of learning, and it is important to manage and train children's use of media at home.

- **Audio** — Audio is the safest media source and includes cassettes, CDs, and digital audio. The strength of audio media is that it is not entirely passive—it requires your children to listen to and process what they are hearing and direct other senses to other tasks at the same time. Your children can listen to an audiobook while drawing or coloring in a picture or moving around the room. Although not as powerful as a parent reading aloud, it is a good alternative. Audio also includes listening to and enjoying all forms of recorded music, dramatized books and audio drama, and recorded historical events, as well as admiring a good storyteller or learning from a good teacher or preacher. Audio should be your first-choice form of home media.

- **Video** — Broadcast or cable/satellite television should be limited or avoided altogether for young children. There are no truly safe channels on television for children. Any discussion of video home media needs to begin with two caveats: (1) video viewing can quickly become a sinkhole of wasted time and a poor babysitter, and (2) unwanted video images, even briefly viewed, can implant in a child's brain for a lifetime. So first, be wise and cautious with your use of video, especially with young children. A thoughtfully managed home media library will have a wide selection of video topics—education, creation science, nature, history, great movies, how-it-works, how-to, do-it-yourself, documentaries, and much more. Video viewing as part of your home learning should be infrequent in the younger years, increasing with age. Don't use video as a training medium for early reading—the brain processes words on a screen as moving images that are passively consumed (the image moves, not the eye). Reading fixed print requires the eye to track the words on a page and actively decode them. Stick with books, not videos, for reading.

- **Digital** — Digital media at home includes computer software, the Internet, and mobile media and apps. Nearly all forms of fixed media for children are migrating in some way to the Internet and mobile apps. As audio, video, and digital media converge into one home system that is connected continuously, digital media will become the primary delivery channel for much of home media. The Internet offers an almost limitless selection of learning opportunities, and many are interactive to allow a child to become more engaged in the learning process or presentation. However, the Internet is a dangerous place, so if there is something on the Internet you want to use, be sure you install a filter such as CovenantEyes, bSafe, or SafeEyes to prevent any unwanted or unintentional intrusions on your monitor. For young children, it is best to avoid the Internet and purchase software or apps to load on your home computer or mobile device. There are many child-friendly educational applications, interactive history programs, creative programs, and much more you can use. As your children get older, you will need to determine if and when to allow more access to the Internet for research, social interaction, interactive learning, and self-directed learning.

Average is way too much!

Most Christian homeschooling families reading this will be way below average when it comes to media consumption. Nonetheless, it is good to know what is going on in millions of other families, just for perspective. However, the data seem to change as quickly as the seasons as teens and young adults expand their participation in the growing markets of social media (Facebook, Twitter, YouTube, MySpace), mobile media (smart phones, tablet computers, MP3 players, book devices), and entertainment media (video games, digital video, online games). Whether it is traditional media or new media, usage will likely increase in the future the more connected and plugged in to the digital grid we become.

- American teens and adults in 2007 spent an average of 3,518 hours consuming media—TV, movies, music, Internet, newspaper. (U.S. Census Bureau)

- Among 8-18-year-olds, average total media exposure per day is 10 hours 45 minutes to TV, music/audio, computer, video games, print, movies. (2010 Kaiser Foundation report)

- Americans watch TV an average of 4 hours 49 minutes per day, up 20% from 1999. (2009 Nielsen report)

- The average cell phone user age 18 and under sends or receives 2,779 text messages per month. (2010 Nielsen report)

- Among 8-18-year-olds, 76% own an iPod/MP3 player, 66% a cell phone, and 29% a laptop. (2010 Kaiser Foundation report)

- The average child will spend 18,000 hours in front of a TV by the time they graduate high school. That's 5,000 hours more than they will spend in school for 12 years.

Listen, my son, to your father's instruction and do not forsake your mother's teaching.

— Proverbs 1:8

[M]ethod is natural; easy, yielding, unobtrusive, simple as the ways of Nature herself; yet, watchful, careful, all-pervading, all-compelling...The parent who sees his way—that is, the exact force of method—to educate his child, will make use of every circumstance of the child's life almost without intention on his own part, so easy and spontaneous is a method of education based upon Natural Law. Does the child eat or drink, does he come, or go, or play—all the time he is being educated, though he is as little aware of it as he is of the act of breathing.

— Charlotte Mason, *Home Education*, 1886.

Methodical Attitudes

Your attitude toward whatever method you are using is at least as important as your skill in using it. If you project a negative attitude toward a method, your children will sense it and reflect your own negativity. It is better to use a less-desirable method with a smile than a great method with a scowl! Your attitude should be enthusiastic and positive about the methods you choose and use.

Use a Variety of Methods

Methods are all the things you do to teach your children. Your methods may even be defined by things you don't do. They are how you teach what you teach. In section 3, we'll go into detail about several dozen representative methods you can use in a Whole-Hearted Learning approach to homeschooling, but before drilling down into that detail, you should see methods as one of the elements that contribute to creating a wholehearted learning home. You may not be consciously aware of it, but you are using a method whenever you read aloud to your children, help them with a math problem, or tell them to go work on the computer. How you do the tasks of teaching are your methods, whether you are systematic and predictable, intuitive and spontaneous, goal-oriented, or nonstructured. It is impossible to teach without using methods.

No matter how you teach, understanding teaching methods will help you become a better home educator. As you discover the methods that reflect your philosophy of teaching and learning or that just seem to work better with your children, it makes sense to try to understand and master those methods so you can be more effective. However, your goal is always to master the methods without letting them master you. The methods you use should never become more important than what is being learned. Use specific methods only if they work for you and your family and only if they are serving your purposes (instead of you serving them). Different methods work differently in different families. You will have to discover for yourself what works best for your family.

The methods discussed in section 3 are not just classroom teaching techniques carried over to a homeschool setting—they are personal tutoring skills that you can use with your child. They emphasize the relational process inherent in home learning, as opposed to the instructional procedures of a classroom setting. The relationship you enjoy with your children is, by God's design, the most powerful factor in their education. In many ways your are patterning your teaching after the relationship of Jesus to his disciples, so you can even call it "Christ-like instruction." The methods we describe in the next section will reinforce that relational quality. In fact, many of the methods we suggest have the positive result of not only helping your children learn the subject matter but also helping both you and your children learn how to relate to one another better. They are family-building learning methods.

IN OUR HOME

Both of us came to Christ in college in the mid-1970s, became involved with the discipleship ministry of Campus Crusade for Christ, and brought those principles with us into adulthood and marriage. We cut our teaching teeth on the Crusade model of personal relationship and discipleship, and it was very natural to apply that to parenting and then to homeschooling. We tried some formal methods early on but could sense when relationship started to become secondary to a method or formula. It was then that we began to develop our own convictions about the power of personal relationship in our children's hearts and lives, not only in parenting, but also in homeschooling. Those convictions became WholeHearted Learning.

Thinking about Methods

When I think of teaching methods, I think of the bread recipes we use at home. Each kind of bread—whole-wheat loaf, dinner rolls, pizza dough, cinnamon buns, herb bread—shares the same basic ingredients, but proportions and seasonings differ, and the way each one is put together differs. And yet they all make bread. It's the same with teaching methods. There are some basic methods you will always use, there are less common methods you will use only occasionally, and the mix you use will vary depending on the result you want to achieve. With standard curriculum, it's the same recipe and the same old plain white bread every time. But you are a master baker, an inspired teacher. Think about methods as the ingredients for creating a mind-watering, soul-fulfilling, heart-stirring learning experience for your children. Your special recipes will leave them asking for more because what you serve up is so good. That is your goal as a home educator: using your creativity to make learning delicious!

- **Think simple and natural.** Like the rest of us, your thinking about learning has probably been deeply influenced by a formal, institutional model of education. It may take a step of faith for you to leave the familiar old world and false security of textbooks, workbooks, and classrooms and step into the new world and freedom of real books and real life. Once you do, though, you and your children will be able to relax and genuinely enjoy learning. The old way will seem like so much regulated drudgery; the new way will turn homeschooling into a natural part of family life. Don't be afraid of methods that are simple and natural—that is how learning should be.

- **Think informal and creative.** Once you have converted to an informal, whole-book approach to learning, it's not uncommon to slowly slip back into the old ways of formal classroom and curricular education. You can avoid that, though, if you train yourself to think creatively about the methods you are using and to maintain an informal learning atmosphere. Remember, God has put your children into a home to learn, not into a school. Use methods that reinforce the natural strengths of your home and appeal to the home-centered interests and desires of your children.

- **Think confidence and success.** The more comfortable you become with Whole-Hearted Learning, the more you can relax and focus attention on your children rather than on curricular demands. Your goal is to build their confidence in their own learning skills and abilities. By selecting methods that encourage them to do their own learning and thinking, you are training your children to be independent learners—not dependent upon your teaching or curricula for them to learn. You are also guiding their learning by setting them up to succeed, not to fail or to settle for mediocrity. Use methods that encourage good effort, challenge weak areas, and reward progress and accomplishment, not just right answers.

- **Think Jesus and his disciples.** Jesus said, "A student is not above his teacher, but everyone who is fully trained will be like his teacher" (Luke 6:40). You are a teacher like Jesus, discipling your children, showing them the way to maturity not only in Christian living but also in learning, and preparing them to live wholeheartedly for God. Jesus constantly used methods to teach his disciples so they would be prepared to lead the new church. His goal was to make them like him—to become like their Teacher. Relational methods will help you raise a fully trained child for Christ.

For some children and for some of the time, certain books will happen to be just right. But if you find yourself struggling to mold your child to a book, try reversing priorities. It's the child you are teaching, not the book. Bend the book, or find another; make the studies fit the child.

— Ruth Beechick, *You Can Teach Your Child Successfully*, Arrow Press, 1993

Let's see that our children have daily opportunities to have an opinion, to make a judgment, no matter how crude, to develop a train of thought and to use their imaginations.

— Karen Andreola, Charlotte Mason Research & Supply

Scope and Sequence

The concept of scope (subjects of study) and sequence (order of study) arose when age-grading became the norm in conventional schools. In that closed learning environment, a standardized system was needed to make sure the teacher covered the right material in the right sequence in the right grade level. Scope and sequence was not created for the children, but rather for the teachers and administrators. There is no such thing as a universal scope and sequence that applies to all children at all times. Since you do not march lockstep in the age/grade parade, you do not need a scope and sequence. Nonetheless, a scope and sequence can be a handy tool to help you evaluate what your children know and don't know at any given point. It's for the parent's benefit, though, not the child's. Use a scope and sequence primarily to evaluate past learning, not to plan future learning. Upon reaching an age or grade milestone, check the scope and sequence to see if you've covered most of the material considered necessary up to that point.

Evaluate Curricula and Workbooks

If you have ever wandered the aisles in a large curriculum fair, you know the temptations of formal, packaged, age-graded curricula. Whether it is full-color products from a big publishing house or a photocopied and hand-bound product from a small family business, the lure is the same. It's a neat, clean, just-add-child learning resource. By its nature, curriculum holds the promise of easy teaching, but that promise—whether or not it should be considered desirable—is not always fulfilled. Even if it is, it brings with it the potential to cultivate curriculum dependence, either by default because it is what you were raised on, by accident because you haven't yet broken the curriculum habit, or even by fear because an underlying lack of confidence accuses you of needing more than what God has enabled you to give.

If you have made the switch to a whole-book, wholehearted approach to home education or you are somewhere on that journey, you don't need to be tempted by curriculum. You're beginning to discover that books are a much better investment of your educational funds than yet one more curriculum that equates learning with filling in blanks and selecting from multiple choices. Part of the liberation of learning in your home will be throwing off the tyranny of textbooks and breaking the grip of curriculum. It is finding the freedom to not choose curriculum because you realize that you are able to teach your children with or without that curriculum. You are free to choose to use a curriculum or not. You do not need to be curriculum-dependent!

There is a lively and well-stocked cottage industry among homeschoolers selling all of the used curriculum that has been cleared from others' libraries. Many times, the curriculum was never really even used, but simply purchased and passed over. You might save a few dollars shopping at the used curriculum tables at homeschool book fairs, but you can save even more by observing what is on those tables. It is nearly a rite of passage for new homeschooling families to buy curriculum that ends up gathering dust on the shelf. Usually it turns out to require more preparation and involvement than they are willing to invest, or when they get it home they realize it just doesn't fit their lifestyle. It becomes an investment in experience. What we all learn, though, is that any curriculum is only a tool—it doesn't really teach anything. The attitude and commitment of the teacher are far more important than the real or perceived effectiveness of the tool. So if it doesn't work, don't worry. Put your unused used curriculum on the table with everyone else's and buy real books next time. You're experienced now.

You and your children need never be enslaved by curriculum again. That doesn't mean you won't ever use curriculum as part of a wholehearted, whole-book homeschool, but only that you will never have to feel that you *must* use curriculum. You may choose to use curriculum, but you will do so knowing you are the master of it, not the other way around. You are also free to choose not to use a curriculum but instead to find a real-book and real-life way to teach your children. The most important factor in choosing a curriculum is not the reputation or promise of the curriculum—it is your own sense of direction and confidence as a homeschooling parent. If you have a clear purpose and plan for your children's learning and you have asked God to lead you, then the question of curriculum is a spiritual issue, and you can trust the Holy Spirit to guide your decision.

What to Ask Yourself When Considering Curriculum

When you are considering a formal curriculum, take a moment to ask yourself the questions below. They are not intended to create a de facto argument against using curriculum but rather to provide questions you may not otherwise ask—to help you evaluate whether and when to use a curriculum, discern quality and content, remind you that there are other ways to look at the curriculum decision, and reinforce your desire to pursue a more wholehearted approach to your homeschooling.

- Can I teach this subject naturally without a curriculum? What will this curriculum do for my children that they or I cannot do without it? Is it really necessary?

- Does this curriculum complement my personal teaching style and my child's learning style? Will it be a delight or a duty to complete this curriculum?

- Do I really need this curriculum, or is it just another safety net to spread beneath my unresolved insecurity and uncertainty? Am I curriculum dependent?

- How much teacher preparation does this curriculum require? Will the result really be worth the time and energy costs? Is this curriculum really cost-effective?

- Does this curriculum fit into my life and my child's life right now? Does it make sense to be adding it in light of our current studies, commitments, or constraints?

- What good books on the subject could I buy with the money it would take to buy this curriculum? What whole books would allow my children to learn about this subject?

- Am I just attracted to the curriculum's packaging and promotion? Am I judging the book by its cover or by it contents? Does its packaging promise too much?

- Do I personally know anyone who is using or recommending this curriculum? Have I read any good reviews of it? Do people I like and agree with endorse it?

- Does the tone of the writing appeal to my children's maturing appetites or to their immaturity and childishness? Does it speak up to or down to my children?

- Is this product really creative or just clever? Am I letting cost and complexity suggest effectiveness? Is this educational gimmickry, or is it an effective learning tool?

IN OUR HOME

One of the most liberating realizations we came to in our early homeschooling, at a time when we were a bit more curriculum dependent than we would later be, was that we were in charge of the curriculum. It did not have to be completed to be useful and effective. (That's a hard sell for perfectionist husbands.) We learned how to skip large parts of a math text that were just post-summer review for returning classroom students. We learned that we could pick and choose from lessons and move ahead if material had been covered elsewhere or was already understood. We learned that we could skip some of the repetitive, mind-numbing drill questions. We learned that we were the masters of the curriculum. We learned freedom.

Curricular Minimums

For most studies in a Whole-Hearted Learning approach, curriculum is unnecessary. However, there is a legitimate need for some curriculum in the early years when studying the basics (Disciplined Studies). We recommend using a written curriculum for math and for language arts, although it is possible to do either without curriculum. Workbooks are generally more child-friendly than textbooks, but you can decide. The key is to remember that you are in control and that God will direct you to determine what is best for your family and children. Don't listen to the guilt-driven message that you might be depriving your child of the best education if you don't use a particular curriculum. You might be depriving them of the best wholehearted education if you do!

Select the Text

As a general rule, stay away from textbooks and workbooks that are written specifically for the institutional school classroom. School is not a home, and classrooms are about generalization and conformity, not individuals. Trying to retrofit a curriculum written for a classroom into your home learning model will be frustrating at best and distracting and counterproductive at worst. There are plenty of curricula that have been written for the home with the individual child in view. They will serve you better. Also, remember that every curriculum is written by someone with a worldview. Be sure you agree with the beliefs and values that are either explicit or implicit in the curriculum text. You are always safer choosing curricula created by Christian publishers, but you should still know the theological views that underlie what is in their texts.

Art-Quality Colored Pencils

There is a noticeable difference between inexpensive colored pencils (such as Crayola and RoseArt) and more costly art-quality colored pencils (such as Sanford Prismacolor). Art-quality pencils use a special formula of wax, binder, and pigment that yields a softer "lead" and richer, truer colors (no lead is actually used in colored pencils). Unlike typical colored pencils, which use a harder color core, art-quality pencil colors can be more easily and effectively blended and shaded. They are responsive to pressure, so a light touch yields a soft, gentle hue, and a firmer stroke leaves a bold, strong hue, giving your children far greater flexibility and range of expression in their artistry. Artists also use quality erasable colored pencils (such as Prismacolor Col-Erase) for sketching and greater detail. Consumer-grade colored pencil sets, which once were known as "map colors" for elementary students, are certainly easier on the budget, but if you want to create an appetite for artistic expression in your children start with art-quality colored pencils.

Basic Supplies

- Pens, pencils, colored pencils, felt-tip markers, crayons, chalk, sidewalk chalk, water-colors
- Rulers, scissors, tape, glue, hole punch, pencil sharpener, erasers, compass, shape templates, stencils, stapler, paper clips, rubber bands
- Paper—white bond, lined writing paper, colored construction sheets, large and small sketch pads, newsprint
- Poster board, foam board, felt, cardboard sheets
- Loose-leaf notebooks, report covers, ringed binders
- Chalk board (chalk, erasers), white board (dry erase markers, eraser), bulletin board(s), art easel

Maintain Materials and Supplies

There is always the temptation to recreate the classroom in the home. If you've ever browsed through one of those classroom supply catalogs or stores, you surely know the lure of all those cute, brightly-colored, creative, and expensive educational doodads. The math section is particularly enticing with all those counters, attribute blocks, base ten boards and interlocking cubes, and the countless books and workbooks for using them all. The bottom line is that schools have lots of money (yours!) to spend on those things...you don't. Just keep in mind all the great books you could buy with the same money.

There is also the temptation to think home education happens only within the four walls of your home. But the reality is that learning can happen everywhere, including outside and when you are in the car. When you are planning how to create a home where learning happens, don't forget to plan for extending that home learning environment beyond your walls to the yard and car. Here are some inside, outside, and roadside ideas.

Inside Supplies

- **Do It Yourself** — The basic principle governing all this stuff is that you can nearly always (1) do just fine without it, (2) find an inexpensive alternative, or (3) duplicate the stuff at no cost using materials you have at home. An obvious example: You don't need cute little rubber bears for counting. Marbles, beans, candy, or any number of things will do just fine. Construct your own rods or counting cubes with the jillions of plastic interlocking blocks you probably already have. Be creative!

- **Enough Is Enough** — Some educational stuff can be good and useful, to be sure. However, it is rarely necessary. So don't buy too much of a good thing. A nice set of shape and attribute blocks is interesting and fun. However, you don't need a 200-piece set—that's for a whole elementary classroom! Just get the basic starter set.

- **Colored Pencils** — Colored pencils are better than crayons and markers. European kids, who've known this for years, carry theirs in nifty little pencil boxes with pop-up pencil holders. They last a long time, sharpen easily with less mess, allow for much more precision and artistic expression, don't smear, provide truer and blendable colors, don't dry out like felt-tip markers, and don't break in half like crayons (or melt in the car in summer). Start with inexpensive map colors for everyday drawing or discover the delight of art-quality colored pencils.

- **Paper** — If you have children who enjoy drawing and doodling, buy your paper in bulk or look for sources of discarded paper. If you have a source of used computer paper (copy centers) or newsprint (newspapers), you can collect and use it for everyday drawing. Don't forget to recycle your own computer paper discards—your children can use the unprinted side for when they are doodling or sketching.

- **Organize** — Supplies can get quickly out of hand, so include some organizers in your plan—boxes, files, notebooks, binders, drawer units, plastic bags, and anything that can hold things and be labeled. Unfortunately, you still have to train your children to actually use the organizers to keep your supplies organized.

Outside Supplies

- **Sand** — While a sandbox sounds like a toddler recreational area, a sandlot can become a creative play area for both younger and older children. If you are able, create a large area bordered by landscape timbers filled with good sand that packs well. Make sure it's drained and have water available. If you build it, they will play.

- **Plants** — Create a small garden area with a small storage box or shed. Provide garden tools, seeds, watering equipment, and books. Then watch them grow!

- **Fun** — Kids love to climb on things and be active. If you don't want them in your trees, provide some climbing areas, rope swings, a zip line, and more.

- **Gear** — Provide sports gear: balls, gloves, basketball backboard, tetherball, volleyball net, pitch-back screen, soccer goals, horseshoes, and more.

- **Games** — Provide supplies and ideas that keep them outside when there are friends and nice weather—laser tag gear, capture the flag, reenactment equipment, and more.

- **Nature** — Provide all sorts of nature discovery tools—field guides, collection boxes and displays, magnifiers, binoculars, telescope, sketchbooks, and more.

Roadside Supplies

- **Creativity** — Think creatively about the backseat of your car and the time that your children sit there when you are on the road. Give them interesting things to listen to, look at, read, and do rather than just zoning out. Redeem that time. Be creative.

- **Audiobooks** — Always keep audiobooks in the car to listen to a book or drama whenever you'll be on the road for more than ten minutes. Load an inexpensive MP3 player with audiobooks that will be exclusively for listening in the car.

- **Travel Bag** — Put together a car travel bag of educational and entertaining resources: illustrated storybooks, drawing materials, challenging puzzle books, favorite magazines, educational activity books, supplemental disciplined study workbooks, and the like. Leave it in the car or take it with you where you are going. Assemble a travel bag for each child that will be used only in the car.

Travel Study

Your car is more than just transportation—it is also a mobile learning environment. Most families spend more time in the car than they care to admit, but it doesn't have to be wasted time. You have the advantage of a captive audience for a defined period of undistracted time in a controlled environment. Use it! Make the most of any trip you take as a family, even if it is just for a weekend. Find out in advance about any special history of the city or region and plan some time for a driving or walking tour. If it is a well-known historical or natural site, plan a unit study or a book and context study. Do extra research and ask local residents about any special out-of-the-way museums, interesting businesses, unusual architecture, or hidden historical sites you might otherwise miss.

IN OUR HOME

We have taken many long trips together as a family for our ministry events and conferences. On one particularly long drive that would take us from Nashville to southern California and back, I (Clay) wanted to make sure our four children had things to do on the road but also some way to stay organized. I bought four fabric attaché-style bags and carefully filled each with an assortment of creative and educational supplies— sketchbooks, notebooks, new colored pencils, pens, pencils, maps, a personally selected Klutz book, audiobook and music CDs, an inexpensive portable CD player, a disposable camera, and other personalized stuff. It was fun for me to do, and it was fun for them to get.

Gaps Are Normal

Don't become anxious because of what your child hasn't covered or does not yet know. If your child is reading widely, whatever holes there may be will be filled in over time. Remember, you are not marching to the beat of the age/grade drum. If you find a topic not yet covered in your reading and other studies, you can simply work it into discussions, nature study, or wherever it most naturally fits, and quickly move on.

Decide about Tests and Grades

Most of us are so indoctrinated by conventional school methods that the fundamental law of classroom instruction is etched on our minds: Thou shalt test and grade thy children. Only it is not a fundamental law of homeschooling. In fact, it is not a fundamental law of education at all—only of classroom teachers. Testing and grading have gained ascendancy only since the advent of public schooling in the last 150 years or so, more as a matter of administrative expediency than instructional necessity. Before that, students were tested orally to determine whether or not they knew a subject—the ability to discuss a concept was as important as the ability to remember a fact. Tests and grades reduce the learning process to getting the right answer. But your children can become highly educated and go to most colleges without ever taking a paper test or receiving a grade. The bottom line is that unless your state law requires it, you don't have to test and grade any more than you have to take roll everyday. You're free to do what is best.

- **Useful?** Grades measure both what your children have learned and what they have *not* yet learned. However, does it make any sense to grade your children for what they have not yet completely learned or understood? Wouldn't it be just as effective simply to continue teaching until they have learned or acquired the skill?

- **Accurate?** If lack of self-discipline is a problem, a poor grade will do nothing to motivate your child to be more diligent. If character is the problem, then your child needs to be properly disciplined and trained, not academically shamed by a poor grade.

- **Motivating?** Standard grading (A, B, C, D, F) can create a motivation to do better or to not do badly. But does allowing mediocrity as an acceptable grade in your home encourage excellence? Your children's best should be judged by their ability, not by an arbitrary or even a curricular standard. When you take away grades, the standard becomes personal excellence in order to please God, parents, and self.

- **Effective?** Testing is just the vehicle for grading. If you tell your child to complete an assignment, does it make it any more effective to call it a test? If you want to know what your child has learned, just ask.

- **Necessary?** There simply is no real need for a record of grades in elementary and middle-school years. Keep one if it is required by your state, but keep it private and confidential.

IN OUR HOME

Our children never worry about tests and grades...they're too busy learning. If anyone asks, we'll tell them our kids are straight-A, honor-roll students! Learning is not a competition to win the most A's in our home. Rather, learning is like any other responsibility we give to our children. One of Our 24 Family Ways *says, "In our family, we do our work promptly and thoroughly to the very best of our ability." That applies equally to the work of learning. The standard is always personal excellence, which is why the only "grade" given for work is "well done" when it is correctly completed. We always expect "best of my A-bility" work in our home.*

Use Age-Integrated Studies

The instructional methods you choose should allow you to do as much as possible in as little time as possible with as much integration of learning as possible. That means minimizing textbook- and workbook-based studies, which are inherently more teacher- and time-intensive, and maximizing whole-book studies, which naturally integrate all age levels. In a whole-book, literature-based approach to home education, all ages can be involved at their own level of ability. It is roughly analogous to the age-integrated one-room schoolhouses of the nineteenth century, except that home and family provide a far better learning environment than a school. When children of varying ages in a family have been trained to listen and learn together, more can be done in less time, leaving more time for other pursuits. It also creates a sense of unity and togetherness that independent, individual study does not. When siblings are all on the same page in their studies, that shared experience will strengthen their family bonds.

- **Focus on books.** Age integration can be easily and effectively used for reading aloud, history and geography, fine arts, science and nature, and other areas of study. Obviously, though, it is not as useful for disciplined studies such as math and language arts studies. Schedule your day to allow your children to accomplish the disciplined studies first so you can focus on book-centered discussion studies without distraction.

- **Think young.** The success of most age-integrated study depends on your providing an age-appropriate way for 4-6-year-olds to participate, especially during a reading time. It might be giving them a specific task to accomplish or just something that will engage their hands yet leave them free to listen and interact. You also need to develop a tolerance of the wiggles, especially in little boys. Allow younger children to move around as long as they do not become a distraction and as long as they are listening to what you are reading or discussing.

- **All can narrate.** Younger children (under age six) can be included in narrations if they volunteer on their own. Have your children narrate starting with the youngest (of listening age) and progressing up in age. If a younger child wants to narrate like his older siblings but needs help, ask one or two simple questions about the reading to prompt his narration. Older children do not need questions to prompt their narrations.

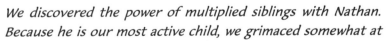

IN OUR HOME

We discovered the power of multiplied siblings with Nathan. Because he is our most active child, we grimaced somewhat at the prospect of integrating him into our normal reading routines. We discovered that even though he needed to move and wiggle much more than Sarah and Joel, he was developing a habit of attention just by being there and listening during reading times. At age six, Nathan could sit still and listen to a reading for an hour just like his older brother and sister. He is bearing the fruit of Sally's patient tolerance of his small interruptions, his wiggly energy, and his budding extroversion. She also trained him early by reading shorter books and storybooks to him and then gradually moving up to chapter books. Patience and progress are the keys with younger children.

Small Suggestions

Age-integrated study requires both spontaneity and patience on the part of the parent. You need to be prepared to respond spontaneously as needs arise but also to be patient with your younger children. The following are some ways to make it work.

- **Start with the youngest.** Start family reading aloud times with a good illustrated storybook of your younger child's choosing.

- **Provide activities.** Give younger children something to do while sitting and listening to a reading, such as drawing, coloring a relevant picture, or making a salt-dough sculpture.

- **Allow alternate input.** If older children draw and label a map for a history reading, have the younger ones color a copy of the same map.

- **Encourage interaction.** Have your children illustrate on a blackboard or marker board what you are reading (visual narration).

- **Involve older children.** Have an older child read to the younger children if you need time to prepare or to work with another child individually.

- **Create quality distractions.** Have a favorite illustrated storybook ready for a child to read in a favorite chair; wait for the right time.

- **Provide positive reactions.** If the younger child becomes tired and distracted during a reading, give him a task to do; don't scold him.

- **Include visuals.** If you are working through a unit study, always include some pictures and storybooks that will appeal to your younger children.

Unless the LORD builds the house, its builders labor in vain. Unless the LORD watches over the city, the watchmen stand guard in vain. In vain you rise early and stay up late, toiling for food to eat—for he grants sleep to those he loves. Sons are a heritage from the LORD, children a reward from him. Like arrows in the hands of a warrior are sons born in one's youth. Blessed is the man whose quiver is full of them. They will not be put to shame when they contend with their enemies in the gate.

— Psalm 127

Work with Your Home and It Will Work with You

Your house is not just a material shell of bricks and boards in which homeschooling will happen. Ideally, your house is meant to be where home will happen—a dynamic environment where living and learning go on all the time. It is in some way telling that in both biblical Hebrew and Greek there is no specific word for the small social unit that we call family. Rather, the same words used to refer to a house (the physical dwelling place) are also used to refer to the household within it (those who are bound together by sharing the same dwelling place). In other words, Scripture seems to suggest a symbiotic relationship between the house and the people in the house. In English, we use the word "home" to capture the extended meaning of that relationship.

It is similar to the biblical truth that God requires a dwelling place among his people—the tabernacle, the temple, the believer's body (1 Corinthians 6:19). When John said of Jesus, "The Word became flesh and made his dwelling among us" (John 1:14), he was literally saying that Jesus "tabernacled" among us. Jesus told his disciples, "In My Father's house are many dwelling places; if it were not so, I would have told you; for I go to prepare a place for you" (John 14:2, NASB). There is a natural longing in our spirits to be part of God's household and to live in our eternal home with him. Perhaps it also parallels the truth that even our spirits need a place to live and dwell (1 Corinthians 15:35-49).

What does all this mean for you and your house as a homeschooling family? We have found in our nearly three decades of parenting and homeschooling that our home—the physical place where we dwell as a family—is not just a structure. It is, by God's design, a dynamic and critical component in cultivating the spiritual life of our family. We believe that God designed the home to work with us, especially as a homeschooling family, if we will work with it. It is not just passive walls but a kind of lived-in assistant—a nearly living entity that comes alive with the Spirit of God if we will pay attention to all the ways God designed us to live in and interact with our dwelling place with him.

Deuteronomy 6:1-9, as we have mentioned before, is the most important passage to the identity of Israel—it is a command and a call to follow God and teach future generations about him. Parents are commanded to diligently teach the words of God (the Law) to their children all the time in every place, which Moses described as sitting, lying down, and rising up "in your house." The words of God were also to be carried on their bodies. And, in the final verse of that passage, they were to "write them on the doorposts of your house and on your gates" (NASB). A house is not a neutral structure in God's design for our spiritual life as a family; it is integral to our life in Christ.

As a homeschooling family, it is very easy to fall into thinking about your home in a very utilitarian way. It fulfills a function, but not much else—it keeps you warm and dry and provides a place to keep your stuff, eat, sleep safely, and live your lives. Frankly, that is probably how most think about their home by default. But let us challenge you to see your home in a new way as an active entity waiting to be involved in the spiritual life of your family. Your home is waiting to help you with your homeschooling too. God designed the home to be the place where your children live and learn most naturally. That is part of the vision that drives our concept of cultivating a wholehearted home. If you work with your home, it (and God) will work with you.

— Chapter 8 —

The WholeHearted Learning Child: Understanding Your Child

Personality and Learning Styles

It doesn't require a college degree to know that children come fully fitted with personality right out of the womb. Time, growth, and life experience will not add new aspects of personality to the new person but will only gradually reveal and add new layers of expression. The big question is not whether there really is a thing we call personality but whether there are distinct kinds of human personalities that can be described, differentiated, limited, and categorized. Beyond that, there is the question of how personality might affect the learning process and even the teaching process. Those questions have spawned a multitude of opinions and a multifaceted educational consulting industry.

Though Scripture is filled with many different and distinct personalities, there is nonetheless no discernible doctrine of personality. Scripture nowhere speaks directly to the issue, yet there are numerous indirect and anecdotal references which indicate that God does indeed shape personality. Cain and Abel, Moses and Aaron, Jacob and Esau, Peter and Paul are all biblical examples of conflicting and complementing personalities with unique traits that often directly shaped their stories in biblical history. Psalm 139:13-16 is a poetic picture of God's handiwork in the womb that seems to include personality. David observes that God "made my mind and heart" (v. 13, NET) and that "all the days ordained for me" (v. 16, NET) were known to God before David knew even one of them. Spiritual gifts in the New Testament seem somehow associated with personality.

Anecdotal biblical references aside, it is reasonable to say that personality is best considered an extrabiblical subject of study, based more on subjective observations of people than on biblical inferences and insights. However, as long as an attempt to understand personality does not violate Scripture or promote a distorted view of man's sinful nature, it can reasonably be assessed and used on its own merits as a helpful tool for better understanding how we are made. It is simply part of God's observable created order.

For the home educating parent, personality will be a constant factor in the learning process, touching on every aspect of family dynamic and child raising. How a child lives and learns—and how a parent teaches and trains—will be unavoidably shaped and affected by personality. It may be difficult to quantify or define it, but it is not difficult to observe that personality is a real and undeniably influential human characteristic. With everyone at home all the time, homeschooling is a personality laboratory that will give your children the best opportunity to test and discover their personality gifts and to understand how God has equipped them to invest their lives for his kingdom. On the following pages, we'll discuss personality and how others have applied it to teaching and learning, and then offer our own model that integrates personality and learning dynamics.

For you created my inmost being; you knit me together in my mother's womb. I praise you because I am fearfully and wonderfully made; your works are wonderful, I know that full well. My frame was not hidden from you when I was made in the secret place. When I was woven together in the depths of the earth, your eyes saw my unformed body. All the days ordained for me were written in your book before one of them came to be.

— Psalm 139:13-16

The boys grew up, and Esau became a skillful hunter, a man of the open country, while Jacob was a quiet man, staying among the tents.

— Genesis 25:27

For since the creation of the world God's invisible qualities—his eternal power and divine nature—have been clearly seen, being understood from what has been made, so that men are without excuse.

— Romans 1:20

The Reality of Personality

The study of personality, despite the appearance of scientific credibility, is really very subjective. At this point, what we know about personality is based primarily on empirical study and observation, not from laboratory proofs derived from scientific method. There is, so far, no reliable way to prove personality, much less a limited range of distinct personality types. Yet most people would agree that personality exists and that there are probably a limited number of identifiable types of personalities.

You are in good Christian company if you accept the reality of personality. Most homeschool families who take personality into account would generally agree that personality is God-given and that children's personalities reveal something about how God designed them to live and learn best. However, though understanding personality is helpful, it should always be a secondary issue in your home education. You can study it and use it because it is helpful and even fun, but you can give your children a good home education with or without knowledge of personality-shaped learning styles. Whole books and real life will work with any child's personality, whether you know what it is or not.

The Personality behind the Person

Personality, though difficult to define, is certainly easy to observe—quiet vs. outgoing, visionary vs. details, leader vs. follower, analytical vs. relational, organized vs. unorganized, and so on. However, those kinds of differences comprise only a small part of the intricate creatures called man and woman that God created in his image. We are much more than our personalities in God's eyes. We are first and foremost persons, eternally stamped with the image and likeness of our Creator. Yet each person is original and unique—a testimony of God's infinite creativity. Each of us has a distinct personality that sets us apart from every other person and, in part, define who we are.

However, studying personality is like studying butterflies. We initially appreciate the natural wonder and beauty of the delicate creatures themselves. Soon, though, we are drawn into separating them into groups according to unifying elements of intricate design and observable behaviors. Among the wide variety of butterflies, we discover not randomness and infinite variety but rather order and categories of common characteristics. In the same way, we initially see all persons as a unified whole—humanity. But soon we are drawn into seeing God's personal handiwork in individuals. We begin to observe and soon discover elements of unity within what appears at first glance to be random diversity. We begin seeing patterns of behavior and common traits. We see personalities.

God is a God of order, so it should come as no surprise to see order expressed in his creation of human beings through common characteristics of personality, just as it is expressed through common physical traits such as eye and hair color, body build, and vocal range. When we talk about personality, we are simply taking part in the great shared exercise of observing, studying, and classifying God's creation. It is a little like nature study—it helps us not only to learn more about ourselves but also to know more about the infinitely creative God who made us (Romans 1:20; Psalm 8).

The Person beyond the Personality

Though we can observe personality and attempt to discover and categorize patterns, any attempt to actually define personality can be no more than a limited effort to understand the mystery of our humanity better. There are simply too many other factors and influences that shape our own human behavior and that shape even our own "objective" observation and evaluation of human behavior in others. These variables don't negate or change personality, which is innate and God-given, but they affect the expression of one's personality. It is these kinds of variables that can create the impression of a seemingly random diversity of types or expressions of personality. Even though a theory or model might try to define four, or eight, or however many kinds of temperaments or personalities, these variables of human experience can create even more apparent diversity.

- **Character Training** — Christian maturity shapes how personality is expressed. A strong aspect of personality might be tempered or a weak one strengthened. Maturity can sometimes soften the edges of personality.

- **Biblical Values** — What a person values can shape behavior that otherwise would be shaped mostly by strength of personality. A strong sense of duty for a particular kind of behavior might override personality preferences.

- **Weaknesses, Temptation, Sin** — Patterns of sinful behavior and the effects of past sin can distort personality.

- **Spiritual Gifts** — God gives each Christian spiritual gifts for ministry in the body of Christ. Spiritual gifts may in fact be related in some way to a person's personality gifts, but they are distinct concepts in Scripture.

- **Life Experiences** — Childhood experiences, both positive and negative, can either sharpen or distort personality.

- **Masculine and Feminine Traits** — How a person understands and expresses their masculinity and femininity can affect their personality.

The Personality of Your Child

You don't need someone to tell you that your children have personalities—it's readily apparent in the way they think, play, and relate. One child loves to read and entertain himself quietly; another is always moving and always wants to be with someone. One child excels at routine tasks such as sewing; another dreams up new and interesting projects. One child is very systematic and orderly but not so relational; another is very relational but not so organized. One child loves music; another loves sports.

In many ways, young children can often seem like pure personality because they freely express it without the restraints of maturity. By early adolescence, they will be more comfortable and more careful with their personalities; by adulthood, they will have developed a full and mature personality, normally with confident personality preferences. During childhood, though, they are still learning to be what they are—they are still growing into their personality. Part of your role as a parent is to understand, encourage, and direct the emerging personality development of each individual child.

Type development starts at a very early age. The hypothesis is that type is inborn, an innate predisposition like right- or left-handedness, but the successful development of type can be greatly helped or hindered by environment from the beginning.

— Isabel Briggs Myers, *Gifts Differing*, Consulting Psychologists Press, 1980

Birth Order Remix

Birth order does not give birth to personality. It is certainly another variable of human experience that may affect how a child's innate and God-given personality is shaped or expressed, but personality is already in place prior to birth order influences. In our view, birth order may shape but it does not create personality. The idea that birth order actually creates personality is more consistent with the tenets of radical behaviorism, which asserts that the brain is a "blank slate" at birth on which all cognitive development (such as personality) is the result solely of external stimuli and behavioral conditioning. It is the pure nurture side of the nature vs. nurture debate. In contrast, the nature side of the argument asserts that certain aspects of who we are and will become are innate at birth—the slate has already been written on. Of course, we believe that God is the author of that writing. Birth order can be a fun and entertaining idea to enliven a family discussion. However, always affirm to your children that their personality was created and given to them by God, not formed out of a cognitive void by their place of birth in the family pecking order.

Suggested Reading

There are many good books on personality type written from both a secular and a Christian perspective. If you are interested in personality type and learning styles, these are some of the books we have found helpful and interesting.

- *Gifts Differing* (Isabel Briggs Myers)
- *Please Understand Me II* (David Keirsey)
- *LifeKeys: Discover Who You Are* (Jane A. G. Kise, David Stark, and Sandra Krebs Hirsh)
- *The Way They Learn: How to Discover and Teach to Your Child's Strengths* (Cynthia Tobias)
- *Nurture by Nature* (Paul D. Tieger and Barbara Barron-Tieger)
- *One of a Kind* (LaVonne Neff)
- *Multiple Intelligences: New Horizons in Theory and Practice* (Howard E. Gardner)
- *In Their Own Way* (Thomas Armstrong)
- *Mother Styles: Using Personality Type to Discover Your Parenting Strengths* (Janet Penley)

The Reality of Learning Styles

Nothing is new under the sun, and no personality theory—regardless of how clear or clever or Christian it may appear—is truly original. Nearly every popular approach to personality can be correlated to some degree with the four temperament types originally postulated by Hippocrates (c. 400 B.C.)—Sanguine, Choleric, Phlegmatic, and Melancholy. The personality model presented in this chapter is no different. It is simply a creative way of understanding observable personality types. The striking similarities among the various models serve to reinforce and strengthen the validity of their common elements. The four most common personality descriptions weren't discovered by primary research and statistical analysis—they were simply observed in human behavior, generalized into four categories, and reported.

For all the efforts to define personality, there is no clear consensus on exactly what elements constitute a person's personality. However, there seems to be agreement that a starting point for talking about personality may be the way you think—that is, how you gather information, organize it, and make decisions with it. So while there are certainly other factors that contribute to your personality, it is your mental processes—the way you think and the mental tasks you prefer to use—that could be considered the first cause of personality. If how you think is somehow intricately bound up with what you are like, then the personality God has given your children will help you understand the way he has designed them to learn. As a homeschooling parent, you can maximize your teaching efforts by understanding your children's personality-shaped learning styles. The following is a sampling of some of the better known personality models that have been applied to education in general and homeschooling. This is a representative, not comprehensive, list.

Survey of Learning Styles

- **Natural Learning Styles** — This is a widely used traditional approach to learning theory. Children learn by one or more natural processes. Most natural models include visual (see it), auditory (hear it), and kinesthetic (do it) learners. Some models also include print (read it) and social (relate it). These styles have also been correlated with other temperament and personality models.

- **Right/Left Brain** — This approach is more physiology than it is personality, but it does offer valuable insights on modes of thinking and learning. The brain is divided into two hemispheres, each with its own mode of thinking. You predominantly use either one side or the other. Some people are predominantly right-brained, global thinkers—they think more intuitively, subjectively, and conceptually. Some people are predominantly left-brained linear thinkers—they think more analytically, objectively, and factually. This is the closest science has come to a physiology of personality, although it does not go far enough to explain the empirical data.

- **Innate Aptitude** (Howard E. Gardner, Thomas Armstrong) — Children are born with one of seven intelligences or innate aptitudes that determine what and how they will learn best (musical, artistic, logical-mathematical, linguistic, bodily-kinesthetic, interpersonal, intrapersonal). If given maximum opportunity and cultivation, they will excel naturally in their area of innate aptitude and intelligence.

- **Bible Models** — Some Christian authors have attempted to create personality models based on various biblical concepts such as spiritual gifts, ways to show love, or Bible characters. These models can be interesting and provide a good teaching outline, but they tend to read too much into the biblical text.

- **Temperaments** (Tim LaHaye, Florence Littauer) — Pastor Tim LaHaye popularized the concept of temperaments by putting them into a Christian framework. He described four temperaments based on the categories originally developed by Hippocrates. He later combined and differentiated each of those even further. Florence Littauer (*Personality Plus*) and others have followed his lead with differing terminology.

- **Personality Type** (Katherine Briggs, Isabel Briggs Myers) — Isabel Briggs Myers proposed sixteen personality types based on four preferences for thinking and living. The sixteen are often generalized into eight types or four temperaments. Numerous educators and writers, both secular and Christian, have used Myers's type theory as a model for their own learning and personality approaches. The Myers-Briggs Type Indicator (MBTI) is widely used in education. Although some are concerned about the Jungian roots of type theory, the MBTI is not a diagnostic instrument and does not measure pathology. The MBTI is a psychological indicator, not a test, and measures only the strength of preference for four areas that Myers believed defined personality or type: how one focuses mental energy, gathers information, makes decisions, and orients to life. Her book, *Gifts Differing* (1980), summarized a lifetime of work in developing her personality type model and the MBTI instrument. The book contains extensive sections on the applications of type to education and parenting.

- **The Gregorc Model** (Anthony F. Gregorc) — Children have one of four learning styles based on their Perceptual abilities or how they prefer to take in information (Concrete or Abstract thinking) and on their Ordering abilities or how they prefer to use that information (Sequential or Random thinking). Gregorc's temperaments are based on the mental processes preferences of the Myers-Briggs model.

- **Temperament Types** (David Keirsey) — Keirsey's personality and character model is based on variations of Myers-Briggs types. His book, *Please Understand Me II* (1998), is popular in government, church, corporate, and academic circles. Keirsey identifies four temperaments: Artisans, Guardians, Idealists, Rationalists. He also identifies four kinds of correlative intelligences: tactical, logistical, diplomatic, strategic. His view is extensively developed, including applications to parenting.

- **Learning Temperaments** (Keith Golay) — Dr. Golay developed a model of learning and teaching styles for use in the public schools (1982). Children fall generally into one of four temperaments or learning styles: Actual-Spontaneous, Actual-Routine, Conceptual-Specific, Conceptual-Global. These temperaments are derived from the Myers-Briggs and Keirsey models of personality type.

- **The 4MAT System** (Bernice McCarthy) — Children have one of four learning styles: Dynamic, Imaginative, Common Sense, Analytic. This educational model includes four learning activities—experiencing, conceptualizing, applying, creating. It is based on a synthesis of major personality and learning styles theories, modifying the Myers-Briggs personality model integrated with Right/Left Brain theory.

A Type of Homeschool Success

A little-known homeschooling success story is the life of Isabel Briggs Myers, co-author of the MBTI (Myers-Briggs Type Indicator). Whatever opinion you may have of her personality type theories, her life is certainly a shining example for home educators. Born in 1897, she was home educated by her mother, Katherine Briggs, who had also been instructed at home. (Isabel's father was a world-renowned scientist.) She entered Swarthmore College at the age of sixteen and graduated first in her class in 1919 with highest honors in political science. Her sixty-one-year marriage began her junior year of college. Until the outbreak of World War II, she was a dedicated mother and homemaker and a prize-winning author. In 1942, with her children grown, she tackled the MBTI with the help of her mother (who had inspired the idea) and her family. Isabel had no formal training in the field, no professional sponsorship, and no grants, yet she would nearly single-handedly go on to create the quintessential home business success story. In 1962, after twenty years of self-instruction in the field of psychological testing and measurement, and countless hours of self-directed research, writing, testing, and validating, her type indicator was finally accepted and published as a professional psychological instrument. It has gone on to become the most widely used personality inventory in the world. From biblical quotes in her writings and from the quality of her life and character, it is clear that Isabel was motivated by her faith and her deeply held Christian values. Friends have noted her phenomenal memory for poetry and biblical passages. Although the MBTI is a belief-neutral instrument, Isabel Briggs Myers believed and wrote that personality is innate and God-given. Concerning education, she was a strong advocate of phonics and encouraged reading widely. She also held biblical views on child training and discipline.

"The human race," someone once said, "is made up of two groups of people: those who divide people into groups, and those who don't." People who study personality development divide people into groups...The number (of groups) isn't important. What's important is the enormous improvement in family happiness that can result when family members understand themselves and each other.

— LaVonne Neff, *One of a Kind*, Multnomah, 1988

WholeHearted Learning Styles

As part of the WholeHearted Learning model, we are including a WholeHearted Learning Styles model. Like many of the other personality type and learning styles approaches described on the previous pages, our model is a theory based on observation and practice. It is not a formula and certainly not a just-revealed secret for unlocking your homeschooling success. It is just our insights on learning styles based on our own study and twenty-five years of parenting and homeschooling. Our learning styles model is best understood as a lens with which to view your children and your homeschooling. The better you understand how your children think and behave, the better you will be able to fine-tune their learning experiences and respond to their needs more confidently. Our model simply offers you accessible language you can use to better understand how your children live and learn and insights that will help you be a better teacher. The rest of this chapter will explain and explore the different facets of the WholeHearted Learning Styles model.

Modes of Thinking

Observation, research, and common sense indicate that our minds operate in at least two definable modes of thinking—investigation or seeking out information to gain knowledge, and determination or sorting out information to reach conclusions. These two modes of thinking can be further broken down by mental tasks—investigating by facts or investigating by insights, and determining by logic or determining by values. Practically, we exercise whichever of those mental tasks are needed most for a given situation and in whatever order they are called upon. In reality, each of us prefers and uses more skillfully only one of the mental tasks from each mode of thinking. The learning style of your child is defined by the two mental tasks they most prefer using.

Thinking Mode: INVESTIGATION

Purpose: Seeking out information to gain knowledge.

- **Investigating FACTS** — You seek out information based on your objective five senses. You favor the practical—you look to the proven way. You are comfortable with routine and details. You are a concrete, linear thinker.

- **Investigating INSIGHTS** — You seek out information based on a subjective sixth sense. You favor the idealistic—you look for a better way. You are comfortable with theory and the big picture. You are an abstract, global thinker.

Thinking Mode: DETERMINATION

Purpose: Sorting out information to reach conclusions.

- **Determining by LOGIC** — You sort out information based on impersonal logic. You are systematic, analytical, and task-oriented. You strongly value competence and being correct.

- **Determining by VALUES** — You sort out information based on personal values. You are relational and people-oriented. You deeply value social skills and harmony in relationships.

Implications for Teaching

Although we haven't defined actual learning styles yet, you can put your knowledge of thinking modes to immediate use in your homeschooling. Your children need to exercise all four of the mental tasks, not just their preferred ones that will define their personal learning styles and also not just the ones you prefer teaching because of your own learning style. Your challenge, regardless of your children's actual learning styles, is to exercise and give each child experience in all four modes of thinking. In providing a balanced mix of teaching methods that will exercise all four mental tasks, though, don't become formal and rigid. The WholeHearted Learning model, if implemented fully, should exercise all four mental tasks naturally without requiring special planning. Knowing the four mental tasks, though, will help you think about providing variety and avoiding inadvertently limiting your methods to those that reflect your own preferred modes of thinking. The following are just a few suggested methods and learning situations to illustrate how to think about the four mental tasks.

Teaching Methods for the Investigation Mode

- **Investigating FACTS** — Research, context study, hands-on science, planning the logistics for a project, manipulatives, audiovisual aids, using any or all of the five senses.

- **Investigating INSIGHTS** — Reading, role-play, using imagination, considering long-range goals for a project, considering solutions to a problem, brainstorming, independent work.

Teaching Methods for the Determination Mode

- **Determining by LOGIC** — Analyzing, computing, categorizing and classifying, debate and discussion, question-and-answer sessions, solving problems, thinking skills exercises.

- **Determining by VALUES** — Group discussion and problem solving, relational skills, presentation skills, creative writing, meaningful projects, lecture with personal insights and stories.

IN OUR HOME

We have always worked to vary our teaching styles as parents, but our own learning styles always rise to the top. Sally is driven by insights and values, so our children have come to expect books that inspire and discussions about ideals, Bible stories, history, and visionary ministry. She is a natural inspirer of hearts. Clay is driven by insights as well, but also by logic. The kids can expect discussions and analysis of Bible concepts and passages, historical ideas, visionary ideals, and ministry plans. He is a natural challenger of minds. That's a good combination for a rich verbal home learning environment, but we also have to get the facts into the process—all the detail and data we aren't as good at. That's the real homeschooling part. The rest is just doing what's natural.

Modes and Methods

Plan learning activities for study projects that will engage and exercise all four mental tasks. Some examples might be:

Unit Study of Rome

- **Facts:** Read a chapter from a children's reference book on the history of the Roman Empire; make a salt-dough map.
- **Insights:** Role-play a scene from Shakespeare's *Julius Caesar*; read aloud a historical novel on Rome.
- **Logic:** Evaluate the reasons for the fall of the Roman Empire; write a short report.
- **Values:** Discuss "What would I have done as Caesar?"; present a comparison of Rome then and America now.

Nature Study of Trees

- **Facts:** Study a field guide to determine types of trees in your area.
- **Insights:** Determine the best way to map the area and record the trees; design mapping materials.
- **Logic:** Classify and categorize the trees; use leaf samples; evaluate growth patterns.
- **Values:** Discuss what new trees should be planted; present reasons; discuss ecological issues of tree planting.

Study of Vivaldi

- **Facts:** Read aloud a story of Vivaldi's life; listen to the Classical Kids CD; listen to *The Four Seasons*.
- **Insights:** Imagine what Vivaldi was picturing in each movement of his work.
- **Logic:** Chart and time the movements; note tempo and feel of music in each one.
- **Values:** Create dramatic scenes to go with each movement, or select appropriate Bible readings.

Notes:

Living Styles: Adding Living to the Learning Styles

The two modes of thinking—seeking out information to gain knowledge (investigation) and sorting out information to reach conclusions (determination)—will be the best indicators of your children's preferred ways to actually learn things. Simply stated, how your children think is how they will learn. We will define four learning styles based on those modes of thinking, but there is more to learning than just what happens in the mind. Your children's learning styles are also affected by their living styles—how they orient to the world around them. They have a mental energy that will tend to be focused either internally or externally, and they will seek a life orientation that will tend to prefer either predictability or spontaneity. While these factors are not directly related to thinking, they directly affect the mode of life within which your children's thinking will take place. Learning styles and living styles are two sides of the same coin.

Mental Focus

It is not unusual to hear someone say about a talkative, gregarious child, "What an extroverted little boy he is!" or about a quiet, introspective child, "She really is quite introverted, isn't she?" Each is trying to describe a child's mental focus and whether their mental energies are directed more externally or internally. However, these big but common psychological terms used to describe the direction of that focus can become somewhat cumbersome, especially when describing children. To simplify those terms, we choose to describe the extroverted child as having an active mental focus and the introverted child as having a reflective one.

- **Active** — Active children focus their mental energies and attention on the external world of people and events. These children tend to think with their mouths; whatever is on their minds is on their tongues. Active children are easily distractible but tend to finish their work quickly in order to move on to something else. They are not as quick to pick up on abstract concepts and ideas but rather are good with concrete facts. They are drawn to and derive energy from being with people and engaging in discussion and activity.

- **Reflective** — Reflective children focus their mental energies and attention on the internal world of thoughts and ideas. These children think before they speak, and they tend to be a bit mysterious because so much goes on inside them that they never let out or get out. Reflective children have strong powers of concentration and are slower to call an effort finished. They more easily pick up on abstract concepts and ideas. They are drawn to and derive new mental energy from being alone with themselves and being able to think and reflect.

Understanding your children's mental focus will help you more easily engage them in learning activities. An Active child needs the freedom to think out loud without having their thoughts-in-process judged too quickly. A Reflective child needs the freedom to think it through before being expected to answer. If you have both Active and Reflective children in your home, you will need to ensure sufficient time in discussions for Reflectives to fully express their thoughts and yet keep the discussion moving so as not to frustrate the Actives who are ready to move on to the next idea or subject.

Life Orientation

For most of the hours of our lives, we are faced with managing the balance between work and play. That lifestyle choice, like so many other things in life, finds its purest expression in children. The preference conflict is the same, whether for children or adults: Do the work first and then enjoy life, or enjoy life and the work will always get done. Your child has a preferred way to orient to the world, which we call here their "life orientation." It is expressed as a preference for either time or experience. Those words are simple, but the differences they spotlight are profound.

- **Time** — Time-oriented children value predictability, order, structure, schedules, and plans. They are motivated to move toward conclusions and decisions so they can know just what to expect and can plan for it. They tend to think they know what other people ought to do and are not shy about saying so. They are less tolerant of others and aim to be right. They tend to regard those who prefer an experience orientation as being aimless or lazy. Time-oriented children believe they (and others) should get the work done first and then play.

- **Experience** — Experience-oriented children value spontaneity, openness, flexibility, and curiosity. They are motivated to put off decisions as long as possible to avoid making wrong ones and to get more input. They tend to know what people around them are doing and want to see results. They are tolerant of others and do not want to miss anything. They tend to regard those who prefer a time orientation as being rigid and missing out on life. Experience-oriented children believe it is best to enjoy life and the work will get done.

Knowing how your children look at the world around them will change the way you look at your children. This life orientation can manifest as an actual conflict of preferences in how your children relate to one another and how things are done and why. Time-oriented children want a predictable schedule that Experience-oriented children will either ignore or try to neutralize. Experience-oriented children want a spontaneous schedule that Time-oriented children will either condemn or try to control. On a field trip, the timers will want to stick to the plan and schedule, and the experiencers will want to be free and unfettered. Your job as a homeschooling parent, regardless of your own life orientation, is to manage the balancing act so everyone is affirmed.

IN OUR HOME

Joel is an Experience-oriented Reflective—the only one in the family. His life orientation is very internalized and unstructured. From the time he was a little boy, his uniqueness as the only reflective experiencer in the family has been legendary. Everyone in the family has had the experience of talking to Joel for a while, only to have him turn and ask, "What did you say?" He was there all the time, but his mind was just somewhere else. It would drive the timers a little nuts, yet Joel was always so open, flexible, and eager to please others that it rarely turned into a life orientation preference issue. Joel was always easygoing when it came to plans and schedules. Now he's a musician and a composer, and his preferences suit him well for the unstructured world of making music.

Notes:

Putting the Learning Style Pieces Together

If you are a student of other personality type theories, such as the Myers-Briggs model, you probably have already observed that the WholeHearted Learning Styles model employs a similar model of four scales, each with two dichotomous preferences (one or the other). Those eight variables could yield up to sixteen combinations, although we limit our model to four combinations. Here are the four preference scales discussed so far:

ACTIVE — or — **REFLECTIVE**   (Mental Focus)

FACTS — or — **INSIGHTS**   (Thinking Mode: Investigation)

LOGIC — or — **VALUES**   (Thinking Mode: Determination)

TIME — or — **EXPERIENCE**   (Life Orientation)

The Myers-Briggs model introduced a new way to think about personality that identified preferences using eight letters (EISNTFJP), which yielded sixteen four-letter personality types (ESTJ, INFP, ESFP, INTJ, and twelve more). It is a complex model that uses often unfamiliar terms, so it can be difficult to discuss meaningfully unless all parties in the conversation have some knowledge of the model. In the WholeHearted Learning Styles model we have attempted to reduce complexity by limiting it to four core personality types created from the two preferences in each of the two thinking mode scales (Facts and Insights from Investigation, and Logic and Values from Determination). To simplify further, rather than using letters or psychological terms, we gave each personality type a descriptive name to make it easier to understand and remember. Here are the four types:

DOER   (Facts + Logic)

HELPER   (Facts + Values)

MOVER   (Insights + Values)

SHAPER   (Insights + Logic)

The other variables in the WholeHearted Learning Styles model (Active or Reflective from Mental Focus, Time or Experience from Life Orientation) are purposely not integrated directly into the four personality types, but rather are used indirectly to provide additional insights about the type. For example, a Doer child will be motivated to get the job done, but one who is Active and Time-oriented will get it done differently than one who is Reflective and Experience-oriented. That fuller picture of your child's personality gives you more insight into how they live and learn best. Our hope is that it is an easier, less complicated, and more memorable way to account for all the personality variables without getting bogged down in too much detail.

In the world of personality theory, types based on selected core elements from a model, commonly generalized as four, are often called temperaments. The WholeHearted Learning Styles model does not identify temperaments simply to avoid adding yet another layer of terminology and to focus on living and learning styles. If you know your child is a Doer, Helper, Mover, or Shaper, you will have an immediate personality profile to help you direct or respond to their living and learning needs quickly and effectively. It's not about putting them in personality boxes; it's about setting them free to be who they are.

Factoring in Growth and Development

Notes:

We believe that personality, whatever it really is, is innate and God-given. However, in the same way that the physical body grows and develops, personality also matures over time. Children under 13 years old generally have not yet had enough experience with life to know with confidence which mental tasks they prefer and use most skillfully. Around the time of puberty (about seventh grade), however, they begin to differentiate which tasks they most prefer to use. Before that time, since your children are not able to accurately identify their preferences on their own, you can observe them in order to determine patterns of preference that are emerging throughout childhood.

During the elementary years, your children will routinely use all four mental tasks. They are trying everything on to see what fits best. This is a necessary step in learning development since all four tasks will be used throughout their lives. Avoid the temptation to isolate their preferred mental tasks, label them, and then focus your teaching methods exclusively on those emerging preferences. That is not the purpose of knowing your children's learning styles! Your goal during the elementary years is to plan your methods so as to give your children a balanced experience of all four mental tasks while allowing them to develop confidence and skill in their emerging preferred tasks. As preferred mental tasks emerge, you can begin to use that knowledge to understand your child's learning patterns and frustrations, to increase their motivation for certain subjects, or to make difficult subjects more understandable for them. In Discovery Studies, for instance, you can direct your children to explore selected subjects in a way that you know will help them to develop skill and competence in the use of their preferred mental tasks.

Don't label your children too soon—the label might not fit in another few years! It's fun to talk about personality and learning styles, but keep it general. Let them tell you what they think they are. Resist the temptation to evaluate everything they do or say through the grid of their learning style or personality. Be especially careful not to show favoritism for certain mental task preferences or personalities. If you are a Mover, you might find it easier to work with a child who is a Mover and inadvertently give that child more affirmation than, say, your Doer child. It is important for you to learn to value all preferences and personalities equally in your children.

IN OUR HOME

Our family is a real study in personality types. Mom is an Active-Time Mover driven by ideals, and Dad is a Reflective-Time Shaper driven by ideas, which possibly explains why we started our own ministry and write books. Each of our children is in full bloom of personality. Sarah is a Reflective-Time Mover; Joel is a Reflective-Experience Mover; Nathan is an Active-Experience Shaper; and Joy is probably shaping up to be an Active-Time Shaper. We have spent many interesting hours identifying and analyzing one another's personality preferences. It has helped us as parents think about how to better love and appreciate each of our uniquely designed children, how to better motivate them to learn and succeed, and how to touch their joys and delights in life. Besides all that, it's just a lot of fun.

Disclaimer

Please note that this indicator has not been tested or validated professionally in any way. It is simply a tool to help you observe your children and better identify and understand their living and learning styles. It is based entirely on our own observations of children, our ministry and formal training, and our use of other similar personality inventories. We make no claims concerning either the effectiveness or validity of this indicator as a tool to identify learning styles.

Siblings

It is best to observe your children in relationship with other children their own age outside of your family setting. Basing your observations only on how your children relate to one another might give a skewed result. Sibling relationships are often unique and might not give a true indication of your child's personality.

Changes

Your children will seem to change over time, and your observations of their personalities will change as well. Though their personalities are God-given and innate, it takes time for children to become comfortable with who God has made them to be. It is part of the growing and maturing process. You can record observations over several years, which is why there are three spaces for each child in the indicator. It is difficult to say with any certainty at what age to begin recording your observations, but your children will not begin differentiating personality preferences with any confidence or consistency much before their late elementary years.

WholeHearted Learning Style Indicator

An indicator is simply that—a tool to indicate what you think your child's learning style might be. It is based entirely on your own observations of how your child thinks and orients to the world around them. An indicator is not a test, but simply a tool to reveal preferences. It's like putting on reading glasses to bring words into clearer focus that before were fuzzy and undefined. With or without an indicator, you are the best and most accurate judge of your child's personality preferences. Use this or any other indicator to help you better understand your children's living and learning preferences, but trust your own instincts concerning your children. In the end, it is not what the indicator says that counts, but what you say. You can make the call.

Instructions for Using the Indicator

Evaluate each child's personality using the following scale for all forty characteristics. (Rate all ten items in each of the four columns.) Use the number corresponding to the answer that best describes how consistently your child exhibits each characteristic.

Rating   **Explanation**

1 = Only occasionally..........................*This doesn't really describe my child.*

2 = Fairly often...................................*This describes my child some of the time.*

3 = Most of the time ....*This describes my child most of the time.*

When you have placed a 1, 2, or 3 value in all forty boxes, add the numbers in each column and place the total in the box below it. For each mode, one of the two mental tasks should be stronger. The two predominant tasks (one from each mode) indicate the learning style of your child's personality type. For instance, if a child scored 24 for Facts and 14 for Insights in the Investigation Mode column and 16 for Logic and 22 for Values in the Determination Mode column, that child's learning style would be the combination of the high score from each column, or FV (Facts+Values). Look at the personality types table to determine that your child is a Helper. Once you have determined your child's indicated personality type, turn to the appropriate page in the section following the indicator to read a profile of that type. If you somehow end up with the same number in the total boxes at the bottom of a mode, you will need to make a personal judgment as to which best reflects your child's own preference. For example, in the Investigation Mode column, your total might be 22 for Facts and 22 for Insights. You could either adjust some of the ratings in both columns to be more accurate or you could be the tiebreaker vote and simply make an informed personal judgment.

Record your child's name and age, the date of the evaluation, your child's learning style, and corresponding personality type. Mental Focus and Life Orientation are personal observations, not scored items, but it is very helpful to record them to enable you to see changes in perceptions through the years. Simply decide which mental focus and life orientation best describes your child—either Active or Reflective and Time or Experience. Record the first initial of each. For example, if you believe your child's mental focus is Active and life orientation is Time, you would record A/T in the M/L space.

Thinking Mode: INVESTIGATION
Seeking out information to gain knowledge.

Investigating FACTS		Investigating INSIGHTS	
Enjoys familiar activities and regular routine.		Enjoys trying new ways and learning new things.	
Wants to know the right way to do things.		Enjoys being different.	
Carefully observes and remembers lots of details.		Learns quickly but tends to forget details.	
Asks, "Did that really happen?"		Enjoys pretending and making up stories.	
Is curious about how things work.		Looks for new ways to do common tasks.	
Enjoys books with lots of facts and information.		Enjoys imaginative books and stories.	
Cares about clothes and how they look.		Likes to invent and design things.	
Is good working with their hands.		Is good with words and ideas.	
Enjoys puzzles and coloring books.		Uses toys in new and original ways.	
Is known to be steady and reliable.		Goes quickly from one new interest to another.	
TOTAL: FACTS		TOTAL: INSIGHTS	

Thinking Mode: DETERMINATION
Sorting out information to reach conclusions.

Determining by LOGIC		Determining by VALUES	
Asks "Why?" a lot.		Likes to talk or read about people.	
Insists on logical explanations.		Wants to be praised for caring for others.	
Likes to arrange things in orderly patterns.		Shows concern if someone is unhappy.	
Shows more interest in ideas than in people.		Tells stories expressively in great detail.	
Holds firmly to their beliefs.		Tries to be tactful, even if it means avoiding truth.	
Not always comfortable with affection.		Shows more interest in people than in ideas.	
Wants rules in games established and kept.		Generally agrees with opinions of friends.	
Likes praise for doing something competently.		Wants physical and verbal expressions of love.	
Can be perfectionistic.		Relates well to other children and adults.	
Controls his or her emotions.		Is upset by conflict with family or friends.	
TOTAL: LOGIC		TOTAL: VALUES	

Ratings: **1** = Only occasionally   **2** = Fairly often   **3** = Most of the time

Records: Learning Style (LS), Personality Type (PT), Mental Focus/Life Orientation (M/L)

Child: _____

Date _____ Age _____ LS _____ PT _____ M/L _____

Date _____ Age _____ LS _____ PT _____ M/L _____

Date _____ Age _____ LS _____ PT _____ M/L _____

Child: _____

Date _____ Age _____ LS _____ PT _____ M/L _____

Date _____ Age _____ LS _____ PT _____ M/L _____

Date _____ Age _____ LS _____ PT _____ M/L _____

Child: _____

Date _____ Age _____ LS _____ PT _____ M/L _____

Date _____ Age _____ LS _____ PT _____ M/L _____

Date _____ Age _____ LS _____ PT _____ M/L _____

Learning Styles:
- FL: Facts + Logic
- FV: Facts + Values
- IV: Insights + Values
- IL: Insights + Logic

Personality Types:
- DOER (Facts + Logic)
- HELPER (Facts + Values)
- MOVER (Insights + Values)
- SHAPER (Insights + Logic)

Mental Focus:
- ACTIVE (outward on people and activities)
- REFLECTIVE (inward on thoughts and ideas)

Life Orientation:
- TIME (predictability, planning, order, structure, schedule)
- EXPERIENCE (spontaneity, openness, flexibility, impulse)

Notes about DOER children

The DOER Child

Thinking Modes: Facts + Logic

Description: The industrious child who gets things done

Life Motto: "I can do that!"

Personal Encouragement

If God has given you a Doer, he knew you could meet the challenges of educating this industrious and practical child. God designed your boy or girl to get things done, make decisions, and make things work. God will someday use your Doer child to take on difficult tasks and challenges and, through personal determination and persistence, get the job done.

If your Doer is a boy, his biblical role model might be the apostle Peter, who took on the challenge of starting and organizing the church in Jerusalem. He preached, baptized, taught in the temple, organized the people, and solved problems. He took on challenges and did what needed to be done.

If your Doer is a girl, her biblical role model might be Esther, who saved Israel through her resourcefulness and determination. She laid out a plan, carried it out carefully, and accomplished her goal by winning the king's favor. She met the problem head-on and solved it by doing what she knew needed to be done.

Personality Profile

- **Summary** — Your Doer child is practical, resourceful, and especially good at routine physical tasks and details. This realistic child does things the proven way, learns from and relies on experience, and enjoys organizing and making things work. This child is consistent and reliable, uses logic and objective analysis to solve problems, is good with technical tasks, and values fairness (logic) over feelings.

- **Learning Style of a Doer** — Your Doer child learns best primarily by investigating facts and determining by logic. This child prefers hands-on subjects and activities, is good at learning facts and remembering details, values clear and direct instructions, and enjoys mastering and using skills. This child is quick to understand ideas, wants decisions to make sense, values fairness and logic over feelings, and respects competence in the quest to make sense of things.

- **Mental Focus** — Active Doers focus their mental energy on the people, activities, and events in their lives. These children organize and direct activities and people. Reflective Doers focus their mental energy on their thoughts and ideas. These children are very thorough, responsible, precise, and good at routine work.

- **Life Orientation** — Time-oriented Doers value predictable routines and plans that enable them to be decisive about accomplishing their tasks. They want to settle matters promptly. Experience-oriented Doers value flexibility that allows them to explore options for accomplishing their tasks. They want to be open to new challenges.

- **Teaching a Doer** — This child is the most hands-on and concrete. The Doer child prefers studying subjects that require specific skills but not subjects that require a great deal of disciplined study. Give them something to do or accomplish now. Assign tasks that require practical or repetitive skill, analysis, and organization. Fully explain instructions or directions step by step. Your teaching must be factual, organized, and orderly to be useful to the Doer. Ask questions that require specific, concrete answers and knowledge. This child likes to accomplish his own work but can become impatient if a lesson takes too long to complete and can be inflexible in how to complete a task or lesson. A Doer will not stay confined to a desk for long, so give them lots of room to move and freedom to do their work in other places.

- **Reading with a Doer** — This child will enjoy action books and dramas but especially real stories about real people and events such as history and biography. Fantasy is not as appealing to a Doer. They are interested in detailed, realistic illustrations. When reading aloud to a Doer, be sure to provide a task to do, such as drawing or coloring. Reading alone may be better accomplished in shorter reading times.

- **Motivating a Doer** — Demonstrate why a task or skill will be useful to this child right now; show what function it will play in the child's life. Recognize manual and practical skills. Affirm them for how reliable, resourceful, competent, and skilled they are. Rewards must be concrete and immediate to be motivational for this child.

- **Correcting a Doer** — Retrace any steps taken in order to find the exact point at which a mistake was made. Start again at that point. Express your confidence in the child to do it correctly the second time. The Doer child often is very active and needs encouragement to develop disciplined study habits.

DOER	Strengths	Weaknesses
LIVING	Practical, productive, self-driven. Oriented to what can be done in the here and now.	Suspicious of change and unproven ways. Can be rigid about schedules and expectations.
LEARNING	Self-disciplined and competent. Enjoys completing assigned tasks. Thorough in project details.	Over-reliant on structure. May need a specific assignment to motivate learning desire.
LOVING	Calm, loyal, and diligent at actively doing things for loved ones. Loves by actions.	Not always able to express affection. May seem remote. Can be inflexible in an argument.
LABORING	Diligent and thorough at tasks. Will work on an assigned task with total devotion until completed.	May be perfectionistic and overly concerned or worried about the details of a task.
LEADING	Strong logical orientation. Sees what needs to be done and will galvanize others to practical action.	Task-focused. May lose sight of the big picture and get bogged down in small details. Can be insensitive.
LISTENING	Hears immediate facts, needs, and information about the present and forms a plan to deal with it.	May miss subtle emotional clues in conversations. Can be resistant to abstract ideas.

Notes about HELPER children

The HELPER Child

Thinking Modes: Facts + Values

Description: The serving child who encourages others

Life Motto: "How can I help you?"

Personal Encouragement

If God has given you a Helper, he knew you could meet the challenges of educating this serving and encouraging child. God designed your boy or girl to help and appreciate others. God will someday use your Helper child to serve others, organize people, and, through appreciation, encouragement, and relational skills, help them work together to help others.

If your Helper is a girl, her biblical role model might be Ruth, whose quiet life of service and loyalty to Naomi was rewarded by God. Ruth gave up her life in Moab to follow Naomi and be a daughter to her. Her servant heart and practical skills eventually led her to become the wife of Boaz and the great-grandmother of David.

If your Helper is a boy, his biblical role model might be Barnabas, who was a behind-the-scenes servant who helped establish the new church. He was the Son of Encouragement who knew how to work with people and help others become successful. When Paul rejected John Mark, Barnabas took him and turned him into a leader.

Personality Profile

- **Summary** — Your Helper child is practical, resourceful, and especially good at meeting existing needs that involve people. This realistic child does things the proven way, learns from and relies on experience, and enjoys working with tasks and details to make people fit together more harmoniously. This child uses relational skills to solve problems, likes to please, avoids conflict, and values feelings over logic.

- **Learning Style of a Helper** — Your Helper child learns best primarily by investigating facts and determining by values. This child prefers hands-on subjects and activities, is good at learning facts and remembering details, values clear and direct instructions, and enjoys mastering and using skills. This child values knowing and mastering social skills, works well in relational settings, likes to please others, values others' feelings over thoughts, and cares about creating harmony.

- **Mental Focus** — Active Helpers focus their mental energy mostly on the people in their lives. These children love either to serve others or to make sure others are served. Reflective Helpers focus their mental energy on their thoughts and ideas. These children thrive working on projects related to the values they hold dear.

- **Life Orientation** — Time-oriented Helpers value predictable routines and plans that enable them to better serve others in their lives. They want to solve personal issues. Experience-oriented Helpers value spontaneity that allows them to respond to new and unanticipated personal needs of others. They want to be flexible to meet needs.

- **Teaching a Helper** — This child is the most willing to serve and appreciate others. The Helper child prefers informative subjects such as reading and history but not impersonal subjects that require much independent study and imagination. Give them something to do or to accomplish that will involve other people. The Helper child is good at practical skills that will benefit others. Create group projects for this child that allow them to offer practical ways to achieve harmony and cooperation. This child wants to be liked and accepted by others and is naturally driven to create harmony but can become passive and resistant to change and can also resist by attempting to avoid conflict. A Helper generally likes to do things in the company of others, so create learning spaces for them that keep them in proximity of others.

- **Reading with a Helper** — This child will enjoy books and dramas based on real events that involve real people working together harmoniously, whether fiction or nonfiction. They are interested in detailed illustrations of real people. When reading aloud to a Helper, emphasize that the reading is something special you are doing together. Reading alone is not nearly as appealing as reading with someone.

- **Motivating a Helper** — Warmly affirm your personal relationship with your Helper child. Work with them or create group situations that are relationally comfortable and nonthreatening. Recognize their ability to get along with others. Affirm their effectiveness in social skills and their friendliness and caring for others.

- **Correcting a Helper** — Express your love and appreciation for the Helper before correcting. Put the subject (especially a difficult one that is resisted) into the context of how much it pleases you to see them learn and grow. The Helper child might need encouragement to become more creative.

HELPER	Strengths	Weaknesses
LIVING	Highly relational and attuned to the present moment. Sensory with a high appreciation for beauty.	Resistant to change or novelty. Attuned to others' feelings, but may hide their own to keep harmony.
LEARNING	Detail-oriented. Interested in subjects dealing with people and life. Diligent in completing assignments.	May need clear instruction to motivate them. Easily frustrated by abstract ideas and subjects.
LOVING	Deeply loyal, openly affectionate. Thrives on affirmation. Accepting, sensitive, compassionate.	Will do anything to avoid conflict. Need for affection may make them insecure or clingy.
LABORING	Excels at hands-on tasks, especially if they involve tangible beauty or people. Great as co-workers.	Can get bogged down in details. May lose interest in a project if people are not involved.
LEADING	Relational and highly aware of others' emotions. Can persuade people to cooperate.	May abdicate leadership for the sake of harmony. Does not like to upset people.
LISTENING	Hears relationally and literally. Highly attuned to picking up on others' needs.	Slow to pick up on subtleties in conversation. Can become frustrated by abstract ideas.

Notes about MOVER children

The MOVER Child

Thinking Modes: Insights + Values

Description: The inspiring child who influences others

Life Motto: "Let's do it together."

Personal Encouragement

If God has given you a Mover, he knew you could meet the challenges of educating this influential and engaging child. God designed your boy or girl to influence others to do great things. God will someday use your Mover child to exercise their strong verbal and relational skills to motivate and move others to join in important ministries and causes and to accomplish great things.

If your Mover is a girl, her biblical role model might be Deborah, who used her personal influence to lead Israel to victory over the chariots of Sisera. She envisioned what could be done and influenced the people to follow her. She persuaded Barak to take up the battle against nine hundred chariots. Because of her vision and plan, Israel routed Sisera.

If your Mover is a boy, his biblical role model might be David, who unified Israel under his leadership. He was a visionary who knew how to move people to action and loyalty through building relationships. Though he had weaknesses, his strength was his close relationship with God, evidenced in the Psalms that still move people today.

Personality Profile

- **Summary** — Your Mover child is inventive, imaginative, and especially good at seeing what might be done with, by, or for people. This idealistic child naturally finds new ways to motivate people to aspire to personal ideals and enjoys promoting worthy causes and persuading others to join in. This child uses relational skills to solve problems, likes to please, avoids conflict, and values feelings over logic.

- **Learning Style of a Mover** — Your Mover child learns best primarily by investigating insights and determining by values. This child is drawn to hearing and creating new ideas, thinks globally about tasks, would rather learn a new skill than use an old one, and naturally looks for the new way to do things. This child values knowing and mastering social skills, works well in relational settings, likes to please others, values others' feelings over thoughts, and cares about creating harmony.

- **Mental Focus** — Active Movers focus their mental energy on the people and events in their lives. These children might organize their friends to pursue a cause or make changes. Reflective Movers focus their mental energy on their thoughts and ideas. These children tend to try to influence others with their deeply felt ideals.

- **Life Orientation** — Time-oriented Movers value predictable routines and plans that provide structure for them to pursue their ideals. They want to purposefully influence others. Experience-oriented Movers value flexibility that allows them to pursue new ideas and ideals that matter to them. They want to stay open to new possibilities.

- **Teaching a Mover** — This child is the most idealistic and possibility-oriented. The Mover child prefers interesting subjects such as reading, writing, and performance arts but not impersonal subjects that require routine work such as drill or workbook studies. Give them something to believe in—a meaningful reason for learning. Create new, nonroutine learning opportunities that enable this child to persuade others to action. Allow them to express their natural leadership abilities. Look for ways to give lessons from an inspirational perspective. This child loves learning ideas and ideals but can become impulsive and imprecise when completing a routine task or lesson and can be overly optimistic about goals and plans. A Mover will create an ideal learning space but will be drawn to interaction with others.

- **Reading with a Mover** — This child enjoys imaginative books and drama that are inspiring accounts of people pursuing a cause, including imaginative books with ideals. They are interested in imaginative and inspiring illustrations. When reading aloud to a Mover, seek out their impressions of the relationships in the book. Movers enjoy reading alone if the book appeals to their sense of ideals and meaningful relationships.

- **Motivating a Mover** — Look for the sparks of inspiration and ideals in this child and draw them out. Recognize their verbal and leadership skills. Affirm their insight, enthusiasm, and commitment. Affirm your relationship with them and how much they mean to you. This child is motivated by recognition from respected individuals.

- **Correcting a Mover** — Engage this child in a discussion of incorrect material. Always offer verbal, interpersonal correction, working through the material with them conversationally. The Mover child is very relational and needs to be encouraged to pay attention to nonpersonal details.

MOVER	Strengths	Weaknesses
LIVING	Highly imaginative. Sees life as meaningful. Driven to communicate ideas and inspire others.	Impractical. Impatient with things that don't captivate interest. Overly sensitive to negative criticism.
LEARNING	Motivated by meaning. Loves the arts and history. Driven by ideas and ideals and loves to discuss.	Easily discouraged by too many details. Hates learning that seems pointless.
LOVING	Deeply devoted and highly aware of others' feelings. Thrives on giving and receiving affirmation.	Hates conflict and avoids it at all costs. Can be defensive and overly sensitive to criticism.
LABORING	Can be very diligent once they are convinced of a project's beauty, worth, or meaning.	Easily discouraged by mundane tasks. May abandon a project if feeling overwhelmed.
LEADING	Strong values and relational skills. Naturally persuasive in enlisting support for a cause.	May back down in the face of conflict. Can be rigid about ideals and values.
LISTENING	Hears conceptually and relationally. Always aware of new ideas and others' needs.	Values orientation may lead to missed or ignored concrete, practical information in conversations.

Notes about SHAPER children

The SHAPER Child

Thinking Modes: Insights + Logic

Description: The imaginative child who conceives new things.

Life Motto: "I have a better idea."

Personal Encouragement

If God has given you a Shaper, he knew you could meet the challenges of educating this creative and innovative child. God designed your boy or girl to be the architect of new ideas and concepts, new ways of doing things, and unthought-of possibilities. God will someday use your Shaper child to conceive, envision, design, and plan new and effective ministries for God.

If your Shaper is a boy, his biblical role model might be the apostle Paul, whom God chose to envision and build his church among the Gentiles. Paul communicated the vision and gave his life to seeing the church grow. He led by the strength, clarity, and logic of his ideas and purposes.

If your Shaper is a girl, her biblical role model might be Mary, the mother of Jesus, who saw God's plan for the child in her womb. Mary's song reveals her grasp of what God was doing in and through her. She committed herself to that plan and to all it entailed. Her obedience would shape eternity.

Personality Profile

- **Summary** — Your Shaper child is inventive, imaginative, and especially good at any mental task that requires ingenuity. This idealistic child naturally finds new ways to do things, looks for new skills to learn, and envisions future possibilities and strategies to accomplish them. This child uses logic and objective analysis to solve problems, is a visionary thinker and planner, and values fairness (logic) over feelings.

- **Learning Style of a Shaper** — Your Shaper child learns best primarily by investigating insights and determining by logic. This child is drawn to hearing and creating new ideas, thinks globally about tasks, would rather learn a new skill than use an old one, and naturally looks for a new or better way to do things. This child is quick to understand ideas, wants decisions to make sense, values fairness and logic over feelings, and respects competence in the quest to make sense of things.

- **Mental Focus** — Active Shapers focus their mental energy on the people and events in their lives. These children draw others into their visions. Reflective Shapers focus their mental energy on their thoughts and ideas. These children are the conceivers and architects who envision and design new ways to do things.

- **Life Orientation** — Time-oriented Shapers value predictable routines and plans that enable them to think about possibilities. They want to solve problems with new solutions. Experience-oriented Shapers value spontaneity that allows them to respond to new and unexpected challenges. They want to stay open to new possibilities.

- **Teaching a Shaper** — This child is the most theoretical and abstract and consequently also the most independent. The Shaper child prefers creative and theoretical subjects such as math, science, and thinking skills but not subjects that require review, lots of written work, or group work. Give this imaginative child assignments that allow him to analyze and synthesize a broad range of ideas, concepts, and information. Create opportunities that exercise their desire to find new ways to do things. You need to tap into their natural creativity and quest for knowledge. This child has very high standards for their work but can become perfectionistic and negative about the work's quality and be generally pessimistic. A Shaper will create an orderly and logical learning space and will be quite content to do their work alone.

- **Reading with a Shaper** — This child will enjoy fiction and imaginative books and drama that provide new ways to look at the world, including complex and interesting literature. They are interested in imaginative, creative illustrations. When reading aloud to a Shaper, ask for their opinion about concepts and ideas in the book. Shapers enjoy reading alone if they find the book thought-provoking.

- **Motivating a Shaper** — Explain how an assignment fits into the big picture of learning. Recognize this child's creativity in analyzing and systematizing facts and information. Affirm their competence, intelligence, and ingenuity. A challenge met is its own reward for this child, but so is recognition for competence and innovation.

- **Correcting a Shaper** — When possible, direct this child to find and correct their own mistakes. Appeal to their sense of competence. Create new assignments or challenges to correct an area of learning. This child tends to be very individualistic and will need to be encouraged to participate in group activities and work with others.

SHAPER	Strengths	Weaknesses
LIVING	Highly independent and inventive. Driven to create and implement new ideas. Values competence.	Very internal and individualistic. Can be unaware of the needs of others.
LEARNING	Always seeking new ideas. Is bright and grasps new concepts. Self-driven in areas of interest.	Can lose interest in a subject once understood. Deeply perfectionistic and may condemn own good work.
LOVING	Loyal, devoted, and deeply committed to trusted loved ones in a quiet, steady way.	Uncomfortable with too much affection. Not naturally attuned to others' feelings.
LABORING	Self-motivated and highly competent. Will work tirelessly on a project that is of interest.	Hates to fail. May get bogged down in minutiae and quit if loses interest in the project.
LEADING	Natural leader through strong convictions, creative and clear ideas, and impartial logic.	May need help being sensitive to others' feelings. Finds managing group relationships tiresome.
LISTENING	Possibility, big-picture thinker. Hears, thinks, and plans in realm of possibilities and ideas.	Doesn't easily catch relational clues. May dismiss mundane details as unimportant.

Deep down, all of us just want to be understood and accepted for who we are. This understanding is the greatest gift we can give our children. It's the real essence of self-esteem.

— Paul D. Tieger & Barbara Barron-Tieger, *Nurture by Nature*, Little, Brown & Co., 1997

Understanding Your WholeHearted Child

This book is written for Christian homeschooling parents, so this chapter has been all about the advantages of understanding personality and learning styles for you, the parent. But there is more to the personality story. There are also advantages for your children. They probably will not come to understand those advantages by reading a book but rather by reading you. Your understanding and conversations about their personality types will seep into their minds and hearts and become a part of their self-understanding and self-image. Over time, in concert with their growing relationship with Christ, that additional insight into who they are will give them a great advantage in how they perceive themselves and in finding their place in the world. Let me close this chapter by considering just a few of the advantages for your children.

- **Self-Confidence** — The world of secular education has decided that self-esteem is a priority of public school philosophy. But that kind of feel-good goal for children or teens is misdirected. The real goal should be self-confidence that grows out of a deepening understanding of who your children are in Christ and how God has uniquely made their personalities for a purpose. The more your children or teens understand who they are, both spiritually and personally, the more confident they will become. Self-confidence is a powerful maturing quality.

- **Acceptance of Others** — Part of our sinful nature, especially while we are growing up, is to compare ourselves with others and judge one another by our differences. Understanding that God has made different personalities, each with a unique set of preferences, can help to neutralize conflicts with others and even encourage the appreciation of differences. Your children can begin to see how personality gifts are often closely related to spiritual gifts in the body of Christ and that God's command for us to "love one another" includes personality.

- **Life Focus** — If your children have a good understanding of their own personality traits and how to maximize their strengths and strengthen their weaknesses, they will be better able to discern a work, career, or ministry direction for their lives. The teen years of moving from young adulthood into adulthood can be a time of great uncertainty and confusion. When your children understand how God has made them to be motivated and driven in certain ways, that knowledge and insight can help them evaluate life-path choices with more discernment and confidence.

IN OUR HOME

We have talked personality in our home since our children were young. They grew up with a seasoned understanding of their own types and an appreciation for the types of others in the family. Everyone likes to defend their own type preference and give humorous examples of why others in the family are so obviously what they are. Some of our most memorable late-night discussions have been about personality type. When Joel headed to college, it was his understanding of his personality type that helped him realize a traditional degree was not for him, which led him to quit one college in order to go to Berklee College of Music. And he was right.

— Chapter 9 —

The WholeHearted Learning Youth: Beyond the WholeHearted Child

Diving into the Ocean

Swimming in the ocean can be scary. I don't mind hanging out on the beach and getting my feet wet in the shallow surf, but diving into a breaking wave and coming up farther out in deep water with nothing under my feet but more water—well that seriously tweaks my anxiety meter. As do all the mysterious dangers lurking unseen just beneath the surface. But once I start swimming I forget about my fears, and I just go with the flow and ride with the tide. It can still be scary at times, but it's better than sitting on the beach.

For many homeschooling parents, that is a fitting analogy for the transition from educating a wholehearted child to educating a wholehearted youth. As your children emerge from childhood and enter into young adulthood (their teens), swimming in the ocean of their culture will be natural to them. However, it probably won't be for you. When you dive into the wave of young adulthood with your children, you will soon find yourself in what can seem like a roiling ocean of changes, challenges, and choices. It can be scary. And that is when you will either start swimming with them or try to take them back to the safety and security of the beach. Swim!

Yes, you will need to study and understand the ocean that you will learn to navigate with your children. It's not at all like the waters you grew up swimming in, and there really are dangers lurking beneath its surface, but it's the water your children will grow up swimming in. That ocean of young adulthood is far too vast and deep and the waves of culture far too unpredictable to explore them in the ten short pages of this chapter. That's why this chapter is not about the ocean; this chapter is about you. It's simply about helping you think biblically and boldly about the critical years of young adulthood so you can have the greatest impact on your children's hearts while they are still in your home.

Educating the WholeHearted Child is about the ten amazing years between the ages of four and fourteen. After raising four wholehearted children using the WholeHearted Learning model, though, we are confident that the model will continue to work for raising wholehearted youth. The principles don't change when your children enter their teens. All of our children are intelligent, mature, motivated, and spiritual. They are all wholehearted children grown into wholehearted young adults who follow God with purpose and passion. This chapter is not about which high school curriculum to choose, what activities and cultural choices are acceptable or not, or how to prepare for the SAT, college, and a profession. The Holy Spirit will guide you in those areas, but keep this in mind: Your children won't remember all of the classes, textbooks, and tests of their teen years, but they will remember whether or not you chose to swim with them through the waters of their youth. We just encourage you to dive in. For their sakes, don't stay on the beach. Swim!

He who walks with the wise grows wise, but a companion of fools suffers harm.

— Proverbs 13:20

Far better it is to dare mighty things, to win glorious triumphs, even though checkered by failure, than to take rank with those poor spirits who neither enjoy much nor suffer much, because they live in the gray twilight that knows neither victory nor defeat.

— Theodore Roosevelt (1858-1919), 26th President of the United States

I write to you, dear children, because your sins have been forgiven on account of his name. I write to you, fathers, because you have known him who is from the beginning. I write to you, young men, because you have overcome the evil one. I write to you, dear children, because you have known the Father. I write to you, fathers, because you have known him who is from the beginning. I write to you, young men, because you are strong, and the word of God lives in you, and you have overcome the evil one.

— 1 John 2:12-14

Train a child (naar) *in the way* (derek) *he should go, and when he is old he will not turn from it.*

— Proverbs 22:6

Folly is bound up in the heart of a child (naar)*, but the rod of discipline will drive it far from him.*

— Proverbs 22:15

The Cult of Independence

Secular sociologists view the teen years as a time when young men and women separate from their parents to seek independence as preparation for adulthood. Many see it as part of an evolutionary process. Biblically, however, it is not a time of independence but of interdependence. The child is dependent; the youth is interdependent; the adult is independent. Don't allow culture to tell you that rebellion and independence are just to be expected in the teen years. God has a better way.

What Is God's View of Youth?

The teenager is not just an invention of modern American culture. Scripture affirms youth as one of three major stages in a person's life—childhood, young adulthood, and adulthood. Perhaps the clearest New Testament example of this progression is in 1 John 2:12-14 where John directly addresses his readers as children, fathers, and young men. Whatever the actual ages of those being addressed, the pattern of words John chooses to use would have been familiar to his readers, just as it still is to us today: Children become youth who become adults. Though physiological maturation is certainly a natural part of that process, John's pointed comments to each group suggest that each of the three life stages is also characterized by different aspects of spiritual maturation.

To understand the nature of the young adult phase of spiritual maturation, a fresh look at two familiar proverbs will be helpful. You've likely quoted Proverbs 22:6 countless times as a parent, yet never stopped to ask yourself, "How old is the child to be trained in this verse?" Well, the child here is a *naar*, a young man. In the context of the book of Proverbs, he is like the young man of chapters 1-9 who is tempted by wayward friends, sexual sins, and violence. In the same way, Proverbs 22:15 translated literally reads, "Foolishness is bound up in the heart of a *young man* [a *naar*]" (my translation). Foolishness, or folly, in this verse is not just childish immaturity but the willful rejection of God's wisdom by an untrained young man. The fool in Proverbs is not a child but one who knows enough to reject what is right (wisdom) and choose the wrong (folly). Solomon's point is that the foolishness of a young man is serious and must be disciplined, even with a rod if necessary, as a master would make a slave submit.

But there's more to consider in Proverbs 22:6. The term translated "train" is the Hebrew word *chanak*. It is used only three other times in the Old Testament, always in reference to dedicating the completed temple to God's intended purpose for it. The term translated "way" is the Hebrew word *derek*. Others read a variety of meanings into the word, but the most natural understanding of "the *way* he should go" within the context of Proverbs is simply the way of God or the path of righteousness. The trained young man will follow God. With those insights in mind, listen to a literal rendering of Proverbs 22:6: "Dedicate a young man to following God's way of wisdom. When he is grown, he will not turn aside from that way" (my translation). Here's the picture Solomon is painting: When the building of childhood has been completed, it is time to dedicate a young man (or woman) to God's intended purpose for their life. This is Solomon's call to godly parents to get serious about discipline and training that will put their young adult's feet firmly on God's path—the way of life. It is not a time to let go, as culture suggests, but rather to take hold of them and lead them into their full purpose as godly, mature adults.

John said he was writing to the young men "because you are strong, and the word of God lives in you, and you have overcome the evil one." John's words should become a clear goal as we walk with our teens through young adulthood—to be strong in faith, to know God's living Word, and to resist Satan's temptations. Many well-meaning parents make the mistake of thinking that young adulthood is just a transitional phase in growing up—a time of becoming less of a child and more of an adult. But that misses the biblical reality that it is a God-designed season of life and you must treat it seriously. Young adulthood is the time to rededicate yourself to dedicating your child to God.

What Is Culture's View of Youth?

Culture is complex and constantly changing, perhaps more rapidly than ever before, but you do not have to become a sociologist to navigate young adulthood with your child. You do, however, need to understand the one, primary, primal force that will always be tugging at your child during those years. No, not *that* one, but rather...conformity. To return to the earlier analogy, conformity is the riptide in the ocean of culture. If you don't understand and respect its power, it can pull your child far out into the ocean of culture quickly and without warning. We have seen too many Christian homeschooled young adults get pulled deep into culture's waters. Some get back but are beaten and scarred; some are still lost; some drown. More often than not, those young adults were sent out by well-meaning parents to swim in the ocean alone or without sufficient training. If you go into the water knowing the power of cultural conformity and you are with your child training them how to avoid its dangerous currents, then it is nothing to fear. They are not meant to sit on the beach but to swim in the ocean. That is where people need to be saved.

That's why not all cultural conformity is bad or evil. Your child will make choices about clothing, music, styles, tastes, and more that will not be about rebelling, as sociologists like to suggest, but only about belonging. It will simply be about your child's natural and legitimate desire to identify with the culture in which they find themselves by birth and to which they will belong as adults. You can help them to be wise and discerning in making those choices, but you should minor on the outward symbols of culture that are mostly only temporary badges of belonging and major instead on the inward growth of character that reveals who they are becoming. If their hearts are good and open to you and they are seeking God, then those outward cultural issues will pass by like so much flotsam and jetsam on the waves. The real issue will not be what they look like outside but who they look like inside. If they are becoming like Christ, then you're doing your job. And they will be able to do their job to take Christ to their own culture.

We want to think it's all about the danger of our children conforming to culture, but that's only half the problem. It's also about well-meaning Christian parents conforming to culture—even homeschooling parents. For over a hundred years, the social order of home and family in America has been dominated and shaped by public and private schooling. Everything in the life of a family is expected to conform to the juggernaut of institutional learning—preschool, primary, secondary, college. The system promises security, success, and a decent living for your child. That promise, though, comes with a catch. It's good only if you do it their way. Choose a different path and you're on your own.

Homeschooling has been a different path, and it has proved culture wrong for over a generation. However, conformity is making a comeback. Many homeschool parents who started out as biblical idealists in the primary years are becoming cultural conformists in the secondary. As their children enter the high school years, the constant drumbeat of conformity and the siren song of cultural promises drowns out their idealism, and they subtly slip back into the system. They put their children in school, or they begin teaching to the SAT for the college track, or they focus solely on academics and credits. And it is this well-intentioned parental conformity ("I only want to be sure my child has the best") that throws their child into the cultural ocean, often alone and without sufficient training, to battle the riptides and figure out how to swim. We need a new ideal.

Prolonged Adolescence

Adolescence is the period of time between puberty and maturity. The idea of maturity, though, has become quite fluid. With the fixed age/grade structure of public schooling, and the four-year college plan following it, the end of adolescence has become a moving target culturally. As a result, many teens and young adults now postpone adulthood until well into their twenties, psychologically enabled by a system that allows them to be considered a pre-adult long beyond the time previous generations would recognize the entrance into adulthood. Adulthood is a state of mind and maturity, not a grade level. A young man or woman who is considered and treated as adult will more likely rise to that perception, regardless of cultural practice.

The Truth about Civilization

The American culture is all about education. The prevailing view is that education ensures civilization—that our system of schooling guarantees the success of our civilization. The idea of Horace Mann's common school was to unify social classes and cultures to create a unified society. Biblically and historically, just the opposite is true. Civilization ensures education. It is the Christian influence of families that created our American civilization, and that is what ensures that children will learn. Families who value their children ensure they are educated.

Therefore, I urge you, brothers, in view of God's mercy, to offer your bodies as living sacrifices, holy and pleasing to God—this is your spiritual act of worship. Do not conform any longer to the pattern of this world, but be transformed by the renewing of your mind. Then you will be able to test and approve what God's will is—his good, pleasing and perfect will.

— Romans 12:1-2

The god of this age has blinded the minds of unbelievers, so that they cannot see the light of the gospel of the glory of Christ, who is the image of God.

— 2 Corinthians 4:4

The weapons we fight with are not the weapons of the world. On the contrary, they have divine power to demolish strongholds. We demolish arguments and every pretension that sets itself up against the knowledge of God, and we take captive every thought to make it obedient to Christ.

— 2 Corinthians 10:4-5

The map of humanism leads to a loss of the true humanness of man. The map of the New Age directs man toward a false spirituality. The Biblical world view leads to the personal infinite God. Only as man bows to God as both Creator and Savior will he find ultimate fulfillment.

— David Quine, *Let Us Highly Resolve*, The Cornerstone Curriculum Project, 1996

The Cultural Challenge: Conform or Transform?

The confrontation with conformity is not new, nor is our twenty-first-century version of it especially unique. It goes way back, but the apostle Paul got to the heart of the matter best in two short verses in his letter to the Romans. Before we move on to exploring a different ideal for young adulthood, it is critical to understand Paul's charge to followers of Jesus in Romans 12:1-2. In the first eleven chapters of his letter, Paul lays out his doctrinal magnum opus covering sin (1-3), salvation (4-5), sanctification (6-8), and sovereignty (9-11). In the final section of Romans, Paul will talk about service (12-15). But first, Paul lays out a pivotal truth that is critical to the entire letter. In Romans 12:1-2, Paul asserts that if Christ in you doesn't change how you view every aspect of your life, then you really aren't listening to God's view of reality. Jesus changes everything.

Paul makes clear in the first verse that we have only one reasonable response to all that God has done for us—to offer ourselves to him as "living sacrifices." We are not dead sacrifices but alive in Christ and able to yield our lives to his will and to place ourselves on the altar as a "spiritual act of worship." It's the same offering that Paul enjoins earlier in his letter to "offer yourselves to God, as those who have been brought from death to life" (6:13). That can only happen, though, if the two commands in the next verse are obeyed. The first command is to stop letting the world tell you how to think. In our day, Paul might say, "Stop being passively conformed to the way the world thinks!" In other words, stop letting the current "isms" of your time shape how you think about your life and about your children—secularism, materialism, pragmatism, educationalism, whateverism. When those patterns replace God's truth in your thinking, you've conformed. The second command is to go to God's Word to keep your mind renewed by truth. The real power of God's Word is not just that it's true and trustworthy, but that it transforms—it is the "living and active" Word that penetrates and changes "soul and spirit" and "thoughts and attitudes" (Hebrews 4:12). The only way to know you are doing God's will as a parent is to constantly renew your mind with God's truth. You become a conformist to the world's ways of thinking by default; you become a biblical idealist only by design.

Romans 12:1-2 is a critical passage for parents of young adults. It is an uncomplicated description of God's design for what it means to be a disciple of Jesus Christ. I have taught it to parents and youth as the three signs of a disciple. Think of them as traffic signs along God's path of life: YIELD to God; STOP the world; GO to the Word. Uncomplicated, but also uncompromising. When high school and college issues start flooding into your world at home, along with all the world's opinions about what is best for your children, don't take one step forward until Romans 12:1-2 is deeply ingrained in your and your teens' hearts and minds. Paul promises that when you follow those three signs of a disciple, "Then you will be able to test and approve what God's will is—his good, pleasing and perfect will." In other words, you will be transformed rather than conformed. Don't risk having to taste the bitter fruits of conformity because you passively accept the world's way of doing things rather than actively transforming your life by faith. Don't risk the faith of your children by betting on the world's promises of security and success rather than proving that God's will is "good, pleasing and perfect" by stepping out in faith to choose a transformed way of living and learning. It's just two simple verses. But in them is the way to the new ideal. It's time to transform young adulthood!

The Parenting Challenge: Transformed Youth!

Ask yourself this question: "In an ideal world, how would I as a Christian homeschooling parent want to prepare my young adult child for life?" Would your ideal world include textbooks and tests, entrance exams, unknown professors, student loans, dorm life, and leaving home at seventeen or eighteen for the college experience? If you did not feel caught in and rushed by the conforming patterns of the American educational system, what would you do differently? There's no single right answer, but as our children approached young adulthood, we knew what we wanted that time to include—lots of great books, long discussions, message making and refining, discipleship and ministry, freedom to explore emerging gifts and abilities, walking with wise people, strong parent and child relationships, doing real things, and time to become. What we wanted, in essence, was more WholeHearted Learning, only self-directed, deeper, and more intense. We knew we didn't live in an ideal world, but by faith we chose to resist conformity and pursue instead a transformed approach to education in our children's young adult years.

The camel of institutional schooling poked its nose into the tent of the American family beginning in the mid-1800s and just kept moving in. But homeschooling is a whole new tent. With new economic realities forcing many families to pull back on spending and with rising tuitions putting campus-based college education out of reach for growing numbers, true alternatives to traditional secondary and campus-based college education are emerging. The digital revolution of personal computing, the Internet, Web 2.0 (and soon 3.0), Google, cloud computing, web conferencing, streaming audio and video, tablets, apps, e-books, mobile devices, and so much more are coalescing into a cost-effective, competitive alternative to the old-school ways of education. Online learning and degree programs, trade schools, ministry and missions opportunities, apprenticeships, and many others are expanding the tent even more with evolving independent learning options that will eventually reshape the paradigm for college and perhaps even for high school.

If you believe that God's design for family can be trusted just as much as and more than man's design for education, then you have options now that have never existed before that can free you to follow your ideals with your teen. You have the opportunity to choose a different path—one that can literally transform your child's young adult years, both experientially and spiritually. It's easy and convenient simply to follow the cultural norms. The ruts in that path run deep from generations before you. Just understand that those ruts also make it very difficult to turn back once you head down that road. Be sure that path is God's will before your child enters it. It takes faith to resist the pull of culture and to trust God with your ideals.

God is always ready to direct your path (Proverbs 3:5-6) and to reward your faith (Hebrews 11:6). Your reward will be to share in your children's spiritual transformation as you walk with them on the path to adulthood. If God leads you to take the traditional path of education and college preparation, just be sure to carefully evaluate both what you are getting and what you are giving away. If you feel like you are falling into educational ruts by default, then step on the brakes and take some time to think about it all. We are not writing this chapter to tell you what to do but rather just to share what we've done and to encourage you to think outside the cultural box before you jump into it. It will be worth it.

It is better to fail in originality than to succeed in imitation.

— Herman Melville (1819-1891), American novelist and essayist

The Age/Grade Trap

Institutional schooling has programmed how we think about children. Culture has created an identity trap that prejudges a child's development based on the arbitrary and meaningless standard of "What grade are you in?" Rather than assessing a child's knowledge and maturity based on who they are and what they know, the assumption is that a ninth grader is less knowledgeable and mature than an eleventh grader simply because of the age/grade difference. It is false assumption that reinforces the cultural commitment to conformity as a desirable norm. Reject the age/grade paradigm. Let your children learn at their own pace in their own way without regard to culture's opinion of their conformity. Conform to Christ, not to culture.

The Costs of Education

We all know the escalating tangible costs of a four-year, on-campus college education—tuition, room, board, books, transportation, and more. Even with some scholarships and grants and working during learning, the college loan debt can become staggering. The specter of that debt and the need to win whatever scholarships are possible are what drive many parents to conform early to the system and to play the educational game in order to acquire a college degree for the least money. But few take the time to calculate the intangible costs of taking that path—lost time with children in their critical teen years, reduced focus on spiritual life in order to focus on educational goals, increased stress from the need to achieve, greater influence of school and peers than family, lost opportunities for real life, fewer books read and enjoyed. Count all the costs.

And without faith it is impossible to please God, because anyone who comes to him must believe that he exists and that he rewards those who earnestly seek him.

— Hebrews 11:6

The tragedy in life doesn't lie in not reaching your goal. The tragedy lies in having no goal to reach. It isn't a calamity to die with dreams unfulfilled, but it is a calamity not to dream. It is not a disaster to be unable to capture your ideal, but it is a disaster to have no ideal to capture. It is not a disgrace not to reach the stars, but it is a disgrace to have no stars to reach for.

— Benjamin Mays (1894-1984), American minister and educator

Hearing God's Call in Youth

Childhood is the time to train and instruct your child in the words and ways of biblical Christianity. Young adulthood is a time for your child to examine what they were taught in childhood. It is a critical phase of moving from receiving truth in childhood to perceiving it in young adulthood to believing it in adulthood. It is a process of ownership and internalization that will shape how your child thinks about life and faith. Here are some of the issues and topics we study, discuss, and examine with our teens to bring their calling into sharper focus.

- Identity in Christ
- Kingdom mentality
- Walking by faith
- Biblical worldview
- Theological perspectives
- Philosophical perspectives
- Apologetics
- Spiritual gifts
- Masculinity/femininity
- Personality gifts
- Skills and abilities
- Circumstances
- Resources available
- Relationships
- Family heritage

Preparing Your Child for a Calling

We have become convinced—not just in theory but by actual practice with four teens—that our primary purpose with our children in the high school years is not just to prepare them for college but rather to prepare them for a calling. It is the calling of God on their lives that should guide your children to decide what to do about college, not the other way around. By calling we don't mean some mysterious and subjective divine directive but rather a settled conviction about vocation. It is the confidence that comes from testing and knowing the unique abilities, messages, and experiences that God has entrusted to your child and the commitment to use them for God's kingdom. Calling is about stewardship—investing God's gifts for God's glory. Our commitment is to prepare our children to make a life that will please God and then prepare them to make a living with God's help.

It has been only a little over a century that American families have been lulled into accepting by default an educational paradigm that not only supplants the God-designed role of family but can even subvert it. Before the advent and domination of the public and institutional school movement, family was the controlling paradigm for education. Public schooling changed that, but the homeschooling movement has reasserted the primacy of the family in the education of a child. However, although many families will homeschool through high school, far too many will not, conforming instead in the young adult years to the cultural paradigm of formal classrooms, textbooks, tests, grades, and performance. But why? What causes so many families to abandon the ideals that brought them to homeschooling at the very time in their child's life when they are needed the most? Some will do so out of familiarity—everyone else is doing it, it's what they grew up with and they turned out fine, so it's a reasonable choice. Some will do so out of formula—it's considered the most proven method to ensure their children's success as adults and probably their own perceived success as parents. Some will do so out of fear—they simply are afraid of doing the wrong thing so they listen to and conform to the prevailing culture rather than "taking any chances" with their children's lives.

The few years of your children's lives between the end of their childhood and the beginning of their adulthood are too critical to the rest of their lives to be guided by anything other than faith. If you abandon their hearts to culture out of familiarity, formula, or fear, whether intentionally or unintentionally, you risk losing the brief window of opportunity you have during their young adult years to dedicate and direct them to understand and own the calling of God on their lives. Too many Christian and homeschooling parents unintentionally begin to act as though God does not exist as their young adult children grow older, and they become narrowly focused on transcripts, GPA, SAT, ACT, and getting into a prestigious college. No matter what decisions you make about their education and career, the simple reality is that you cannot dedicate and direct them into their calling except by faith. If you focus on faith in those years, your reward will be to know that you and your child will be focused on believing in and pleasing God, not just on conforming to culture. If Scripture is the fuel that will transform your and your child's minds, then faith is the spark that will keep it ignited. That kind of faith is not just passive belief, though, but active believing. God-pleasing faith not only "believes that he exists" but also "that he rewards those who earnestly seek him" (Hebrews 11:6). God has a calling on your young adult's life. You can believe him for that. Faith is simply taking God at his word.

Preparing Your Child for a Career

As the calling of God on your child's life becomes more clear, the choice of a career should become a more natural process. But let's rethink that term. By etymological coincidence, the origins of the word "career" mean a road or a race track. To put it in Old Testament perspective, a young adult's career would be about finding their place on the path of life with God—getting on the right track in life. Our goals as parents during the teen years should be to help each child follow their calling and find their career. That is not the same as saying our goal is to help them find a profession, a job, or a business. Choosing a career path is finding the most suitable course for your calling, however that career then leads you to make a living. For our purposes here, determining calling and career is about making a life; creating income is about making a living. Each has a distinct purpose, and each is a critical part of your child's successful transition from young adulthood to adulthood.

Here's how you might look at the young adult years differently if you focus on helping your child make a life before thinking about making a living. Making a living is about learning a skill, trade, or profession that is in demand and being financially rewarded for your particular knowledge or service that meets a need. There are many ways to make a living, and the required skills can be learned and mastered by many means. To make a living well and honorably in a way that pleases God, though, is also about relationships, responsibility, hard work, resourcefulness, and wisdom. Those things cannot be learned in a classroom. And that's where making a life comes in. If all of the focus when your child turns fourteen or fifteen turns to "How can you make a living?" then the real need to help them first determine their calling and career will never get in focus and you will never be able to go back for a do-over. That's why we determined to focus in those years on who our children would become rather than only on what they would do.

- **Maturity** — Christian maturity is Job One during the teen years. Biblical character and godly virtues do not just happen by accident. We are growing disciples of Christ, which requires strategic training and concerted effort over a limited period of time.

- **Ministry** — Serving God by serving others in the family, church, and community is the primary training ground during youth for later serving employers, customers, clients, and even a spouse. Ministry is a barometer of growth in Christian maturity.

- **Message** — We believe God has written a message on every person's heart. It's our privilege as parents to discover and release that message in our children's hearts and to help them learn how to express it effectively. We are training communicators.

- **Marriage** — Training to be a desirable spouse begins in earnest in youth, when attitudes about marriage and children, relational skills, and life habits are formed.

- **Motivation** — Self-motivation, self-direction, and self-confidence are keys to future success in life. Youth is the ideal time in life to begin practicing those traits.

- **Management** — Life management skills are best learned and habituated in youth—time management, project planning, setting/achieving goals, resource management.

- **Manners** — Manners and graciousness are the language arts of relational skills. What is trained and habituated in youth becomes a lifetime advantage and vice versa.

The Indie Learner

There are many options now that make thinking outside the cultural box a positive option.

- Community college
- Distance learning
- Online learning and degree programs
- Internships
- Apprenticeships
- Entrepreneurial opportunities
- Trade schools
- Industry training

Academy of Communication

The learning years from fourteen to eighteen are a critical time for developing competence and confidence. It is an ideal time to begin to identify and release the message God has placed in your child's heart. An academy of communication arts once a week can provide a social environment with other teens in a context of learning and doing meaningful projects. It can include Bible study, history study, Christian worldview, communications skills, writing, speaking, drama, blogging, performing, and more.

Homeschool Outliers

In his 2008 book *Outliers*, Malcolm Gladwell challenges the notion that exceptionally successful people possess inherent genius and talent. He shows that instead, "They are invariably the beneficiaries of hidden advantages and extraordinary opportunities and cultural legacies that allow them to learn and work hard and make sense of the world in ways others cannot." He cites the "10,000 Hour Rule" of practicing a task as the key to success in any field. We've seen that in our children. Sarah has put in 10,000 hours reading countless books, revealed in her profound insights into story. Joel has put 10,000 hours in composition, expressed in his success in school and his musical abilities. Homeschooling, especially in the formative high school years, is uniquely suited to allowing a child a shot at 10,000 hours.

Why We Graduate Early

We graduate our children from high school around age fifteen or sixteen. Here's why. By that age, it is usually clear to us that they are beyond being mommied anymore and are ready to move on in life and take on new challenges. The desire and ability to learn was instilled in childhood, so we are confident in graduating our children from formal schooling and moving on to intentional, self-directed learning. The next two years are a time to fill in learning gaps, explore possibilities, develop gifts and skills, read widely, write, discuss, and have the freedom to learn without classroom walls and borders. In those two years, we are giving each child time to add real-life experience to their learning so the decision about college will be based on who they are (their calling) and what they are meant to do (their career), rather than on the arbitrary next step on the age/grade education treadmill.

Projects and Possibilities

Each child has a senior project—write a book (Sarah), create a CD of original piano compositions (Joel), write and perform original songs (Nathan), create a CD, book, and performance (Joy). We explore all of our children's gifts and talents.

Classes, Co-ops, and Camps

Our teens loved being in home education co-ops to learn with friends, in special classes for subjects and skills (piano, photography, dancing), in worldview camps (Summit Ministries, MasterWorks), in arts camps and projects (community theater productions, musicals), and in church and community events (holiday programs, historical re-enactments). We also created groups of friends that provided purposeful fellowship—mother/daughter group, video production club, Inklings discussion group, boys nights out, book clubs, Bible studies, and many others.

Our Story: Learning and Living with Youth

All the ideas and ideals of the previous pages are just a first step. The real journey will be wherever they take you with your teen children. That will be *your* story. If you wait for instructions, you might miss the opportunity. Even if an "Educating the Whole-Hearted Youth" book were on the agenda (it's not), you don't need a manual to live by faith. We can tell you what we did as a family, but we can't tell you what to do for *your* family. We can only challenge you to think differently and to step out in faith.

Learning with Our Wholehearted Youth

We looked beyond the cultural paradigms to think about what a commonsense, family-centered, biblical approach to educating our teens would look like. These priorities became what WholeHearted Learning by faith looked like in our home with our teens.

- **Word: Learn from God.** In childhood, our children learn from us as we learn from God. In youth, we expect them to learn directly from God and to begin to own their relationship and walk with him. We suggest Bible studies; offer books to read, audio to listen to, videos to watch; and talk regularly about what they are learning from God in their personal Bible study and devotions.

- **Wisdom: Learn from others.** We want our children to know that we don't know everything and to seek out wisdom from other godly, trusted people. ("He who walks with the wise grows wise," Proverbs 13:20.) We bring men and women into our home, encourage our children to make appointments, and listen to great speakers.

- **Walk: Learn from life.** This is addressed on page 177, but we use life as a classroom. We talk about people and events in the news; discuss messages in media, songs, and movies; and think critically about political and social issues.

- **Ways: Explore the possibilities.** We give our children freedom and opportunity to explore their gifts, abilities, drives, and desires. Youth is a critical time to test and discover the "real me" as they move toward an uncertain future. They need freedom, direction, and encouragement to try and to learn from both success and failure.

- **Words: Read more books.** WholeHearted Learning still works in high school. The core of our learning model is still books and reading, only now we expect the reading to become wider and deeper. We direct some reading choices and give freedom for the rest, but reading is a constant expectation in their teen years. We make an effort to start a library of books for each child—fiction, nonfiction, arts, and reference.

- **Words: Discuss more ideas.** Narration in childhood reading becomes discussion in youth. We create a highly verbal environment in our home where ideas and insights are routinely discussed with interest. It is a crucible for developing communication skills—the ability to present and defend personal views and opinions effectively.

- **Words: Write more essays.** We also encourage a highly scribal environment in our home, where the ability to write well is valued and affirmed. Essays and opinion papers help our children learn how to write clearly and effectively about topics of interest and also provide an opportunity to critique mechanics and style.

Living with Our Wholehearted Youth

You cannot separate learning from living—they are two sides of the same coin. We put just as much effort, maybe more, into creating a rich living experience for our teens as we put into creating strategic learning goals. Life is more than education.

- **Family** — We place a high priority on family in our children's teen years. We want to give them reasons to prefer family and to see it as both a launching pad and a safe place. We make our home available for them to use for events, meetings, groups, and entertainment with their friends. We stay in their lives, connected and aware.

- **Friends** — Friendships and relationships are an important part of any teen's life. We look for families, groups, events, and classes to provide a pool of friends, as well as create study groups that meet in our home. We want each child to learn how to get along with others, be committed, make moral choices, and be a leader.

- **Church** — We know the arguments about youth groups, but by the time our children are fifteen to sixteen, we are moving into a trust relationship with them and expect them to make good choices. Church will be a part of their adulthood, and it should be a part of their youth, especially for ministry, leadership, and special events.

- **Culture** — We respect culture, but we do not fear it. We believe God has brought our children into this world to be lights for him in their culture. We interface with culture together in order to help them learn to think critically about their place in it.

- **Work** — We encourage our children to find part-time jobs during their teens to learn the disciplines of work—responsibility, dependability, punctuality, and excellence.

- **Trips** — There is so much that can be gained from trips—history, government, important people, ministries, and much more. As we travel we also listen together to audiobooks and talk about them, discuss many subjects, and grow closer as a family.

- **Events** — We stay alert to special events that can broaden perspectives and create new relationships—conferences, seminars, concerts, retreats, and more.

- **Media** — Our children will grow up in a media-dominated culture. We help them walk through the minefield of media with a biblical worldview.

IN OUR HOME

Sarah, our firstborn, is a good example of taking a transformed, Indie learning path. She was raised wholeheartedly as a child and youth, graduated early at sixteen, and began writing. Due to family moves, travel opportunities, and health issues, she put off college. Instead, she wrote two books, developed a speaking ministry, was mentored by a retired professor of English literature, traveled to five continents, wrote and edited for our ministry, interned with an apologetics ministry in England, developed blogs and was invited to be a guest author on a popular faith and arts blog, and much more. Now, at twenty-six, she is considering an accelerated bachelor's degree program in writing and literature.

"In Your Life" Parenting

An important part of our homeschooling strategy in the teen years is what we call "in your life" parenting. We stay involved in every aspect of our children's lives. We want (and expect) to know about friends and activities. We ask about feelings, fears, moods, and conflicts. Nothing is off limits. It works because they know our questions are out of love, concern, and care, not out of rules and regulations. We are in their life with grace, not law, and that keeps us there. We give up our lives so we can be in their lives.

Saying Yes to Friends

It is healthy and natural for your teenaged children to want friends and a bigger life beyond the walls of your home. There is nothing wrong or disrespectful about that kind of desire. However, we also know that they won't look for life outside the home if they feel there is life inside of it. That is why we sacrifice to make sure our home is a place of life and light where they can bring their friends. We open our home, hearts, and lives to them. Of course, we pray they find good and godly friends, but we also know that friendships can occasionally be challenging. When there is a good friend who makes bad choices, we don't panic, but we open our lives to our child and the friend. We work through it together as a ministry and as a learning bridge to adult relationships.

The Youth Group Quandary

We approach the issue of youth group with caution. We do not fear that our children will be caught up in youth group culture, and we want our teens to be able to meet, worship, and minister with friends from church, but we don't want a group that disagrees with our beliefs and convictions about family and ministry. We discuss, discern, and pray, but encourage and trust our children to make those assessments.

Parents in the Picture

The key to transformed parenting in the young adult years is to stay in the picture. We know that whatever we want our children to become and do, they need to see it in some form in our lives. It's the discipleship principle of Jesus in Luke 6:40, "A student is not above his teacher, but everyone who is fully trained will be like his teacher." Many parents we hear just want to get out of their teen children's way and let them go. We also want to give our children freedom to grow, but we want to take hold of their lives, not let go, and stay in the picture in their teen years. The more we are in their lives, the more we will earn the right and the privilege to speak into their hearts the things of God and challenge them to walk with him and serve him.

Children on the Launch Pad

Our children have never heard us say that we longed for the day when they would leave home so we could get our lives back. We have only longed for the day when we could send our children from our home as mature Christian men and women to be lights in the world for God and his kingdom. We want to be in their lives as long as it takes to know we did all we could, by faith and God's grace, to launch them into adulthood ready to follow and serve God.

The Bigger Story: Changing the World

Perhaps you're thinking, "There are a lot of easier ways to do high school!" No argument there, but our decision to do high school differently is about something more than efficiency. After pouring ten years of our hearts and lives into each of our children, high school for us is about preserving and continuing that commitment as our children reach the most exciting and strategic time in their lives. It's about completing the vision that started us on this WholeHearted Learning journey—to raise wholehearted children for Christ who will be leaders in their generation. The days of their youth are the critical years for making that happen. Let me explain with the story of two strategic youths in the Bible.

Josiah was eight years old when he became king of Israel. The northern kingdom had fallen to the Assyrians eighty years before, and after fifty-seven years of wicked rule in Judah by his father and brother, Josiah would rule righteously in Jerusalem for thirty-one years. At age sixteen, "while he was still a youth [a *naar*], he began to seek the God of his father, David" (2 Chronicles 34:3, NASB) and cleansed the land of pagan worship. At age twenty-six he set about to repair and restore the forgotten and neglected house of God, the temple, and there the Law of God was discovered in the rubble. As it was read aloud to him, Josiah was deeply convicted by Israel's years of disobedience, and he sought the Lord. His repentance in 621 B.C. began a revival in Judah for the rest of his reign.

Now imagine for a moment there was among the nobles in Josiah's courts a young couple who responded to his call to repentance and obedience and who loved God with all their hearts just as their king Josiah did. And imagine that young couple had a child at that time, and they raised him during Josiah's revival. When the child was twelve years old, in 609 B.C., Josiah died at age thirty-nine. Suspecting that Judah's days were few, the child's righteous parents began to teach him and train him in all the Law and the ways of God—to pour into him their very hearts and lives out of obedience to God. Just four years later in 605 B.C., King Nebuchadnezzar would enter Jerusalem, raid the temple, and deport the best and brightest young Israelite nobles back to Babylon. Among them was a handsome sixteen-year-old young man named…Daniel. And you know the rest of the story. Daniel, like Josiah in Judah at age sixteen, took a stand for God in Babylon. He distinguished himself before Kings Nebuchadnezzar and Cyrus and before the people of Babylon. God was with Daniel, and he became a powerful witness for God's presence and righteousness in a pagan land and culture. He was prepared in King Josiah's courts by godly parents and was ready in his youth when God called him to follow him and stand for him.

We all live like we think we know what the future holds. We assume life will go on as we have known it, our children can count on a certain amount of predictability, and we as parents can sort of ease on down the road as our teens navigate a familiar path through life. All that may be true, but the biblical reality is, "You do not even know what will happen tomorrow. What is your life? You are a mist that appears for a little while and then vanishes" (James 4:14). That's why we resist conforming and choose instead what we consider a transformed approach to high school for our young adult children. We are jealous for the hearts and souls of our children. We don't want to let go of them right when our parenting can have the greatest impact on who they become and how they live their lives for God. Whatever the future may hold, we want to face it knowing that we did all we could to put them on God's path. We want them to be in the bigger story.

Section 3

Methods

WholeHearted Learning Methods

DISCIPLESHIP STUDIES METHODS

DISCIPLINED STUDIES METHODS

DISCUSSION STUDIES METHODS

DISCOVERY STUDIES METHODS

DISCRETIONARY STUDIES METHODS

— Chapter 10 —

Discipleship Studies Methods: The Study of the Bible

Go into Your Home and Make Disciples

"The fear of the Lord is the beginning of knowledge; fools despise wisdom and instruction" (Proverbs 1:7, NASB). Solomon was setting the theme in this verse for his entire 915-verse collection of wise sayings, but he was also speaking directly to the heart of his young adult son (1:8, *naar*). Here's what Solomon might have said in person: "Son, you must fear the Lord before anything else—all knowledge for living wisely and well begins with God. It is what I believe and live, and if you turn away from my wisdom and instruction, you will show you do not fear God, and you will be choosing to live as a fool. Listen to my instruction!" Solomon was exhorting his son to follow God.

If that sounds like the father of Ephesians 6:4 in the New Testament—the father who is to bring up his children "in the training and instruction of the Lord"—that's no coincidence. God is consistent, and though the terminology may change over time, the methodology does not. What these fathers are described as doing is the same as what Jesus commanded us to do in his Great Commission in Matthew 28:18-20—to "make disciples" of our children and to teach them "to obey everything I have commanded you." It's all discipleship. It's the process of making your child a follower of Jesus.

We start our WholeHearted Learning model with Discipleship Studies because a disciple is a follower—literally a learner. That is why your responsibility to disciple your children is so foundational to your ability to educate them. If you desire to teach your children effectively, their hearts must first be turned to God. One way young children do that is by learning how to honor and obey their parents "in the Lord" (Ephesians 6:1). Until your children submit their hearts to God and to you, you cannot effectively educate their minds. In fact, in view of eternity, it is far more important that your children become wholehearted disciples of Jesus Christ than it is that they become well educated. A mature disciple of Jesus Christ with the will and skill to learn is much more useful to God and his kingdom than a well-educated but immature Christian.

True biblical discipleship is not a responsibility you can put off or turn over to your church or to someone else. Jesus commanded his followers to "make disciples," and that certainly should include your children. In our homeschooling model, Discipleship Studies focus on the study of God's Word. Now that we have the full revelation of God in the Old and New Testaments, the Bible has become the "wisdom and instruction" of Solomon's counsel and the "everything I have commanded you" of Jesus' commission. We have a Great Family Commission now to make disciples of our children. That is the foundation of our homeschooling model—the solid rock upon which, like the house of the wise man in Matthew 7:24-27, the whole house of learning you are building will stand strong.

I have hidden your word in my heart that I might not sin against you...I will never forget your precepts, for by them you have preserved my life...Your word is a lamp to my feet and a light for my path...You are my refuge and my shield; I have put my hope in your word.

— Psalm 119:11, 93, 105, 114

Let the word of Christ dwell in you richly as you teach and admonish one another with all wisdom.

— Colossians 3:16

For the word of God is living and active. Sharper than any double-edged sword, it penetrates even to dividing soul and spirit, joints and marrow; it judges the thoughts and attitudes of the heart.

— Hebrews 4:12

Bible reading is an education in itself.

— Alfred, Lord Tennyson (1809-1892), Poet Laureate of Victorian England

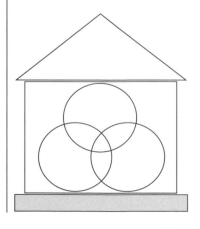

Bible Facts

The Bible is the best-selling printed book of all time. An estimated 61 million copies, in whole or in part, are distributed annually worldwide. It has been translated into over 1,200 languages and dialects. The first English translation of the Bible was made by John Wycliffe in 1382. The Bible was divided into chapters in 1228, Old Testament verses in 1488, and New Testament verses in 1551. The Gutenberg Bible was the first book printed with movable type in 1456 in Germany. William Tyndale's was the first printed English Bible (partial) in 1526. The Geneva Bible was the first printed with both chapters and verses in 1560 in England. The 1611 King James Version became the standard English Bible.

- The Bible was written over a span of about 1,500 years (1400 B.C. to A.D. 100), covering 40 generations, by 40 authors, on 3 continents (Asia, Africa, Europe), in 3 languages (Hebrew, Greek, Aramaic).
- There are 39 Old Testament books—17 historical, 5 poetical, 17 prophetic.
- There are 27 New Testament books—4 gospels, 21 epistles, Acts, and Revelation.
- There are 1,189 chapters and 31,101 verses in the Bible—929 and 23,214 in the Old Testament; 260 and 7,957 in the New Testament
- The shortest book in the Bible is 2 John (1 chapter, 13 verses); the longest is Psalms (150 chapters, 2,461 verses).
- The shortest chapter in the Bible is Psalm 117 (2 verses); the longest is Psalm 119 (176 verses).
- The shortest verse in the English Bible is John 11:35; the longest is Esther 8:9. In the original Greek, the shortest verse is 1 Thessalonians 5:16.
- The longest word in the Bible is "Maher-Shalal-Hash-Baz" in Isaiah 8:1.
- But the most important fact is that the Bible is God's revelation of himself to us.

Bible Knowledge

The Bible is God's wholly inspired revelation to mankind. In it, God has spoken, and we must listen. But it is also an inspired whole-book library in one volume. God has spoken through great historical literature, compelling storytelling, beautiful poetry, inspiring ideas and ideals, stimulating biography, and a wide variety of creative writing styles. In other words, the Bible is a holy whole book. It should be your first, last, and best resource for whole-book reading and the standard against which the content of all other literary works is judged. It is the starting point for giving your children an appetite for books because it is the book of books.

Of all the appetites for life and learning that you instill in your children's hearts, let a love for God's Word be one that you feed and stimulate every day. Let all others be minimized until you see the signs in your children's hearts of a godly hunger and thirst for righteousness. As you cultivate your children's appetite and love for the Word, be careful to avoid two extremes that will leave a bad taste, or no taste, for Scripture in their mouths. On the one end, avoid treating the Word primarily as a collection of inspiring stories and moral ideals to be enjoyed and valued. At the other end, avoid treating the Word primarily as a book of rules and principles that must be learned and obeyed. The correct attitude is found in the middle, where "grace and truth" meet in the person of Jesus Christ, who is "the Word [who] became flesh" (John 1:14). You should treat the Word of God, the Bible, as a personal message from the heart of God to you and your family.

Knowledge of Scripture has been in decline for decades, and research by The Barna Group, Gallup, and others suggests that it could soon be in freefall. Much of the present generation is rejecting the objective truths of biblical Christianity in favor of a subjective experience of spirituality. Increasingly, organized religion and the Bible are no longer trusted, as personal experience detached from divine revelation becomes the new norm. Your children will grow up in a culture that no longer knows Scripture or considers it to be revealed truth from God. The absolute truths of God's Word will find less and less traction in the minds of a new generation of postmodern Christians who see no irony in holding to the firm belief that truth is relative and feel no conviction from a Bible they personally value, but only for its religious thoughts and wisdom for living. Rich Mullins expressed in his powerful song "Creed" in 1993, a musical version of the Apostles' Creed, that it is not we who create the truth that shapes our lives, but rather it is God's truth that forms our very being. That has been the central belief of Christians since the birth of the church. There will still be churches, movements, and Christians faithful to the truths of God's Word, but the larger culture will no longer identify with them as in the past.

The concept of a Christian culture is rare in history. It is possible we are at the start of a time of decline of American Christianity. You must prepare your children to be faithful in their generation, when faith could be questioned or even rejected; to be "children of God without fault in a crooked and depraved generation, in which [they will] shine like stars in the universe as [they] hold out the word of life" (Philippians 2:15-16a). Teaching them the Bible is not just one more academic subject to check off—it is putting God's Word into their hearts and minds and preparing them to hold out that Word to others in the darkness. It is making them light. Bible knowledge is God's life and light.

Knowing the Bible as God's Truth

Your children will accept the inspiration, authority, and reliability of the Bible during their childhood years because they trust you, their parents. They will be confident in the Bible's truth because you are. However, as they move into their young adult years, they will need to come to their own convictions about the Bible's accuracy and truthfulness. They will need to find and own their own reasons to accept Scripture as divinely-inspired, reliable, and trustworthy. That is not always a process you can control, and it will likely take place over a period of time, but it is a necessary process of maturity and faith. Perhaps the most effective way you can be a part of that process is to make sure you don't neglect teaching and talking about the reasons throughout their childhood. That is part of that solid foundation you are building with Discipleship Studies. The more your children hear and learn about the Bible's reliability, the clearer and easier their path will be as young adults to a full confidence in Scripture as God's revealed Word.

- **How We Got the Bible** — The study of the origins of the Bible, even apart from matters of canon and textual criticism, can get very deep very quickly. There are some excellent printed resources for children that demystify the history of the Bible with easy text and colorful illustrations. Review them periodically to keep them fresh.

- **How the Bible Is Put Together** — The idea of Bible drill may not seem like a high priority, but the reality is that a solid knowledge of books of the Bible, how the Bible is organized (History, Law, Prophets, Poetry, Gospels, Epistles, etc.), and who wrote what and when is a strong factor in confidence-building as your children grow older.

- **What's in the Bible** — Bible storybooks can give your child an early familiarity with the major stories, events, and people in the Bible. That knowledge and understanding of the Bible as a record of actual historical events and people can become a foothold for them as they go on to consider the Bible's spiritual claims.

- **What the Bible Is About** — Above all else, be sure to teach the major truth claims in the Bible—the big ideas of Scripture. There are good child-friendly resources that cover doctrinal truths. The caution is not to turn this into an academic exercise but to read, study, and discuss what the Bible teaches about God, Jesus, the Holy Spirit, man, salvation, and other doctrines in a personal, even informal way. Strive to create opportunities for those truths to be learned together rather than only taught.

IN OUR HOME

Despite bookshelves loaded with Bible reference works, study resources, and devotionals, our grown children now say that it was our dinner-table discipleship that had the most lasting impact on their knowledge of and confidence in the Bible. We took every opportunity to create a highly verbal home environment, and there was no better time than when we all gathered at dinner, enjoying food and facing one another across the table. Most times a topic was raised intentionally, sometimes it came up accidentally, but always it was taken seriously and pursued vigorously from all angles. There was always plenty of meat on the table.

Recommended Resources

In order to give your children confidence in the authority and accuracy of the Bible, you should have a firm grasp on the origins of canon (the selection of books considered inspired), the transmission of texts used for translation, and the history of English translations. If the authority of Scripture is settled in your mind, you will be able to confidently answer when your children ask how we got our Bible and why we believe everything it teaches. Following are some good resources both for you and your children.

- *How the Bible Came to Us* by Meryl Doney (David C. Cook) — excellent children's illustrated book with lots of child-friendly detail

- *How We Got the Bible*; *Bible Translations Comparison*; *Bible Time Line* (Rose Publishing pamphlets) — color, laminated and highly detailed charts for teens and up

- *What the Bible Is All About for Young Explorers* by Frances Blankenbaker and Henrietta C. Mears (Gospel Light) — informative Bible handbook for 9-12-year-olds

- *How We Got the Bible: A Visual Journey* by Clinton E. Arnold (Zondervan) — full-color visual history of the Bible using short text blocks and vivid images

- *How We Got the Bible* by Neil R. Lightfoot (Baker) — easy-to-read text summary of the Bible's origins from an evangelical view

At the Heart of the Bible

Here are some fascinating Bible facts that will fill your children with wonder about God's Word. The shortest chapter in the Bible is Psalm 117, the longest chapter is Psalm 119, the middle chapter is Psalm 118, and there are 594 chapters before and 594 chapters after, or 1,188 chapters. The center-most verse of the Bible is Psalm 118:8: "It is better to take refuge in the LORD than to trust in man."

But as for you, continue in what you have learned and have become convinced of, because you know those from whom you learned it, and how from infancy you have known the holy Scriptures, which are able to make you wise for salvation through faith in Christ Jesus.

— 2 Timothy 3:14-15

If there be any thing in my style or thought to be commended, the credit is due to my kind parents in instilling on my mind an early love of the Scriptures.

— Daniel Webster (1782-1852), American statesman

But if you love your children, let the simple Bible be everything in the training of their souls; and let all other books go down and take the second place.

— J. C. Ryle, *The Upper Room*, 1888

The study of God's Word, for the purpose of discovering God's will, is the secret discipline which has formed the greatest characters.

— James Waddel Alexander (1804-1859), American Presbyterian minister

Placing Value on the Bible

There has never been a time in history when more Bibles, in more versions, with more added content, in more styles, for more age groups, with more marketing angles have been published. Most Christians are likely to say that is a good thing—that we should rejoice that God's Word is saturating culture. Granted, to a degree, but perhaps it's time to step back and get a different perspective on the Bible publishing phenomenon, especially about how it might affect how our children think about and value God's Word.

Mass marketing has made Scripture available to anyone who wants a Bible, but there has been a downside. Let's be honest—the Bible has become a lucrative publishing commodity and Scripture a product used for financial gain. Commercial tie-ins, cartoon characters, celebrities, and every other imaginable product angle are used to sell Bibles. The incessant fragmentation of Bible content into booklets, condensations, Bible stories, Bible products, software, websites, greeting cards, Biblezines, ad infinitum unfortunately trivializes and devalues Scripture rather than making it more valuable. It's no wonder so many no longer think of it as God's Holy Word. Your challenge as a parent is to guard against that cultural attitude and to give value to the Bible in your home. It is a deliberate choice you make to ensure your children grow up valuing the Bible as God's revealed Word, not just consuming it like another Christian product. Here are some thoughts:

- **God is speaking.** When you read and study the Bible with your children, remind them you are carrying on a conversation with the God of the universe. When you open the Bible to read God's words, remind them to open their hearts to hear God's voice. Remind them often that the Bible is not just an inspired curriculum about God and the Christian life, nor is it just a heavenly storybook, but it is God speaking to the world and to them through his revealed Word.

- **Resist commercialized Bibles.** Be very selective in purchasing a Bible for your children. Don't give in to the latest kids' Bibles full of cartoons, wacky graphics, or the latest teen celebrity's wisdom. When your children are reading confidently, give each one a real leather-bound Bible. (Bonded leather is just fine.) Ideally, give them the same translation you choose as a family. Encourage them to think of their Bible as special so it doesn't become just another Christian book to them. Limit the number of Bibles they own or use. Make sure they take their Bible to church each week.

- **Display Scripture.** Moses told the people of Israel to "tie [God's commands] as symbols on your hands and bind them on your foreheads. Write them on the doorframes of your houses and on your gates" (Deuteronomy 6:8-9). The principle is to keep the Word of God close at all times and to let your home show that you value Scripture. We have art-quality framed calligraphy hanging throughout our house. The beauty and skillfulness of each piece honors Scripture and suggests its high value.

- **Talk about Scripture.** The best way to ensure that your children know you value the Bible is to use it and talk about it. If your children hear you quoting a verse that spoke to your heart, applying a relevant Scripture to a circumstance or piece of news, counseling and encouraging a friend with a verse, using a Scripture when praying for the day, discussing what Scripture says, or reciting some memorized Scripture, they will see and hear clearly that you greatly value God's Word.

Choosing a Bible Translation

With the growth of the Christian bookselling industry beginning in the 1960s, every major Christian publisher has sought a translation to carve out its corner of the Bible market. The chief motivation for English Bible translation since the Reformation, beginning with William Tyndale (1494-1536), has been to make the Scriptures available to all people in their own common language. The 1611 King James Version, though it sounds so formal to our ears now, was considered the common language of seventeenth-century England. However, the explosion of competing English-language translations in the second half of the twentieth century is unprecedented, expanding the idea of common language to include age and grade reading levels, literal versus vernacular, theological traditions, cultural and demographic distinctions, gender sensitivity, and many other defining factors. The Bible now reaches more English-speaking people than at any other time in history, yet with that success has come choice fatigue, comparison confusion, and even biblical brand loyalty ideology. Choosing a Bible translation translates into a lot of research and work. As you navigate the crowded waters of Bible choice, consider the following:

- **Choose early.** If your children are still young and you are undecided, consider finding a translation that you can use for your whole family. Children can understand much more than they can read, so don't be afraid to choose a translation that might seem too much for children. Even if you use child-friendly translations occasionally with them, use the family Bible for reading, discussion, study, and memorization.

- **Lead the way.** If both parents use the same translation, go with that one for your children. They will more naturally follow your lead, and you will be more motivated to use Scripture with them from the translation you are using. If you use different translations, choose one of the two for the family Bible translation.

- **Study helps count.** If you feel strongly about systematic Bible study, choose a translation that has enough history to have a full range of study helps—exhaustive concordance, word studies, commentaries, and more. Also, make sure your translation of choice will be represented on any Bible study websites that you might use.

- **Try out others.** Always stick with and promote your chosen family Bible translation, but have other trusted translations in your library you can draw on for more insight. Comparing translations will provide other views of a passage and also reinforce to your children that you consider other versions to be God's Word too.

IN OUR HOME

We both grew up with the KJV and each individually adopted the NASB in college after becoming involved with Campus Crusade for Christ. After we were married, Clay used the NIV for a decade, beginning in seminary, but came back to the NASB when the 1996 update version finally dropped the arcane Thee's and Thou's. For their thirteenth birthday each of our children receive a full-grain leather NASB and for their eighteenth birthday an NASB Study Bible. Even though they may choose a different version later in life, having the NASB as our family translation gave us common language when we talked about, memorized, and studied the Scripture.

Modern Bible Translations

The most popular current translations and Bible versions arranged by translation standard and by year of release:

Word for Word

- *King James Version* (KJV) — traditional preferred text; difficult to read; grade 12 reading level; 1611/1769
- *New King James Version* (NKJV) — new translation based on KJV text; grade 9 reading level; 1982
- *New American Standard Bible* (NASB updated) — widely used; valued for accuracy for Bible study; grade 11 reading level; 1971/1995
- *New Revised Standard Version* (NRSV) — balanced approach; gender neutral; grade 10 reading level; 1989
- *English Standard Version* (ESV) — considered literal and readable; in wide use; grade 8 reading level; 2001
- *Holman Christian Standard Bible* (HCSB) — Southern Baptist; considered highly accurate and readable; 2004
- *New English Translation* (NET) — independent translation valued for accuracy and extensive translator notes; 1996-2005

Thought for Thought

- *Good News Translation* (GNT) — created to provide a Bible for nonnative English speakers; also for children; grade 6 reading level; 1976
- *New International Version* (NIV) — bestselling Bible translation; easy to read and understand; widely used; grade 8 reading level; 1984
- *Contemporary English Version* (CEV) — simplified English; gender sensitive; grade 5 reading level; 1991/1995
- *New Living Translation* (NLT) — translation using modern language equivalents and idioms; grade 6 reading level; 1996/2004
- *The Message* (MSG) — a modern paraphrase loosely based on original languages; grade 6 reading level; 2002

We know that no finer literature exists [than the Bible], that poetry and pathos, grandeur and tender beauty, all the thoughts of the human heart and the glory of earth and heaven are expressed in language matchlessly vivid and simple. Will any one give a good reason why this language should be turned into common-place English for children who particularly delight in rhythmical, poetic sound?

— Clara Whitehill Hunt, *What Shall We Read to the Children?* 1915

Best Bible Reads

Young children enjoy some parts of Scripture more than others. Stick with what will stick with them—the rest will come later.

- Genesis and Exodus
- Historical narrative (stories)
- Gospels and Acts
- Parables (selected)
- Proverbs (selected)
- Psalms (selected)
- Key passages

Stories to Tell

There are many excellent story Bibles. Here are a few good ones, new and old:

- *The Child's Story Bible* by Catherine Vos (1939) — Bible stories with literary power; great for reading aloud
- *The Children's Illustrated Bible* by Selina Hastings (1996) — good text; illustrations bring stories to life
- *Jesus Storybook Bible* by Sally Lloyd-Jones (2007) — Bible narrated as one unified story about the Savior
- *Egermeier's Bible Story Book* by Elsie E. Egermeier (1927) — classic and beloved traditional story Bible
- *Hurlbut's Story of the Bible* by Jessie L. Hurlbut (1904) — classic collection; 138 stories
- *Aunt Charlotte's Stories of Bible History* by Charlotte M. Yonge (1898) — 100 narrated stories; includes questions

Bible Reading

Bible reading used to be a mainstay in Christian families. The entire family would gather together in the evening to listen to the Bible read aloud, usually by the father. Unfortunately, in a culture characterized by too many activities, distractions, and 24/7/365 media options, it is rare to hear of Christian families who take the time for family Bible reading. In an age of information fragmentation and saturation, though, our children need to have their hearts and minds trained to listen to long readings of God's Word. They may have quality in their devotions and Bible study, but they also need quantity in their Bible reading. Television and video have progressively shortened attention spans with rapid scene changes, commercial breaks, and thirty-minute programming. Listening to longer Bible readings requires the same training as listening to other books read aloud.

- **The Book of Books** — Above all other books, the Bible should be honored in your family as the best of books. It is the very Word and words of our God. Make it a regular part of your required reading for your children. And when you read the Bible aloud, always read it with expression, energy, and pacing that says to your children, "You'll want to hear this. It is worth listening to!"

- **Enjoying the Bible** — Your children will value the Bible as a source of reading pleasure only if they see that you do. Make Bible reading a regular part of your daily routine. Set aside special time to read longer passages of the Bible. Talk about the Bible to your children the same way you talk about favorite books.

- **Selective Reading** — Give your children realistic, age-appropriate Bible reading assignments. Be selective in suggesting which books and passages they should read. Focus on historical narrative, selected Psalms, Proverbs, the Gospels, Acts, and selected passages from the Epistles. Assign blocks of reading but allow them to read at their own pace or create Bible reading goals for a quarter or for a year.

- **Children Reading** — Be sure to provide opportunities for your children to be the ones who read the Bible aloud. Let them read long passages (chapters or short Bible books), but guide them in reading with expression, energy, and pacing. Reading thoughtfully is a form of interpretation, so it's good Bible study training.

- **Audio-Bible** — An audiobook version of the Bible is an effective way to expose your children to long readings of Scripture. It's OK to let their attention be focused on some other project while they listen—schoolwork, Bible story coloring book, letter writing, or whatever keeps their ears open and their hands busy (not computer, though). It will reduce distractions and increase passive listening and learning.

- **Bible on Video** — Be very choosy about watching Bible video products. Animated Bible stories are very entertaining for children and can even teach, but the power of images can override the simple Bible story itself in a child's mind and memory. In the same way, dramatized Bible stories with real actors can provide historical context and insight but can add more to the plain reading of the Bible than is really there. A young child cannot distinguish which parts of a movie about a Bible story are real and which are made up or added. Be sure you know what they are seeing, talk about it, and limit Bible video viewing. And be sure to read aloud the story they watch.

Bible Devotions

It has always been our conviction that the primary goal of a family devotional should be not only to learn the Bible but even more to love the Bible. Children can learn the Bible and not love it, but they cannot love the Bible and not learn it! Our goal is to create a spiritually-enriching atmosphere in which we all genuinely love to open the Word and listen to God and to talk and think and laugh and pray because something in his Word touches our spirits. We have great confidence that if our children grow up loving God's Word, then the learning of God's Word will take care of itself.

A good family devotional allows you to model for your children how to hear God speak through his Word and how to respond to him in prayer. You are training your children how to relate to God and how to appropriate his grace for daily living through personal Bible reading (God speaking to us) and prayer (us speaking to God). Many parents (especially dads) wrongly assume that Bible instruction is a substitute for Bible devotions, but it is not. With instruction, your focus is on the mind. In devotions, your focus is on the heart—it's about knowing God, not just knowing about him.

- **Model a devotional time.** If your children never see you reading the Bible, hear you say how a verse has ministered to you, or share how God's Spirit spoke to you in your own devotional time, then you should not be surprised if they don't make the step from participating in a family devotional time to developing their own personal devotional time. The most effective method for developing the personal devotional habit in your children is for them to see you have personal devotions. If they observe you reading and praying regularly in the morning or evening, they will more readily agree to begin doing it for themselves with your help.

- **Share what you learn.** Turn your own personal devotion into a family devotional. Read the verse or passage from your own devotional time to your family, share with your children how the Spirit of God spoke to your heart, and then pray about the passage. Give them a pattern to emulate.

- **Have family devotions.** The next best method for developing the personal devotional habit in your children is to have daily family devotions at a regular time (such as breakfast, dinner, or bedtime). Choose a time (or times) that allows for the greatest consistency and priority. Don't go too long in your daily family devotional time, and focus more on seeking God rather than teaching about God.

- **Give your child a Bible.** Soon after your children begin reading, give them an inexpensive Bible of their own. Encourage them to take it to church each week. Teach them proper Bible care and respect, but be careful not to make the Bible itself an object of veneration (bibliolatry). We take care of the container because the contents are holy, not the container.

- **Teach your child devotional disciplines.** Once your child is reading confidently, encourage them to have a daily personal devotional time. Select an age-appropriate Bible-based devotional guide or create your own readings and prayer list for them on a one-month calendar. Ask them to spend five to ten minutes daily in reading and prayer. Be sure to ask them what they learned from God in their devotional times.

The Family Devotional ARTS

Create a family devotional on a minute's notice with this simple ARTS outline. Select a paragraph or passage suited to the ages of your children, such as David and Goliath. First, ask (A) a personalized question to create interest. ("If you were a giant, what would you eat for breakfast?"). Read (R) the passage and have your children narrate. Talk (T) about what principles can be learned and applied, such as courage and trust, and share a brief family story to illustrate. Finally, speak (S) to God about the passage—pray for courage and trust.

- **A — Ask a question.**
  Ask it personally.
  Ask it simply.
- **R — Read the Bible.**
  Read it persuasively.
  Read it slowly.
- **T — Talk about it.**
  Talk about principles.
  Talk about stories.
- **S — Speak to God.**
  Speak with praise.
  Speak with submission.

Devoted to Devotionals

Family devotional products can often be: (1) childish, with cartoon tie-ins or dumbed-down text; (2) schoolish, with topics aimed at public school teens; or (3) adultish, in a wide variety of non-child-friendly formats. There are more, but here are our favorite family devotional books.

- *Our 24 Family Ways* — Clay's "just add Bible" family devotional workbook built on Scripture and biblical values
- *Leading Little Ones to God* by Marian M. Schooland — good doctrine for 4-6-year-olds and older, from 1965
- *My Time with God* — NT readings and OT verses with book excerpts and prayers
- *Step into the Bible: 100 Bible Stories for Family Devotions* — excellent for ages 4-8; from the Billy Graham family
- *My Utmost for His Highest* by Oswald Chambers — classic of 365 devotions

Do your best to present yourself to God as one approved, a workman who does not need to be ashamed and who correctly handles the word of truth.

— 2 Timothy 2:15

But in your hearts set apart Christ as Lord. Always be prepared to give an answer to everyone who asks you to give the reason for the hope that you have.

— 1 Peter 3:15

But because learning is viewed [in the OT] as shaping values, character, and lifestyle itself, the content must be processed in a life-transforming way. It is not enough to gain mental mastery of biblical information. The divine word must be taken into the very heart of the learner and expressed in his every choice and act.

— Lawrence O. Richards, *Expository Dictionary of Bible Words*, Zondervan, 1985

Bible Study Helps

Online Bible study helps abound, but nothing can substitute for a library shelf full of Bible reference books and resources.

- Variety of Bible versions
- Exhaustive concordance
- Word study guide
- Bible encyclopedia
- Bible dictionary
- Commentaries
- Topical Bible study guide
- Bible study software
- Bible handbooks
- Study Bibles
- Reference Bibles
- Online Bible study sites

Bible Study

The primary purpose of Bible study for your children is not simply to pour knowledge about the Bible into their brains. It is, first and foremost, to instill in them a respect and love for the Word of God and to teach them how to acquire wisdom from it. You are training your children how to search the Scriptures in order to find answers and guidance for their lives. You are showing them that "the word of God is living and active" and "judges the thoughts and attitudes of the heart" (Hebrews 4:12-13). Knowledge *about* the Bible is important, too, but knowledge *from* the living Bible is the goal.

- **Study the Bible.** No matter how many colorful, illustrated, child-friendly Bibles, Bible supplements, and materials are created and marketed, there is no substitute for direct interaction with the Word of God. Despite a flood of children's Bible products, we have found very little that takes our children seriously in Bible study. Even the few that do a good job can tend to become a substitute for the Bible rather than a supplement to it. Give your children the real thing—study the Bible, not Bible books.

- **Teach Bible knowledge.** Bible knowledge of books, authors, people, events, general doctrines, and key passages is a necessary foundation for meaningful Bible study. However, whatever isn't picked up in read-aloud and devotions can be easily learned through discussion, assignments, and self-study.

- **Written study comes later.** Because writing is necessary to Bible study, wait until your child's handwriting has developed enough so that it is not a frustrating experience (nine or ten years old). Buy or create a simple Bible study form for your children to use in recording their own Scripture discoveries.

- **Use Bible study tools.** Teach your children as soon as possible how to use some of the basic Bible study tools: Bible dictionary, concordance, topical Bible, encyclopedia of the Bible, Bible handbook, and a Bible atlas. There are good child-friendly versions available to get them started, or they can use simplified teen and adult versions.

- **Start with topical.** Teach your children how to do a topical Bible study as soon as they achieve some biblical literacy. This is the easiest and most fundamental form of Bible study to learn. The purpose of this study is to train your children how to search and survey the Scripture with a concordance to gain wisdom concerning a specific topic (faith, love, patience, friendship, Christ's return, baptism, and so on).

- **Then do inductive.** Teach your children how to do an inductive Bible study as soon as they show readiness for deeper, more systematic study of the Word. Start your children on individual verses and work them up to paragraphs, passages, and chapters. It's the pattern of study that counts, not just the product of it.

- **Do the application.** Teach your children how to synthesize what they are learning from topical or inductive Bible studies into a guiding principle or principles. In other words, show them how to define a personal application that is derived from several passages, not just one. Give them a Bible study notebook to record all their studies and applications. They will be more accountable to a written application. You are teaching them to be doers of the Word, not hearers only (James 1:22).

Bible Study Methods

Teaching your children formal Bible study methods is important. However, in the four-to-fourteen-year-old window your priority should be not to academicize the Bible but rather to read, use, study, do, and enjoy it. Expose your children to Scripture through Bible reading and reading aloud, give them a good foundation of Bible knowledge through discussion and living books, and help them develop a daily devotional time to learn how to listen to and learn from God and his Word. If those are in place, then you can begin to explore Bible study methods. But do it informally, not as a new subject area for your homeschooling. Too much formality risks turning the inspired Word of God into just another curriculum. Rather, present Bible study as an exciting journey of discovery, and plan to do it along with your child. Serious, systematic Bible study is important, but it can wait until the high school years. In the childhood years, you are building spiritual appetites and habits for the Bible that will become personal commitments to serious Bible study later. That said, you can certainly introduce your children to basic Bible study methods whenever they show interest. As a general rule, though, master the use of print resources before using digital or online Bible study helps. Here are some suggestions:

- **Topical Bible Study** — Topical Bible study is about investigating what the Bible teaches. It is the best starting place for your children because it simply asks the "What does the Bible say about _____?" questions they are already asking. Just show them how to use a concordance or topical Bible to find verses and passages about a topic, and they're on their way. Use a one-page form to walk them through a simple study: topic, key verses, key words, summary of teaching, and personal application (see Resources C: "My 'Check It Out' DiscipleSheet").

- **Bible People and Events** — Your children are also naturally interested in the people and events of the Bible. Bible storybooks are universally popular because children love stories. Use that interest and delight to demonstrate how to study a Bible person (Moses, Joseph, Joshua, Paul) or story (the Flood, the Exodus, Jericho, the early church). Show them how to use a Bible handbook to find the best references and how to create a simple outline of the person's life or the event, then have them write their own Bible story narrative and collect them in a notebook.

- **Inductive Bible Study** — Inductive Bible study is, in the simplest terms, interpreting scripture with scripture. It is letting the Scripture speak for itself and then letting it speak to you. If topical Bible study is about investigation, then inductive study is about interpretation—understanding the meaning of a Bible book, chapter, section, or passage. There are good Bible study guides based on the inductive method designed for children, but they don't need a guide to learn the basics of the method. The inductive method is characterized by three actions applied to any passage: (1) Observation—What does the passage say? (2) Interpretation—What does the passage mean? (3) Application—What does the passage teach? Following these three steps will enable your child to extract the big idea from any passage of Scripture.

- **Historical Context** — Always study the historical context surrounding a Bible story or passage. Where was the author writing? Why and to whom was he writing? What were the cultural conditions at that time? What other people are involved? Help your children listen to the passage as though they were there.

Books on Bible Study

These books are good sources of help for a parent wanting to teach Bible study methods and for children and teens wanting to learn how to study the Word.

- *Discover 4 Yourself Inductive Bible Studies for Kids* by Kay Arthur and others (Harvest House) — guided inductive book and topic studies
- *Handbook for Personal Bible Study* by Dr. William W. Klein (NavPress) — excellent overview by a favorite Denver Seminary NT professor
- *How to Study Your Bible for Kids* by Kay Arthur and Janna Arndt (Harvest House) — introduction to inductive Bible study for kids 10-12
- *Parenting with Scripture* by Kara Durbin (Moody) — 100+ two-page topical Bible studies for "training and instruction" with children and teens
- *Rick Warren's Bible Study Methods* (Zondervan) — 12 methods of Bible study to unlock God's Word, with useful outlines and forms
- *Truth Trackers* series by Evelyn Wheeler (Liberty Books) — guided inductive studies for children in larger workbook format
- *Unlocking the Scriptures* by Hans Finzel (Cook) — easy-to-understand introduction to the basics of inductive Bible study method for teens and up

Websites on Bible Study

These online Bible study sites offer search on multiple translations, and study helps:

- www.Bible.com
- www.Bible.org
- www.BibleGateway.com
- www.BibleStudyTools.com
- www.BlueLetterBible.org
- www.eBible.com
- http://NET.Bible.org
- www.SearchGodsWord.org
- www.StudyLight.org
- http://Unbound.biola.edu
- www.ZondervanBibleSearch.com

But the goal of our instruction is love from a pure heart and a good conscience and a sincere faith.

— 1 Timothy 1:5 (NASB)

All Scripture is God-breathed and is useful for teaching, rebuking, correcting and training in righteousness, so that the man of God may be thoroughly equipped for every good work.

— 2 Timothy 3:16-17

These three phases—experiencing, teaching, and applying the principle [just learned]—used by Jesus to teach the twelve will provide structure to our teaching and at the same time provide a greater degree of understanding for our children. It is not coincidental that research studies during this century have shown this type of instruction to be the very best for truly understanding what is being taught. Real learning is then taking place!

— David Quine, *Let Us Highly Resolve*, The Cornerstone Curriculum Project, 1996

Bible Instruction

Instruction runs like a strong thread through the entire Bible. Truth must be passed along, and instruction is the means—person to person, parent to child, generation to generation. At the heart of the *shema* (Deuteronomy 6:4-9), the verses that start every pious Jew's day, is the command for parents to diligently instruct their children. At the heart of Christianity is the command to make and teach disciples or learners (Matthew 28:18-20). At the heart of the church is instruction in the Word (2 Timothy 3:16-17). At the heart of the family is bringing up children "in the training and instruction of the Lord" (Ephesians 6:4). If you are not instructing, you are in need of instruction.

Every major scripture that deals directly with bringing up children touches on the idea of instruction. However, instruction is about more than just the transmission of information about God to your children. The goal of biblical instruction is righteous living, not just right answers (1 Timothy 1:5; James 1:22-27). It is about godly relationships, not just religion (Luke 6:40). Your instruction will prevent your children from being "conformed to this world" and transform them "by the renewing of [their] mind" so they will do God's will (Romans 12:1-2). You are instructing your children in the spirit of Psalm 78:1-8 so that they "would put their trust in God and would not forget his deeds and would keep his commands." True biblical instruction always results in changed hearts and minds.

Of course, you first must be a student of the Word instructed by others before you can be the kind of instructing parent that God pictures in Scripture. The truths of God's Word must "be upon your hearts" before you will be able to "impress them on your children" (Deuteronomy 6:6-7). But you also must know how to "impress" those truths or to "teach them diligently" (NASB) in a way that will reach your children's hearts. You may know how to tell your children biblical truth, yet not know how to show it to them. We know the function of truth but have lost touch with the forms that would allow us to instruct effectively. Consider just a few of the ways that Jesus, the master teacher, instructed others to reach their hearts, then use them to help you instruct your children.

- **Storytelling** — Jesus told stories. The parables are timeless examples of how much spiritual truth can be transmitted in a story. Children are drawn to stories because they help them visualize and respond to truths they may not yet fully comprehend.

- **Illustration** — You probably remember your pastor's sermon illustrations more easily than the sermon teaching. A well-chosen illustration or anecdote can powerfully summarize and picture a truth you want your child to understand.

- **Questions** — Jesus asked poignant questions that went right to the heart of what he wanted to teach. There is an art to asking good questions, but the right one can draw out a response, test understanding, stimulate discussion, and convict the heart.

- **Persuasion** — Persuasion can be manipulative, and that should be avoided completely. However, it can also be influential as an appeal to the heart and conscience. Let your children sense passion and conviction in your biblical instruction.

- **Object Lessons** — Jesus often used nature for object lessons (birds, flowers, mustard plant, pearl). The power of object lessons is that your child will never again be able to see the object you use without associating it with your biblical instruction.

— Chapter 11 —

Disciplined Studies Methods: The Study of the Basics

Teaching Your Children to Learn

We don't seem to hear as much about the three Rs anymore—Reading, 'Riting, and 'Rithmetic. The idea is not that old, probably dating back to the early 1800s in a less-literate England that likely produced the phonetic misspellings. However, it soon caught on and stuck for the better part of two centuries in England and the U.S. as a handy slogan for the priorities of primary education. In the modern primary school system, though, educational theorists and industry leaders believe we have outgrown such an outdated and limited concept. They assert that young children need much more than just the basics of a traditional education. The three Rs are 'rong for the modern school child.

The three Rs now must compete with science, geography, history, social science, music, and PE instruction, among other subjects, added to the educational mix in a typical primary classroom day. Traditional educational goals also get pushed aside by the latest trends, such as standards-based educational reform. One proponent of the latter repurposed the venerable three Rs for his own standards-based program to a more grammatically correct, but educationally baffling, "Relating, Representing, and Reasoning." Fortunately, there are still strong proponents of traditional education and the three Rs, not the least of which are homeschooling families. All the other subjects for elementary study are certainly worthwhile, but never at the expense of those basic three Rs.

It's not likely that the five Ds of the WholeHearted Learning model will ever catch the ear of educational theorists, but we are satisfied that those five focused study areas capture the full spectrum of learning in the primary years. We naturally integrate the three Rs into the second D of our model—Disciplined Studies. We describe that area as the study of the basics for learning. There simply is no learning apart from the foundational skills of reading, writing, and arithmetic. In fact, a strong case can be made that if primary education consisted only of the three Rs, Scripture, whole books on a wide variety of subjects, and a thoughtful mix of real-life learning experiences, there would be absolutely no need of other subject areas of formal study. None.

Children raised on such a natural educational experience would be well-equipped by the time they graduated from childhood into young adulthood to learn whatever they needed to learn in the secondary school years to follow. But even more than that, they would be excited about learning, not burned out by eight years of formal, structured classroom and textbook schooling. The new models of learning will never improve on the effectiveness of a traditional approach, whether it is by the three Rs or by the five Ds. When it happens in a loving, Christian home, everything is in place for a child to grow up to be not just educated, but truly learned. Traditional is the way to learn to learn.

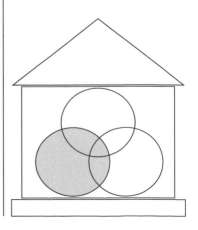

193

Many persons consider that to learn to read a language so full of anomalies and difficulties as our own is a task which should not be imposed too soon on the childish mind. But, as a matter of fact, few of us can recollect how or when we learned to read: for all we know, it came by nature, like the art of running; and not only so, but often mothers of the educated classes do not know how their children learned to read...Whereby it is plain, that this notion of the extreme difficulty of learning to read is begotten by the elders rather than by the children.

— Charlotte Mason, *Home Education*, 1886

Beginning Reading Resources

- *Reading Made Easy: A Guide to Teach Your Child To Read* by Valerie Bendt (Greenleaf Press, 2000)
- *Teach Your Child to Read in 100 Easy Lessons* by Siegfried Engelmann and others (Fireside, 1986)
- *Noah Webster's Reading Handbook* by Darrel Trulson (Christian Liberty Press, 2007)

Before Beginning Reading

- Read aloud favorite illustrated storybooks every day with your child.
- Read alphabet books that contain pictures of a variety of objects for each letter.
- Play with alphabet blocks and magnetic letters to familiarize your child with the alphabet.
- Label important things in your child's life and read them out loud every day.
- Teach your child the letters of their name, especially the beginning letters.
- Make reading books aloud with you a wonderful, pleasurable time for your child.
- Create a library shelf in your child's room to encourage ownership of books.

Beginning Reading

Reading is a mysterious process. Although various schools and experts defend their respective theories and methodologies of how to teach a child to read, no one fully understands how a child actually does learn to read. We simply do not understand all the physiology, neurology, biology, and other possible processes involved that interact and, at some unknowable point, all come together to enable a child to read. It might as well be a metaphysical process for as little as we fully comprehend the physical one! If scientists really understood that process, there would be no debate on how to teach a child to read—science would settle the method. As it is, though, two methodologies get the most attention—phonics and whole language (sight method, look-say).

Though we emphasize phonics in learning to read, we also recognize that whole-language learning is part of the process. Our starting point is that God has created every child with intelligence and an innate ability to learn language. The ability to read is already there—it is not something that you will teach your child but something that you will release in him. In other words, the power to read is not in the theories, the rules, or the methods—it is in the child. In helping your child learn to read, you are simply cooperating with God's design. Too many new homeschooling parents put pressure on their young children to learn to read early, wrongly perceiving reading ability as a gauge of their own success as homeschooling parents. They inadvertently turn what should be the delightful, enjoyable, rewarding adventure of learning to read into a stressful, burdensome, and wearisome task. That is not by faith, and it is not of God. Relax! Enjoy! Read.

- **Learn to read by reading.** The goal of a good reading program should be to lead your child to read, and then get out of the way. Don't burden your child with memorizing dozens of phonics rules—an emphasis which can turn learning to read into a tedious, frustrating effort and result in a child who only deciphers words instead of reading for meaning and enjoyment. Reading is not that difficult! Phonics *principles* will enable your child to read well. Phonics *rules* can help them spell better, but the rules can wait until they are 10 or 11, and then only if they are needed.

- **Focus on phonics.** Choose a phonics-based reading program that focuses on reading, not just on phonics rules. It will teach your child naturally, in the process of actual reading, how to decode the actual letter and word symbols on the page. However, don't be surprised when your child reads by pattern memory (look-say) too. It is a natural part of learning to read, especially in the exception-ridden English language. In many ways your child's learning processes are out of your reach and will develop on their own, with your child's own internal adaptive learning processes being used as needed. Don't fret. This is by God's design.

- **Keep it simple.** Prior to the entrenchment of public schooling in American life, the ability to read was learned at home. There were no expensive and complicated beginning reading programs then, only the Bible, books, and simple reading primers. Parents taught their children to read by reading, not by studying reading. You don't need gimmicks to teach your child to read. The simple, inexpensive methods work. Don't be intimidated into thinking complexity means effectiveness—it doesn't. Complicated games, flashcards, songs, and colors do not teach reading—you do!

- **Relax and don't push.** Some children start reading later. Don't worry and don't push if your child is a late reader—just keep reading aloud to them until they signal their own readiness to read (asking about words, reading signs and boxes, "reading" books). If you encounter resistance, put away the lessons until the child is ready to try again. When the time is right, the process will be natural and enjoyable. Resist the cultural pressure to be sure your child learns to read on schedule. Your child may read much earlier or much later.

- **Be your child's reading coach.** The most important role you play as your children's reading teacher is not just teaching them to read—it is making each individual child feel successful as a reader. Offer lots of praise and encouragement during the learning process, even if there is only a little progress. Always tell your child what he is doing well when learning to read; don't focus on areas of struggle or on what he is not yet able to do. And never use reading as a threat—"You may not ride your bike until you read this to me well!" Always present reading as a wonderful, pleasurable experience that your child is going to enjoy greatly.

- **Be consistent in practice.** Reading skills are developed progressively and incrementally, so make it a habit to practice with your child a little bit every day. And just as important, read aloud to him every day. Research confirms that hearing language is an important part of learning to read. There is always a certain amount of tension when a child is learning to read. He will be coming up against barriers that can be frustrating, even though they are not that formidable. It is the tension that draws a child forward in the learning process. As a parent, your job is to discern when that tension is healthy and normal and when it is becoming unhealthy and counterproductive. When it does, you need to be ready to ease up and take a break. Be sure to affirm your child's progress when you do.

- **Create a verbal home.** Before teaching reading became an industry, children learned very naturally with no formal curricula. In a more literate time, they grew up immersed in language and books, and reading was simply taught in a natural, common-sense way. Reading was learned by reading, not by learning reading skills. If you want to give your child the best reading curriculum possible, fill their world (your home) with language. Let them explore books with you. Talk with them often. Explain something to them. Tell them what you are learning. Show them what you are writing. You will be preparing them to read.

IN OUR HOME

Like so many other new homeschooling parents, we spent $500 trying out various multisensory beginning reading packages. Then we found Teach Your Child to Read in 100 Easy Lessons, *a $20.00 phonics-based book with no flash cards, games, rules, or gimmicks. Just scripted lessons to be read with the child. And it worked just fine. In fact, Sally never made it all the way through the 100 lessons before each child was off and reading. We learned that our children were ready to learn by God's design. We did not need to be anxious because God had already prepared them to learn to read, and we just needed to walk along with them in the process.*

Even speaking with scientific logic, it is an impossibility for the mind of man to search and understand the mind of man. Thus we Christians, more than others, ought to be humble about our knowledge of teaching and learning language. The answers are not all in. They likely never will be.

— Ruth Beechick, *The Language Wars*, Arrow Press, 1995

In concentrating exclusively on teaching the child how *to read, we have forgotten to teach him to* want *to read...Somehow we lost sight of the teaching precept: What you make a child love and desire is more important than what you make him learn.*

— Jim Trelease, *The Read-Aloud Handbook*, Penguin, 1985

Learning with Phonics

Phonics-based beginning reading programs will emphasize common aspects:

- Learning letter sounds before words
- Writing out block letters
- Learning short vowel sounds
- Blending consonants and vowels
- Reading short vowel one-syllable words
- Learning long vowel sounds and general rules
- Reading simple sentences
- Learning two-syllable compound words
- Adding clusters, endings, silent letters, exceptions

How much time for the fluency stage? Two years. One full year at the least. For instance, if children learn basic phonics in first grade they can spend second and third grades reading widely in easy books...Even with good readers, there is no need to push on with what textbooks call reading skills. When children read real books, they get practice in the skills. Reading is learned by reading.

— Ruth Beechick, *The Language Wars*, Arrow Press, 1995

Illustrated Storybooks

A well-written, creatively illustrated children's storybook can imprint positively on a young child's heart and mind for a lifetime. Unfortunately, many modern children's storybooks present fragmented and alternative family structures as normal and desirable or promote a diversity of values unanchored by biblical truth and morality. Though harder to find, there are still many well-written, illustrated storybook treasures that celebrate the traditional family, promote biblical virtues, and reinforce family values. When you find them, make them a regular part of your reading times with your young children.

Good Early Reading Books

- Meet... historical series by various authors (Landmark Books)
- Billy and Blaze series by C. W. Anderson
- *Little House on the Prairie* series by Laura Ingalls Wilder
- *Chronicles of Narnia* series by C. S. Lewis
- Henry and Mudge series by Cynthia Rylant
- Books by Marguerite D'Angeli
- Books by Ingri and Edgar Parin D'Aulaire

Early Reading — The First Year

Teaching your children *how* to read is only the first step. The real challenge is influencing them to *want* to read. The first year of your child's reading life will be critical to leading them into a life of reading. You must whet their new appetite for reading with books that will be so tasty and satisfying that they will naturally want more. Create a reading plan with them and keep as many first-year books on hand as possible. Continue reading aloud to them, but gradually increase their time of reading alone.

- **Choose real good real books.** Create a mini-library of books for early reading practice. Choose readers that will stimulate an appetite for real books. Avoid basal readers, which are usually just twaddle, and oversimplified primary readers. Provide books that are well-written, with larger print, fewer words on a page, and challenging vocabulary (can be a little beyond your child's reading level).

- **Repetitive reading is OK.** When children discover a book they like, they will want to read it over and over. Repetitive reading reinforces reading development and should be encouraged, not discouraged. Your child's confidence grows as he masters a book through repetitive readings, just as he would master getting a basketball in the goal by repeatedly throwing the ball.

- **Begin book ownership.** It is never too early to create your child's own shelf of reading books in their room or study area. Give them their own copies of favorite and requested books on birthdays, holidays, and for special reading rewards. The books should belong to your child, not be loaners from the family library. Teaching your child how to care for books will also encourage them to care about books.

- **Always be supportive.** If your child is slow at becoming a confident reader, don't make the mistake of fretting and worrying about their lack of progress. If your child senses that you are stressed by their inability to do as well at reading as you think they should, they will naturally become stressed by it as well, and reading will become an unpleasant activity. Your pressure will become counterproductive rather than helpful. Just give it time, and always be supportive and affirming when they read for you. They will catch up quickly when their brain gets on track with reading.

IN OUR HOME

We realized early on that the first year of reading needed to be a really positive experience for our children. So we got out the poster board and made a very simple and rather crude chart with a segmented road leading to a building. Each of the 100 segments represented one book, or about 30 pages of reading. We let Sarah, who was nearly seven, decide on the reward. She wanted to spend the night at a hotel with her mother and eat out for dinner and breakfast. As a typical first child, she got the best deal. Joel got a day at Opryland with his dad; Nathan got a night out for dinner and a baseball game; Joy an overnight with mom. It didn't really matter what the reward was, just so it seemed special to the rewardee. Those reading challenges set the pace for what would become a steady run at reading. Try it!

Language Arts

The art of language is the expression of thoughts and ideas through speaking and writing. Language arts, on the other hand, are the skills that help you speak fluently, read proficiently, listen carefully, and write clearly. The terminology usually encompasses phonics, grammar, punctuation, spelling, vocabulary, and handwriting. Your children learn to speak fluently without any formal instruction because God designed their minds for language. If your home environment is rich in language and good books, your children will, in much the same way, naturally pick up language arts without the necessity of formal instruction. However, at this point many parents fall prey to their fears and spread the curricular safety net—comprehensive, age-graded grammar curriculum, spelling lists, phonics workbooks, and so on. There is a much better way.

It is unnatural and burdensome to segregate each language arts discipline to study it separately and out of the context of its use in real language. A better way is to immerse your child in reading and writing, creating an environment rich in language usage. If you want to use a curriculum, choose materials that integrate several areas of language arts studies, incorporate real literature, provide examples of language used correctly and well, and parallel the natural learning methods already in place in your home. However, whether you choose a more natural and literature-based approach or use a written language arts curriculum, one thing will always be true—the single best way to strengthen your children's minds is making sure they read lots of good books. You'll want to have them repeat that exercise often. Whether it is the Bible, literature, history, fine arts, poetry, or anything else, good books are the food and fuel of the mind.

Before the advent of public schooling, language arts were learned naturally within the context of a family. You can still easily and effectively teach language arts without any age-graded curricula. For example, select a section of quality literature or a Bible passage. Have your children read the selection aloud (reading). Write new and difficult words from the passage on a marker board (vocabulary). When completed, have each child narrate the passage to you, from the oldest to the youngest (speaking). Define the new and difficult words and have each child use each word in a sentence (vocabulary). Dictate a passage from the selection that was read for your children to write down (handwriting), then check and correct their work (spelling, grammar, and punctuation). Collect each child's work in a personalized notebook. The language arts lesson is complete.

Whatever knowledge your children attain, it will be of little consequence if they are unable to use it to communicate their thoughts clearly and convincingly. Language arts provide that ability. The more immersed they are in language through reading, discussing, and writing, the more confident they will become in their ability, whether by speaking or writing, to express an idea, teach a truth, defend a belief, argue a point, promote a cause, comfort a friend, or share the gospel. There simply is no textbook or curriculum that can make that happen. Again—and it bears repeating many times—the best language arts curriculum for your child is a language-rich home environment. Don't become dependent on an impersonal structured curriculum and end up failing to do what God has already enabled you to do naturally at home. Be sure that creating a language-rich environment at home is the first priority in your lesson plan before turning to other language arts helps.

What Goes into the Heart...

"For the word of God is living and active. Sharper than any double-edged sword, it penetrates even to dividing soul and spirit, joints and marrow; it judges the thoughts and attitudes of the heart" (Hebrews 4:12). The writer of Hebrews could have just said, "The Bible is convicting." But instead, he showed that truth using words skillfully and employing the powerful and very visual metaphor of a sword piercing the human body that would be well known to the readers from their experience with Roman soldiers. He makes us see the truth in our mind's eye. That is the power of language used skillfully. Whatever is in your children's hearts will come out in their words. Fill their hearts with Scripture, great books, challenging ideas, and time discussing the things of God and life with you. Have them narrate books they are reading and explain ideas they are thinking. Give them language skills, but even more fill their hearts so those tools of language will be used to reveal goodness, truth, and beauty in the words they speak and write.

Keyboarding

In our computer-based modern culture, keyboarding (typing) is a form of language arts. The ability to use a keyboard will remain the entry point for computer use for a long time to come. In a way, it is electronic handwriting. Get your children started early on a simple "typing" computer program.

Life is tons of discipline. Your first discipline is your vocabulary; then your grammar and punctuation, you see. Then, in your exuberance and boundless energy you say you're going to add to that. Then you add rhyme and meter. And your delight is in that power.

— Robert Frost (1874-1963), American poet, *Life*, December 1, 1961

When a thought takes one's breath away, a grammar lesson seems an impertinence.

— Thomas Higginson (1810-1884), American author

Grammar, which knows how to control even kings.

— Molière (1622-1673), French playwright

I have no patience with the stupidity of the average teacher of grammar who wastes precious years in hammering rules into children's heads. For it is not by learning rules that we acquire the power of speaking a language, but by daily intercourse with those accustomed to express themselves with exactness and refinement and by the copious reading of the best authors.

— Erasmus (1466-1536), Reformation-era Catholic theologian

Grammar Disciplines

In the primary schooling years, grammar is a term of convenience to describe a wide range of disciplines related to the proper use of spoken and written language. It really is more a language art that changes and evolves over time than it is a language discipline with relatively static rules that regulate correct usage, but both are true. For instance, the terminology of the grammar school originated in the Middle Ages for Latin studies but evolved over the ensuing centuries of use into an exclusive form of schooling in Great Britain, then into a form of classical schooling in the Victorian era, then into primary public schooling in America, and has since fallen out of use in American culture. It now means whatever the hearer thinks it means by context. Even though the English language has its rules that will help children get a good start, it also is fluid and changing as it moves through time, cultures, and history.

There are two general groups among those who actually study grammar for a living: (1) descriptive grammarians who study how language is actually used with less concern about its correctness and (2) prescriptive grammarians who study and formulate language rules to promote widespread correct usage. Some use the collective term "mechanics" to refer to all the inner workings of language that apply to the study of grammar in the primary schooling years. We prefer "grammar disciplines" as the collective term, while "grammar" refers more narrowly to syntax and usage. Other grammar disciplines include punctuation, spelling, handwriting, and vocabulary. The challenge in the primary schooling years is to find the balance between your child's informal process of learning grammar by hearing and using language in the context of everyday life and the formal process of systematically studying and mastering the accepted rules that regulate proper grammar use. That balance often gets tipped to the side of studying about how to use language as opposed to actually using language. The goal of studying the grammar disciplines in the primary years is not mastery of grammar rules; it is using the English language properly.

The temptation is always strong to rely on systems and programs to teach language arts. Mostly that's by default, sometimes because the parent-teacher is insecure but often because many parents strongly believe that teaching must be measurable to be meaningful. Textbooks, tests, and assignments objectify language arts for those who don't trust the subjective nature of much of language learning. For those, a caution: Don't become a grammar cop in your home, jumping in to make an arrest every time your child breaks a law of language. All you will do is teach them that it's better to do only what they know will be acceptable than it is to explore and enjoy language and get busted.

Whether you find yourself more in agreement with the descriptive or the prescriptive side of the English language aisle, English is a complex language. For all of its strengths, it also is dogged by more exceptions, irregularities, and challenges than a first grader can shake a number-two pencil at! The simple reality is that there is no workbook, program, or formula that will teach your child all the language arts and grammar disciplines they need to know. Don't trust a program to do for your child what God has designed your home and family to do better. Many great men and women of history learned how to use language with no formal training, workbooks, textbooks, or programs. They simply grew up in a language-rich environment. The more they listened, spoke, read, and wrote, the better they became. That's how God designed it to happen.

Grammar

Grammar is to writing what phonics is to reading. The goal is to learn how to write well, not to learn how to be a good grammarian. The best way to help your children acquire a good grasp of grammar is reading good literature and hearing it read aloud. The more language your children are exposed to in the early years, the more they will naturally acquire good grammar. Grammar rules, which will never by themselves make any child good at grammar, can wait until your child is writing easily and well at around age ten, and then only if they are needed. Grammar studies, like phonics, should move aside once your child is actively writing. Your children will learn grammar by using it, not just by studying it. In fact, too much emphasis on grammar will quickly kill an appetite for writing by turning it into a technical, academic exercise.

- **Young Children** — Once your children are writing easily, they will want to begin communicating by writing. Release that desire with real writing assignments rather than shackling it to tedious grammar workbooks. Have them write every day. Choose one or two assignments each week to review with them. Write it on a marker board or read it aloud, and allow your child to try to find the errors before correcting.

- **Older Children** — Require more complex writing more often from your older children. Move from their real writing efforts, which you can still review occasionally, to more creative writing assignments that require more grammar usage. Include specific instructions about using nouns, verbs, adjective, adverbs, and other parts of speech. Include issues of plurality, time, point of view, and others to stretch them.

Punctuation

Although it may seem redundant, the best method for teaching punctuation is to have your children read many good books. The more they read, the more they will see sentences, capitalization, and punctuation at work. Punctuation is learned best by writing, not just by studying about it. Whenever your child writes in a journal or creates a report, scan the page for punctuation errors. Never simply tell your child what the error is—mark the line or paragraph in pencil (lightly, so it can be erased) and have your child find and correct the errors. Of course, you can also check for grammar and spelling errors in the same way. Dictation is an excellent way to drill for punctuation. Read a selected paragraph which your child copies and do the same as above. Choose a selection rich in age-level punctuation to get an indication of how your child interprets what is heard.

- **Young Children** — Learning punctuation for a young child is a little like learning manners—you want to get it right, but something is always wrong. Overcorrecting early writing can frustrate your child. Give your child the opportunity to find errors, then gently point out the bigger issues of capitalization, periods, commas, and such. Have the child rewrite the sentence using the correct punctuation.

- **Older Children** — As your child progresses in writing longer assignments, begin to be more thorough in identifying and correcting punctuation errors and having them rewrite the piece with correct mechanics. This is also a good time to introduce a workbook to focus on editing punctuation errors using short writing samples. This kind of workbook can be not only challenging and instructive, but also enjoyable.

Grammar is the logic of speech, even as logic is the grammar of reason.

— Richard C. Trench (1807-1886), English philologist, Christian, and educator

Parts of Speech

Knowing the names of basic parts of speech won't make you a better writer, but it will enable you to learn grammar better to make you a better writer.

- **Noun** — names a person, place, or thing
- **Pronoun** — takes the place of a noun
- **Verb** — identifies action or state of being
- **Adjective** — modifies a noun
- **Adverb** — modifies a verb, adjective, or other adverb
- **Preposition** — shows a relationship between a noun (or pronoun) and other words in a sentence
- **Conjunction** — joins words, phrases, and clauses
- **Interjection** — expresses emotion
- **Article** — identifies and specifies a noun

Marking Punctuation

It is a relief to remember that there are a limited number of punctuation marks to master.

- Period .
- Comma ,
- Question mark ?
- Exclamation mark !
- Colon :
- Semicolon ;
- Hyphen -
- Dash —
- Parentheses ( )
- Brackets [ ]
- Ellipsis ...
- Apostrophe '
- Quotation marks " "
- Slash (Virgule) /

To say that phonics does not solve all spelling problems is not to say that spelling comes naturally. Phonics is one element in spelling. There is also a strong visual element, and a rote memory element, as well as the need for a good knowledge of English language—its homonyms, contraction rules, rules for possessives and plurals, and other grammatical rules. Spelling needs a many faceted approach.

— Ruth Beechick, *Dr. Beechick's Homeschool Answer Book*, Arrow Press, 1998

My spelling is Wobbly. It's good spelling, but it Wobbles, and the letters get in the wrong places.

— Winnie-the-Pooh, *Winnie-the-Pooh* by A. A. Milne (1882-1956), English author

Boys and Girls

In general, boys are slower to develop in fine motor and verbal skills than girls. Parents who understand this will adjust their expectations of their sons to prevent unnecessarily frustrating them by expecting more than they are capable of doing or expressing. If you have a boy who is slower, don't worry about it, just give him space to grow and time to mature. Fill that space and time with lots of good books and real-life experiences.

Spelling

Common sense indicates that some children are naturally good spellers and some are not. We believe that good readers will be generally better spellers because they are constantly reviewing words visually in their reading. If your child is having difficulty spelling, don't panic. First, give your child freedom and encouragement to keep writing. Spelling is learned best by writing, not by the tedium of memorizing word lists. The last thing you want to do is discourage them from doing the one thing that will give them the most practice at spelling! Then, start to focus only on words your child is misspelling, not on isolated lists of words they might someday misspell. Memorizing spelling lists is tedious, distasteful, and not all that effective if the words are not used regularly in writing after they are memorized. Instead, have your child start a notebook to record misspelled words. Newly misspelled words can be written correctly three to five times to reinforce the correct spelling, although be cautious about turning this into a tedious exercise that becomes counterproductive. It is not necessary to put every misspelled word in the notebook—a representative sample of the more common words will provide a spelling pattern that will carry over to similar words. Good spellers often are able to see words in their minds, so have your child pronounce the word correctly and then spell it out loud to strengthen the ability to visualize a word before spelling it. Review selected words once or twice a week from the notebook. Have your child use those words in a written sentence.

The question naturally arises, "Should I continue teaching phonics in order to teach spelling?" The bigger question, of course, is whether or not your child should be required to learn and master all the phonics rules for their own sake. The purpose of phonics is to teach reading, so if your child is reading well, it's perfectly alright to put aside the phonics, even if you never made it through all the rules. When your children are writing easily and well at around nine or ten years old, you can review the rules of phonics with them then, but only if they are helpful. Phonics will not magically turn your child into a good speller. If misspelling patterns emerge in your child's writing that reflect certain phonics rules, then study those rules with them if that makes sense.

- **Young Children** — Early spelling experiences are tied closely to learning to read by phonics (shorter words, simple sentences). You can dictate and correct easily at this stage. However, when your child begins reading bigger words than they know how to spell, that's when spelling becomes a discipline. Don't panic at the outcropping of creative phonetic spellings—they are a good thing and a natural part of the process. Gently correct the phonetic attempts at new or harder words, but allow for some latitude and flexibility. Encourage your child to find the misspelled words in a sentence before you identify them for them.

- **Older Children** — If your child is a naturally good speller, just watch for patterns of misspelling and encourage them to self-correct. If your child struggles with spelling, you can create a more individualized approach to studying spelling by using a notebook. Organize the misspelled words in a way that makes sense to your child—word families, phonics rules, alphabetical order, usage. Review the lists periodically with your child, spelling only selected words. Encourage your child to sound out and spell words a syllable at a time. Then discuss with them how they are hearing and seeing the word in their head and why they misspelled the word.

Handwriting

In the same way that some children are naturally good spellers, some children are naturally going to excel at having a good hand, while others will work long and hard to be acceptable. The goal in handwriting is legibility, not perfection. The purpose of good handwriting or penmanship is to be able to communicate clearly, effectively, and quickly in writing; it is not about looking better than others. There are generally three approaches to handwriting: (1) Palmer Method ball-and-stick printing and traditional cursive (different forms), (2) D'Nealian manuscript-precursive and simplified cursive (similar forms with joins), and (3) Getty-Dubay italic print and connected cursive handwriting (identical forms with joins). If you are just starting out or even if your child has started another handwriting method, italic is the easiest method to learn and master. The elliptical forms of italic are more natural than rounded ones, and there is no need to learn different letter forms in order to move to the italic cursive. It produces a good hand that is fast and legible with less stress because of the simple print-to-cursive transition.

- **Young Children** — Italic handwriting begins in kindergarten, but you can start your child at any skill level and allow them to progress at their own pace. Help your child develop a proper three-finger grip. Many handwriting problems are the result of un-corrected irregular grip and positioning of the writing instrument in the early years. You want to help your child develop good muscle memory for acceptable handwriting so they have a good foundation to build on from there.

- **Older Children** — As your children make the transition from basic to cursive italic (grades 2-3), closely monitor their use of joins to try to avoid inconsistencies that can habituate easily. Also continue to observe and correct writing grip irregularities.

Vocabulary

A good vocabulary is indicative of mental strength and yields two distinct advantages: (1) your children will understand more of what they are reading, and (2) your children will be more effective communicators. If you are reading quality literature, there is no need to wonder if you need to be drilling your children from vocabulary lists. You will find so many new and infinitely more interesting words in your reading than a curriculum could ever offer. Whenever you come upon an unfamiliar word in reading, stop reading and ask if the children know what it means. Write the word on a marker board, then define it for them or have them look it up in the dictionary. Have them say the word out loud and then use it in a sentence. Identify some synonyms for the word (use a thesaurus). Then continue reading, which is the priority activity. Keep the words on the board for a few days to review them periodically. For fun, challenge your children to use the word during the day without getting caught. Bottom line in vocabulary: words learned in context increase working vocabulary; words learned in lists increase only potential vocabulary.

- **Young Children** — Have fun with vocabulary. Introduce a few new words each week and then use them during the day. Have your children look for new words.

- **Older Children** — Expand their vocabulary by reviewing selected words in subjects they are studying or are interested in. Investigate word origins and learn Greek and Latin roots, prefixes, and suffixes. Make vocabulary an adventure in learning.

That Sounds Right

Language arts can also be studied orally and often should be. A child's mental ability to understand concepts typically far exceeds his physical ability to write. If writing is tedious and difficult for your child, simply have them answer questions orally. Oral examination is much more accurate as a means of determining if your child knows or has learned something. This can be an especially helpful method for boys, whose fine motor skills (handwriting) develop more slowly than those of girls.

Reading Research

A vocabulary-rich environment at home is one of the best indicators of a child's success in all areas of learning. The "Matthew Effect" in childhood development is, in simple terms, the equivalent of the economic concept that "the rich get richer and the poor get poorer" (and the spiritual concept of Matthew 25:29). The concept was applied to reading by Dr. Keith Stanovich of the University of Toronto, a respected research scientist in the area of cognitive development and childhood reading. He suggests that children raised in a home rich with printed books and materials (as well as discussion, conversation, and reading aloud) begin formal education with a literacy foundation that enables them to advance quickly in every school subject, while those who lack exposure to words will lag behind. This kind of research simply confirms that God designed your child to learn naturally from books, reading, and discussion—the core elements of the WholeHearted Learning model. We didn't need the research to know what Scripture and common sense had already taught us, but it's nice to have those convictions confirmed.

Write Reasons

Give your children a reason to write. Writing on topics that have no meaning to them will not help them become better writers. If the topic interests them and they know the reason to write, they will write with a purpose. Ask them to write for one of these reasons:

- **Descriptive** — to describe actions, things, and people
- **Narrative** — to tell a story about events and people
- **Informative** — to discuss or inform about a subject
- **Persuasive** — to convince or persuade about a topic
- **Creative** — to express an idea in an artistic way

Write Reasoning

Writing is thinking on paper. The process of writing any kind of report or story is perhaps the best tool in the parent educator's toolbox to develop a child's intellect and spirit. There is truth in Edward Bulwer-Lytton's saying that "the pen is mightier than the sword." You are putting that might into your children's hands to fight the wars of words waged on the world's stage. But remember, too, that there will be writing in eternity. The written word is central to God's eternal plan, and by writing your children take up the power of written language that God himself built into our human experience. When we enable our children to write well, we release them to think well about God and to share those thoughts with the world. The more they write, the better they will reason. The better they reason, the more they will write. The more and better they write, they more they will have the power to influence the world for God. That's reason to write.

Writing and Composition

Writing is the highest expression of language. It is the ability to communicate thoughts and ideas in a medium that is both permanent and transferable. John wrote "For God so loved the world..." one time two thousand years ago, but it is still changing lives today. Giving your children the ability to write clearly and powerfully will allow them to communicate far beyond the range of their spoken words, perhaps even to future generations. Most writing, of course, is purely utilitarian—lists, forms, information, and the like—and for that your children need know only handwriting. Writing to communicate, though, requires much more—orderly thinking, proper mechanics, good vocabulary, creativity, and imagination. It will also require more of you as a parent. But you do not need to resort to a formal, structured curriculum to guide your children in developing the ability to write well. In fact, trying to reduce writing to an academic exercise may be counterproductive, giving your children technical proficiency yet failing to give them reasons to write and a voice to write well. Good writing begins long before your child ever picks up a crayon to scribble his name and an "i luv yu."

The essence of good writing is clear thinking. The best way to prepare children for writing is through oral composition, or what is more commonly referred to as narration. The practice of reading aloud good literature and then having your children narrate back to you what they have heard is foundational to good writing—it is the first step in ordering thoughts to communicate clearly and logically. The same process can also be applied to narrating personal reading and life experiences. You are training your children to think about what is best to say and how to say it best—that is composition. If a child learns to think clearly and logically about speaking, it is a natural step to think the same way about writing. The grammar, mechanics, and spelling may not be perfect (and probably won't be until a later stage of their maturity), but that is a minor concern that can be fixed or improved over time. However, if a child does not learn early how to think clearly and logically, it is very difficult to remedy that deficiency. It is critical to create an environment rich in good books, writing, and language in order to lay the foundation for your children's writing abilities. If you want writing to be important to your children, it must be important to you first.

- **Don't rush writing.** It is difficult and frustrating for young children to write very much until they have developed the necessary hand strength and coordination. Early writing experiences should be short—notes to friends, copywork, short dictation, Scriptures to memorize, a nature journal, a commonplace book, or other similar writing activities. Older children can take on longer writing exercises and projects—written narration of a book or experience, an article for a family newsletter, an imaginative story, poems, longer letters, and such. The more natural and personal the subject of the writing experience, the more motivated your children will be to write.

- **Learning to write well is a gradual process.** Writing well takes time and practice—lots of both. Have your children do some kind of writing regularly—daily if possible—whether it is a note, in a journal, a list, or whatever it might be. Be sure to allow time for mental composition—time to think. If you want your children to write well, give them time to think well. Be sure that the environment is conducive to writing—quiet, low distraction level, comfortable, and not rushed.

- **You are your children's writing coach.** One of the most important things you do is keep your children motivated to write. They need to feel confident that their communications are acceptable, even though you know they are full of errors. Whenever your children make errors in an emerging skill area, be very slow to correct. (If it is something they already know, correct it.) For instance, there is no need to correct preschoolers' invented spelling. They will soon pass out of that phase and want to become proficient at spelling. At first, though, they are simply motivated to communicate and will attempt phonetic reconstructions of the words they do not know. Focus on the communication, not on the mechanics. Don't be overly concerned about older children who aren't getting all the mechanics quite right yet. Focus first on the content and quality of the composition itself.

- **Natural writing is the best.** Forcing a child to write a generic report about Rome may not be as effective as tying it to an interest—Roman transportation for a boy who likes cars or Roman homes for a girl who loves homemaking. In creative writing, encourage your children to write from personal experience or knowledge. Keep good reference materials handy, especially a child-friendly dictionary and thesaurus, for help in making their writing more precise and descriptive. Take time to dialogue with your children about the subject to draw out impressions and perspectives. Direction is always more positive than correction. Have younger children dictate a story which you write down word for word.

- **Avoid too much structure.** Guiding your children in becoming good writers requires you to maintain a delicate balance of freedom and structure. You want to give them maximum freedom to express themselves with the voice God has given to them, not to you. But that freedom will be expressed through a structure—grammar, mechanics, spelling, and the rest. Your goal is to build a solid structure on which their expressive freedom can stand—too much will overpower it, too little will undermine it, the right balance will release it. Avoid workbook-style curricula that keep your children dependent on tedious writing exercises. Write what is real and meaningful.

- **Give writing time.** Good writing is not learned by formula or rules. It is not a skill that can be obtained from workbooks but an art form that must be developed over time. It is a process, not a procedure. Give your child plenty of time to write, and be sure to allow for it in your homeschool schedule. Prepare to practice patience!

IN OUR HOME

Writing is a time-intensive exercise for children, no matter how good they are. We try to personalize the process to make writing something they actually choose to do. We keep a collection of rubber art stamps and inks, decorative paper, quality writing paper, and a generous selection of card stock which our children know how to use to make their own cards and notes. Writing a note on a handmade card doesn't seem like a writing assignment to them, but just one more step in the creative process. They also make their own stationery, stamped all over with boy stuff (cars and planes) or girl stuff (flowers and cute animals). Since they already want to write to their friends, we just consider that to be another writing exercise.

Write Now!

There is no shortage of possibilities for natural writing opportunities for your children. Some will need to be assigned, but most can simply be encouraged. "Have to" writing can be more focused; "want to" writing is more general but is self-motivated and rewarding. Here are a few ideas to get started:

- Letters to friends and family
- Personal thank-you notes
- A handmade greeting card
- An article for the family Christmas letter
- An international chain letter (yes, it's legal)
- Writing to new pen pals
- How-to instructions for a newly learned skill
- Making a book
- Creating and illustrating a story on the computer
- Favorite recipes cards
- Directions to your home or favorite restaurant
- Create an eBay page to sell something
- Favorite Scripture passages
- Greeting cards
- Best memories journal
- Descriptions of family photo album pictures
- Personal or devotional journal entries
- An opinion letter to a magazine or newspaper
- Comment on a blog
- Write on your Facebook wall

Write Night

Gather around the dining room table once a week for a creative writing time. Have several topics ready to suggest. Poll the family as to their choice of topic. Everybody writes something for a set amount of time. Everybody then reads their writing aloud. Parents offer suggestions on grammar, style, and content. Parents can also ask other children for their thoughts. Everyone edits or rewrites until their composition is polished. Keep a binder of all your Write Night creations.

Write Brain Writing

Brain hemisphere study is not an exact science, but it can provide helpful insights into the writing process. The theory is that most people tend to favor and use one brain hemisphere over the other (though some are bimodal and use both sides equally well). However, both sides of the brain can be exercised and strengthened for use as needed, and both are used in composition of any kind. Childhood is the best time to exercise both modes of thinking, and writing is the best way to selectively exercise each hemisphere. Descriptions of both right- and left-brain functions are at best generalizations, but they are helpful guides.

- **Left-Brain Writing** — The left brain is associated with sequential thought processes that are logical, linear, and analytical. It is characterized by literal concreteness in the use of language, is more verbal (propositional), and focuses on the present and past (What does work or has worked?). The left brain is exercised best with expository writing that requires verbalization of facts, practical insights, and logical thinking. For example, have a younger child write a descriptive essay about how a bakery makes bread; have an older child write an essay about how a bill is passed in Congress.

- **Right-Brain Writing** — The right brain is associated with simultaneous thought processes that are intuitive, global, and holistic. It is characterized by contextual nuance in the use of language, is more visual (imaginative), and focuses on the present and future (What could or would work?). The right brain is exercised best with creative writing that requires visualization of ideas, imaginative insights, and intuitive thinking. For example, have a younger child write an imaginative fable about an adventurous rabbit; have an older child write a fictional account of a historical event.

Expository Writing

Beginning composition skills for children fall mostly into the descriptive and narrative categories—describing things, people, and events they know about. But your children's ability to think more critically and systematically about things that matter to them will increase along with their ability to write about those things. Expository writing refers to composition that moves into explanation and even persuasion. True persuasive essay writing will come later in high school, but the same thinking patterns begin with expository writing in later elementary and middle school. Expository writing takes what has been learned in reading, grammar, and writing—word usage, vocabulary, sentences, paragraphs, content, structure, and voice—and begins to weave them all together into an organized, thoughtful piece of writing that makes a point.

Learning how to have a message and communicate it effectively with their own voice is an important period in your children's lives. Your critical role is to begin to release the message and voice that is within them by God's design. That means helping your children identify subjects about which they have something they want to say. This is a perfect time to help them formulate thoughts about God, his Word, and the Christian life. Their voice will not emerge immediately, but you can shepherd it and coax it out as a parent and coach. Writing is the most powerful means in their life at this point to give expression to their nascent message and voice, and you can give it birth.

In simplest terms, an expository composition—whether it is a single paragraph or several pages—should have a beginning (the introduction), a middle (the body), and an end (the conclusion). The beginning introduces the topic, sets the tone, and creates a natural transition into the body. The middle expands and explains the topic. If it includes more than one point, it moves through them logically, showing how each relates to the topic. The end ties the composition together by summarizing or concluding the topic. As you review compositions with your children, look not only for how well they write (grammar, punctuation, paragraphs, spelling) but also how well they think on paper (structure, content, vocabulary, voice). Address both, but be careful that the technical issues of writing don't overshadow the execution of the idea or content of the composition. As you guide your children in developing the ability to explore and explain a topic logically and clearly, you are giving them the power to one day change lives, shape culture, and perhaps even influence the course of history. What they know will make them knowledgeable; writing well about what they know can make them influential. Expository writing is a step in your children's lives toward becoming influential for God and his kingdom.

IN OUR HOME

Writing came naturally to Sarah, our firstborn child. Her first attempt at creative writing was a fairy tale about a talking, flying pony. Cute, fanciful, a touch of redemption, but nothing life-changing. Eight years later, at age sixteen, she wrote Journeys of Faithfulness, *twelve chapters of historical fiction retelling the stories of four single women in Scripture. That book of redemptive stories of faith has touched and encouraged the hearts of thousands of young women with God's truths. Mature writing for only sixteen, but she really started writing it when she was eight years old.*

Creative Writing

Creative writing is generally considered a right-brain-oriented activity. Home-educating parents who are strong left-brain thinkers might consider it an optional and unnecessary use of their children's writing time, perhaps even frivolous. Creative writing, especially by younger writers, can often seem childish, overly fanciful, or like pointless flights of the imagination. But don't miss the bigger point of creative writing—it will make your children better expository writers! Exercising the right-brain functions of intuition and global thinking will help your children go beyond the logic and linear thinking of pure exposition to explore big-picture ideas of their topic. It can help them add visual insight to the verbal information—add showing to the telling. In a video-saturated culture trained to process information visually and therefore less skilled at processing verbal information, the ability to visualize concepts for future readers will add power and effectiveness to your children's written communication skills. Don't neglect to give them a full toolbox of writing skills because you believe that expositional writing is all they need.

The essence of creative writing is story. To borrow a concept given life by our writer-daughter Sarah, we are a "story-formed" people. We bear the image of our Creator, who is a God of story. The divine narrative has formed the very way we think about life and shaped our ability to understand that we need a savior, Jesus. History is truly "his story," and whether or not every person realizes it, all are part of that story. All of human experience is part of a divine story arc encompassing creation, fall, and redemption. Those story elements are woven into and through every part of the whole tapestry of life, and we are all the colors. No thread of that grand tapestry is unneeded or isolated; all are connected. History is not a random chain of disconnected events but the telling of a story that is bigger than life and is imprinted on our very natures. Creative writing, at its best and most powerful, is retelling that story in infinite variations and combinations of the original story elements. It is tapping into the intuitive right-brain ability to imagine new ways to reflect different facets of the story within which we exist, whether tiny fragments or large curves of the arc. It is not just retelling God's stories, the Bible stories, but telling new and imaginative stories that tell something of the God of all stories, reflect bits of his truth, goodness, and beauty, and enable readers to see themselves in them.

That bigger picture, though, will not be where your children start as creative writers. More likely, they will start with a story about friends being loyal, a tale about a mystery solved, a fable about talking animals, a fairy tale about lost treasure, or a fantasy about an imagined world—creative stories that are entertaining, interesting, and maybe even meaningful. At first, they may simply create a story with no particular point, but soon they will tell a moral to their story and then learn how to show the moral or meaning. Each of those steps of creative storytelling exercises the imagination, and every attempt at telling a story that emerges from their divinely story-formed imagination will be a step toward creative writing that one day will reach into the heart of a reader to turn on the "Aha!" light in a dark corner. And perhaps it is that light that will shine on some piece of that child's then mature expository writing that will allow their reader to understand a truth about God or life for the first time. Let your children tell their stories. Let them exercise their imagination with creative writing. A creative story is told just like an expository explanation—it must have a beginning (introduction), a middle (body), and an end (conclusion). But most of all, creative writing must have imagination (story).

The Write Order

It helps to have a roadmap to follow when trying to steer your thoughts from brain to paper. On selected compositions, help your children work through each step of this APEx writing model. The process will be abbreviated and more compressed at first, and only a few compositions will need a presentation, but every part is important. As your children get older, have them use the model regularly in their writing.

Access

- **Think** — Take time to reflect about the chosen topic. Write down random thoughts, ideas, and sources of information.
- **Research** — Gather information about your topic from books, the Internet, dictionary, the encyclopedia.
- **Refine** — Organize the information that you will use for your composition; select and highlight the best.

Process

- **Outline** — Create a simple outline of the composition summarizing what each main section or paragraph will say.
- **Write** — Working from the outline, write a first draft of the composition, adding transitions and more detail.
- **Revise** — Read it through several times to evaluate flow of thought, clarity of ideas, voice, tone, and form.
- **Rewrite** — Correct and rewrite the composition using revision notes and input from others on style and form.

Express

- **Polish** — As you are able, format the composition for printing (typeface, font size, line spacing, indents).
- **Publish** — Publish the composition in a form that is neat, clean, and attractive, whether written or printed.
- **Preserve** — Archive the composition in notebook, folder, or file, with date and place indicated clearly.

Who has measured the waters in the hollow of his hand, or with the breadth of his hand marked off the heavens? Who has held the dust of the earth in a basket, or weighed the mountains on the scales and the hills in a balance?

— Isaiah 40:12

Branches of Math

In the four-to-fourteen-year-old window of learning, you should go as far as your children want to go, but you only need to cover what is required by your state.

Required

- **Arithmetic** — study of the basic computation of numbers using the four arithmetical operations of addition, subtraction, multiplication, and division, including positive and negative numbers, fractions, and decimals
- **Algebra** — study of problem-solving calculations using a mathematical language of symbols to represent unknown numbers in calculating the relationship between known and unknown numbers
- **Geometry** — study of the properties, measurements, and relationships of points, lines, angles, surfaces, and solids, in either two (plane geometry) or three (solid geometry) dimensions

Elective

- **Trigonometry** — study of the relationships (ratios) between the sides and angles of plane (two-dimensional) or spherical (on the surface of a globe) triangles and the calculations based on them
- **Calculus** — study of calculating rates of change (differential calculus) and determining functions from information about their rate of change (integral calculus)
- **Applied Mathematics** — study of mathematics applied to practical problems in the physical, biological, and sociological worlds, including engineering, mechanics, statistics, astronomy, computing, electronics, and others

Math

In the same way that your children are prewired by the God of the spoken and written Word to learn and use language, they also are prewired by the God of space and time to learn and use mathematics. Math is a big bugaboo for many new homeschooling parents, but it doesn't have to be. Always keep in mind that God has set you up to succeed as a math teacher. Your job, with his help, is simply to release and guide your children's inherent ability to use numbers and arithmetic functions that is already burned into their being by God. Every child bears the image of God, who created everything in seven days, who counts the number of stars, who measures the span of the heavens, who numbers our days, and who knows the number of hairs on every head. Math is as much a part of God's nature stamped on our being as is language. It's there. Count on it!

Math should and will undoubtedly play a large role in your children's lives. However, not every child needs to learn higher math. Yes, that's what I said—not every child needs to learn higher math. You have no doubt heard the dire and drastic news reports about the failure of American education to teach higher math and how we lag behind other industrialized nations. Whether or not that is true, I would suggest that there has been a greater failure to guide young minds to major in subjects where they will excel and to minor in subjects not related to their developing gifts, rather than a systemic failure to teach every child higher math (that is, if you don't take calculus and trig, you're part of the problem). If your child has a proclivity for math, let them go as far as possible with it. If it doesn't appear that your child needs years of higher math, then there is no reason for them to go beyond algebra and geometry. The goal should be familiarity and experience with common mathematical concepts, not mastery of every discipline of higher math. Let your children excel where they are strongest and most motivated. If math, great. If something else, it's OK. Don't let math become a source of stress and anxiety because you're afraid you're going to handicap your children if you don't push them. You won't.

Aside from being required study and from the guilt-driven fear that your children will be part of the problem of falling math scores (they aren't), there are good reasons to study math strictly for its own merits. Math is empowering—it strengthens logical thinking, which can contribute to real-life problem-solving skills. Math is rewarding—there is a certain feeling of pride and accomplishment in getting the right answers to challenging math problems. Math is necessary—the bottom line of math study is acquiring abilities that enable us to function successfully and independently in society. Math is affirming—the beauty, elegance, and exactness of math reflect the nature and faithfulness of God (unchanging) in contrast to the corruption and confusion of sin. Math is the most disciplined of the Disciplined Studies, but that discipline yields good results.

Computational terminology is often interchangeable, but here's how we use the terms: "Arithmetic" is the term we use for basic mathematics (numbers and operations); "mathematics" (or "math") is the global term we use for all branches of computational study, including arithmetic. We will not delve into the nuts and bolts of any of the branches of math studies but rather provide only a very broad overview. The subject is simply too large for the limits of this book and far too specialized for us to provide any kind of meaningful detail. For that reason, we also will not suggest that any of the many good math programs is better than another. You can make that call for your family.

Arithmetic

If language arts is the foundation for reading and writing, then arithmetic is the foundation for mathematics. Your goals for the arithmetic of childhood are easily defined: the ability to add, subtract, multiply, and divide quickly and easily; the ability to understand and use positive and negative numbers, fractions, and decimals; and the ability to tell time and count coins. If you invest the time and effort to make sure basic arithmetic understanding and skills are solid and second nature before moving ahead to higher math, it will pay huge dividends in reduced frustration and less stress. Don't be afraid to postpone advancing if more time is needed to master the basics. Your children will catch up quickly, and you won't have to backtrack.

- **Arithmetic Curriculum** — Once you choose a curriculum or approach, if you stick with it, your children will learn. In most cases, the curriculum chosen probably has less to do with the children and more to do with what the teaching parent is willing to use. No matter what approach your primary arithmetic curriculum takes, you should try to use a variety of methods in your instruction.

- **Your Children's Pace** — Let your children set their own pace for learning. If a lesson is too easy, let them work ahead as they are able; if it is too difficult, slow down for a while. Due to learning lost over summer break, classroom math curricula can contain a large amount of review material. If you homeschool year-round, this is unnecessary and tedious repetition. If your children already know the material, move on.

- **Learning Speed Bumps** — Most children will hit occasional roadblocks when new mathematical concepts or functions are introduced (multiplication, fractions, geometry, etc.), but that is natural and to be expected. If progress slows to a halt, just go to another area of study. Come back to the other area after a while and try again.

- **Early Math Strategies** — You can teach math in casual conversations with preschool and early school children. Focus first on quantities up to ten, counting things in the process of normal life ("Let's count the carrots") and including concepts of more vs. fewer, bigger vs. smaller, and other comparisons. Next, begin associating quantities with number symbols ("Which number goes with the carrots?"). Finally, illustrate simple arithmetic operations ("One carrot and one more carrot..."). Introduce math manipulatives when your children begin to initiate their own math observations.

- **Maturing Math Strategies** — Once your children are settled into whatever math study materials and routines you choose for them, the temptation will be to relegate math to a homeschooling corner where you talk about it only in relation to problems in textbooks or workbooks. Instead, redouble your efforts to integrate math teaching into your real-life activities—have your children double or halve a recipe; measure a room onto graph paper and make scaled cut-outs of each piece of furniture; calculate how many gallons of water are used for each bath and figure the cost per bath; figure the gas mileage for each of your cars. Make the problems real and challenging.

- **Real Math Problems** — Math can require a frustrating amount of abstract thinking for young children. Numerals and operation signs are symbolic and abstract. Rather than frustrate your children with mathematical abstractions, translate the problem into familiar concrete images—apples to count, pizza fractions, cups of milk.

Math Tools to Count On

Math teaching tools are effective and fun and are often just what you need to help your child grasp a difficult concept. A box or shelf of math tools ready to use as needed is a good homeschooling investment. However, before you spend a lot of money in a teacher supply catalog, be creative with what you have at home. Good tools to keep on hand:

- Workbooks — Keep a few colorful math workbooks around to pull out as needed.
- Applications — Whether software or webware, there are lots of good math programs.
- Legos & Duplos — Perfect for counters, base 10 blocks and rods, cubes, and much more.
- Counters — Beans, coins, popsicle sticks, yogurt cups, or anything countable.
- Flash Cards — Make your own 3x5s or computer printouts for any drill material.
- Charts & Posters — Make your own wall posters and charts to visualize math facts.
- Number Lines — Make a template on your computer and use for any number sequence.
- Attribute Blocks — Make your own shapes out of colored poster or foam board.
- Peg Board — Make or buy a peg board for numbers, geometry, math, and more.
- Measuring Tools — Keep rulers, measure cups, thermometers, and such on hand.
- Clock — Find an old analog alarm clock with manual time setting known for easy use.
- Calendar — Design and print out blank calendar pages or make a large poster board.
- Hundred Chart — Use 10x10 large graph paper or create a chart on your computer.
- Calculator — Find a calculator with large number keys and a large screen area.
- Games — Make some up (it's not that hard) or look for good manufactured games.

Higher Math Teach-niques

There are many ways you can teach math, dozens of math systems, and a limitless well of supplemental resources, websites, and tools. Your challenge is to tailor a math program for you and your children, keeping in mind that math is only one part of your homeschooling plan. Reading, writing, and books are still the priorities while you have access to your children's hearts and minds. Do the math, but do the reading more! Here are some ways to teach math:

- Learning it yourself — You may find you can relearn algebra and geometry quickly in order to teach then.
- Team learning — You can work with your child to help one another over the learning speed bumps.
- Independent learning — Your child can study independently using texts, worktexts, and answer keys.
- Distance learning — Your child can take a correspondence course that adds accountability and feedback.
- Personal tutoring — You, a friend, or a private tutor is available to help your child when needed.
- Learning by teaching — In a role reversal, your child can teach you what they are learning to reinforce the concepts.
- Mixed traditional — Use a core textbook along with a selection of workbooks from several sources.
- Digital learning — Your child watches and interacts with a teaching presentation on video, DVD, or online.
- Eclectic — You and your child choose a variety of resources and tools to a create a custom math study program.
- Co-op or tutorial — Your child combines a homeschool co-op or tutorial class with home learning for math.

Higher Math

Math is a metaphor of the process of maturity. During the childhood years of elementary math, it's all about exactness—addition facts never change; multiplication tables are like math laws; it's either correct or incorrect. In the same way, character and morality in childhood are very either-or, black and white, right or wrong. But then puberty happens, and some of the moral blacks and whites begin to blend into grays. Character and morality are suddenly more nuanced by new and less-defined factors, and what once was all about doing the right thing becomes more about becoming the right person. At the same time, math studies segue from the simple security of arithmetic into the less certain realms of algebra and geometry. What once was concrete quickly becomes more abstract. What once was all about the product (knowing the right answer) soon becomes more about the process (finding the right solution). As you move from the security of elementary arithmetic with your children into the complexities of higher math with your young adults, just remember that it's a picture of the process of maturity. Becoming frustrated with math or giving up is not the answer. Just stay with it and move through it, until you emerge on the other side with new understanding. Just like you will with your children. Find a good math program, learn it along with your children, and don't give up.

- **Plan your path to math.** Moving from arithmetic into algebra can be unsettling to some children. The decision about when to make that move is not about arbitrary age and grade levels determined by the education industry; it's about readiness determined by you and your children. If you are satisfied with your children's arithmetic skills, try out a pre-algebra program. If it's hard and frustrating, go slowly until you sense readiness; if it is not too difficult, move forward, or even move to Algebra I.

- **Try before you buy.** Since higher math study will be more self-directed on your children's part, don't choose a math program just because you like it or because it's the same publisher as their arithmetic. Ask other homeschooling parents what they have used, read reviews, and let your child try out the materials at a book fair. Listen to your children's thoughts about which materials or program they think they might like best. Keep their learning styles in mind, but pick a program they will use.

- **Expect speed bumps.** When your young teens hit the inevitable speed bump in studying higher math (most do at some point), it is not unusual for them to be discouraged and feel that they aren't smart enough to do the work. Affirm their intellect, let them know it's not unusual, and let them take a break for a couple of days. Then, select a relaxed time to sit down with them, pick up at the speed bump, and work together on the problem or concept.

- **Accentuate the positive.** If your children are good at math, then affirm their ability and give them freedom to pursue their own pace. If your children struggle with math, then affirm their effort and encourage them to give it their best.

- **Co-op classes and tutors.** Homeschool co-op or tutorial classes, if not too large, can be helpful, especially when moving into a new concept or preparing for testing. For more focused instruction, a private tutor is still the best. You can also use DVDs or online helps, but they are less effective because they are impersonal. If you have an accelerated math student, a private tutor will always be the best option.

Practical Math

Whether a child eventually needs the full range of math studies to go into science or engineering or needs only the basics to go into writing or the arts, one thing is absolutely certain—each of your children will need to learn practical math skills. Using math effectively in your daily life is not the same as theoretical or applied mathematics. A math-whiz mechanical engineer is not necessarily better equipped for handling personal finances than a math-challenged English teacher. Both will have to learn how to think wisely and accurately about using math in real life. The sooner you begin training your child in "way of life" math, the easier it will be for them to orient and adjust to the math challenges of adulthood. You can set the learning bar higher for later in high school, but the goal in the four-to-fourteen window is regular exposure to and practice with practical math.

- **Personal and Family Finances** — The best place to begin is a personal budget. It may be only "save, give, keep, spend" to start, but that will build understanding for the more complex family budget categories. Use a simple spreadsheet program to allocate funds together, track actual expenses, and generate charts to visualize budget and spending. Show how to use a checkbook, ATM, and online banking.

- **Consumer Math** — Do online comparative shopping together for special items (electronics, clothing, appliances, etc.), analyzing cost and features to make a decision. For services (car, home, yard, etc.), check mail-order coupons and call to compare prices, experience, and materials. For groceries, analyze cost (make sure serving sizes are equivalent) and nutritive value of various foods.

- **Small Business Finances** — Start a simple home business that you can let your child manage. Create a business plan and a simple spreadsheet for tracking expenses and revenue, cash flow, inventory, profit and loss, and net worth. Be sure to include tax requirements (estimated income tax, Social Security, sales tax collections, etc.).

- **Home Ownership** — Compare the costs of renting vs. buying a home and the value of accelerated mortgage payments. Study utilities bills to understand the charges, and evaluate twelve-month usage patterns together to determine ways to reduce costs. Chart home maintenance costs and when they occur (AC, landscaping, filters, etc.).

- **Other Areas to Consider** — Investments tracking (stocks, bonds, funds), insurance costs (auto, home), transportation costs (gas, upkeep, maintenance), college expenses (room, board, tuition, loans), food preparation (following recipes).

IN OUR HOME

God has made us good at words, but not so much at numbers. We rely on formal curricula to get the job done. We also harness our children's love of computers to math. They love climbing a ladder to higher levels of recognition or racking up points for accuracy and speed. (We monitor skill levels to keep the problems challenging.) We work together with them as much as possible but have at one time or another used video helps, supplemental resources, math-savvy friends, classes, and tutors. A private tutor helped our children do much better on SAT math.

Mathe-Metrics

The U.S. may never fully convert to the metric system, but the pharmaceutical industry, the U.S. Army, NASA, the automobile industry, the food industry, and others are either fully or partially metric already, and many jobs and industries require some level of metric proficiency. It is not difficult to teach the metric system at home, if only to give your child a good working knowledge of the system. There is no need to teach all the arcane conversion formulas for moving between our custom units and metric—everyone resorts to a table of formulas for that tedious chore. Instead, teach the metric system separately and directly. It is a very logical measurement system based on multiples of 10, and it can be quickly understood and mastered. Your children will enjoy knowing the system, measuring in metric, and understanding the terms when they see them or hear them in use. It will give them confidence if they ever have to use metric.

Metric Units
- Kilo (k) = 1000
- Hecto (h) = 100
- Deca (dk) = 10
- Deci (d) = .1 (1/10)
- Centi (c) = .01 (1/100)
- Milli (m) = .001 (1/1000)

Length
- Meter
- Centimeter (1/100 meter)
- Decimeter (1/1000 meter)
- Kilometer (1000 meters)

Volume
- Liter
- Deciliter (1/10 liter)
- Decaliter (10 liters)

Weight
- Gram
- Kilogram (1000 grams)
- Tonne (1000 kilograms)

Your adult thinking is on a higher level than your children's, so you teach a lot just by conversing with them. Thinking is a language skill and one way to simplify your schooling is to let children think in content subjects and daily activities, and avoid spending too much time with courses on the latest trendy theories.

— Ruth Beechick, *A Biblical Home Education*, B&H, 2007

Thinking Skills

Exercising and strengthening your children's thinking skills will help them learn how to use their mental capacities more effectively—thinking clearly about ideas and issues; solving problems on paper or in real life; expressing their thoughts in written and spoken words with clarity, logic, and persuasiveness. Logical thinking skills (left brain) enable your children to address issues and problems based on facts and accuracy of thought. Evaluative thinking skills (right brain) enable your children to reach conclusions based on values and clarity of thought. Generally, a child will have a natural preference for one brain side or the other, but both are needed for thinking well.

- **They can work it out.** Avoid the temptation to always tell your children what to think or to play the Answer Man to all their questions. Encourage and help them to think through their questions to allow them to reason or research their way to an answer. Validate their thinking process even if you can't always validate the conclusions they reach.

- **Look for good workbooks.** Bookstores, educational stores, and teacher supply stores offer a good selection of helpful thinking skills workbooks that exercise problem-solving and logical skills, visual skills, and mathematical reasoning skills. Children usually enjoy the mental challenges they offer.

- **Think about real-life problems.** When there is a real-life problem at home, involve your children in finding a solution—deciding how to plant the garden, fixing something that is broken, making room for more books on the bookshelf, or rearranging furniture in a room. The purpose is not necessarily to have them solve the problem but to play a role in *thinking* about solving the problem.

- **Think out loud.** Develop evaluative thinking skills through the use of discourse and discussion. Ask open-ended questions that allow for opinion and evaluative thought. Create hypothetical situations, talk about current events, or discuss a real experience. Stay away from topics that will be morally vague or ambiguous. Children need practice in thinking about and applying the moral principles and precepts they are learning. However, fill-in-the-blank questions looking for the right answer do not train thinking skills. Dinner time and long trips in the car are natural opportunities for this kind of discussion.

IN OUR HOME

Opinion is not in short supply at our house. We have to guard against parental intimidation when it comes to opinion formation in our children. The dinner table is a good place for discussion since eating keeps everyone in one place. We try to elicit opinions on various subjects, track their reasoning, and interact about the topic. Humor keeps the discourse enjoyable and blunts the intimidation factor. The value in these times is not in the conclusions they reach but in the process of reaching them. We keep the discussion general and discourage argumentativeness, but verbal interaction is just a part of our home atmosphere...and our meals.

— Chapter 12 —

Discussion Studies Methods: The Study of Ideas

Speaking of the Heart of Learning

Discussion Studies are the heart of the WholeHearted Learning model. In a human body, if the heart isn't beating constantly to keep blood flowing to all the other parts of the body, the life will soon go out of it. In the same way, if Discussion Studies are not the constantly beating heart at the center of WholeHearted Learning, pulsing the life-blood of new thoughts and ideas to every part of the model, then the life will soon go out of your homeschool. Without the strong, steady beat of Discussion Studies, your homeschool can quickly become a lifeless routine of educational duties and tedium. After doing Discipleship Studies, there was never a debate in our home about which study area to choose if we could not get everything done on some days—we always, without exception, would choose Discussion Studies. We believe now, with four children graduated, the life-giving learning of Discussion Studies made the difference in our children's hearts and minds.

On a linear scale (similar to the LifeGIFTS scale on page 48), the five focused study areas of WholeHearted Learning move deliberately from mostly parent-directed head learning on the left (Discipleship and Disciplined Studies) to more child-directed hands learning on the right (Discovery and Discretionary Studies), with family-centered heart learning in the middle (Discussion Studies). That center point is the fulcrum that keeps everything in balance. In some ways, the WholeHearted Learning model is a picture of the natural process of growth and maturation for a child—from dependence (parent-directed in childhood) to interdependence (family-centered in young adulthood) to independence (self-directed in adulthood). The family-centered interdependence phase is critically important to helping your child make the passage from dependence to independence in their process of maturation. Discussion Studies during childhood will do more to prepare your child for that coming phase of young adult interdependence than perhaps anything else you do in your homeschooling. It is the heart of your homeschooling that can help you to win the heart of your child so they will give you their heart as a young adult.

When you think of Discussion Studies, picture Jesus and his disciples reclining at a table and discussing the Scripture together. It was a verbal, vital atmosphere—the Word was read or recited, or Jesus would teach, and everyone had a thought or an opinion. It was in the talking and discussing that they learned, grew, and matured. It's the same with your children. When you read a book (or the Scriptures), let it be the fuel for discussion. Never read a book (or study art or listen to music) that you don't give your children the opportunity to discuss. It is in the verbalizing of thoughts and ideas that their brains will grow and their spirits will be enriched. We believe that a strong verbal environment is critical to developing intelligence in children. Discussion Studies are the part of WholeHearted Learning that contributes most to that verbal experience. Talk about it!

What better way to nourish this love of books than for the mother to gather the children about her in the long winter evenings and read to them and talk over with them the legacy of great minds?

— Ella Frances Lynch, *Educating the Child at Home*, 1914

We ought to reverence books; to look on them as useful and mighty things. If they are good and true, whether they are about religion, politics, farming, trade, law, or medicine, they are the message of Christ, the maker of all things, the teacher of all truth.

— Charles Kingsley (1819-1875), English pastor, author, professor, and historian

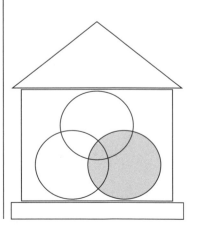

I read to live. Every book I've read and every story that has made itself a part of my imagination has taught me something about what it means to live life well. I'm passionate about reading because I'm passionate about life.

— Sarah Clarkson, *Read for the Heart*, Apologia Press, 2009

Reading Christians are growing Christians. When Christians cease to read, they cease to grow.

— John Wesley (1703-1791), founder of the Methodist movement in England

The man who does not read good books has no advantage over the man who can't read them.

— Mark Twain (1835-1910), American author and humorist

Reading for Life

The ability to read is foundational to all education. Literacy is the power to acquire knowledge and learn. But your efforts at giving your children the *ability* to read will be in vain if you do not also give them the *desire* to read. If you do nothing else in home education, raise your children to love reading. A heart for reading is the key to self-education, your ultimate goal for your children.

In a home where parents value reading and reading is a natural part of life, the question "Why should I read?" is rarely asked. But the reasons are plain to see. First, we read because that is how we can know God's truth. In the early years of our country, the main reason parents taught their children to read was so they could read the Bible on their own. God has revealed himself through the written Word—the one who "correctly handles the word of truth" (2 Timothy 2:15) must first be able to read it. Second, we read in order to learn and grow intellectually. Reading is a nonnegotiable essential of WholeHearted Learning to help your children become strong learners with strong mental muscles. Third, we read in order to grow and mature. Reading will enable your children to continue throughout their lives the education you begin while they are at home. You are equipping them to grow and mature on their own through books and Scripture. Fourth, we read because God has put within us a thirst for knowledge and equipped us to meet that need through reading. To paraphrase Descartes, "I think; therefore, I read." Finally, we read because it is personally enjoyable and fulfilling. Reading is an adventure of the heart and the imagination. A well-written book is a joy to read, whether it is fiction, inspiration, biography, history, poetry, or any of a multitude of writings. Rather than being a passive pleasure like most media, reading is an active pleasure that engages, enlivens, and enriches the whole inner person. It is a wholehearted activity.

Your children will naturally imitate you and adopt your values. If you want them to have a heart for reading, then they must see that *you* have a heart for reading. If you love to read, your children will love what you love. The best way to create a desire to read in your child is by modeling a genuine interest in a wide range of reading materials—the Bible, history and biography, inspiring fiction, interesting magazines, letters, poetry, reference resources, newsletters, and on and on. And don't be only a passive reader. Whenever you have the opportunity, involve your children in what you are reading—read a passage out loud, ask them to read selections, explain what you are reading and why, share an interesting insight you just learned. Always emphasize that reading is not just something you *have* to do, it is something you *want* to do—that you can't imagine what it would be like to live without reading. Become a dedicated promoter of books in your family, always talking positively about them and pointing out their benefits.

This call to a life of books and reading is not about living to read, as though that should be your highest pursuit. However, it is about reading to live and being sustained and enlivened by books for the rest of your life. It is not too strong to say that to the degree you fail to enrich your children's lives and spirits with good books, you run the risk of leaving them spiritually impoverished for life. It doesn't have to be that way! Reading good books will enrich your children's spirits, and the best book, the Bible, will give them life. We all know the negative warning "Run for your life!" But your children should also hear the positive warning "Read for your life!"

Reading to Live

Reading is much more than simply an academic discipline. It is the doorway between a life of dependence on other people on one side and a life of spiritual and personal freedom on the other. If you cannot read and think about the Bible for yourself, then you must depend on someone else who will read it and interpret it for you. If you cannot read reference books to gain firsthand information about a subject, then you must depend on others for that information. If you cannot read an instruction manual, then you must depend on someone else who can. Without literacy, there is no liberty. But even worse is the growing plague of functional illiteracy—being able to read but choosing not to. Why take the time and effort to read when visual and audible media provide so much? By instilling deep in your children's hearts both the ability to read and the desire to read, you are leading them through the doorway to a life of personal freedom. You are giving them the assurance that, with God's help and good books, they can succeed in life.

Some parents worry that a whole-book approach will leave holes in their children's education. But it's really just the opposite—personal reading fills in so many holes that you will never be able to cover as a teacher. It is often said that a netted hammock will support you even though it is full of holes. However, if the cords used in the netting are weak, then the hammock will fail. A whole-book approach creates strong cording that will not fail; the absence of reading and books in children's learning will leave the hammock cords of their lives weak and subject to breaking. The reality is that homeschooled children who read widely and deeply will have fewer and smaller holes and have stronger minds than conventionally schooled children who read or are read to alarmingly little. Another difference that has even greater impact on the future success of a child—children raised on good books will know how to close the holes in their learning.

Reading is life-giving. Most mothers think that to be a truly life-giving mom means making sure your children are well fed, clothed, happy, and protected, and that is certainly true. But the life-giving list is incomplete without the idea of making sure you read to your children and raise them on a steady diet of good books. There simply is no substitute for the power of books in shepherding children's hearts and minds during their developing years. Most educators will acknowledge books and reading as a consistent factor in the lives of children identified as successful students. Consider just a few of the advantages:

- Reading is the foundation of all knowledge and education.

- Reading exercises and strengthens the mind for great thoughts.

- Reading cultivates a love for knowledge and self-education.

- Reading contributes to moral development and godly character.

- Reading provides patterns for noble, heroic, and righteous living.

- Reading increases understanding of the world's views and values.

- Reading instills a broad understanding of history and its influences.

- Reading models correct grammar and the best uses of language.

- Reading contributes to a wide vocabulary and good word usage.

Good Books on Good Books

There is no end to the making of books (Solomon), and no end to the making of book lists. Here are our favorite booklist books.

- *Read for the Heart* by Sarah Clarkson (Apologia Press) — whole books for wholehearted families; Sarah's insights on classic children's books and the gift of reading from growing up in our home

- *Books Children Love* by Elizabeth Wilson (Crossway) — reading list for children; companion book to Susan Schaeffer Macaulay's *For the Children's Sake*

- *Who Should We Then Read?* Volumes 1&2 by Jan Bloom (BooksBloom) — excellent book lists of authors and series that capture the hearts of children

- *All through the Ages* by Christine Miller (Nothing New Press) — exhaustive guide to over 7,000 quality living books: history, biography, historical fiction, literature, and culture

- *Let the Authors Speak* by Carolyn Hatcher (Old Pinnacle Publishing) — a guide to worthy books for children based on historical setting

- *Honey for a Child's Heart* by Gladys Hunt (Zondervan) — good insights on reading, with a recommended reading list for children

- *How to Grow a Young Reader* by Kathryn Lindskoog and Ranelda Mack Hunsicker (Shaw) — quality reading list from a Christian perspective

- *Books That Build Character* by William Kilpatrick and others (Simon & Schuster) — recommended books for children and youth that reinforce character and virtue

- *The Children's Literature Lover's Book of Lists* by Joanna Sullivan (Jossey-Bass) — lists by categories and subjects for children's books (pre-K to grade 6); no descriptions or opinions

Reading is a habit. It may take a little ingenuity and a sprinkling of discipline to get the habit formed in a child; but once it is, it becomes a regular, centering beat in the life of a home. If you teach children from their youngest days to expect and enjoy the daily rhythm of reading, it will quickly become a settled routine. A huge part of this habit is to establish family read-aloud times. Hearing a parent read books aloud is one of the central forces that will shape a young child into an active reader.

— Sarah Clarkson, *Read for the Heart*, Apologia Press, 2009

I had a Mother who read me the things
That wholesome life to the boy heart brings—
Stories that stir with an upward touch.
Oh, that each mother of boys were such!
You may have tangible wealth untold;
Caskets of jewels and coffers of gold.
Richer than I you can never be—
I had a Mother who read to me.

— From "The Reading Mother" by Strickland Gillilan (1864-1954), American poet

Laugh-Aloud Favorites

There is nothing like reading aloud a great book that is also laugh-out-loud funny. Laughter is God's memory glue.

- *Winnie-the-Pooh* and *The House at Pooh Corner* by A. A. Milne
- *The Wind in the Willows* by Kenneth Grahame
- *Summer of the Monkeys* by Wilson Rawls
- *Rascal* by Sterling North
- *The Treasure Seekers* by E. Nesbit
- *From the Mixed-Up Files of Mrs. Basil E. Frankweiler* by E. L. Konigsburg
- *Holes* by Louis Sachar
- *Cheaper by the Dozen* by Frank B. Gilbreth, Jr. and Ernestine Gilbreth Carey

Reading Aloud

It is impossible to overstate the influence you can have on your children simply by reading aloud to them regularly. Apparently, God has designed the minds of children to grow when watered with words from good books—his words being the best—that cultivate intellectual, emotional, moral, and spiritual development. It seems that just hearing a book read aloud, regardless of content, can be helpful, but better books will undoubtedly yield better results. Reading aloud stands alone as an educational activity that is nearly universal in its appeal, unquestioned in its effectiveness, and unequaled in its ease of use and bang for the book. Beyond that though, there is also a bonding that takes place when a family shares the experience of reading aloud. It is a unifying experience. Some are apt to be suspicious that such an uncomplicated means can produce such complex ends, but sometimes God uses the simple things to confound the wise. Reading aloud is just that.

- **Read to be heard.** The art of listening is inextricably linked to the art of reading aloud. If you want your children to learn to *listen* well, you must learn to *read* well. You must learn how to read aloud so as to capture and hold your children's attention, interest, and imagination. The reason you read interpretively is not merely to entertain your children, but rather to train their attention and to teach them by example how to be expressive in speech and mannerisms.

- **Read to be enjoyed.** If the passage is sad, sound sad. If a person is angry, show anger. If there is joy, be joyful. Use your voice to interpret. Try to give characters different voices and personalities—high voice, low voice, accents, fast and slow. Vary the speed, intensity, tone, inflection, and volume with which you read. Set a moderate pace to begin with so you can slow down or speed up from it. Vary other elements to reflect the atmosphere and literary tone of the story.

- **Establish eye contact whenever possible.** It keeps your children more alert and enables you to gauge their attentiveness. Put your entire body into the reading—facial expressions, hand and arm movements, body movements. If you do all that and interest in the story seems to be waning, set that book aside. Select another book more attuned to their interests or reading levels. If you have both sons and daughters, read a girl book or boy book occasionally.

- **Choose read-aloud books carefully.** Immerse your children in a rich pool of living books from all streams of knowledge: fiction, history, historical fiction, biography, science, nature, myths and legends, essays, and of course the Bible. Because we are awash in books in our day—many good, multitudes not—be especially discriminating of the books you promote at home. Cultivate your children's literary appetites with only the best in age-appropriate whole, living books.

- **Establish regular read-aloud times.** Make read-aloud times a routine part of your family experience. Select times that work best for your family—morning, mealtimes, bedtime. Select locations where distractions will be at a minimum and where the children can be comfortable. Set aside a time when you can read undisturbed for up to an hour or more. Also, set aside an evening for a regular extended read-aloud time together as a family.

- **Always begin with narration.** Whenever you return to a story, have your children review (narrate) what has happened so far—characters, plot development, setting. There's no need to retell the entire story—just enough to catch up. Before reading, have them imagine what they think might happen next.

- **Pass the reading around.** Have your children read aloud from time to time to develop their oral reading skills. Reading aloud is excellent training for speaking and presentation. Expect them to read aloud expressively and dramatically. Be sure they read the Bible aloud regularly.

- **Learn the moral of the story.** Select read-aloud books that are morally and spiritually inspiring. Discuss the characters in the story—their moral character, their choices, and their companions. Look for Christian types, symbolism, and metaphors. Identify principles of wisdom and life found in the book. Use the characters and events of the stories as illustrations for teaching and talking about scriptural principles and truths.

- **Let them wiggle.** Younger and active children can become distracted during reading aloud. Allow them to play quietly with something that will engage their hands yet leave them free to listen—a toy, a ball, colors. It will actually help them to concentrate on the reading. Even if you have a terminally wiggly child, the key is whether or not they are listening and paying attention to what you are reading. Whatever position they assume for listening—sitting down, lying down, or standing on their heads (common for little boys)—it's OK as long as they can narrate back to you what has been read.

- **Build attention span**. Attention spans vary greatly, but all children can be trained to listen attentively to progressively longer and more advanced readings. Don't wait to start training until they start school—start reading very early in your children's lives with interesting picture and story books. They will progress naturally to chapter books.

- **Create a read-aloud memory.** Create a read-aloud experience that your children will never forget. For example, pick a winter weekend night, get a nice fire going in the fireplace, snuggle up with comforters on the couches, make hot chocolate and a snack, dim the lights, and make an evening of it. Unforgettable.

IN OUR HOME

The simple, venerable bedtime story is great for dads. We read a children's adventure novel about a boy from Greece who is captured by slave traders and sold. Not great literature, but a good historical story. Then came Trumpet of the Swan *by E. B. White, a rich, allegorical fantasy about a voiceless trumpeter swan. After that a historical children's novel set in colonial America, and one of our favorites,* Rascal, *about a memorable raccoon. It is very satisfying to see my children enjoy this time because I enjoy the childlike reactions when I read descriptive narrative expressively and add dramatic character voices. It's exciting to see the kids hurry to get ready and to get comfortable when they know I'll be reading.*

If children haven't been read to, they don't love books. They need to love books, for books are the basis of literature, composition, history, world events, vocabulary, and everything else.

— Edith Schaeffer

Read-Aloud Favorites

These are some of our favorite read-aloud books that are enjoyed by everyone in the family.

- *Treasures in the Snow* by Patricia St. John
- *Chronicles of Narnia* series by C. S. Lewis
- *Dangerous Journey* (John Bunyan's *Pilgrim's Progress* arranged for children by Oliver Hunkin)
- *All Things Bright and Beautiful* and others by James Herriot
- *Little House on the Prairie* series by Laura Ingalls Wilder
- *Little Women* by Louisa May Alcott
- *Little Men* by Louisa May Alcott
- *Heidi* and others by Johanna Spyri
- *The Secret Garden* by Frances Hodgson Burnett
- *Freckles* by Gene Stratton Porter
- *A Girl of the Limberlost* by Gene Stratton Porter
- *Just David* by Eleanor H. Porter
- *Pollyanna* by Eleanor H. Porter
- *Black Beauty* by Anna Sewell
- *Hans Brinker, or the Silver Skates* by Mary Mapes Dodge
- *Where the Red Fern Grows* by Wilson Rawls
- *Benjamin West and His Cat Grimalkin* by Marguerite Henry
- *Johnny Tremain* by Esther Forbes
- *Caddie Woodlawn* by Carol Ryrie Brink
- *Great Dog Stories* by Albert Terhune

We all know the story of the illiterate man who, after assuring the pretty book-agent that her wares would be of no use to him, as he could not read, still further excused himself from purchasing, by answering: "Oh, yes, my darter—she can read; but she's got a book." We also know the story of the very new millionaire who ordered four yards and six inches of books bound in red leather like a sample of wall paper! It is a far cry from the daughter's "a book" to the millionaire's "four yards and six inches"; but it is safe to say that the daughter came nearer to possessing a library than did the millionaire; for her book was probably read, and lived with, and loved. And it is the book that we read and live with and love that really counts—for us. After all, never to own a book is like trying to go through the world without friends—merely acquaintances. And always to depend on a circulating library for brain sustenance is very much like trying to satisfy one's stomach at a perpetual quick lunch.

— Eleanor H. Porter, author of *Pollyanna* and *Just David*, from *The Boston Herald*, ca. 1916

First Year Reading Chart

Rewards are not necessary to get your children to read, but they can be an effective source of positive motivation. Get your children off to a strong start with a simple first year Reading Challenge chart. Decorate poster board with a creative progress chart, such as a segmented road leading from a start to a picture of the reward to be received as the goal. Establish a reachable goal (number of books or pages to be read) and a meaningful reward for accomplishing the challenge (that will be special to your child). Your children will enjoy marking off their progress on the road to completion of the challenge.

Reading Alone

You will read many wonderful books aloud in your home, creating wonderful memories and feeding your children's growing minds with nutritious words. However, it is also true that your children will read more books during their years at home than at any other time for the rest of their lives, and most of them they will read alone. With their minds set by God for peak learning, they can learn more from reading good books on their own than you can ever hope to verbally teach them. The patterns of reading alone established in your home will stay with your children for a lifetime of reading, so you are investing in their future adult learning. In a whole-book approach, personal reading is the primary source of learning. But you have to purposely plan to make reading alone a strategic part of your homeschooling.

- **Provide structure and freedom.** To ensure the best use of personal reading times, you need to provide both structure and freedom. You provide structure—a scheduled reading time and selected books to read—to make your children accountable to you for what they are reading and learning. You provide freedom—to make their own choices for some of their reading as long as they are age-appropriate and acceptable to you—to encourage your children to follow their own interests in reading.

- **Make it a habit.** For personal reading to become habitual, you need to create designated daily reading times. Make it a priority for your children to read during these times. With so many competing options vying for your children's attention, you must be consistent at keeping the reading time a priority, or else it will be pushed aside by lessons, activities, field trips, or whatever other option comes along. Reading alone should become an unquestioned expectation. When your children are young, require them to read or rest quietly for an hour. (Which do you think they'll choose?) During the reading times, be sure to keep noises and distractions in your home to a minimum. Choose a time that is generally quiet when all (or most) of the children can participate.

- **Make it a delight.** Help each child create their own reading spot that will be their special place to read. Give them a private corner, a nice overstuffed chair, or a special spot on a couch that is comfortable for them. And be sure to let them have a cup of tea (in the tradition of C. S. Lewis) and a snack to savor during their private literary hour. Make it delightful and they will want to go there every day. Create a reading spot in their bedroom near a window if possible. Give them their own bookshelf and keep it stocked with chapter books and other interesting reading material. Frame and hang on their walls some interesting art prints about books, children reading, or illustrations from favorite children's books.

- **Make it easy to find a book.** Make your house a place where books are inescapable—where there is no place in the house that a good book is not within easy reach. When children are idle and books are available, it is natural for them to pick one up to read or browse (without being told). Place book baskets strategically next to couches and chairs throughout the house. Put stacks of classics on bookshelves so your children can easily see and grab them. Put visual books out on coffee tables for easy browsing.

- **Keep a required reading list.** Each child should always have a required reading list to work on. These are books that can be read during the daily designated reading time, so you do not need to establish a time frame for completion of the list. Only required books should be read during that time. Any other time, they may read any approved books (including from the reading list) of their choice. For the list, three might be selected by the parent and two by the child (with the parent's approval, of course): one history or biography; one science or nature; one fiction; one Christian history; one Bible-related.

- **Engage with the book.** The natural result of reading great literature and experiencing an engaging, well-told story is a heightened sense of creativity in the reader's own thoughts and ideas. Your children may not know how to express that sense, but you should assume that it is there and can be cultivated. Encourage them to respond to what they have read in a creative way—write a letter to the author or main character; create a poem outlining the events of the story; write a creative composition on specific ideas, quotes, or characters presented in the book. You do not need to look in a study guide for ideas. This sort of creative discipline is much more natural and real, and it trains your children to interact and engage with stories and ideas as living things. It also helps you to train them to see themselves as thinkers and writers in their own right. Never let a good book be closed or put back on the shelf without encouraging your children to engage with it in some way, large or small.

- **Encourage book ownership.** Do everything you can to cultivate in your children a love of books. Give them their own copies of special books they read on their own, illustrated storybooks that capture their hearts, series of books that they especially enjoy, classics that every child should have, informational books about subjects that are special to them, and even books that they are not quite ready for but will be soon. Go to bookstores regularly (they are the new libraries) and let your children select and buy new books. Go to library sales and community book sales to look together for loved-and-left bargain books. Visit antiquarian and used bookstores to spy out hidden treasures valued by your family that others might not know about. (For us, it was Eleanor Porter, Norman Macleod, Johanna Spyri, and others.) Be generous with books. It is an investment that will return hundredfold rewards in your children's lives.

IN OUR HOME

With all the baskets lying around our house, someone might think we like to shop at the local Farmers' Market. Except for one thing—they are all filled with books! Next to just about every comfortable couch or overstuffed chair, there is a big cane or wicker basket of fruits and vegetables for the mind. The baskets were originally filled with random or topical selections of books (holiday, illustrated stories, heroes, preschool, etc.). Later we turned them into personal reading baskets—one for each child and one for library books. We change the selection periodically with input from the children. It's so fulfilling to see our children grab books to read alone or together stretched out on the couch or stuffed into the overstuffed chair. Now if we can just find a good Farmers' Market for books.

Play-Aloud Books

When you need some extra time, let an audiobook read aloud for you. You can use this option occasionally as well for reading alone. Just remember that an audiobook can never replace the power of a parent reading aloud. They're great for a change of pace but should never become a substitute. Long drives are also good times for listening to an audiobook. We listened to the following books during about a six-month period:

- *Where the Red Fern Grows*
- *The Trumpet of the Swan*
- *Silas Marner*
- *Les Miserables*
- *Great Expectations*
- *The Call of the Wild*
- *The Swan Princess*
- *The Secret Garden*

Act-Aloud Favorites

Some books naturally stimulate more active imagination and creativity. It's very rewarding and delightful to see a book read in the morning and then acted out in the afternoon. Here's a sample of books to act on:

- *Roxaboxen* by Alice McLerran — Children create an imaginary town made of rocks and boxes, with pebbles for money.
- *Little Women* by Louisa May Alcott — Creative exploits of the March sisters inspire a theatrical play, a family newsletter, a neighborhood postal system, and more.
- *The Golden Road* by L.M. Montgomery — Six cousins write and publish a newspaper of their doings.
- *The Story of the Treasure Seekers* by E. Nesbit — The Bastable children's inspired attempts to raise the family fortune includes writing poetry and digging for treasure.
- *Tales from Shakespeare* by Charles and Mary Lamb — These 1807 prose adaptations for children of Shakespeare's plays provide easier material for them to act out creatively.

As knowledge is not assimilated until it is reproduced, children should "tell back" after a single reading or hearing; or should write on some part of what they have read.

— Charlotte Mason, *Towards a Philosophy of Education*, 1925

Narrating is an art, like poetry-making or painting, because it is there, in every child's mind, waiting to be discovered, and is not the result of any process of disciplinary education. A creative fiat calls it forth...and the child narrates, fluently, copiously, in ordered sequence, with fit and graphic details, with a just choice of words, without verbosity or tautology, so soon as he can speak with ease.

— Charlotte Mason, *Home Education*, 1886

A single reading is a condition insisted upon because a naturally desultory habit of mind leads us all to put off the effort of attention as long as a second or third chance of coping with our subject is to be hoped for. It is, however, a mistake to speak of the "effort of attention." Complete and entire attention is a natural function which requires no effort and causes no fatigue... the concentration at which most teachers aim is an innate provision for education that is not the result of training or effort.

— Charlotte Mason, *Towards a Philosophy of Education*, 1925

Narration

Narration is telling back or writing down in your children's own words what they have heard or read. It is the best way for children to acquire knowledge from books. As a teaching method, it is as old as language itself. Through the centuries, cultures that relied on oral tradition were using a form of narration—telling back and writing down accurately and clearly what had been heard. Until relatively recently in history, Bible knowledge was primarily passed along orally—hearing, internalizing, memorizing, and repeating. The Hebrews relied on oral tradition to transmit God's truth from one generation to the next; Jesus relied on his followers to hear and remember his teachings; and in the early church, Scriptures and Epistles were read aloud and remembered.

In our media-flooded times, oral skills have declined, but the practice of narration from books of literary quality can reclaim them for your children. And not just oral skills, but the powers of attention and retention that are fundamental to learning and to the ability to sort, sequence, select, connect, reject, classify, visualize, synthesize, and communicate knowledge from books. This uncomplicated method releases powers of reasoning, attention, and self-expression in your children left untapped by textbooks, worksheets, and lectures. In the use of narration, Charlotte Mason revived the forgotten simplicity and power of telling that teachers from Socrates onward have known. It should be a part of every homeschooling method, no exceptions.

- **Narration is a necessary skill.** An oversimplified version of the mental process of learning from hearing a book read aloud can be summarized in five steps: listening, processing, retaining, accessing, and expressing. No matter how much you think you know what is happening, the reality is that you cannot know which, if any, of the first four steps are happening in a child's mind or to what degree without the last step. Expressing is narration. The quality of narration will tell you clearly if your child has heard, comprehended, remembered, and recalled what was read.

- **Narration is a progressive skill.** Before age six, let your children simply talk—do not ask for narrations. At around age six, though, your children can begin narrating shorter readings of children's stories, Bible stories, and the like. From age seven, provide the best classic children's literature for reading material. As your children age and mature, you can progressively increase the amount and complexity of material to be narrated. By age nine or ten, the narrative ability is well developed.

- **Narration is a creative process.** Some children need more time than others to think and to express themselves. Be patient and allow your children sufficient time and freedom to narrate as creatively as they desire. At first, your children may have difficulty recalling all the details or getting them in their proper order. The more narration they do, however, the better they will become at attention and retention. If a book has a lot of detail, have your children narrate less material more frequently.

- **Narration builds language skills.** Narration develops language skills in the ability to express whole thoughts and complete sentences well before the ability to write is developed. When mechanical writing skills are more fully developed, compositional skills are already in place from verbal narration—the ability to mentally organize. From about age nine or ten and on, written narrations can be included.

- **Narration requires discipline.** Parents are often tempted to help out their children's narrations just a little. It takes discipline to stick to a single reading with no prompting for the right answers. To heighten their attention, gently remind your children before reading that they might be asked to narrate. Upon finishing the reading, simply ask your children to tell you the story. No further prompting is necessary. Charlotte Mason insisted upon a single reading. She believed children are naturally endowed with a great power of attention, and that re-readings, questioning, and summarizing would only dissipate rather than strengthen their developing attentiveness. You don't need to ask your children to narrate everything that is read, but they will often narrate it anyway simply by talking about it. That's the best kind of narration.

- **Narration can be directed.** Without taking away anything from the previous point, narration can also be directed by the parent. It's not about directing your child to a right or desired answer, but rather directing them to think about what has just been read in a new or different way that will help them think differently about the reading. For instance, you might direct a child to narrate a reading of fiction as though they are the protagonist or antagonist. Directed narration should be used sparingly, but it is a useful and effective way to keep narration disciplines fresh and fun.

- **Be flexible.** Narration is not a strict standard that must be adhered to with legalistic fervor. It is a method and a process. Through it, you are helping your children learn to learn from real books. It begins as a formal method, but the more it becomes a natural habit to your children, the more informal it can become. Corrections, if necessary, should be offered sparingly, and only after the narration. Before discussing corrections with a child, offer some positive affirmations about the narration, both about the content (what is expressed) and the delivery (how it is expressed). Never interrupt a verbal narration, especially if it is to offer a correction. Give them space and freedom to be able to verbally express what is in their head. Some children do mental editing while they speak, so letting that happen is critical to their thinking process.

- **Help with the hard content.** Some books or readings may include words, names, dates, and places that would be difficult to remember when narrating back the reading. This is especially true for younger children. You can list those pieces of information on a marker board and note them before the reading. Encourage your children to refer to the board, if it is needed.

IN OUR HOME

When Nathan was about four years old, he was all mouth and movement. Getting him to pay attention to anything for more than a few minutes was a challenge. When Sally wanted to read The Children's Homer *to his two older siblings, she told him he could draw or play quietly, but he had to be there with them. He did those things, in addition to squirming, wiggling, and literally standing on his head. She assumed he would be glad when she stopped reading. But Nathan did not want her to stop, and he began to narrate all the details of the story he had just heard. He perfectly recounted the adventures of Odysseus and the main people involved. He wanted to hear more! It was a good reminder that narration comes naturally.*

Given books of literary quality the mind does for itself the sorting, arranging, selecting, connecting, rejecting, classifying...The day a child begins using narration is the day he begins to become an independent learner. With narration the mind poses questions to itself. It is independent of the questionnaire.

— Karen Andreola, "Tips for Teachers on Narration," *The Parents' Review*, Summer Issue, Vol. 4

Narration Requests

There are numerous ways to ask for a narration. The following are suggestions adapted from an article by Karen Andreola in her quarterly magazine, *The Parents' Review*:

- "Tell me all you know about _____."
- "Explain to me how..."
- "Describe our _____."
- "Describe anything new you learned from this chapter."
- "Tell me five things you learned about _____."
- "Tell me the story back in your own words."
- "Ask six questions about the material in this chapter."
- "What did you learn about _____ in this chapter?"
- "Draw a picture, map, or likeness of _____."

Now this art of telling back [narration] is Education and is very enriching. We all practise it, we go over in our minds the points of a conversation, a lecture, a sermon, an article, and we are so made that only those ideas and arguments which we go over are we able to retain... Further, we not only retain but realise, understand, what we thus go over. Each incident stands out, every phrase acquires new force, each link in the argument is riveted, in fact we have performed The Act of Knowing, and that which we have read, or heard, becomes a part of ourselves, it is assimilated after the due rejection of waste matter.

— Charlotte Mason, *Towards a Philosophy of Education*, 1925

Reading for Writing

Young, aspiring canvas artists have long learned the basic skills of creating great art by copying the works of master artists of the past. By recreating the strokes and colors of a masterpiece, they learn how the master created it. Though the discipline is different, the same principle is true for writing. By imitating the language, syntax, and style of a great author, a budding writer begins to learn what makes some writing great and timeless rather than average or common. Whether or not your children become great writers, the practice can help them become better writers and heighten their appreciation and understanding of good literature. A written narration after hearing or reading a classic work of literature is a small step in the direction of imitating that author. As your children get older, encourage them to notice the particular techniques of descriptive narrative, character development, and writing style that characterize the writing of classic authors. Encourage them to copy some of those techniques, using them creatively in their written narrations. They will learn more than just what was written—they will learn why it is still being read.

Written Narration

Written narration is not a composition assignment. You are simply redirecting the process of telling back what has been heard from spoken words to written words. Too much formality will rob the process of spontaneity and vitality.

- **Be flexible.** Let your children know you are not as concerned about grammar and mechanics as you are about the content, vocabulary, and organization of their thoughts. Correct the writing issues later, but while the reading is still fresh in your children's minds, let them let the words flow onto paper without the burden of grammatical precision. Adjust the length of a written narration to each child's age and abilities—it is better for them to feel successful with a paragraph than overburdened by a page. Don't rush the writing—allow extra time if needed. Encourage creativity and originality. When your children are young or not yet adept at handwriting, you can become their scribe and write out their narration for them. Write it out just as they say it, then review it with them for corrections they (not you) want to make.

- **Vary the narrations.** Add some interest and enjoyment to written narration by allowing your children to select their favorite section of the book and having them write a narration of how it fits into the rest of the story. If there is a particularly interesting character in the story, ask your children to write out their narration as though they were that character. Choose a spiritual or character theme, either positive (courage, sacrifice, faithfulness, resourcefulness) or negative (anger, deception, envy), and have your children write a narration about that particular quality in the story.

IN OUR HOME

The following is an example of a short written narration. Sarah wrote this one at age ten, narrating the first chapter of Where the Red Fern Grows. *"One day, a man whose name was Billy was walking home from work. It was a beautiful day, and Billy was perfectly happy. As he was nearing his house, he heard the sounds of a dog fight. As he rounded the corner, Billy saw a lot of neighborhood dogs fighting against one old redbone hunting hound. Billy could tell that the dog did not live around there. A hunting hound would have come from the mountains in the country. The hound brought beautiful, sad and happy memories to Billy's heart. He felt sorry for the dog and, taking off his coat, he shooed the other dogs away. He took the dog home with him. As Billy was giving the dog a bath, he found a little tag on which was crudely marked, 'Buddy.' It was a little boy's handwriting. Buddy must have been sold for much needed money, or maybe he had to be left behind when his family had moved. Whatever it was, Buddy was going home to the master he loved. After the bath, Billy fed Buddy. He ate every last scrap of meat in the house! Billy had to go down to the store to get some more. Later than night, Buddy started out for the rest of his journey. After he had gone, Billy took two beautiful prize cups down from the mantelpiece. One was large and gold, the other was smaller and made of silver. They stirred boyhood memories of two redbone hounds and a red fern."*

Why Read to a Reader?

Reading aloud is an effective educational method at all ages, even into adulthood. Rather than diminishing your older children's reading skills or boring them, as some fear it will, reading aloud improves their skills and captivates their imaginations. It is an effective antidote to the effects of video. Video trains the brain to passively receive images and content with no mental interaction required. Reading aloud requires the brain to engage in attending, receiving, processing, imagining, sorting, and evaluating what is heard. Reading alone also requires complex interaction, but reading aloud is a unique learning exercise. The following are just some of the reasons to read to readers, no matter how old they are.

- **Emphasis** — When you are reading, you are able to emphasize words and concepts that your children would not always understand if reading alone. You can also point out recurring themes, symbolism, and types in literature that might otherwise go unnoticed by an immature reader.

- **Insight** — As a seasoned reader, you will know much better than your child what portions of a book to read interpretively, when, and how. The way you read will make the book more understandable and interesting to your child.

- **Vocabulary** — Listening vocabulary, especially in children, is much larger than speaking vocabulary, so you can choose books that have more difficult vocabulary. Reading aloud enlarges their listening vocabulary by allowing them to hear new words in the context of well-written language.

- **Variety** — Children develop their own appetites for reading which often do not include challenging new types of reading materials. Making them read a book is not always effective, but reading a new kind of book aloud with your children expands their reading horizons in an enjoyable way.

- **Discussion** — Reading aloud sparks conversations at all age levels. A good story provides examples to discuss godly character, good and bad choices, the uncertainty of life, and the importance of family and friends.

- **Appetite** — You can stimulate your children's appetites for quality literature through reading aloud. Your reading can set the standard for excellence, especially with older children as they begin to make their own reading choices.

- **Comprehension** — Through directed narration and evaluative questions (those that ask for an opinion), you can raise your children's level of reading comprehension. You are modeling how to understand an author's intent.

- **Togetherness** — Above all, your children will never grow too old to enjoy the warm feeling of gathering together as a family to read aloud a good book. The shared memories of those hours will build strong bonds of parent-child relationships that will last a lifetime, and the story will become a part of your shared family language.

- **Model** — The biblical pattern for learning how to live is to read the Word of God. (Until recently in history, the Bible was mostly read aloud.) Reading aloud models the priority of reading as a natural part of living and learning. Children who value reading will value reading the Bible if they see their parents regularly reading the Bible.

When mother reads aloud, the past
Seems real as every day;
I hear the tramp of armies vast,
I see the spears and lances cast,
I join the thrilling fray;
Brave knights and ladies fair and proud
I meet, when mother reads aloud.

When mother reads aloud, far lands
Seem very near and true;
I cross the desert's gleaming sands,
Or hunt the jungle's prowling bands,
Or sail the ocean blue;
Far heights, whose peaks the cold mists shroud,
I scale, when mother reads aloud.

When mother reads aloud, I long
For noble deeds to do—
To help the right, redress the wrong;
It seems so easy to be strong,
So simple to be true.
Oh, thick and fast the visions crowd
My eyes, when mother reads aloud!

— "When Mother Reads Aloud" by Hannah G. Fernald (1875-1967), New Hampshire librarian and poet, poem from 1904

Children benefit from working steadily through a well-chosen book. And if they narrate it to you, it will become theirs. But more happens. Because they've tackled a complete book, they become acquainted with its flow and its use of language. They are students of another person—the author.

— Susan Schaeffer Macaulay, *For the Children's Sake*, Crossway, 1984

Types of Study Guides

To paraphrase Solomon, "Of making many study guides there is no end, and much study wearies the body" (Ecclesiastes 12:11b). For the purposes of this book, we can focus on a limited section of the vast study guide universe—literature-based study guides. To narrow that selection even further, most of the study guides in our field of view will reinforce whole-book or Charlotte Mason principles and methods. Here is what you're most likely to find in that galaxy of study guides.

- **Single book study guides** — These typically are dedicated to a single piece of literature. Some provide useful and interesting background information but they should be used rarely, if at all, to direct the reading of a whole book.

- **History study guides** — These typically incorporate several works of history and literature to flesh out a historical unit study. As long as they do not fragment the reading of the books, a good history study guide can provide useful and interesting insights. (See page 230.)

- **Topical study guides** — These typically incorporate several works of literature into a subject unit study. As long as they do not fragment the reading of the books, a good topical study guide can provide an enjoyable way to learn about a subject of interest through whole books.

What about Study Guides?

There is nothing magical about study guides for individual books. Even though the best ones are built around good literature, they can still become a curricular safety net. The more confident you become in the book, the whole book, and nothing but the book, the less you will feel a need for written curricula. Study guides always contain useful insights about a book, to be sure, but that information is usually readily available elsewhere, sometimes in the very text of the book being read. You just have to be looking for it.

The unfortunate effect of a study guide, even though it is usually not the writer's intent, is to take a whole book and dissect it into a number of discrete lessons, usually one per chapter. Rather than training your children to read the whole book, you can end up inadvertently training them to think of a book in terms of its parts rather than as a whole. The book's author did not intend for each chapter to be reduced to a formal lesson any more than a poet would intend that each stanza of his poem be studied separately. Using a study guide also has the unintended effect of reducing the amount of reading aloud that you actually do. The literary math is simple—the more time you spend reading and using a study guide, the less time you spend reading and discussing real books.

There may be good and useful information in a study guide, but you need to ask how much of that information is really necessary to enjoy the whole book and how much of it could be called curricular filler. Be confident, read the whole book first, and then you can fill in any holes once you know where they are. Keep in mind that a study guide can perpetuate a dependence on experts rather than on your own insights. If you feel you need to use a study guide to start reading a new book, you are telling your children that you need someone else to guide you through a book rather than reinforcing their own confidence in being able to understand a book. Just read the book!

The implied promise of a study guide to turn a book into an educational tour de force is probably based more on perception than reality. Any kind of structured curriculum tends to promise more than it can actually deliver, and it is usually packaged and promoted to reinforce that perception. In reality, the practice of narration is a simpler, more natural, more powerful, and proven method for reading and learning from a book. It does not detract from the unity of the book, it allows maximum reading time, and it affirms the natural intelligence of your child. The intent of study guides is right, but the method is often unnecessary. You don't need a study guide safety net—just a good book.

IN OUR HOME

When we used study guides, it was usually for the recommended reading lists. That was the most helpful part of the study guides we had in our library. However, our children often found the guided questions obvious, tedious, or just unnecessary. Some of the better study guides provided some extra insights and information, but most of the time we just read the books and enjoyed them, letting them speak for themselves, create their own questions, and guide us to find our own answers. We found that the interest level of our children was our best study guide for reading, narrating, discussing, and learning from books.

History

There are many good reasons for your children to become students of history. From a strictly cultural perspective, a person who does not know basic historical facts might be considered not well-educated in some circles, limiting access and opportunity where a working knowledge of history would open doors. Also, knowledge of history increases comprehension in reading and media consumption. Historical literacy is necessary to understanding the meaning of content that includes historical names and places, nations and events, metaphors , anecdotes, quotes, and assumptions. Similarly, history study is part of a liberal arts education that creates a whole, well-rounded individual.

However, there is another overriding reason for you, as a Christian family, to study history—to give your children confidence to follow God. The psalmist exhorted parents to teach their children the history of Israel and the commandments of God so that generation after generation would "put their confidence in God and not forget the works of God, but keep His commandments" (Psalm 78:7, NASB). When you study history, you are giving your children reasons to be faithful to God by showing them the faithfulness of God in the affairs of men and nations. As they come to understand that God has been faithful in the past, they can grow in confidence that God will be faithful in the future.

All of history is "His story"—the study of God's providence and sovereignty and of the obedience and disobedience of men and nations to his righteous standards that bring either blessing or judgment. History is full of true heroes used by God who can be examples to your children of godliness, faith, courage, resourcefulness, integrity, sacrifice, perseverance, and vision. But history study gives your children more than just good examples to emulate—it also gives your children hope. The apostle Paul said, "For everything that was written in the past was written to teach us, so that through endurance and the encouragement of the Scriptures we might have hope" (Romans 15:4). Your teaching goal is not just to impart historical facts but to help your children see that history is more than just the passage of time—it is the progress of God's plan that will culminate in an eternal kingdom. Seeing history through the lens of Scripture will give them hope.

How should you begin? With whole, living books. Historical periods are best studied by reading whole books about real people and real events. Biography is the most interesting to a child, especially when told as a story with realistic dialogue and descriptive narrative. Other living books can be used to fill in the context with historical color and detail. History textbooks can take the life out of history, leaving only bare facts; but literature-based study through whole books can make history come alive. The stories of great men and women told well will stir the hearts and stimulate the minds of everyone in the family. You can integrate almost any area of study into your historical reading with context and unit studies—literature, science, fine arts, Bible, character, language arts, social studies, and others naturally relate to history with very little effort. Where should you begin? The Bible is the best place to start a study of history because Genesis begins at the beginning of recorded history. The account of the Fall, the origins of language and governments, the Flood, and the birth of Israel all provide the context for evaluating the rest of world history. Even the seeds of our American and western civilization were planted in the beginning in Genesis. For American history, start with Columbus or with the Pilgrims, showing that God used his people in the founding of our country.

There is no history, only biography.

— Ralph Waldo Emerson (1803-1822), American poet

History is a mighty drama, enacted upon the theatre of times, with suns for lamps and eternity for a background.

— Thomas Carlyle (1795-1881), Scottish historian

History isn't just something that ought to be taught or ought to be read or ought to be encouraged because it's going to make us better citizens...It should be taught for pleasure. The pleasure of history, like art or music or literature, consists of an expansion of the experience of being alive, which is what education is largely about.

— David McCullough, American biographer and author, and Pulitzer Prize winner, *Imprimis*, Hillsdale College, 2003

The Lenses of History Study

Think of history study as a set of three magnifying lenses through which you can not just study what happened long ago but also see how it keeps happening here and now.

- **Events** — Chronology or "What happened?" Look at the context and impact of historical events. How are we still experiencing the results of those events? What events today are like them?
- **People** — Biography or "Who made it happen?" Look at the lives of famous people through biographies and historical accounts. Is the person a good example or a bad one? Who is like them today?
- **Ideas** — Ideology or "Why did it happen?" Look at ideas and their movements that have changed and shaped history. How have those ideas shaped our lives today? What ideas today are like them?

History is a vision of God's creation on the move.

— Arnold J. Toynbee (1889-1975), British historian

The moral principles and precepts contained in the scriptures ought to form the basis of all our civil constitutions and laws...All the miseries and evils which men suffer from vice, crime, ambition, injustice, oppression, slavery, and war, proceed from their despising or neglecting the precepts contained in the Bible.

— Noah Webster (1758-1843), American lexicographer and author

Likewise an introduction to World History, the characters and places in which are utterly unknown strangers to the child, must be something more than a mere name introduction, and there must be very few introductions given at a time or both names and faces will be instantly forgotten.

— V. M. Hillyer, *A Child's History of the World*, The Century Co., 1924

Periods of World History

Identifying the great eras of world history is an exercise in generalization. However, generally agreed upon eras include:

- The Ancient World (up to 500 BC) (Old Testament)
- The Classical World (499 BC to AD 500) (Greece & Rome)
- Early Middle Ages (501-1100) (or Dark Ages)
- The Middle Ages (1101-1460)
- The Renaissance (1461-1600) (and Reformation)
- Trade and Empire (1601-1707) (Exploration)
- Revolution and Independence (1708-1835) (Enlightenment)
- Unification and Colonization (1836-1913) (Industrial Age)
- The World at War (1914-1949) (Great Depression)
- The Modern World (1950-present) (Information Age)

World History

World history is not a limited territory with defined borders that can be contained, conquered, and controlled. It is instead a vast and limitless ocean that can only be explored and charted. The farther you sail into the ocean of world history, the more you realize it is a journey with no end. However, you can drop anchor at any point and probe the depths of world history where you are, and those anchors can become permanent places in your children's minds. People, events, and ideas are the anchors that will hold history in place for your children. Your goal is not to try to cover the entire ocean surface of world history, which would require a very fast and shallow trip, but rather to pick some specific routes, stop at the most interesting places, and put down as many historical anchors as you can. The more anchors you can create, the easier it will be for your children to begin to sort out and make sense of world history. The best way to create those anchors is through reading whole, living books that make history come alive.

Many parents start out with very high ideals, determining to study history comprehensively and chronologically. The reality, though, is that there is far too much world history for any child to absorb, and it is rarely experienced chronologically. Your goal is the exploration of the whole of world history, not just the inculcation of selected facts and details. Whole books that tell the stories of world history are your best tools for navigating that vast ocean. If your children love the stories, they will love the history within the stories. In the process of exploring and dropping anchor often for deeper study, you will be cultivating in your children's hearts a love and appetite for learning about history through books that will stay with them for their entire lives. It is the love of history, not just the knowledge of facts, that will anchor understanding in their hearts.

- **Tell the stories.** The term "history" is derived from a Greek term that means "one who knows or sees." The implication is that history is written by those who know about it firsthand or have seen the event. History is, at its core, personal. It is not just facts and details, but it is a person recounting what they know or what they saw. It is someone telling a story. The most effective history study you can do is to tell the stories of history to your children, and whole books are your best storytellers. Find books that make the people come alive, that transport your child into a literary window of real history, and that explain the ideas with personal interest and insight.

- **Start with roots.** In the elementary years, focus on your own historical roots. Follow the streams of history that flow most naturally into your children's lives—the great civilizations of the Old and New Testaments (Egypt, Medo-Persia, Greece, Rome), European history (Middle Ages, Renaissance, Reformation, Enlightenment, Revolution), American history (Colonial, Revolutionary, National, Pioneer, Civil War, and Slavery), and others (Vikings, Exploration, and Conquest). If your ethnic background is not European, you might also study Asia, Africa, or South America.

- **Focus on people.** Children have a natural curiosity about the olden days of world history and how people used to live. They want to know what they were like, what they did, and what happened to them. The key to your children's interest in world history is not archaeological but biographical—they want to hear about real people. Young children do not have enough experience with events in their own history to understand events in past history, but they can understand people.

- **Connect the dots.** Children also have a natural desire to know who and what came during, before, and after. Chronological study of world history allows your children to see the steady progress of history across centuries instead of just disconnected bits and pieces. Chronology presents world history to children in a logical, understandable sequence. However, because any time period of world history is so layered with different civilizations, continents, cultural developments, languages, arts, religion, and so many other layers, overly strict chronological study can easily become forced and artificial, robbing world history study of exploration, interest, and joy.

- **Sequence history.** Chronological study can be useful for certain historical periods and places, but always remember that it is a servant, not a master. Be flexible, and by all means don't become compulsive about chronology. The underlying principle is to study history sequentially. In other words, follow the sequence of events in any area or period of history study. You will naturally break into any chronological study of world history throughout the year to study parts of American, European, or church history for holidays, trips, or just because your child is interested in something else. When you do, don't be concerned. Your children are learning both globally and linearly in the elementary years. They will put it all together in their own time anyway. So enjoy your historical side trip and then simply return to the sequence where you left off. A simple, visual timeline will help your children orient to the chronological relationship of different historical sequences that you study.

- **Follow the ideas.** One of the benefits of studying some history chronologically is to be able to see the history of ideas, which develop linearly in history. Ideas (whether right or wrong) about origins, science, technology, liberty, the church, or whatever develop gradually over time. Chronology allows you to study the history, development, and impact of ideas on civilization more effectively.

- **Make timelines.** Post historical timelines on the wall at your children's eye level. Use a published one or make your own using drawings and clip art. The purpose of a timeline is not to memorize names and dates but to help your child visualize where an event being studied fits in history by seeing what comes before and after it and what else was happening in the world at that time. Be sure to use drawings or pictures for every idea, event, or person you want to emphasize. Those will be the visual anchors your children will remember and visualize in their minds for putting together the pieces of history.

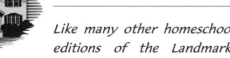

IN OUR HOME

Like many other homeschooling families, we collect original editions of the Landmark history series for children. Landmark books are those venerable (and sometimes valuable) hardback history books for children from the 1950s and 1960s. We have many of the over 200 books in the series, most of which are in their original jackets. It's a fun treasure hunt, and they are perfect for U.S. and world history read-aloud or personal reading. Our children have become very good at spotting Landmark spines in book vendor stalls, used bookstores, and library sales. They're getting harder to find at the once-lower prices, but easier to trade.

Homemade Timelines

Fan-folded computer paper works well for a timeline. Divide it vertically along the lines of major periods of history. (Have your children learn the names and order of those periods.) You can divide the line by whatever date intervals work best, but keep in mind any length limitations. You can also create multiple timelines for more detail. You might consider starting out with a timeline divided by centuries. You can also divide the paper horizontally into three to five areas of influence, such as the Church, the Arts, Ideas, and so on (or use parallel timelines). The center horizontal section or line is the core timeline with the events of history written onto it. Whenever you start a new history study, stick a piece of clip art or a symbolic picture on the line to represent what you are studying. Timelines can be hung on the wall, folded, or rolled and stored.

History on a Roll

If wall space is at a premium and you're willing to be creative, try making a scrolling timeline. Find two cardboard tubes and cut them to the height of whatever continuous paper you will use for your timeline, or you can find shipping or wrapping paper already on tubes ready to use. Just connect each loose end to a tube and mount the tubes on two vertical poles (closet rod, PVC). Create your timeline on the paper and scroll through history. You have an almost limitless ability to grow your timeline as long as you want, and it can be kept in a small amount of space without permanently using the wall space.

Dress (Up) Rehearsal

Keep a role-play locker full of costumes and clothing for different periods of world and American history. Use them as teaching and learning aids to dramatically rehearse key events from history.

If religious books are not widely circulated among the masses in this country, I do not know what is going to become of us as a nation. If truth be not diffused, error will be; If God and His Word are not known and received, the devil and his works will gain the ascendancy; If the evangelical volume does not reach every hamlet, the pages of a corrupt and licentious literature will; If the power of the Gospel is not felt throughout the length and breadth of the land, anarchy and misrule, degradation and misery, corruption and darkness will reign without mitigation or end.

— Daniel Webster (1782-1852), American statesman and orator, *America's God and Country*, William Federer (AmeriSearch, 2000)

Periods of American History

Although historians will debate dates, the following represent the generally accepted eras of American history.

- Pre-Columbian (pre-1492)
- Colonial (1493-1763)
- Revolutionary (1764-1789)
- The New Nation (1790-1828)
- Western Expansion & Reform (1829-1859)
- Civil War (1860-1865)
- Reconstruction (1866-1877)
- Industrialization & the Gilded Age (1878-1889)
- Expansionism & the Progressive Era (1890-1913)
- The Great War (WWI) & the Jazz Age (1914-1928)
- Depression & the New Deal (1928-1940)
- WWII (1940-1945)
- Postwar America & the Cold War (1945-1960)
- Vietnam Era & Civil Rights (1960-1980)
- Reagan Era & the Digital Age (1980-2000)
- Bush Era & the War on Terror (2000-2008)
- New Era & the Clash of Ideologies (2008-present)

American History

If world history study is like exploring and charting a vast and limitless ocean, American history study is more like surveying and defining the boundaries of a limited territory. World history study, by its nature, requires more global thinking; American history study, though, can be much more linear. There are well-defined periods of American history of reasonably limited scope that can be studied chronologically or sequentially. Unlike world history, there is a sense in which American history study can be conquered and contained. Because your children's lives revolve around American history—holidays, traditions, freedoms, language, symbols, museums, geography, pictures, songs, movies, stories, events, and more—there are fewer language and cultural barriers to impede study, and they have already internalized more information. America is naturally their own history—they are already a part of it and will want to find their own place within it. It is the most intensely personal realm of history study for your children.

You have the privilege of filling in your children's American identity with a view of American history that includes God's hand of providence in our past, present, and future. You will also find yourself correcting false, misleading, incomplete, and de-Christianized versions of American history often purveyed by secular media. But more than that, you will be able to positively present a view of America as a country founded on biblical principles of personal and religious freedom that have provided liberty, opportunity, and prosperity for more people than any other nation in the history of the world. Your goal is to help your children find themselves in the story of American history and then see American history as part of world history. That does not mean teaching them a narrow nationalism, nor does it mean avoiding the less-honorable and even bad parts of our American history. It simply means teaching them from their closest reference point to history—that they are Americans. As your children find their place in American history, they will be able to make sense of world history and even biblical history.

One of the great advantages of homeschooling is the freedom you have to teach your children about our unique historical heritage from a Christian worldview. In an increasingly secularized public school system, the Christian and biblical foundations of America are often glossed over, ignored, or even excised out of a misguided view of separation of church and state. But you have the freedom, secured by the sacrifices of our forefathers, to tell your children the whole story of America's Christian beginnings. From its earliest days, our country's identity was shaped by Christian beliefs and ideals and formed by the impulse of those driven to find individual and religious freedom.

Our founding documents affirm the "self-evident" truths that our equality as people and our rights to "Life, Liberty, and the Pursuit of Happiness" as individuals come from our eternal Creator, God, not from temporal kings or man-made governments. The documents assent to or assume our dependence on God for our existence and preservation. Our founding fathers often gave testimony to their trust in God and their belief that our survival as a nation would depend on our continued adherence to the truths of God's Word. The stories of our beginnings include countless incidents of God's mercy, intervention, and providence in overcoming seemingly insurmountable unfavorable odds to give birth to a nation "conceived in liberty." You have the freedom and the privilege to preserve those stories in the hearts of your children for future generations.

- **Study great Americans.** In the elementary years, the theme of study for American history is, predominantly, personal and religious liberty. Your children need to understand the costs, privileges, and responsibilities of the freedoms they enjoy as American citizens, as well as the threats to those freedoms. Study the historical roots of our liberties and the men and women who fought and died for our right to be free. The principles of liberty embodied in our national documents and heritage are solidly rooted in a biblical worldview. Regularly read biographies of great Americans, patriots, leaders, and heroes, especially those with a Christian testimony. They are the antidote for the antiheroes of today's pop culture. They will inspire your children to greatness of character and endeavor.

- **Study the original documents.** Even though they may not understand all of the content, you should expose your children to original American documents. Read them aloud and stop to discuss important words and concepts. Hearing the language and words repeatedly during their formative years will gradually increase their familiarity, understanding, and historical literacy. Read a biography at the same time to increase interest—read a Landmark biography about Thomas Jefferson and read the Declaration of Independence, or read a biography of Abraham Lincoln and read his Gettysburg Address.

- **Acknowledge the good and the bad.** In our desire to give our children reasons to be patriotic and positive about America, it is easy to simply minimize or skip over the bad parts of our history. But it does not diminish America's strengths for our children to know that America is only as strong and good as its leaders and that some leaders have rejected God's laws, resulting in decisions, events, and policies that do not honor God. If they know that "righteousness exalts a nation," then they also will understand that "sin is a disgrace to any people" (Proverbs 14:34).

- **Provide biblical context.** Examine issues of American history through the lens of biblical truth. Even though God will not directly judge nations again until Christ returns, the principle of blessing or curse (Deuteronomy 11:26-28) still holds true for nations today—God's ways bring blessing to a nation; sin brings a curse. On the blessing side, consider what the Scriptures say about freedom, generosity, the poor, self-discipline, and other qualities and apply them to America. Then consider what the Scriptures say about slavery, abortion, greed, and other matters and apply them.

IN OUR HOME

We turn American holidays into history lessons. On Independence Day, we talk about our freedoms, the founding fathers, our Christian heritage, and other American themes. We read the Declaration of Independence. We might watch a movie, such as Johnny Tremain. *On Thanksgiving, we tell the story of the Pilgrims and their pursuit of religious freedom. We read from Governor Bradford's journals and retell the stories of Squanto and Pocahontas. On Memorial Day, we take time to recall that "all gave some, and some gave all" to defend and die for the freedoms our family now enjoys. On all these holidays, we see the hand of God's providence in the founding and preservation of America.*

American Documents

Documents are history in situ, written in process. Visit www.ourdocuments.gov for "100 Milestone Documents." These are just a few to start with.

- Mayflower Compact (1620)
- Declaration of Independence (1776)
- Articles of Confederation (1777)
- Constitution of the United States (1787)
- Washington's First Inaugural Speech (1789)
- Bill of Rights (1791)
- Washington's Farewell Address (1796)
- Monroe Doctrine (1823)
- Homestead Act (1862)
- Emancipation Proclamation (1863)
- Gettysburg Address (1863)
- Lincoln's Second Inaugural Address (1865)
- 13th Amendment: Abolition of Slavery (1865)
- 14th Amendment: Civil Rights (1868)
- 15th Amendment: Voting Rights (1870)
- 19th Amendment: Women's Right to Vote (1920)
- Civil Rights Act (1964)
- Voting Rights Act (1965)

History on the Road

Plan family vacations to include visiting historical sites. Coordinate the trip with reading a book about the site or event, as well as a context study. Use the visit as a starting point for broader study and reading about the associated period of American history

- Washington, DC
- Colonial Williamsburg, VA
- Freedom Trail in Boston, MA
- Concord & Lexington, MA
- Philadelphia, PA
- Gettysburg, PA
- Valley Forge, PA
- Plimoth Plantation, MA
- Mount Vernon, VA
- Monticello, VA
- Fort Sumter, SC

American History Readers

There are many well-written but easy-to-read American history books for younger readers.

- Childhood of Famous Americans (Aladdin, ages 9-12)
- Landmark Books American history series (Random House Books for Young Readers, ages 9-12)
- Landmark Books Meet… biography series (Random House Books for Young Readers, age 9-12)
- American Story series by Betsy & Giulio Maestro (HarperCollins, illustrated, ages 4-8)
- Biographies by Jean Fritz (Putnam Juvenile, illustrated, ages 9-12)
- Biographies by Ingri and Edgar Parin D'Aulaire (Beautiful Feet Books, illustrated, ages 9+)
- Histories by Cheryl Harness (National Geographic Children's Books, illustrated, ages 9-12)

American History Anchors

People

- William Bradford
- George Washington
- Thomas Jefferson
- Benjamin Franklin
- Samuel Adams
- John Adams
- Patrick Henry
- Paul Revere
- Henry Clay
- Daniel Webster

Events

- Pilgrims & Plymouth Colony
- Boston Tea Party
- Concord & Lexington
- The Revolutionary War
- Constitutional Convention
- War of 1812

Ideas

- Religious freedom
- The Mayflower Compact
- Slavery
- Declaration of Independence
- *Common Sense* (Thos. Paine)

- **Event Celebrations** — Your children's lives revolve around American history, so it will be difficult to teach it chronologically. An American history timeline is especially helpful to put people and events in time and place whenever American history is being discussed. Cycle American history into your studies regularly, especially biographical studies of Christian colonists and founding fathers. Teach periods of American history sequentially, but don't worry about the chronology.

- **Presidents** — Studying American history by presidents is simple, fun, and comprehensive. Create a notebook with a form for each president for your child to fill in with common information (dates, events, people, laws, decisions, issues, controversies, etc.). Create a presidential timeline divided by the presidents' terms and show other events happening in America and in the world. Create a simple rating system and rate each president with your children. You create the criteria, assign one to five stars for each of the criteria, and then calculate an overall average rating.

- **Government** — Your children cannot fully understand American history without a basic understanding of our representative form of constitutional government—the relationships among the three branches of government (executive, legislative, judicial), the role of the president and the executive branch, how laws are enacted in a bicameral legislative system (Senate and House of Representatives), what the Supreme Court does, how states function, how elections work, and more. Don't rely on workbooks, but include discussions of government in your daily conversations.

- **Economy** — The history of America is inseparable from the economic principles of free-market capitalism that are expressions of personal liberty that have driven the growth and development of America as the greatest wealth-producing country in history. There are positives (self-reliance, personal success) and negatives (greed, corruption) to that history, but it must be studied. Understanding the basic principles of a free-market economy will help make better sense of many historical events and eras.

- **Freedoms** — Study the history of America through the lenses of the rights enumerated in the Constitution and Bill of Rights (Amendments 1-10). The concept of personal liberty is at the core of our American experience, so study how rights have been expanded or limited—religion, press, speech, civil rights, assembly, right to bear arms, and others. It a great way to show that the American government works.

- **Wars** — Like it or not, wars have defined major periods of American history—the French and Indian Wars, the Revolutionary War, the War of 1812, the Civil War, WWI, WWII, the Korean War, Vietnam, and the wars in Iraq and Afghanistan. What America is willing to fight and die for has defined much of our existence. However, studying the history of American wars can wait until late elementary.

- **Local American History** — Local and state histories are also American history. Identify historical sites that you can visit and create simple unit studies for them. Your local library should have plenty of good books and resources to get you started. Call ahead to the historical sites to find out if they have resources you can obtain and study prior to your visit. They often have unique books and publications about the history surrounding that site that are difficult to find elsewhere.

Church and Christian History

It is easy to get lost in church and Christian history, especially when you try to follow the countless streams and tributaries that make up the flow of the Christian church, not just in world history but also in American history. Yet your children will benefit greatly from knowing which stream of church history your family is in and how you came to be in it. If they know where they are now, it will be an anchor to see where they have come from and where they are going.

- **Keep the kingdom in view.** In world and American history, you are studying about the kingdoms of the world and its people. In church history, you are studying about the kingdom of God and his people. The church is a spiritual institution that must be studied historically through the eyes of faith.

- **Focus on biography.** For children, the emphasis in church history should not be on chronology (what and when) but on biography (who). Read stories and biographies of great men and women of the faith—ministers, missionaries, and martyrs. As in other history studies, locate those you read about in both place (map) and time (timeline). Trace their influence to the present day.

- **Keep church events general.** Study the events of church history in very broad strokes, emphasizing the early church, the medieval church, the Reformation, the church in early America, and the church today. Your goal is not to teach and test the details of church history but to give your children a sense of continuity with the church through the past two millennia.

- **Study the history of Christianity.** Study Christianity as a movement of belief from its founding in the book of Acts up to today. Observe how it has spread and how it has influenced cultures around the world. Compare it to the origins and spread of other world religions. Normally, comparative religions would be high-school-level study, but with so much about other religions in the media now, late elementary is not too early to begin with a general overview and discussion of other religions.

- **Learn the history of the Bible.** The story of Christianity is inextricably connected to the story of how the Bible came to us, how it was preserved, and how it has been translated and distributed around the world. It is still the best-selling published book of all time, and Christian history is incomplete without its story in the telling.

IN OUR HOME

Like many others, we have traveled quite a few church streams to be where we are now. Neither of us stayed in our parents' stream, but we both found ourselves as new believers in the seventies in the conservative evangelical stream that flowed out of the student discipleship movement of the fifties and sixties. However, mobility (fifteen homes in twenty-five years of marriage) did not allow us to settle into a particular church tradition, so our children understand that they are in a stream of beliefs about the Bible, truth, grace, and Jesus. We go wherever that stream flows, finding fellowship in churches that worship in spirit and truth.

God's People

Include a separate line for God's people on your historical timeline to place and trace the great men and women of faith in secular historical context. Trace your own church's leaders and historical roots and shoots.

Periods of Christian History

This outline of Christian history is adapted from *Church History in Plain Language* by Dr. Bruce Shelley (my professor at Denver Seminary):

- The Age of Jesus and the Apostles (6 BC to AD 70) — Jesus, the early church, gospel to the Gentiles
- The Age of Catholic Christianity (70-312) — persecution, canon and the Bible, bishops, rise of orthodoxy, Alexandria
- The Age of the Christian Roman Empire (312-590) — Constantine, councils and creeds, monasticism, papacy, Augustine
- The Christian Middle Ages (590-1517) — Gregory the Great, Christendom, Crusades, scholasticism, Thomas Aquinas, Wycliffe and Hus
- The Age of the Reformation (1517-1648) — Luther and Protestantism, Anabaptists, John Calvin, Church of England, America and Asia, Puritanism, denominations
- The Age of Reason and Revival (1648-1789) — the Enlightenment, pietism, Wesley, Methodism, the Great Awakening
- The Age of Progress (1789-1914) — Catholicism, England and social reform, Protestant missions, Christian America, Protestant liberalism
- The Age of Ideologies (1914-1996) — American Evangelicals, Fundamentalism, ecumenism, Vatican II, third-world missions, individualism, global Christianity
- The Age of Assessment (1996 -present) — youth leaving, gender issues, women in leadership, megachurches, emergent church, new worship

It was in reading [The Lord of the Rings trilogy] that I first understood that life—my life—is a story. The entire history of the world is an epic written by God and told throughout the colorful drama of each advancing generation. We are the heroes and heroines, the villains and knaves that people the pages of this one true tale. Our actions and our decisions contribute as much to light or darkness as any prince or princess in a fairy tale.

— Sarah Clarkson, *Read for the Heart*, Apologia Press, 2009

History Study Guides

There are numerous Charlotte Mason and literature-based history and unit study guides. The best ones are high-quality, thoughtful resources, but be sure they will reinforce and supplement your WholeHearted wholebook reading and narration, not supplant it.

- Greenleaf Guides (Greenleaf Press) — literature-based "Famous Men of…" world history study guides for Old Testament history, ancient Egypt, ancient Greece, ancient Rome, Middle Ages, Renaissance & Reformation, and more
- History Revealed (AIG) — Diana Waring's history books and CDs covering *Ancient Civilizations & the Bible: From Creation to Jesus Christ* and *Romans, Reformers, Revolutionaries*
- History through Literature Study Guides (Beautiful Feet Books) — literature-based study guides for ancient history, early American history, world history, geography, and other subjects
- TruthQuest History Study Guides (TruthQuest History) — sequential history study for all periods focusing on God's truth, historical literature, and ThinkWrite exercises

Family History

Family history is all relative…literally and figuratively. Some families have more relatives to find in their past than others; some have more appealing relatives than others; and some have more spiritual relatives than others. It's all relative as to just how deep and wide you choose to make your study of family, but it is unquestionably important for your children to know something of their own family history and heritage, even if only for a few generations back. Connecting them to direct family members in their past who actually lived through the times and events of history that they are studying will turn "How much more?" impersonal textbook history into "Tell me more!" personal living history.

- **It's up to you.** No matter how many names and abstracts you can put into your genealogical record, how many new branches you can add to a family tree, or how many presidents or princes or paupers pop up in your family line, just keeping track of ancestors and descendants can easily become a meaningless exercise. On the other hand, if it reveals to your children a Christian heritage and legacy that has been passed from one generation to the next, then it has great value.

- **Focus on the stories.** Much more important than facts and data about relatives are their individual stories. Collect interesting stories and insights about your relatives and ancestors—Christian testimony, childhood incidents, history witnessed, impressions about progress, what it was like when they grew up, insights on other relatives now deceased, hopes and dreams. Video or record interviews with older family members to capture their stories in their own words. Create a notebook for storing all your genealogical notes chronologically for easy browsing. Include the stories, photographs, and memorabilia in your own homeschool history study.

- **Trace your family tree of life.** Uncover any Christian heritage and ancestry of your family. Trace the various religious traditions and denominations of your family members over the last one or two centuries. Look especially for Christian testimonies and reports. This is an expression of Psalm 78:1-7 to help your children see a history of generational faith. Due to increased mobility over the past hundred-plus years, we have lost the sense of family community and continuity that defined generational faith for centuries. We have to work hard to create it now or else lose it entirely.

IN OUR HOME

Before our children's great-grandmother died, Sally's mother (Mimi) taped an interview with her about her childhood, her memories of being in a wagon train attacked by Indians, and other fascinating insights about her life. Sally's great-aunt gave her a genealogy of the Bone family line that traces back to Eleanor of Aquitaine, mother of John and Richard, kings of England. Clay's mother (Nana) compiled piles of files about the Clarkson family line, tracing our direct lineage back to Thomas Boston, a seventeenth-to-eighteenth-century Scottish pastor whose books are still in print. The line also includes Thomas Boston Clarkson (William Wilberforce's fellow abolitionist), as well as South Carolina relatives whose mansion was burned by Sherman and a doctor who tended the wounded of both sides at Gettysburg.

Geography

Geography is all the rage these days, and our society has decided that the truly educated child can name every country and capital in the world. While there's nothing wrong with such geo-trivia, it has little to do with true education. Geography is not just land masses and borders, but also people and events. The importance of geography is not just in being able to identify a country and its capital, but also in knowing its role in history and current events. To say that Vienna is the capital of Austria is a bare fact of little interest. To talk about the classical music associated with Vienna, or its strategic location during wars, or its one-time prominence as the center of an empire makes the geography of Austria worth learning. The study of history provides a natural bridge for the study of geography—they are almost inseparable. When continents, countries, cities, rivers, mountains, and such are part of a book or story that you are reading, then the study of geography comes alive with new meaning. World geography studied for no other reason than to fill in maps quickly becomes tedious and tiresome, but when geography is studied in the context of history and current events it doesn't even seem like a geography lesson. It's natural and enjoyable.

- **Study the people.** Geography is as much who as it is where. Study the people in a geographical area: What are they like? What do they eat? How do they dress? How do they worship? What do they do for work? Study the people living in the various countries where missionaries from your church are ministering.

- **Study geographical context.** Geography should be a part of any context study when you are reading a whole book on history. To see what the geography was like at the time of the story, check the encyclopedia, a historical atlas, or a historical reference book on that period.

- **Study current geography.** Whenever you hear a country mentioned in the news or encounter it in reading, take a minute to find it on the map. Use a reference atlas to discover more about the people, their customs and culture, the topography of the land (mountains, rivers, deserts, forests, etc.), and more. Keep a world globe handy to visualize the location of the country. (The globe does not have to be precisely current.)

- **Study Bible geography.** For Bible reading, always keep wall maps or a Bible atlas close at hand so you can quickly locate cities, land masses, bodies of water, and travel routes. "Then and Now" overlay maps are especially helpful. Map study makes the Bible much more visual and interesting.

- **Study missionary geography.** Start praying as a family for people groups around the world and for missionary outreach to them. Check with missionary groups such as the U.S. Center for World Mission for resources. This is a natural and effective way to make the study of current world geography meaningful to your children.

- **Focus on macro-geography.** In the elementary years, focus your studies on macro-geography—the study of larger elements such as continents, oceans, land masses, deserts, major rivers, large cities, and such. Your goal is to give your children a basic geographic literacy so they will be able to understand what parts of the world are being talked about in books, discussions, and news.

The teaching of Geography suffers especially from the utilitarian spirit...to strip the unfortunate planet which has been assigned to us as our abode and environment of every trace of mystery and beauty. There is no longer anything to admire or to wonder at in this sweet world of ours...Perhaps no knowledge is more delightful than such an intimacy with the earth's surface, region by region, as should enable the map of any region to unfold a panorama of delight, disclosing not only mountains, rivers, frontiers, the great features we know as "Geography," but associations, occupations, some parts of the past and much of the present, of every part of this beautiful earth.

— Charlotte Mason, *Towards a Philosophy of Education*, 1925

Place in History

Whenever you come across a geographical reference in reading aloud or studying history, turn it into a mini-geography lesson. Go to a globe, wall map, or atlas to locate the country and its capital. Observe its topography— rivers, lakes, mountains, harbors, deserts, plains, and grasslands. Locate any relevant cities (or their probable locations). Learn more about the customs and culture of the land and its people. It is a natural way to get to know the world.

Beauty interprets itself, whether seen in nature, in a fine painting or building or statue, or in conduct. By a few skillful questions or suggestions that help to reveal the message, we can bring the children under the spell of the beautiful, and then leave them alone to dream their dreams...It is a great mistake to give children only what can be fully comprehended. They need something more.

— Randall J. Condon, *The Atlantic Readers*, Little, Brown, and Co., 1926

The Real Thing

We try hard to give our children appetites for good and godly art, music, and poetry. Culture, though, tries even harder to give them appetites for cartoon and pop-culture art, childish and pagan music, and puerile poetry. If they ask why we don't read a particular book, listen to certain kinds of music, or watch Saturday-morning cartoons, we use the illustration below. The subject is the same in each, but which is more interesting? Which is more real? Which tells a story? We believe our children's minds are made for better appetites. God doesn't want us only avoiding the ungodly things; he also doesn't want us to let mediocrity crowd out excellence in our minds. He wants us to train our appetites for beauty and excellence.

The Fine Arts: Art, Music, Poetry

The fine arts have their origin in God, the Creator of language, color, and music. Fine arts reveal within us an intrinsic need to create and enjoy artistic beauty that is a part of God's image stamped on our being—an attempt to recover a glimmer of what was lost in the Fall. God used all the fine arts to express his nature—the beauty of the artists' creations on the tabernacle and temple, the expression of praise through instruments and songs, the emotion of poetry in the Psalms. In training your children to appreciate the fine arts, you are tapping into and releasing that part of God's creative nature within them.

While history might be described as the record of humanity's actions, the arts might well be called the record of its passions in our quest to make sense of life. Art, music, and poetry reveal the deepest loves and longings in the human heart in its search for and expression of the transcendent in life. Rather than being perceived as a frivolous side subject that is less important than the study of concrete ideas of history or worldview, the arts should be seen as important artifacts of history and culture that express in a tangible form the more abstract thoughts and ideas that both reflect and shape people in different times and places. By exposing your children to the beauty of art, the mystery of music, and the contemplation of poetry, you are teaching them a universal language that God has stamped on every person's nature. It is the study of who we are and what we value.

Philosophers and theologians have long mused about transcendent virtues, which are most often identified as truth, goodness, and beauty. This triad has been mapped in numerous ways to the human experience (mind, will, emotions) and the godhead (Father, Son, Spirit), but the fine arts can uniquely express all three at once. Those otherwise abstract words are given meaning by scriptures such as Philippians 4:8 and many others, but as believers we instinctively know in the Spirit when a work of art, music, or poetry expresses what is true about life, when it reflects the goodness of God, and when it is a thing of beauty. Fine arts hone our spirits to be sensitive to the transcendent.

In the same way that narration trains your children to hear what an author is saying through a book, you can also train your children to hear and narrate what an artist, musician, or poet is saying through a creative work. In the process, you can train their appetites to hunger after that which is truly fine and beautiful, rather than just common or commercial. Studying the fine arts will sharpen their ability to distinguish between mediocrity and a masterpiece. It is not necessary for you to be knowledgeable about the fine arts in order to enjoy them with your children. Your attitude will set the pace. If you are interested and excited about the fine arts, your children will be, too.

Always provide some background on the creator of a work—not just raw biographical data, but real stories about the person's life, especially as they might relate to the artwork, composition, or poem. The more your children see the real person behind the creative work, the more interesting it will be to them. Put the work being studied in historical context with a timeline and by studying other fine artists of that time—look at the work of a few other visual artists, listen to compositions by other musicians, read other poets. Appreciation of the fine arts is not just about learning who painted, composed, or wrote what and when. It is about learning to listen to the unspoken, hear the spirit, and explore the mysteries of life. It is about recognizing the creative fingerprints of the Creator God.

Art

Art is contemplation—it forces the viewer to slow down, observe, and reflect. A piece of art captures a moment in time that is interpreted and expressed through the artist's skills and perception to emphasize aspects of that slice of reality that say more than the reality itself might say. Good art is a one-frame movie that brings reality, and the transcendent behind and beyond reality, into sharper focus. When you enjoy and study art with your children, you are taking time to look into a window so you can see the world through the artist's eyes and see the creativity of God in the artist's handiwork.

- **Appreciate artistry.** Your goal in the elementary years is to lead your children into an appreciation and enjoyment of art in all of its varied expressions. Train them to observe how the artist uses line, form, composition, color, shading, texture, and style. Ask what the artist is saying through the artwork—what is his subject—and how the various elements help or hinder his message. Ask your children what they like and don't like about the artwork, and why. Teach them to narrate artwork.

- **Understand artists.** In order to really get to know an artist and his work, select one artist and study several of his works over a period of several weeks or even months. Thoroughly examine and discuss one piece of artwork at a time, discovering the artistic signatures that characterize the artist's work. If you can study an artist's work chronologically, look for changes or developments in style and subject matter.

- **Stick to your standards.** You must set your own standards concerning nudity in studying fine art. Much of it can be avoided in the elementary years, and certainly any base or vulgar use of nudity should be rejected. However, nudity is an almost unavoidable fact of life in art, especially if you visit any art museums. Overreacting to nudity can inadvertently create, rather than prevent, more interest in it. Determine what your threshold of comfort is for your family with artistic nudity and decide ahead of time how to respond when an artist exceeds your comfort level.

- **Enjoy picture and art books.** The first form of art your children will encounter will be the work of children's book illustrators, whether in classic literature or just illustrated storybooks. Many children's book illustrators are, or were, also professional artists (Jessie Wilcox Smith, N. C. Wyeth, Thomas Locker, Margaret Early). Art anthologies and artist overviews are helpful for art study. Keep quality art books out and open on tables or displayed on a small easel for easy browsing. Your local library probably has a good selection of art books and posters.

IN OUR HOME

Nathan didn't seem interested in art as a little boy until we found him intently studying a Norman Rockwell mural in one of our oversized art books. He had found in the painting, called The Land of Enchantment *(a wall mural in New Rochelle Public Library), background images of characters from children's literature. It was a joy to hear him tell us about his discovery. In the area of music, it was hard to get our children interested in classical music until we played recordings with dramatized stories about the composers' lives. Once the music became personal, they wanted to hear more.*

Art is contemplation.

— Auguste Rodin (1840-1917), French sculptor

A man should hear a little music, read a little poetry, and see a fine picture every day of his life, in order that worldly cares may not obliterate the sense of the beautiful which God has implanted in the human soul.

— Johann Wolfgang von Goethe (1749-1832), German writer and thinker who rejected Christianity

Windows made of ink and light,
*   of color, note, and line;*
Dim-glass portals fixed within
*   this mortal frame of time.*
On panes of grace we trace the
*   fragile shades of his design:*
Creator God, created and
*   creation;*
Hints of places just beyond our
*   grasping.*
Seeing through the artist's heart
*   we hold the hope divine.*

— "Panes of Grace" by Clay Clarkson, 2007

Art Starts

Your children will learn to enjoy and appreciate art because you do it with them. Child-friendly art books are the best place to start for art appreciation.

- Come Look With Me series by Gladys Blizzard — selected fine art with questions for children
- *Looking at Pictures* by Joy Richardson — excellent introduction to art study
- *Noah's Ark* by Rien Poortvliet — Dutch artist in the masters' tradition
- How Artists See series, by Colleen Carroll — selected artworks on specific subjects to show how artists see
- *Children's Book of Art* by Rosie Dickins — studies of classic artists and their art*
- *A Child's Book of Art: Great Pictures—First Words* by Lucy Mickelthwait — wide range of art styles for study*

(* minor nudity)

Let the word of Christ dwell in you richly as you teach and admonish one another with all wisdom, and as you sing psalms, hymns and spiritual songs with gratitude in your hearts to God.

— Colossians 3:16

The aim and final end of all music should be none other than the glory of God and the refreshment of the soul.

— Johann Sebastian Bach (1885-1750), German Baroque composer and musician

Music expresses that which cannot be said, and on which it is impossible to be silent.

— Victor Hugo (1802-1885), French novelist

Music to Their Ears

Child-friendly classical music appreciation resources are not as plentiful as in other arts. Inexpensive but good classical music collections and MP3 downloads abound, so it is easy to find good classical music for listening. Here are a few other helpful resources for enjoying music with your children.

- Classical Kids series CDs — audio-drama of six composers with their music and other music productions
- Getting to Know the World's Greatest Composers series by Mike Venezia — over a dozen illustrated children's books about great composers
- *The Story of the Orchestra* by Robert Levine — colorful picture book about the orchestra with accompanying CD
- *Peter and the Wolf* by Sergei Prokofiev — there many versions of the music, some with a picture book and CD
- *Spiritual Lives of the Great Composers* by Patrick Kavanaugh — book of essays exploring God's role in great composers' music

Music

If art is about visual perception, then music is about auditory perception. Where a piece of art requires the viewer to cognitively process the artwork, a piece of music requires the listener to emotionally process the musical work. In that sense, learning with your children to enjoy and appreciate classical music trains them to be able to hear and comprehend the less tangible emotions and affective aspects of an art form. Since music is processed in a different part of the brain from where most cognitive activity takes place, it is also strengthening another mental muscle. But even more, it is training your children in God's language of worship. Music is a universal language across all cultures, but western classical music has uniquely expressed the sacred. Music is a special expression of God's creative nature. Don't neglect to give your children ears to hear it.

- **Train the appetite.** There is value, purpose, and beauty to be appreciated in nearly all forms of music across all cultures. However, there is also much music that is at best mediocre and shallow and at worst dangerous and destructive. That is why it is vital that you train your children's musical appetites from the earliest time on the best of classical music. Avoid childish, commercial, and contemporary music when they are young. There will come a time when they will follow their own musical tastes, but they will always have classical music as an anchor in their spirits.

- **Appreciate all music.** As in art, the primary goal of music study is to learn to enjoy music in all of its variety, not just to study it academically. Be aware, though, that due to so much background music in our culture, your children are already trained to ignore music to some degree. Your first priority, then, is taking time to really listen to music—to slow down and to hear the variety of musical nuances that distinguish one piece from another, listening for what the musician was attempting to say through music, feeling the emotions expressed in the composition.

- **Study classical composers.** Listen to several compositions by a composer before moving on to another. Try out all kinds of music—symphonic, ensemble, solo instrumental, string quartet, choral, opera, and so on. Baroque and classical period music are the best place to start for children because the music is more structured and predictable. Read a story of the composer's life to pique your children's interest. Whenever possible, go to classical concerts so they can hear the real thing. Look for free and inexpensive concerts or recitals in churches and smaller facilities.

IN OUR HOME

Throughout the elementary years and even later, we would always listen to the Classical Kids musical dramas whenever we had a longer car trip. The child-friendly dramatic stories about a composer, combined with musical excerpts from the composer's works as the sound track of the story, made the music come alive. We were amazed at how perceptive our children became at recognizing a composer's work when they would hear it in another context. Each child had a favorite, and would identify "their" composer when heard—Vivaldi (Sarah), Beethoven (Joel), Bach (Nathan), or Handel (Joy). It became a bit of a game for everyone.

Poetry

If art is visual, and music is auditory, then poetry is verbal. There is a very real sense in which poetry must be read aloud to be fully appreciated. The written structure of poetry is, to be sure, a part of its artistic nature, but in its essential form, poetry is spoken art. It is the artistic use of words, rhyme, meter, structure, and thought that goes far beyond just communicating to creating an artistic verbal expression of beauty, goodness, and truth. Poetry is the most complex form of literary expression, not just for the poet but also for the reader. The ability to understand the poet's message requires a higher level of concentration, the synthesizing of abstract thoughts and concepts, and the discipline of maintaining both the lyrical meter of the structure and the emotional expressiveness of the content. Good poetry opens the heart to profound thoughts and concepts expressed in new ways. But even beyond that, as with all of the fine arts, poetry is a unique expression of the creative nature of God, the one who created language. Just as the Psalms express the highest thoughts in the Word about God, classical and quality poetry can do the same and can reveal one more layer of God's creative nature within us.

- **Enjoy poems.** If you give your children an appetite for poetry now, it will stay with them throughout their lives. Start out with simpler verse and work up to longer pieces. Read it aloud expressively and have your children narrate back what they hear and feel. Have them read poems expressively for the rest of family during a tea time or at dinner. Set aside a time for poetry reading—make it a fun, enjoyable activity.

- **Appreciate the poetry of worship.** Training your children to enjoy the lyrical beauty and emotional power of poetry challenges them personally and mentally, and it also prepares them spiritually for reading the Psalms, the primary form and language of worship in the Bible. Poetry is part of God's language.

- **Memorize poems.** Memorizing great poetry internalizes the language, rhythms, and beauty of poetic thought in a way that holds them in long-term memory. It is a powerful learning experience that both strengthens and edifies your children's minds.

- **Value poetry.** In generations before the advent of mass media, poetry was a form of entertainment, comfort, and commentary. Learned men and women were expected to be well-read in the classical poets and to have memorized significant amounts of poetry. There are fewer poets now, but perhaps a greater need for good poetry.

IN OUR HOME

When Sarah was in her early teens, she took it into her head to memorize "The Highwayman," the dramatic story poem by Alfred Noyes famously recited by one of Sarah's favorite literary characters, Anne of Green Gables. Once inspired, it took her just a week to memorize all 103 lines of the poem, all of which she can still recite these many years later. We had the pleasure of her own recitation, although without the Victorian setting of the story. Other poems, such as Kipling's "If" and Frost's "The Road Not Taken," have been memorized and recited in our home, and their words have become a part of our family language.

To introduce young children to poetry is to set a rhythm to their play, a lovely cadence to their discovery of the smallest bits of everyday life. Poetry is the lens through which we find the miraculous in the mundane. It is also the word-woven net in which great writers have caught the whispers of mystery, nobility, and transcendence that invade even the most ordinary of lives. The earlier children are brought into this world, the earlier they enter into a marvelous awareness of cadence in reality, of beauty lurking in normal corners, of delight to be culled from average days.

— Sarah Clarkson, *Read for the Heart*, Apologia Press, 2009

Poetry for Family

Good poetry will enrich your family's spirit with "treasures of the heart." These collections of classic verse and poetry for families are our favorites:

- *Favorite Poems Old and New: Selected for Boys and Girls*, ed. Helen Ferris (Doubleday, 1957) — a popular favorite for family poetry
- *The Best Loved Poems of the American People*, ed. Hazel Felleman (Doubleday, 1936, 2008) — a classics favorite
- *Random House Book of Poetry for Children*, ed. Jack Prelutsky (Random House, 1983) — best poetry collection for younger children
- *The Golden Books Family Treasury of Poetry*, ed. Louis Untermeyer (Golden Books, 1998) — reprint of a popular earlier edition
- *A Treasury of Poems*, ed. Sarah Anne Stuart (Galahad, 1999) — popular poetry gems
- *A Sourcebook of Poetry*, ed. Al Bryant (Zondervan, 1968) — good collection of Christian and inspirational poetry
- *A Child's Treasury of Poems*, ed. Mark Daniel (Dial, 1986) — the best poems for children from the 18th and 19th centuries, with lovely illustrations

Unit Study Tools

Your unit study toolbox is overflowing. But when you're building for learning, you use only the tools you need. If a study tool doesn't really fit the unit and it has to be forced in to make it work, your children will know it and resist that study area.

- Reading books
- Reference resources
- Nature study
- Music
- Art
- Science experiments
- Writing
- Audio/video tapes
- Bible
- Dictation
- Computer
- Arts and crafts
- Food and cooking
- Role-playing and drama

Unit Study Studies

Numerous Christian unit study curricula are available. Many use a literature-based or Charlotte Mason approach at the core but expand widely from there to create a comprehensive multi-subject curriculum.

- Five in a Row
- Heart of Wisdom
- KONOS
- My Father's World
- Sonlight Curriculum
- Tapestry of Grace
- Weaver

Unit Study

At the heart of unit study is a very natural teaching and learning process. When you really want to know something about a subject, you immerse yourself in it to become knowledgeable. Unit study, which takes that natural drive and creates a systematic approach to education with it, integrates several sources and subjects of learning around a common theme or topic. A unit study on bumblebees, for example, might include books (reading), coloring or drawing (art), observing (science and nature), creating poetry or prose (writing), listening to "Flight of the Bumblebee" (music), and so on. Although many use unit study as their primary teaching model, in the WholeHearted Learning model it is best used as a supplemental teaching method. When there is a subject of interest to one of your children or you want to emphasize a certain area of study (history, nature, science, others), you'll find yourself naturally thinking about how you can make that subject interesting for your children, and you will begin to put together a unit. Your children will enjoy the variety of learning methods you include in the unit study, and you as a parent will appreciate the learning reinforcement that results from integrated study activities.

- **Start with your children's interests.** There is a nearly endless supply of units that could be planned, but the ones that will be the most effective are those that take advantage of your children's current interests and desires. If you are planning to study a period of history, plan a unit on that time with your children. Units that your children are most interested in can be accomplished in your Discovery Studies and Discretionary Studies. These delight-directed studies, as Gregg Harris calls them, allow your children to study and explore the delights that God has placed in their hearts.

- **It is tool, not a test.** Unit study is a helpful servant but can be a demanding master. If your children sense that you are more concerned about the structural details of your unit than you are about the joy of learning, they will not be free to learn. If you are uptight, they will be uptight. If it becomes a test of your teaching ability, it's time for a change. Unit study is only one of several methods you will use as a home educator. Flexibility and freedom to change are the keys to keeping it effective.

- **Books are still best.** Many unit studies emphasize hands-on and multisensory activities. However, because they require so much additional planning, effort, and time, they can too often take away from time that could be spent reading aloud. Of more concern, too much emphasis on activity can train your children to expect all learning to be fun and to become less attentive to reading. If you inadvertently train an appetite for activity, you might find it difficult to train it out. If you are strong in hands-on activities, you will do them well. If it is not your area of strength, though, don't do them out of false guilt. Your time will be better spent reading a good book with your children and talking about it. Let your Discovery Studies provide the hands-on and multisensory activities during informal, more child-directed learning times.

- **Keep the activities focused.** Every unit needs a big idea—a subject or theme—that the studies you select will relate back to. Be careful not to add extraneous studies and activities that don't really reinforce the big idea of your unit, such as drinking goat's milk when reading *Heidi*. Although it may seem a clever thing to do, it has nothing to do with the compelling themes of love and forgiveness in the book.

Context Study

One of the many benefits of whole-book learning is the natural way that good books lead into so many areas of study. A good whole book stimulates interest in people, places, ideas, and times related to the story it is telling. Context study takes advantage of that natural interest in knowledge to integrate several areas of study and research. A context study is similar to a unit study, except that it is tied to a single whole book rather than a single theme. Like unit study, it should be used selectively, not as a primary teaching structure or pedagogical method. Context study is reading a book for all that it is worth.

- **Select a few good books.** You cannot create a formal context study for every book you read! However, several times a year at your discretion, choose a book that lends itself well to a context study and do it together as a family. You might select a good historical novel that corresponds to your current history studies, such as *Johnny Tremain* if you are studying the American Revolution.

- **Stay centered on the book, not the context.** The number of contexts to study is limitless: social, political, religious, scientific, geographical, historical, technological, to name just a few. You can focus on one, some, or a lot of them. Context studies always return to the original book that is the focus of the study.

- **Make it a habit naturally.** Context study is a natural way to develop habit patterns that will help later in doing research. Most of the time, context study should be informal, natural, and transparent—your children shouldn't even realize they are doing it. You simply suggest they find out more about something you are reading and then steer them in the right direction. ("Go find out about...," not "Go do a context study on....") You are helping them to develop a habit pattern of searching out knowledge for greater understanding and insight.

- **Make a book a context project.** You can also design a more formal context study with a book to read and specific contexts to research. However, your purpose in designing formal context studies is never just to give your children research assignments. Rather, it is to create a pattern they can follow on their own by using the library, the computer, the phone, or other resources you make available. You are helping to build their learning confidence and competence. Context studies reinforce the idea that your children can find out what they need to know on their own.

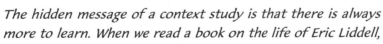

IN OUR HOME

The hidden message of a context study is that there is always more to learn. When we read a book on the life of Eric Liddell, we didn't plan to do a context study. But as we read more, the desire to know more drove us very naturally to the encyclopedia and atlas to find out more about China. Nobody groaned or complained about having to do a research study on China because the desire to know more was already there. There was almost a race to be the one who could report back with something new to illuminate our reading. Our children learned more because they knew there was more to learn.

Context Study Examples

Start with your own home library and the Internet for context studies. Take a trip to the public library or a local bookstore to find more. You can also use other physical resources to build on a context, such as field trips, museums, historical artifacts, foods, role-playing, period clothing, musical recordings, poetry readings, and the like. Context will make the book come alive for you and your children.

Little House on the Prairie
- Geography — map study of 19th-century midwest
- Political — president(s), number of states in the union
- Social — games children played, popular books
- Economics — cost of basic items, personal incomes
- Religion — pioneer churches and Christianity
- Arts & Music — songs of the day, artists, and musicians

Johnny Tremain
- Geography — colonial America, roads, waterways
- Political — history of English rule in the colonies
- Geopolitics — King George, colonialism, revolution
- Economics — British trade, taxation, capitalism
- Military — English Navy, armaments, battles
- Social — colonial rural and city life, trades
- Government — parliamentary, republic, democracy

Contextual Books

Some books are better than others at providing opportunity for interesting context studies, such as biographies and historical literature. The following examples are rich in context:

- *The Bronze Bow*
- *Adam of the Road*
- *A Tale of Two Cities*
- *Heidi*
- *Caddie Woodlawn*
- *The Witch of Blackbird Pond*
- *Johnny Tremain*
- *Amos Fortune, Free Man*

Commonplace Book

Students and adults alike used to keep a commonplace book of proverbs, maxims, aphorisms, quotes, Scriptures, and other such short, pithy sayings. Have your children begin to collect wise words for life in their own commonplace books. Encourage them to read them and memorize some of them.

Heart Treasures Book

A more literary variation on a commonplace book is collecting longer works of literature, essay, and poetry in a heart treasures book. Find a nicely bound 8.5x11 journal or sketchbook with clean white pages. Whenever you find a piece of prose or poetry that touches your child's heart or that they find especially interesting or meaningful, have them copy the piece into their heart treasures book. Encourage them to be creative and artistic and to illustrate and decorate the pages to make it a personal keepsake. Use their special word treasures for memorization and recitation.

Good Memory Stuff

In addition to Bible memorization, there are many excellent speeches, texts, and poems worthy of your children's memorization. Here are a few favorites.

- Preamble to the Declaration of Independence
- Patrick Henry's "Give Me Liberty" speech
- Abraham Lincoln's Gettysburg Address
- Martin Luther King's "I Have a Dream" speech
- "If" by Rudyard Kipling
- "The Road Not Taken" by Robert Frost
- "A Psalm of Life" by Henry Wadsworth Longfellow
- "There Is a Tide" from *Julius Caesar* by Shakespeare
- Sonnet CXVI by Shakespeare
- "Paul Revere's Ride" by Henry Wadsworth Longfellow

Memorization and Recitation

Memorization is a way to fill up the deep reservoirs of your children's hearts and minds with word treasures of beauty, wisdom, inspiration, and truth. Recitation is the opening of those reservoirs to let their contents flow out through the expressiveness of speech and emotions. Memorization and recitation not only strengthen your children's mental muscles, but they also shape their hearts and fill up their spirits with words that go deep inside and stay there. A person will never again be able to memorize as much as easily and as quickly as they can in childhood. The brain is at its peak for memory work, and what goes in then will likely stay in for a lifetime. Memorization is also the best antidote to the brain-cell-killing, mind-numbing effects of passive television and video viewing. There is perhaps no other exercise that can strengthen the brain and the mind as well as memorization and recitation. It is like daily neural calisthenics for the developing mind.

- **Make memorizing count.** If ever there were a place to be twaddle-free, it is in memory work. Keep your children's minds free of useless clutter. Memorize for meaning, not just for the sake of memorizing. Carefully select what you want your children to memorize based on its value for their lives: Scripture, poetry, prose, great words of great men and women, historical writings. Memorization is not for impressing others but for impressing truth, goodness, and beauty onto the heart.

- **Work at memory work.** Start with short passages and build up to longer ones. In addition to assigned memory work, let your children make some selections on their own to memorize. Create a special notebook for all of their memory work, complete with pictures and histories of the authors. Have your children make a recording of themselves reading the piece and then use that for memory practice, or let them listen to a recording of the material recited by a parent or a professional reader.

- **Recite what is memorized.** Memorization should always have an audience. Incorporate recitation into your family worship (Scripture), holidays (poems), and history study (speeches and documents). Let your children recite into a tape recorder and send the recording to friends or family. Whenever you have a live audience for your children's recitations, make sure that your children know ahead of time and that the audience will be affirming and supportive.

- **Keep it simple.** Avoid memory gimmicks that only add another layer to the memorization process. Association techniques using pictures and symbols might help adults, whose childhood memorization capacities are long gone, but they are unnecessary distractions for children. Children have an almost limitless capacity to memorize in the elementary years. If a child needs a little help, you can use key words or hand movements, but keep it simple and uncomplicated.

- **Dramatize recitation.** Who can forget Anne Shirley's dramatic recitation of "The Highwayman" in *Anne of Green Gables*? You can create your own dramatic recitation event for your children and their friends. Get several families to take part, and set aside a special day for the event. To add to the drama, encourage the children to dress up in a period or relevant costume. Create special prizes so everyone gets some kind of recognition (best dramatizer, best costume, longest piece, most confident, most eloquent, and so on). And of course, be sure to film it and post the video online.

Scripture Memorization

If we're being honest, we all know that the child who has memorized and can recite publicly on demand some undisclosed number of Scripture passages has earned an unofficial but undeniable homeschooling merit badge for spiritual achievement—not for the child, but for the parents! Memorizing and reciting Scripture is a good thing to encourage your children to do, both for the value of the words and for the discipline required. However, don't confuse what is good for your child with what is good for your reputation! Scripture memory is not about performing; it is about transforming. Here's the unseen spiritual merit badge you really want to earn—children who can quote Scripture to help them make a tough decision, to pray God's promises into a situation, to offer Psalms of praise to God, or to encourage a parent or sibling with wisdom. It's not about performing Scriptures for others but about being informed and transformed by God's truth. Be an example to your children by memorizing and quoting scriptures throughout your day.

- **Memorize verses for life.** Your children need concrete, practical scriptures that apply to life as they know it when they are young, not only the more abstract scriptures about theology and doctrine. Identify scriptures that you want your children to put into practice at home, organize them into meaningful and useful topics (promises, wisdom, speech, relationships), and then create your own Scripture memory cards on your computer. Whenever you memorize a verse, also study and talk about it so your children will know it as truth, not just a memory verse.

- **Go for the whole passage.** It is good to memorize lots of Scripture verses for how to live, but it is great to memorize Scripture passages. God has spoken to us in whole thoughts, which we now find in paragraphs and chapters. Help your children memorize some significant, longer passages of Scripture. There will never be an easier time for them to put large sections of God's Word into their minds and hearts.

- **Memorize what counts.** If verse references are a roadblock in memory work, remove them. Verse references are not inspired by God. It is more important for your children to know the inspired Scriptures and to have the Word in their hearts at this point than it is to get every verse reference right by memory. Try a graduated learning method. Start out with knowing what book of the Bible the verse is from. Then add chapter references. Then add verse references.

- **Recite with might.** Don't let your children recite memorized Scripture in a passionless exhaling of words. It not just words, but God's words. Teach them to recite their verses expressively (with emotion) and even interpretatively (with emphasis).

IN OUR HOME

We memorize Scripture at home, but sometimes a little child-friendly competition can move the mind and spirit to even greater challenges and achievements. For our family, AWANA Bible Clubs did that. When Sarah was eleven, she started in AWANA in our small Bible church. Despite a late start, she determined to catch up and then pushed herself even harder to achieve. She finished four books, had a bunch of pins on her vest, and won the Timothy Award that year. Way to go, Sarah!

I have hidden your word in my heart that I might not sin against you...Your word is a lamp to my feet and a light for my path.

— Psalm 119:11, 105

Bible Memory Passages

If you want your children to memorize longer passages of Scripture, you can't miss by starting with the best-known and most-loved passages. They will be reinforced throughout their lives by references in literature, movies, politics, and culture.

Most Popular

- Genesis 1 (in the beginning)
- Exodus 20:1-7 (the Ten Commandments)
- Psalm 1 (the blessed man)
- Psalm 23 (the Lord is my shepherd)
- Psalm 90 (God our dwelling place)
- Psalm 100 (praise the Lord)
- Matthew 5:3-16 (the Beatitudes)
- Matthew 6:9-13 (the Lord's Prayer)
- John 1:1-18 (the Word)
- 1 Corinthians 13 (love)
- Ephesians 6:10-18 (the Christian's armor)
- 2 Peter 1:3-11 (Christian virtues)

Extra Credit

- Psalm 19
- Psalm 139
- Ecclesiastes 3:1-10
- Isaiah 40
- Luke 8:4-15
- John 15:1-17
- Romans 8:28-39
- Philippians 2:1-18
- Hebrews 11:1-12:2

But in your hearts set apart Christ as Lord. Always be prepared to give an answer to everyone who asks you to give the reason for the hope that you have. But do this with gentleness and respect.

— 1 Peter 3:15

Let your conversation be always full of grace, seasoned with salt, so that you may know how to answer everyone.

— Colossians 4:6

Play 'n Speak

On slips of paper, write a variety of speaking situations— interview with the president, commercial for a favorite book, Sunday School class, receiving an award, introducing a famous person. Put all in a bowl. Each family member draws one in turn and acts it out.

Literary Night

Have several families over for a literary night. Each child prepares a reading, recitation, or presentation based on literature. For fun, have them dress to match their presentation.

Call to Action

When your child is ready, help them write a persuasive speech for a cause of their choice.

- **Attention** — First, use an opening that will grab your audience's attention.
- **Interest** — Next, give them a reason to be interested in your subject.
- **Desire** — Then, show why it is a desirable cause for the audience to adopt.
- **Action** — Finally, call the audience to action.

Speaking and Presentation

Your children will reach adulthood surrounded by generally literate but inarticulate peers. In a world of sound bites and media images, those who are able to present their ideas articulately, succinctly, and persuasively will lead; those who cannot will follow. You can give your children an enormous advantage in life simply by developing their speaking and presentation skills. It will put them out in front in every area of their lives— family, ministry, occupation, public service, public speaking, and others. Even more than that, you are preparing them biblically to do what God expects *all* believers to do: proclaim Christ and defend the faith. The very heart of the Christian faith is speaking and presentation. Your role as a parent is to release the message that God has put in your children's hearts and to give them a voice to speak confidently for God.

- **Expect narration.** Narration is the foundational method for cultivating your children's speaking and presentation skills. Let them know that you expect them to narrate confidently and expressively. Don't accept a lazy narration that is mumbled and disjointed.

- **Encourage presentation skills.** It is important for your children to be themselves when they speak or present—to be natural and sincere. However, also teach them that there are four basic elements to an effective presentation, no matter what kind of speaking situations they might face: (1) eye contact, (2) enthusiasm, (3) clear speech, and (4) relaxed posture. These are easily trained habits of speech, whether for daily discourse or for speaking before an audience.

- **Practice at home.** The very best early preparation for speaking is to create lots of opportunities to talk at home. Whenever your children have an opportunity to present a paper, idea, thought, recitation, or song, view it as a learning experience and work on their presentation skills. Verbally affirm your children's speaking abilities. Speaking ability is mostly just the confidence and competence resulting from growing up in a verbal environment. Skills just polish the words.

- **Make it family fun.** Drama and music are excellent training grounds for speech and presentation. Find a simple play or musical and assign parts. Get together with another family or your support group to put on a dramatic presentation. It's not only educational; it's also great family fun!

- **Look for presenting opportunities.** Most presentations by children in our home are spontaneous—a play someone has created, a nature project to explain, or an opinion to express. We readily affirm these mini-presentations, knowing that they are the building blocks for more developed and structured presentations. At homeschool support group meetings, we often provide time for the children to offer presentations or readings. At homeschool science fairs, they are able to present their projects. All these opportunities build confidence in speaking and presenting.

- **Show a story.** Since they share the same three-part structure as a speech (introduction, body, and conclusion), have your child write a creative story (real or imagined) and then present it to the family. Older children can choose a topic and write a speech. Encourage them to be prepared to be expressive.

Storytelling

Storytelling is the same as reading aloud, only without a book. You are using your memory and imagination to create an interesting and meaningful story with characters, settings, and events that are familiar to your children. Your children are prepared by God to be your audience, so their attention level is high. (Narration is not necessary.) Like reading aloud, you are demonstrating speaking skills, and you are also modeling creativity, imagination, and composition. Both storyteller and audience experience excitement as they listen to a story unfold that they know is being created right under their ears. And stories are not just for entertainment. In the same way that Jesus told stories (parables), your stories have the power to shape the hearts and spirits of your children. You are using the oral tradition to teach them just like Jewish parents have done for centuries.

- **Know the elements of story.** A story can be short or long but should always have a clearly discernible structure: It starts with a beginning (introduce characters, set the scene, arouse interest), builds through a succession of events (story moves toward the climax in a smooth flow of action), reaches a climax (the point of the story, the moral, the meaning), and concludes with an ending (resolution, closure, conclusion).

- **Personalize your stories.** Use your children's names in imaginative stories. Create a setting with familiar places and activities or a historical or imaginative setting. Make your child the clear hero who exercises character and virtue.

- **Put your children in known settings.** Use a book or story you have recently read to your children as the basis for a story. If you're studying history, put them into the historical setting or event and have them interact with great men and women in history. Let them play a part in influencing history in your story.

- **Tell your own stories.** Tell real stories about your own life. Events from your own childhood are especially effective for storytelling, illustrating a point, or illuminating a lesson. Include family stories about parents, siblings, grandparents, and other family and friends when they were children.

- **Tell stories of faith.** At holiday gatherings, tell family stories of faith and of God's faithfulness. Make favorite stories an annual tradition at those holiday events. After a few years, the children can tell the stories.

IN OUR HOME

It was a dark and stormy night. We had just moved to the country. In a new and unfamiliar setting, fears had surfaced. So Dad told a story for bedtime. It was a simple little story about a boy called Joel (coincidence?) and his faithful dog Brownie. Joel was hiking the ravine on the property when he slipped down an embankment and sprained his ankle. He was afraid, but he didn't panic. He knew he had to practice self-control. He sent his dog to get help. He had his pocket knife, a walking stick, and rocks to protect him. He was a resourceful lad. Soon he was rescued. Joel was recognized in the local paper for his courage and self-control. The end. A simple story (very condensed) that helped Joel over his fears.

Stories are the natural soul-food for children, their native air and vital breath; but our children are too often either story-starved or charged with ill-chosen or ill-adapted twaddle-tales...Let me tell the stories and I care not who writes the textbooks.

— Edward Porter St. John, *Stories and Storytelling*, 1910

Tell It to the Microphone

Get out your laptop or a digital recorder whenever you're going to tell a story. The kids will love listening to it many times over, especially if they are a part of the story. And you will have a family heirloom and memory to pass on to future generations.

Sharable Parables

The parables of Jesus provide a rich source of story outlines. Just substitute the biblical names and places with ones familiar to your children. Afterward, you can read the real parable and watch their lights come on.

Serial Storytelling

On the first night, introduce all the characters, create a minor problem/conflict, and resolve it, but don't conclude the story. Let them know a series of adventures will follow. On subsequent nights, continue the story but leave them with an unresolved conflict or situation to be concluded the next night. Repeat that cycle until you are ready to conclude the stories.

Chain Story

Get everybody involved in telling a story. Decide together what kind of story it will be—life, relational, adventure, history, mystery. You can also create a main character, if you choose. Draw numbers, then let the story roll. Each person has a set amount of storytelling time to pick up the story wherever the last person leaves off and take it wherever they want it to go. Turn on the digital recorder!

That's a Good Question

Think before you ask to be sure you will get what you ask for.

Good questions should be:

- Simple — asking for one thing with clear and precise words
- Short — a concise query with a minimum of elaboration
- Sweet — asked invitingly and gently, without challenge
- Strategic — you know what you want it to accomplish
- Stimulating — your child will enjoy thinking about it

Good questions should not be:

- Closed — answerable only with yes or no, I don't know, or an either-or response
- Loaded — asked with a hidden agenda, such as to admonish, correct, or raise an issue
- Rhetorical — raising theoretical and abstract questions a child cannot easily answer
- Confusing — morally or ethically vague or allowing relativistic values or beliefs

Good questions should ask for:

- Opinions and views
- Feelings and impressions
- Knowledge and facts
- Analysis and interpretation

I'm Glad You Asked

Discussion starters are not difficult to write. The key is to think like a child and be creative. They can be general questions or tied into a current area of study. A few examples to get you started:

- If you were [name of the family pet] and you could talk, what would you want to say?
- If you were Squanto, how do you think you would feel about the Pilgrims?
- What is the most beautiful thing you have ever seen?
- What person in history would you most like to meet or be, and why?
- If you could be the child of any person in history, who would you choose and why?

Asking Questions

There is an art to asking good questions. Whether you are trying to draw out a response, test understanding, or stimulate a good discussion, everything depends on the quality of the question. Put thought into asking good questions if you want to draw good thoughts out of your children. A well-crafted question will generate stimulating conversation; a poorly thought-through question will elicit only awkward silence, uncertain responses, or hopeful is-that-the-right-answer-daddy looks. When interacting with children, a question should be more *invitation* than investigation or interrogation. If invited properly, your children will gladly respond to your question.

- **Keep questions relevant.** When used with a whole-book approach, the purpose of asking questions is to stimulate your children's mental processes. Questions should be used sparingly, only to assist your children's understanding of a book, not to subvert or circumvent their own thoughts about it. Always have them do narration before you ask questions.

- **Keep questions focused.** Build on levels of content understanding when asking questions. Start with concrete facts (Who did what? When and where?), move to abstract concepts (Why did they do it?), and then to general principles (How should they have done it?). By walking your children through a summary of a book (after they have narrated it), they can see how the pieces make up the whole of the book.

- **Ask them to ask.** Give your children the opportunity to come up with their own questions about a book or story. It can be a kind of reverse narration that causes them to think about what is important in what they have heard. Be careful not to default into the questioning mode too quickly, though. Give them time to think. When you ask a question, give them time to answer. Don't override their thinking process.

- **Ask for opinions and insights.** Apart from whole books, challenging or thought-provoking questions can become a way of helping your children learn to think and talk on their feet. It is a little like narrating in that they are synthesizing and expressing their own thoughts rather than an author's, but the mental processes have to work a little harder since there is no book. Well-crafted questions will challenge them to think well and speak clearly.

- **Engage in table talk.** Good questions about current events will come up naturally during the process of normal conversation. However, it's always good to have some discussion-starter questions ready at meal times. It is easy and natural to pose a hypothetical situation and ask, "What would you do?" Also ask them to evaluate the choices leaders make—whether biblical, historical, or living—to sharpen their ability to discern right from wrong, true from false, and so on.

- **Start a question box.** Keep a 3x5 file box near the dining table. Keep 3x5 cards with you to write down good questions that come to mind.

- **Ask, don't interrogate.** One or two well-formed questions can generate long and interesting answers and discussion. Too many questions can weary and frustrate your children and cause them to give short, perfunctory answers. Don't interrogate.

## Chapter 13

Discovery Studies Methods: The Study of Learning

Recovering the Joy of Discovering

Christianity can often seem like a closed system, defined by settled beliefs on one side and settled behaviors on the other. There seems nothing really left to discover, and the suggestion that there is can be met with suspicion. We forget, though, that life with God has always been characterized by a spirit of discovery—Abraham "did not know where he was going" when he left Ur (Hebrews 11:8); Jesus said "follow me" (Matthew 4:19) and called his followers to "make disciples of all nations" (Matthew 28:19); Paul pressed on while "forgetting what lies behind" (Philippians 3:13, NASB); and many others found themselves on similar new paths of discovery. We are called as Christians to "live by faith, not by sight" (2 Corinthians 5:7), a faith which is defined as "being sure of what we hope for and certain of what we do not see" (Hebrews 11:1). We have the "Spirit of God" within us (Romans 8:9), we "seek first his kingdom" (Matthew 6:33), and we "keep in step with the Spirit" (Galatians 5:25), though we cannot see God, his kingdom, or his Spirit. The Christian life is a journey of continual discovery, moving ahead in faith, learning new things by doing, and doing new things we learn.

The ultimate goal of the WholeHearted Learning model is to prepare our children for that journey—to raise them to be self-directed and self-motivated learners who will move confidently into a life of faith and discovery with God. That is why our model moves from parent-directed learning (Discipleship and Disciplined Studies) to family-centered learning (Discussion Studies) and then to self-directed learning (Discovery and Discretionary Studies). True education is not indoctrination, as can happen in a closed system, but liberation. The purpose of Discovery Studies is to provide methods of learning that allow and encourage our children to begin to direct their own learning experiences, to build confidence in gaining knowledge and insight, and to learn the personal freedom and fulfillment of discovery. We provide plenty of raw materials and resources for their exploration, and we are always involved in their learning processes, but the *intent* of Discovery Studies is just as important as the *content*—we want to instill in our children the awareness and understanding that they are responsible for becoming self-directed learners.

You might be tempted to control Discovery Studies more than is necessary, either out of a subtle distrust in your children's ability to discover what you feel they need to discover about a subject or even out of fear that they might discover something you cannot control. But the alternative should cause concern too—that they will limit themselves to learn only what they feel they have permission to learn, which is the opposite of discovery. Resist that urge to control, and show your children the joy of discovery instead. You might even recover the freedom and joy of discovery for yourself in the process.

Imagination is also necessary to education. The goal of a truly excellent education ought to be a whole person with a soul driven by a potent dream and a mind equipped with the knowledge and skill necessary to pursue it. Thus, it is absolutely necessary that children be given the means to dream. Children can be filled up with facts, equipped with a wide knowledge, and trained to embrace a correct understanding of reality. But if their imagination has died in the process, they will have no energizing dream on which to base a vision-driven life.

— Sarah Clarkson, *Read for the Heart*, Apologia Press, 2009

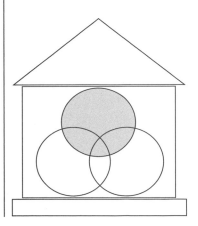

You could not find a major education writer or thinker from Plato onward who did not emphasize the importance of the arts in our Western education. The ancient Hebrews also supported musicians and artisans in their culture. People are not fully human without art in their lives.

— Ruth Beechick, *You Can Teach Your Child Successfully*, Arrow Press, 1993

Chorale Your Kids

If your homeschool support group is large enough, form a children's choir. Teach the kids a selection of songs or purchase a children's musical or musical drama with an instrumental accompaniment track. Perform the music at a nursing home, orphanage, or church.

Play It Again, Kids

Kids love to make music. The more instruments you have on hand for them to experiment with, the more likely it is that music will be a part of their lives. Look for used starter instruments at garage and estate sales, thrift shops, and similar sources.

- Piano, keyboard
- Guitar, ukulele
- Recorder
- Flute, piccolo
- Violin
- Trumpet
- Clarinet, saxophone
- Xylophone, vibes
- Autoharp
- Drums, bongos
- Rhythm instruments

The Creative Arts: Music, Art, Drama, Movement

In addition to studying and appreciating fine art, music and poetry, children should be given the opportunity for doing them. In public schools, the arts historically have included music, art, theater, and dance. Because of the independent nature of homeschooling and the lack of facilities and resources, though, these creative arts are often not emphasized. However, they should be considered a viable part of home education in developing a well-rounded, wholehearted child. The goal is simply exposure and experience, not mastery. If there are budding artists in your family creative troupe, creative arts activities will let their talents come out in the open.

Music

- **Sing as a way of life.** Singing is the most basic form of making music. Create ample opportunities to try a wide variety of musical styles, rhythms, and even harmonies. Sing hymns, praise songs, folk songs, or whatever music interests you and your children the most. Form a homeschool singing group to learn how to sing music from books. Put together a mini-musical or choral presentation.

- **Be instrumental.** Every child enjoys the immediate feedback of a musical instrument, even if it is not always beautiful. For an introduction to musical instruments, try a recorder or ocarina (end-blown flute), ukulele, 3/4 size guitar, or autoharp. A piano or inexpensive digital keyboard will give them the greatest opportunity for musical exploration. Even if they are not musically inclined, be sure your children are grounded in basic music theory at some point during childhood.

- **Get on track with tracks.** If you want to try singing but you lack a family instrumentalist, get a small karaoke (sing-along device) and purchase accompaniment collections of different kinds of music. It's great fun for family sing-alongs (there are lots of Christian and hymns CDs) and perfect for any future family performers.

Art

- **Encourage art work.** There is no better way to stimulate artistic expressiveness than with the canvas arts. For children, that means lots of opportunities to draw and paint in a variety of media—colored pencils, watercolors, charcoal, colored markers, tempera, pastels, and others. Your goal is not necessarily artistic skill at first, but exposure and experimentation. If artistic skill emerges or there is special interest in a particular medium, then you can consider further art training or lessons.

- **Explore art making.** Pursue each medium for a long enough period of time to allow your children to become proficient and confident at using it. Give them several different subjects to draw and color so they can experience the range of expressions for each media. Explore each subject by using a variety of perspective, composition, and lighting. Always display the best works of your budding artists.

- **Try it all.** Be sure to include other visual arts in your experiments with expression. Sculpting with clay, making pottery, mosaic art, and others are great for children who may not excel with brushes and colors but love more tactile and hands-on art.

Drama

- **Be dramatic about drama.** Drama is an opportunity for your children to learn to express themselves verbally and emotionally. Whereas music and art are generally third-person expressive arts, drama is decidedly first person. Your *child* is the artistic medium—voice, emotion, attitude, posture.

- **Read aloud dramatically.** Dramatic expression is really an outgrowth of narration and reading. In addition to its mental benefits, narration is also an oral exercise in articulation, and reading aloud is the first step in dramatic expression. If you read aloud dramatically, your children will read aloud dramatically. Start with some books rich in good dialogue—have your children perform dramatic readings with the rest of the family playing the part of an audience.

- **Start with improvisation and role-playing.** Acting out Bible stories or historical scenes and stories is an easy way to ease into drama. If your children enjoy dramatic expression and want to go further, try some simple one-act plays written for church or the narration and dialogue from a church musical, especially ones with humor. You might even want to stage a small play or musical with other homeschooling families.

Movement

- **Get moving.** God gave us bodies to use for creative expression too. Traditionally, public schools have taught dance—folk and square dancing—as an area of creative expression. Gather other families to explore dance, or find some group lessons, but also engage your children in creative expression using movement—reflecting feelings and attitudes, doing pantomime, interpreting classical music, and others.

- **Say it in movement.** Your goal is to help your children learn that how they use their bodies communicates even more than what they say with their voices. You are training them to use their physical voices as expressively as they would use their spoken voices. They are freer to explore movement while young, so let go of adult inhibitions and move freely with them. Have fun! Avoid the sensual, but give movement a try.

We write, we make music, we draw pictures, because we are listening for meaning, feeling for healing. And during the writing of the story or the painting or the composing or singing or playing, we are returned to that open creativity which was ours when we were children. We cannot be mature artists if we have lost the ability to believe which we had as children. An artist at work is in a condition of complete and total faith.

— Madeleine L'Engle, *Walking on Water*, Shaw Books, 2001

A robust imagination must, in large part, be carefully culti-vated. Children are born with the raw material of imagination, the conception of the world as being unfettered in its possibilities. But it is an ability that must be nur-tured, coddled, and nourished daily if it is to become a source of inspiration that will drive the goals and dreams of a growing soul.

— Sarah Clarkson, *Read for the Heart*, Apologia Press, 2009

IN OUR HOME

When we lived in Nashville, our children were in Sally's homeschool children's choir and even did some professional voice-over work on a musical project. When we moved to rural Texas, we all missed those Music City performing arts opportunities. So when we heard about auditions for The Promise, *a professional contemporary musical production of the life of Christ at a new 3,500-seat outdoor amphitheater, we were ready. By faith, we worked with Sarah (10) and Joel (7) for several weeks on their audition songs, rehearsed them on their lines from the script, and coached them on expression and projection. Not only did they learn from the audition process, but they actually won the lead parts! They performed forty weekends per year for three years. Mom and Dad got in on the act too. We even all performed the show at the Kremlin Palace Theater in Moscow, Russia.*

Sketchbook Expressions

Whatever your children can envision with their eyes and imagine with their mind's eye can fill the pages of their sketchbooks. They are visual journals.

- Nature — trees, flowers, plants, leaves, rocks, fruit
- Landscape — fields, lakes, forests, oceans, mountains
- People — kinds, ages, nationalities, dress, settings
- Bible — characters, events, places, battles, miracles, objects, stories
- Still life — whatever is fun to arrange on the table
- Animals — horses, dogs, cats, birds, fish, jungle animals, farm animals, ad infinitum
- Transportation — cars, trucks, emergency, planes, jets, rockets, trains, bikes, motorcycles
- Habitats — buildings, houses, huts, tents, teepees, cities
- Careers — farms, machines, offices, stores, police and firefighters
- Historical — colonial, Revolutionary War, knights, castles, American west, space age
- Military — soldiers, weapons, jets, boats, tanks, cannons
- Imaginary — worlds, animals, buildings, fairy-tale creatures, dragons (no space aliens!)
- Doodles — geometrics, free-form lines and shapes, boxes, circles, stick figures
- Cartoons — panels, storyboards, Bible stories, humor, family life

Drawing and Coloring

In a culture like ours that is increasingly visual and nonverbal, your children will have a distinct advantage if you enable them to acquire the ability to communicate through drawing and color. Unfortunately, most parents—if they think about drawing at all—wrongly equate learning to draw with studying art, so their initial impulse that their children should learn to draw usually results in the purchase of an expensive art curriculum. That is like giving your children a dictionary because you want them to learn to read! Most children will not become artists, so an expensive art curriculum is often overkill. However, every child needs to know how to draw and how to use color. A well-rounded child should be able to express and communicate ideas visually as well as verbally. Your goal is to give your children visual arts skills (line, form, perspective, color, and so on) in the same way that you are giving them language arts skills (alphabet, phonics, writing, and so on). Teach them how to show as well as tell, to illustrate as well as explicate.

- **Let your children draw.** You do not need to prompt your children to draw—it is as natural for them to draw about their world as it is for them to talk about it. Unfortunately, we try to turn them into artists as they get older, and our desire for them to do it right takes away their desire to do it at all. The first rule of teaching drawing is: Let your child draw. Respond to and appreciate a drawing; don't try to correct it. Your children are communicating...listen to them.

- **Keep moving forward.** At around age five or six, introduce your children to an incremental drawing guide that will lead them through the seven to ten basic elements that make up all drawings. At age seven or eight, introduce them to color with art-quality colored pencils, watercolor pencils, and a simple book on color. Let your children know that you love to see them draw and thought they would enjoy learning some new ways to express themselves. Treat it as an enjoyable Discovery Studies area, not as a Disciplined Study.

- **Draw and color for real.** Give your children real-life drawing and coloring opportunities. Have them make their own thank-you notes and greeting cards, write and color an announcement poster, create a wordless book, make place cards for the dinner table, or illustrate and color a letter. Real-life projects reinforce the idea that drawing and coloring are a natural part of communicating.

- **Draw on nature.** Nature is a perfect subject for drawing and coloring. Give your children good sketchbooks and art-quality colored pencils and have them draw and color a variety of plant life, trees, and flowers. Use drawing to spotlight the variations in different items within a class, such as what attributes makes leaves different. Some nature coloring books have line-art depictions of wildlife to color (animals, birds, butterflies, and so on), with full-color examples on the inside covers.

- **Draw on their interests.** As they find subjects that they enjoy drawing more than others—cars, rabbits, rockets, horses, cartoon people—find a simple, step-by-step "I Can Draw" resource that will let them add variety to what they have already learned. Mastering how to draw one subject with a variety of styles, techniques, details, and perspectives will transfer easily to other drawing subjects.

Creative Play

"When you finish your studies, then you can play." It's an innocent statement we all use, but it reveals an underlying cultural assumption that education and recreation are distinctly different activities. We are telling our children in so many words that when they start playing they can stop learning. Yet if God designed children to be learning from all of life, then play is an important part of that learning process. In fact, if God has built into children the drive to play, it may be the best way for them to learn. With that in mind, then, your goal is to provide creative play opportunities that will be mentally stimulating as well as fun and enjoyable. Loving to learn and loving to play are not mutually exclusive drives in your children—they can naturally complement one another and work together.

- **Keep it real.** Fill your children's playtime with real things as much as possible or lifelike imitations of real things. Whether they are doing historical dress-up, playing house or store, building a fort in the backyard, or whatever, the more real things they have to play with, the more closely their play will resemble real life. If you fill their playtime with plastic and toys that have no real-life counterpart, their play will tend to become more escapist and will not reinforce real life for them.

- **Keep the creative impulse supplied.** Provide creative modeling and building materials that let them use their imaginations: wood building blocks, cardboard bricks, Lincoln Logs, Legos, wood for carpentry, paper products, and similar items. The process of visualizing, designing, and building creations is a high-level learning process. Even the couch and chair pillows can become a learning experience in building a pillow tent or maze.

- **Record creativity.** Give your children access to electronic media: video camera, digital audio recorder, computer, electronic keyboard, and so on. Let them create movies, recordings, musical productions, and whatever else their imaginations come up with. They can also use other creative play options in their productions, such as historical dress-up, sword play, medical mimicry, and such. When all is said and done, you will have a great memory recorded for later viewing.

IN OUR HOME

When we give our children freedom, time, and materials for creative play, we're sometimes amazed at the results. Our imaginative middle child Joel loved to fiddle around with the thousands of Legos we acquired at garage sales. One afternoon he brought in five Lego houses he had built representing different historical periods: a pyramid and Sphinx, a Roman villa and bath, a medieval castle, a contemporary home, and a home of the future. Around the same time, Nathan, our organizationally gifted third child, surprised us by showing us the restaurant he had made on the front porch: tables and chairs, table settings, flowers and decor, a sign, a menu, and a waiter outfit. In both cases, the boys had initiated their projects with no prompting from us, but just because it was fun for them. That's how learning should be—as natural as having fun.

The most effective kind of education is that a child should play amongst lovely things.

— Plato (428-348BC), Greek philosopher

Work or Play?

There is no apparent theology of leisure or doctrine of play in the Bible. The few references to children playing are prophetic, with the millennial kingdom in view. It seems that the Old Testament feasts are the only God-ordained recreation in Scripture, and their purpose was worship, not just undirected recreation. The rhythm of life most evident in Scripture would seem to be *worship*, *work*, and *rest*—a trinitarian pattern that can encompass all of life's activities. In our modern culture, though, the concept of leisure or play has been appended to that balance because of the unprecedented amount of free time we enjoy, not because of clear biblical teaching. In God's original design, worship and rest fulfilled the recreational needs of adults. Play is attributed naturally only to children in Scripture—children play, adults work. It would seem reasonable to suggest that play as a child becomes work as an adult. In other words, child's play is the antecedent to adult work. With that understanding, play is an important developmental time in your children's lives. It is, in a way, rehearsal for a life of work, that will find its balance in worship and rest.

God blessed them; and God said to them, "Be fruitful and multiply, and fill the earth, and subdue it; and rule over the fish of the sea and over the birds of the sky and over every living thing that moves on the earth."

— Genesis 1:28 (NASB)

For since the creation of the world God's invisible qualities—his eternal power and divine nature—have been clearly seen, being understood from what has been made, so that men are without excuse.

— Romans 1:20

I love to think of nature as an unlimited broadcasting system, through which God speaks to us every hour, if we will only tune in.

— George Washington Carver (1864-1943), American educator, scientist, and inventor

Nature Basics

A whole-book approach to nature study will normally provide the basic language and facts your children need to know about nature for grade level. Any gaps can usually be quickly and easily filled in through fact books, family discussion, selected media and online resources, and other products for nature study.

The Nature of Media

There is a growing supply of excellent books, resources, media, and websites for nature study. However, you need to keep an eye and ear open for the inevitable evolutionary dogma that permeates nature books. Many Christian publishers produce high-quality print and digital resources that study nature through a creationist lens.

Nature Study

Your children are supernatural naturalists. There is a God-given, built-in curiosity about creation in their hearts that naturally wants to observe, ask questions, and seek understanding. Your goal in nature study is more than just to inform your children about the details of creation. You greater task is to form in them eyes that can see the Creator in his creation (Romans 1:20), an abiding sense of wonder and appreciation of what God has made (Psalm 8; 19), and a passion to care for, subdue, and rule over this earth as the handiwork of the Creator God (Genesis 1:28; Job 38-39). Nature or creation is the most natural realm of science for your children to study because it is an ideal laboratory for studying the things that have been made in their created contexts. God defined the major areas of nature study for us in Genesis 1 ("In the beginning God created the heavens and the earth"), and he created living things and human beings.

The Heavens (Astronomy, Weather)

- **Look up.** Get in the habit of getting your children to look up at night (especially when you are in the country). The best way is flat on your back or in tilt-back chairs. Start pointing out constellations, observe the different moon phases, look for the Milky Way, try to spot planets and other heavenly bodies, and look for meteors. Any field guide to astronomy will orient you to the night sky.

- **Plan ahead.** Always plan sky-watching parties for special events such as the annual Perseid meteor shower, a solar or lunar eclipse, or an unusual conjunction of planets. Plan a unit study on the event the week before and have your children write a report about it afterwards. It will be a special experience and memory.

- **Keep a log.** Have your children keep a night sky log to chart the changes during the different seasons of the moon (rise, set, phase), the constellations, and the planets, including unusual phenomena such as halos around the moon. They can also keep a day sky log to chart the changes in weather patterns through the seasons. Studying weather is a door into a wide variety of nature study areas—atmosphere, oceans, planetary motions, vegetation patterns, temperatures, and many more.

- **Scope it out.** If possible, purchase the best telescope you can afford for stargazing. A refractor telescope is usually more powerful but with a narrow field of view. A reflector telescope is usually less powerful but clearer (brings in more light from distant objects) with a much wider field of view. Use an astronomy field guide to check off all the heavenly bodies you are able to locate and view.

- **Consider time and space.** As your children ponder the heavens and the earth, they will come face to face with the imponderables of infinity and eternity. When they look to the heavens, beyond the stars, they will soon ask, "How far does space go?" When they look to the earth, at the mystery of life, they will soon ask, "When did everything begin, and when will it end?" These are profound questions and can be disturbing even to a young child. When they ask, you need to be prepared to give a satisfactory answer from Scripture about the nature of God, time, and space. It's OK to say that some things are mysteries that God tells us simply to accept by faith.

The Earth (Land, Rocks, Water)

- **Nature is a natural.** Take nature walks as a family. Rather than teaching about nature, simply talk about things you and your children observe. Stimulate nature conversation with questions: Have you noticed that some trees lose their leaves and others don't? Why do you suppose God made worms? What makes some rocks sparkly? Have each child keep a nature journal in which they can record their thoughts and impressions and draw sketches of objects found or observed in nature.

- **Listen for spiritual lessons.** God has built lessons into nature. Jesus often illustrated spiritual truths from nature. Nature metaphors abound in Scripture. You don't need to look for a spiritual insight every time you talk about nature! Just be ready to note a spiritual insight when the Spirit gives you one. It might be just what your children need to understand a biblical principle.

- **Observe the seasons.** Have your children keep a seasons log in a nice notebook by a window that allows observation. Identify a selected number of things to observe—temperatures, tree leaves, flowers, garden growth, sunrise/sunset times, location of the sun, and stars in the sky. On the first day of each month, have them make a record of changes they observe.

- **Collecting is in order.** Encourage your children to start simple collections of inanimate objects in nature: leaves, wildflowers, rocks, shells. Use the collections for lessons in observation and classification. Look for Scriptures about the collected objects, as well as about wildlife that is caught or observed. Display the collections at your support group science fair.

- **Build a nature library.** Collect a good assortment of child-friendly field guides (focus first on current interests), quality children's reference books (see column), good literature about nature and animals (such as books by Ernest Thompson Seton), nature media (software, videos, audiotapes), posters, and nature magazines.

- **Get good gear.** Equip your children with a good set of tools for nature study in the field: pocket field guides, field binoculars (7x35), compass, magnifying lens, good insect net, walking stick, small pickax, multipurpose pocket knife, notebook, specimen collection bag. Supply them with display materials too: collection boxes and boards, insect pins, killing jar, holding jars, aquarium (for fish) or herpetarium (for reptiles and amphibians), a plant press, and notebooks.

IN OUR HOME

Nature is a natural in our home. We like to take long walks to observe and talk about all that God has made. We recently found a washout that was rich with marine fossils which our children have enjoyed collecting and classifying. They also contribute to our "nature museum" displays of butterflies, fossils, and rocks. When the weather is nice, Dad takes the kids to browse a local nature center or to the zoo for a nature walk and picnic. It is a good way to combine learning time, Dad time, and free time for Mom. And, of course, we never miss a good sunset.

"Where were you when I laid the earth's foundation? Tell me, if you understand. Who marked off its dimensions? Surely you know! Who stretched a measuring line across it? On what were its footings set, or who laid its cornerstone—while the morning stars sang together and all the angels shouted for joy? Who shut up the sea behind doors when it burst forth from the womb, when I made the clouds its garment and wrapped it in thick darkness, when I fixed limits for it and set its doors and bars in place, when I said, 'This far you may come and no farther; here is where your proud waves halt'?"

— Job 38:4-11

Nature Library

Stock up on good field guides and reference resources:

- Audubon Pocket Guides
- Peterson First Guides
- Peterson Field Guide Coloring Books
- Usborne Spotter's Guides
- Eyewitness Books
- Usborne Books
- Golden Press Guides
- Field Guides to Wildlife Habitats
- *Kingfisher Encyclopedia of Animals*
- *Reader's Digest Guide to North American Wildlife*
- *Usborne Illustrated Encyclopedia of the Natural World*

Whole-Book Nature Readers.

- *Parables from Nature* by Mrs. Alfred (Margaret Scott) Gatty, 1855
- *Wild Animals I Have Known* and other books by Ernest Thompson Seton, ca. 1900
- *Handbook of Nature Study* by Anna Botsford Comstock, 1911
- Christian Liberty Nature Readers
- *Pocketful of Pinecones* by Karen Andreola, 2002

O LORD, our Lord, how majestic is your name in all the earth! You have set your glory above the heavens. From the lips of children and infants you have ordained praise because of your enemies, to silence the foe and the avenger. When I consider your heavens, the work of your fingers, the moon and the stars, which you have set in place, what is man that you are mindful of him, the son of man that you care for him? You made him a little lower than the heavenly beings and crowned him with glory and honor. You made him ruler over the works of your hands; you put everything under his feet: all flocks and herds, and the beasts of the field, the birds of the air, and the fish of the sea, all that swim the paths of the seas. O LORD, our Lord, how majestic is your name in all the earth!

— Psalm 8

For you created my inmost being; you knit me together in my mother's womb. I praise you because I am fearfully and wonderfully made; your works are wonderful, I know that full well. My frame was not hidden from you when I was made in the secret place. When I was woven together in the depths of the earth, your eyes saw my unformed body. All the days ordained for me were written in your book before one of them came to be.

— Psalm 139:13-16

A Flood Changes Everything

A worldwide flood, as described in Genesis 6-8, would affect many of earth's systems normally considered uniform and unchanging. They could include:

- Landscape erosion
- World population
- Vegetation distribution
- Animal distribution
- Atmospheric changes
- Weather patterns
- Geologic layers
- Continental drift

Living Things (Plants, Animals, Fish, Fowl, Insects)

- **See God in nature.** Studying the heavens and the earth helps children understand the greatness of God—his transcendence, beauty, eternality, power, and other qualities of his divine nature. Study of living things will help them understand the goodness of God—his care, creativity, provision, love, and other qualities of his moral nature. All of creation reveals the God who created—his fingerprints are on everything.

- **Name and classify things.** Living things are the ideal place to begin studying nomenclature (the names of things) and taxonomy (classifying and grouping things). Plants are the best starting point for children—for instance, collecting leaves, naming the trees they come from, and grouping them by type or region. Or pursue bird watching—observing birds, naming them, and classifying them by kind and region. Moths and butterflies can be a good nature study. Not all living things can be easily studied in actual nature, but you can study them through books and media. (There are many excellent nature DVD sets and websites.)

- **Observe nature naturally.** The key to nature study is observation. Be sure to regularly plan long walks in nature (mountains, forests, nature centers, etc.) with no other goal than simply to observe and enjoy nature and to be alert to anything interesting. Take a camera and sketchbook along to record your findings. Have your children take a digital recorder or journal to record their thoughts about discoveries and observations. Explain that the goal is not to collect anything, so you won't be looking for specimens. The goal is simply to listen to what God has to say through nature.

Human Beings (Man and Woman)

- **We are a special creation.** In-depth study of human physiology can wait until high school, but your children should understand that we are in the living things category, yet we are a special creation of God—we have a God-breathed soul that no other living thing has, and we are made in God's image. It is why we alone, of all the things God created, can relate personally and purposefully with our Creator.

- **Getting to know ourselves inside-out.** Most children will be curious to know how their physical body works and why boys and girls are different. It's best to focus on the major systems early on—skeletal, muscular, nervous, digestive, respiratory, circulatory, and such. You should be sensitive to your children's threshold of comfort for studying about things that can seem a bit creepy and strange. If there's any sign of resistance or discomfort, just put it all off until later.

- **Keep reproduction in balance.** You will need to determine when and how to explain where babies come from for your children. However, be sure to talk about the miracle of birth and the sanctity of life in the womb. Your children do not need to understand the physiology of reproduction to be able to appreciate the biology of gestation and birth and the special design of a mother's body (womb, breasts, etc.). There are many good books by Christian publishers you can use to open the discussion of reproduction generally and gently. As your children approach adolescence, you should be prepared to begin to explain issues of sexuality and reproduction.

Creation Science

If nature study helps your children see the pieces of God's Creation up close, creation science helps them fit those pieces into the big picture within the framework of the book of Genesis—God created the heavens and the earth in six creative days; people are created beings with eternal souls, not just evolved, intelligent animals; the flood of Noah was a worldwide, catastrophic event that reshaped the earth's surface and altered its atmosphere. With the study of creation science, you are providing evidences to your children to show that the biblical account of creation is true and defensible and that facts do not support all of Darwinian evolutionary theory. You are laying the foundations in their minds for a biblical worldview of the origins of life, the nature of man and woman, the results of the Fall, and our need for a Savior.

- **Study science by creation days.** Use the six creation days of Genesis as an outline for science studies: day 1, energy (light); day 2, atmosphere (pre-Flood water canopy); day 3, land, seas, and vegetation; day 4, sun, moon, and stars; day 5, fish and fowl; day 6, land animals and man. This will reinforce Scripture and show the natural order and progress of God's creative acts.

- **Take on the big questions.** Don't be afraid to engage your children in lively conversations about the bigger issues of biblical creationism vs. secular naturalism. If the universe started with a bang, where did the stuff that exploded come from in the first place (first causes)? If we evolved from lower forms, why aren't there any ape-men or man-apes running around today (fossil record)? How can there be such obvious design in creation unless there was a Designer (teleology)? Study Romans 1 to show that people who close their eyes to the God of Creation are blinded to the truth. Their refusal to acknowledge God means they must make up explanations based only on the teachings of sinful man, such as unexamined Darwinian evolutionary theory.

- **Be clear about creation.** Creation science does not have to be black-and-white dogma for children. They can understand that ideas about how creation happened must be tested against our understanding of what Scripture says and against empirical data and known facts. Although godly, Christian men agree that God created the universe and man, many disagree over whether the Creation is young (thousands of years) or old (billions of years). Teach your children what you believe, but don't callously label believing Christians who disagree as false teachers or deceivers.

- **Be clear about evolution.** Train your children to discern truth and error in the matter of evolution. You cannot escape evolutionary references in many of the otherwise very desirable nature and science books, audio, video, and software. If you refuse to buy such products, you will have a very thin library shelf. Wisely use helpful resources, but monitor them and avoid obvious evolutionary propaganda.

- **Explore dinosaurs and more.** A study of dinosaurs (always a big hit, especially with boys) can lead into a number of creation science study areas. Use some of the excellent illustrated children's books on Creation and creation science by Christian authors and publishers to help your children better visualize and understand the place of dinosaurs in a creationist view. Make sure creation science resources are age-appropriate.

While you can find many text-books on science that teach you very important details about the world around you, most of them never give you the foundation for the science you are learning: the fact that all you are studying has been created by an omniscient, omnipresent, omnipotent God. Without that foundation, you are woefully unprepared to understand the "big picture" when it comes to science.

— Dr. Jay L. Wile, Apologia Catalog, 2009

Apologia Science

Apologia Educational Ministries' series of science books cover the gamut of science studies for the elementary years and are built on the foundation of belief in a Creator God.

- *Exploring Creation with Astronomy* by Jeannie Fulbright
- *Exploring Creation with Botany* by Jeannie Fulbright
- *Exploring Creation with Zoology 1, 2, and 3* by Jeannie Fulbright
- *Exploring Creation with Human Anatomy and Physiology* by Jeannie Fulbright
- *Exploring Creation with General Science* by Dr. Jay L. Wile
- *Exploring Creation with Physical Science* by Dr. Jay L. Wile

Creation Mural

Take seven poster boards and label the first six Creation Day 1 through Creation Day 6. Write the respective verses from the Genesis account for each day at the top of each poster. While you do a study of Genesis 1-2, draw and cut out pictures to illustrate what God created on each of those days (1-6). Be sure to include a poster for Day 7, the Sabbath, when God rested from creation. Be creative for Day 7 with illustrations and pictures of the church, family, heaven, and other spiritual ideas and subjects. When the posters are full, get really creative—find a place to display them!

How Much Science?

First principle of science instruction: You are raising a child, not a scientist. Despite hand-wringing in the public schools over their failure in science, your priority is to focus on training your children to be confident, self-motivated learners in all areas. Once that is in place, learning about science will take care of itself. If science has been a natural part of your elementary homeschooling years, then by around age fourteen (grade 8), you should know whether or your children are inclined toward science as a particular field of study. If they are inclined, then provide the books, tools, tutors, classes, and resources needed and point them in the right direction. They will set their own pace. If they are not inclined, you don't need to try to make them be. You can provide a solid foundation in the sciences, but keep it in balance. More important is for you to find out what they are inclined to—what God has gifted and motivated them to be and do—and point them in that direction.

Hands-On Science

All children enjoy the pop-fizz, whiz-bang, ooh-ahh nature of physical, hands-on science. It's interesting and fun, and it captures their attention and curiosity. However, the focus of their attention is nearly always on the secondary effect, not the primary cause. Physical science—which deals primarily with the inanimate world, such as chemistry, machines, heat, light, electricity, sound, magnetism—is better studied in later grades when the issue of causes can be better understood. Experimental science can be lots of fun, but you have to determine whether it is better to invest in time-consuming experiments that produce mostly short-term effects or in life-enriching nature study that produces great memories, collections, drawings, photographs, and journals that will last a long time. It is certainly true that the process of observation and discovery in experimental science can stimulate in children a curiosity and desire to know more, but don't let it be a substitute for reading. Your children will receive most of what they need in the four-to-fourteen window if you are laying a solid foundation in nature study and reading.

- **Stay focused on one experiment.** When you do hands-on science projects, limit your focus to a single and simple principle, idea, or concept that you want to demonstrate. Avoid lots of information, data, and details. Let your children's hands, not just yours, be on the experiment. Encourage them to observe effects, ask questions, and postulate explanations about causes. Know what you want them to learn from the experiment. Emphasize useful vocabulary terms, facts, and principles.

- **Make it a group project.** Increase your audience to make the most of your experiments. Create a monthly study group to which each family brings a hands-on science project to do that the rest of the group can observe. You can choose a topic, coordinate the experiments to avoid duplication, and rotate the homes (to share the mess). Also, have your children prepare hands-on science projects of interest to them for your support group science fair.

- **Learn science naturally.** Ours is a words-and-music family, so whatever our children learn about the physical sciences is primarily from books, media, and life, not from hands-on science experiments. We constantly use real books and real-life situations to talk about physical sciences—the nature of water, how a car works, what's in a computer, how gears work, the principle of displacement, how a flashlight works. These kinds of real-life lessons are much more instructional than the entertaining experiments and razzle-dazzle of much of children's hands-on science resources.

IN OUR HOME

Sarah was the object of most of our hands-on science experiments. Among other projects, she created a papier-mâché volcano for a homeschool science fair that erupted reasonably well, and worked with igneous rocks for a display. As the boys got older, we put our hands on many experiments, including a popular one at the time—making giant bubbles. We tried to discuss the science of it all, but everyone was much more fascinated by the results than by the reasons. We were never sure how much of the science would stick, but we were always sure the fun memories would.

Foreign Language

Scientists believe that the first ten years of a child's life are the peak time for learning language. A child's brain in those years is wired by the sounds of language—neural pathways are constructed from what is heard and used, and other factors contribute to make learning a foreign language easier and more natural than at any other time in life. However, it is also true that children will not learn a foreign language in those years just because they are able. Capability and accessibility do not automatically become ability. Some parents introduce a structured curriculum in elementary years because they believe it will give their child access to a second language early. However, if children have no real reason to learn that language, there is no reason to assume they will. However, you can take advantage of your children's language capabilities with some commonsense actions.

- **Create a reason to learn.** If you want your children to learn a foreign language, you should create a reason for them to want to learn it. For instance, if you want them to speak Spanish, get your family involved in a short-term mission in Mexico or a local Spanish-speaking ministry. Be sure they are exposed to Spanish speakers.

- **Pursue immersion learning.** Most language teachers agree that immersion learning is an effective way to learn a language. It is especially effective for children because hearing large amounts of language in their peak language learning years builds strong neural pathways. Your children will learn more quickly if they have language immersion opportunities (in a setting where only the foreign language is being spoken).

- **Make the language a family project.** This should go without saying, but if you really want your young child to learn a foreign language, then you need to be learning the language and using it at home. If you are motivated, then they will be too.

- **Make language enjoyable and fun.** Don't turn language learning in the elementary years into an academic tedium that must be endured rather than enjoyed. Keep it light and fun. Introduce vocabulary and simple phrases, and look for ways to use them during the day. If you make the language something that is enjoyable and interesting to them, then you'll be able to introduce more structured learning sooner.

- **Don't neglect English language.** It would be the height of irony for parents to neglect the development of their children's native language skills in order to make sure they get a foreign language early. Read copiously, create a verbal and language-rich home, and even expose them to Greek and Latin roots before trying on a new language. Build their own language foundation first, then add another language.

IN OUR HOME

We lived in Austria for several years as a young family, so our children naturally wanted to learn German. The BBC Muzzy cartoon videos were dated and very unusual even then, but our children really enjoyed watching them and learning German. Their simple narrative and storytelling style made them easy and enjoyable, and our now-grown children still remember some of the German they learned from the big, blue, furry creature called Muzzy (not sure what he is, but he's friendly).

Foreign Language Resources

There are probably as many approaches to foreign language instruction for children as there are, well...languages. Which product you choose to use depends on too many factors to factor in here. The best advice is that if you enjoy using a particular instructional resource, then your children will be more likely to enjoy it too. If foreign language study becomes something you look forward to together, it will become something you'll more easily move forward on. Here are a few recommended programs:

- *JumpStart Languages* (Vivendi) — introduction to basics of language learning, games and puzzles, pre-K-3 (4 languages)
- *Learnables* (International Linguistics Corporation) — popular for homeschool, uses word-image association, K-12 (9 languages)
- *Muzzy* (Early Advantage) — very popular BBC-produced cartoon video series, K-6 (8 languages)
- *Rosetta Stone* — popular resource with a homeschool program, uses immersion and word-image association, K-12 (31 languages)
- Usborne Books — wide selection of language books and resources, colorful word-image association, K-12 (12 languages)

(Home) Educational Software

Some categories of educational software are better suited to the home than others. Most software you will use falls in one or more of the following categories:

- Drill — to test and reinforce math, spelling, etc.
- Reference — encyclopedia, Bible, history, nature, etc.
- Creativity — art, storybooks, music, writing, etc.
- Discovery — interactive with several areas to explore
- Productivity — child-friendly versions of real programs
- Tutorial — digital curriculum for specific subjects
- Edutainment — game-based learning of any kind

The Devil in the Details

A disturbingly large number of programs for children draw upon occult, demonic, alien, and distorted depictions of men and women. There are many wonderful programs that are free of that kind of culture crud, but you have to do your homework before you do your shopping to keep your computer sanctified and your conscience clean. Read the reviews and visit the websites before you buy.

The Key(board) to Computer

The sooner your children develop good keyboard (typing) skills, the sooner they will be able to tap into the computer's potential as a tool for creativity and productivity. Since children begin keyboarding at a very young age now, it is critical to get them on a typing program early to prevent the forming of bad typing habits. A good program will build proper touch-typing muscle memory that will prepare them for a lifetime of confident keyboarding. There are many child-friendly typing programs to help your child learn finger and key positions, any of which would work, but many are visual twaddle. As your children get older, the Mavis Beacon series can help them increase in typing speed and accuracy.

Computer

Your children are growing up in a digital world and culture. Even as digital technologies expand and converge, computers and connected devices become necessary home and business utilities, and broadband becomes as ubiquitous as electricity, the digital age is still very young and will grow exponentially in the coming decades. After buying books for your library (always the priority), a computer is the best investment of your educational dollars. However, you need to be clear how a computer will fit into your home education goals. Many parents use a computer only to augment, reinforce, or computerize their Disciplined Studies, such as language arts and math. If that is the only reason you want a computer for the children, save your money. The real value of a computer for home education is as a tool for Discovery and Discretionary Studies. A computer is unequaled as an interactive medium for creative expression, mental challenge, and multisensory learning; it is irreplaceable as an instrument for exploring the expanding universe of information; and it is unchallenged as a tool for creativity, productivity, and real-world work. Computer competence is now an essential learning skill.

- **Get a good computer.** Don't handicap your children's digital learning experience by giving them an underpowered, outdated, or low-quality desktop or laptop. Give them a tool that will work as well as their brains want to work. Your children can be productive and creative equally well on either a PC or a Mac computer. It's largely a matter of preference and cost. When budgeting for a computer, be sure to include useful peripherals. An all-in-one color printer will give your children all they need with a printer, scanner, and copier. Be sure to research the cost of replacement ink cartridges to determine the actual cost of printing per page. It can vary significantly.

- **Get the best applications.** Good applications are to your computer what good books are to your library. Be as choosy as you would be for any other books or media your children consume. There is just as much digital twaddle as there is paper-and-ink twaddle. Look for applications that allow your children to be creative and expressive in writing and art or to explore useful information and knowledge stored in words, sounds, and images. Don't automatically assume your children will need dumbed-down, child-friendly software. Give them a chance to try the real thing first.

- **It's a tool.** Keep in clear view your ultimate goal in providing a computer for your children—to train them to use it as a productivity, research, and communication tool. Teach them keyboarding skills early and train them to use a word processor, database, desktop publishing program, web page editor, and other tools. Give them meaningful tasks to accomplish—a family newsletter, posters, a video database, family mailing-list maintenance. They'll be exercising writing, thinking, logic, reading, art, and other learning skills, and they will build confidence to keep learning.

- **It's not a game box.** Make it clear from the start that your family computer or your children's computer is an educational tool for your homeschool, not just an electronic game box. Many educational applications and websites have game-style features that increase learning. Good ones can be an enjoyable, even mind-challenging, diversion for your children, but they can also become insidious time thieves that create hard-to-sate appetites. A computer can be a lot of fun, but keep it in balance.

Internet

Say what you will of the Internet, but this one thing is certain— the Internet cannot be ignored. The technology that created the Internet dates back to the 1960s, and the World Wide Web online environment to about 1991, but the Net did not have a public face (or interface) until 1994 when Mosaic, the first popular web browser, was released. In the brief moment of time since that birth of the Information Age, the Internet has changed forever the world as we know it. Every place on earth is closer, vast knowledge is available at a keystroke, communication is revolutionized, and information is ubiquitous and immediate. With the advent of mobile media and devices, the expanding universe of the Internet is as personal and portable as a cell phone. It can be praised for the good it enables or pilloried for the evil it inflames, used by those who value God and people or abused by those who value only sin and self, provide a forum for truth or a channel for deception. The Internet itself is neutral, not evil, but its potential to do harm is just as strong as its potential to do good. It will become what we make of it, but as it becomes more entrenched at every level of our daily lives, we will have to work hard not to become what it makes of us. That is the challenge parents face in interfacing with the Internet— how to raise wholehearted children who understand and can use the Internet but who are not shaped and controlled by it. Here are some principles to help.

- **Use it.** It is an incredible tool for learning. Use it wisely, responsibly, and for sure cautiously, but by all means use it. It is a deep and wide ocean of knowledge about any and every topic your children might express an interest in. Explore it with them.

- **Enjoy it.** Searching the Internet can become a fascinating treasure hunt for information. There is something very enjoyable and satisfying about being able to find what you want to find on the Web. And there is much there just for fun too. Enjoy!

- **Distrust it.** It is common sense to not fully trust anything that has potential to harm you or your children There is no question that the Internet can slime your children with ideas and images harmful to their innocence, so always monitor the monitor.

- **Respect it.** The temptation is to have a negative attitude toward all things Internet because of the harm that it might do. Instead, acknowledge the good it does do. Respect it for new ways it provides to teach truth, spread the gospel, and help others.

- **Restrain it.** The Internet can seem like a living thing that grows, learns your ways and habits, and very quietly insinuates itself into your life. Putting restraints on its presence and your use of it in your home is not only wise but also necessary.

- **Control it.** There is no reason for the Internet ever to become something that is out of your control. There are countless programs to give you full control over your access to and experience of the Web—filters, portals, timers, and more. Just use them!

- **Master it.** Like it or not, your children will grow up in a Web-centered world. It is not an optional subject for preparing them for real life in the Information Age. Like any academic subject, if they gain mastery over it, they will not be dependent on others when it is needed. There is great confidence that can come from knowing what the Internet can and cannot do and from knowing you are its master, not its servant.

The Interesting Internet

Be creative in how you use the Internet in your homeschooling.

- Research topics of interest.
- Visit virtual museums.
- Search out free e-books.
- Play family-friendly games.
- Join in homeschool forums.
- Read other homeschool blogs.
- Search for good supplies.
- Find, trade, exchange books.
- Explore the world.
- Find international e-penpals.
- Network with homeschoolers.
- Start a blog for a cause.
- Build a family website.
- Create videos for YouTube.
- Search for old books.
- Sell stuff on eBay.
- Start a viral video.
- Explore Google Earth.
- Follow Facebook groups.
- Start a family e-letter.
- Visit missionaries on Skype.
- Research fields and missions.

Web Content Filters

A software-based filter installs on your computer's hard drive and requires manual updates by the user. A proxy filter installs a small application on your computer that sends every search through a content filter on a remotely-located server. Proxy filters are easy and accurate, and they update automatically. Every filter offers slightly different features, so you have to determine which one offers what your family needs—parental controls, accountability, time controls, user-definable filter categories, coverage, and more.

- Safe Eyes — proxy filter, Windows and Mac (www.safeeyes.com)
- Bsecure — proxy filter, Windows and Mac, Christian (www.besecure.com)
- Covenant Eyes — proxy filter, Windows only, Christian (www.covenanteyes.com)
- Integrity Online — proxy and hardware filters, Windows and Mac (www.integrity.com)

Getting Started

Many parents make the well-intentioned mistake of overestimating creative talent and overreacting to a creative interest. If a child draws a face that actually resembles something human, Mom or Dad thinks it may be a gift, and within days there is a full battery of art tools and supplies ready for any artistic impulse from the six-year-old future artist. But all the child really needs, and what he ends up using, is a good pencil and decent paper. This happens with audio/video production, too. If a child creates a simple slide show online that shows some creative promise, parents can find themselves talking about Apple MacBook, video camcorder, DSLR, video editing software, a digital MIDI keyboard, and on it goes. Rather than releasing creativity, though, all that expensive gear can just as easily become an intimidating barrier to creativity that discourages rather than motivates. Creativity is its own motivation. Let your children start with natural, uncomplicated projects and tell you when they want to take another step forward. Many A/V home projects require very little additional gear beyond a computer. Let creativity grow naturally.

Audio

- Create MP3 interviews.
- Make GarageBand music.
- Create a musical slide show.
- Write and record a song.
- Record an audiobook.
- Tell a story with sound FX.
- Record music as a DJ.
- Write and record an audio drama.

Video

- Edit digital home movies.
- Create a music video.
- Create a family video collage.
- Make a kids' video blog.
- Make a short documentary.
- Make a short movie (story).
- Create a how-to video.
- Create a YouTube viral video.
- Record a visual Bible lesson.

Audio/Video Production

In today's digitally democratized world of media creation, anyone—including your children—can become a producer of video, music, websites, and more. Creating any kind of audio, video, or digital media is a tour de force of learning activities, all bundled into one endeavor that results in a product that flexes developing creative muscles. It is positively affirming for your child and gives you a digital family heirloom. If other children are involved, it also is a natural way to create socializing events where all involved can contribute to something bigger than any alone could make and that will require teamwork, cooperation, and shared skills to produce. If the production has a message, they will learn how to express important ideas creatively. Eventually, if an interest in A/V matures, you may need more gear. Here's a short list of media tools to consider:

- **Computer** — Since the computer is the *sine qua non* for all media creation, provide one with a reasonably fast processor, extra memory, a large-capacity hard drive, and a dedicated video card. Either a PC or a Mac will get the job done.

- **Peripherals** — As needed and as you are able, add some selected and helpful peripherals: laser printer (for writers), color laser or inkjet printer, flatbed scanner, color disc printer (for CDs and DVDs).

- **Software** — Good software is a must. The best video and audio creation and editing programs have lite or limited editions of the full version. Depending on the projects, you might need a video editor, sound editor, photo editor, graphic design app, website design app, or others. Start with entry level and work up. Mac bundles many of these in iLife; Windows apps are available as free or inexpensive shareware.

- **Recording Gear** — An inexpensive computer microphone is fine for basic speech but inadequate for recording music. A USB condenser microphone is minimal; a USB mixer, large diaphragm condenser mic, and quality headphones are better. There are many good, inexpensive audio editors for PC; GarageBand is free with the Mac.

- **Video Gear** — A consumer camcorder, video tripod, and even minimal lighting gear will get your videographer up and going. Or start at the low end with an inexpensive flash memory digital video recorder—fun and easy to use.

IN OUR HOME

We moved back to the Nashville, Tennessee, area just as our boys were in their peak creative early teen years. It was a difficult two years, but one of the things that made it a good memory was the many hours our boys and the Price family children spent working on video productions. They took hundreds of photos and video clips and then created photo slide shows with original music and music videos for songs they liked or had written. They wrote, produced, acted, directed, scored, and edited a variety of creative video shorts, as well as a complete fantasy story. None of them had done that before, but they learned how to do it together. And now they are pursuing many of those same arts—film scoring, acting, and film production.

## Chapter 14

Discretionary Studies Methods: The Study of Living

Becoming a Student of Your Children

By now, it probably goes without saying that a homeschooling parent needs to become a student of their student...their child. However, in our years of experience, we have seen far too many loving and well-intentioned homeschooling parents who, rather than being students of their children, could probably be better described as being students of homeschooling. Their homeschooling lifestyle is defined and driven by a studied concern about methods, curricula, plans, schedules, tests, and scores rather than by a studied pursuit of their children's emerging personalities, gifts, skills, desires, spirituality, and dreams. It's certainly important to get the educational model correct (which is why we wrote this book), but not at the expense of becoming a serious student of all that makes each child unique and special.

What we call Discretionary Studies is the roof on the house of our WholeHearted Learning model. The roof holds everything together. The foundation makes the house stable; the roof makes it secure. The roof represents all the things you do as a student of your children, who are made in the image of God and gifted for use in his kingdom and church. You use your discretion to determine what your children need beyond the academic side of homeschooling in order to become whole and mature. You are a serious student of who and what your children are becoming. The stronger you build the roof, the better and tighter all of the other pieces of your homeschooling will hold together, and the more confident your children will become as they move toward adulthood as whole persons, secure in who they are, what they know, and who they know is with them.

Too often, our hearts have been broken to see homeschooled children graduate and leave home only to get lost in a determined search to find out who they are apart from homeschooling. Of course, there is no simple answer to why that happens, but our observation is that it is rarely because there was a lack of education. The parents were almost always good students of homeschooling, but perhaps not always good students of their children. God has given you as a parent the Spirit-led discretion to study your children and discover with them the unique and special gifts and callings of God on their lives. The ultimate goal of your homeschooling is not just good SAT scores and college—it is to help each of your children answer the question, "What does God want me to do with my life?" Discretionary Studies in the four-to-fourteen window of your children's lives will keep your homeschooling balanced and will begin to build in your children's hearts a confidence in God's design and purpose for their lives that will carry them through adolescence and into adulthood. There is far more to Discretionary Studies than we can cover in this section, so...just use your discretion.

For you created my inmost being; you knit me together in my mother's womb. I praise you because I am fearfully and wonderfully made; your works are wonderful, I know that full well. My frame was not hidden from you when I was made in the secret place. When I was woven together in the depths of the earth, your eyes saw my unformed body. All the days ordained for me were written in your book before one of them came to be.

— Psalm 139:13-16

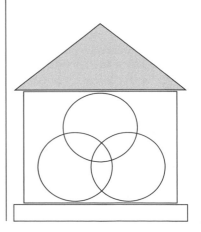

257

Give A Life

Make practical life skills a regular part of your homeschooling. Have your children:

- Plan and prepare (or help with) one meal each week, including shopping.
- Plant and tend a garden patch and sell the produce.
- Help prepare a music and drama presentation to offer to nursing homes.
- Plan one hour of childcare activities for a Bible study or support group.
- Do their own washing, folding, and sorting.
- Create and manage a computer database for videotapes or DVDs.
- Keep the tool shed/room neat and organized.

Lessons from Life

Your children can take lessons other than in a class. Life offers a wide range of great lessons, especially as your children get a little older.

- Volunteer at a hospital or nursing home to learn about caring for others, medicine, nursing, and hospitals.
- To learn about nature and animals, volunteer to help at a nature center, veterinary clinic, or the zoo.
- If you have a mechanically-minded child, arrange for him to help at a garage.
- Put together a backyard Bible club for neighborhood children. Have your children give their testimonies or teach a lesson.
- Help with a political campaign or work with your party precinct organization.
- Host an international exchange student in your home.
- Get involved in a moral or social issue as a family. Write letters, hand out materials, and help with mailings.

Real-Life Learning

Everyone learns through life. Real life is immeasurably rich as a source of learning experiences. It is the best method in your teaching toolbox for developing general living, avocational, and even vocational skills in your children. Your home should provide your children an apprenticeship in real living that exposes them to the kinds of experiences and responsibilities they will face as adults. When they graduate from your homeschool, they should have a clear sense of direction and a confidence that they can handle the basic responsibilities of adulthood. The goal is to give them a sense that they can be independent and self-sufficient whenever they leave home.

Every family will bring a slightly different perspective to the kinds of life skills they want on their "don't leave home without it" list. It is a good idea to begin creating such a list as your children approach the point where they will turn the corner from childhood into young adulthood. You can then work on the list during their final years of homeschooling. Before then, especially during late childhood, you can begin to introduce your children to the areas on your list, talk about the kinds of skills you would like them to gain, ask what kinds of skills they would like to gain, and begin to work in some of the areas. The following are just a few examples of live-and-learn activities.

- **Business** — Start a business for your children that will enable them to learn the basics of manufacture, sales, and service. Examples: make and sell greeting cards, handmade crafts, or specialty foods; develop an in-home pet care service; publish a neighborhood newsletter; cut and sell kindling and firewood; grow and sell produce.

- **Ministry** — Get involved in a church ministry or community service. Examples: instead of going to Sunday School, let them help you teach a younger grade; take them to help on church work days; involve them in whatever ministry you are doing; do Meals on Wheels; visit nursing homes and shut-ins.

- **Homemaking** — Train your children to take care of a home inside and out. Examples: all areas of housecleaning; laundering and ironing all kinds of clothing; planning, buying for, and preparing nutritious meals; decorations and table settings; babysitting; mowing and trimming the lawn; flower bed and garden care.

- **Maintenance and Repair** — Train your children how to think about appliances, machines, and cars so they will be able to run them and discuss problems knowledgeably when repair is needed. Examples: keep maintenance records for cars; know how to check basic fluids (oil, wiper, coolant); clean and detail the interior.

- **Computer** — Train your children how to think about computers and peripherals (printer, scanner, etc.) so they will be able to diagnose and possibly fix problems and system conflicts. Examples: know how to reboot; organize and manage files; change printer toner; clear a printer jam.

- **Finances** — Involve your children early on in the family finances. Let them participate in the entire process. Examples: establishing a family budget; evaluating purchases; paying bills; making deposits; reconciling checking accounts; tracking investment values; entering income and expenses in an accounting program.

Private Lessons and Mentors

Lessons outside the home can be a good way to expose your children to a wide variety of new skills and experiences. Group lessons can also provide opportunities for interaction with other children. However, because groups must be controlled and it is difficult to study a topic in depth in a group, group lessons can be disappointing both for your children and for you. If you are truly serious about giving your children lessons for an emerging interest or skill, then private lessons, if affordable, are always to be preferred over group lessons. Individual tutoring is the ideal lesson format for learning. In contrast, the nature of a classroom greatly limits what can be accomplished—too many children for one teacher to give personal attention to them (impersonal), everybody works on the same things (conformity), lecture (detached), and a very slow pace of instruction (boring). Once a class gets larger than three or four children, it begins to become more formal and regimented, and the advantage and benefits of tutoring are lost.

If your child has an exceptional or emerging skill or interest, consider trying to find an older mentor or coach in their area of interest. This kind of one-on-one relationship is the most effective form of tutoring because the mentor usually will offer time and input not out of a commercial motivation but purely out of a love for the subject and your child. Even when payment is involved, it is still well worth the investment for the more intense personal attention your child will receive. This type of mentoring relationship is not an apprenticeship, which would be a formal working relationship for an older teen. The mentor is more like a coach who is committed to helping, developing, and encouraging your child in their interest area. If you can find this kind of mentor-coach for your child, consider yourself very fortunate.

Lessons will work best when four factors are in place: (1) your child is interested in the subject and already motivated to learn more or master the skill; (2) your child's teacher or mentor-coach has a good reputation, is motivated, and is good with children; (3) the teacher is known as being knowledgeable in the subject area; and (4) something real or tangible is accomplished or produced as a result of the lessons. If any one of those factors is missing, it could become a less-than-great learning experience. If a friend is taking the lessons too, that can somewhat compensate for one of the factors being absent, but it is still not a guarantee of a good experience. A homeschooling co-op can be a wonderful adjunct to your homeschool, but only if the teachers of the classes are motivated, qualified, capable, and good with children. Don't waste your money and your child's time in a class just because it is there. Make sure your child will benefit.

IN OUR HOME

Dancing was not Joy's passion, but as a musical theater enthusiast she wanted to be a triple threat (acting, singing, dancing). She took lessons first from a homeschool mother who helped her choreograph a routine for a national competition. Then she found a great local studio to learn basic dance moves. When she was in a musical production of Pride and Prejudice *at age fourteen, she was asked to choreograph three major production numbers for thirty-plus dancers. All because of a few lessons!*

Lessons to Learn

If you can come up with a skill that can be taught, there is probably a class somewhere for it. Here's a list of both common and uncommon lesson ideas:

- Drawing
- Painting
- Piano
- Violin
- Guitar
- Harp
- Computer skills
- Graphic art and design
- Desktop publishing
- Photography
- Videography
- Video editing
- Audio editing
- Creative writing
- Needlework
- Dressmaking
- Knitting
- Horseback riding
- Drama and theater
- Speech and debate
- Singing
- Songwriting
- Dance and movement
- Physical education
- Team sports (basketball, etc.)
- Individual sports (tennis, etc.)
- Carpentry
- Crafts
- Pottery
- Wood carving
- Gardening
- Many more

Limit Private Lessons

Limit lessons to one per child at a time. If you try to do more—especially if you have other young children—you will crash your calendar and take time away from your homeschooling, especially from reading. Lessons are an important part of a full homeschool experience but should always be considered optional and expendable. What happens at home is always the priority.

There is not such a cradle of democracy upon the earth as the Free Public Library, this republic of letters, where neither rank, office, nor wealth receives the slightest consideration...It was from my own early experiencee that I decided there was no use to which money could be applied so productive of good to boys and girls who have good within them and ability and ambition to develop it as the founding of a public library.

— Andrew Carnegie (1835-1919), Scottish-born American industrialist and philanthropist

Wrong Way ALA

The American Library Association (ALA) is a private member trade association that indirectly controls most public libraries through its accreditation of full-time librarians. Members are expected to support and implement the ALA-created Library Bill of Rights, a statement of library policy that considers community or parental standards on what a library offers to be censorship. The ALA believes that whatever a child wants to see should be freely available without restrictions on its display and without parental notification on its accessibility and use. Ask if your library has adopted the Library Bill of Rights and speak out if they have.

The Library

Going to the library with your children tells them that you value books and reading. It also instills in them the attitude that the library is an enjoyable, exciting place of learning. While you are building your own home library, a public library can be your best source for new and varied reading materials. Family library days should become happily anticipated events as your children's appetites for reading whole books grow. If your children know you'll be going to the library in the morning and then going out for a fun lunch afterwards, they'll always look forward to library day.

- **Learn the library people and system.** Get to know your reference librarian by name. Then get to know your library. Familiarize yourself and your children with the different sections of the library. Each area holds its own treasures to be mined. Create a regular library time when you will go there with your children. Obtain library cards for your children when they can write their names or when the library allows.

- **Become a confident library user.** Learn how to use the library research tools and services: card catalog, Dewey Decimal System, computerized search, printed indexes, periodical guides, interlibrary loan service, Books in Print, and so on. Involve your children in the processes so they learn how to use them. Then give them assignments that will require them to use the research skills they are learning. Always ask the librarian if you need assistance with anything—they are generally very helpful and knowledgeable.

- **Go with a list of books.** Select books that are on Christian and homeschool recommended children's reading lists. Award-winning books (usually designated on the cover) can also be good, but always check for objectionable content. Award-winning books are selected for many reasons, most dealing with illustration, literary style, overall excellence, and relevance. However, you will not find many books in the library with awards that recognize traditional, moral, or family values. Such books are there, but they will rarely be the award-winning titles.

- **Make the most of your trip.** Select a variety of books on each trip (fiction, history, biography, science, nature, etc.). Give your children guidelines and allow them to choose what they would like to read, but let them know you will make the final decisions. Help them learn how to discern whether or not a book they are looking at is appropriate. Look at the book with them and explain why it does or does not meet your family's standards for reading material. Allow your children to check out as many books as they would like to try to read. In many cases, you (and other homeschoolers) will be the only families checking out books, so don't be concerned about checking out the maximum number of books allowable.

- **Separate library books.** Keep a dedicated basket, bag, or box to take to the library for carrying books. When you get home, keep the library books in it or in another designated place that is easily accessible for all your children. This will keep them from getting misplaced before the next trip to the library. Be sure everyone knows how to properly care for the borrowed books. Write the due date and the number of books checked out on your calendar.

Field Trips

Field trips expose your children to the real world, reinforce current areas of study, and provide opportunities for social interaction with other families and children. A field trip can be either a memorable learning experience or just a fun outing with family or friends, depending on how educational you want to make it. The better the planning for a field trip, the greater the return on your investment of time will be.

- **Keep it relevant.** Plan to go on only those field trips that will be compatible with the age and interests of your children. If you can link a field trip with something you are reading or studying about, all the better.

- **Plan and prepare.** Before the field trip, read to your children from some living books that are related to the subject of the trip. Have them do some research and reading on their own so they will know what they are going to see.

- **Expect questions.** Encourage your children to plan to ask questions at the field trip and to go with questions in their minds from their own research. Their questions and the answers they receive can be recorded in a report and saved. Coach younger children with questions they can ask; counsel older children about how to ask good and thoughtful questions and what kinds of questions not to ask.

- **Review trip manners.** Before leaving for the field trip, review expected behavior at the location, especially if other children will be there. Remind them that the time for play is before and after, but not during, the field trip. Review with them how you expect them to behave during the tour and how they should respond to any leaders. Train them to have a good testimony whenever in public.

- **Debrief and report.** After the field trip, have your children write a brief report about what they saw and learned. Keep a notebook of those reports with any pictures taken or materials collected. Have your children write thank-you notes to the field trip leaders and to anyone who helped out at the location. It's a small way to train them in graciousness, and it is a meaningful writing assignment.

IN OUR HOME

Rather than always going to the field, sometimes we bring the field to us and invite other homeschooling families to join us. We asked a knowledgeable creation scientist to come to our home in rural central Texas to talk to us about the fossils in our area and how they fit into a creation model. We had a lot of fossil samples for the kids to examine, and we took them via tractor and trailer to some limestone washouts where they could go on their own fossil dig. We also want our kids to be exposed to a variety of social settings, so we've had tea parties for the mothers and daughters to provide training in social graces and manners. Everyone dresses up and is on their very best behavior. During political campaigns, we'll invite local and state candidates to come and speak to us. We'll plan some government and civics learning activities and maybe even stage a mock election.

Field Trips to Go

A few ideas to get you going:

- Airport
- Auto garage
- Bakery
- Bank
- Bottling plant
- Central post office
- City/county offices
- Dairy
- Farm or ranch
- Fire department
- Homeless center
- Magazine publisher
- Manufacturing plant
- Museums
- Nature center
- Newspaper
- Nursery
- Park and recreation programs
- Police department
- Print shop
- Recording studio
- State capitol
- Symphony or theater
- TV or radio station
- Water treatment plant

Field Trip Rules

For the Children

- Stay with your group, buddy, parent, or teacher at all times.
- Listen quietly when any adult is speaking.
- Touch only what is permitted; ask before you touch.
- Raise your hand to ask a question in a group.
- Look your best and be on your best behavior.

For the Adults

- Honor calendar deadlines for keeping field trip coordinators informed.
- Arrive 10-15 minutes early.
- Be sure you and your children are clean and dressed appropriately.
- Keep your children with you and under control at all times during a tour.
- Guard your testimony.
- Never use a field trip for babysitting.

Discussion, especially with adults, is the best known way for children to raise their level of thinking, which raises their test scores.

— Ruth Beechick, *You Can Teach Your Child Successfully*, Arrow Press, 1993

Group Example

You are leading a study group on Egyptian civilization with two other mothers and their young children. Before the study group, you could assign responsibilities to the other mothers. Children would either dress up or bring an Egyptian "artifact." You could do any of the following:

- Read aloud *The Egyptian Cinderella.*
- Build a Lego pyramid with burial chamber and sarcophagus.
- Read aloud and role-play parts of the confrontation between Moses and the Pharaoh.
- Make a colored, salt-dough map of Egypt.
- Color a line-art drawing of King Tut's sarcophagus.
- While reading about Egyptian burial chambers, draw objects described on the chalk or marker board.
- Create hieroglyphic messages that the children must translate.

Study Groups

A study group is simply a small group of parents and their children who get together to study a mutually agreed-upon subject—history, science, art, music, literature. Typically, leadership of the study rotates to a different family for each meeting. The parent leading the group each session plans the lesson, the involvement of other parents, and learning activities for the children. It is essentially a group unit study with shared teaching responsibilities. In addition to the educational component, the study group also provides enjoyable and meaningful social interaction, especially if the children know each other. What they learn together as friends they will more likely talk about outside the group. The social nature of a small study group of friends can make it a much more effective learning environment than a class in a larger, more impersonal homeschooling co-op.

- **Smaller is better.** A smaller study group is more easily planned and managed. If there are too many families or children in the group, interaction and presentations become unwieldy. Three or four families is an ideal size.

- **Be selective.** Choose families for your study group with the children in mind. If they enjoy their friends, they will enjoy the study group. Look for families who share your values in order to avoid unnecessary conflicts and disagreements.

- **Make it interactive.** Study groups work well for context and unit studies where each child can personally prepare and present a report on some aspect of the study or creatively contribute in some other way to the group learning experience. Participation and interaction are the keys to the success of the study group.

- **Focus on unit study.** Historical books make good fuel for study groups, as do any topics that lend themselves to a unit or context study. Assign study projects prior to the group meetings. At the group, read the chapter aloud or introduce the subject of the unit, then have the children do their presentations, followed by a learning activity or lesson. In a good study group, both the book and the children will come alive.

- **Include social interaction.** A study group provides a unique social activity in addition to the learning. Try to plan the study group around a meal. For instance, meet as a study group in the morning, followed by a lunch together. That will provide an extra incentive for the children to participate in the group (lunch is the reward!), and it will associate learning with fellowship and fun.

- **Keep a record.** Compile a notebook of handouts, reports, materials, photos, and journal pages with notes about the meetings. When completed, have the notebook printed or put on a disc (if it is a digital notebook of some kind) or have it photocopied and bound with a nice cover (if it is a physical notebook) and give a copy to each child.

- **Keep it informal.** You do not need to make your study group a formal learning environment. Because many homeschool parents grew up learning only in structured, formal classrooms, there is a natural suspicion that informality in a group learning situation is a sign of ineffectiveness. If informality encourages more interaction, questioning, and debate, then just the opposite is true. Formality is used to keep a classroom of children under control, but it also keeps them passive and docile.

Home Workshops

A normal frustration for homeschooling families is how to get Dad involved as a teacher. Often, he is not there during the day when most of the learning and instruction take place, and it doesn't work to put off some subjects until after dinner just so Dad can be a part. A much more natural way for Dad to get involved is through family workshops. In a workshop, Dad can direct a hands-on study of a specific topic that will be of interest to all the family. It's like a family night for learning. It reinforces his role as the head of the home and gives him the opportunity to be an expert in his children's eyes and to enjoy the learning process with his children. Mom can help him by pulling together materials and resources. Of course, Mom can lead workshops, too.

- **Schedule your family workshop.** Workshops can be worked into your schedule at random times. However, it is more likely they will get done if you set aside a workshop night on a regular basis (usually bimonthly or monthly) and promote it to your children as a special time. Plan an early dinner (one the kids will really like) to leave the evening as free as possible.

- **Be a prepared workshop leader.** Although many workshop subjects can be taught with very little planning, some advance thought and planning will make the time go much more smoothly. You can lead a series of workshops on a single subject if there is too much to cover in one session, but be sure to plan the entire series with different emphases and activities for each session. Repetition and too much lecture (signs of underplanning) will kill a workshop.

- **Plan for needed materials.** Know what you want your children to learn in the time allotted for each workshop, then create a simple lesson plan. Find creative visual aids and hands-on projects. Have handouts with learning games. Plan the kinds of questions you can ask. Use a marker board for illustrating. Think ahead about examples and personal illustrations that will clarify areas that might be difficult for children to understand. If you have a friend who is knowledgeable in a particular subject, invite them to be a part of your workshop.

IN OUR HOME

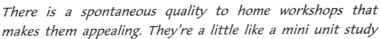

There is a spontaneous quality to home workshops that makes them appealing. They're a little like a mini unit study and lesson combined. Our children reached a point with computers where they could use the jargon of motherboards, hard disk drives, memory, and so on, but they had never actually seen any of these things, so we had a computer home workshop. While Mom was out teaching a Bible study, Dad cracked the case on the home computer and gave the kids a circuit-level view of what's inside. We talked about where images on the monitor come from and how they get there, the operating system and how Windows works, and other parts. Of course, there was a lot of hands-on experimentation. More computer workshops are being planned for the future, but we're off to a good start by demystifying the thing. And the kids love having Dad for some one-on-four time.

Working on Workshops

Workshops are more useful for practical and skill-based subjects than for academic subjects, but they are versatile enough for either. The following list suggests just a few of the subjects that can be taught in workshops.

- Writing — creative writing projects with input from parents
- Computer — learning about hardware, software, and operating systems
- Internet — how to use the Internet safely, how to search, how to find what you need on a website
- Family Newsletter — how to plan and design a family newsletter, writing articles, layout, printing
- Business — how to start and run a business, business financing, management issues, ideas for a business
- Tools — what different kinds of tools are for and how to use them
- Drama — theater basics, acting, directing, producing
- Speech — writing and delivering effective speeches, talks, opinions, devotions
- Machines — principles of machines; demonstration of some simple machines
- Electricity — kinds of current, circuits, switches, breaker boxes, wires
- Political Action — issues, election process, political parties, writing letters to Congressmen
- Sewing — practical sewing, creative sewing, different stitches and techniques
- Manners — rules of etiquette for eating, telephone, out in public, at others' homes, in church, with adults
- Electronics — how to operate various components (DVD, VHS, TV), devices, gadgets
- Personal Finance — how to create a budget, keeping records, savings, checking
- Songwriting — qualities of a good song, lyric structures, melody, harmony, rhythm

Notable Notebooks

We find it helpful to think of two kinds of notebooks—living notebooks about personal interests and learning notebooks about homeschooling subjects.

<u>Living Notebooks</u>

- Bible (study, devotions)
- Hobbies and sports
- Special interest topics
- Field trips
- Holidays (Christmas, July 4)
- Commonplace book
- Personal notebook
- Vacations (landmarks, cities)
- Special research or project
- Homeschooling

<u>Learning Notebooks</u>

- History (world, American)
- Church history
- Geography
- Literature (books read)
- Unit or context studies
- Creative writing
- Handwriting
- Music/art appreciation
- Nature (plants, animals)
- Astronomy (planets, stars)
- Weather (seasons, extreme)

Notebook Supplies

Notebooking, like scrapbooking, requires keeping a good supply of basic materials on hand.

- Binder, notebook, presentation folder, report cover
- Variety of paper for writing, drawing, mounting
- Sheet protectors, pocket inserts, dividers, labels, etc.
- Pens, markers, colored pencils, rubber stamps, ink, etc.
- Scissors, staplers, glue, tape, hole punch, etc.
- Computer, digital camera, scanner, color/photo printer

Digital Notebooking

There are numerous software applications and online websites and resources that can create a digital notebook. Children, though, will benefit most from the analog tangible kind.

Living and Learning Notebooks

In the great new-millennium tradition of verbalizing nouns, the homeschooling world can apparently claim exclusive rights to originating the term "notebooking." As of this writing, the verbal form has not made it into any known reputable dictionary, and a Google search on the term pulls up only homeschooling-related results. The concept is certainly much older than the term, but homeschooling has elevated notebooking almost to an educational model, similar to the concept of unit study. In the WholeHearted Learning model, notebooking is simply a wonderful method to keep in your educational toolbox. It is an easy, natural, tangible way to enrich your children's learning experience.

In the absence of an official definition, here's a working one: Notebooking is the act and art of creating, recording, collecting, and organizing selected content and media about a subject of personal interest onto pages stored within a binder or notebook. Pretty simple, yet every family will approach notebooking differently, with different subjects, interests, materials, standards, priorities, drives, and expectations. And still, every family is doing the same thing—making a notebook on a subject. In our model, we create notebooks in two broad categories—living and learning. Here are some benefits:

- **Record Keeping** — Notebooks are an easy way to create a tangible record of your children's learning activities and progress. Simply keep representative samples of written lessons or projects in language arts, handwriting, composition, math, and other subjects. You have a portfolio of work if needed, and your children will enjoy seeing their own progress. It is both a keepsake and a permanent record of learning.

- **Creative Learning** — Notebooks are fun and fruitful tools for releasing your children's natural creativity and harnessing it to learning. They will be naturally motivated to research the notebook topic, select and sort the content, design and decorate the pages, and make it their own. Each notebook becomes a creative expression that they will take pride in owning and showing off. Learning happens...with a notebook.

- **Personalized Learning** — Whatever type of personality your children may be— Doer, Helper, Mover, Shaper—their notebooks will allow them to exercise and reflect their own personal living and learning styles. Give each child freedom to follow their own personality in choosing how to investigate and determine (see chapter 8) what is important to them about the subject of their notebook. In the process, you will affirm their personality and create a love for learning that will stay with them for a lifetime.

IN OUR HOME

My mother keeps everything. "Europe, by Clay Clarkson" was my first notebook effort from sixth grade (1962). Inside the bright red report cover are one hundred pages, front and back, of reports, clippings, lists of information, drawings, pictures, and my thoughtful eleven-year-old insights on the famous Renaissance European artist, "Michael Angelo." The content appeared copied right out of the venerable World Book *encyclopedia, but it was all done in my own hand, which apparently brought my grade down. "Clay, you do such nice work, but try to be neater. A-." Indeed!*

Standardized Tests

Standardized achievement tests can be helpful for you, as the parent educator, to evaluate your children's progress. However, it is possible for the results of the tests to wrongly become either a source of over-concern if your children don't get above grade level or of false pride if they're way above grade level. Since the major tests are currently normed against a public-school student population, there is no way to know the actual validity of your children's scores. It is reasonable to assume that most homeschooled students, especially those raised in a verbal and print-rich environment, should score higher than the public-school-based norm.

- **Tests help the teacher.** The best use of standardized tests is to help *you* better ascertain where you need to put more emphasis in your teaching. Testing every year or two gives you a reasonably objective means to measure your children's development. Nonetheless, tests will more than likely only confirm what you already know to be true about your children. In the end, you are the best measure of their development.

- **Explore testing options.** In addition to the public and private school testing times, many homeschooling umbrella schools and support groups administer standardized tests for members. If you have a teaching certificate or are a graduate of a four-year degree program, you may be able to administer certain tests for your own children and others. Check with the testing service or with the test publisher.

- **Evaluate testing factors.** A low score does not necessarily mean low comprehension in an area. Take other factors into consideration: Is he a poor test taker? Was she not feeling well, or was she overly anxious? Had you covered the area in which he scored low? Was there a readiness for the subject? (Tests do not take into account the concept of learning readiness.) In the end, you—not an impersonal test—are the final judge of your children's comprehension. Trust your own God-given insight into your children's minds.

- **Practice with pretests.** Pretests are available from testing services and catalogs to prepare your children for the test. If you don't use written tests in your homeschool, a pretest will familiarize your children with the mechanics. Buy the test early so you can incorporate the testing methods and concepts into your teaching, but wait until the week before the actual test to give your children the pretest.

- **Coach your children.** Instruct your children how to take the test: Read directions carefully; look for clue words; answer the questions they know first; don't spend too long on one item; if there is time, go back and answer unanswered questions (a logical guess is usually better than a blank, but check with the administrator); be sure test item and answer sheet numbers match; mark only one answer per test item; fully erase errors and stray marks.

- **It's your call to tell.** Your children will naturally want to know the results of the tests. You should discern whether to give them generalities ("You're doing very well in... We need to work on...") or specific results in each of the tested areas. Whichever you choose, be especially careful not to compare your children's results ("When Susie was your age, she scored..." or "Wow, Jack is as smart as Jill in math!").

[Y]ou can let most children in on test scores and how they are interpreted. This is usually better than being secretive, as though test results are only for parents and teachers. On the profile page of your children's achievement tests they can easily see where their higher and lower scores are, and they can plan with you which scores they should try to raise before the next testing. The scores can be viewed something like golfing or bowling scores, and used for motivation.

— Ruth Beechick, *You Can Teach Your Child Successfully*, Arrow Press, 1993

Testy Terminology

It is helpful to understand some of the technical terms used on the test reports you'll receive.

- **Raw Score** — The number of test items your child answered correctly.

- **Percentile** — Refers to your child's relative ranking to all other tested children; it does not refer to the percentage of correct answers. In a room of 100 children, a 75 percentile ranking means your child did better than 75 other children. Highest is 99 percentile.

- **Grade Level** — Indicates the grade in which your child's score would be average. A 6.4 grade level means sixth grade, fourth month (based on ten months). It is the score a child at 6.4 grade level would score on the same test. It does not mean your child would score average on a sixth-grade test.

- **Stanine** — Ranking on a scale of 1-9 based on the percentile groupings. In general, 1-3 is below average achievement, 4-6 is average, and 7-9 is above average. The middle stanine represents about half of the group (based on a bell curve of standard distribution).

This Is Only a Test

There are several standardized achievement tests for grades K-8. Depending upon state requirements, each is an acceptable measurement device. It is advisable to stay with the same test from year to year to make it easier to compare results and evaluate progress.

- **Iowa Test of Basic Skills (ITBS)** — Testing time in grades 3-8 is 4-5 hours. Tests are timed. No listening tests in grades 3-8. Qualified parent may administer.
- **Stanford Achievement Test (SAT)** — Testing time in grades 3-8 is 5-6 hrs. Tests are not timed. Listening tests and subtests included in all grades. Stricter qualifications for administration.
- **California Achievement Test (CAT)** — Testing time in grades 2-8 is 2-3 hours. No listening tests. No subtests. Reflects more traditional values. Parent may administer test in home.
- **Metropolitan Achievement Test (MAT)** — Testing time in grades K-8 is 1.5-4 hours. Tests language and math skills and reading comprehension. Group administered.
- **Personalized Achievement Summary System (PASS) Test** — Developed specifically for homeschoolers. Tests reading, language, and math for grades 3-8. Test is untimed. No degree is required, and parent may administer the test at home.

Testing Information

- Bob Jones University Press, Testing and Evaluation Service — ITBS, SAT, MAT
- Christian Liberty Academy, Christian Liberty Press Testing — CAT
- Hewitt Homeschooling Resources, Testing — PASS
- Independent testing services
- State and regional homeschool associations

Putting a Roof over Your Children's Lives

Webster's Dictionary defines discretion as "the power to decide or act according to one's own judgment." It is derived from a Latin term that means to separate or distinguish. In the WholeHearted Learning model, Discretionary Studies are those areas of homeschooling that you as a parent decide to provide based on your own judgment of what your children need. Going back to the roots of the word, you become a student of your children in order to determine what separates and distinguishes them—what makes them unique. The other four study areas of our model are about subjects, knowledge, and skills that every child needs; this study area is about what each individual child needs.

Some suggest that the four-to-fourteen window is too early in the maturation and mental development process to discern anything really useful about a child's innate and internal gifts, abilities, and drives. They argue that everything is in flux during childhood and can and often does change dramatically in adolescence, so what is most important during childhood are basic learning skills and core knowledge. But the idea of a whole-hearted child is not just about the mind—it is about a child whose spirit is being shepherded to long for God, whose heart is being shaped to live for God, and whose mind is being strengthened to learn for God.

Too many parents are satisfied if they can educate children who demonstrate they have learned how to learn and are able to be good students. It's a measurable outcome. But failing to give equal emphasis to the developing spirits and hearts of those children can handicap them in adolescence when it becomes apparent that they must also learn how to live. At a time when they enter a peak learning phase of life as young adults, they can find themselves *searching* for who they are rather than *becoming* who they are. Building a strong roof of discretionary learning over their life throughout their childhood can give them a developing confidence in who they are as they enter adolescence. That roof will help hold everything together.

IN OUR HOME

Joel is a perfect example in our family of using discretionary studies. From the time he could begin making noises, it was obvious he had an extra dose of musical genes. We had no idea where it would lead, but we encouraged his interest in music as a child—piano lessons, boys' choir, musical theater, and guitar lessons. He went to a school of worship at our church and then headed to college. It took only one semester of liberal arts studies for him to realize his love was music. Even though he had never learned to sight-read music (he always played by ear), he decided to audition for Berklee College of Music, a highly respected Boston music conservatory. He and Sarah drove three days, and he played an original composition written for the audition. Four months later he was accepted, and soon he will graduate with high honors with a degree in Composition. (He's created two CDs of original music.) Because we studied Joel as parents and recognized and developed his music, he has found his opportunity to excel in his gifts and calling. Music is the roof over his life that holds in place everything else we put into him.

Section 4

Living

— Chapter 15 —

Family: Keeping the Vision Alive

Looking Back to Keep Moving Forward

We live in a culture that is rapidly redefining the term "family" to mean almost anything that anyone wants it to mean. When "family values" first entered the cultural vocabulary in the seventies and eighties, there was no argument about what it meant—it was about traditional, biblical family values. It is still a positive thing to be "pro-family," but what it actually means two generations later is a moving target. But family means something to God, and it is up to us, his family, to keep the biblical idea of family alive and defined by our lives. We give definition to the biblical concept of family by being one.

Critics of the biblical view of family are quick to point out the many varieties of human relationships, especially in the Old Testament, that were practiced both by the enemies and the followers of God. While God did not whitewash his Word to avoid the messiness and brokenness of life in this fallen world, he also did not fail to uphold the monogamous family as the core and cornerstone of human relationships. Family is always assumed and honored in Scripture as God's ideal design for men and women—in the creation account, the fifth commandment ("Honor your father and your mother"), the parental charge in Deuteronomy 6:4-7, the wife of Proverbs 31, the loving couple in Song of Solomon, the birth narrative of Jesus, Paul's instructions to households, the church family, adoption, and many more. The language God chooses to use about his own divine nature and about our relationships with him and with one another—father, mother, children, sons, brothers, sisters, bride, bridegroom—reveals God's eternal purpose and design that we should understand him, and indeed our very being and experience, through the analogous language of our earthly family relationships.

Family is the only institution in Scripture that was created before the Fall. God designed one man and one woman to join together, to have children, and to rule over and subdue the earth. Family was the pinnacle of God's creative work and the center of his created order for the world. The fall of that perfect world into sin would result in distortions and perversions of God's perfect will for man and woman, but it would not distort the reality that God's ideal for family is what we see in his creation of Adam and Eve. The world may change, but God's intent never changes. Jesus affirmed that very concept in an argument with the Pharisees over divorce. They wanted to litigate the law of Moses, but Jesus said, "Moses permitted you to divorce your wives because your hearts were hard. But it was not this way from the beginning" (Matthew 19:8). Jesus based his response on God's intention for marriage "in the beginning." In other words, he told them if you want to know God's heart and ideal for marriage and family, look at Adam and Eve. If we want to keep the family moving forward we, too, need to look back at Genesis.

For everything that was written in the past was written to teach us, so that through endurance and the encouragement of the Scriptures we might have hope.

— Romans 15:4

Do not move an ancient boundary stone set up by your forefathers.

— Proverbs 22:28

Christian parenting is a journey. The destination is clear—raising godly children—but the roads to get there are not always clearly marked. We have God's perfect road map, the Bible, but He has not taken a divine highlighter pen and marked the single route that leads to where we want to go. He expects us to study the map and chart a wise course to the desired destination.

— Clay Clarkson, *Heartfelt Discipline*, WaterBrook Press, 2003

269

What has been will be again, what has been done will be done again; there is nothing new under the sun. Is there anything of which one can say, "Look! This is something new"? It was here already, long ago; it was here before our time...I know that everything God does will endure forever; nothing can be added to it and nothing taken from it. God does it so that men will revere him. Whatever is has already been, and what will be has been before; and God will call the past to account.

— Ecclesiastes 1:9-10, 3:14-15

Homeschooling from the Beginning

Homeschooling is much more than just an educational movement. At its core, it is a family movement—a new expression of what it means to be and to live as a family in modern culture. It's not new in the sense of "never seen before" but in the sense of "what's old is new" (Ecclesiastes 1:9-10; 3:14-15). In a rapidly secularizing culture, the old idea of family as God designed it "in the beginning" is new to those not attuned to Scripture and the Genesis narrative. Perhaps biblical marriage and family—certainly when expressed within a homeschooling family—is becoming part of the "foolishness of God" that is "wiser than man's wisdom" articulated by Paul (1 Corinthians 1:20-31).

This is not the place to dive deep into doctrine, but it is worth thinking for a moment: What is it about God's "in the beginning...in the image of God" design for family that will set ours apart in an "in my opinion" world remaking family in its own image? We'll look at the roles of fathers and mothers in particular next, but consider first a few of God's family values that were revealed in the beginning before the Fall of mankind and the entrance of sin into the perfect creation. The creation account in Genesis 1-3 reveals expressions of God's heart in his perfect, pre-Fall work of creation. Because of the corruption of sin, we cannot expect to fully express those "in the beginning" ideals of marriage and family. However, we can acknowledge those ideals as a goal, and though we will not reach it in this lifetime, those ideals provide a fixed point toward which to move. Homeschooling is a unique expression of biblical family life aiming for the ideals.

- **Image Bearers** — In all that was created, only man and woman bear the image of God. We are made to be like God: rational, creative, and relational. Marriage and family are an expression not only of God's eternal purpose, but also his divine nature.

- **Male and Female** — Male and female are part of God's created order. Each bears the image of God, and each is imbued with divine purpose. They are equal in value in God's eyes, yet unique in their roles. A marriage is between one man and one woman.

- **Procreators** — Our created purpose as men and women is to marry and have children. Sex is not just a pleasurable end in itself, but the pleasurable means to an end—to have children, fill the earth, and subdue it.

- **Co-Regents** — God gave the charge to subdue and rule over the earth to man and woman together. Husband and wife share the mandate equally as partners in the task of subduing (bringing order to) and ruling over (maintaining order in) the earth.

- **Domain Subduers** — Implicit in the creation account and in the mandate to subdue and rule over the earth is the idea of unique domains over which to rule—man outside the home, woman inside. Both are serving the goal of a whole, healthy family.

- **Complementary Roles** — Man alone was incomplete. Woman was created to be a "suitable helper" for the man. Together, man and woman can accomplish what neither can do alone. They complement one another in God's plan for his creation.

- **Freedom** — God gave Adam and Eve freedom. Although he gave them one restriction, they were otherwise free to explore and enjoy Eden. It is a foreshadowing of the freedom in the Spirit we have in Christ and will enjoy again one day in the new earth.

FATHER — The Head of the Home

Even though the specific terminology is not found in Scripture, we commonly think of dad as being the "head of the home." For our purposes, it's just a good, biblically informed description of a father's unique role in the family, just as the "heart of the home" describes a mother's unique role. Unfortunately, the terminology often gets weighted down with notions of authority that don't fit the biblical picture of being head. Being the head of your home is not about being the autocratic leader of an organization called the home; it is about being the servant-leader of an organism called the family. If you miss that distinction, your experience of being the head of your home can devolve into a set of man-made rules that override the very uncomplicated roles that God designed. God has not defined in Scripture a one-size-fits-all model of family. Instead, he has given us a one-Spirit-guides-all model for living out the biblical principles and patterns of family. Whatever your homeschooling family looks like and however you live out the biblical principles, pictures, and patterns of family, God wants you to do it by his Word, by faith, with grace. It's about freedom in the Spirit, not rules.

The best picture in Scripture for what it means to be the head of your home is in Paul's instructions to husbands and wives in Ephesians 5:22-33. He compares the husband's role in marriage to that of Christ and the church. When he declares that "Christ is the head of the church, his body" (23), he is describing the organic relationship of a head and a body. A body cannot exist without a head; and a head cannot function if the body to which it is attached does not respond to it. Paul's teaching throughout his letters is that Christ is the head of his church, not as a CEO is the head of an organization, but as the head of a body naturally gives life and direction to it. The body is dead without the head; the head needs a body to fulfill its purpose. The ideal church body naturally submits to Christ, its head, because he is their source of spiritual life and sustenance.

The idea of submission in this passage is not about obeying positional authority but rather about the body willingly aligning with the head so the whole body can live. It is an organic, symbiotic relationship because, at the same time, "husbands ought to love their wives as their own bodies...After all, no one ever hated his own body, but he feeds and cares for it, just as Christ does the church—for we are members of his body" (28-30). The term for "feeds" is *ektrepho*, which means literally to feed from or nourish. In other words, the husband's role is to nourish his body so it will live; the wife's role is to willingly receive that life and nourishment from her head. It is an organic relationship, not an organizational one, based on the servant-leadership of the husband: "Husbands, love your wives, just as Christ loved the church and gave himself up for her" (25).

This organic concept is extended to the entire family when Paul tells fathers to stop frustrating their children, but rather "bring them up in the training and instruction of the Lord" (Ephesians 6:4). The word for "bring...up" is *ektrepho* again. Dad, you are to feed and nourish your children as the head of your home, just as you are to feed and nourish your wife. By God's design, your "training and instruction *of the Lord*" feeds your family body; you are uniquely a source of Christ's life and sustenance to them. Your family is held together, nourished, and growing by the life of Christ that comes from you, its head. Your role as head of the home is a work of faith, grace, and Spirit.

In giving us the place and the name and the power of father, God has in a very real and solemn sense made us His image-bearers. He asks and expects us, in doing our work as such, in every way to copy Him, to act as like Him as possible. The parents who desire to bring a full blessing to their children must make God's fatherhood their model and their study.

— Rev. Andrew Murray, *The Children for Christ*, 1887

For I have chosen him, so that he will direct his children and his household after him to keep the way of the LORD by doing what is right and just, so that the LORD will bring about for Abraham what he has promised him.

— Genesis 18:19

As a father has compassion on his children, so the LORD has compassion on those who fear him.

— Psalm 103:13

He who fears the LORD has a secure fortress, and for his children it will be a refuge.

— Proverbs 14:26

Children's children are a crown to the aged, and parents are the pride of their children.

— Proverbs 17:6

The Godly Father

God has spoken succinctly but directly to dads in Scripture. The relative economy of instruction is not because fathering was low on God's priorities—after all, he is God the Father! Perhaps he knew dads would choke on "101 Ways to Be a Better Dad." The Heavenly Father put only a few choice admonitions in his Word directed specifically to earthly fathers, but they are enough. Taken together, they can be expressed in seven simple biblical admonitions to dads or "dadmonitions" (also expressed with the acrostic FATHERS). The seven dadmonitions are all a dad needs to know for becoming the godly father that God the Father wants him to be and to open and win his children's hearts. These are not formulaic rules for fathering but biblical principles that express the organic nature of fatherhood just described on the previous page. It's how to be a godly dad.

F — FAITH

Be a dad who intentionally influences his children.

Moses told the parents of Israel before entering the Promised Land: "These commandments...are to be upon your hearts. Impress them on your children" (Deuteronomy 6:6-7). This command, still repeated daily by pious Jews, established the truth that passing righteousness on to your children is an intentional parental process and that whatever you intend to "impress...on" your children or "teach them diligently" (NASB) must first be on your own heart. Your spiritual influence as a father starts with your heart. It's intentional.

A — AUTHORITY

Be a dad who faithfully instructs his children.

Paul commanded the Ephesian fathers—stop exasperating your children by failing to nurture them with the "training and instruction of the Lord" (Ephesians 6:4). Your children, by God's design, are looking to you for training and truth. If you are passive as a father and neglect to give your children what God has divinely designed you to give, that failure will leave them frustrated and angry. Your faithfulness in being a godly father will have a direct influence on your children's faith. Be faithful to instruct your children "in the Lord" so they will know God's truth. (Proverbs 22:6)

T — TRAINING

Be a dad who lovingly disciplines his children.

In the same way that God the Father disciplines his children so that we may "share in his holiness" (Hebrews 12:10), we discipline our children so that they may share in our love for them. An undisciplined child is by nature self-centered and self-serving, unable to fully enjoy the benefits and blessings of loving and being loved. But your loving, gentle discipline is a powerful tool of formation on their spirits that will help them to become self-controlled in order to love God and love people (Matthew 22:37-40). Biblical discipline is more than just correction—it is the process of gently and lovingly guiding your children along the path of life. (Proverbs 29:17-18; Proverbs 3:11-12; Hebrews 12:7-13)

H — HUMILITY

Be a dad who tenderly sympathizes with his children.

When Paul wrote to the Colossian dads, "Fathers, do not embitter your children, or they will become discouraged" (Colossians 3:21), he was affirming a common truth—dads can be harsh. We know how to control our children with strong words, actions, and expressions. But is that how God the Father relates to his children? A careful reading of Scripture will reveal a sympathetic God who is loving, tender, gentle, kind, longsuffering, and patient as our Father. Paul describes a godly dad as "encouraging, comforting, and urging" his children to godliness (1 Thessalonians 2:12). Sympathy is counterintuitive for many dads, and that's why it requires tenderness and an attitude of humility. (Psalm 103:13)

E — ENCOURAGEMENT

Be a dad who graciously provides for his children.

Jesus reminded his followers that God is generous and gracious, ready to encourage his children when they come to him in prayer. "For everyone who asks receives, and he who seeks finds, and to him who knocks it will be opened" (Matthew 7:8, NASB). He reminds them that a good father will not give a stone to a son who asks for a loaf, or a snake for a fish, but rather gives "good gifts to those who ask him" (Matthew 7:11). God doesn't want fathers providing grudgingly for their children, but rather graciously and generously, just as he, our Father, provides for us. (1 Timothy 5:8; 2 Corinthians 12:14; Proverbs 19:14)

R — RESPONSIBILITY

Be a dad who confidently guides his children.

It's easy to give your children biblical information; very little is required of you as a father to indoctrinate your child. However, it requires a godly confidence to use that truth to give them biblical guidance and direction in life. Abraham is a model of godly confidence, as is the man who fears the Lord in Psalm 112. Paul taught that a man's ability to "manage his own family well" (1 Timothy 3:4) and to have believing, respectful children is a barometer of his ability to lead the church. Self-confidence is good, but Paul is describing a God-confidence. As a father, your confidence to guide your children should come from your confidence in God and his Word. (Genesis 18:19; Psalm 112:1-2; Titus 1:6)

S — SERVICE

Be a dad who purposefully pursues his children.

The father who purposefully pursues his child for God says with Solomon, "My son, give me your heart and let your eyes keep to my ways" (Proverbs 23:26). A godly father will pursue the heart of his child. He says with the psalmist about God's truths, "We will not hide them from our children; we will tell the next generation the praiseworthy deeds of the Lord, his power, and the wonders he has done" (Psalm 78:4). A godly father will serve God in pursuing not just his own children, but also children of generations to come.

Open: Three Good Dadittudes

"Dadittudes" are good and godly attitudes that will open your children's hearts.

- **Love** — "The only thing that counts is faith expressing itself through love" (Galatians 5:6).
- **Humility** — "Be completely humble and gentle; be patient, bearing with one another in love" (Ephesians 4:2).
- **Spirit** — "But the fruit of the Spirit is love, joy, peace, patience, kindness, goodness, faithfulness, gentleness and self-control" (Galatians 5:22-23).

Win: Seven Simple Do-Dads

"Do-Dads" are tangible and practical actions that will win your children's hearts.

- **Intentionally Influencing** — Spend time regularly with God, and then share with your children what you learn and pray with them about it.
- **Faithfully Instructing** — Have a daily family devotional time of reading and discussing Scripture and life and praying together with your children.
- **Lovingly Disciplining** — Take responsibility for biblical discipline in your home, whether direction, correction, or protection is needed.
- **Tenderly Sympathizing** — Make special times to connect with each child's heart and to talk about their life, questions, hopes, and concerns.
- **Generously Providing** — Practice random acts of giving to demonstrate that you are generous and gracious because God is to you.
- **Confidently Leading** — Encourage and affirm each child's unique gifts and skills and help them discover and develop their life's messages.
- **Purposefully Pursuing** — Plan an annual getaway with each child to talk about God's plan for their life and to record their hopes and dreams.

Therefore, I urge you, brothers, in view of God's mercy, to offer your bodies as living sacrifices, holy and pleasing to God—this is your spiritual act of worship. Do not conform any longer to the pattern of this world, but be transformed by the renewing of your mind. Then you will be able to test and approve what God's will is—his good, pleasing and perfect will.

— Romans 12:1-2

The Transformed Dad

Romans 12:1-2 is Paul's prescription for being a disciple of Christ. There are three simple signs of a disciple in his words that can become an anchor for you as a father and for your children to keep you from drifting as disciples of Christ. Study and memorize the passage together, and then learn the signs. You will burn into your children's minds and hearts a visual and memorable model of what it means to live as a follower of Christ.

- **Yield to God** (12:1) — In light of all that God has done for you, to save you and sanctify you (Romans 1-11), you must present your life to God to serve him. It is your only reasonable response.

- **Stop the World** (12:2a) — Once yielded to God, Paul commands you in effect to stop allowing your mind to be passively programmed by the times in which you live. Stop being conformed to its untruths!

- **Go to the Word** (12:2b) — Instead of listening to your world, listen to God's Word. Allow God to transform your life by renewing your mind with his truth. Then you can know and do God's will.

The Teaching Father

If you are a Christian homeschooling father, you may or may not teach your children some of their homeschooling subjects. You have lots of options. However, you *must* teach your children the Word of God. For that, you have no options. God speaks directly to fathers throughout Scripture and instructs them to teach their children, especially in the pivotal passages such as Deuteronomy 6:4-9, Psalm 78, and Ephesians 6:4. Your responsibility to teach your children is distinct from any gift of teaching—God simply expects you to teach your children. Period. Moms instruct their children, too—the mother of Proverbs 1-9, the Proverbs 31 mother, the Titus 2 mothers, Timothy's mother and grandmother teaching him the Scriptures. However, God the Father gives fathers special exhortations and instructions to teach their children. In fact, to be a Christian father is to be a teaching father. God's Word does not allow you to separate those identities.

At this point, some fathers will resist God's instructions because they are not confident with all the doctrine and theology they think they will have to learn and understand in order to teach their children. A father might think, "I don't really know that much about the Bible, and I don't have enough time to study it that much, so there's no way I can ever teach the Bible to my children" and then just defer to the teaching programs of the church, relying on Sunday School and Bible club attendance. But God did not intend for his church to become a surrogate parent; its role is to equip parents, not replace them. A father is competent to teach his children not because of what he knows but because of who he is.

Your role is not to indoctrinate but to incarnate. You are not just giving your children information about the Bible, as though it is a textbook on Christianity, but you are taking in and living out its truth and then showing your children how God's truth can live in them too. That is the heart of godly instruction. Remember, the Scripture is "living and active" (Hebrews 4:12) and "inspired by God," able to make you "adequate, equipped for every good work" (2 Timothy 3:16-17, NASB), which certainly must include the work of teaching your children. Teaching the Bible to your children is about relationship and interaction, not about religion. When Paul says fathers are to nurture their children "in the training and instruction of the Lord," he uses very relational terms. If you do nothing else with your children, simply open the Word with them and let it come alive.

IN OUR HOME

Since I (Clay) have an advanced seminary degree, I suppose I should be confident about teaching the Bible to my children. There's no doubt that I love teaching the structured instructional content of the New Testament, digging into word studies, uncovering historical nuance, and outlining passages to reveal meaning. However, I am much less confident when it comes to teaching from the narrative and historical content of the Old Testament—I can never remember all the people, places, and events or get the chronologies right. Sally, though, knows every story and person and how they all fit together. The kids (and I) love hearing her teach them. When I teach the Old Testament, I've learned to enjoy the reading, let the narratives speak for themselves, and trust the Holy Spirit to bring them alive.

Seven Secrets of the Home TEACHER

Studies have affirmed about teaching what Jesus modeled—the smaller the group, the larger the retention of information and the greater the personal impact. Jesus often taught the multitudes in parables, but he taught his disciples the "knowledge of the secrets of the kingdom of God" (Luke 8:10). But here's the important thing to remember—Jesus did not teach his disciples everything they would know about him and his kingdom. There simply was not enough time in just three very busy years of ministry. But there was enough time for Jesus to win and influence their hearts so they would be fully committed to him and to his kingdom after he was gone. The Holy Spirit would keep the learning going after that (John 14-17; Acts 1:1-9), and now we have the complete Bible.

You cannot teach your children everything they need to know about the Word of God. Even if you could, it probably would be to the neglect of other aspects of their lives. You can, though, open and win their hearts and model for them what it means to follow Jesus as a committed disciple. There will be many Bible truths and insights you won't get to in that process, but you can trust the Holy Spirit to continue to teach them. Jesus influenced his disciples to turn the world upside down. I've tried to capture key elements of his teaching model in an acrostic using the word TEACHER. It's just a helpful reminder that as a teaching father, it's not just about what you know, but about who you are and what you do. To raise world-changer children, make sure you are a teacher.

- **T = Time to Talk** — The first priority is to make time with your children to talk about the things of God. Remember, you'll reach their hearts through their ears. Learn the art of asking and listening whenever you open the Word with them.

- **E = Enthusiasm to Explain** — You must be ready and willing to enthusiastically explain the answer to any question. Your response will feed your children's desires to know more and to ask more. Your enthusiasm gives them freedom to be curious.

- **A = Ability to Apply** — The Bible is not just information to be learned but divine truth that leads to transformation. God's truth is never static; it is always dynamic, changing the learner. Show your children how the Word changes you for good.

- **C = Confidence in Christ** — This secret of teaching is the fulcrum that keeps all the other secrets in balance (TEA head qualities on one side; HER hands qualities on the other). Your confidence in Christ is always the heart of your teaching.

- **H = Humility to Help** — Be ready to humble yourself as a teacher when your children seem slower to learn. Your children want to know that—like Jesus washing his disciples' feet—you can sympathize with their weaknesses and help them learn.

- **E = Encouragement to Explore** — Don't be afraid of your children's thirst for knowledge. It is there by God's design and needs only your direction and protection. Encourage them to explore. Lead them to explore. Trust the Holy Spirit to work.

- **R = Responsibility to Remind** — Peter said, "So I will always remind you of these things, even though you know them…" He knew, from being with Jesus, the power of repetition. Accept the responsibility to be a reminder of truth to your children.

All Scripture is God-breathed and is useful for teaching, rebuking, correcting and training in righteousness, so that the man of God may be thoroughly equipped for every good work.

— 2 Timothy 3:16-17

For the word of God is living and active. Sharper than any double-edged sword, it penetrates even to dividing soul and spirit, joints and marrow; it judges the thoughts and attitudes of the heart.

— Hebrews 4:12

Fast Four-Words Bible Time

Use this simple four-question model to teach your children any passage of Scripture. Not only is it an easy instructional method for you to follow, but it also provides a simple inductive learning pattern that your children can follow in their own Bible reading and study.

- **Know** — Is there something in this passage God wants me to know? Is there truth, doctrine, principle, wisdom, or insight to understand?

- **Be** — Is there something in this passage God wants me to be? Is there a character quality, example, or virtue to grow in or to practice?

- **Do** — Is there something in this passage God wants me to do? Is there a command, admonition, exhortation, or advice to obey or follow?

- **Believe** — Is there something in this passage God wants me to believe? Is there an issue of faith, trust, or surrender that must be spiritually accepted?

These commandments that I give you today are to be upon your hearts. Impress them on your children. Talk about them when you sit at home and when you walk along the road, when you lie down and when you get up. Tie them as symbols on your hands and bind them on your foreheads. Write them on the doorframes of your houses and on your gates.

— Deuteronomy 6:6-9

The Homeschooling Father

Scripture instructs you as a dad to make sure you understand and cultivate your organic relationship to your wife and family. If you are not spiritually feeding and leading them, anything else you do will be gradually reduced to activities disconnected from the life and vitality of Christ. Just as Christ is the source of life to his body, the church, as the head of your home you are a vital source of Christ's life in the life of your family. However, the church is not only a living organism; it is also an organization. In the same way, your family has both organic and organizational qualities. No matter how well it is functioning on the organic level, an unorganized family will be less effective and productive. Homeschooling requires some organization.

It's no secret that mothers are the engines of industry when it comes to the education of their children. After all, the home is their natural domain. For most families, the day-to-day responsibilities of homeschooling and homekeeping are managed by mothers at home. Every committed homeschooling father wants to be involved, but the organizational responsibilities of fathers in the actual homeschooling program remain largely undefined and vary greatly from home to home. Whatever subjects dad may step into the program to teach, there are some organizational roles that every homeschooling dad can readily fulfill that every homeschooling mom will thankfully welcome.

- **Homeschool Principal** — As the principal of your homeschool, you represent and oversee the whole program. You make sure your "teaching staff" has all she needs to do her job, and you love and discipline your students. As the God-appointed head of your home, you take personal responsibility for the effectiveness of your homeschool. Your teacher and students are looking up to you for leadership. You must take the initiative to be involved in planning and evaluating your homeschool, fixing problems, and offering input on fine-tuning it. You do not need to micromanage your homeschool—your wife is a capable manager of the day-to-day responsibilities. Just be available and be involved. Also, as the head of your family, you represent your homeschool. You are its spokesman in the community, at church and, if ever called upon, before government officials. The buck stops with you.

- **Adjunct Teacher** — As an adjunct teacher, you are available to step in as needed to teach areas of special interest and knowledge. You can plan special evening workshops for your children on areas that you personally are interested in (such as computers) or for which you have special insight or ability (such as math or science). Or you can plan a short nature outing to observe wildlife, stars, or creation. Best of all, you can read books aloud at meals and bedtimes. However it is possible, you help carry some of the teaching load with your wife, not just for your wife's sake but for your children's sake as well. They need your fatherly involvement, instruction, and perspective as much as your wife needs your help.

- **Daily Reviewer** — Your job as daily reviewer is to listen to your children tell what they have learned that day. By proudly and patiently hearing their presentations and reports, encouraging them in their new skills, and affirming their projects and progress, you can give them a sense of worth they can get only from you, their dad. They are looking and listening for your approval.

- **Teacher's Helper** — Even the best teachers need helpers. You can be there for your homeschooling wife to offer real, practical help when it is really needed. It may require sacrificing some of your own desires or plans, but you are called to be your helper's helper. Whether with academics (reading, writing, math, science), logistics (taking some children so she can work with others, driving children to an activity), projects (working on art or science fair projects with children, directing an outdoor project, guiding a child through a computer project), or some other area (organizing the learning room, systematizing the library), you can actively look for ways to help.

- **Recreational Director** — You can't lose with this job. Just have fun with your children. Teach them sports, play outside with them, take a walk, play a board game, go on an extended outing. Schedule regular times throughout the week to be actively involved with your children, especially when they are young, whether they are planned activities or just doing whatever the children want to do. Just before dinner, while mom is in the kitchen, is a good time for dads to take over for a while.

- **Guidance Counselor** — Your children want to spend time with you alone. They need guidance and counsel that God has designed you alone to give to them, especially from the ages of about seven years old and up. Their development as healthy young men and women is largely dependent upon your involvement in their lives during the formative years before adolescence. Set aside special times with each of your children to talk. Think ahead about some areas of interest and concern that you can probe in their lives. Offer personal affirmation and encouragement for ways they are growing up and maturing. Share your vision for their lives as your children.

- **Spiritual Instructor** — It is easy for any homeschool to fall into a task orientation of just getting the schoolwork done. But WholeHearted Learning as described in this book is not just an educational program—it is, we believe, a full expression of what it means to be a Christian family. Whether you wear your spiritual instructor hat in the morning or in the evening, your words of blessing, encouragement, inspiration, prayer, and instruction will help your children know that their homeschooling is about more than just schoolwork...it is about God's work. Speak that into their hearts.

Just as in the OT era, the teaching that Scripture finds significant is not that which provides information alone, but also the teaching that creates disciples who live in responsive obedience to God's will...[To] be a teacher one must have taken the external Word into the heart, so that it finds expression in a godly life.

— Lawrence O. Richards, *Expository Dictionary of Bible Words*, Zondervan, 1985

IN OUR HOME

There is a nearly universal experience shared by homeschooling dads. I (Clay) call it the "so many hours, so little time" syndrome. What I find happening in my own life is an acceleration of projects that need to be done yesterday or sooner and steadily expanding needs for me to be involved in the lives of my children. It seems there are always too many things to do and too little time to do them. The only solution I have found is a business management approach. If I don't actually schedule activities, I end up getting involved in whatever is most urgent or visible. So I put my kids on the calendar and show them when and what I'll be doing with them. Then I am almost certain to do it because I have made a specific commitment. You may not be that structured, but if you find you are more involved in projects than with your children, try the calendar. It can help!

Train a child in the way he should go, and when he is old he will not turn from it.

— Proverbs 22:6

Fathers, do not exasperate your children; instead, bring them up in the training and instruction of the Lord.

— Ephesians 6:4

The Life-giving Father

Way back in section 1, we talked about "The Biblical Case for Home Nurture" (page 46). Earlier in this chapter we examined Ephesians 6:4 to reveal a nuance of meaning not apparent in the common translation (page 271). "Fathers...bring up your children" can just as well be rendered "Fathers...nurture your children." Paul's admonition to fathers was to feed and nourish their children with godly training and personal instruction that was to be "of the Lord." Children need the life of Christ not just from the Word of God, the Scriptures, but also from the Word of God, the Savior, who lives in their father's heart. It's usually the moms who are called life-givers because of Eve's name meaning "the mother of all the living" (Genesis 3:20). But according to Paul, dads are also life-givers.

Life-giving is not the natural motivation of most dads, though. Notice that Paul has to rebuke the Ephesian fathers and command them to be life-givers to their children. They apparently were being passive about being a new kind of father, and they were failing to feed their children spiritually. Perhaps they were still following the Roman custom of *patria protestas*, the "power of a father" that gave them absolute authority to do whatever they wanted with their children with impunity. Paul corrects their unbiblical thinking, reminding them that their parenting is now "of the Lord," that God has authority in their lives, and that they have an obligation to their children as Christian fathers. Perhaps we fathers today can inadvertently slip into a similar of-the-father parenting mindset, rationalizing our passivity and laziness as a dad by whatever excuses the non-Christian culture around us uses. "When in Rome, do as the Romans do." But may it never be!

Let me suggest a very simple way to think about what it means to become a life-giving father. In the New Testament, God's grace is his goodness expressed to mankind. In many ways, grace is our spiritual food, and we cannot live as Christians without it. You need God's grace, your children need God's grace, and as a father you can feed them with God's grace. There are three biblical ways by which we can personally and regularly receive God's grace. If you simply look for ways every day to open your children to these channels of God's grace, you will be a life-giving father, and you will have the satisfaction of seeing your children nourished and growing in the Lord.

- **God's Word (God speaks to you)** — Make it a daily habit to read your Bible and then to share with your children a verse or passage from your reading and how God spoke to you through it. You don't need to teach it; just talk about it. Write out a special verse on an index card as your verse for each child.

- **Prayer (you speak to God)** — Invite your children to pray with you. Let them hear what you talk to God about so they can learn from you how to relate to God. Let your words be words they can use to talk to God. If you are comfortable praying while they listen in, they will become comfortable praying.

- **Fellowship (God speaks through others)** — Practice biblical fellowship with your children—talk with them about the Lord, ask questions, share testimony of God's grace in your life. Include them in spiritual fellowship in your home, both to be encouraged and to share encouragement. Engage them with others in Christ's body.

MOTHER — The Heart of the Home

The connection of a mother and a child is deeply physical, emotional, and even spiritual. When her egg is fertilized, a new life is conceived, and it begins to grow within her, that new mother's body begins to change and adapt from the first moments of cellular mitosis. The mystery of conception, gestation, and birth is not just about the new life growing within her but also about her body becoming a life-giving vessel for her baby. To say that a baby changes everything is true on every level of a mother's life. It changes not just things, but it also changes her—she will never be the same. Once the baby is born, hormonal and other physiological processes will create a natural bond between the mother and her child. It can be resisted, even rejected, but it cannot be denied.

That bonding, though, goes both ways. By God's design, children will always sense at some level a special connection to their mother that gives her a unique voice and influence in their lives and hearts. If properly cultivated, developed, and understood within the context of God-given personality drives (see chapter 8), it is a powerful source of influence. It might be said that a father must ask for a child's heart (Proverbs 23:26), but a mother already has it. It is not biblical terminology, but it makes sense to us to call a mother the "heart of the home." In the homeschooling home, she has the unique opportunity to be the relational heartbeat of the family as she interacts with her children throughout the day. She has nearly constant access to their hearts.

However, your influence as a homeschooling mom won't come from reading all the right books on motherhood, listening to the latest parenting experts, using the "best" homeschooling materials, or being the best homemaker. It will come because of your faithfulness—because your "mom heart" is open to God and seeking what he wants you to do as a woman, wife, and mother. Faithfulness is simply learning to see with God's eyes and seize with godly hands the hundreds of small opportunities you have every day to influence your children—to shape their values and attitudes, build their faith, discipline their disobedience, inspire their genius, nurture their emotions, train their habits, cultivate their character, and set their feet on the path of righteousness. It is those seized moments of godly influence in your children's hearts that will make you the heart of the home.

Being that faithful mother may seem like an idealistic goal, but it is really a very realistic challenge. That is why so many mothers confess that the homeschooling lifestyle is so much harder than they had imagined. It is demanding and constant, and with only a few exceptions, there is little time off from the day-to-day responsibility of caring for your children from the time they get up in the morning until the time they go to sleep at night. The reality of homeschooling is that God is asking you to become a servant to your children—to be willing to sacrifice your time, body, energy, emotions, and expectations for them. That takes more than natural strength—it takes supernatural strength. It takes the kind of faithfulness that comes only from trusting God and depending upon his grace every day. It takes you being willing to become the heart of your home. But that's exactly how God wants you to live! Faithfulness is simply saying, "I can do everything through him who gives me strength" (Philippians 4:13). It is knowing that "the eyes of the Lord range throughout the earth to strengthen those whose hearts are fully committed to him" (2 Chronicles 16:9) and wanting to be one of those he sees. Being the heart of your home is having God's heart for your family and serving their hearts for God.

She speaks with wisdom, and faithful instruction is on her tongue. She watches over the affairs of her household and does not eat the bread of idleness. Her children arise and call her blessed; her husband also, and he praises her: "Many women do noble things, but you surpass them all." Charm is deceptive, and beauty is fleeting; but a woman who fears the LORD is to be praised. Give her the reward she has earned, and let her works bring her praise at the city gate.

— Proverbs 31:26-31

If I could only encourage mothers to follow one principle of wisdom in their relationship with their children, it would be that of cultivating fervent, intimate love with each of their children. When children feel loved and cherished by the parents who brought them into the world, they have enduring stability and a security that provides them with groundwork for understanding the God of the universe who so loves us. Love is the most important foundation for learning to believe in God.

— Sally Clarkson, *The Mom Walk*, Harvest House, 2007

There is no nobler career than that of motherhood at its best. There are no possibilities greater, and in no other sphere does failure bring more serious penalties...To attempt this task unprepared and untrained is tragic, and its results affect generations to come. On the other hand there is no higher height to which humanity can attain than that occupied by a converted, heaven-inspired, praying mother.

— Anon., quoted by Elisabeth Elliot, *The Shaping of a Christian Family*, Word, 1992

The mother's heart is the child's schoolroom.

— Henry Ward Beecher (1813-1887), American clergyman and reformer

So God created man in his own image, in the image of God he created him; male and female he created them. God blessed them and said to them, "Be fruitful and increase in number; fill the earth and subdue it. Rule over the fish of the sea and the birds of the air and over every living creature that moves on the ground."

— Genesis 1:27-28

The task of building our homes into places of beauty and life that will feed the hearts, souls, and minds of our children is the most comprehensive task to which God has called us as mothers. We are called quite literally to be "home makers"—to plan and shape a home environment that provides our families with both a safe resting place and a launching pad for everything they do in the world.

— Sally Clarkson, *The Mission of Motherhood*, WaterBrook Press, 2003

Your Mission of Motherhood

If you have children, you have a mission from God. You are a missionary. Your mission is so necessary, so critical, that God has entrusted it to you alone. No one else can accept the mission or fulfill it in the way that you alone can do. God has sent you not to a place that will be foreign and fearful to you but to a place that you already love and cherish—a place that you want to know and influence more than anywhere else in this world. God has sent you on a mission into the heart of your child.

When you became a mother for the first time, you probably sensed that mission of motherhood but may not have been able to put words to it. In a Christian culture that has neglected the high calling of motherhood for too long, that should not be a surprise. A good starting place is a short verse in Proverbs that is like a preamble to the mission: "The wise woman builds her house…" (14:1a). With that new child in your arms, you know you want to build a house for him or her—not a literal structure, but a spiritual home. It's your house to build, but you know you need a blueprint. This section is a heartfelt attempt to put that plan into words and to show how it can be fulfilled by loving, teaching, training, and modeling the reality of God for your children in your home.

The mission for every godly mother, though, requires continual refreshing. The mission-minded mother knows that what she does with her children in her home domain will affect generations to come. If her heart is not constantly turned to God's design for her life, her mission can be easily sidetracked. Satan knows this, and that is why he has used feminism, culture, peer pressure, materialism, and media to tempt mothers away from God's design. To keep focused on the mission, you need to strengthen your heart.

- **Your Heart for God** — Loving God is not just a strong desire or feeling for him; it is seeking to know and please him. It is your love for God that will fuel your ability to love your children as God calls you to do. Your heart for God will drive you to him every day to fill up your spirit with his presence and Word so you will have the emotional, physical, and spiritual resources needed to fulfill your mission of motherhood.

- **Your Heart for Children** — Children are an expression of the heart of God. He loves them and created mothers so they would love them too. Your body and biology are divinely designed to bear, nurture, bond with, and love your children. As you understand that perfect design and accept it as God's blessing for you and your children, you strengthen your heart for them and reflect the heart of God to them.

- **Your Heart for Home** — Your home, by God's design, is where your children will experience the reality of God and grow into adults who know and follow him. As you learn to value your home as God does, you will discover limitless possibilities for expressing his creativity and bringing his life into your family—delightful meals prepared, books read and cherished, traditions celebrated, relationships cultivated.

- **Your Heart for Eternity** — The heartbeat of the mission a motherhood is a heart for eternity. It is the realization that being a mommy is not just a temporal role to fulfill, but rather that it is a strategic part of God's kingdom work in this world. You are not just raising children so they can make a living but so they can make a life for God. If you want them to be world-changers, they need to see your heart for eternity.

Your Ministry of Motherhood

If mission is your calling as a mother, think of ministry as your doing. Jesus had an overarching mission for his life—to reconcile God and man—but he lived it out every day in hands-on ministry. "For even the Son of Man did not come to be served, but to serve, and to give his life as a ransom for many" (Mark 10:45). He had a mission to fulfill that would take him to the cross, but it is his ministry done in people's hearts and lives that we imitate now—loving, touching, forgiving, healing, teaching, praying, encouraging, inspiring, leading, and more. Nowhere is that better seen than in how Jesus related personally and purposefully to his disciples. His mission drove his ministry in their lives—all his doing was intentional, focused on building close and loving relationships and on giving them wisdom and understanding, all so they would be willing to give their lives for his gospel and his kingdom. He won their hearts through ministry so he could win their minds for his message and mission. Isn't that what we want to do with our children? If so, then you can model your own ministry of motherhood after Jesus and his disciples. Following are just a few ways to be like Jesus:

- **Jesus was gracious.** Jesus touched those who were considered untouchable to show them grace—the poor, the broken, lepers, prostitutes, tax collectors, women. We model Jesus for our children by reaching out to the poor and oppressed, serving the homeless, helping those in need. We give our children the same grace.

- **Jesus was a servant.** Jesus served all people, especially his disciples—he knew their needs, he washed their feet in the upper room, he cooked breakfast for them after the resurrection. We show our children his servant nature by anticipating and providing for their needs, serving special meals, and giving up our expectations for them.

- **Jesus was compassionate.** Jesus saw the crowds and felt compassion—he met their needs, taught them, and was with them. We model Jesus for our children by taking meals to shut-ins, helping neighbors, and serving the community. We show our children his compassion by soothing hurts, having sympathy, and meeting their needs.

- **Jesus was encouraging.** Jesus encouraged his disciples—he spoke words of truth and life just to them, encouraged Peter when he failed him, affirmed their hearts and abilities, believed in them. We show our children his encouragement by believing in them, affirming gifts and abilities, and cheering good character and godly choices.

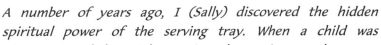

IN OUR HOME

A number of years ago, I (Sally) discovered the hidden spiritual power of the serving tray. When a child was struggling with an issue or needed special attention, the serving tray became a special tool for ministry. I would carefully select a favorite decorated tray and load it up with love—colorful napkin, tiny lit candle, a cup of hot chocolate or tea in a special mug, buttery cinnamon toast, a Scripture or quote, and a mommy card of loving thoughts. Of course, I would be "on" the tray, too, for a "Mom & me" tea time. It was an opportunity to serve my child and be Jesus to them by telling them how much I loved, appreciated, or believed in them.

Likewise, teach the older women to be reverent in the way they live, not to be slanderers or addicted to much wine, but to teach what is good. Then they can train the younger women to love their husbands and children, to be self-controlled and pure, to be busy at home, to be kind, and to be subject to their husbands, so that no one will malign the word of God.

— Titus 2:3-5

In the end, the measure of my success as a mother will not be how well I have taught my kids or cared for them but whether I have been faithful in helping them respond to God's call on their lives. Seeing my children develop a heart for God's service and begin to find their own place of ministry in the world is a reachable goal for me as a mother, because God has designed me to fulfill this purpose.

— Sally Clarkson, *The Ministry of Motherhood*, WaterBrook Press, 2004

For this reason also, since the day we heard of it, we have not ceased to pray for you and to ask that you may be filled with the knowledge of His will in all spiritual wisdom and understanding, so that you will walk in a manner worthy of the Lord, to please Him in all respects, bearing fruit in every good work and increasing in the knowledge of God; strengthened with all power, according to His glorious might, for the attaining of all steadfastness and patience; joyously giving thanks to the Father, who has qualified us to share in the inheritance of the saints in Light.

— Colossians 1:9-12 (NASB)

We were made to enjoy life and our Creator, and we were meant to choose to live in His beauty and provision...When I choose to notice, every day, the beauty of my children instead of the duties my children bring my way, I am worshipping God.

— Sally Clarkson, *The Mom Walk*, Harvest House, 2007

I approach God's throne so he can give me all the grace I need to give my children all the life they need.

— Sally Clarkson, *Seasons of a Mother's Heart*, Apologia Press, 2009

Walking with God as a Mother

Walking with God as a mother is like setting out on a long walk in the mountains in real life. Your walk can be refreshing and exhausting, delightful and difficult, inspiring and tiring. It may not always be what you expected when you started out, but it will always move you forward, deeper, higher. You never stay in one place when you walk with God, and you're never quite sure where you're going, but you know you are never lost. It will be a longer, harder walk than you anticipated, but it will be worth it. When you purpose to walk with God as a mother, you are choosing to live spiritually and supernaturally. You determine that you are going to "walk by faith, not by sight" (2 Corinthians 5:7, NASB). You acknowledge every day that motherhood is a life of faith and that you need God to be with you, not just for your sake but also for your children's sakes. If you follow these signs on the path that is your "mom walk," God will be with you all the way.

- **P = Purpose** — The mom walk is purposeful. No matter what obstacles and challenges you encounter on your walk as a mom, you can know that God has a purpose for your life—to make you more like Christ. If you know God is with you, challenges can become opportunities to trust him rather than reasons to be depressed or discouraged. As you grow in Christ, you will be a testimony of faith to your children.

- **A = Assurance** — If purpose is knowing where you're going, then assurance is knowing who is with you. There will be times of difficulty or darkness on your walk, but that is when you can rest in the assurance of God's promises to you in his Word— to be with you, to give you wisdom, to strengthen you, to give you grace in every situation. Assurance is knowing that God sees you, even when you can't see him.

- **T = Trust** — If assurance is knowing who walks with you, then trust is knowing that you can depend on him. Trusting God is taking hold of his hand, letting him lead you on, waiting for his provision, and believing in his ability to get you safely to wherever you should be. Trust is the attitude of complete dependence that will produce the peace in your spirit that you long for as a mother. It's believing that God is in control.

- **H = Heart** — If trust is depending on God, then heart is living fully in his presence. Your heart is a complex spiritual place of trust, fear, love, anger, belief, and doubt. You long for many things, but God alone can truly satisfy those needs. He knows your heart and all of its limitations, dreams, and desires. As you live in his presence and find his grace and love, your heart will find the fulfillment it longs for...in him.

IN OUR HOME

In order for me to have the heart for my mom walk with God, I realized very early that I needed to make the habit of my daily time in his Word something that would encourage me to be faithful. I put a comfortable Queen Anne recliner near a window with a nice view. I filled a beautiful basket with lovely books, magazines, and Bible study guides for moms. I placed a small vase of flowers, a favorite picture of my family, and a special tea cup on a small table next to my chair. I made a special place that invited my heart to come every day and meet with God in that place.

Following God's Heart for Moms

Mothers were in the heart of God at the Creation. Motherhood is not just the necessary byproduct of marriage and becoming "one flesh" but is the very heart of God's design for the family—the pinnacle of his creative work that he blessed and declared to be "very good" (Genesis 1:28, 31). Sin would soon distort his perfect design, but it remains part of his image that is stamped on our spirits. Adam acknowledged a mother's special place in God's creative work when he "named his wife Eve, because she would become mother of all the living" (Genesis 3:20). She was divinely designed to fulfill with the man God's creation mandate to "be fruitful and multiply, and fill the earth" (Genesis 1:28, NASB). Every part of the female body that God designed is an expression of his heart for the special creature called "woman" and her pivotal role in his eternal plan for mankind.

But American culture no longer considers motherhood to be a divine calling, strategic in God's biblical plan and invested with eternal significance. Now motherhood is simply a biological option to consider (whether in marriage or not) or just one commitment of many in a modern woman's life. As a Christian homeschooling mother, though, you are pursuing a higher calling for motherhood. The world around you, and even Christian culture, no longer supports or affirms God's design for mothers. It has lost its heart for biblical motherhood. To keep your own mom heart in this time, you need to have a clear understanding of how the design for motherhood was in the heart of God at the creation, before the Fall. Look at Genesis 1-3 to find the heart of God for mothers:

- **It's a heart that bears and declares the image of God.** Motherhood is an expression of the very nature of God himself. The image of God in you, though distorted by sin, makes every act of motherhood meaningful and strategic. (1:26-27)

- **It's a heart that colabors for God with her husband.** The man and woman receive God's mandate to "rule over" creation together. They share in his purpose for their lives as a couple and colabor to fulfill his charge to them. (1:26)

- **It's a heart that values having and embracing children.** God values children. The purest essence of biblical motherhood is a heart for children. They are a blessing from God to be desired. (1:28)

- **It's a heart that works to influence and subdue her home and world.** Within the co-conservatorship over the earth shared with her husband, the woman's primary domain to rule over and subdue will be her children and her home. (1:28)

- **It's a heart that looks for God's blessing and affirms his goodness.** God called his new family "very good" and blessed them. The mother who looks for, expects, and sees God's blessings will bring his presence and reality into her home. (1:28, 31)

- **It's a heart that wants to be a godly wife and good partner.** A woman who fulfills her role as a godly wife will create a lasting and positive impact on the lives and hearts of her children to prepare them for marriage and family. (2:29-31)

- **It's a heart that seeks to give and celebrate life.** Life-giving is about giving birth biologically, but it also about a mother bringing God's life to her children and even to the world around her. It is about being a channel of God's grace. (3:20)

Can a mother forget the baby at her breast and have no compassion on the child she has borne?

— Isaiah 49:15

As apostles of Christ we could have been a burden to you, but we were gentle among you, like a mother caring for her little children.

— 1 Thessalonians 2:6-7

God blessed them and said to them, "Be fruitful and increase in number; fill the earth and subdue it."

— Genesis 1:28

When entering the corridors of heaven, finally meeting Jesus face to face, I do not want to arrive gasping, out of breath, desperate, barely making it over the finish line. Instead I want to enter resiliently with a hopeful, loving heart.

— Sally Clarkson, *Dancing with My Father*, WaterBrook Press, 2010

So I counsel younger widows to marry, to have children, to manage their homes and to give the enemy no opportunity for slander.

— 1 Timothy 5:14

There is a tension that God is asking me to acknowledge and accept—the tension between ideals and realities. True joy is found by living somewhere between the ideal life and daily realities. That is where Jesus meets me, where his Holy Spirit empowers, and where I learn how to live the Christian life with supernatural joy. To celebrate life is simply a choice.

— Sally Clarkson, *Seasons of a Mother's Heart*, Apologia Press, 2009

The Life-giving Mother

Most woman can give life as a mother, but not many will then become life-giving mothers. How often do you see a mother who has given life but then seems to do nothing to add living to the lives of her children? Her home is lifeless, and her children are just existing within its walls. It breaks your heart. As descendants of Eve, whose name means "life-giver," it could be argued that the quality of life-giving is a part of every woman's spiritual DNA. If that is the case, though, sin has corrupted it, and selfish living now gets in the way of selfless life-giving. To be a life-giving mother is to choose to give life to your husband and children by becoming a source of God's grace and freedom to them and by bringing his life into your home in any way you can. Being a life-giving mother will be a daily, even momentary, decision. You know a life-giving mother when you see one (and when you are one), yet you don't know exactly how to define her. To help you become more life-giving at home, here is a simple descriptive acrostic for the life you give:

- **L = Love and Liberty** — The first and strongest mark of a life-giving mother is love. There is life in loving acceptance, appreciation, forgiveness, patience, and gentleness. Children long to be loved just as they are, and with that love comes liberty. Life-giving sets people free to be what God wants them to be.

- **I = Inspiration and Imagination** — A life-giver fills her home with inspiring truth and rich stories of God's greatness, heroes for Christ, what God can do, and all that is good in life. She frees and feeds the imagination to fly to new skies through inspiring art, poetry, and music. No good and godly thought is off limits to ponder and discuss.

- **F = Fun and Feasting** — God has given us all things to enjoy, which includes food, drink, and laughter. A life-giving mother makes her home a place of feasting, sharing wonderful food around her dinner table. She fills her home with fun, frivolity (to balance unrelenting seriousness), and adventures that fill and delight the senses.

- **E = Engaging and Enjoying** — A life-giving mother uses her home to engage the hearts and minds of her family and enjoy the life God has given them. With so many ways to stimulate the mind, the senses, and the spirit, she sees her home as a God-given domain into which she brings the art of living and the God of life.

IN OUR HOME

I (Sally) remember always wanting to be a life-giving mother. I have had to overcome my own selfish nature, but choosing to make my home a place of life and seeing my children prefer it over any other place in the world (and we've been to a lot of them) has been the most rewarding part of my motherhood. I have gone through many seasons in my spirit as a life-giving mother—sunny springs, easy-going summers, gentle falls, and dark winters—but wherever my emotions led me, I never gave up on reading aloud, hot chocolates on the couch, singing loudly as we worked, family walks in the woods, talking until past midnight, playing games together, watching favorite movies, and making my home the "bestest place" of all.

— Chapter 16 —

Structure: Keeping the Homeschooling Together

Subduing Your Home Domain

A lovely garden is a delight. Civilization started in a garden, planted for Adam by God in Eden, which in Hebrew means "delight" (Genesis 2:8, 15). There is something delightful about a well-organized, freshly tended, carefully cultivated, and bountifully fruitful garden. However, we wouldn't have reason to know that it was delightful if we hadn't also seen unkempt, overgrown, weed-infested, unfruitful plots of vegetation and found them not so delightful. We know intuitively that carelessly throwing seeds onto unprepared ground and then just waiting for things to grow will not make a garden. Things may grow, but they probably won't be delightful or fruitful. A garden is created. A true garden says that someone loved the soil and seed enough to invest time and to make a serious effort to make things grow orderly and well. Someone is committed to that garden.

Your home is the garden God has prepared for you, and your children are the seeds God has placed in your hands. The world is full of children whose parents simply cast them to the winds and hope they will find roots and grow. Their gardens too often are not delights. You have the opportunity to care for and cultivate your home garden so that it will be a delight to others who see its bountiful fruit (Psalm 128). Genesis 2 is all about a garden, how God created Adam and Eve and placed them in it, and gave them the mandate to "subdue it" and "rule over" it (Genesis 1:28). It is a picture of our challenge even to-day—to subdue our homes (to prepare the soil for the seeds by bringing order) and to rule over them (to work the soil to make the seeds grow well by maintaining order).

As a Christian homeschooling parent, you are already committed to growing a bountiful and fruitful garden in the lives of your children. But growing a delightful garden will require you, like Adam, to "work it and take care of it" (Genesis 2:15). No one has to remind you that your home domain can quickly get out of control and need to be subdued. That's why you need some principles, priorities, and convictions that will help you bring order and structure to your lifestyle. It's like laying out a garden so you'll know what goes where, when, how much, and what will be needed to keep it all healthy. You cannot cultivate an orderly home garden until you define some grids and lines for your life.

Will every homeschool parent's grids look the same? Of course not! Every home will be different because God works with different personalities, backgrounds, resources, and circumstances. You have freedom in the Holy Spirit to figure out what is right for your family and to follow his lead confidently in faith. Every home garden is different and reflects the unique creativity and purpose of its gardeners, but if a garden is cultivated, tended, and cared for with love and commitment, it will all be healthy, fruitful, and delightful. Homeschooling should be delightful not just to you but also to the world.

The wise woman builds her house, but with her own hands the foolish one tears hers down.

— Proverbs 14:1

By wisdom a house is built, and through understanding it is established; through knowledge its rooms are filled with rare and beautiful treasures.

— Proverbs 24:3-4

God almighty first planted a garden, and indeed, it is the purest of human pleasures.

— Francis Bacon (1561-1626), English philosopher, statesman, scientist, and author

There are many varieties of personalities and possibilities of home organization. Each of us simply has to find the combination of routines that suits our lifestyle and desires. I tend to be artistic and visionary—in other words, organization is not my strong suit. I love developing the ambience in my home, but keeping everything under control has been a challenge for me.

— Sally Clarkson, *The Mission of Motherhood*, WaterBrook Press, 2003

285

I know I can't neglect the basic educational foundations my children will need for a full and meaningful life—reading and understanding the written word, thinking clearly and wisely, communicating ably in speech and in writing, being competent in math. But I am determined not to neglect the basic spiritual truth that will undergird and give meaning to that education—seek first the kingdom of God and his righteousness (see Matthew 6:33). A well-educated person will be useful to God only if he is focused on God's purposes.

— Sally Clarkson, *Seasons of a Mother's Heart*, Apologia Press, 2009

Homeschool on Purpose

If you don't take some time each year to remember and renew your reasons to homeschool, you may soon find yourself going through the motions by default rather than living in faith by definition. When you homeschool by default, you put yourself on a downward path to defeat. When you lose sight of the "Why" of homeschooling, you will lose touch with the "Who," and you'll soon find yourself wondering, "What is the point?" That's when moms who started with such high ideals and desires end up giving up in defeat and despair. The best way to avoid that destructive downward spiral is to take time before each school year to review and renew your purpose for homeschooling. Take some time away in a quiet place to pray that God will clarify your vision as a mother for homeschooling and renew your purpose for doing it for him. If it helps, write out a personal purpose statement for your life as a homeschooling mother. You can even sign and date it as a tangible expression of your commitment to doing God's will. When you hit a low time during the year, you can reread it to renew your faith. Don't fall by default into defeat! Be definitive in faith about your life. Decide each year to homeschool on purpose.

Know Your Purpose

As a Christian homeschooling mother, you need to have a very clear sense of your purpose in life—why God has given you a husband and children and why you are at home doing what you are doing. The reason for knowing your purpose is not just to be able to explain or defend your lifestyle to others but to be able to better express it in your day-to-day living. Your husband and children will be blessed if they know that your life is directed by a biblical purpose. Your confidence as a mother after God's heart will be a source of strength for them. What you believe about God's design for mothers will determine how you live, and how you live will be the expression of whatever you consider to be God's path of greatest blessing for you. Consider the following biblical purposes for mothers as you define God's purpose for your life.

- **To Bring Order to Your Home** — You have a mandate from God to bring order to your home (to "subdue" it). By God's perfect design, it is your primary domain of influence, and your divine calling is to bring all aspects of your home life—marriage, children, meals, decor, schedule, environment—into subjection to the design for living that God has revealed in his Word. If you want to find fulfillment as a mother, you will find it only in the biblical pattern of motherhood. It's the only way you'll ever feel at home as a mother.

- **To Nurture Your Children** — Like Eve, the "mother of all the living," you have the God-given ability to impart life to your children—not just physiological life, but joyful, abundant, and eternal life. You will help place them on the path of life in Christ and teach them how to walk it in faith. You will help gently guide them into a living relationship with Jesus, train them in godly character, and instruct them in biblical truth. What your children become will be in large part because of your nurturing, life-giving influence in their lives. Your children will look to you for sustenance, and God has given you the privilege of caring for their needs.

- **To Cultivate Relationships** — God has uniquely equipped women for relationship. Your children will learn much about how to love God and especially how to love others through you. Ministry begins with a commitment to relationship that can be modeled in your home—through opening your home in hospitality, ministering to others in need, or even just through kindness shown in Christ's name.

- **To Grow in Maturity and Obedience** — Your example of being "self-controlled and pure" (Titus 2:5) not only creates a pattern for your children to follow but also results in a home that is peaceful and Christ-centered. A mother growing in maturity and in obedience to God will have a tremendous impact on her children. Your example of virtue will live on in your children and even your children's children.

- **To Respect and Help Your Husband** — The Christian life is based on the principle of submission—husbands to God, wives to husbands, children to parents, church members to church leaders, citizens to government, employees to employers. By submitting to your husband, you become a living illustration for your children of what submission looks like. God wants you to love your husband by showing him respect and being his helper. Your attitude toward your husband (and his towards you) will say more to your children than a hundred lessons.

Know Your Priorities

Everyone has priorities. If someone wants to know your priorities, they need only observe how you spend your time. It makes little difference what you say your priorities are—it's what you do that reveals your true priorities. Of all the opportunities and options before you, your priorities are the ones you should and must do, so you do. The essence of setting priorities is limitation—you must voluntarily limit some things of less importance to accomplish the things that are most important. Your most pressing limitation is time. You have only one opportunity to "train a child in the way he should go" (Proverbs 22:6), and once the window of opportunity closes as your child enters young adulthood, you can never open it again. However, if you invest yourself in your child's life, shining as much light as you can in the open windows of his heart during childhood, then you can count on God's plan that "when he is old he will not turn from it." It all comes down to priorities, and setting priorities means accepting some limitations.

- **Limit your expectations.** There are always other things that you would love to do—working, eating out with friends, a sport or hobby, shopping—things that other mothers with their children in school have time to do. But as a homeschooling mother you have chosen a different set of priorities. Your priorities now revolve around doing everything you can to raise wholehearted Christian children. Your expectations about life must change accordingly.

- **Limit your commitments.** Knowing that your priorities are different will limit what you will commit your time and family to doing. Your priorities will lead you to say yes to some things and no to others, even if those others are attractive, desirable things. You are simply maximizing your efforts and reducing unnecessary commitments in order to do God's will for your life. Whatever you give up will be compensated for by the blessings you gain.

- **Limit your objectives.** There will never be enough time to do all that you want to do in your homeschool, so don't even try to! It will take everything you can muster just to stick to your priorities and still live a balanced Christian life. It takes time—lots of it—to build close, productive relationships with your children. You need time to communicate, build trust, and love them; to listen, talk, and answer their questions; to offer counsel, advice, comfort, and encouragement. Limiting your objectives allows you more time to do fewer things more effectively.

- **Limit your activities.** You need to be at home building an atmosphere that is calm, secure, and inviting. It is too easy to become distracted by too many outside activities that rob you of the brief and fleeting time you have to influence your children's minds and hearts. Put personal goals, desires, and activities on hold for a later season of life—this is the time (while they're young) and the place (at home) that your children need you most. Limit your activities and spend your time at home.

- **Limit your complaints.** This is perhaps the most difficult limitation. It is certainly tempting to want your friends to know the limitations you are experiencing as a homeschooling mother, but the more you give yourself permission to complain about your life, the more you will give yourself reasons to give up if things get too hard. Train yourself to limit those complaints and express the blessings instead.

...But one thing I do: Forgetting what is behind and straining toward what is ahead, I press on toward the goal to win the prize for which God has called me heavenward in Christ Jesus.

— Philippians 3:13-14

Homeward Bound

New homeschooling moms are often over-concerned about what their children might be missing by being home. This insecurity often leads a mom to overcompensate by getting her children involved in too many activities. The result, of course, is even less time at home and, therefore, even less direct influence on her children—the very reason most begin homeschooling in the first place!

This One Thing

Try to use the "this one thing I do" principle—one church ministry, one lesson, one sport, one night out, and so on. Limit unnecessary distractions in your home—telephone, television and video, e-mail and the Internet, magazines, frivolous meetings—that compete with your highest "this one thing" priorities.

Just Say "I'll Let You Know"

Make it a habit not to commit to anything on the first hearing. Simply say, "Let me ask my husband." This one little phrase will reap bushels of time by keeping you from making those regretted, hasty commitments that are neither purposeful nor strategic. Learning not to say yes at the first hearing is the first step in becoming proficient in the homeschooling skill of strategic under-commitment.

To man belong the plans of the heart, but from the LORD comes the reply of the tongue. All a man's ways seem innocent to him, but motives are weighed by the LORD. Commit to the LORD whatever you do, and your plans will succeed.

— Proverbs 16:1-3

Planning Help

The planning forms included in the appendix will help you get a handle on weekly, monthly, and quarterly planning. There is also a calendar/planner blank that you can use. The forms will help you get in the habit of planning and help you establish educational goals and routines.

All in a Year's Work

Flexible year-round schooling allows you to strike while the iron is hot. During the indoor seasons when the weather prevents going outside as much, focus more on drill and workbook work. During the outdoor seasons, focus more on field trips, nature walks, and outdoor learning experiences. The key is flexibility. Teach several weeks, then take a break when life demands it. Take breaks for holidays, out-of-town company, short trips, and catch-up weeks, then return to teaching. Steady progress is the measure of your success: Have you accomplished in a year what you planned to finish?

Plan Away

Plan a way to get away to plan. Find a time when you can leave the children with someone and you and your spouse can go for an extended breakfast, evening, or overnight to plan for the coming weeks or months. Trade off with another homeschool family for overnight childcare. It's good for your family and good for your marriage!

Know Your Plans

When you take the time to plan your life, it is a tangible expression that you are confident and secure enough about your priorities to actually do something about them. By making and following plans, you are making yourself accountable to what God has put on your heart to do. It is an act of faith, so always cover your planning in prayer, asking for God's guidance and wisdom. You'll never be able to perfectly judge all your own motives, so just do the best you can and then move ahead in faith. As the Proverb says, "Commit to the LORD whatever you do, and your plans will succeed" (16:3).

Plan your life to accomplish your purposes.

- **Plan with your husband.** Whether you can do the day-to-day micro-planning together or you just review your individual plans regularly together on a macro-planning level, make it a habit to be partners in planning with your husband. It will affirm his role as head of the home, provide accountability and teamwork in your role as heart of the home, and strengthen your marriage.

- **Plan and evaluate as a way of life.** In order to be effective in home education, planning is a necessity. That does not mean every fifteen-minute segment of the day must be scheduled! It simply means that you should know at any time most of what you want to accomplish with your children and how you're going to do it this week, month, quarter, or year. Planning also lets you evaluate the things that haven't been accomplished so you can adjust your plans accordingly.

- **Use flexible year-round schooling.** Real life is not divided in neat little calendar blocks like in school. Flexible year-round schooling means letting real life set your schedule rather than trying to fit real life into a rigid schedule of weeks on and off, semesters, quarters, or whatever. Home is not school! Real life at home requires flexibility—don't create a rigid schedule that will set you up to fail!

- **Make small adjustments as you go.** Life changes, so count on the need to make adjustments to your plans along the way. It's better to make them earlier rather than put them off. It's just like adjusting the trajectory of a slightly off-target missile—the longer you wait to correct its course, the bigger the adjustment must be.

- **Keep a long-term perspective.** Learning is a process, not a procedure. Steady progress, not constant success, is the goal, and that takes time. Progress seems slower when your children are younger, but the reality is that they grow in spurts mentally just as they do physically. Learning to discern their pace and rhythm of learning takes time—time to see what comes easily to your children as well as what is slow to develop and time to give them individual attention. Perseverance, persistence, and patience are the keys to success in homeschooling. Keep your eye on the ultimate goal, not on each stride to be run.

- **Plan your work and work your plan.** Keep an eye on your plans so you'll know if you're making progress, but don't be a slave to them. Know what you want to accomplish, plan how to do it, then relax, live, learn, and enjoy your children. The goal is steady progress toward your goals, not doing it all at all costs.

Plan your home for homeschooling.

In order to homeschool well as a mother, your home must be at the center of your life—the hub of the wheel of life in your family. If you and your husband know what you want to accomplish in your children's lives and you are clear about your priorities, then your home will reflect that. Though it is the center of your life, your home should always be a means to an end, never an end in itself. In other words, it is a tool that you use to build and bless your family. It is your domain to rule over, but it's about more than just managing all the things you do there. You want your home to be the air you breathe as a homeschooling family. When your children think about home, it should be the same feeling as when they are in a lovely, outdoor setting on a beautiful day. You want the atmosphere and environment in your home to be just as inviting and soul-pleasing.

- **Atmosphere** — Atmosphere is the attitude of your home. It determines how your children feel about being at home—either uptight and anxious in an adult's world or free and relaxed in a child-friendly world. If you are holding onto *House Beautiful* ideals, they must inevitably give way to House Bountiful realities—the dinner table gives way to a craft, wall space gives way to papers and timelines, floor space gives way to a creative project, and shelf space gives way to books and creations. Every room, in some way, at some time, will be affected by the activities related to home education. You cannot avoid it—homeschooling is messy because children are messy. If you learn to accept messes, your children will feel more accepted too. Your relaxed attitude will determine the atmosphere.

- **Environment** — Environment is the setting of your home. It is whatever is around you that influences you or your children. We believe that children grow intellectually in an enriched home environment where they are surrounded by easily accessible books, creative options, music, and art. Intellectual curiosity is naturally cultivated in a home environment that encourages a child to read, explore, discover, question, observe, and learn. Wherever they turn, your children should run into something that is interesting, challenging, or stimulating. But the home environment also needs to be characterized by personal warmth and beauty so your children come to value the special place they'll remember as home. As with atmosphere, you are the key to creating a unique, personal environment in your home.

IN OUR HOME

When the Lord moved our young family to property in the country, he gave us the exciting opportunity to remodel a home to complement our home-centered approach to learning and life. A garage was transformed into our learning room, with floor-to-ceiling built-in bookshelves and desk units, a deep-shelved closet for games and creative stuff (the Lego Lab), and room for a large couch and computer corner. An enclosed porch became a combination breakfast nook and craft center (vinyl floor, of course). We invested, too, in an outdoor playground, especially for our two boys. And, just as important, we carved out a "tea and talk" sitting area in our bedroom. It was such a blessing to be in a homeschooling-friendly house.

Adapt-a-Home

If you have a home and don't plan to move, take a fresh look at your floor plan through a homeschooling lens. Ask what you need and then evaluate how your present house can meet those needs. If you decide to remodel, ask what you can do to improve both the atmosphere and the environment of your home for homeschooling. If you can't add a room, convert a garage (children are more important than cars!). Keep in mind that remodeling is an investment in your children.

House Plans

If you are in the market to build or to buy an existing home, establish some criteria for evaluating the house plans or houses you look at. Decide (1) what features will make the home work for you in homeschooling and (2) what features would work against you. You'll make trade-offs on the final decisions, but you'll move in knowing it is a homeschooling home.

Home for the Holidays

Use this annual calendar to plan monthly themes for teaching or devotions and for holiday celebrations.

January
- Sacrifice of Christ Month
- New Year's Day

February
- Love of Christ Month
- Presidents' Day; Valentine's Day

March
- Life of Christ Month
- St. Patrick's Day

April
- Lordship of Christ Month
- Easter/Resurrection Sunday

May
- Motherhood Month
- Mother's Day; Memorial Day

June
- Fatherhood Month
- Father's Day

July
- American Heritage Month
- Independence Day

August
- Family Heritage Month
- Family Day

September
- Missions Month
- Labor Day

October
- Christian History Month
- Reformation Day

November
- Christian Heritage Month
- Thanksgiving

December
- Birth of Christ Month
- Advent/Christmas

Plan your year around holidays, special days, and traditions.

Holidays, special days, and traditions should stand out as the bright yellow high-lighter-marked sections of your life story. They illustrate and accentuate the messages, values, and gifts that are unique to your family's Christian heritage. They also emphasize and reinforce the truths and convictions that you want to take root in the hearts of your children and provide them with rich food for their memories. Everything associated with holidays and traditions—decor, food, child-made crafts, music, readings, sharing, and more—creates an emotional anchor to hold memories deep in your children's hearts for a lifetime. Those anchors also become sources of stability and security for your children as they navigate the sea of life. Here are a few ideas for lowering anchors in their hearts.

- **Plan a Family Day.** Establish an annual Family Day to remember and celebrate God's faithfulness to your family (see facing page). Make it a special day that your family always looks forward to. Invite other family members or friends to be a part of your day. Show them how to have their own.

- **Tell family stories.** At all holidays and special days, encourage family members to tell stories about their lives, especially the older members of the family who are present. Tell stories of faith that relate to the holiday or even just add color and warmth to it. Tell stories of history or just humorous family stories. Encourage the children to share stories and memories too. Mealtime is a convenient time for storytelling. Always turn on a recorder when a family elder shares a story—you never know if you'll hear it again!

- **Plan a monthly theme.** Select a holiday or special theme for each month. Decorate your dining table accordingly and plan devotional projects around those days and themes. Use the weeks before certain holidays for an extended study or reading of a longer book. Holidays best suited for extended studies include Christmas (Advent), Easter, Independence Day, Reformation Day, and Thanksgiving.

- **Celebrate birthdays.** Turn birthdays into family celebrations. Invite families you are close to to join you for each child's birthday breakfast or dinner (whichever works best for you). Serve that child's favorite meal and have some special presents to commemorate their year. Then have everyone at the table share how they have seen the birthday child grow in maturity during the previous year, new skills and talents they have noticed, and what they especially like about him or her. Then spend some time praying for that child for the coming year. If you start this tradition early, be sure to record these times for their memory boxes.

- **Study holidays.** Use holidays and special days to reinforce current study emphases in history, Bible, or other subjects. Save special books and tapes for those times. For example, when studying the Civil War, read a biography about Lincoln for Presidents' Day.

- **Get everyone involved.** Create ways for everyone in the family—from the oldest right down to the very youngest—to have a significant role in any holiday celebrations. Everyone should be involved in some way. And always try to give special honor and recognition to the family elders (parents and grandparents).

- **Store the decor.** Make and use centerpieces and decorations that can be used every year. Whatever you purchase or make for a holiday, carefully store it in a clearly labeled box with a lid (such as a Bankers Box). You'll save yourself the energy of thinking of something all over again the next year! Just pull it out of the box, and you're ready for the season.

- **Make holiday crafts.** Holidays provide a meaningful opportunity for your children to do crafts that everyone will see and admire. Have them make decorations, decorate their rooms, make special place cards for the table, puff-paint t-shirts for everyone, or make special posters. And rather than buying overpriced greeting cards, have your children make their own cards for birthdays and holidays.

- **Build on past traditions.** Build on traditions whenever possible by repetition and familiarity. Use the same decorations, play and sing familiar songs, serve the same food, and do the same things. Repetition is a fundamental principle of learning. Repeated traditions become the moments which your children will remember most clearly and vividly and which will define their memories of childhood and you. Beyond just reinforcing memories, though, the assurance that "we do this every year" also creates a sense of stability and security in children.

IN OUR HOME

When our children were still young, we started the tradition of having an annual Family Day. We decided to make ours the Saturday before Labor Day. It was inspired by the account of Joshua's memorial stones which were to remind the Hebrew children of coming generations of God's power, faithfulness, sovereignty, and love (Joshua 4:19-24). We make it a whole day of family togetherness. We start off the day with a special breakfast (Mom's homemade whole-wheat cinnamon rolls). We read some scriptures on family and take a little time to affirm all the things we like about our family and one another. Then we get out the photo albums from the previous year or two and spend time just remembering the events of our lives. We normally prepare a fun picnic lunch and then go on an outing for the rest of the morning and into the afternoon. Later in the day we might play games or watch a good family movie. Then we have a special dinner to lead into our Family Day memorial stone time. First, we read the account of Joshua and the memorial stones to teach the principle of taking time and making a way to remember all the ways that God has been faithful. After the story, we all begin to share and discuss all the ways we see that God was faithful to us as a family in the year since the last Family Day. Each thing becomes a memorial stone of God's faithfulness written at the top of a piece of paper. Those are parceled out to different family members, who draw pictures on those papers to illustrate each of the memorial stones. We keep those memorial stones in a Family Day notebook and review them each year. We also select annual verses for each family member. We then write down prayer requests for the year ahead, pray, and end the day with a fun activity and a favorite dessert.

Holidays and Holy Days

Holidays are God's idea. He created several for the Jews to celebrate and reinforce the memory of what he had done and to teach the children. The Jews also created other holidays to celebrate God's work in their lives as a nation. Whatever the reason for the holiday, though, they were always more than just recreational—they were first and foremost educational. In the same way that the Jews followed God's pattern for new holidays, Christianity has developed its own holiday traditions. Holidays such as Christmas and Easter have no biblical mandate, but they are patterned after God's use of holidays as a way to remember and learn about God's actions in history and in our lives. Since the principle of the holiday is transcultural and universal, the Christian family can benefit from it as well. For the Christian homeschooling family, holidays can be an effective way of using the God-given seasonal cycles to remember and to learn. God is never opposed to traditions per se—only to empty traditions that serve no purpose for him. When our lives—including our holidays and traditions—reflect his reality, then he is honored (Romans 14:5-6a).

Future Moms and Dads Days

Use Mother's and Father's Days to talk about the joys of parenting and to talk to your children about being future parents. On Mother's Day, include your daughters as future mothers, with both Dad and sons honoring them. On Father's Day, include your sons as future fathers, with both Mom and daughters honoring them. Recognize your children's future roles as extended family and as the recipients and guardians of your family's heritage and values. Pray for their future spouses and children, that they would pass on your legacy.

Center on the Table

Plan ahead to make meaningful seasonal centerpieces for your table, such as:

- February/Presidents' Day — Lincoln Log cabin, picture of President Lincoln, pennies, books on Lincoln. Also for President Washington.
- July/Independence Day — Minutemen cut-outs, American flags, Declaration of Independence, books about the Revolutionary War.
- September/Missions Month — Globe, foreign stamps and coins, foreign artifacts and crafts, pictures and biographies of famous missionaries.

Set the Theme

Start making a list of theme ideas that you can use to make meals memorable. Creatively customize the meal and the table to emphasize the theme. A few ideas to get you started:

- When I Grow Up Night — Put a variety of doodads on the table to represent different professions, pursuits, and callings. Brainstorm occupational names for the meal (ex.: Fireman's Feast, Police Plate, etc.). Each child shares one or more thoughts of what they might want to be or do when they grow up. Parents also share what they think their children could become or do.
- Secret Mission Meal — Decorate your table with a secret agent, spy, or detective motif. First night, put everyone's name in one hat and missions (clean room, fix a treat, etc.) in another. Each person draws out a name and a secret mission. Each tries to fulfill the mission without being detected. Report on their missions the next night.
- God's Hands Night — Have everyone share how they have seen God's hands at work in their family during a one-week period. Decorate your table with a Bible/prayer theme and motif. Serve a simple meal.

Plan your days around mealtimes.

You have to eat every day, so make that time count. Use those 1,095 opportunities to be together each year to enhance your homeschooling and to impart your family's values and beliefs. Turn meal times into servants to accomplish your goals rather than just "eat and run" breaks. Whether it's cheese and crackers or pot roast and potatoes, each meal can be turned into a strategic learning session in your homeschool schedule—a memory-making hour of discussion, laughter, debate, Bible discovery, narration, book-talk, and life-in-progress wisdom and counsel.

Mealtime Memory Making

Our future fellowship with Jesus in heaven is pictured as a feast we will never forget. Make each meal a feast of food and fellowship your children will never forget.

- **Meals are anchors.** Every family's schedule is different, but it is important to sit down together to at least one leisurely meal each day. It's another one of those anchors in your children's lives that they will remember and cherish. When you do eat together, it only takes a little effort to enhance your time together.

- **Make each meal special.** When you eat at the table, whether the meal is casual or formal, show that it is an important occasion by setting a clean, attractive table with a full place setting. Be sure the dining area is clean and neat too.

- **Add personal touches.** Create an occasion with candlelight in the winter, a variety of background music, place cards with Scriptures or notes, a "You're special today!" red plate, or other memorable touches. Get in the habit of changing your centerpiece periodically to reflect study or holiday themes.

- **Be creative.** Create special theme nights, with or without advance notice to the rest of the family. Make them different, fun, and meaningful—"What I want to be when I grow up" night, Secret Mission Meal, "God's hands in our family" week, and so on. Decorate the table accordingly.

IN OUR HOME

While living in Europe, our family developed a taste for tea and for tea time! It followed us back to the States, and now Sunday afternoon tea time has become a regular, anticipated, rarely missed fixture in our week. Whether we're just having tea and cinnamon toast or a full-blown high tea with sandwiches, fruits, and a special dessert, we take time to set the table nicely and use our special Austrian tea set (a bit beaten now, but still beloved). We always put on some beautiful or interesting music to provide the proper ambience. Sometimes, we even practice being civilized, as though we were taking tea with the Queen and must at least appear that we know how to behave. To make it more enjoyable, we save some special books to be read only during tea time, such as James Herriott's stories, new illustrated storybooks we have discovered, or an intriguing novel. Everyone in the family looks forward to our Sunday afternoon tea time.

- **Keep books on the menu.** Keep several books nearby that can be read aloud. You will cover a lot of extra pages of good literature in a year just by getting in the habit of reading a chapter at the table occasionally. Linking good food and good stories is a good way to create a good memory! Have Dad read.

- **Make meals personal.** Regularly prepare special meals that your children will remember as "our family meals" (desserts, too!). Come up with fun, original meals and creative variations to old dishes. It puts the focus on the meal and not the food. Give names to the special dishes your family likes—Mama Mia Meatball Casserole, Papa's Pizza Bread, Shepherds' meal, Mom's Polish eggs, spaghetti pie, and such.

Dinner Table Discipleship

Mealtime is a natural time for Dad to lead family devotions or share some biblical thoughts and insights, whether they are planned or spontaneous. For a short time, he has a captive, quiet, relaxed audience, and they are all are in a listening state because they are eating. You can help to enhance those times by managing the table environs.

- **Word at Hand** — Keep a Bible, a Bible storybook, and devotional materials in sight and in reach. Accessibility helps to create both a devotional habit and spontaneity.

- **Questions at Hand** — Make a habit of writing down spiritual discussion questions or Scriptures with discussion questions on 3x5 index cards. Keep them in a handy file box so you can put them on the table with the rest of the meal. Then just have a child pick one randomly, read it out loud, and let the discussion begin.

- **Prayers at Hand** — Keep a prayer reminder list or prayer journal handy to stimulate prayer times. Also keep missionary letters at hand. When you pray for the meal, pray also for something from your list and for a missionary or ministry.

Tips for Table Talk

Good conversations don't just happen—they grow in well-cultivated soil. The following tips will create good soil for your table talk.

- **Be courteous and mannerly.** Being courteous and gracious toward others is an act of humility, honor, and service. Even proper table manners show that you respect others. Basic civil behavior is a prerequisite for civil, fruitful conversation.

- **Speak graciously.** All conversations should be with grace. Whatever is said should be said in love. Graciousness edifies. Always consider other people at the table. Be sensitive to what might offend, embarrass, or hurt someone's feelings.

- **Seek to build up others.** The goal of a discussion is never to make points or win arguments—it is to build up and encourage one another. A critical or contentious attitude can quickly poison a conversation. If it starts, don't let it continue.

- **Be respectful of all.** Each person at the table is due the same respect. No one's thoughts or opinions are better than another's. Everyone at the table should be able to participate in the topic of conversation—young children, teens, elders, visitors.

Table-talk ought to be such, in every family, as to make the hour of home meal-time one of the most attractive as well as one of the most beneficial hours of the day to all the children.

— H. Clay Trumbull, *Hints on Child Training*, 1890

Check My Manners

Make and photocopy a list of table manners you want your children to practice. Give them a copy of the list as a reminder. Occasionally, check off the manners on the list that are good and the ones that need improvement, and give it to them. Each family has its own standards for table manners. Some of them might include:

- Place your napkin in your lap before eating any food.
- Don't ever lean your elbows on the table.
- Sit up straight in your chair.
- Use your bread or a knife, not fingers, to push food.
- Clear your mouth completely before speaking.
- Take small bites of food.
- Chew quietly with your mouth closed.
- Sip your drink; don't gulp it.
- When something is needed, ask for it; don't reach.
- Keep your eating utensils on your plate.
- Always ask to be excused before leaving the table.
- Keep your free hand in your lap, not on the table.
- Always offer the last item on a food plate to others first.
- Eat whatever is put in front of you without complaint.
- Break your bread before eating it.
- Don't play with your food.
- Use a clean utensil, not your own, for serving.
- Wait for your mother or the hostess to eat before you begin eating.

Binder Minder and Finder

Forget files and folders for your basic homeschooling records and forms. Keep them all in a three-ring binder. It will be much easier to mind your records and to find them when needed if they are all in one place. Use tabbed dividers to organize your records either by categories of kinds of forms or by names of your children—whichever way makes more sense to you. You can either create a new binder for each school year (label the spines by year and store on a shelf), or you can empty and reuse the binder each year (remove the previous year's contents, put in a large manila envelope labeled by year, and store in a Bankers Box). You will feel much more in control of your home school if your most important records are always in one place and in easy reach.

Plan how to keep adequate records.

Keeping records won't necessarily improve the effectiveness of your teaching, but they will make you more credible to certain education officials. Records are an important defense against government intrusion into your homeschool. In some states, homeschoolers are required by law to make and keep certain records. Even so, you should feel obligated to keep only as much as what is or may be required by law. If you have administrative gifts or you actually enjoy keeping records, do what suits you the best. For nonadministrative home educators, though, as long as you are compliant with the law, there is really no compelling need to become compulsive about keeping educational records. Record-keeping should serve your needs, not the other way around.

- **Attendance** — An attendance record shows that your child was "in homeschool" on a given day and that some minimum level of schooling was done. As to the number of daily hours some states require, count anything that has educational value—actual study time, field trips, cooking, fixing things, computer, piano class and practice, sports, and arts and crafts. If it has a public school counterpart or equivalent, you should be able to count it toward your hours.

- **Curricula and Reading** — Keep each child's finished workbooks or a record of their progress and completion. Also, keep a list of books read by each child. In addition to its possible use to defend the credibility of your homeschool, your children will be greatly encouraged to see how many books they have read and to see the list growing. An informal record of field trips and real-life experiences might be useful too, especially if your child writes a report about it, but they are not necessary.

- **Health** — Keep a minimum record of family health care including vital statistics, check-ups, shot records, and so on. Check with your state as to what is required for your children. If your children have annual physicals, keep a file with those records.

- **Standardized Testing** — Keep a file for each child with the results of any standardized tests they have taken. Unless your state requires annual tests, every two years is sufficient to track your children's development.

IN OUR HOME

There is, of course, no such thing as a typical day in our home, or in any homeschooling home for that matter! Daily routines are routinely subverted by unexpected distractions, teachable moments, lessons from living, the unrelenting unpredictability of the human child, and even the occasional sinfulness of the all-too-human parent. And yet a very definite rhythm characterizes the homeschool lifestyle. It is the rhythm of purpose. It is the rhythm of real life. The schedule on the facing page is really just one of several "typical" days that might characterize our homeschool lifestyle. However, it is not meant to be the expression of an ideal WholeHearted Learning lifestyle day, nor is it offered as a template to copy for a best day. It is only illustrative, but it gives a sense of the kind of purpose and rhythm that we hope characterizes most of our homeschool days.

What a WholeHearted Learning Day Looks Like

The homeschooling day pictured below is only a highly generalized snapshot. It is not a perfect or ideal model to try to emulate every day, but only a slice of life to give you a taste of what a WholeHearted Learning homeschool day might look like. Ask the Holy Spirit to guide you to create the homeschooling schedule that is just right your family.

TIME	ACTIVITY
7:30 - 8:00	Get up, make bed, get dressed, read Bible, and do morning chores.
8:00 - 8:30	Breakfast: Eat breakfast and have family devotions.
8:30 - 9:00	Clean up and prepare materials. Children prepare for their day.
9:00 - 12:00 *Discipleship Studies* *Disciplined Studies* *Discussion Studies*	Structured homeschooling activities. Scripture memory, Bible reading, and Bible study. Math, language arts, and composition. Read-aloud and narration. Daily: Literature and history. Alternate Days: Fine arts (art, poetry, music) and nature/science.
12:00 - 1:00	Lunch: Prepare and eat lunch, read aloud at table, and do chores.
1:00 - 4:00 *Discovery Studies*	Free time for reading, computer, educational or instructional videos, projects, lessons, correspondence, library, drawing, and writing. Special projects and assignments, lessons, field trips, and activities.
4:00 - 6:00 *Discretionary Studies*	Play time and dinner preparation. Lessons and personal projects, field trips, and activities. (Discretionary Studies often require flexibility with the daily schedule.)
6:00 - 7:00	Dinner: Prepare and eat dinner, review, discuss, and read aloud.
7:00 - 7:30	Clean dishes and kitchen, pick up, clean up, and tie up loose ends.
7:30 - 8:30	Winter: Relax as a family, read aloud, Bible stories, and pray. Summer: Play outside, take long walks, play yard games/sports.
8:30 - 9:00	Bedtime: Younger children: Lights out. Older children: Listen to music or read.
9:00	Parent talk time, review homeschooling, relax.

The faith which you have, have as your own conviction before God. Happy is he who does not condemn himself in what he approves.

— Romans 14:22 (NASB)

The only true, biblical path of blessing for a mother is to reach out to the children God has given her, to raise and nurture them to become godly adults. Fulfillment will come only when a mother is willing to do God's will.

— Sally Clarkson, *Seasons of a Mother's Heart*, Apologia Press, 2009

I believe it would be much better for everyone if children were given their start in education at home. No one understands a child as well as his mother and children are so different that they need individual training and study. A teacher with a roomful of pupils cannot do this. At home, too, they are in their mother's care. She can keep them from learning immoral things from other children.

— Laura Ingalls Wilder, *Little House in the Ozarks*, Thomas Nelson, 1991

Know Your Principles

The principles that guide your life as a home educator will be constantly challenged. The vast majority of parents choose conventional schooling for their children, and many will adamantly argue that homeschooling is an inadequate educational choice. Some people will perceive your choice to homeschool as a passive judgment of their choice of public schooling. Your decisions about activities, media, playmates, and other issues will inevitably create some conflicts, even with other homeschooling families. In all these situations and more, you must know your own principles and be ready to defend them when necessary, with confidence and graciousness. You cannot change your convictions and lifestyle simply to accommodate those who do not agree with your principles—it will only diminish your choice and deplete your spiritual and emotional energy. Be prepared to stand on principle.

- **About Home Education** — Although many non-homeschoolers support homeschooling, it is not a neutral issue for some. Just accept it—you will be a threat to some people. You may not want to be or feel like one, but you will be. However, when confronted by opposition, you don't have to be falsely humble about your choice. You can confidently testify why homeschooling is right for you. Be assertive, not aggressive, but above all be gracious in your attitude and words.

- **About Church Activities** — Homeschooling is a quietly divisive issue in many churches. In a church that is not supportive of homeschooling, realize that you will be viewed with suspicion and that you and your family will stand out. Choices you make about your children's activities and companions might cause controversy. If you have the energy to fight for change, do as the Lord leads. However, you, your children, and the church might be better served by your attending a church with other homeschooling families that will be supportive of your choice.

- **About Companions** — If you have strong principles about the kinds of companions you allow your children to have, they will be a source of conflict. This will be an issue for you whether in your neighborhood, church, or homeschool support group. Proceed with caution with new friends for your children until you know the family and their values. You must be prepared to limit your children's relationships if you begin to see negative influences. Getting control is better than damage control.

- **About Media Exposure** — Prevention is the best means of avoiding a conflict of principle when it comes to media—don't put your children in tempting situations. However, since you don't always know the media standards of other families, train your children to discern when to "just say no thank you" to media your family has decided is unacceptable or to media that they aren't sure is acceptable, wherever it is encountered and whoever is in charge. Let them know you're always on call.

- **About Learning Methods** — Homeschooling families can be very loyal and highly committed to whatever learning methodology they choose for their children, even to the point of judging their choice as the best way and others as inferior. Whatever teaching and learning methodology you choose, be quietly confident that it is the right one for your family. You don't need to get into an educational duel over whose method is better, more biblical, or most proven.

Know Your Personality

Take it on faith—your personality is suited for homeschooling. Your character may need some work, but there is no such thing as a homeschooling personality that somehow qualifies some to be better homeschooling parents than others. There is no ideal homeschool parent model that you need to become like. It is a phantom, especially for homeschooling mothers. If your husband and children love you, don't worry about what everyone else is supposedly doing or judge yourself against what others are saying or begin to think you need to do more to be more acceptable to "them" (whoever they are). Just be yourself. Listen to God. You will never really relax and enjoy homeschooling with your children until you free yourself to be who you are before God, not who you think you should be for other people. Consider the following to give you perspective.

- **Accept yourself.** God made you and accepts you unconditionally, and he knew what he was doing when he gave your children to you. Your strengths, skills, knowledge, and abilities are what God knew your children would need—he doesn't mismatch parents and children! Beware of comparing your weaknesses with other mothers' strengths. Remember that they may have weaknesses in areas of their lives where you are strong. Every homeschooling mother has flaws. Whatever you see as your own limitations, God knows them and will work more powerfully in you because of them. God is not limited by your limitations!

- **Be yourself.** God gave you your personality for a reason. Because of it, you have a special relationship with your children that is totally distinct from every other mother and child. No one else can nurture your children the same way you can. It is natural and normal, then, that you will homeschool differently than other mothers. So don't compare yourself with other homeschooling mothers, and don't compare your children with other homeschooling children! If what you are doing is working, don't worry about what others are doing that you are not. Just be yourself and enjoy your children. They will enjoy the relaxed, real you much more.

- **Help yourself.** Homeschooling is hard. Determine whatever it is you need that will help you persevere in the homeschool lifestyle, and then give yourself permission to have it, especially if it provides more rest and energy. You don't have to feel guilty about thinking of ways to help yourself, especially if it makes you more effective as a homeschooling mother. Give yourself the freedom to spend time and money on the things that you need to be more effective and that you and your children will enjoy the most—lessons, occasional help with cleaning, an afternoon out, pool passes for the summer, zoo or museum memberships, and so on.

- **Enjoy yourself.** If homeschooling is God's will for you and your family, then you will have a sense of joy and freedom in it. If, however, home educating your children seems like a joyless burden, then you need to make adjustments. Study what God says in his Word about joy, thankfulness, contentedness, patience, and waiting. Do whatever you need to do to cultivate and keep the joy of the Christian life alive in your life. Learn what it means to live each day in the power of the Holy Spirit, whose fruit is love, joy, and peace (Galatians 5:22). You cannot homeschool for long without the joy of the Lord. With his joy, though, you can go the whole distance.

...for I have learned to be content whatever the circumstances. I know what it is to be in need, and I know what it is to have plenty. I have learned the secret of being content in any and every situation, whether well fed or hungry, whether living in plenty or in want. I can do everything through him who gives me strength.

— Philippians 4:11-13

Trust in the LORD and do good; dwell in the land and enjoy safe pasture. Delight yourself in the LORD and he will give you the desires of your heart. Commit your way to the LORD; trust in him and he will do this: He will make your righteousness shine like the dawn, the justice of your cause like the noonday sun.

— Psalm 37:3-6

Homeschooling is not an introverted lifestyle....Your children need to know that you accept them as God made them, not as your personality wants them to become.

— Sally Clarkson, *Seasons of a Mother's Heart*, Apologia Press, 2009

This above all: to thine own self be true, And it must follow, as the night the day, Thou canst not then be false to any man.

— William Shakespeare (1564-1616), English poet and playwright, from *Hamlet*, Act 1, Scene 3

I know what it is to be in need, and I know what it is to have plenty. I have learned the secret of being content in any and every situation, whether well fed or hungry, whether living in plenty or in want. I can do everything through him who gives me strength.

— Philippians 4:12-13

No temptation has seized you except what is common to man. And God is faithful; he will not let you be tempted beyond what you can bear. But when you are tempted, he will also provide a way out so that you can stand up under it.

— 1 Corinthians 10:13

Do you not know? Have you not heard? The LORD is the everlasting God, the Creator of the ends of the earth. He will not grow tired or weary, and his understanding no one can fathom. He gives strength to the weary and increases the power of the weak. Even youths grow tired and weary, and young men stumble and fall; but those who hope in the LORD will renew their strength. They will soar on wings like eagles; they will run and not grow weary, they will walk and not be faint.

— Isaiah 40:28-31

Not only so, but we also rejoice in our sufferings, because we know that suffering produces perseverance; perseverance, character; and character, hope. And hope does not disappoint us, because God has poured out his love into our hearts by the Holy Spirit, whom he has given us.

— Romans 5:3-5

Know Your Breaking Point

Homeschooling is not easy. Though its outward blessings and advantages are evident, they often hide its dark underside—it can be mentally and emotionally demanding, physically exhausting, and spiritually frustrating. Most homeschool mothers at one time or another find themselves struggling with burn-out—the feeling that says, "I can't do it! It's too much! I quit!" Their flame for homeschooling is either flickering or seems to be extinguished. Whatever the source of those feelings may be—weariness, defeat, immaturity, insecurity—the important thing is what you do with the feelings. Here are some ways to prevent your homeschool flame from burning out.

- **Lean into God.** Proverbs are wisdom for living—not just "getting by" living but "getting blessed" living because you are on God's path of life. An apt proverb can be a handle to hold onto to help you keep your spiritual balance through the tough times. "Trust in the LORD with all your heart and lean not on your own understanding; in all your ways acknowledge him, and he will make your paths straight" (Proverbs 3:5-6). Sometimes it just helps to have a verse that helps you lean on God.

- **Lower your expectations.** The phantom homeschool mom keeps your expectations unrealistically high—orderly home, schedule under control, children who do all their work, lots of field trips, baking bread, keeping a garden, ministry with children, and the ability to leisurely read all the homeschooling magazines and books on your shelves. But she doesn't exist! In reality, all you can do is accept each day from the Lord, live it as wisely as possible, and stay flexible. Learn to expect inconvenient interruptions, incomplete goals, and time-eating bouts of immaturity in your children. Don't expect more of yourself than God does—faithfulness.

- **Accept life's limitations.** You'll never accomplish in one lifetime everything you want to do, much less everything you think others want you to do. You will always run into limitations—sinful attitudes (yours, your husband's, and your children's), insufficient time, inadequate resources, weak skills, poor relationships, ad infinitum. No matter how strong you are in some areas, you will be weak in others. Yet God is not limited by your limitations—he will accomplish by his grace all that he intends to accomplish in your life and in the lives of your children, if you trust him. "With man this is impossible, but not with God; all things are possible with God" (Mark 10:27).

- **Learn to wait.** Time lifts burdens. Whatever is overwhelming you today will probably not seem so burdensome tomorrow, in a week, or in a month. Trusting God is, in essence, waiting—patiently depending on him to meet your needs. Many times, it is through the waiting that God works to make you stronger. As you grow in faith and perseverance, what once was overwhelming may actually become a normal way of life. Sometimes God changes your circumstances; more often he changes you.

- **Expect adversity.** The Baby Boomer generation was raised to expect prosperity and the good life. If life didn't provide that, we could simply quit and do something else. Scripture, though, reminds us that was never true. God wants us to experience, prepare for, and learn from adversity and difficulty. It is part of his plan for our maturity. If you are not surprised by it, then God can use it to strengthen you even more.

Know Your Provider

The better you know your Provider, the easier it will be to trust him to provide for your needs, including the grace and strength to home educate your children. If you really believe that the God of Creation has called you to homeschool your children, then he will supply your need and sustain your faith. He knows your needs, and he knows your children's needs. However, be aware that God will also use homeschooling to bring you to maturity as a parent. Those times when God doesn't answer your prayers as quickly as you'd like or in the way you'd like will test how well you know your Provider.

When the new Jewish Christians of the Jerusalem church were persecuted and scattered after the stoning of Stephen (Acts 7), they found themselves suddenly separated from all the familiar things that had given them stability and identity for generations—the temple, the sacrifices, the festivals, the holy city, the people of God. After a while, they were weary and ready to go back. The book of Hebrews was written to encourage those believers not to give up and go back but to stay strong and live by faith because God is faithful. Homeschooling can feel like living in a foreign land, separated from cultural norms that can seem attractive and secure. If you ever feel tempted to give up and go back to that culture, the same two simple truths the scattered Christians needed to hear can also help you persevere—faithfully trust God because you can trust God's faithfulness.

- **Faithfully trust God.** "And without faith it is impossible to please God, because anyone who comes to him must believe that he exists..." (Hebrews 11:6a). Regardless of the circumstances you face, you have the ability to remain faithful to God. In the end, the measure of your success in homeschooling will not be how well your children perform on achievement tests but how faithful you have been to trust God for his grace and strength in the process of discipling and educating them. Be faithful!

- **Trust God's faithfulness.** "...and that he rewards those who earnestly seek him" (Hebrews 11:6b). Regardless of the circumstances you face, you can trust God because he is faithful. Do a Bible study on God's faithfulness to his people. Then take some time to take inventory of all the ways he has shown his faithfulness to you in the past. He has been faithful to his people in every generation. He is looking for faith in your generation, and he will bless it when he finds it. Trust God!

IN OUR HOME

Our diaspora experience was in 1993. We had been in Nashville, Tennessee, for two years when God put it on our hearts that we should pray about moving to family property in rural central Texas to start a ministry to parents. One day later, God sent a buyer for our home, and in three weeks we were unpacking in Walnut Springs, Texas, population 701. For the next year, we felt alone and lost in the wilderness. We had a vague idea of what God wanted us to do, but nothing solid. There were times of fear and discouragement, but we simply chose to be faithful, believing that God would guide our future because he had been faithful to us in the past. By faith, we stayed and waited, and in 1994 God started Whole Heart Ministries.

So do not throw away your confidence; it will be richly rewarded. You need to persevere so that when you have done the will of God, you will receive what he has promised. For in just a very little while, "He who is coming will come and will not delay. But my righteous one will live by faith. And if he shrinks back, I will not be pleased with him." But we are not of those who shrink back and are destroyed, but of those who believe and are saved.

— Hebrews 10:35-39

Be still, and know that I am God; I will be exalted among the nations, I will be exalted in the earth.

— Psalm 46:10

A daily, regular quiet time when I read the Bible, seek His wisdom, and pray to Him for my needs each day has been the means through which I am able to stay faithful as a mom.

— Sally Clarkson, *The Mom Walk*, Harvest House, 2007

Homeschooling should be a blessing to us, not an unbearable burden. If it has become such a burden, then perhaps we have required things of ourselves that the Lord never asked us to do. Perhaps the standards we are trying to follow are not God's standards but man's. Perhaps we are living by formula rather than by faith.

— Sally Clarkson, *Seasons of a Mother's Heart*, Apologia Press, 2009

Know Your Path

The saying has been attributed to Yogi Berra, who is probably better known now for his memorable malapropisms than for his illustrious baseball career, but its origin is probably unknown: "If you don't know where you're going, you'll get there every time." In other words, if you don't have any path to follow, you'll follow any path. You won't know where you're going, but you know you're going somewhere. You would be following Yogi's directions to get to his home: "When you come to the fork in the road, take it." If you are a homeschooling mom and you don't really have a path you are following for subduing your home domain, you'll end up taking any path and taking any fork in the road. You'll get somewhere, but you may find it's not really where you wanted to go.

When it comes to subduing your home domain and creating a structure that will enable you to do the things that are on your heart to do, you have to know where you're going if you want to get there. To quote another maxim, "If you fail to plan, you'll plan to fail." If you want to succeed in the homeschooling lifestyle in order to grow your children into mature adults, the path to that end will be much more difficult if you're always looking at your feet to try to figure out the next step. If every challenge or opportunity requires you to rethink and realign your path, then you're just letting life plan you rather than you planning life. The sooner you can see the path that leads to the biblical goal of a whole and healthy family and the more clearly you can envision the kind of homeschooling home and family life you want to create, the sooner you can move toward that goal.

This kind of proverbial wisdom is also rightly applied to your children—envision the kind of adults you want them to be and then plan your life to achieve that end. However, relationships are unpredictable and dynamic, so it's more realistic when applying this idea to children to set the larger goals of Christian maturity that Scripture holds up as the goals of life, and then begin to make the kinds of choices that will put your family on the path of life to realizing them. That's really what this whole book is all about. This chapter, though, is about one thing—subduing your home to create the kind of structure and patterns that will allow you to effectively stay on the path to realizing those larger goals. It's about defining the purposes, priorities, plans, and principles that will get you where you want to go. The path is there; it's up to you how you walk it with your family.

IN OUR HOME

We began to define our path when we lived in California. Our children were five, two, and newborn, and we were fully committed to homeschooling. We were leading a singles ministry (Clay was on pastoral staff of a large church) in which ten of the eleven leaders on our team came from broken homes. One day Sarah said, "When I grow up and get divorced, I want to come live with you." That got our attention! We thought of how all our Campus Crusade for Christ training taught us to disciple adults well, but we had never heard about parents discipling children. We realized then that we had one chance to get it right for our children. We began to define the goals we wanted for them so we could begin to build the kind of home and family life that would give them a better end than our singles leaders.

— Chapter 17 —

Order:
Keeping the Home Together

Ruling Over Your Home Domain

The idea of a home domain really begins at the beginning. When God created man and woman, he blessed them and instructed them to "fill the earth and subdue it" and to "rule over" the new creation (Genesis 1:28). Later in the narrative, in a proleptic retake on their creation (2:18-25), God declares that the man whom he created first was incomplete and needed a "helper suitable for him" (2:18). God created the woman to be man's helper to fulfill the creation mandate, not only for filling the earth (procreation) but also for subduing and ruling over it (having dominion). It was an implicit prefiguring of future roles that would be made more explicit after the Fall. Any creation ideals have been distorted by sin, but the intent of God's pre-Fall design for the family has never changed.

As a homeschooling mother, your home is your domain—it is the part of creation that God has uniquely designed and delegated to you to subdue and rule over. In his ideal design for the created order here on earth, home is your realm and stewardship, and you have the privilege to bring order to it, which will bring honor and glory to God. Sin creates disorder, and that disorder creates anxiety, and that anxiety can make being "workers at home" (Titus 2:5, NASB) seem like a burden rather than a blessing. But "God is not a God of disorder but of peace" (1 Corinthians 14:33). Bringing order to your home domain is not only a biblical stewardship that can bring honor to God; it is also a biblical principle that can bring peace, a fruit of the Holy Spirit (Galatians 5:22), to your family.

When your home is under control, the resulting peace is a powerful testimony of God's living presence in your family. When order brings peace to your home, it also frees you to fulfill more effectively your God-given role to nurture and care for your family. When your home gets out of control and becomes characterized by stress and anxiety, the testimony of God's life and presence is distorted. The stress becomes a distraction from your life in Christ and a constant drain on your spiritual and physical energy that detracts from your ability to give your family the life of peace that they need. Bringing peace to your home through order is a powerful ministry of the Spirit to your family.

This chapter is written primarily to the experience of a homeschooling mother because the home is the domain over which you rule all day, every day. The principles of home management in this chapter can help you bring order to your home domain and peace to your family. Of course, the life of God will not automatically come into your family life just because your home is in order. However, order will be a key that will allow you to lay the critical foundation of Home Nurture (chapter 3) in creating a home where you and your husband can shepherd your children's spirits to long for God. Having an orderly home is not just a burdensome duty; it is a spiritual act of life-giving.

The wise woman builds her house, but with her own hands the foolish one tears hers down.

— Proverbs 14:1

By wisdom a house is built, and through understanding it is established; through knowledge its rooms are filled with rare and beautiful treasures.

— Proverbs 24:3-4

For God is not a God of disorder but of peace.

— 1 Corinthians 14:33

Most worthwhile endeavors— whether they involve housework and chores, schoolwork, serving outside the home or providing hospitality within it, or training our children to be servants of the Lord—end up taking more time, energy, effort, and character than we ever thought they would.

— Sally Clarkson, *The Ministry of Motherhood*, WaterBrook Press, 2004

Because the responsibilities of maintaining a home, especially a home with children, are so varied and unrelenting, the pressure to get it all together and keep it together is constant. Doing laundry, cleaning messes, cooking, washing dishes, shopping, organizing, keeping clutter under control—the tasks can be daunting. That's why effective home management is an important part of making a home into a nurturing environment. A perfectly ordered home isn't necessarily a haven, but neither is a messy, chaotic one. Coming up with a plan for subduing the messy details of our domain is essential to maintaining a peaceful atmosphere, teaching children to take care of themselves, and simply keeping the work from overwhelming anyone.

— Sally Clarkson, *The Mission of Motherhood*, WaterBrook Press, 2003

To be organized is not synonymous with meticulous. To be organized means you do things for a good reason at the best time and in the easiest way...It doesn't mean that you never get behind, rather that you can stick to it until you have recovered.

— Bonnie McCullough, *Totally Organized*, St. Martin's Press, 1986

Keeping It All Together All the Time

Whoever says homeschooling is not a full-time career obviously has not applied for the job lately. As a homeschooling mom, you teach and train your children and plan lessons and field trips, but you also manage your home, shop for and prepare meals, clean and organize, do laundry for your entire family, counsel your children, spend copious amounts of time on the road between errands and activities, take care of planning and record keeping, and multitask all day long. You may even add a home-based business to the mix in your home and all that it takes to manage it and involve the children. Then, of course, you spend time with your husband, enjoy his company both with and away from the children, plan and dream with him, and do all the things that build and strengthen a good marriage. The point is, there is nothing remotely part-time or easy about the homeschooling lifestyle. It requires a great deal of confidence, competence, commitment, and coordination. You are a woman, wife, mother, and manager every day.

Because your responsibilities are so varied and unrelenting, the pressure to get it all together and keep it all together is constant. You feel it all the time, and it affects your effectiveness. If you ever hope to be both more effective (doing the right things) and more efficient (doing things right) as a homeschooling mother, you must start by getting more systematic about it—creating systems and then making those systems work for you so you can manage your home and responsibilities.

Personality factors definitely come into play in home management. You should re-read chapter 8 to develop a better understanding of how the dynamic of your personality will affect the way you attempt to bring order to your home domain. If you are a Doer mom, you probably already have some practical systems in place, but your kids may wonder if they are just pieces in the system to get things done. If you are a Helper mom, you probably have some systems developed where your children are involved in a meaningful way, but the nonpersonal aspects of your home that require attention are in various states of disarray. If you are a Mover mom, you're probably so busy interacting with, influencing, and personally challenging your kids that the house and the schedule are in a constant state of flux because things are just not as important as people. If you are a Shaper mom, you probably are spending much more time thinking about, creating, designing, and improving your home systems than you are actually making use of them, but you are convinced they are right. The reality is that no personality is the perfect homeschooling mom, so every personality type has something to learn about home management.

This chapter explains management by the box, a home management approach that will help you move toward the ideal of keeping it all together, all the time. Keep in mind that there is a big difference between reaching for the ideal and actually reaching it. The approach outlined in this chapter is a doable but imperfect way to reach for the ideal. It is purposely uncomplicated, even simplistic. It is easy to understand and implement, but it covers all the major areas of your home management responsibilities. We try to approach this area with a sense of humor because, let's face it, it's better to laugh at the foibles of disorganization in your life than it is to get knots in your stomach because of them. But beyond all that, the concept of boxes can help you get the clutter under control, whether it is stuff, information, time, or other areas. Whatever your home situation, whatever your personality, whatever your mess—home management by the box can help.

Characteristics of an Orderly Home

When it comes to home management, every mom has a different set of priorities and abilities, every dad has a unique combination of strengths and weaknesses, and every family has its own challenges and limitations. There is no one-size-fits-all goal for what an orderly or organized home should look like. Only one thing should be true for every mother when it comes to her home: Do not judge yourself by someone else's standards of home organization. God does not judge your specific home management skills—he does not grade your calendaring, housecleaning, and filing abilities. Rather, God's standard for homemaking is about the condition of a mother's heart, not the condition of her home. He wants mothers with children at home to "love their husbands and children, to be self controlled and pure, to be busy at home, to be kind, and to be subject to their husbands, so that no one will malign the word of God" (Titus 2:4-5). He wants them to be wise rather than foolish: "The wise woman builds her house, but with her own hands the foolish one tears hers down" (Proverbs 14:1). An orderly home will help you achieve those biblical ideals.

That said, though, the main question still remains for this chapter: What is an orderly home? There are definite practical advantages and personal benefits to an orderly home for a homeschooling family. In addition to the idea of a mother subduing disorder and ruling over her home domain to bring order and peace, organization is also a characteristic of the wise women in Proverbs (9:1-6; 14:1; 24:3; 31:10-31), and it is certainly a quality of being a good steward of all that has been entrusted to her (Matthew 25:21). The list below is limited and only suggestive (definitely not inspired), but it is an attempt to describe some of the characteristics of an orderly and organized home. You will be stronger at some things than at others, and some you may have already given up on, but most of the following characteristics will be true in an organized home. If three or more of them are out of whack in your home, consider it a red flag and take some time to consider how you could improve your home management. Don't do it because you think you need to be more acceptable to anyone else; do it to give yourself a better opportunity to really enjoy homeschooling, with less stress and more success.

- There is unrushed time to hear from God as a family in prayers and devotions.

- Clutter is under control, stuff is subdued, and the kids know where things should go.

- There is a basic weekly schedule for chores, schoolwork, shopping, and activities.

- Household routines create a realistic rhythm for your daily family life.

- Important household and homeschool items can be easily located.

- Important books, information, and papers are readily accessible.

- Incoming information is handled with minimal effort.

- Meals are on the table in a timely fashion.

- Children are ready for bed at a reasonable hour.

- You are in bed at a not-too-unreasonable hour.

- You have 15-30 minutes for a coffee or tea break in the afternoon.

Great Dad Tips

Some dads will be more involved in hands-on homeschool instruction than others, but the reality for most families is that Mom is the primary homeschooling parent. No matter how much Dad is involved in the lessons, though, the more he is involved in his children's lives, the more supported and encouraged Mom will feel, and that will make the stresses of home management even lighter. Here are a few tips for dads for how to be sure to be involved in the children's lives.

- Initiate regular family devotional times, Bible study, and family nights.
- Make it a habit to read to your children at meals, bedtime, or other special times.
- Take regular planning times alone with your wife to discuss family life and schedule.
- Take the kids regularly for several hours on planned, fun, and meaningful outings.
- Defend and protect your wife's schedule against controllable time consumers.
- Schedule specific times to be with your children during the week (Dad dates).
- Step in when the kids need to be distracted from their mother (ex.: dinner prep).
- If life gets crazy, give your wife freedom to find and hire a paid housecleaner.
- Prepare an arsenal of ideas that you can do with the children on a moment's notice.
- Be sensitive to end-of-the-day stress levels, stepping in to help even if you are tired.
- If you are an organizer, help keep things organized without comment or complaint.

But seek first his kingdom and his righteousness, and all these things will be given to you as well. Therefore do not worry about tomorrow, for tomorrow will worry about itself. Each day has enough trouble of its own.

— Matthew 6:33-34

The Laws of Home Systems Management

Just as there are natural laws that govern the natural universe, so are there home laws that govern the home universe. These laws are a part of the warp and woof of daily life in your home universe. You are either working with them or against them. The astute home manager understands these laws and submits to them. You cannot escape them, but you can learn to use them to your advantage.

Home Thermodynamics

- First Law: In home systems, all things tend toward disorder and disarray.
- Second Law: In home systems, a finite amount of energy is being dissipated at a constant rate.

Home Systematics

- Law: Systems work.
- First Corollary: If you don't work your systems, your systems won't work.
- Second Corollary: The more you work your systems, the less you'll work.

Home Cause and Effect

- Law: In home systems, every undesirable effect has a proximate cause.
- First Corollary: To eliminate an undesirable effect, you must change the cause.
- Second Corollary: Causes can be changed only through the application of time and effort (complaining about effects will not change causes).

The FIRST Five Priorities of Home Management

There is no perfect system for managing your home, and there is no such thing as a stress-free home environment, especially for homeschooling families. The idea of a stress-free home is a myth because the disorderly sources that cause stress—that gnawing feeling that you need to keep it all together all the time, but you're not—are constant and unavoidable. You can't control the reality of those stress factors, but you can reduce the level of anxiety you feel from them. The WholeHearted Learning model attempts to reduce the educational stress that comes from homeschooling parents trying to bring school into the home. This chapter addresses how to manage the home part of homeschooling. It's about how to be a better "keeper at home" ruling over the five priorities of home management that attempt to address the primary sources of stress in your homeschool life: family, information, rest, stuff, and time (FIRST).

- **F = Managing Family** — It's good that Family is first in the FIRST acrostic. This entire book is actually about managing the family, but it's here in a discussion of home management as a reminder that it is not just about tasks and duties, but it is always about family first. Family is the organic and living part of home management that is the random element for even the best manager moms. Home management is not about command and control but about relationships and reality. It's just life.

- **I = Managing Information** — Information is pernicious and persistent. You are daily flooded with papers, forms, records, e-mails, ads, magazines, catalogs, and more. Useful information gets lost only because it is hard to find. If your filing system consists mainly of the top of your desk, the bookshelf, random piles, or the always-full "everything" drawer in your kitchen, your information is probably out of control. If you're going to stay above the information flood, you've got to manage your information flow.

- **R = Managing Rest** —It is significant that Rest is at the center of the FIRST acrostic. Rest is not the reward for having done good home management; it is the requirement for doing good home management. You will not be able to manage all the responsibilities and tasks of a homeschooling lifestyle unless you ensure that you get sufficient rest every day. Call it a kind of micro-Sabbath. Sufficient rest is an essential component in managing homes and stress. Rest in that!

- **S = Managing Stuff** — Stuff is the most easily identified constant in your life because it is so frustratingly visible: clothes, toys, books, games, junk, doodads, sports gear, kitchen stuff, garden stuff, and so on. The more it accumulates, the more burdensome it becomes just to have it and to keep track of it, even if it is never used. It can progressively becomes a permanent weight and distraction in your family's life. If you don't want your stuff to control you, you need to get your stuff under control!

- **T = Managing Time** — Time is the least visible of the five priorities but by far the most demanding and hardest to manage. In the homeschool home, it seems like time is the least available commodity and the most in demand. The time-eating onslaught of scheduled activities, unexpected distractions, unwanted interruptions, and little and big crises provides few breaks from the demands of time. The only way to "make" more time is to make better use of the time you have. That means time management.

Home Management "By the Box"

Why the "box"? Simply because it is the most natural way to think about organization. At some point, everything in your life goes into a box, so it seems reasonable to elevate it to an organizational principle. Its beauty and strength are its simplicity. It provides a minimalist approach to organizing—no expensive materials to purchase, no fancy hardware to install, no complicated instructions to decipher, no confusing systems to maintain, no thick books to read. It is really just a metaphor that you apply to life. As long as you don't get hung up on the term "box," the principle will serve you very effectively to help you bring your home environment under control and, with systems and routines, keep it in under control.

We have simply applied the organizational principle of the box to the FIRST five priorities of home management—family, information, rest, stuff, and time. Whether it is a physical box or a figurative one, the box serves as a useful organizational tool—for family you'll use task boxes; for information you'll use file boxes; for rest you'll use personal boxes; for stuff you'll use real boxes; for time you'll use time boxes. The suggestions for each of the five areas of home management by the box will not be comprehensive, as the actual range of possibilities is huge. The suggestions and ideas that follow are just starting points—some thoughts and suggestions to help get you thinking about how to apply the principles to your own home. Once you get in the habit and rhythm of thinking about these five areas of home management by the box, you'll soon find yourself promoting the power of the box to others.

Now most of us, especially as nonconformist homeschooling types, probably experience a bit of a conditioned reflex reaction to so much talk about boxes. You may be thinking (or even saying out loud), "Don't put me in a box!" But don't worry—this is not about putting you in a box, but about putting your life in boxes so you can get out of one. It's boxing up the parts of your life that, if left uncontained and uncontrolled, would make you feel like you're trapped inside a box that just keeps getting smaller and more crowded. The intent of this attempt to get at some kind of boxology of home management is to give you freedom. It's not about narrowing the scope of your life but broadening it.

IN OUR HOME

Most of the Clarkson family members are not organizers by nature. Only Clay seems to have the gift of organization (which he often considers a curse since it seems to be regularly challenged). Everyone in the family, especially the girls, values orderly rooms and clean living areas and will work as needed to bring outward order to the immediate living environment so it is civilized and delightful, but that's where it often stops. Clay, on the other hand, is driven to create systems of organization, not just outwardly but inwardly as well. Whether it is the twenty-four hinged-lid crates for holiday decor (different color lids for different holidays), the organized and labeled pantry shelves (which never stay that way), the four drawers of family files with color-coded hanging files and dividers, or the organized garage, it is his burden to organize.

Do not store up for yourselves treasures on earth, where moth and rust destroy, and where thieves break in and steal. But store up for yourselves treasures in heaven, where moth and rust do not destroy, and where thieves do not break in and steal. For where your treasure is, there your heart will be also.

— Matthew 6:19-21

Boxes Known and Loved

If you've ever had a favorite box, then you'll understand this list. The contents vary tremendously, but the usefulness of a good box never changes.

- Rubbermaid small and medium lidded storage boxes
- Bankers Boxes (the heavy-duty, double-walled kind)
- Hinged, cardboard records boxes (9x12x2)
- Magazine holders
- Portable hanging file box with hinged lid and handle
- 3x5 card boxes (metal hinge on wood or heavy plastic)
- Check boxes (only the sturdy kinds)
- Mini-crates (small plastic "milk" crates)
- Hinge-lidded storage crates (15 gallon and smaller)
- Cigar boxes, all sizes
- Humidors and other small all-wood boxes
- Military ammunition boxes (a guy thing)
- Jewelry boxes (a girl thing)
- Polish boxes (decorative wood boxes from Poland—a Clarkson family thing)

Box Mania

Between 1982 and 1992, the value of one share of Rubbermaid stock rose from $2.41 to $31.00. That is an increase of 1186%! Why did it rise in value so dramatically? The answer in one word—BOXES! Rubbermaid became the leading home storage and container maker in America. Over-stuffed American baby-boomer consumers bought them by the caseload.

Quick & Easy Meals

Keep a supply of low-prep, high-value, good-taste meals on hand.

- Snack Dinner — popcorn, fruit, raw veggies, cheese and crackers, muffins, cereal
- Toasty Tostados — chips, refritos, meat, cheese, tomatoes, onions, sour cream
- Shepherds' Meal — veggie or potato soup, wheat or herb bread, cheese, nuts, and fruit
- That's a Wrap — pita or flat bread, tasty spread, meat, veggies, cheese, more to fill
- Tater Plate — baked potatoes and green salad with as many toppings as you want to add
- Mix & Mex — flour and corn tortillas, meat(s), cheese, refritos, and other fixings
- Breakfast Dinner — cold cereal, fruit, omelet and toast, or waffles

Cooking to the Max

You don't need to reinvent the meal every day. Depending on your freezer space, use one of these strategies for making the most of your cooking time.

- 30 Meals Plan — Set aside one day each month to shop for, prepare, cook, and freeze thirty main-course meals for your family. Doing it all at once saves time, energy, clean up, and money. There are several good books that explain how to do this quickly and efficiently.
- 30-Minute Meals Plan — Create some 3x5 card recipes for several enjoyable meals you can prepare in under 30 minutes using ingredients that are easy to store or freeze. Keep a list of the ingredients for those recipes that you can keep in stock in special places in the pantry and freezer.
- Multiple Meals Plan — Whatever you are cooking, always double or triple the batch and freeze the extra in meal-size containers. It's a simple way to cut your cooking and cleaning time by half or more. Keep a good supply of plastic freezer bags on hand. Always date and label.

FIRST: Managing Family

Life will always be unpredictable—your schedule will fall apart, homeschooling will occasionally grind to a halt, and the house will at times seem like someone detonated a megaton stuff-bomb inside your walls. If that puts your heart in conflict with the Lord, then no amount of organization, planning, or scheduling is going to make you the godly homeschooling mother that you envisioned becoming. If, though, you are trusting God and depending upon his grace, you can still be the mother you want to be, which includes managing your family and your home. If you are regularly seeking God, strengthening your faith in the Word, letting the Spirit control your attitude, and being as faithful as you know how to be, then you can be assured you are fulfilling your role as a mother and as a family manager. God is not asking any more of you than your faith and your faithfulness.

But let's just be honest at this point...on a practical level, there really are few other things in your homeschooling life that will challenge your attitudes and spirit more than the daily duties of domesticity and the tasks of homemaking. They never go away, at least not completely, and will be a constant and demanding drain on your already limited time and energy if you don't find some way to contain them. You must find some way to make managing your family manageable. Families with children in school often seem to have it easier when it comes to home management—fewer hours when children are at home, and more undistracted time to manage it during the day. Homeschooling is 24/7/365.

The idea of using task boxes is not a perfect solution, but it might help you begin to contain your family management puzzle. There are really just a few pieces to that puzzle, and they really will fit together if you work at it. A task box is simply a mental or physical box to contain certain kinds of management tasks needing to be done. Rather than having to manage an unlimited number of tasks that seem to be unrelated, task boxes enable you to group all those discrete duties into a limited number of boxes. We have identified five (that's not too many) areas of family life that generate most of the work: things, dirt, food, kitchen, and clothes. If you can contain those five areas in five task boxes, it will make your life more manageable. Here are a few suggestions:

- **Things** (Straightening) — An undeniable law of home thermodynamics is that all things tend to disorder and disarray. No matter how much energy you expend to bring order, the natural state of a homeschooling home will be disorder. Create regular times each day for your children to bring order to the most lived-in parts of your house. Make it a habitual, nonnegotiable routine to stop every day at a set time before lunch and before dinner to straighten the house. Assign a specific task to each child. Less public areas will require strategic planning but must also be tamed.

- **Dirt** (Cleaning) — Few people really like all the dusting, wiping, vacuuming, sweeping, mopping, scrubbing, and polishing required to keep a house clean, but no one wants to live in a dirty-dusty-muddy-smudgy home. If you can't afford a maid service, then set aside a task box of time as a family and just get it done. Keep all the necessary cleaning gear, rags, and fluids in one place so you don't have to search. Assign specific tasks—no whining allowed. Put on some fun music, turn it up loud, and sing and dance as you clean.

- **Food** (Cooking) — We believe in good food and memorable meals in our home, so cooking is a big deal, especially for dinner. If you are like us, breakfast and lunch will go pretty easily, but you'll definitely need task boxes to contain the tasks of shopping for, preparing, and serving those special evening meals. Those meals are important memory-makers, but even more, they are strategic times for building bonds of unity as a family. (Good food is a great unifier.) Putting the whole process into a mental task box will elevate the meal's importance not only to you but also to your family.

- **Kitchen** (Eating) — It's amazing how we can spend so much time preparing for and cleaning up after a meal and so little time actually eating the meal. Every tasty meal generates the need to clean up after it. Doing the dishes is such a disdained duty in our house that we have to enforce discipline, or else it might never get done. Every family has to come to grips with its own strategy for kitchen clean-up—how many task boxes (dishes, countertops, put away), who does what when ("do by" times), and how it's done (standards of cleanness). Make the meal worth all the work!

- **Clothes** (Washing) — Life would be much easier if we all didn't have to wear clean clothes every day. Other than wearing fewer clothes more often, the best strategy for keeping the dirty laundry under control is to teach your children early how to wash their own clothes. Keep it efficient by enforcing a few washroom rules: create a washing task and time box for each person (avoid random wash times); wash, dry, fold, and remove clothes ("no clothes left behind"); give everyone their own personalized clothing basket (different color baskets work best).

IN OUR HOME

We found in our home that I (Clay) could help with family management both directly and indirectly. When I came home from the office, it was a good time to direct the children to pick up toys and straighten the main rooms before dinner. I could help direct kitchen clean-up after dinner and later help with bedtime routines. However, it was the indirect help that often made the bigger impression. Sally would often say that it helped her on Saturday mornings when I would not just take the kids, but take them away. That habit would give Sally some undistracted time at home to get some family management things done more efficiently or just to be alone to get personally and spiritually refueled, and it gave me some memorable times with my children. Every child needs time with Dad, so I would use the "take them away" times to build some wonderful memories with them. We had some special breakfast places that would become highly anticipated outings. I made sure to use the time to talk and laugh as much as we would eat (no newspaper or Day-Timer allowed). We had several places we could go on a moment's notice—a favorite park, a special playground, a lake area, a nature center. A picnic meal or snack would extend our time. I would often take the children with me on special errands and get them involved in whatever task was before me (buying an appliance, getting the car fixed, shopping for something special). It wasn't so much about what we did as what it did for Sally.

Child Chores

Here is a short list of chores that your children can do around the house. For older children, define exactly what you mean by the chore ("The kitchen is clean when..."). For younger children, give them one or two specific tasks at a time ("Organize your toy closet").

- Make bed
- Clean room
- Set the table
- Clear the table
- Do the dishes
- Clean the kitchen
- Empty dishwasher
- Fold/distribute laundry
- Change bedding
- Feed pets
- Clean sinks/mirrors
- Scrub toilet
- Straighten any room
- Vacuum

Homemade Task Boxes

You can easily create your own task box system.

- Chore Cards — The 3x5 card is still around. Use an index card box with dividers for main areas, and write tasks, times, and names on the cards. Index cards are easy to pull, distribute, and check.
- Chore Sheets — A personalized printed sheet for each child with assigned chores, and an attitude review. Ours is called "My Check Me Out List" and is reviewed each night with a parent.
- Chore Chart — Usually a single, full-page printed weekly chart to assign chores and check off when done. Color-coding, symbols, and special stickers will help make it more fun and useful.
- Chore Board — Similar to a chart, but using a whiteboard and colored dry erase markers. You can add lines and categories with tape or a permanent marker. Just erase and start over each week.

Parents can help to discipline their children in the important character trait of orderliness by providing their children with routine work responsibilities; and by seeing that the duties that are assigned to their children are performed satisfactorily.

— Jacob Abbott, *Training Children in Godliness*, ca. 1850

Analog to Digital

The highly-touted paperless office of the early 1990s never materialized (irony intended), but those early years of the new Information Age laid the groundwork for an inevitable, although ongoing, transition—from being a culture dependent on analog information (stored and retrieved in physical formats) to becoming one dependent on digital information (stored and retrieved in digital formats). Communications that once were dominated by paper, landline phones, cassettes, fax, VHS tapes, and TV now are dominated by e-mail, messaging, cell phones, texting, PDFs, online video, the "cloud," flash drives, and more. (Even physical media for digital information, such as CDs and DVDs, are on the way out.) Older homeschool parents will make peace with the digital information invasion in a wide range of ways, depending on their comfort levels with technology and their resistance to change. Younger homeschool parents will be much more likely to fully embrace the new digital era in all its forms and naturally integrate new technologies into their homeschool lifestyle.

FIRST: Managing Information

We are awash in information. Just consider how much more printed matter is generated and injected into your life now than in past generations in every category—magazines, newspapers, hard copies of e-mails and Internet pages, direct-mail advertising, brochures, documents, business letters, church communications, coupons, books, and more. You can never really control it, but you can try to contain it.

- **File Cabinet** — A traditional filing cabinet is nothing more than a divided information box with moving parts. File folders simply let you subdivide your box for storing information. Create file categories to direct the information flow—home, homeschool, action, financial, topical, and such. Work with whatever works for you.

- **File Drawers** — Many filing options are available—portable file boxes, one-drawer file units, crates with hanging file channels, among others. You might choose different kinds for different tasks—portable file for financial records, a crate for homeschool papers, and a one-drawer file for topical research.

- **Storages Boxes** — The venerable Bankers Box is great for storing bulk information, old files, seldom-accessed papers, memorabilia, and the like. Label the box clearly and store it where you can get to it if you need it. At warehouse stores you can buy packs of Bankers Boxes that are inexpensive, store flat, and assemble easily.

- **Files Piles** — Create a holding area where new information can be stored until boxed (filed). Use whatever method of files or piles works best for you. Look at it as a kind of paper waiting room, where all unfiled papers patiently await their appointment, either to being saved in the files or lost to the wastebasket.

- **Digital Files** — Some things are just beyond the scope of this book or even human understanding. How you structure and store digital information on your hard drive or in your e-mail or web browser folders is a bridge too far for this discussion. Most are very organic systems that cannot be explained or duplicated. You're on your own!

- **Or NOT!** — Just a final encouragement (at Sally's behest). If you just can't get the information flood under control with filing strategies yet you somehow just know intuitively where all the most important information is when it is needed, then don't stress over this section. Do what comes easiest or just delegate it all to your husband.

IN OUR HOME

We're still trying to tame the paper beast. We have files that work well, as well as files that don't. I (Clay) manage several filing systems and a stack of flat files where all the "to be filed" stuff gets stuffed. I may be the only one in the Clarkson family who actually cares about filing papers, but everyone else seems very happy that I do (so they don't have to think about it). Of course, even I resort to shoebox filing systems for some papers. In fact, the handy Bankers Box is my default "filing angst" option—fill it, label it, lid it, store it, forget it. There are times when you can definitely just file everything under "Arrrrrgh!"

The Best Filing Systems for Home Management

A home filing system is, in essence, just a very fancy divided box for papers. A seemingly never-ending river of printed materials constantly flows through our lives—if we don't control it, we get buried in its flood waters. A good filing system (that is, one that you actually use) is like a dam on a river that controls that flow of print. Whatever filing system you use will be, in essence, an extension of your mind. It needs to reflect the way you think about information—how you organize it and keep track of it in your mind. A mismatch will result in misplaced and missing files because your filing system thinks differently than you do. Following are some popular ways to file:

- **Intuitive File (Bills/Correspondence/Pending...)** — This is everybody's default file system, best for a filing system with random categories of information that you want to be able to access quickly. The trick with this system is to have enough files but not so many that you forget what and where they are. Identify the categories of information you need to keep at hand, and then create a file for each one. Arrange the files in whatever order works for you. You can subdivide the file by larger categories using a different color of hanging files for each category. Categories might include Action file (Bills, Current, Pending, To Do, etc.), Homeschooling, Correspondence, Finances, Consumer Information, Projects, and the like...you decide.

- **Alphabetical File (A/B/C...)** — A slightly more organized step up from the Intuitive File system. You need a file folder divider for each letter of the alphabet (or 25, with Mac and XYZ files) to separate your folders. Your divider can also be a file for keeping miscellaneous materials that don't need a separate folder. File new material alphabetically behind the file divider corresponding to the first letter of the topic. To prevent the file from looking like it is totally disorganized, place all file labels in one position (usually left or center, or dividers center and topics left).

- **Alpha-Numeric File (1-Reading, 2-Writing, 3-Math...)** — Best for large files containing multiple topics, such as a research or topical file. File folders are numbered sequentially starting with 1 and followed by the topic description. Enter each new topic on the next unused file folder in sequence, typically with five labels across the drawer. Whenever you assign a new topic to a file number, create a new 3x5 index card with the topic written in the upper left and the file reference number in the upper right of the card. Arrange file cards alphabetically in a 3x5 card file box. To find filed material, look under the topic in the card file box to obtain the file number. Cross-referenced and topically-related files can also be included on the 3x5 card. This method will hold as many files as you have room for.

- **Consonant-Vowel File (Aa/Ae/Ai/Ao/Au/Ba/Be/Bi/Bo/Bu...)** — A research-style file without the need for a separate 3x5 card file. Use 129 file folders (all must be 1/5 cut). Label each set of five using a letter of the alphabet followed by a vowel (see above for example), for all 26 letters of the alphabet. Identify and file material by the first letter and first vowel of its topic (ex.: Family under **Fa**, Children under **Ci**, Internet under **Ie**, and so on). This system is very quick and easy for filing, but it requires you to be able to recall what topic you would file something under. You can place cross-reference sheets in other folders to indicate the file where the material is located. Always write the assigned topic at the top right of the filed material.

Hang It All, Get the Best!

Yes, hanging file folders are more expensive, but they are worth the extra money. They are incredibly versatile since you can move the plastic label holders to any of nine positions. Add colored folders and you can create categories or file systems within file systems. They actually can be more economical in the long run since you can easily change the paper file labels that slip into the plastic holders. They almost never wear out, and the metal top edges make them very durable and easy to handle. They come in standard office-green or a variety of different colors. Most file cabinets and portable files are designed now to use them without any modification, or a simple metal frame will fit right in and get you hanging.

File Folder Mashup

Another approach that works well for an Intuitive file is to combine hanging file folders and full-cut manila file folders. I use different colors of hanging files for different kinds of material (red for action, blue for information, yellow for projects, etc.). I then use the full-cut manila folders that are labeled for the contents and placed in a hanging file folder. (Some hanging file folders contain more than one manila folder.) I can also use the hanging file folder tabs for dividers or labels.

Periodical Control

Periodicals (magazines, newsletters, newspapers) are just paper weeds—they will overtake your home and choke out all signs of new organizational growth if you don't keep them weeded out. Do not save low-priority magazines, mail, newspapers, or other paper information unless you are certain you will recycle it, clip it or file it. If you're not going to, toss it!

My heart is not proud, O LORD, my eyes are not haughty; I do not concern myself with great matters or things too wonderful for me. But I have stilled and quieted my soul; like a weaned child with its mother, like a weaned child is my soul within me. O Israel, put your hope in the LORD both now and forevermore.

— Psalm 131

Because my life is rarely neat and together, I attempt to make my devotional spot a regular place where I can spend my quiet, holy moments resting in beauty and having a sense of civility. This gives a sense of order to the rest of my life, even when the other edges of my life are seemingly out of control. Life in our home with four kids, a dog, and people in and out rarely provides composure. Yet when my inner life is composed, my outer life feels manageable.

— Sally Clarkson, *The Mom Walk*, Harvest House, 2007

How many a woman's life is spoilt by the fret and fever of a disquieted spirit waiting for "more time," and feeling the overwhelming claim of home life, upon every moment of her day, she gets in the stream of ceaseless work and worry, and denies herself the necessary leisure for physical recreations and spiritual rest!...Duties never clash. If thoughtful mothers would remember their "previous claims" upon time and energy and strength, they would not rob their lives of the quiet and rest which health of soul and body alike demand by accepting responsibilities which are too often burdensome and at best but ill-discharged.

— Mrs. G. S. Reaney, *Mothers and Motherhood*, 1896

FIRST: Managing Rest

The real heart of motherhood is not found in those deep, but often sentimentalized, feelings of maternal love for our children, but rather in the very real and demanding random acts of giving that fill a mother's life. Getting married is wonderful, but as you move into motherhood and then into homeschooling, a fuller picture of God's plan for family comes into focus. God is asking you to give much more than just your heart as a mommy—he asks you to give your time, energy, freedom, expectations, resources, plans, emotions, body, and more. A homeschooling mother's days are a litany of giving—cleaning, cooking, washing, driving, teaching, talking, training, explaining, correcting, writing, helping, preparing, resolving, e-mailing, calling, meeting, leading, participating, serving, entertaining, discussing, listening. Motherhood is not a sentimental journey but a challenging marathon characterized by acts of giving—giving to, giving over, giving away, giving in, giving out, and occasionally, when not enough is taken in, giving up.

And that last one is the real challenge of the homeschooling lifestyle—how to stay refreshed and replenished as a mother so you can keep giving out, without giving up. Perhaps it is no accident that Rest is in the middle of the FIRST acrostic. You can keep the other aspects of keeping your home together in balance—Family, Information, Stuff, and Time—but only if you keep Rest at the very center. Rest is the fulcrum of a fruitful life at home. It is part of God's created order for mankind and the fourth of his Ten Commandments. In the same way that God created for six days and then rested, we are to rest from our work, and that certainly should include a mother's work at home. It's a command, a divine principle, and part of the image of God imprinted on our souls.

The principle of rest is all through Scripture—God "rested from all His work" at creation (Genesis 2:2) and commands his people to rest in the same way (Exodus 20:11); the psalmist said, "Be still, and know that I am God" (Psalm 46:10); Isaiah said, "In repentance and rest is your salvation, in quietness and trust is your strength" (Isaiah 30:15); Jesus said, "Come to me, all you who are weary and burdened, and I will give you rest" (Matthew 11:28); the writer of Hebrews said, "for anyone who enters God's rest also rests from his own work, just as God did from his" (Hebrews 4:10). Rest is biblical! It is part of the divinely-designed process of bringing order and peace to your home. You know instinctively that your children laugh and smile more when their mommy is refreshed and replenished, and they probably frown and mope when she is weary, tired, and grumpy. Your getting enough rest will put smiles on your children's faces.

Paul talks about the principle of reaping what we sow, and he even acknowledges that a good Christian can become "weary in doing good" even to the point of being willing to "give up" (Galatians 6:7-10). Weariness can disable you from doing the good you want to do for your children. But if you sow rest into your life at home, "at the proper time [you] will reap a harvest if [you] do not give up" (6:9). Being a mom who is able to bring a harvest of order and peace into her home does not happen by accident—it is an intentional process. Getting enough rest involves much more than just lying down for a few minutes—you need rest not only physically, but spiritually, mentally, and emotionally as well. Rest is about your life and needs as a whole person, not just about the busy mommy part. Following are a few suggestions to help you start the process of integrating rest into your life at home.

- **Use personal boxes.** You can use the box as a principle to ensure that you get the rest you need. Think of rest as your personal time box, a place of solitude and quiet in your day. It will also help your children visualize your rest time and respect it. Remember that it's a time for rest, not for work. Make the most of your personal box.

- **Children rest or read.** The focus of this section is on you getting rest as a homeschooling mother, but your children need rest too. So make their rest the time for your rest. We have a rest-or-read time every afternoon when children may either read a book or take a nap (rest). Make it a daily, nonnegotiable, 30-60-minute time.

- **Seek solitude.** In a house full of children, you need to insist on regular solitude and quiet, even if just for a few minutes each day. You need a time in the midst of the tumult of life when you can say with the psalmist, "But I have stilled and quieted my soul" (Psalm 131:2). Restoration begins with rest and quietness (Psalm 23:1-3).

- **Subtract distractions.** This may be the hardest part about getting rest. Assuming your children are reading or resting, make a commitment to limit outside distractions—put aside work, unplug the telephone, silence your cell phone, close the laptop, turn off the TV or talk radio, shut your door. It takes discipline. Just don't do it!

- **Add comforts.** Rest is personal. Add whatever creature comforts will make the time in your personal box more restful and relaxing—Scripture, books, beauty, music, tea or coffee, favorite food, plants, flowers, magazines, poetry. Customize your box.

- **Live wisely and well.** Beyond the personal box time at home, you cannot ignore all of the commonsense lifestyle factors that affect your ability to find rest and restoration—diet, exercise, stress, relationships. You need a balanced diet rich in whole grains, fresh fruits and vegetables, low-fat dairy, vegetable oils, lean meats, complex carbohydrates (not refined sugars and flour), and water. Your body needs good fuel to run well. You need daily exercise, such as walking, to help regulate your metabolism. You need to learn some simple ways, such as meditation on Scripture and deep breathing, to counter the physiological effects of stress and anxiety. You need seven to eight hours of sleep. You need close friends with whom you have freedom to share whatever is on your heart and who can carry your burdens and pray for you.

IN OUR HOME

As the homeschool mother of the house, I (Sally) know that adequate rest is a key priority because there is never a time to catch up on lost sleep. An important time of my day is my midafternoon, private, "do not disturb!" take-the-phone-off-the-hook, one-woman tea time. It is during the kids' rest-or-read hour, so I take as long as that lasts for my own rest-and-read time. Another great rest period for me is when Clay takes the kids for weekend outings so I can have the house all to myself! I also make it a habit to go to bed early so I get plenty of sleep since I like to get up early for my morning "tea-votional" time. These little things may not seem like much, but they can add up to a weary sigh of resignation when they're missing and a contented sigh of relief when they're there. I rest my case.

The LORD is my shepherd, I shall not be in want. He makes me lie down in green pastures, he leads me beside quiet waters, he restores my soul.

— Psalm 23:1-3a

Whatever your personality, be sure you allow yourself the time to be refreshed in a way that is right for you. There is no single, one-size-fits-all formula for how and where that happens, but you need enough time with yourself to determine how and where it will happen for you.

— Sally Clarkson, *Seasons of a Mother's Heart*, Apologia Press, 2009

Dads: Give Mom a Rest

Easy things to do with the kids to give mom a rest.

Out-ings (away from the house)

- Take them to the park.
- Take them to a nature center.
- Take them to a lake or beach area.
- Take them to a museum.
- Ride bikes in the country with them.
- Take them on a mini field trip.
- Go on a hike with them.
- Go swimming with them.
- Take them to the library reading time.
- Play tennis with them.
- Take them to special events.
- Take them to local seasonal festivals.

In-ings (in and around the house)

- Read books to them.
- Play a game with them.
- Throw a ball or shoot baskets with them.
- Take a walk around the block with them.
- Teach them something new.
- Clean up the yard together.
- Make a tent with them.
- Build something with them.
- Play table tennis with them.
- Overhaul bicycles (clean, tighten, etc.) together.

Do not love the world or anything in the world. If anyone loves the world, the love of the Father is not in him. For everything in the world—the cravings of sinful man, the lust of his eyes and the boasting of what he has and does—comes not from the Father but from the world. The world and its desires pass away, but the man who does the will of God lives forever.

— 1 John 2:15-17

I spend a lot of time straightening my house and attempting to keep a peaceful, orderly environment that soothes and blesses my family. However, I am a passionate, philosophical, artistic person. I am very relational but love to have time to think, read, write, and drink lots and lots of tea and coffee.

— Sally Clarkson, *The Mom Walk*, Harvest House, 2007

FIRST: Managing Stuff

Homeschooling is a stuff magnet. Much of the stuff that accumulates in an average public or private school classroom now accumulates instead in your living and learning rooms—books, supplies, curricula, materials, visual aids, media, projects, displays, collections, and so much more. And then there's the stuff that accumulates because your children are in your home 24/7/365—and the more children you have at home, the more stuff there is to manage. You cannot ignore the reality of stuff in the homeschooling lifestyle—either you must manage it or it will manage you. It may sound simplistic, but the stuff in our homeschooling life would have buried us but for the principle of the box. Here are some thoughts on managing stuff in your home by the box.

- **Stay alert for boxes.** First, become a box lover. Learn to look for boxes and storage containers that you can put to use in your home. If they're in a store, wait until they go on sale and then buy what you need. If they are discards, grab them quickly before a more dedicated box-er comes along.

- **Keep boxes consistent.** Whenever possible, use a consistent size and type of box for each stuff piling area (a place in your home where large amounts of stuff accumulate or are stored). Stackable boxes are by far the most space-efficient way to box stuff in a closet. Be sure they can be labeled. Transparent boxes are even better.

- **Store like things together.** Keep the contents of boxes generally homogenous (the same kinds of stuff)—crafts, holiday, special papers, little toys, extra homeschool supplies, and so on. Be sure to label every box with a large removable label that can be read when the boxes are stacked.

- **Box everything.** General rule for loose stuff in the house: If it's loose and has friends, box them all! In other words, as you go around the house, find all the stuff that's loose and make general-purpose storage boxes for it if you can.

- **Get rid of old stuff.** Purge your possessions annually. Be merciless. If you haven't used something in 2-3 years, it's not likely that you're ever going to use it, so why hold on to it? Give it to Goodwill, the Salvation Army, or a local thrift store while it's still useful before you have to throw it away when it's useless. Always try to make space when you take space. You cannot displace space infinitely in your home—you've got to make room for more, especially as your family grows.

IN OUR HOME

No matter how messy the rest of our learning room is, parents who come by (especially moms) nearly always comment on the closet. Their object of interest is a converted eight-foot closet with three deep shelves. In the closet are about thirty small plastic lidded and labeled boxes filled with the kids' toys, educational stuff, rubber stamp collection, and so on. There are also wing-lidded boxes on the floor full of stuff and medium and large plastic boxes full of Legos. There are Bankers Boxes on the top shelf full of holiday stuff and boxes with small games on two shelves. There are still messes, but now they are containable.

Good Boxes for Home Management

You can find discarded boxes free to get better organized. However, buying good storage boxes will be an investment that you will be able to use for many years. The are some definite advantages to better storage boxes: they will last longer; they are easy to stack and use space much more efficiently; they are easier to label; they often allow you to see what's inside them; they are easily repurposed for a variety of storage uses; and they can be sold (although you probably never will). Here are some of the boxes we've used the most, most of them for many years.

- **Bankers Boxes** — The venerable Bankers Box is easily the most versatile box for things, papers, and longer-term storage. They are easy to stack (5-6 high), label (write on the sides of the box), and get into (removable lid). You can store them in closets or along walls in a dry area. The heavy-duty, double-walled style is best. (Staples, Office Depot, Walmart, Sam's, Costco)

- **Mover's Book Boxes** — If you have more books than bookshelves, as we do, you'll eventually need to store books. The standard mover's book box is a good, inexpensive way to store books. Be sure to seal (two-inch shipping tape) and label them well. If you think you might reuse them, label them using removable (not permanent) 4x3 shipping labels. (U-Haul Moving Center, www.Uline.com, Sam's, Costco)

- **Small/Medium Lidded Clear Plastic Boxes** — These small boxes are good for little things that can be collected and grouped. They're usually stackable, so you can store a lot in a small space. Clear plastic lets you see inside, and colors let you organize by category. (Walmart, Target, Sears)

- **Large/Shallow Lidded Clear Plastic Boxes** — These are useful for under-the-bed clothing storage, but also for many other kinds of items. If your kids have lots of Legos or Duplos, the shallow design makes it easier for your child to look for pieces. Good for larger papers and artwork, too. (Walmart, Target, Sears)

- **Hinged-Lid Crates, Clear** — These crates are good for any items you want to be able to store away quickly but identify easily. Just right for blocks, Legos, multi-piece building sets and toys, crafts, supplies, decor, and more. Quick and easy access, stackable, and durable. (Home Depot, Lowes, Sears)

- **Hinged-Lid Crates, Heavy Duty** — These solid, sturdy boxes are good for large, heavy items, books, heavier craft materials, and garage/shed storage. The heavy-duty style is a commercial crate that will not break or crack and will last a lifetime. (www.Uline.com, www.Globalindustries.com)

- **Milk Crates** — Plastic milk creates are good for keeping things that you want to move around the house (cleaners, supplies, books, etc.). Sturdy construction, stackable, and easy to carry with built-in handles. (Walmart, Home Depot, Lowes)

- **Mini Milk Crates** — These are harder to find, but really great for organizing CDs, supplies, letters, and little stuff. Sturdy and stackable. (Walmart, Target)

- **Wood Fruit Crates** — If you know a grocer, the wood fruit crates are useful for collecting all the children's outdoor stuff in one place.

Tour de Boxes

Here is a very brief tour of some of the home box-works at the Clarkson house.

- Small lidded plastic boxes with all the kids' little stuff, rubber stamps, supplies, etc.
- Bankers Boxes for closet organization, storage, kids' keepsakes, financial records, and lots of other stuff
- Mini milk crates for storing CDs, cassettes, office supplies, etc.
- Medium and large lidded plastic boxes for games, Legos, crafts, modeling clay, blocks, hardware and tools, supplies, etc.
- Small milk-crate-style boxes for loose stuff in the boys' toy closet
- Portable hanging file boxes for homeschool papers, music, records, maps and travel information, manuals, etc.
- Clear wing-lidded crates for holiday decor, large crafts, books, etc. (easy to ID through the clear plastic)
- Large, heavy-duty, wing-lidded storage crates for hardware, garden, garage, and large items

Managing Time: Analog

Analog, paper-based organizers are not surrendering to the digital invaders. Every major retail chain seems to have its own selection of organizers, calendars, add-in sheets, accessories, and binders. And if you don't like what's on the shelf or in the catalog, design and print your own pages with your home computer and printer. Every organizer has its own unique look and feel, so you have to kick the pages and slam the binders to find the one that's right for you.

- Day-Timer
- DayRunner
- Franklin-Covey
- Quo Vadis
- Filofax
- At-a-Glance
- Moleskine

Managing Time: Digital

Digital, Internet, and electronic systems will inevitably win the war of the organizers. Inconvenient, slow, eco-challenged, static paper is losing ground to convenient, fast, eco-friendly, dynamic technologies. A new class of young homeschool parents, the first wave of the digital generation, will adopt and integrate new software and hardware technologies to manage the time in their lives at home.

- Android phones
- Apple MobileMe
- Blackberry
- Google Calendar
- iPod Touch
- iPad
- iPhone
- MS Office Outlook

FIRST: Managing Time

No matter how much you might decry the accelerated pace of life or how much you try to simplify and declutter your calendar, it seems that some kind of planner or organizer—paper, digital, mobile, or cloud—has become a necessary accessory in our time-obsessed and time-challenged culture. When you add the stay-at-homeschooling lifestyle to the already crowded calendar of the average American mom, the need for planning becomes even more acute. For the homeschooling parent, an organizer or planner is more than just a convenience; it is a trusted tool to help you keep making the most of every opportunity every day in your home and family. A calendar is about finite increments of time, but this chapter is about the principle of time boxes. This principle gives you a new way to think about and visualize the blank pages of days and weeks in your organizer or planner waiting to be filled up. It's a way to use your time more wisely.

- **Choose what you will use.** No matter what kind of digital or printed calendar, planner, or organizer you own, the real test of effectiveness for any of them is this: Will you use it? A simple weekly planning calendar and an ordinary to-do list may be all you need to get started in managing time. Or you may want a nice leather organizer with detailed calendars and extra planning pages. Or you may be fully digital, using your PC with Microsoft Outlook, or Mac with apps, or Google Calendar and Android, or a iPhone or iPad, or whatever works for you. You can spend a lot of money on any kind of organizing system, but if it does not "think" the way you do—if it does not fit your own mental patterns—you probably will not use it. Use what you will use.

- **Choose how you will use it.** Unless you are a veteran organizer and planner, it is probably best to start with some paper planning sheets for homeschooling lesson plans and records. Use your personal calendar or organizer to map out your week into time boxes, schedule appointments, keep a running to-do list, and keep other notes and information you need handy (phone directory, grocery list, meeting notes, etc.).

- **Keep time in a box.** Any calendar or daily planner is just a box for time. To be a good home manager of time, you need to train yourself to think of your week in terms of time boxes. A time box is a two-to-four-hour segment of time that can either be filled with specific tasks, activities, or goals or be left empty. It is a single unit of time, not a series of discrete time segments. For example, Tuesdays from 8:30 to noon is a box for homeschooling, 1:00-3:00 is a box for discovery studies, 3:00-6:00 is an unscheduled box, and so on. Each day is different, but the principle remains the same.

- **Put lids on your time boxes.** Think of mealtimes and bedtimes as lids for your time boxes. Divide each period of time before and after the lids into one or two time boxes (for example, a lunch lid, followed by two two-hour time boxes in the afternoon). Avoid the temptation to open time boxes ahead of their time.

- **Don't reopen what you've closed.** Group similar events and commitments into each time box whenever possible (errands in a box, homeschool lessons in a box, etc.). Once a time box is closed for that day, don't go back to what you had planned in it until the next day. In other words, don't borrow time from other boxes. If you're behind, it's better to close that box and just wait until the next day to try to catch up.

- **Don't overplan.** Don't try to plan activities by time segments within your time boxes, such as what you will do every fifteen or thirty minutes. Rather, plan your general goals for that time box, estimating the time it will take you to complete each goal (so you don't plan four hours of goals for a three-hour time box), and then place them all in that time box without regard to segments of time. Again, see the box as a single unit of time, not as a string of time segments.

- **Leave some boxes open.** Always leave at least two time boxes empty each week for flexibility and spontaneity. You should always build unscheduled time into your schedule to relax, catch up on missed work, do something new and unplanned, or whatever. The basic principle is don't overplan. Keep a sheet of "things to do to fill an empty time box" in your organizer. You'll be surprised at what you can get done.

- **Avoid media time thieves.** Media can include TV, radio, and film, but TV is the main culprit. Although many homeschooling families wisely bypass it, cable and satellite TV is pervasive and ubiquitous in our twenty-first-century lives. Most homes have a television of some kind, and home theaters are growing in popularity. Anyone with a remote knows how quickly hours can be lost in channel surfing, but even "good" video viewing can ruthlessly consume time. If you choose to have cable, satellite, or a large video library, you must exercise strong discipline to prevent it from becoming a giant hole into which you or your children pour time.

- **Avoid digital time thieves.** The computer and the Internet have revolutionized the world, but those advances have also grown time-thieving tentacles of technology that reach into every part of our lives—e-mail, social media, cell phones, smart phones, cellular Internet, cloud computing, streaming audio and video, MP3 players, e-book readers, DVDs, digital photography and video, GPS devices, tablet computers, netbooks, and on and on. Though the digital and gadget universe will change rapidly and often, the basic advice will never change—parents must control their own use of technology so they can teach their children how to control theirs. Every new gadget represents one more potential time thief to reduce the time your children can spend reading books, discussing great ideas, exploring their gifts, and living real life. You're the one in control of the digital invasion of their lives. Guard your children's hearts.

Top Ten Time Eaters

In no particular order, these are the time consumers that subtly nibble away at the precious minutes and hours of your day. They may be very good things that are also blessings, or they may be things that you could do without. In either case, they all eat away at the minutes of your day. They are the things that leave you wondering at the end of the day, "Where did all the time go?!"

- Unscreened incoming phone calls from friends during homeschooling time
- Unoccupied children, especially when they are young and inside the house
- Emotional breakdowns of children (favorite thing lost, soiled, touched, or broken)
- E-mail, blogs, Facebook, and other digital distractions
- Interruptions of a home business in the daily routine (if new, quadruple the effect)
- Unexpected, uninvited friends dropping by (especially if they bring young children)
- Multiple messes, unfinished projects, and piles of papers in the house
- A new baby, a sick child, or both
- Plumbing and appliance disasters of any kind
- Telemarketers and programmed phone calls

IN OUR HOME

We are definitely a family of planners. For years, until parental demands no longer allowed it, we would go out as a couple for breakfast once a week with Day-Timer and Quo Vadis planners in hand, even though most of the time we didn't really need to. Now we really need to do planning, but we have to do it whenever we can—before breakfast, driving in the car, late at night. We do, however, try to set aside a half day together about once a quarter to do major planning and to set goals for ourselves and our family. I (Clay) created a "My Days and Ways" binder organizer for kids with pages for calendar, planning, financial stewardship, spiritual, correspondence, and even life goals and plans. With the advent of the digital age, there's not as much need for paper planners anymore, but it's a legacy I leave anyway. Now I'm planning how to digitize all those planners.

Routinize Your Kids

The goal of routines in your children's lives is to train them to be responsible and to take initiative without being told. In other words, the more routine there is in their lives, the more they should begin to take initiative in other areas, independently and without prompting. Routines also give your children a certain sense of stability and feeling of security that is important in a homeschool setting.

- **Schedule** — Any recurring daily event should be cultivated into a daily routine—rise-time, educational activities, mealtimes, bedtimes, chores, and responsibilities.

- **Delegate** — Age-appropriate responsibility for routines (all or part) should be transferred to your children as soon as possible—collecting and putting out the trash, mowing the lawn, vacuuming and mopping, and other areas of housecleaning.

- **Expect** — Don't keep or take over an area of responsibility that your children are able to do. Make your children masters of their own routines. While it is not necessary to reward children when routines are maintained, you should be sure there is a cost of some kind for broken routines.

- **Structure** — Use routines as anchors to stabilize your children's days. The more they know what is expected of them or what is allowed at all times of the day, the more they will follow the patterns of living you create. Routines become automatic so your children are not always looking to you for direction.

- **Recover** — When life throws your routines off temporarily, always get your children back on them as quickly as possible. The longer you delay, the more time and effort that will have to be applied to re-establish them.

The Invisible Energy of Routine

There is a physics of homemaking. Just as there are natural laws that govern the natural universe, there are home laws that govern the home universe. The most obvious would be the natural laws of home thermodynamics: All things tend to disorder and disarray, and a finite amount of energy is being dissipated at a constant rate. And you thought physics just applied to science studies! Similarly, there are also invisible powers in the home universe that hold everything together. In the physical world, there are subatomic powers that keep   thing from flying apart. In the home universe, there is a correlative invisible power that keeps everything from flying apart—it is called routine.

Routine is simply a habitual pattern of living created by effort applied regularly over time. Once a pattern of living is established in one area of your lifestyle and schedule, it becomes an invisible, self-generating force to hold that part of your home universe together and keep it from coming unraveled. The more you learn to harness and use the power of routines, the more efficient you will become and the more energy you will actually conserve. That extra energy can be applied to other areas of your home, creating new efficiencies and ultimately more energy reserves. However, if routine is ignored, inefficiency will begin to rule, and energy will rapidly dissipate in wasted efforts to regain lost equilibrium. The elements within your home universe will naturally begin to disintegrate at rapidly increasing rates of decay. When that happens, even greater amounts of time and effort are needed to regain and maintain stability. Routine is the stabilizer.

Like the laws of home thermodynamics, there are also cause-and-effect laws of routine: For every action taken to establish routine, there is an equal and similar reaction generating greater amounts of routine energy; and for every action not taken to establish routine, there is a corresponding decrease in total home routine energy. All that is to say that it takes a lot less energy to live with established routines than it does to live without them. Most children will not naturally be driven to develop routines on their own, so you will need to create them for them, but it will be worth the effort. If your children see you establishing routines in your life (devotions, exercise, house cleanup), they will be more likely to imitate your example in their own (Bible reading, home-school assignments, cleaning up their room, chores). Routine will return more than it requires.

IN OUR HOME

Morning at our house is the most important time for routines. If the children get off to a good start with their morning routines—get dressed, make bed, straighten room, read Bible, set breakfast table, clean dishes—then they do better at remembering other routines throughout the day. A good start really sets the pace! Bedtime is another routine time, but somewhat of a wild card time in our day. We're not very consistent on the "time" of the bedtime, so we focus on training in the routine of getting ready for and into bed. If it's early enough, Dad keeps up a reading routine by reading aloud. The beauty of routines, theoretically anyway, is that once they become set patterns, you won't have to ask...as much. Our goal is always to use routines as a source of guidance, not guilt.

The Routine Ups and Downs of Home Life

There will be days in your homeschool journey when you'll be tempted to think that enduring to end will not be as big a challenge as just enduring to the end of that day. The homeschooling lifestyle can at times become personally challenging, yet it is a path of greater blessing with God, and he is always ready to walk through it with you. The charts below provide some simple wisdom and ways to think about the "ups and downs" of the homeschooling lifestyle and how you can navigate them with God's grace.

Home Management Uppers: Staying UP on Top of It All

UPPER	What?	When?	Who?
Putting Up	Messes	As You Go	Whoever makes the mess or benefits from it (meals) helps.
Picking Up	Things	Daily	Everyone picks up and puts away clutter at set time every day.
Cleaning Up	Dirt	Weekly	Everyone cleans the house with and without assignments.
Keeping Up	Information	Monthly	Parents do e-mail maintenance, filing, and piling. Kids help.
Catching Up	Organization	As Needed	Everyone helps, but it helps to have at least one organizer.

Home Management Downers: Getting DOWN from It All

DOWNER	Source	What to Do	Comment
Lying Down	Laziness	Get going. Get organized.	Ask God for strength to do his will at home. **Philippians 4:13**
Winding Down	Inactivity	Get healthy. Get fit.	Ask God for help to be healthy and fit. **1 Corinthians 9:27**
Slowing Down	Overcommitment	Get free. Get realistic.	Ask God for wisdom to guard your time. **Philippians 3:13-14**
Falling Down	Weariness	Get rest. Get help.	Ask God for personal and spiritual rest. **Galatians 6:6-10**
Getting Down	Hopelessness	Get counsel. Get support.	Ask God for faith and hope in the Spirit. **Hebrews 10:35-39**

It is natural to whine and complain or to be selfish and unloving—but it is supernatural to praise and be thankful and to choose to express love and faith—even when my feelings don't agree. When we choose to practice praise, joy, and love, when we cultivate celebration even as God did, we then find that we experience the love of God to a greater degree in our own lives.

— Sally Clarkson, *The Mom Walk*, Harvest House, 2007

Allowing for Allowances

Every family has its own philosophy when it comes to money. Here are some of the principles that we use.

- **Give Allowance** — Allowance is s given. It should not tied to chores or responsibilities. It is given just for being part of the family—no strings attached.

- **Expect Chores** — Chores are performed without remuneration. They are simply a responsibility attached to being part of the family. Chores are generally defined by daily use—the child helped generate the mess or benefited from it (meals, room, etc.).

- **Reward Extra Help** — Extra help, on the other hand, is rewarded, usually financially. Extra help is generally defined as work that the child did not generate or that does not directly benefit the child (yardwork, straighten attic, clean garage). The parent decides when a task should be remunerated. Extra help tasks can also evolve into chores as the children get older.

Teach us to number our days aright, that we may gain a heart of wisdom.

— Psalm 90:12

By organizing my life to make time to dwell in the light and beauty of the Lord, everything else seemed to fall into place. I became a happier, more joyful mom, and my children and husband benefited from me taking life as a gift, not as a job or duty to complete. This journey is a marathon, which requires pacing myself and making sure I don't burn out before the end of the race.

— Sally Clarkson, *The Mom Walk*, Harvest House, 2007

Managing Your Home or Just Managing?

Most stay-at-home homeschooling moms would readily agree that if ever there were a part of the homeschooling lifestyle that needs to be redeemed, it would be housekeeping. The apostle Paul encourages us to do just that. In Ephesians 5:15-16, he exhorts his readers to be "very careful, then, how you live— not as unwise but as wise, making the most of every opportunity, because the days are evil." Literally, he tells them they are to be "redeeming the time" (NKJV). The Greek word for redeeming is the same term used for the price Christ paid on the cross for our freedom; it was also the term used for buying a slave out of slavery and setting him free. But here, it is "the time" (*kairos*) that is enslaved that we are to redeem. How does that apply to the Christian home?

God wants us to redeem even the housekeeping time in our busy lives—to buy that time back from slavery to the world and set it free for God's use. Here's the point— housekeeping should not be wasted time! It is valuable time just waiting to be freed for God. We can squander it, and fail to "make the most of every opportunity" God gives us, including housework. But that is God's time just as every other minute of your day is his, and it is your choice whether it will be left enslaved to the world or set free for God's purposes. You can think of all the practical suggestions in this chapter only as coping strategies for surviving the mundane tasks of housekeeping, or they can be powerful tools for redeeming your time at home for God. It's your choice.

Moses said much the same thing in Psalm 90: "Teach us to number our days, that we may present to You a heart of wisdom" (90:12, NASB). It's all too easy to let large portions of our days slip through our fingers, leaving behind only meaningless minutes. But Moses calls on God to teach us that we have a limited number of days on this earth that can be used wisely or unwisely. If we learn how to number our days and redeem the time we are given, we can present to God at the end of our days a heart of wisdom. That is the real goal of learning to bring order to your home domain and to keep your home together—not just to get through the housework faster and more efficiently so you can get to the "real" parts of the homeschooling life, but to learn wisdom even from the necessary housework part of life at home. God will use that redeemed time to build wisdom in your life and in your children's lives. That is the ultimate purpose of ordering your home.

IN OUR HOME

We have dedicated to God's use every house we have owned as a homeschooling family when we moved in. We decided early on that a House Beautiful *home was probably a home largely unused by God. When you open your home to God and ask him to use it for his glory, the reality is that it tends to be in various states of disorder. When we clean, it's not just about subduing dirt and messes, but it is about making our house ready for ministry or restoring order after ministry. Housework is a work of ministry. We have regularly opened our homes for large groups of children and teens, fellowship dinners, people needing a place to stay, travelers, three years of a Bible study for forty to fifty women, church prayer and worship meetings, neighborhood gatherings, and much more. The mess is the ministry.*

— Chapter 18 —

Support:
Keeping the Spirit Strong

Feeding Your Spirit to Keep Going

Homeschooling, by its nature, can be a lonely lifestyle, both for you as a parent and for your children. Even though more families are homeschooling every year, it will be a very long time, if ever, before the movement can generate the same kind of communal identity inherent in almost any expression of institutional schooling. Of course, along with that kind of school-centered community identity come other intractable problems that mitigate against its appeal, but it can and does provide some sense of belonging even so. Homeschooling, on the other hand, is still in essence a countercultural decision. You are choosing not to go with the flow of everyone else in the river of culture. It is a decision not so much to swim upstream against the flow of that river as it is to swim in a slow-flowing tributary apart from it. Even though others are in your tributary with you, the sense is still that you are swimming alone, and you have to swim pretty hard just to keep moving. It's not as easy to keep swimming when it's just you and your kids.

It's the same thing the Jewish Christians probably felt when they were forced out of Jerusalem at the persecution of the new church following the stoning of Stephen. They were no longer swimming in the cultural river of Judaism, and they were getting tired of swimming alone in the new tributary of Christianity. The author of Hebrews encourages them to stay strong in faith with admonitions to "spur one another on toward love and good deeds," to "not give up meeting together," and to "encourage one another" (10:24-25). It echoes the many "one another" statements of the New Testament that affirm a critical truth for all believers—we cannot live the Christian life alone. That is especially true for Christian homeschoolers; you need others to help you stay faithful.

But there's another side to that coin of truth. Paul admonished the Colossian believers to "let the word of Christ dwell in you richly as you teach and admonish one another with all wisdom, and as you sing psalms, hymns and spiritual songs with gratitude in your hearts to God" (Colossians 3:16). We think of that verse for the church, but why not also for the Christian homeschooling home, where that picture of one-anotherness can be lived out all day every day instead of only once or twice a week? Our independence requires a lonelier life on some levels, but it also provides the opportunity for that richer and fuller spiritual life centered on Christ as a family. We are each other's best "one another" to enjoy the blessings of life in Christ. This chapter is about how to make sure you don't swim in the stream of homeschooling alone, so you can enjoy the wonderful richness of the homeschooling lifestyle. We offer just a few ideas, but there are many more ways you can find support and fellowship. They generally will not find you, so you'll need to find them and then make the effort to connect and engage with them. It's a lot more enjoyable swimming with others, so begin to find your own support groups.

Two are better than one, because they have a good return for their work: If one falls down, his friend can help him up. But pity the man who falls and has no one to help him up! Also, if two lie down together, they will keep warm. But how can one keep warm alone? Though one may be overpowered, two can defend themselves. A cord of three strands is not quickly broken.

— Ecclesiastes 4:9-12

Humans are created to be God's hands of comfort, God's words of affection and appreciation, God's face of love, and God's works of service and help. We are created to be one of the venues in which the Spirit of God demonstrates the reality of his own unconditional love. Friendships and other close relationships provide opportunities for people to feel the love of God through words and touch, given by real people who are prompted by his Spirit.

— Sally Clarkson, *Dancing with My Father*, WaterBrook Press, 2010

Support Group Unity

In a typical small and informal homeschool support group, there will often be a wide range of church and cultural backgrounds. Even though the real source of unity is Jesus Christ and a common commitment to home education, the diversity can foster interpersonal conflicts. To guard against conflict, following are some suggested guidelines for small support groups:

- **Annual Goals** — Group goals should be determined and evaluated each year at a meeting of the group members, not by one person. A group leader can be recognized then.
- **Group Leader** — All planning and general communication should go through the group leader. That person oversees the group calendar and coordinates with other members in charge of events or field trips.
- **Volunteer Workers** — All involvement should be voluntary. If there are no volunteers for an event, then there is not sufficient interest in it. Mandatory attendance and assigned responsibilities don't work. Legalism will kill a small group.
- **No Drop-offs** — Group activities should never be used as passive childcare opportunities. Allow for flexibility, but establish and enforce a "no drop-off" policy.
- **No Gossip** — Group members should agree together not to gossip among themselves about each other. Encourage one another to never start, and to always stop, gossip.

Get Involved in a Support Group

Wherever two or more Christian homeschoolers are living in an area, there they will be gathered in that name. A homeschool support group is not the church, but the same need for fellowship and support in community with other like-minded Christians that drives believers together drives Christian homeschool families together as well. Support groups can even be a bit like denominations—some organizing around a shared curriculum or approach to home education (such as whole books, unit studies, or classical education), some to provide classes and activities, and others coming together primarily for fellowship and field trips. Most groups, though, recognize the reality that a homeschooling parent without a support group can become isolated and vulnerable. The perceived need of educational support is what brings groups together at first, but it's the felt and real needs of encouragement and social contact that keeps them going. A group can also become an important source of group identity, friends, and activities for your children. However, keep in mind that even though everyone in the group is a homeschooler, it won't necessarily mean all in the group will share the same values. Still, don't stay home without one!

A small, informal support group (ten or fewer families) is easy to establish and lead, so there are often many of these groups in an area, although not all will be open to new member families. If you can't find a group that suits your needs, you can start your own group. Invite several homeschooling families to meet together, and put announcements about the meeting where other likeminded families might see them. Poll the group to identify common needs and desires for support—fellowship, field trips, activities, cooperative learning. Determine the scope of the group and requirements for participation. Make a calendar, ask for volunteers, and get started. Leadership usually flows to the one most willing to create a calendar or a newsletter for the group. An alternative small support group is a whole-book or similar study group (history, science, etc.). It is an informal fellowship that meets regularly to review and discuss topics, books, and resources. Planned activities give the children a regular social outlet, but they can also do special readings, recitations, and presentations as part of the group meeting. These smaller groups tend to be more informal and to meet less frequently than a formal homeschooling support group.

A large support group of dozens or even hundreds of families has some distinct advantages over smaller support groups. In the same way that a larger church can provide more services, a larger support group can offer more classes, special events, special speakers, graduation ceremonies, contests and awards, large social events, and other services. There are often smaller sub-groups within the large one that offer additional options for fellowship and involvement. Larger groups also, by necessity, have many leadership and volunteer needs through which you can get involved and get to know others in the context of ministry. There are, though, disadvantages inherent in the large group model. Not surprisingly, all the attractive benefits typically require a significant financial commitment in the form of membership, class tuition, and event fees. Larger groups unfortunately can also provide increased potential for disagreements, personal conflicts, unwanted influences on your children (usually by other children), and other negative experiences. Before you join a large support group, get to know the leadership and learn as much as you can about the inner workings and culture of the group. The best support group will be the one your children look forward to attending because of the friends and activities.

Homeschool Support Group Etiquette

There's nothing quite like a homeschooling support group meeting with children to stir up the troubled waters of the sin nature. Aside from everyone just choosing to walk in the Spirit, sticking to a few basic, commonsense rules of support group etiquette can help keep the waters calm. It's mostly just about thinking of the needs of other first.

- **Be early.** In order to be sure to be on time, plan to be early; being late is rude.

- **Be engaged.** Control your children in the meetings so others won't feel they have to.

- **Be brief.** When speaking or sharing, be brief so others will have an opportunity.

- **Be positive.** Complaining is a sign of immaturity, not insight; it can be corrosive.

- **Be discreet.** Gossip of any kind should be off limits, even for "prayer requests."

- **Be helpful.** Help pick up and clean up before leaving; make children do the same.

- **Be courteous.** Don't be the last one to leave; encourage others to depart on time.

- **Be available.** Volunteer to help with activities and projects when there is a need.

- **Be faithful.** Come to meetings every time you are able; it shows respect to others.

- **Be humble.** Personal humility is a sure antidote for personal conflict and discord.

- **Be loyal.** Even if you disagree, support and encourage your fellow homeschoolers.

IN OUR HOME

We have participated in an amazing variety of support groups in our twenty-five years of homeschooling. These are the highlights, but not all the lights. Our first support group was a formal umbrella school in southern California in 1988 (when we were the only homeschool family in our church of 1,500). When we moved to Nashville, Tennessee, in 1991, we started our own church-based support group with a moms' Bible study and educational co-op that quickly grew to 40 families and 120 children (later renamed Whole Heart Academy and still going in 2011 after twenty years). When we moved to rural central Texas in 1993, we joined a small, home-based support group of about 10 families and later made our own connections. In 1997, we were part of a small church in Fort Worth that was predominantly homeschoolers. In Colorado in 1999, we were involved in a local support group in our community, and then we planted a church with all homeschool families. We moved back to Tennessee in 2002 and created our own mini-support group with friends. We moved back to Colorado in 2004 and became involved in High Country Home Educators at New Life Church, an umbrella school, support group, and educational co-op with up to 800 children at all grade levels. Sally has been a Bible study teacher and small group leader there. More recently, we have started our own history study group of four families, all close and personal friends with children who know and enjoy one another. Our weekly meetings are a highlight for all of us. It doesn't get better than friends.

Starting a Larger Group

If you are in an area with a sufficient population and you see the need for a larger support group, or if you have a vision and desire to create a group, here are some abbreviated tips for how to get started.

- **Don't rush.** Homeschool full-time 2-3 years before attempting to start a group. Leadership will be very demanding.

- **Plan ahead.** Plan 6-12 months in advance. Create a leadership team to share the responsibilities.

- **Find a facility.** Try to find a homeschool-friendly church with rooms for classes, nursery, Bible study, and more.

- **Promote the group.** Promote over the summer for fall. Set a maximum group enrollment. Create a waiting list if needed.

- **State beliefs.** Create a simple statement of faith to ensure leader agreement on areas of essential doctrine.

- **Create policies.** Create a support group policies statement that all must sign, as well as a group info notebook.

- **Create positions.** Create a clear and complete job description for any leader or volunteer positions.

- **Set tuition.** Charge fairly. Pay well for good teachers. Offer reduced fees for leaders and volunteers.

- **Set up accounting.** Make sure accounting is done professionally, especially if your group is church-based.

- **Get financial advice.** Consult an accountant. If nonprofit, be sure you know the law and the expectations.

- **Get legal advice.** If you are an independent group, be sure you understand legal liabilities and constraints.

Books for Help and Hope

We love books that feed and encourage us as homeschooling parents. After all, those are the kinds of books we've written for other parents.

Parenting

- *Heartfelt Discipline* (Clay Clarkson)
- *Hints on Child Training* (H. Clay Trumbull)
- *The Ministry of Motherhood* (Sally Clarkson)
- *The Mission of Motherhood* (Sally Clarkson)
- *The Mom Walk* (Sally Clarkson)
- *Seasons of a Mother's Heart* (Sally Clarkson)
- *What Is a Family?* (Edith Schaeffer)

Homeschooling

- *A Biblical Home Education* (Ruth Beechick)
- *Beyond Survival* (Diana Waring)
- *For the Children's Sake* (Susan Schaeffer Macaulay)
- *The Heart of Home Schooling* (Christopher Klicka)
- *Let Us Highly Resolve* (David & Shirley Quine)

Resources

- *A Charlotte Mason Companion* (Karen Andreola)
- *Books Children Love* (Elizabeth Wilson)
- *How to Grow a Young Reader* (Kathryn Lindskoog & Ranelda Mack Hunsicker)
- *Our 24 Family Ways* (Clay Clarkson)
- *Read for the Heart* (Sarah Clarkson)
- *Seven Tools for Cultivating Your Child's Potential* (Zan Tyler)
- *You Can Teach Your Child Successfully* (Ruth Beechick)

Get Out Books to Read

The homeschool lifestyle, by its nature, is more home-centered. A certain degree of loneliness—of feeling separated from the social norms of other parents in your community and church—comes with your choice to stay home with your children. You will need regular encouragement to strengthen your convictions and stay motivated as a home educating parent, so do what you tell your children to do—look to your books. Start building a library section of books on Christian parenting and homeschooling. Even though they're just paper and ink, they'll become some of your best friends the longer you homeschool.

- **Family and Parenting** — There are only a few family and parenting books around that reflect or affirm the values of a home educating family. When you find one, it is a rare jewel—you'll find yourself going back often for more encouragement and insight. *Hints on Child Training* is a must-read from 1890.

- **Christian Life** — As we have tried to express in this book, the homeschooling lifestyle is not just about an alternative education but about striving for the fullest expression of biblical ideals of family and the Christian home. Read books that will help you live the Christian life with grace and freedom, in the power of the Holy Spirit.

- **Homeschooling Introductions** — These are the homeschooling primers that give you the "why to" from a variety of perspectives. They reinforce and sharpen your convictions and remind you why you are homeschooling. The best are Christian models that reinforce a real-life and literature-centered approach to learning.

- **Homeschooling Testimonies** — Reading real-life war stories from the homeschooling front lines can be a shot in the arm when you're feeling a bit battle-weary yourself. The methods and even the spiritual values may vary, but the commitment is the same. It helps to hear what others have gone through.

- **Teaching Methods** — Read books that will reinforce your own preferred methods of teaching your children. If you adopt a WholeHearted Learning approach, look for books that promote a whole-book or literature-based method and that emphasize learning through real-life experiences.

- **Educational Resources** — Even if you don't need any new resources, reading about all the resources available is a learning experience in itself. Major on books with good reading lists and full-service catalogs and magalogs that specialize in whole books. They usually have many helpful articles in addition to the resources.

- **Life Management** — Proverbs is, in essence, the first "book" on life management. There is a never-ending flow of books with new insights about how to live and work more efficiently and effectively. Some are biblically-based, most are not, and yet there are good insights to be found. Minor on these books.

- **Personal Motivation** — There are many motivational books that will move you, stir your spirit, and push you in a new direction. Great literature and stories can do that, but so can a wise person with life experience and a gift of writing. When considering one of the latter, make sure their spirit is biblical and their testimony is credible.

Get On the Internet

First, the bad news: The Internet is not going away. But here's the good news: The Internet is not going away. You heard that right. The Internet is an enormous cultural advance that we love, love to hate, and hate to love. As a medium for finding support as a homeschooling parent, it can connect you with an exciting online world of homeschoolers you would never otherwise know. However, the Internet is a values-neutral tool that can open up an attractive virtual world on the one hand while shutting out the difficult real world on the other. For some lonely homeschooling moms, that virtual reality can become very enticing, even to the point of escaping into it to the neglect of children. That doesn't mean the Internet is bad; it just means to be cautious about how you use it. The best that we can say here is this: Don't be afraid of it, but be careful and be disciplined. It's impossible to cover this topic in less than a book, but here a few thoughts as you go online.

- **Blogs** — There are many excellent blogs that will help you and feed your soul as a homeschooling parent—too many, to be honest, so limit the number of blogs you follow. To manage your time reading posts from your favorite blogs, use an RSS feed reader (such as Google Reader) and read all new blog posts at once at a set time during the day. If you want to comment, keep it short and to the point.

- **Social Media** — Social media is still young and evolving. On its face right now, it is an easy, personal, and immediate way to connect and communicate with other homeschoolers. However, it can also quickly devolve into a world to itself that demands constant monitoring. If you don't know someone, you don't have to friend them; if you do, you can hide their posts on your feed. Use social media wisely.

- **Websites** — Websites are somewhat old in some ways, and yet they are still the heartbeat of the web. There is an ocean of useful information on websites for you as a homeschooling parent, and you can spend hours searching, surfing, and scrolling through pages. It's easy to become "digistracted," getting lost in link detours taken along the search. Stay ruthlessly focused when searching. Get in, get out, get on.

- **Forums** — Forums are no longer as popular as they once were, but they are still a useful tool to get answers to questions or to seek advice. Avoid the temptation to get into long discussion strings about controversial topics. Minutes can quickly become hours of pouring words into a digital black hole. Use forums wisely to gain wisdom and insight to help you, not to engage in or win arguments or, worse, to gossip.

IN OUR HOME

If you have something to say that might help or encourage other homeschooling moms, then you might be a blogger waiting to happen. I (Sally) never thought of myself as a blogger until I started blogging on www.ITakeJoy.com and began to see moms being encouraged. My heart is to be a source of spiritual encouragement to moms, and all of a sudden I was communicating with moms around the world. I try to write a blog post twice a week, which I find doable early in the mornings. Now I'm connected with many other blogger moms who encourage me.

Safely Networking the Net

Know some basic rules to stay safe and secure on the Internet.

General

- When not online, disconnect from the Internet.
- Set up a personal firewall.
- Keep your antivirus software updated and automated.
- Change important passwords periodically with a combo of alpha-numeric characters.

E-mail

- Never open attachments from unknown sources.
- Never open attachments with an ".exe" extension.
- Never send credit card information as e-mail text.
- Don't include sensitive info in e-mails—username, password, PINs, SSN, DOB.
- Don't respond to e-mails requesting personal data.
- Don't click any links in any suspicious e-mails.
- Use BCC (blind copy) to send private bulk e-mails so you don't expose friends' e-mails.

Websites

- Look for HTTPS in the address bar to know it's secure.
- Don't click links from unknown sources; type the URL in your browser address bar.
- If a website seems unprofessional or unusual, leave it.
- Never provide personal info to a website for access.
- If on a public, unprotected network, don't make purchases or send private info.

Social Media/Blog/Website

- Post only what personal information is needed, no more.
- Don't post address, phone numbers, places of work, or children's names.
- Use a disposable e-mail address, not your primary e-mail address, on public sites.
- Don't post anything that could be gossip, personal about others, venting, controversial, or slanderous.
- Download only from reputable sites or known sources.

Annual Tune-Up

Summer is a good time for an annual tune-up of your home and homeschool. Set aside a week and get everyone involved. Here are a few suggestions for tuning up the home front for a new year of homeschooling.

- **Purge** — Get rid of all the books, papers, used workbooks, unused workbooks, broken pencils, and useless stuff that is just taking up space in your learning room.
- **Organize** — Systematize your storage so everything has a place (at least for a while). Use whatever organizers and boxes will help.
- **Arrange** — Put the library back together with an accessible arrangement. Arrange desktops for maximum efficiency and minimum clutter potential. Give each child a study area all their own.
- **Plan** — Determine your first-quarter goals for each child, write them out, and post them. Plan for any new materials you need to acquire.
- **Schedule** — Fill in monthly calendars with all known event and commitment dates. Post the calendar where all can see it and add to it as necessary.
- **Shop** — Set aside a day to shop for school supplies and clothes. Stock up on often-used items and materials. Go to the teacher supply store to get supplemental resources.
- **Simplify** — Take stock of commitments and determine which ones can be dropped. Consider simpler ways of doing things at home—meals, clean up, chores, etc.
- **Relax** — Don't be so hard on yourself. Keep long-range goals in mind, not just short-range plans. Resolve to find some time each day to relax.
- **Refocus** — Review with your spouse why you started homeschooling and why you want to continue. Refresh your vision and purpose.

Get Off to a Good Start

Whether you are a newbie or a veteran, it is not necessary to approach homeschooling each year as though you are completing the pre-flight checklist for a Boeing 757—books, check!...materials, check!...blackboard, check! All you really need to do is get oriented and headed in the right direction. If you can overcome the initial inertia and get started moving in the right direction, momentum will build to keep you going from there, and all the details will begin to take care of themselves in due time. Here are some commitments that will help you get off to a good start. The rest is up to you.

- **Agree and pray with your spouse.** Christian home education is a ministry to your children. You and your spouse must be of one heart and mind—not just that home education is God's will for your family but also about your philosophy of homeschooling. If you are divided on either of those issues, see that as a "slow down" flag. Set aside a day to get away together to talk and pray about your family.

- **Set goals and make plans.** Once you are on the same page as a couple about homeschooling, begin to determine together some general goals for your children—academic, spiritual, social, physical. Then write out some simple plans for how you could begin to accomplish those goals. Don't be overly detailed with the actual plans—just create something you can (and will) use to keep you on track.

- **First, work on devotion and discipline.** Discipleship is the foundation of education. Your first priority of home education is to establish patterns of family devotion, Bible study, and Bible reading. Decide the what, when, and who of discipleship activities and get them on the calendar or planner. At the same time, you should also define together your convictions about childhood discipline and training. Be sure you agree on discipline so you can be consistent and supportive of one another.

- **Next, begin reading to your children every day.** Reading is the lifeblood of the WholeHearted Learning model. Make it a daily priority to read aloud to your children and to have them practice the habit of regularly reading alone. Reading aloud a wonderful work of children's literature at mealtimes or bedtimes will become a highly anticipated activity. Even if the rest of your day falls apart, always try to spend some time with your children reading aloud and narrating.

- **Then, establish routines for living and learning.** Determine what your days will be like as you organize them around the five focused study areas of the WholeHearted Learning model. Establish a daily routine so your children know what you expect of them throughout the day and week. Train your children in self-control and responsibility by encouraging them to become the regulators of the routine. If positively affirmed, they will make it their young mission to keep you on track.

- **Set up your learning room and discovery corners.** Your learning room and discovery corners should be like an educational garden for your children. If you plan that garden well, then wherever they plant themselves at home, they should be able to grow a little more inside because they are drawing nourishment from a little spot of soil that has been enriched just for them. If you cultivate the soil of a learning environment throughout your home, growth will happen naturally.

- **Build a quality home library.** Your library will become the heart and soul of your homeschool. Start filling it up with all kinds of whole and living books, as well as child-friendly reference books. The more books you have on your library shelves, the more likely it will be that your children will naturally reach for a book to satisfy their natural hunger for knowledge without your prompting. Good children's literature, quality illustrated storybooks, and photo-illustrated Eyewitness-style books that invite browsing are all especially inviting. Good books are an investment in your family.

- **Choose your instructional materials carefully.** Some learning activities, such as language arts and math, just take more diligence and discipline than others. However, be careful that your learning materials do not create unnecessary work. The basics take work, but they should not be drudgery.

- **Enjoy life with your children.** Above all, relax. Take time just to enjoy your children and get to know them. Begin to enjoy family the way God always intended it to be. You were designed to be living, learning, loving, and growing together at home. Homeschooling is a natural extension of the family—it brings back into the home what never should have been given away. If you and your children are feeling tense, stressed, and burdened by homeschooling, then you probably are trying to do too much or you are trying to use burdensome textbooks and workbooks. Homeschooling does not have to be complicated or overwhelming. The WholeHearted Learning model will liberate learning in your home.

- **Care for yourself and your children.** Take care of your kids. Make sure they get plenty of exercise and fresh air. Give them a healthy, balanced diet with plenty of energy-feeding and body-building whole grains, fresh fruits and vegetables, lean meats, nuts, and water. Limit foods that are known to make them sluggish physically and mentally, such as sugars, refined carbohydrates, saturated fats, processed foods, and empty-calorie junk foods. Be sure they get sufficient sleep and outdoor exercise. Healthy children will be happier children, and healthy, happy children make much better students. Set a good example by taking care of yourself in the same way. Eat, exercise, and rest wisely—you'll need all the energy you can get to keep going.

IN OUR HOME

We homeschool year-round, but September always starts a new "school year" for us. One of the things our children noticed early on is that their schooled friends always got a bunch of new stuff when they started school. We're not ones to imitate the world, but we both had fond memories of those early school days of shopping for new notebooks, paper, stuff to fill up the plastic pencil pouch, a lunchbox, and new school clothes. We decided it was a worthwhile investment in homeschool motivation, so every year we would brave the crowds and take our children shopping for the new school year. We would give them a list of the things they could buy and head for Target or Walmart. We would also let them pick out a new outfit and maybe a new pair of sneakers. It was a fun way for them to start the school year and gave them the same fond memories.

Get on Good Mailing Lists

Whether you get p-mail (paper mail) or e-mail, get on the mailing lists of organizations that you value. Hearing from them regularly will be an encouragement and a help.

<u>Organizations</u>

- Whole Heart Ministries
- Home School Legal Defense Association (HSLDA)

<u>Publications</u>

- *The Old Schoolhouse*
- *Home School Enrichment Magazine*
- *Practical Homeschooling*
- *Homeschooling Today*

<u>Catalogs and Suppliers</u>

- Beautiful Feet Books
- My Father's World
- Timberdoodle
- www.ChristianBook.com
- Rainbow Resource

<u>Activity Calendars</u>

- Chambers of Commerce
- Churches, ministries
- Local newsletters, newspapers, periodicals
- Colleges, seminaries
- Library
- Recreational facilities
- Museum, zoo, nature center
- Tourist areas or attractions
- Symphony, theater
- Local professional associations, clubs

<u>Groups</u>

- State/regional homeschooling organization(s)
- Local support group(s)
- Informational organizations

Let us not give up meeting together, as some are in the habit of doing, but let us encourage one another—and all the more as you see the Day approaching.

— Hebrews 10:25

Mom Heart CPR

In the physical world, a heart that stops beating needs CPR—cardiopulmonary resuscitation. In the spiritual world, we believe God's heart for motherhood needs some CPR—celebration, preservation, and restoration. Mom Heart small groups are our attempt at spiritual CPR to restore moms' hearts to God's design for biblical motherhood.

- **Celebration** — communicating and cultivating a positive, affirming, attractive vision of biblical motherhood
- **Preservation** — keeping biblical motherhood in the cultural and ecclesial conversation about children
- **Restoration** — fueling and feeding a renewal movement centered on the biblical priority of motherhood

Get Together with Other Mothers

Going to a homeschool support group is a little like the experience of going to church on Sunday morning—you look forward to it, you want to fellowship with others, it gives you and your family a sense of belonging and mission, and you are reminded of why your choice is important to you and to God. But the same thing that church leaders know Sunday morning alone cannot provide church members can also be missing in a homeschool support group—spiritual and biblical accountability, encouragement, and support throughout the rest of the week. That's why churches create small group ministries, and that's why we encourage homeschooling mothers, if at all possible, to have a small group of like-minded mothers with whom they can meet regularly, study the Word of God together, and encourage, pray for, and support one another as mothers. Without that kind of group, you might be tempted to believe that your driving goal is to be a great homeschooling mother. But it's not! Homeschooling is a means, not an end.

Your goal is to become a great *biblical* mother, one who reflects and lives out God's design for motherhood. You need a small group to strengthen your mom heart so you can live confidently and faithfully to the beat of God's heart for mothers (pp. 279-284). You may be thinking, "Well, I get together with several mom friends during the week for a play day, usually more than once, and we have great fellowship together, so that's enough for me." There's no question that those kinds of relaxed friendships and activities are critical to the homeschooling lifestyle, but you do need more, even if you don't realize it. Many highly committed homeschooling moms are not able to see what's missing simply because their lives are so full of activities and people. What they really need is not more homeschooling activity, but one simple biblical activity.

Christian homeschooling mothers live in a culture that no longer values the biblical design for motherhood. In 2010, more women were in the workforce than men for the first time in our country's history. In every area of American secular culture that shapes values and beliefs—media, government, education, entertainment—the biblical vision for motherhood is routinely ignored, ridiculed, or simply rejected as outdated and even oppressive. Even the church has found it hard to affirm the biblical design for motherhood when so many of the mothers in its congregations are part of that prevailing culture.

As a Christian homeschooling mother, you are choosing a lifestyle that will have you swimming against the rising tide of secular culture. Nothing in culture, and frankly very little in the church, is going to affirm and validate your decision and lifestyle. You may not realize it, but you are a countercultural warrior holding the hill of homeschooling against a vast army of educational secularists—a nonconforming rebel breaking ranks and marching to your own drum. It's good to have comrades in arms—your homeschooling friends, who will celebrate your decision with you—but that's not enough. If you plan to stay in the battle, you will need to think strategically. What is missing and what you will need is a small group of moms who will study God's Word together to keep one another accountable, refreshed, renewed, and committed to the biblical design for motherhood. Homeschooling is not your strategy for staying strong in the battle to be a biblical mother; following God's eternal plan for motherhood is the only strategy that will help you stay strong as a homeschooling mother. You need a small group.

How to Start and Lead a Small Group for Moms

You need one small group for two big reasons—to be encouraged as a mother by other moms and to encourage other moms. That's the heart of any small group. However, a small group that exists only for itself will eventually become ingrown and die. That's why a small group also needs a spirit—to train mothers to start and lead new groups. That's the 2 Timothy 2:2 principle of multiplication—teaching faithful believers who can then teach others. You can easily start a small group with other moms by following five simple steps: ask, meet, read, talk, and pray. But two more simple steps will move your group from being a meeting to becoming a ministry: train and send. That's our vision for Mom Heart small groups for mothers—to train moms how to start and lead small groups and how they can train and send others to do the same. That's biblical ministry in its most basic expression, and you can do it. The following outline, an acrostic of HEART, is a small group meeting model we use to train mothers how to lead an effective small group. Additional instruction and resources are in the *Mom Heart Group Leader Guide*.

- **H = Hear the Spirit** — Ask a question or read a quote that allows the Spirit of God to open hearts and minds (not about Scripture content, but to raise interest level).

- **E = Engage the Word** — Read and discuss the Bible study passages and questions in whatever lesson you are using. Discuss together God's voice and intent.

- **A = Affirm the Truth** — Help the group identify together one big idea (a one-sentence summary) that captures the truths discussed in the lesson.

- **R = Respond to God** — Give the group a few minutes of quiet reflection time during which each mom can write out a brief personal response or application to the lesson.

- **T = Take it to Heart** — Briefly share some responses to the lesson (not personal prayer requests) and then pray together as a group about the truths learned.

IN OUR HOME

Starting a new homeschool support group was challenge enough—coordinating facility, teachers, registration, classes, volunteers, and everything else was more than a handful of responsibility. I (Sally) trained a team of four women to be my leaders, and it was still a challenge when we started with over 100 children. So it was probably a bit perplexing to some that I insisted that the group also include a required Bible study time for all moms when they weren't volunteering in the classes. From my own experience from the previous seven years of parenting and from my background in ministry, I strongly believed that even if they did not know it, homeschooling mothers needed more than just a convenient drop-off educational co-op. They needed spiritual support, not just as homeschoolers but even more as Christian mothers. That time of fellowship and encouragement became an anchor in the week for all of us. It is a model that I have repeated as a leader in other homeschool groups in the twenty years since that first one— moms supporting one another as moms.

Mom Heart Ministry

Mom Heart Ministry is a ministry initiative of Whole Heart Ministries to cultivate an international movement of small groups for mothers to restore moms' hearts to God's heart for motherhood. To learn more about Mom Heart small group leader training, online resources and networks, and small groups materials, visit the Mom Heart website at www.momheart.org.

Sally's Books for Groups

Sally's books are written and designed with small groups in mind. Find some moms, pick a book, read, meet, talk, and pray.

- *Seasons of a Mother's Heart* — Sally's first book for homeschool mothers and for small group Bible study
- *The Mission of Motherhood* — the big picture of biblical motherhood, with good small group questions
- *The Ministry of Motherhood* — mothering after the model of Jesus, using the LifeGIFTS model of discipleship
- *The Mom Walk* — how to walk with God by faith, in his Spirit, on the path of life and motherhood

Keeping Your Group ALIVE

Every small group can become dull and seem dead spiritually. Here is a helpful acrostic to keep your group alive.

- **A = Affirm** — Affirm each woman's unique personality, strengths, gifts, and abilities.
- **L = Listen** — Listen to each woman's story of her journey, children, concerns, dreams.
- **I = Inspire** — Inspire each woman to embrace her story as God's to use for his glory.
- **V = Validate** — Validate each woman's thoughts, fears, and feelings as important to God.
- **E = Encourage** — Encourage each woman with biblical words of faith and confidence.

Search me, O God, and know my heart; test me and know my anxious thoughts.

— Psalm 139:23

And whatever you do, whether in word or deed, do it all in the name of the Lord Jesus, giving thanks to God the Father through him.

— Colossians 3:17

...continue to work out your salvation with fear and trembling, for it is God who works in you to will and to act according to his good purpose.

— Philippians 2:12b, 13

For God did not give us a spirit of timidity, but a spirit of power, of love and of self-discipline.

— 2 Timothy 1:7

Get Your Heart Right with God

We began this book by challenging your convictions about home education. In four sections, we looked at topics related to Home, Learning, Methods, and Living—what makes a Christian home, principles of home education and the WholeHearted Learning model, methods for the five focused study areas of the model, and what it takes to live out this model in your home. Now, as we reach the end, we come full circle back to you, the home educating parents. When all the philosophy, methods, and materials are stripped away, it is clear that Christian home education is an issue of the heart...your hearts, your children's hearts, and God's heart. If you really believe homeschooling is a matter of obedience to God's will in your family, then you should do it with your whole hearts—driven by the conviction it is right, with confidence that the full authority of God and his Word is behind you. As a couple, get your hearts right together so you are of one mind when you share your vision for your family with others. Keeping your hearts right will not be because this book or any other is so convincing or persuasive but because you have turned your hearts together to God, made a decision in faith, and will keep it by his grace. That point of faith should become an anchor in your life. Keep the following in mind.

- **Children** — If you are making this decision as a young couple, you are blessed that your children will know only homeschooling as their lifestyle. If you have older children (elementary age), give them the freedom to voice their thoughts and opinions with you, but let them know you are obeying God. They will follow your hearts. If you have teens, it will require much more prayer and interaction, depending on their spiritual maturity. God will work in any situation.

- **Family** — Let your parents know about your plans and reasons to homeschool. Hopefully they will be supportive, but even if they are not, it is best to have the matter out in the open. Keep the discussion open as much as possible. You can let other family members (siblings) know about your decision when it seems right and natural.

- **Church** — If you are involved in ministry of any kind in a local church, you should share your plans with your pastor or with ministry leaders under whom you serve. Most church leaders will be supportive, but be prepared to stand on principle if yours are not. Talk to your friends at church and casually let them know your plans.

- **God's Word** — You need to hear God's voice. Don't rely only on all the good arguments for homeschooling, but seek out God's will for your family, his plan for parents and children, his design for the home, and his path of greatest blessing for your family. Go to God's Word together regularly and listen for his voice.

- **Prayer** — When you pray out loud together, you will find God speaking to you through his Holy Spirit as you speak to him. Prayer can be a powerful time of expressing the convictions and desires of your heart and putting real words to them. Pray together often and listen for God in the conversation.

- **Friends** — When you fellowship in the Spirit with other Christian friends that you know, love, and trust, God will speak through them to you. As you share your vision for your family and they respond with biblical encouragement and personal support out of their love for you, you will be strengthened in your spirit by the Spirit of God.

Postscript

— Postscript —

The Challenge: Keeping Faith in the Family

There's No Place Like Home

Who can forget the classic movie moment when a young Judy Garland, playing Dorothy in *The Wizard of Oz*, closes her eyes, clicks her ruby-slippered heels together three times and says with great feeling and teen angst, "There's no place like home." Of course, it didn't happen that way in the 1900 book by L. Frank Baum. There the slippers are silver, and Dorothy simply orders her magic shoes, "Take me home to Aunt Em!" But the movie was in 1939, ten years into America's Great Depression, when people were daring to hope again. The movie scene is a celluloid paean to the sentimental notion of family that has long shaped the American ideal—home as a place of perfected family love, warm feelings, and security in a troubling world.

The movie-Dorothy actually borrowed her famous line from John Howard Payne's 1822 poem and song, "Home, Sweet Home." Payne's lyric has become one of our most oft-quoted and cross-stitched family maxims: "Be it ever so humble, there's no place like home." Seventy-odd years after the movie, most Americans will still affirm in principle that 1939 sentimental ideal of home. The reality, though, is that the story and song of the American home now include dark lines with the sour notes of brokenness, fragmentation, isolation, dissolution, and hidden horrors. "Be it ever so humble" notions aside, cynics today might say there really is "no place like home" as Dorothy envisioned.

But they're wrong. They're looking in the wrong place. The true ideal of home is not defined by human experience but is found in God's design and his Word. Because we all bear the image of God, that ideal is stamped on the inmost being of every person alive. It manifests as a deep spiritual longing for home, but it is corrupted and covered over by sin. Those who will not see and honor God, the Creator, as the author and designer of home will see only a false ideal of home born of poems, movies, and sentimentalized human experience. Without God in the picture, the idealized family portrait is colored by a hopeful, humanistic sentimentalism that simply glosses over the reality of sin.

But that is not your family portrait. You honor God, acknowledge that he is the Creator, and see in his design for home and family a divine institution through which he desires to bless his creatures. You put no hope in the sentimentalized visions of "Hollyworld" but in the God who gives you, your spouse, and your children eternal hope. Your faith paints the portrait of your home with the colors of reality from the palette of God's Word. And it is our mission to help you paint the most beautiful, realistic, inspiring portrait of home and family for all the world to see and desire. We will help you keep faith in *your* family so it never fails or fades and keep faith in *the* family so you have confidence in the God who designed it. There's no place like home...with God in it.

Do not conform any longer to the pattern of this world, but be transformed by the renewing of your mind. Then you will be able to test and approve what God's will is—his good, pleasing and perfect will.

— Romans 12:2

Mid pleasures and palaces
though we may roam,
Be it ever so humble, there's no
place like home!
A charm from the sky seems to
hallow us there,
Which, seek through the world,
is ne'er met with elsewhere...

How sweet 'tis to sit 'neath a
fond father's smile,
And the cares of a mother to
soothe and beguile!
Let others delight 'mid new
pleasures to roam,
But give me, oh, give me, the
pleasures of home!

Home, Home, sweet, sweet
Home!
There's no place like Home!
There's no place like Home!

— From "Home, Sweet Home" by John Howard Payne, 1822, American actor, author, poet, and playwright

331

But seek first his kingdom and his righteousness, and all these things will be given to you as well.

— Matthew 6:33

Jesus replied, "If anyone loves me, he will obey my teaching. My Father will love him, and we will come to him and make our home with him."

— John 14:23

When the disciples saw this, they were amazed. "How did the fig tree wither so quickly?" they asked. Jesus replied, "I tell you the truth, if you have faith and do not doubt, not only can you do what was done to the fig tree, but also you can say to this mountain, 'Go, throw yourself into the sea,' and it will be done. If you believe, you will receive whatever you ask for in prayer."

— Matthew 21:20-22

But the seed on good soil stands for those with a noble and good heart, who hear the word, retain it, and by persevering produce a crop.

— Luke 8:15

But the Counselor, the Holy Spirit, whom the Father will send in my name, will teach you all things and will remind you of everything I have said to you.

— John 14:26

Take a Step of Faith Toward Home

We'll end where we began. This is where you must take a step of faith. Everything is said, and now it remains only for things to be done. However, we are not going to ask you to buy a curriculum, subscribe to a periodical, or join our special co-op. There's nothing wrong with any of those things, but our purpose in writing this book has not been to try to sell you something—it has been to try to convince you that God has provided everything you need to be a Christian home-educating family. You do not need to rely on experts to do what God has already equipped and enabled you to do by the power of his Holy Spirit. Your children already have everything they need to receive a good and godly education—they have you, your home, and God's grace. All that's left is for you, by faith, to do what you are designed by God to do with your children—to "bring them up in the training and instruction of the Lord" (Ephesians 6:4). And, we might add, to do it wholeheartedly. It is up to you to take a step of faith toward home.

The book of Joshua is the historical record of Israel's return to and conquering of the land promised to Abraham and his descendants, but it is more. It is also a picture of faith and salvation. It is no coincidence that Joshua is the Hebrew name for Jesus—Jeshua, which means "Jehovah is salvation." In the first five chapters of Joshua, there is a picture of what it means to step out in faith in the five references to "feet" (NASB).

- **1:3 Promise** — God promised Joshua, just before he would lead the Israelites into the Promised Land, to give him "every place on which the sole of your foot treads." Jesus promises that he will honor our faith when we live for him. (Matthew 6:33)

- **3:15-17 Obedience** — When the priests carrying the Ark of the Covenant obeyed God's instructions and put their feet in the water, God dried up the waters of the Jordan as he said he would. Jesus promises to honor our obedience. (John 14:23)

- **4:9 Faith** — While the priests were standing in the middle of the Jordan as God had directed, Joshua built his own altar there in an act of personal faith. Jesus promises that even the smallest amount of faith can move mountains. (Matthew 21:20-22)

- **4:18 Perseverance** — The priests, who had carried the Ark of the Covenant on their shoulders the entire day, stepped out of the Jordan, and it returned to normal as promised. Jesus promises that our perseverance will produce fruitful results. (Luke 8:15)

- **5:15 Presence** — Joshua confronts the "captain of the host of the Lord" (Jesus) as he stands outside Jericho, where he is told to remove his sandals because God is there with him. Jesus promises the Holy Spirit to be his presence in our lives. (John 14:26)

Wherever you are in the process of choosing homeschooling, God is ready to honor your step of faith toward home. Joshua could have tried to conquer the land by relying on his weapons, warriors, and brilliant strategy as a general, but he would have failed spiritually. God wanted his faith. It's the same for you. You can home educate your children by relying solely on experts, curricula, and "proven" methods, but you will miss part of God's blessing. He wants you to trust in him in your homeschooling. He wants your faith so that he will have the honor of having produced the fruit. Take a step of faith toward home, and then keep walking. God will be with you each step of the way.

Begin with the End in Mind

Do a Google search on "Begin with the End in Mind" and you'll find those words applied to a wide range of careers and circumstances. Perhaps the phrase is most famous as the second of Steven Covey's *Seven Habits of Highly Effective People*, which he defines as "begin everything you do with a clear picture of your ultimate goal." However, it was a popular maxim long before that. The Apostle Paul spoke of "straining toward what is ahead" (Philippians 3:13); Solomon before him said, "The mind of a man plans his way, but the Lord directs his steps" (Proverbs 16:9 NASB); Moses before him said, "Teach us to number our days aright, that we may gain a heart of wisdom" (Psalm 90:12). Families have their own way of saying the same thing. In Sally's home growing up, the family saying was, "Better to shoot for the moon and miss than to aim at the mud and stick." In Clay's home, it was, "Aim at nothing and you'll hit it every time." These expressions of axiomatic truth, whether biblical or just commonsense, all assume a common ideal—that there is an ultimate goal in life that is worth all the effort required to reach for it.

That is the final critical element in home education. It is the shaping force behind everything in this book. Its presence or absence will affect everything you do in home education. Without it, you will likely grow weary and give up too soon. With it, though, you will be more likely to endure, persevere, and overcome, keeping going even beyond the scope of this book until you usher your homeschool graduates into adulthood as followers of Christ and his cause. The critical element is vision. Your vision.

Vision is "beginning with the end in mind." It is how you think about your whole life, not just about today or tomorrow. It is what you see with the eyes of your spirit when you look ahead to the end of your life and then look back to the present from that perspective. Vision is your *raison d'être*, your reason for being. Unfortunately, you cannot learn from a book how to have vision for Christian home education. Vision is the byproduct of your own walk with God and interaction with his Word. The closer your walk with the Lord, the clearer your vision will be for your family's life. The more you are in his Word and his Word is in you, the sharper your vision will become. This book is an incomplete but honest attempt to capture and communicate our own family's vision for home education. Obviously, it is written to influence your vision for the education of your children, but ultimately that vision must come from God working in your own heart and mind. You must find your own vision for your life as a Christian family.

In the midst of a rebuke of King Asa of Judah, God offers a promise of hope for all who seek to do his will. "For the eyes of the LORD range throughout the earth to strengthen those whose hearts are fully committed to him" (2 Chronicles 16:9). The "eyes of the Lord" are looking for you. His perfect vision sees into your heart, seeing what you see with the "eyes of your heart" (Ephesians 1:18) as you try to keep the end in mind. When he sees your commitment to him and to his ways, it is his pleasure and delight to strengthen you for your journey of faith. Your vision—the commitment of your heart to God—is what will cause his eyes, as they range throughout the earth, to land on your heart. But homeschooling is not the vision; it is only a means to reach your vision. God is not looking for the most committed homeschooler; he is looking for a father and a mother "fully committed to him" as Christian parents. Whether or not you choose to homeschool, we pray that God's eyes will see you because of your vision for your family.

For the eyes of the LORD range throughout the earth to strengthen those whose hearts are fully committed to him.

— 2 Chronicles 16:9a

A Good End for Your Child

The end you need to envision for your children is not what they will do with their lives but what they will become. It's not about making a living but about making a life. If the internals (who they are) are strong, the externals (what they do) will take care of themselves. As we have said before, a mature disciple of Jesus Christ with the will and skill to learn is much more useful to God's work than a well-educated but immature Christian. Here are some of the goals that we "C" for our children.

- **Christ** — We will give our children Christ, in the fullness of his reality in our own lives through the Holy Spirit.
- **Calling** — We will give our children an understanding of God's claim on their lives for his purposes and glory.
- **Conviction** — We will give our children biblical convictions to give them hope, renew their minds, and fuel their faith.
- **Commitment** — We will give our children a clear choice and sound reasoning for the truth by which they will live.
- **Character** — We will give our children biblical character that will guide their relationships and choices in life.
- **Confidence** — We will give our children self-confidence to pursue boldly the dreams God puts in their hearts.
- **Competence** — We will give our children competence to accomplish whatever they determine to do for God.

We will not hide them from their children; we will tell the next generation the praiseworthy deeds of the LORD, his power, and the wonders he has done. He decreed statutes for Jacob and established the law in Israel, which he commanded our forefathers to teach their children, so the next generation would know them, even the children yet to be born, and they in turn would tell their children. Then they would put their trust in God and would not forget his deeds but would keep his commands.

— Psalm 78:4-7

Therefore, since we are surrounded by such a great cloud of witnesses, let us throw off everything that hinders and the sin that so easily entangles, and let us run with perseverance the race marked out for us. Let us fix our eyes on Jesus, the author and perfecter of our faith, who for the joy set before him endured the cross, scorning its shame, and sat down at the right hand of the throne of God.

— Hebrews 12:1-2

His master replied, "Well done, good and faithful servant! You have been faithful with a few things; I will put you in charge of many things. Come and share your master's happiness!"

— Matthew 25:23

Final Words and Final Word

There is no more important calling on your life than the parental duty of setting your children's feet on God's path of life and bidding them to follow you as you follow Christ. Your children, though, are not just a task of parenting that can be completed and checked off your "big biblical things to do" list. They are God's gift and reward to you in this life, and they are in turn your gift to the world. But there is an even greater eternal reward to parenting. Through your children, God has given you the privilege of passing on your faith and the truths of Scripture "so the next generation would know them, even the children yet to be born, and they in turn would tell their children. Then they would put their trust in God and would not forget his deeds but would keep his commands."

When you reach your heavenly home and stand before God, he will be waiting to show you the past generations of faithful families and saints who came before you and cleared a path of faith for you to find and follow his son, Jesus—that "great cloud of witnesses" who surrounded and cheered you along your own earthly journey. But then, as the Lord of eternity for whom all is eternally present, he will also show you the generations that are yet to come—all those coming after you who will find his path to their eternal home with him because of your faith and faithfulness and because of what you have done for your children. May that future cloud of witnesses be filled with faithful saints and families—the sons and daughters of your heritage as parents who will follow God and his son, Jesus Christ. And may God, your Father, then welcome you into his eternal present and presence as a "good and faithful servant," and may you "share your master's happiness" forever.

Our Prayer for You!

For this reason I kneel before the Father, from whom his whole family in heaven and on earth derives its name. I pray that out of his glorious riches he may strengthen you with power through his Spirit in your inner being, so that Christ may dwell in your hearts through faith. And I pray that you, being rooted and established in love, may have power, together with all the saints, to grasp how wide and long and high and deep is the love of Christ, and to know this love that surpasses knowledge—that you may be filled to the measure of all the fullness of God.

Ephesians 3:14-19

Resources

— Resources A —

Books for the WholeHearted Family

A Family Sampler of Favorite Books

Every family has its own favorite books. If you asked our children what their favorite books were growing up, you'd probably hear *Just David, Little Women, Heidi, The Chronicles of Narnia, Oliver Twist, Lord of the Rings, Summer of the Monkeys,* and others. Many of the books they'd mention are probably ones we read aloud, and those timeless stories have become part of the story of our family. But hundreds of other books were read alone to become personal favorites indelibly stamped on our children's hearts and spirits. Books have become part of our family, and our literary brood is always growing.

Your favorites will, of course, be different from ours but hopefully no less influential in your children's minds and memories. The list that follows is not a comprehensive collection of books for WholeHearted Learning—not even close (for that, get Sarah's book, *Read for the Heart*). In fact, we expect you to add many more of your own favorites. This list is just a sampler. It's the cream skimmed from the enormous bucket of wholebook milk. It's a tasty sip of the kinds of books that have shaped our family and our children's lives. Call it a starting place for your own list of family favorites for the roughly four-to-fourteen-year-old age window. (Reading and comprehension levels are not included since they vary so widely among children.) They're all good. Read! Read! Read!

Children's Literature

Classic Children's Fiction

- *Adventures of Huckleberry Finn* (Mark Twain)
- *The Adventures of Tom Sawyer* (Mark Twain)
- *Alice's Adventures in Wonderland* (Lewis Carroll)
- *Anne of Avonlea* (Lucy Maud Montgomery)
- *Anne of Green Gables* (Lucy Maud Montgomery)
- *At the Back of the North Wind* (George MacDonald)
- *Black Beauty* (Anna Sewell)
- *The Call of the Wild* (Jack London)
- *A Connecticut Yankee in King Arthur's Court* (Mark Twain)
- *David Copperfield* (Charles Dickens)
- *Freckles* (Gene Stratton Porter)
- *A Girl of the Limberlost* (Gene Stratton Porter)

Read for the Heart

For an extended annotated list of recommended books for wholehearted families, organized by genre and author, Sarah Clarkson's book, *Read for the Heart: Whole Books for Wholehearted Families* (Apologia Press, 2009), is a must-have companion book to *Educating the WholeHearted Child*. It is the book section of this book that needed to be its own book. Sarah shares her thoughts and convictions about the mind- and soul-shaping influence of good books, reading, and the power of story on children. She writes as a twenty-six-year-old woman looking back on the many books she read growing up as the first wholehearted child in the Clarkson home and how they have shaped her life, mind, and spirit. Chapters include:

- Reading to Live
- Reading Lost: The State of Literacy in America
- Life by Books: How to Begin
- A Roadmap for Using This Book
- Picture Books
- The Golden Age Classics
- Children's Fiction
- Fairy Tales and Fantasy
- History and Biography
- Spiritual Reading for Children
- Poetry
- Music, Art, and Nature
- Epilogue
- Appendix (book lists)
- Indexes (Authors, Illustrators, Titles)

Such is the peculiar charm of the children's classics. They have a staying power and a timeless beauty that endears them to adult and child alike. Of the many books I read throughout my childhood, these were the stories that most delighted and formed me. I almost can't imagine childhood apart from these books.

— Sarah Clarkson, *Read for the Heart*, Apologia Press, 2009

- *Hans Brinker, or the Silver Skates* (Mary Mapes Dodge)
- *Heidi* (Johanna Spyri)
- *Ivanhoe* (Sir Walter Scott)
- *The Jungle Book* (Rudyard Kipling)
- *Just David* (Eleanor H. Porter)
- *Just So Stories* (Rudyard Kipling)
- *Kidnapped* (Robert Louis Stevenson)
- *The Little Lame Prince* (Dinah Maria Mulock Craik)
- *Little Lord Fauntleroy* (Frances Hodgson Burnett)
- *Little Men* (Louisa May Alcott)
- *A Little Princess* (Frances Hodgson Burnett)
- *Little Women* (Louisa May Alcott)
- *Mother Carey's Chickens* (Kate Douglas Wiggin)
- *Oliver Twist* (Charles Dickens)
- *Peter Pan* (Sir James M. Barrie)
- *Pinocchio* (Carlo Collodi)
- *Pollyanna* (Eleanor H. Porter)
- *The Prince and the Pauper* (Mark Twain)
- *Rebecca of Sunnybrook Farm* (Kate Douglas Wiggin)
- *Robinson Crusoe* (Daniel Defoe)
- *The Secret Garden* (Frances Hodgson Burnett)
- *The Swiss Family Robinson* (Johann Wyss)
- *Tales from Shakespeare* (Charles and Mary Lamb)
- *Through the Looking-Glass* (Lewis Carroll)
- *Treasure Island* (Robert Louis Stevenson)
- *The Water-Babies* (Charles Kingsley)
- *The Wind in the Willows* (Kenneth Grahame)
- *The Wonderful Wizard of Oz* (L. Frank Baum)

Modern Children's Fiction

- *All-of-a-Kind-Family* series (Sydney Taylor)
- *Because of Winn-Dixie* (Kate DiCamillo)
- *Black Gold* (Marguerite Henry)
- *The Black Stallion* (Walter Farley)
- *Ellen* (E. M. Almedingen)
- *Father and I Were Ranchers* (Ralph Moody)
- Five Little Peppers series (Margaret Sidney)

- *From the Mixed-Up Files of Mrs. Basil E. Frankweiler* (E. L. Konigsburg)
- *Gentle Ben* (Walt Morey)
- *Great Dog Stories* (Albert P. Terhune)
- *Holes* (Louis Sachar)
- *Justin Morgan Had a Horse* (Marguerite Henry)
- *King of the Wind* (Marguerite Henry)
- *Lassie Come-Home* (Eric Knight)
- *Little Britches* (Ralph Moody)
- Little House series (Laura Ingalls Wilder)
- *Man of the Family* (Ralph Moody)
- *Misty of Chincoteague* (Marguerite Henry)
- *The Railway* Children (E. Nesbit)
- *Rainbow Garden* (Patricia St. John)
- *The Runaway* (Patricia St. John)
- *Star of Light* (Patricia St. John)
- *Stormy, Misty's Foal* (Marguerite Henry)
- *The Story of the Treasure Seekers* (E. Nesbit)
- *Summer of the Monkeys* (Wilson Rawls)
- *The Tanglewoods' Secret* (Patricia St. John)
- *Treasures of the Snow* (Patricia St. John)
- *The Twenty-One Balloons* (William Pène du Bois)
- *Tuck Everlasting* (Natalie Babbitt)
- *Twice Freed* (Patricia St. John)
- *Where the Red Fern Grows* (Wilson Rawls)

General Children's Books

Illustrated Storybooks

- *All the Places to Love* (Patricia MacLachlan)
- *The Bear That Heard Crying* (Natalie Kinsey-Warnock, Helen Kinsey)
- *Billy and Blaze* series (C. W. Anderson)
- *The Blue Hill Meadows* (Cynthia Rylant)
- *Blueberries for Sal* (Robert McCloskey)
- *The Boy Who Held Back the Sea* (Lenny Hort, Thomas Locker)
- Brambly Hedge series (Jill Barklem)
- *Bunny Bungalow* (Cynthia Rylant)
- *Dangerous Journey* (John Bunyan; *Pilgrim's Progress* condensed by Oliver Hunkin)

In their early years, children are sensory sponges, soaking up every drop of sight and sound as they furnish the landscape of their minds. With every picture and illustration they encounter, they are building an internal expectation of beauty against which they will measure all future experiences with art. They are also outfitting the realm of their imagination, setting up that secret world of pictures to which they will turn later in life as they come across great literature that will demand them to furnish images out of the stock in their own minds.

— Sarah Clarkson, *Read for the Heart*, Apologia Press, 2009

A book—a well-composed book—is a magic carpet on which we are wafted to a world that we cannot enter in any other way. Yet, in another sense, all true works of fiction have their scenes laid in the same country, and the events take place in the same climate: that country, that climate which we all long for and in our several ways strive to reach—the region where truth is eternal and man immortal and flowers never fade.

— Caroline Gordon (1895-1981), American author and literary critic, *How to Read a Novel*, 1964

- *Does God Know How to Tie Shoes?* (Nancy White Carlstrom)
- *Follow the Drinking Gourd* (Jeanette Winter)
- *From Dawn Till Dusk* (Natalie Kinsey-Warnock)
- *Hattie and the Wild Waves* (Barbara Cooney)
- *Island Boy* (Barbara Cooney)
- *James Herriot's Treasury for Children* (James Herriot)
- *Least of All* (Carol Purdy)
- *Lucy's Summer* (Donald Hall)
- *Make Way for Ducklings* (Robert McCloskey)
- *Miss Rumphius* (Barbara Cooney)
- *My Great-Aunt Arizona* (Gloria Houston)
- *My Mama Had a Dancing Heart* (Libba Gray)
- *Old Home Day* (Donald Hall)
- *One Morning In Maine* (Robert McCloskey)
- *Only Opal* (Barbara Cooney)
- *Ox-Cart Man* (Donald Hall)
- *The Quiltmaker's Gift* (Jeff Brumbeau)
- *The Relatives Came* (Cynthia Rylant)
- *Robin Hood* (Margaret Early)
- *Roxaboxen* (Alice McLerran)
- *The Seasons Sewn* (Ann Whitford Paul)
- *Simeon's Gift (*Julie Andrews Edwards)
- *Song and Dance Man* (Karen Ackerman)
- *Stories That Jesus Told* (Patricia St. John)
- *They Were Strong and Good* (Robert Lawson)
- *Through Grandpa's Eyes* (Patricia MacLachlan)
- *Time of Wonder* (Robert McCloskey)
- *Train to Somewhere* (Eve Bunting)
- *The True Princess* (Angela Elwell Hunt)
- *The Velveteen Rabbit* (Margery Williams)
- *When I Was Young in the Mountains* (Cynthia Rylant)
- *We're Going on a Bear Hunt* (Michael Rosen)
- *Wilfrid Gordon McDonald Partridge* (Mem Fox)
- *William Tell* (Margaret Early)
- *Yonder* (Tony Johnston, Lloyd Bloom)
- *The Young Artist* (Thomas Locker)

Fables, Fairy Tales, and Fantasy

- *Aesop's Fables* (various versions)

- Andersen's Fairy Tales: "The Little Match Girl," "The Little Mermaid," "The Ugly Duckling," "The Brave Tin Soldier," "The Emperor's New Clothes," "The Princess and the Pea," "Thumbelina," and others (Hans Christian Andersen)

- Beatrix Potter Tales: *The Tale of Peter Rabbit; The Tale of Squirrel Nutkin; The Tailor of Gloucester; The Tale of Benjamin Bunny;* 19 others (Beatrix Potter)

- *The Book of Virtues* (William J. Bennett, ed.)

- *Charlotte's Web* (E. B. White)

- *The Chronicles of Narnia* series (C. S. Lewis)

- *The Chronicles of Prydain* series (Lloyd Alexander)

- *Phantastes* (George MacDonald)

- *The Hobbit* (J. R. R. Tolkien)

- *The House at Pooh Corner* (A. A. Milne)

- Kingdom Tales trilogy (David and Karen Mains)

- *The Light Princess* (George MacDonald)

- *The Lord of the Rings* trilogy (J. R. R. Tolkien)

- *The Lost Princess* (George MacDonald)

- *Mrs. Frisby and the Rats of NIMH* (Robert C. O'Brien)

- *The Pilgrim's Progress* (John Bunyan)

- *Redwall* series (Brian Jacques)

- *Stuart Little* (E. B. White)

- *The Tale of Despereaux* (Kate DiCamillo)

- *The Trumpet of the Swan* (E. B. White)

- *Watership Down* (Richard Adams)

- *Winnie-the-Pooh* (A. A. Milne)

- *The Wolves of Willoughby Chase* (Joan Aiken)

- *A Wrinkle in Time* (Madeleine L'Engle)

Poetry and Art

- *Best Loved Poems of the American People* (Hazel Felleman, ed.)

- *A Child's Garden of Verses* (Robert Louis Stevenson)

- *A Child's Treasury of Poems* (Mark Daniel, Ed.)

- *Classic Poetry: An Illustrated Collection* (Michael Rosen, ed.)

- *Come Look with Me* series (Gladys S. Blizzard)

- *Favorite Poems Old and New: Selected for Boys and Girls* (Helen Ferris Tibbets, ed.)

- *The Golden Books Family Treasury of Poetry* (Louis Untermeyer, ed.)

Imaginative, fantastical stories are a gift. While great discernment is imperative in this genre, the right imaginative literature can illumine spiritual reality in such a way that it makes biblical truth clearer. Great fantasy and fairy tales uniquely capture the soul-shaking reality of the spiritual world...In an increasingly secular culture, the point of good fairy tales or fantasy is to prick our souls awake to spiritual reality. These stories can help flesh out what it means to be good into a clear-cut realm of beauty, battle, and the momentous consequences of our moral choices.

— Sarah Clarkson, *Read for the Heart*, Apologia Press, 2009

Moral excellence ought to be inseparable from creative or literary excellence. However, some people are tempted to gloss over the literary excellence (or lack thereof) of a book in favor of its moral content. While certainly some stories are worth reading just because of the virtue they relate, I think it is vitally important that children be raised primarily on books of literary value. The inherent beauty or literary excellence of a story aids in the illumination of the moral and spiritual themes it addresses.

— Sarah Clarkson, *Read for the Heart*, Apologia Press, 2009

- *He Was One of Us* (Rien Poortvliet)
- *The Image of Christ* (Morgan Weistling)
- *Jessie Willcox Smith: America Illustrator* (Edward D. Nudelman, ed.)
- *Looking at Pictures: An Introduction to Art for Young People* (Joy Richardson)
- *Noah's Ark* (Rien Poortvliet)
- Poetry for Young People series (Sterling Publishing)
- *Something Big Has Been Here* (Jack Prelutsky)
- *Talking Like the Rain* (X. J. and Dorothy M. Kennedy, Jane Dyer)
- *A Treasury of Poems* (Sarah Anne Stuart, ed.)

History and Biography

Ancient World

- *Alexander the Great* (John Gunther)
- *Augustus Caesar's World* (Genevieve Foster)
- *The Bronze Bow* (Elizabeth George Speare)
- *The Cat of Bubastes: A Tale of Ancient Egypt* (G. A. Henty)
- *The Children's Homer* (Padraic Colum)
- *Cleopatra* (Diane Stanley, Peter Vennema)
- *D'Aulaires' Book of Greek Myths* (Ingri and Edgar Parin d'Aulaire)
- *The Eagle of the Ninth* (Rosemary Sutcliff)
- *The Golden Fleece* (Padraic Colum)
- *The Golden Goblet* (Eloise Jarvis McGraw)
- *Joel, A Boy of Galilee* (Annie F. Johnston)
- *The Pharaohs of Ancient Egypt* (Elizabeth Payne)
- *Twice Freed* (Patricia St. John)

Middle Ages

- *Adam of the Road* (Elizabeth Gray)
- *The Black Arrow* (Robert Louis Stevenson)
- *Bold Robin Hood and His Outlaw Band* (Louis Rhead)
- *Brother Francis and the Friendly Beasts* (Margaret Hodges)
- *Don Quixote and Sancho Panza* (Margaret Hodges, condensed version of *Don Quixote* by Cervantes)
- *The Door in the Wall* (Marguerite de Angeli)
- *Fine Print: A Story about Johann Gutenberg* (Joann Johansen Burch)
- *Ivanhoe* (Sir Walter Scott)
- *Joan of Arc* (Lucy Foster Madison)

- *The Legends of King Arthur and His Knights* (Sir James Knowles)
- *The Magna Charta* (James Daugherty)
- *The Merry Adventures of Robin Hood* (Howard Pyle)
- *Otto of the Silver Hand* (Howard Pyle)
- *The Red Keep* (Allen French)
- *Saint Valentine* (Robert Sabuda)
- *The Scottish Chiefs* (Jane Porter)
- *Sir Gawain and the Green Knight* (J. R. R. Tolkien)
- *Saint George and the Dragon* (Margaret Hodges)
- *The Story of King Arthur and His Knights* (Howard Pyle)
- *The Trumpeter of Krakow* (Eric P. Kelly)
- *Two Travelers* (Christopher Manson)

Renaissance

- *Along Came Galileo* (Jeanne Bendick)
- *Bard of Avon: The Story of William Shakespeare* (Diane Stanley, Peter Vennema)
- *Good Queen Bess* (Diane Stanley, Peter Vennema)
- *I, Juan de Pareja* (Elizabeth Borton de Trevino)
- *Peter the Great* (Diane Stanley)
- *The Playmaker* (J. B. Cheaney)
- *Westward, Ho!* (Charles Kingsley)
- *The World of Columbus & Sons* (Genevieve Foster)

Reformation

- *The Bible Smuggler* (Louise A. Vernon)
- *The Hawk That Dare Not Hunt by Day* (Scott O'Dell)
- *A Heart Strangely Warmed* (Louise A. Vernon)
- *Ink on His Fingers* (Louise A. Vernon)
- *Morning Star of the Reformation* (Andy Thomson)
- *Thunderstorm in Church* (Louise A. Vernon)

Colonial America

- *The Adventures of Obadiah* (Brinton Turkle)
- *Ben and Me* (Robert Lawson)
- *Benjamin West and His Cat Grimalkin* (Marguerite Henry)
- *Calico Captive* (Elizabeth George Speare)
- *Columbus* (Ingri and Edgar Parin d'Aulaire)
- *The Courage of Sarah Noble* (Alice Dalgliesh)

When history is studied solely through textbooks—disconnected from the particular, colorful stories of individual lives—it loses the luster of its deep emotion and becomes simply a recitation of obscure dates. History is really the epic, true story of the world, and it ought to be told with the same skill and delight inherent in any great tale. Children need to be absorbed by the real drama of history so that they will be able to understand the vast consequences wrought by the actions of a single person.

— Sarah Clarkson, *Read for the Heart*, Apologia Press, 2009

Except a living man, there is nothing more wonderful than a book!—a message to us from the dead—from human souls whom we never saw, who lived perhaps thousands of miles away: and yet these, on those little sheets of paper, speak to us, amuse us, vivify us, teach us, comfort us, open their hearts to us a brothers...

— Charles Kingsley (1819-1875), English pastor, author, professor, and historian

- *Homes in the Wilderness* (William Bradford, Margaret Wise Brown)
- *I Discover Columbus* (Robert Lawson)
- *The Thanksgiving Story* (Alice Dalgliesh)
- *Justin Morgan Had a Horse* (Marguerite Henry)
- *The Landing of the Pilgrims* (James Daugherty)
- *Leif the Lucky* (Ingri and Edgar Parin d'Aulaire)
- *The Light and the Glory for Children* (Peter Marshall)
- *A Lion to Guard Us* (Clyde Bulla)
- *A Little Maid of New England* (Alice Turner Curtis)
- *The Many Lives of Benjamin Franklin* (Aliki)
- *The Matchlock Gun* (Walter D. Edmonds)
- *Mr. Revere and I* (Robert Lawson)
- *Pilgrim Stories* (Margaret Pumphrey)
- *The Pilgrims of Plimoth* (Marcia Sewall)
- *Pocahontas* (Ingri and Edgar Parin d'Aulaire)
- *Pocahontas and the Strangers* (Clyde Bulla)
- *Rachel and Obadiah* (Brinton Turkle)
- *The Sign of the Beaver* (Elizabeth George Speare)
- *The Story of William Penn* (Aliki)
- *Squanto, Friend of the Pilgrims* (Clyde Bulla)
- *Squanto* (Feenie Ziner)
- *Stranded at Plimouth Plantation 1626* (Gary Bowen)
- *Three Young Pilgrims* (Cheryl Harness)
- *Thy Friend, Obadiah* (Brinton Turkle)
- *Traitor: The Case of Benedict Arnold* (Jean Fritz)
- *The Witch of Blackbird Pond* (Elizabeth George Speare)
- *The World of Capt. John Smith* (Genevieve Foster)

Revolutionary America

- *The American Revolution* (Bruce Bliven, Jr.)
- *America's Paul Revere* (Esther Forbes)
- *Amos Fortune, Free Man* (Elizabeth Yates)
- *Ben and Me* (Robert Lawson)
- *Benjamin Franklin* (Ingri and Edgar Parin d'Aulaire)
- *Carry On, Mr. Bowditch* (Jean Lee Latham)
- *Early Thunder* (Jean Fritz)
- *George Washington* (Ingri and Edgar Parin d'Aulaire)

- *George Washington's World* (Genevieve Foster)
- *The Great Little Madison* (Jean Fritz)
- *Guns for General Washington* (Seymour Reit)
- *Johnny Tremain* (Esther Forbes)
- *Of Courage Undaunted* (James Daugherty)
- *Paul Revere's Ride* (Henry Wadsworth Longfellow)
- *Poor Richard* (James Daugherty)
- *Toliver's Secret* (Esther Wood Brady)
- *The Winter at Valley Forge* (F. Van Wyck Mason)
- *Yankee Doodle Boy* (Joseph Martin)
- *Young John Quincy* (Cheryl Harness)

Pioneer America & Expansion

- *Abe Lincoln Grows Up* (Carl Sandburg)
- *Addie across the Prairie* (Laurie Lawlor)
- *The Cabin Faced West* (Jean Fritz)
- *Caddie Woodlawn* (Carol Ryrie Brink)
- *Diary of an Early American Boy* (Eric Sloane)
- *From Sea to Shining Sea for Children* (Peter Marshall)
- *A Gathering of Days* (Joan Blos)
- *Johnny Appleseed* (Steven Kellogg)
- *Magical Melons* (Carol Ryrie Brink)
- *On to Oregon* (Honoré Morrow)
- *The Pony Express* (Samuel Hopkins Adams)
- *Remember the Alamo!* (Robert Penn Warren)
- *The Santa Fe Trail* (Samuel Hopkins Adams)
- *Sarah, Plain and Tall* (Patricia MacLachlan)
- *Thee, Hannah* (Marguerite de Angeli)

Civil War & Reconstruction

- *Abraham Lincoln* (James Daugherty)
- *Abraham Lincoln* (Ingri and Edgar Parin d'Aulaire)
- *Abraham Lincoln's World* (Genevieve Foster)
- *Across Five Aprils* (Irene Hunt)
- *Brady* (Jean Fritz)
- *Gettysburg* (MacKinlay Kantor)
- *Go Free or Die* (Jeri Ferris)

Reading should always thrust us back into the drama of the real world. A healthy love of books gives birth to a renewed enthusiasm for daily living and for the people who shape its stories. A story-formed imagination is naturally driven to real-world action. The great point of excellent stories is to wake us up to beauty, dress down our pride, and teach us how to live with courage, compassion, and creativity.

— Sarah Clarkson, *Read for the Heart*, Apologia Press, 2009

If a book is worth reading, it is worth buying. No book is worth anything which is not worth much; nor is it serviceable until it has been read, and re-read, and loved, and loved again; and marked, so that you can refer to the passages you want in it, as a soldier can seize the weapon he needs in an armory; or a house-wife bring the spice she needs from her store.

— John Ruskin (1819-1900), English art critic, artist, poet, and essayist

- *Rifles for Watie* (Harold Keith)
- *Sound Forth the Trumpet for Children* (Peter Marshall)
- *Unconditional Surrender: U. S. Grant and the Civil War* (Albert Marrin)
- *Virginia's General: Robert E. Lee and the Civil War* (Albert Marrin)

Twentieth Century

- *Around the World in Eighty Days* (Jules Verne)
- *Bully for You, Teddy Roosevelt* (Jean Fritz)
- *The Endless Steppe* (Esther Hautzig)
- *Escape from Warsaw* (Ian Serraillier)
- *Number the Stars* (Lois Lowry)
- *The Singing Tree* (Kate Seredy)
- *War Game: Village Green to No-Man's Land* (Michael Foreman)
- *The Winged Watchman* (Hilda van Stockum)

Miscellaneous Sets, Series, Readers

- Childhood of Famous Americans biography series— *Abigail Adams: Girl of Colonial Days; Abraham Lincoln: The Great Emancipator; Benjamin Franklin: Young Printer; Daniel Boone: Young Hunter and Tracker; Davy Crockett: Young Rifleman; George Washington: Young Leader; Paul Revere: Boston Patriot; Teddy Roosevelt: Young Rough Rider; Thomas Edison: Young Inventor; Thomas Jefferson: Third President of the U.S.;* many more from American history, government, literature, civil rights, sports, science, medicine, and other fields (multiple authors)

- Christian Heroes: Then & Now biography series (Geoff and Janet Benge)

- *Minn of the Mississippi; Paddle-to-the-Sea; Pagoo; Seabird; Tree in the Trail* (Holling C. Holling)

- I Can Read Books Level 3— *The Boston Coffee Party; Buffalo Bill and the Pony Express; George the Drummer Boy; The Long Way to a New Land; The Long Way Westward; Sam the Minuteman; Wagon Wheels;* others (multiple authors)

- Jean Fritz readers — *And Then What Happened, Paul Revere?; Can't You Make Them Behave, King George?; What's the Big Idea, Ben Franklin?; Will You Sign Here, John Hancock?; Why Don't You Get a Horse, Sam Adams?* (Jean Fritz)

- Landmark Books American and World History series (200+ titles, multiple authors)

- Lamplighter Books Collection — Bible stories, historical fiction, moral stories (multiple authors)

- The Sower Series biographies (Mott Media, numerous titles/authors)

- Landmark Books Meet series (also Step-Up Books series) — *Meet Abraham Lincoln; Meet Benjamin Franklin; Meet Christopher Columbus; Meet George Washington; Meet Thomas Jefferson;* others (multiple authors)

- Trailblazer Books Christian historical fiction series (Neta and Dave Jackson)

Additional Books

Additional Books

Books for WholeHearted Learning

A Sampler of Books for Christian Homeschooling

We cover a lot of ground in this book, and we've turned a lot of topsoil to reveal the richness that can be found in many topics with a bit more digging, but it's just not possible for us to stop and dig deep at every point of interest. That's why we've included this list of other recommended books about Christian parenting and homeschooling—to encourage you to dig deeper where we've loosened the soil. We have gone deeper in several other books we've written for Christian parents which are, of course, included in the list, but we can never write all the books we want to in our brief journey here.

There are many more good books that reinforce and reflect our convictions than we can mention here, but this list is a good place to start—a sampler of books about Christian family, parenting, and homeschooling that have encouraged and equipped us on our own journey. We have discovered much wisdom from turn-of-the-century Christian books, from roughly 1860 to 1920. Some may seem dated or irrelevant now, but many read like they were written for today. Look for the wisdom, and any book will reward you. That is good advice for some newer books, too, which can have you grinning in agreement on one page and grimacing with disagreement on the next—glean the wisdom, toss the chaff.

Many of the books below are available from the webstore at www.WholeHeart.org. Some books are out of print. Whole Heart Press titles, both current and future releases, are indicated with [WHP]; Apologia Press titles are indicated with [AP]. Read on!

Home and Parenting

- *The Children for Christ* (Andrew Murray, 1887) [WHP]
- *The Duties of Parents* (J. C. Ryle, 1888) [WHP]
- *Grace-Based Parenting* (Tim Kimmel)
- *Heartfelt Discipline* (Clay Clarkson) [WHP]
- *Hints on Child Training* (H. Clay Trumbull, 1891) [WHP]
- *Parenting Is Heart Work* (Scott Turansky and Joanne Miller)
- *Parenting with Scripture* (Kara Durbin)
- *Praying the Scriptures for Your Children* (Jodie Berndt)
- *Relational Parenting* (Ross Campbell)
- *Seven Tools for Cultivating Your Child's Potential* (Zan Tyler) [AP]
- *What Is a Family?* (Edith Schaeffer)

Blessed be God that hath set up so many clear lamps in his Church; no none but the willfully blind can plead darkness; and blessed be the memory of those his faithful servants, that have left their blood, their spirits, their lives, in these precious papers, and have willingly wasted themselves into the enduring monuments, to give light unto others!

— Joseph Hall (1574-1756), English bishop, writer, and poet

Why are we reading, if not in hope that the writer will magnify and dramatize our days, will illuminate and inspire us with wisdom, courage, and the hope of meaningfulness, and press upon our minds the deepest mysteries, so we may feel again their majesty and power?

— Annie Dillard, *The Writing Life*, 1990

Fatherhood and Motherhood

- *Fathering Like the Father* (Kenneth O. and Jeffrey S. Gangel)
- *King Me* (Steve Farrar)
- *The Ministry of Motherhood* (Sally Clarkson)
- *The Mission of Motherhood* (Sally Clarkson)
- *The Mom Walk* (Sally Clarkson) [WHP]
- *A Mother's Heart* (Jean Fleming)
- *Raising a Modern-Day Knight* (Robert Lewis)
- *Seasons of a Mother's Heart* (Sally Clarkson) [AP]
- *Seasons of a Mother's Home* (Sally Clarkson) [WHP]

Young Men and Women

- *A Girl of Beauty* (Carol Fiddler)
- *Boyhood and Beyond* (Bob Schultz)
- *Fairest Girlhood* (Margaret E. Sangster, 1906)
- *Journeys of Faithfulness* (Sarah Clarkson) [AP]
- *My Young Man* (Louis Albert Banks, ca. 1900) [WHP]
- *Reaping the Harvest* (Diana Waring) [AP]
- *Talks to Boys* (Eleanor A. Hunter, 1890) [WHP]
- *Talks to Girls* (Eleanor A. Hunter, 1891 [WHP]
- *Teen People of the Bible* (Daniel Darling)
- *Wise Guys* (Dan and Carol Fiddler)
- *A Young Person's Guide to Knowing God* (Patricia St. John)

Devotions and Discipleship

- *The Children's Illustrated Bible* (Selina Hastings)
- *The Child's Story Bible* (Catherine F. Vos)
- *Good Morning, God* (Davis Carman) [AP]
- *The Jesus Storybook Bible* (Sally Lloyd-Jones)
- *Leading Little Ones to God* (Marian M. Schoolland)
- *My Time with God* (Thomas Nelson/NCV)
- *Our 24 Family Ways* (Clay Clarkson) [WHP]
- *Our Family Day Celebration* (Clay Clarkson) [WHP]
- *Proverbs Project Wisdom Workbook* (Clay Clarkson) [WHP]
- *Step into the Bible: 100 Bible Stories for Family Devotions* (Ruth Graham)
- *Stepping Stones to Praise and Worship* (Joyce Herzog)

Homeschooling and Books

- *Beyond Survival* (Diana Waring) [AP]
- *A Biblical Home Education* (Ruth Beechick)
- *A Charlotte Mason Companion* (Karen Andreola)
- *For the Children's Sake* (Susan Schaeffer Macaulay)
- *Homeschooling the Challenging Child* (Christine Field)
- *Honey for a Child's Heart* (Gladys M. Hunt)
- *How to Grow a Young Reader* (Kathryn Lindskoog, Ranelda Mack Hunsicker)
- *Mommy, Teach Me!* (Barbara Curtis)
- *Read for the Heart* (Sarah Clarkson) [AP]
- *Reaping the Harvest* (Diana Waring) [AP]
- *The Ultimate Guide to Homeschooling* (Debra Bell) [AP]
- *Who Should We Then Read?*, Vols. 1 & 2 (Jan Bloom)
- *You Can Teach Your Child Successfully* (Ruth Beechick)

Reading and Writing

- *Any Child Can Write* (Harvey S. Wiener)
- *Books Children Love* (Elizabeth Wilson)
- *English for the Thoughtful Child* (Mary Hyde, Cyndy Shearer)
- *Great Explorations in Editing* series (Common Sense Press)
- *Mommy, Teach Me to Read!* (Barbara Curtis)
- *Reading Made Easy* (Valerie Bendt)
- *Simply Grammar* (Karen Andreola)
- *Story Starters* (Karen Andreola)
- *Teach Your Child to Read in 100 Easy Lessons* (Siegfried Engelmann)
- *Wordsmith* writing series (Janie B. Cheaney)
- *The Write Stuff Adventure* (Dean Rea)

Thinking and Speaking

- *The Fallacy Detective* (Nathaniel and Hans Bluedorn)
- *From Playpen to Podium* (Jeff Myers)
- *Secrets of Great Communicators* (Jeff Myers)
- *Starting Points* (David Quine)
- *Stories and Story Telling* (Edward Porter St. John, 1918) [WHP]
- *Thinking Like a Christian* (David Noebel, Chuck Edwards)
- *The Thinking Toolbox* (Nathaniel and Hans Bluedorn)

The Teacher searched to find just the right words, and what he wrote was upright and true. The words of the wise are like goads, their collected sayings like firmly embedded nails—given by one Shepherd. Be warned, my son, of anything in addition to them. Of making many books there is no end, and much study wearies the body.

— Ecclesiastes 12:10-12

[Paul writing to Timothy from prison] *When you come bring the cloak which I left at Troas with Carpus, and the books, especially the parchments.*

— 2 Timothy 4:13 (NASB)

Additional Books

Forms for WholeHearted Learning

Forming Your WholeHearted Learning

Forms will not make you a better homeschooling parent. Some states mandate record-keeping, and you must fill out required forms. However, the personal habit of forms-keeping is not an inherent factor in homeschool success. Those who love keeping forms will probably think those who do not are minimizing something important; those who love *not* keeping forms will probably think those who do are emphasizing something unimportant. Though there are some very good arguments for keeping some forms, the truth is that you can form a well-educated, mature child without forms. Forms are just tools you can use—if you need them, they can help; if you don't, they may not be necessary.

We don't major on forms for two reasons. First, we don't want a form to become a substitute for your instincts as a parent and home educator. WholeHearted Learning is about liberating learning, not formulizing it. Second, forms are very personal and, by their nature, inflexible. That's why we encourage you to make your own forms to reflect your family's priorities and practices. Even if you are not naturally a forms-keeper, here are some good reasons for you to consider forming the habit of keeping a few good forms.

- **Records** — If a state educational or social worker ever questions your homeschooling, good records will become your ally.

- **History** — It's nice to keep a history of what you have studied and done. Your kids will enjoy looking back.

- **Motivation** — A book-reading form can become a motivational tool for reading, especially when milestones are added.

- **Creativity** — If you keep your forms in binders, let your children create a colorful cover insert, decorate the section dividers, and provide other artistic touches.

- **Projects** — Forms for your children can become homeschooling projects. For example, create a My 24 Family Ways binder for each child.

- **Organization** — A simple form or two can help you stay better organized in the flood of homeschooling papers.

- **Planning** — Forms for planning your school year can help you get on track and stay on track in a busy season.

- **Accountability** — In the absence of other people in your life, a simple form can help you stay accountable to your goals.

Go Form It!

Whether you write on forms or write off forms, there is a good argument to be made for the educational value of form making and keeping. Getting your children involved in designing forms that they or your family will use engages them creatively and can give them a sense of accomplishment. Consider how form making can engage your children on several levels of learning:

- Purpose — defining a reason for the form that will guide the process of creating it
- Logic — determining what information should and should not be gathered
- Organization — considering priority of form elements and flow of information intake
- Spatial Reasoning — assigning sufficient space for each element of the form
- Design — creating an efficient design for gathering and retrieving the information
- Art — creating an attractive design with graphics, icons, photos, and more

Getting In-Formed

Computers excel at form design and creation. Word processors, page layout programs, and productivity software packages are the best places to start. They typically include many customizable form templates, form creation tools, and downloadable online resources. There are also good online suites. Once you and your kids get the right tools and get the hang of design, you'll become form-making pros in no time. And if you want to share your form with others, just print it as a PDF and pass it around. Your friends will soon be saying, "Good form!" Following are some good tools to get forming:

Installed Resources

- Microsoft Publisher — desktop publishing, page layout
- Microsoft Works — word processor, spreadsheet, database, and more
- Microsoft Word — advanced word processor
- Apple iWork — Apple Pages word processor with page design, spreadsheet, presentation, and more
- www.LibreOffice.org — free, open-source, downloadable productivity software suite with six applications for use on all platforms

Online Resources

- http://Docs.Google.com — free online word processor, spreadsheet, drawing, forms creation, and more
- www.Zoho.com — online productivity suite with many tools, some free
- www.Live.com — free online Office Web Apps (Word, Excel, PowerPoint)

A Few Good Forms

The forms in this section vary widely in purpose, age-level, design, and content. You may copy the forms for your own personal and family use. If you want to use a form for a group or organization, please contact Whole Heart Ministries for permission. Most of these forms and others are available for download on the Whole Heart Ministries website (www.wholeheart.org).

- **WholeHearted Learning Agenda** — A detailed weekly planning sheet that includes both living and learning aspects of WholeHearted Learning (one child per sheet).

- **WholeHearted Learning Overview** — A universal, simple form for planning and goal-setting WholeHearted Learning by month, week, or day (up to three children).

- **WholeHearted Learning Planner** — A detailed weekly planning sheet for primary subject areas of WholeHearted Learning (one child per sheet).

- **My "Do It Today" Task List** — A simple checklist for your children covering things to do in the primary task areas of their daily homeschooling life.

- **My "Get It Done" Project Planner** — A basic project planner for your children to help them think through what needs to be done to complete a project.

- **My "Books Are the Best" Reading Record** — A simple form for your children for keeping individual records of books that have been read.

- **My "Read for My Life" Book Report** — A simple book report form that can be filled out for each book read, and stored in a binder.

- **My "Check It Out" DiscipleSheet** — Select a topic for study and give this sheet to your child to do a simple topical Bible study (good for training and instruction also).

- **My "Check Me Out" DependableList** — Positive reinforcement for your children in learning to be responsible (intended for training, not for discipline).

- **My 24 Family "Ways to Be" ~ Godly Character** — Character qualities from *Our 24 Family Ways* for memorization and for training (one quality for each Way).

- **My 24 Family "Ways to Go" ~ Biblical Values** — Biblical values statements from *Our 24 Family Ways* for memorizing and applying to daily life at home.

- **LifeGIFTS Discipleship Planner** — Plan discipleship goals using the GIFTS model.

- **Family Devotional ARTS Planner** — Plan family devotions using the ARTS model.

- **Bible Reading Record** — Check off chapters as you read through the Bible.

- **Bible Reading & Devotional Journal** — Personal daily devotional journal form.

- **One Month Calendar Planner** — A universal monthly calendar form.

- **One Week Calendar Planner** — A universal weekly calendar form.

- **Family Chores Assignment Chart** — A form for assigning chores and responsibilities to family members on a quarterly basis (three months of assignments).

WholeHearted Learning Agenda

Child: Week:

Bible Study & Research Topics	Family & Special Responsibilities
Bible Reading:	Mealtime:
Bible Topic:	Afternoon:
Bible Book:	Check Daily:
History Research:	As Needed:
Science Research:	Cleaning:

Reading & Study List	Special Instructions & Calendar
History:	Morning:
Biography:	
Church History:	Afternoon:
Literature/Fiction:	
Science/Nature:	Evening:
Christian:	
	Weekend:

Subject	Book, Resource, Curriculum		MON		TUE		WED		THU		FRI
Bible											
Language Arts											
Handwriting											
Writing & Composition											
Math											
History											
Geography											
Science & Nature											
Art, Music & Poetry											
Computer & Internet											
Government & Civics											
Worldview & Apologetics											

WholeHearted Learning Overview

Quarter: Year:

MONTH WEEK DAY	Child	Child	Child

WholeHearted Learning Planner

Child: Week:

Subject	Book, Resource, Curriculum		MON		TUE		WED		THU		FRI

Discipleship Studies

Subject			MON		TUE		WED		THU		FRI
Bible Reading											
Bible Study											

Disciplined Studies

Language Arts											
Handwriting											
Writing & Composition											
Math											
Thinking Skills											

Discussion Studies

Reading & Narration											
History											
Geography											
Art, Music, Poetry											
Science & Nature											

Discovery Studies

Nature Study											
Computer & Internet											
Creative Arts											

Discretionary Studies

My "Do It Today" Task List

My Name:	Today Is:

#	TO DO TODAY	DO BY	DONE

ASSIGNMENTS

#		DO BY	DONE
1.			
2.			
3.			
4.			
5.			

READING

#		DO BY	DONE
1.			
2.			
3.			
4.			

PROJECTS

#		DO BY	DONE
1.			
2.			
3.			
4.			

CHORES

#		DO BY	DONE
1.			
2.			
3.			

FRIENDS & FAMILY

#		DO BY	DONE
1.			
2.			
3.			

OTHER STUFF

#		DO BY	DONE
1.			
2.			
3.			

My "Get It Done" Project Planner

My Name:	Date Started:

NAME IT ~ What is a good name for this project?

PROJECT:

DESCRIBE IT ~ What do you want to accomplish with this project?

SUPPLY IT ~ What resources will you need for this project?

Books	
Materials	
Digital/Online	
Tools/Gear	
Other	

PLAN IT ~ What steps will you need to take for this project?

#	Steps to Take	Do By	!!!

EVALUATE IT ~ What is your opinion of this project?

My "Books Are the Best" Reading Record

My Name: | Date Started:

FICTION BOOKS

#	TITLE AND AUTHOR	PAGES	DATE
1.			
2.			
3.			
4.			
5.			
6.			
7.			
8.			
9.			
10.			
11.			
12.			

NON-FICTION BOOKS

#	TITLE AND AUTHOR	PAGES	DATE
1.			
2.			
3.			
4.			
5.			
6.			
7.			
8.			
9.			
10.			
11.			
12.			

My "Read for My Life" Book Report

My Name:	Date Written:

BOOK:

Author(s)	
Illustrator	
Publisher	
Details	Copyright:　　　Binding:　　　# Pages:　　　[ ] Fiction [ ] Nonfiction

THE STORY ~ Summarize the story that you think the author of this book wanted to tell.

THE CHARACTERS ~ Describe the main characters by qualities using single-word descriptors.

Character	Description (key words)

THE READER ~ Describe how this book affected your thinking, feelings, understanding, or faith.

Extra: Use the back of this sheet to write a brief review and personal evaluation of this book.

My "Check It Out" DiscipleSheet

My Name:

Date Studied:

TOPIC ~ What Bible subject is on God's heart for me to check out?

TOPIC:

DEFINITION ~ What is a good definition of this topic?

SCRIPTURES ~ What does God's Word say about this topic?

SCRIPTURE REFERENCE	KEY WORDS, IDEA, OR TEXT

INSIGHT ~ What does God want me to KNOW about this topic?

ACTION ~ What does God want me to DO about this topic?

My "Check Me Out" DependableList

My Name:	Date Started:

MORNING ~ Sow your seed in the morning...

DID I...	SUN	MON	TUE	WED	THU	FRI	SAT
Make my bed neatly?							
Dress myself nicely?							
Groom myself well?							
Read my Bible and pray?							
Do my morning chores?							

EVENING ~ And at evening let your hands not be idle...

DID I...	SUN	MON	TUE	WED	THU	FRI	SAT
Pick up all my clothes and things?							
Put up all my homeschool work?							
Clean up all my messes?							
Straighten my room and bath?							
Get myself ready for bed quickly?							

ALL DAY ~ Whatever you do, do it all for the glory of God...

DID I...	SUN	MON	TUE	WED	THU	FRI	SAT
Honor and obey my parents?							
Get along well with others?							
Use my time wisely?							
Guard my tongue (words)?							
Guard my heart (attitudes)?							

END OF THE WEEK ~ Let another praise you...

My 24 Family "Ways to Be" — Godly Character

Name: I started memorizing: I finished memorizing:

AUTHORITIES

1. Godlinesss — Wanting more than anything else to please God in everything that I think, say, and do.
2. Trust in God — Remembering every day that God loves me and will take care of me.
3. Reverence — Honoring God, my parents, and all proper authorities because of who they are in God's eyes.
4. Submissive — Willingly accepting and following the authorities God has placed over my life.

RELATIONSHIPS

5. Love — Wanting only the best for others and showing it in how I treat them and speak to them.
6. Service — Doing for others without expecting them to do anything for me in return.
7. Encouragement — Speaking words to others that build them up and lift them up in the Lord.
8. Forgiveness — Treating someone who has offended me as though I had never been hurt.

POSSESSIONS

9. Thankfulness — Being glad and grateful for my life, and showing it.
10. Contentment — Deciding to be happy with my circumstances, whatever they may be.
11. Generosity — Happily sharing with others all that God has given to me.
12. Stewardship — Using wisely everything that God has given to me—my time, my talents, and my treasures.

WORK

13. Diligence — Working hard on a task and keeping at it until I finish it.
14. Initiative — Doing what needs to be done without needing to be asked.
15. Cooperation — Joyfully working with others to do more in less time than I can do by myself.
16. Responsibility — Choosing to do what I know I should do because it is the right thing to do.

ATTITUDES

17. Joyfulness — Happiness in my heart that comes out on my face and through my words.
18. Peacemaker — Finding a way to avoid or end a disagreement rather than to begin or win it.
19. Patience — Keeping a calm spirit while waiting for God to work out his will.
20. Graciousness — Treating all people with the respect they deserve because they are made in God's image.

CHOICES

21. Integrity — Knowing what is right and living that way.
22. Discernment — Learning to recognize right and wrong so I can choose what is right.
23. Self-Control — Choosing to control my thoughts and feelings so they do not control me.
24. Honesty — Telling what I know is true without any hint of deception or falsehood.

The "Ways to Be" on this page are from *Our 24 Family Ways: A Family Devotional Guide* by Clay Clarkson (Whole Heart Press, 2010).

My 24 Family "Ways to Go" — Biblical Values

Name: I started memorizing: I finished memorizing:

AUTHORITIES — In our family...

1. We love and obey our Lord, Jesus Christ, with wholehearted devotion.
2. We read the Bible and pray to God every day with an open heart.
3. We honor and obey our parents in the Lord with a respectful attitude.
4. We listen to correction and accept discipline with a submissive spirit.

RELATIONSHIPS — In our family...

5. We love one another, treating others with kindness, gentleness, and respect.
6. We serve one another, humbly thinking of the needs of others first.
7. We encourage one another, using only words that build up and bless others.
8. We forgive one another, covering an offense with love when wronged or hurt.

POSSESSIONS — In our family...

9. We are thankful to God for what we have, whether it is a little or a lot.
10. We are content with what we have, not coveting what others have.
11. We are generous with what we have, sharing freely with others.
12. We take care of what we have, using it wisely and responsibly.

WORK — In our family...

13. We are diligent to complete a task promptly and thoroughly when asked.
14. We take initiative to do all of our own work without needing to be told.
15. We work with a cooperative spirit, freely giving and receiving help.
16. We take personal responsibility to keep our home neat and clean at all times.

ATTITUDES — In our family...

17. We choose to be joyful, even when we feel like complaining.
18. We choose to be peacemakers, even when we feel like arguing.
19. We choose to be patient, even when we feel like getting our own way.
20. We choose to be gracious, even when we don't feel like it.

CHOICES — In our family...

21. We do what we know is right, regardless of what others do or say.
22. We ask before we act when we do not know what is right to do.
23. We exercise self-control at all times and in every kind of situation.
24. We always tell the truth and do not practice deceitfulness of any kind.

The "Ways to Go" on this page are from *Our 24 Family Ways: A Family Devotional Guide* by Clay Clarkson (Whole Heart Press, 2010).

LifeGIFTS Discipleship Planner

Child: Date:

#	TRAINING	#	INSTRUCTION

G — GRACE

#		#	

I — INSPIRATION

#		#	

F — FAITH

#		#	

T — TRAINING

#		#	

S — SERVICE

#		#	
#		#	

Family Devotional ARTS Planner

Led by: Date:

Bible Passage / Translation	
Subject or Theme	
Writer or Speaker	
Historical Setting	
Cross References	

A — Ask a question.

Ask a personalized question to create interest in the topic of the Bible passage.

Younger:

Older:

R — Read the Bible.

Read the passage slowly and expressively, and have your children narrate it back.

Key Verses:

Key Words:

T — Talk about it.

Talk about both the content (details) and the intent (principles) of the passage.

Question:

Question:

Question:

S — Speak to God.

Speak to God about what you should know, be, do, or believe from this passage.

Prayer:

Prayer:

Prayer:

Bible Reading Record

Name: Start: Done:

Your word is a lamp to my feet and a light to my path. ~ Psalm 119:105
All Scripture is inspired by God and profitable for teaching, for reproof, for correction, for training in righteousness;
so that the man of God may be adequate, equipped for every good work. ~ 2 Timothy 3:16-17

OLD TESTAMENT

Genesis	1 2 3 4 5 6 7 8 9 10 11 12 13 14 15 16 17 18 19 20 21 22 23 24 25 26 27 28 29 30 31 32 33 34 35 36 37 38 39 40 41 42 43 44 45 46 47 48 49 50
Exodus	1 2 3 4 5 6 7 8 9 10 11 12 13 14 15 16 17 18 19 20 21 22 23 24 25 26 27 28 29 30 31 32 33 34 35 36 37 38 39 40
Leviticus	1 2 3 4 5 6 7 8 9 10 11 12 13 14 15 16 17 18 19 20 21 22 23 24 25 26 27
Numbers	1 2 3 4 5 6 7 8 9 10 11 12 13 14 15 16 17 18 19 20 21 22 23 24 25 26 27 28 29 30 31 32 33 34 35 36
Deuteronomy	1 2 3 4 5 6 7 8 9 10 11 12 13 14 15 16 17 18 19 20 21 22 23 24 25 26 27 28 29 30 31 32 33 34
Joshua	1 2 3 4 5 6 7 8 9 10 11 12 13 14 15 16 17 18 19 20 21 22 23 24
Judges	1 2 3 4 5 6 7 8 9 10 11 12 13 14 15 16 17 18 19 20 21
Ruth	1 2 3 4
1 Samuel	1 2 3 4 5 6 7 8 9 10 11 12 13 14 15 16 17 18 19 20 21 22 23 24 25 26 27 28 29 30 31
2 Samuel	1 2 3 4 5 6 7 8 9 10 11 12 13 14 15 16 17 18 19 20 21 22 23 24
1 Kings	1 2 3 4 5 6 7 8 9 10 11 12 13 14 15 16 17 18 19 20 21 22
2 Kings	1 2 3 4 5 6 7 8 9 10 11 12 13 14 15 16 17 18 19 20 21 22 23 24 25
1 Chronicles	1 2 3 4 5 6 7 8 9 10 11 12 13 14 15 16 17 18 19 20 21 22 23 24 25 26 27 28 29
2 Chronicles	1 2 3 4 5 6 7 8 9 10 11 12 13 14 15 16 17 18 19 20 21 22 23 24 25 26 27 28 29 30 31 32 33 34 35 36
Ezra	1 2 3 4 5 6 7 8 9 10
Nehemiah	1 2 3 4 5 6 7 8 9 10 11 12 13
Esther	1 2 3 4 5 6 7 8 9 10
Job	1 2 3 4 5 6 7 8 9 10 11 12 13 14 15 16 17 18 19 20 21 22 23 24 25 26 27 28 29 30 31 32 33 34 35 36 37 38 39 40 41 42
Psalms	1 2 3 4 5 6 7 8 9 10 11 12 13 14 15 16 17 18 19 20 21 22 23 24 25 26 27 28 29 30 31 32 33 34 35 36 37 38 39 40 41 42 43 44 45 46 47 48 49 50 51 52 53 54 55 56 57 58 59 60 61 62 63 64 65 66 67 68 69 70 71 72 73 74 75 76 77 78 79 80 81 82 83 84 85 86 87 88 89 90 91 92 93 94 95 96 97 98 99 100 101 102 103 104 105 106 107 108 109 110 111 112 113 114 115 116 117 118 119 120 121 122 123 124 125 126 127 128 129 130 131 132 133 134 135 136 137 138 139 140 141 142 143 144 145 146 147 148 149 150
Proverbs	1 2 3 4 5 6 7 8 9 10 11 12 13 14 15 16 17 18 19 20 21 22 23 24 25 26 27 28 29 30 31
Ecclesiastes	1 2 3 4 5 6 7 8 9 10 11 12
Song of Songs	1 2 3 4 5 6 7 8
Isaiah	1 2 3 4 5 6 7 8 9 10 11 12 13 14 15 16 17 18 19 20 21 22 23 24 25 26 27 28 29 30 31 32 33 34 35 36 37 38 39 40 41 42 43 44 45 46 47 48 49 50 51 52 53 54 55 56 57 58 59 60 61 62 63 64 65 66

Jeremiah	1 2 3 4 5 6 7 8 9 10 11 12 13 14 15 16 17 18 19 20 21 22 23 24 25 26 27 28 29 30 31 32 33 34 35 36 37 38 39 40 41 42 43 44 45 46 47 48 49 50 51 52
Lamentations	1 2 3 4 5
Ezekiel	1 2 3 4 5 6 7 8 9 10 11 12 13 14 15 16 17 18 19 20 21 22 23 24 25 26 27 28 29 30 31 32 33 34 35 36 37 38 39 40 41 42 43 44 45 46 47 48
Daniel	1 2 3 4 5 6 7 8 9 10 11 12
Hosea	1 2 3 4 5 6 7 8 9 10 11 12 13 14
Joel	1 2 3
Amos	1 2 3 4 5 6 7 8 9
Obadiah	1
Jonah	1 2 3 4
Micah	1 2 3 4 5 6 7
Nahum	1 2 3
Habakkuk	1 2 3
Zephaniah	1 2 3
Haggai	1 2
Zechariah	1 2 3 4 5 6 7 8 9 10 11 12 13 14
Malachi	1 2 3 4

NEW TESTAMENT

Matthew	1 2 3 4 5 6 7 8 9 10 11 12 13 14 15 16 17 18 19 20 21 22 23 24 25 26 27 28
Mark	1 2 3 4 5 6 7 8 9 10 11 12 13 14 15 16
Luke	1 2 3 4 5 6 7 8 9 10 11 12 13 14 15 16 17 18 19 20 21 22 23 24
John	1 2 3 4 5 6 7 8 9 10 11 12 13 14 15 16 17 18 19 20 21
Acts	1 2 3 4 5 6 7 8 9 10 11 12 13 14 15 16 17 18 19 20 21 22 23 24 25 26 27 28
Romans	1 2 3 4 5 6 7 8 9 10 11 12 13 14 15 16
1 Corinthians	1 2 3 4 5 6 7 8 9 10 11 12 13 14 15 16
2 Corinthians	1 2 3 4 5 6 7 8 9 10 11 12 13
Galatians	1 2 3 4 5 6
Ephesians	1 2 3 4 5 6
Philippians	1 2 3 4
Colossians	1 2 3 4
1 Thessalonians	1 2 3 4 5
2 Thessalonians	1 2 3
1 Timothy	1 2 3 4 5 6
2 Timothy	1 2 3 4
Titus	1 2 3
Philemon	1
Hebrews	1 2 3 4 5 6 7 8 9 10 11 12 13
James	1 2 3 4 5
1 Peter	1 2 3 4 5
2 Peter	1 2 3
1 John	1 2 3 4 5
2 John	1
3 John	1
Jude	1
Revelation	1 2 3 4 5 6 7 8 9 10 11 12 13 14 15 16 17 18 19 20 21 22

Bible Reading & Devotional Journal

Year:

Page:

Today's Passage: | Day: | Date:

Write a one-sentence summary of this section:

Today's Verse: | ☐ Meditated? | ☐ Memorized?

What does God say that I need to KNOW, BE, DO, or BELIEVE?

What are the key words in today's verse?

Today's Passage: | Day: | Date:

Write a one-sentence summary of this section:

Today's Verse: | ☐ Meditated? | ☐ Memorized?

What does God say that I need to KNOW, BE, DO, or BELIEVE?

What are the key words in today's verse?

Today's Passage: | Day: | Date:

Write a one-sentence summary of this section:

Today's Verse: | ☐ Meditated? | ☐ Memorized?

What does God say that I need to KNOW, BE, DO, or BELIEVE?

What are the key words in today's verse?

One Month Calendar Planner

Month: Year: For:

Sunday	Monday	Tuesday	Wednesday	Thursday	Friday	Saturday

Events & Activities

People & Projects

One Week Calendar Planner

Month: Week: Year: For:

	MORNING	AFTERNOON	EVENING
		Weekdays	
Monday			
Tuesday			
Wednesday			
Thursday			
Friday			
		Weekend	
Saturday			
Sunday			
		This Week	
To Do			

Family Chores Assignment Chart

Tasks to Be Done / Months:				

Meal Chores

WASH & DISHWASHER
- Wash all dirty dishes and utensils.
- Rinse and put dishes in dishwasher.
- Leave sink area clean and neat.

TABLE & COUNTERS
- Set and clear table at meals.
- Clean counter and table tops.
- Straighten chairs and settings.

DRY & PUT AWAY
- Dry any hand-washed items.
- Put away all food and cooking items.
- Sweep floors in kitchen and dining room.

Room Chores

FAMILY ROOM
- Pick up and straighten room.
- Organize (books, CDs, DVDs, pencils, paper).
- Take extra items to appropriate rooms.

LIVING ROOM
- Pick up and straighten room.
- Organize (music, magazines, games).
- Take extra items to appropriate rooms.

DINING / UTILITY ROOM
- Pick up and straighten room.
- Organize (table tops, cleaning things).
- Take extra items to appropriate rooms.

Area Chores

YARD / GROUNDS
- Pick up trash and things.
- Pick up loose sticks and branches.
- Police entire lot around house.

DRIVE / WALKS / PATIO
- Sweep and clean entry areas.
- Wash drive and walks as needed.
- Straighten (hoses, outdoor toys, furniture)

ENTRY HALL / CLOSET
- Organize and put away loose things.
- Sweep entry area and closet.
- Organize storage closet.

Special Chores

TRASH
- Put out trash for pickup.
- Empty and take out trash as needed.
- Take out other refuse as needed.

CARS
- Clean and organize cars as needed.
- Regularly remove unnecessary items.
- Clean surfaces and windows as needed.

GARAGE
- Sweep and clean garage as needed.
- Keep it organized (things on shelves).
- Clean any large appliances as needed.

Daily Living Schedule

_____	Out of bed
_____	Parent time
_____	Breakfast
_____	Devotions
_____	Homeschool
_____	Lunch
_____	Homeschool
_____	Free time
_____	Chores
_____	Dinner
_____	Family time
_____	Reading
_____	Bedtime
_____	Lights out

Regular Cleaning

- **Beds** — Strip, wash, replace sheets.
- **Surfaces** — Clean, dust, and polish.
- **Bathrooms** — Surfaces, mirror, floor.
- **Floors** — Vacuum, sweep, mop.
- **Glass** — Windows, entry door, mirrors.
- **Kitchen** — Surfaces, sweep, and mop.

Other Responsibilities

- **Bedrooms** — Everyone cleans and organizes their own room every day.
- **Laundry** — Everyone washes, folds, and removes their own laundry.
- **Dishwasher** — Everyone helps empty the dishwasher whenever it is clean.
- **Children** — Everyone plays with and reads to younger children when needed.
- **Pet(s)** — Everyone decides who will feed, water, walk, groom, and clean after pets.

Wash (W) Bathe (B)	SUN	MON	TUE	WED	THU	FRI	SAT
MORN							
AFTN							
EVEN							

Notes

Notes

Notes

Keeping Faith in the Family

Whole Heart Ministries is a Christian home and parenting ministry dedicated to encouraging and equipping Christian parents to bring up wholehearted children "in the training and instruction of the Lord." Whole Heart Ministries is a nonprofit, family-run faith ministry founded by Clay and Sally Clarkson in 1994. For more information about our ministries and materials, visit our website or contact us directly.

Whole Heart Ministries

P.O. Box 3445 | Monument, CO 80132

888-488-4HOME (488-4466) | 888-FAX-2WHM (329-2946)

www.wholeheart.org | whm@wholeheart.org

Mom Heart Ministry, a ministry initiative of Whole Heart Ministries, seeks to restore mothers' hearts to God's biblical design for motherhood through an international movement of small groups for mothers. Mom Heart provides training, resources, events, websites, and blogs for Christian moms. For more information, visit the Mom Heart website or contact us directly through Whole Heart Ministries.

Mom Heart Ministry

www.momheart.org | mhm@momheart.org

Apologia Educational Ministries has served the Christian homeschooling community since 1996 as a publisher of highly respected creation-based science textbooks. Under new ownership since 2008, Apologia Press has expanded the product line with books and resources for Christian parents, which now includes the Apologia/WholeHeart imprint of the Clarksons' books for Christian homeschooling.

Apologia Press

1106 Meridian Plaza Suite 220/340 | Anderson, IN 46016

888-524-4724 phone | 765-608-3290 fax

Books by the Clarkson Family

Apologia / WholeHeart Books

Seasons of a Mother's Heart
Sally Clarkson (1998, 2009)

Heart-touching essays with Bible studies on the seasons of a homeschool mother's life. Revised and expanded version of the original 1998 book. Good for small group study.

Read for the Heart
Sarah Clarkson (2009)

Sarah both defends and demonstrates, by her own writing skills, the power of books and reading in a child's life. She reviews hundreds of whole books for families.

COMING BOOKS: **Journeys of Faithfulness**, Sarah Clarkson's book for older girls and young women, blending historical fiction and inspirational insight, extensively revised and expanded to speak to the spiritual hearts of young women today.

Whole Heart Press Books

Our 24 Family Ways
Clay Clarkson (2010)

An illustrated family discipleship tool with 120 family devotional outlines, character qualities, and more. Teach your children the language of biblical values.

Just David
Eleanor H. Porter (2002, 2011)

A family favorite novel by the author of *Pollyanna*. Perfect for read-aloud with the whole family. A Whole Heart Family Classics book in a quality paperback edition.

COMING BOOKS: **Heartfelt Discipline**, Clay Clarkson's thought-provoking exploration of biblical childhood discipline and path of life parenting. **The Mom Walk**, Sally Clarkson's inspirational and motivational insights on how to walk with God as a Christian mother. Whole Heart Family and Christian Classics, reprints of public domain books from 1860 to1920.

WaterBrook Press Books

The Mission of Motherhood
Sally Clarkson (2003)

An inspiring, personal portrait of biblical motherhood with a clear vision of God's design and plan for moms today. Includes group study and discussion questions.

The Ministry of Motherhood
Sally Clarkson (2004)

A thought-provoking exploration of following Jesus' example as a mother. Presents a simple model of home discipleship called LifeGIFTS. Good for group study.

Dancing with My Father
Sally Clarkson (2010)

A journey of the heart to learn how to live a life of grace and joy in the Lord, in both good and hard times. Filled with personal anecdotes and scriptural insights.

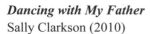

The Clarksons' books are available online through the publishers' websites, at Christianbook.com and Amazon.com, at selected bookstores, and from the Whole Heart Webstore. To find out more, visit our website:

www.wholeheart.org